Donated by
Ian Thomson

Not for loan

# *European Union Law for the Twenty-First Century*

VOLUME 1

CONSTITUTIONAL AND PUBLIC LAW
EXTERNAL RELATIONS

This book is based on the proceedings of the WG Hart Workshop 2003. It contains contributions by leading experts seeking to assess the state of development of EU law some fifty years after the establishment of the Communities and to contribute to the current debate on the European Constitution. The volume concentrates on the theme of European Constitutionalism and analyses the proposed Constitution dealing with, among others things, the division of competence between the EU and the Member States, Community legislation, the role of the national parliaments, democracy in the EU, the Court of Justice, and human rights. It also deals with enlargement and the external relations of the EU.

# European Union Law for the Twenty-First Century

## Rethinking the New Legal Order

*Volume 1*
*Constitutional and Public Law*
*External Relations*

Edited by
Takis Tridimas
*Queen Mary University of London*
*&*
Paolisa Nebbia
*University of Southampton*

·HART·
PUBLISHING

OXFORD AND PORTLAND OREGON
2004

Published in North America (US and Canada) by
Hart Publishing
c/o International Specialized Book Services
5804 NE Hassalo Street
Portland, Oregon
97213-3644
USA



Hart Publishing is a specialist legal publisher based in Oxford, England. To order further copies of this book or to request a list of other publications please write to:

Hart Publishing, Salters Boatyard, Folly Bridge,
Abingdon Rd, Oxford, OX1 4LB
Telephone: +44 (0)1865 245533 Fax: +44 (0)1865 794882
email: mail@hartpub.co.uk
WEBSITE: http//:www.hartpub.co.uk

British Library Cataloguing in Publication Data
Data Available

ISBN 1-84113-456-2 (hardback)

Typeset by Olympus Infotech Pvt Ltd, India, Sabon 10/12pt
Printed and bound in Great Britain by
TJ International, Padstow, Cornwall

# *Foreword*

The contributions contained in this volume are based on papers presented in the 2003 WG Hart Workshop, which took place at the Institute of Advanced Legal Studies, London. The Workshop concentrated on three themes: European constitutionalism in the 21st century, the future of the internal market, and external relations. The aim of the Workshop was to assess the state of development of EU law some fifty years after the establishment of the Communities, contribute to the current policy debate on Europe, and identify likely future trends. The proceedings of the Workshop are published in two volumes. This volume contains contributions in constitutional law and external relations. The second volume contains contributions pertaining to the internal market and Community policies.

We are grateful to Professor Barry Rider, who, as Director of the Institute of Advanced Legal Studies, initiated this project, and the administrative staff of the Institute, especially David Phillips and Belinda Crothers, who worked tirelessly to make the Workshop possible. We are very grateful to all speakers and participants who enabled the Workshop and the resulting volumes, and those who gave their time to chair sessions. We were very fortunate to be assisted by Lord Slynn of Hadley, Advocate General Francis Jacobs QC, Professor Walter van Gerven, and Sir Christopher Bellamy.

We would like to thank Richard Hart and the staff of Hart Publishing who embraced with enthusiasm this project and, as always, have been extremely helpful and efficient in preparing the publication of both volumes. Our thanks also go to Angeliki Mitsolidou for her invaluable assistance in the preparation of the list of cases.

The Workshop was organised by David O'Keeffe and Takis Tridimas. It would not have been possible without David's tireless efforts and inspiration. It is most unfortunate that, due to circumstances beyond his control, David was not able to participate in the preparation of the publications. In his absence, we have taken it upon ourselves to prepare the volumes and our only hope is that the quality of the end product has not suffered too much as a result.

Takis Tridimas
Paolisa Nebbia
*March 2004*

# *Contents*

*List of Contributors* xi
*Table of Cases* xiii

1. Introduction 1
*Takis Tridimas*

2. Three Challenges for European Constitutionalism in the 21st Century 9
*Francis Snyder*

3. Judicial Review as a Contribution to the Development of European Constitutionalism 17
*Koen Lenaerts and Tim Corthaut*

4. Competences of the Union 65
*George A Bermann*

5. The Hierarchy of Norms 75
*Paul Craig*

6. Protecting Fundamental Rights in Europe's New Constitutional Order 95
*Anthony Arnull*

7. The European Court of Justice and the Draft Constitution: A Supreme Court for the Union? 113
*Takis Tridimas*

8. The European Commission: Should it be at the Heart of the Future European Union? 143
*Mike Cuthbert and Sarah Willis*

9. The Role of National Parliaments in the EU's New Constitutional Order 153
*Adam Cygan*

10. For Substantive Constitutionalism in the European Union 171
*Bernard Ryan*

11. Forgetting Law in the European Convention? Europe's 'Hidden' Constitution-Building and its Legitimation 189
*Michelle Everson and Julia Eisner*

12. The Draft EU Constitution and Private Party Access to Judicial Review of EU Measures 209
*Angela Ward*

13. Legality Review of Member States Discretion Under Directives 223
*Chris Hilson*

14. What is the Point of *Francovich*? 239
*Michael Dougan*

15. Lines in the Sand: Between Common Foreign Policy and Single Foreign Policy 259
*Eileen Denza*

16. Which Policy for Which Europe? The Emerging Security and Defence Policy of the European Union 273
*Panos Koutrakos*

17. Gripping Global Governance: The External Relations of the EU Between the Treaty of Nice and the Convention on the Future of Europe 291
*Christoph Herrmann*

18. Squaring the Circle for Tomorrow's World: A Comparative Analysis of the EC and WTO Approaches to Balancing Economic and Non-economic Interests in International Trade 303
*Emily Reid*

19. The Participation of the European Community in the World Trade Organisation: An External Look at European Union Constitution-Building 321
*Antonis Antoniadis*

20. EU Immigration and Asylum Law: Internal Market Model or Human Rights Model? 345
*Steve Peers*

21. A Missed Opportunity? EU Law and Asylum in the 21st Century 361
*Hélène Lambert*

22. Asylum and Immigration in the Context of Enlargement 377
*Catherine Phuong*

23. Enlargement: A Successful Instrument of Foreign Policy? 397
*Marise Cremona*

24. The European Employment Strategy and the Challenges of Enlargement 415
*Samantha Velluti*

25. The EU Charter of Fundamental Rights: Is it a New Accession Condition for the Candidate Countries Especially in Light of the Post-Nice IGC? 437
*Jenö Czuczai*

*Index* 451

# *List of Contributors*

ANTONIS ANTONIADIS is Lecturer in Law, University of Durham and Durham European Law Institute

ANTHONY ARNULL is Professor of European Law and Director of the Institute of European Law, University of Birmingham

GEORGE A BERMANN is Jean Monnet Professor of European Union Law and Gellhorn Professor of Law, Columbia University School of Law

TIM CORTHAUT is Assistant at the Institute for European Law, Leuven University

PAUL CRAIG is Professor of English Law, St John's College, Oxford

MARISE CREMONA is Professor of European Commercial Law, Queen Mary, University of London

MIKE CUTHBERT is Senior Tutor in Law, University College Northampton

ADAM CYGAN is Lecturer in Law, Centre for European Law and Integration, Faculty of Law, University of Leicester

JENÖ CZUCZAI is Associate Professor, Faculty of Law, Károli Gáspár Protestant University, Budapest; visiting Professor, College of Europe, Brugge and Natolin, and Vice-President of the European Law Academy, Hungary.

EILEEN DENZA is Professor of Law, University College London

MICHAEL DOUGAN is Professor of European Law and Jean Monnet Chair at the University of Liverpool.

JULIA EISNER is Research Assistant and PhD Candidate, Birkbeck College, London

MICHELLE EVERSON is Lecturer in Law, Birkbeck College, London

CHRISTOPH HERRMANN is Associate Lecturer at the Chair for Public and European Law of the Ludwig-Maximilians-Universität, Munich

CHRIS HILSON is Reader in Law, University of Reading

PANOS KOUTRAKOS is Professor of European Law, University of Birmingham

HÉLÈNE LAMBERT is Lecturer in Law, University of Exeter

KOEN LENAERTS is Judge at the European Court of Justice and Professor of European Law, Leuven University

PAOLISA NEBBIA is Lecturer in Law, University of Southampton

STEVE PEERS is Professor of Law, University of Essex

CATHERINE PHUONG is Lecturer in Law, University of Newcastle

EMILY REID is Lecturer in Law, University of Sussex

BERNARD RYAN is Senior Lecturer in Law, University of Kent

FRANCIS SNYDER is Professor of Law, Université Aix-Marseille-III; Centennial Visiting Professor, London School of Economics; Professor, College of Europe; Co-director, Academy of International Trade Law (Macao, China)

TAKIS TRIDIMAS is the Sir John Lubbock Professor of Banking Law, at the Centre for Commercial Law Studies, Queen Mary College, University of London and Senior Legal Adviser to the EU Presidency held by Greece (January–June 2003)

SAMANTHA VELLUTI is Lecturer in Law, University of Manchester

ANGELA WARD is Reader in Law, University of Essex and Barrister of the Middle Temple

SARAH WILLIS is Senior Lecturer in Law, University College Northampton

# *Table of Cases*

### *European Court of Justice*

**Judgments**


Cases 15/62 and 17/62 *Producteurs de Fruits v Council* [1962] ECR 449 . . . . . 32
Case 25/62 *Plaumann v Commission* [1963] ECR 95. . . . . 19, 21, 38–39, 121, 212
Case 6/64 *Costa v ENEL* [1964] ECR 585 . . . . . 72, 268
Case 29/69 *Stauder v City of Ulm* [1969] ECR 419 . . . . . 187
Case 64/69 *Compagnie Française Commercial et Financière v Commission* [1970] ECR 221 . . . . . 211
Case 11/70 *Internationale Handelsgesellschaft mbH v Einfuhr- und Vorratstelle für Getreide und Futtermittel* [1970] ECR 1125 . . . . . 90, 187
Case 22/70 *Commission v Council (AETR)* [1971] ECR 263 . . . . . 297, 325, 329
Case 62/70 *Bock v Commission* [1971] ECR 897 . . . . . 121
Case 21-4/72 *International Fruit Company NV and others v Produktschap voor Groenten en Fruit* [1972] ECR 1279. . . . . 333
Case 34/73 *Variola v Amministrazione delle Finanze* [1973] ECR 981 . . . . . 86, 336
Case 41/74 *Van Duyn v Home Office* [1974] ECR 1337 . . . . . 224
Case 100/74 *CAM v Commission* [1975] ECR 1393 . . . . . 211
Case 26/76 *Metro v Commission* [1977] ECR 1875. . . . . 21
Case 41/76 *Donckerwolcke and others v Procureur de la République* [1976] ECR 1921 . . . . . 329
Case 51/76 *Verbond van nederlandse Ondernemingen v Inspecteur der Invoerrechten en Accijnzen* [1977] ECR 113 . . . . . 226
Case 29/77 *Roquette Frères v France* [1977] ECR 1835. . . . . 309
Case 139/79 *Maizena v Council* [1980] ECR 3393 . . . . . 58
Case 811/79 *Amministrazione delle Finanze dello Stato v Ariete* [1980] ECR 2545 . . . . . 34
Case 197/80 *Ludwigshafener Walzmühle Erling KG v Council and Commission* [1981] ECR 3211 . . . . . 309
Case 8/81 *Becker v Finanzamt Münster-Innenstadt* [1982] ECR 53. . . . . 224–25
Case 124/81 *Commission v UK* [1983] ECR 203. . . . . 313, 315
Case 210/81 *Schmidt v Commission* [1983] ECR 3045 . . . . . 21

Case 246/81 *Lord Bethell v Commission* [1982] ECR 2277. . . . . . . . . . 21
Case 11/82 *Piraiki-Patraiki v Commission* [1985] ECR 207 . . . . . 22, 121
Cases 35 and 36/82 *Morson & Jhanjhan v Netherlands* [1982] ECR 3723 . . . . . . . . . . . . . . . . . . . . . . . . . . . . . . . . . . . 352
Case 199/82 *Amministrazione dello Stato v San Giorgio* [1982] ECR 3595 . . . . . . . . . . . . . . . . . . . . . . . . . . . . . . . 220, 241
Case 264/82 *Timex Corporation v Council and Commission* [1985] ECR 849 . . . . . . . . . . . . . . . . . . . . . . . . . . . . . . . . . . . 341
Case 271/82 *Auer v Ministère Public* [1983] ECR 2727. . . . . . . . . . . . 224
Case 14/83 *Von Colson and Kamann v Land Nordrhein-Westfalen* [1984] ECR 1891 . . . . . . . . . . . . . . . 225–26, 245
Case 231/83 *Cullet v Leclerc* [1985] ECR 305 . . . . . . . . . . . . . . . . . . . 138
Case 240/83 *Procureur de la République v Association de Défence des Bruleurs de l'Huiles Usagées* [1985] ECR 531 . . . . . . . 306
Case 294/83 *Parti Ecologiste 'Les Verts' v European Parliament* [1986] ECR 1339 . . . . . . . . . . . . . . 19, 23, 25, 34, 54, 186
Case 44/84 *Hurd v Jones* [1986] ECR 29. . . . . . . . . . . . . . . . . . . . . . . 224
Case 75/84 *Metro v Commission* [1986] 3021 . . . . . . . . . . . . . . . . . . . . 21
Joined Cases 142/84 and 156/84 *BAT and Reynolds v Commission* [1987] ECR 4487 . . . . . . . . . . . . . . . . . . . . . . . . . . . . . . . . . . . 48
Case 152/84 *Marshall v Southampton and South-West Hampshire Area Health Authority* [1986] ECR 723 . . . . . . . . . . . . . . . . . . . . 255
Case 169/84 *Cofaz v Commission* [1986] ECR 391 . . . . . . . . . . . . . . . . 21
Case 222/84 *Marguerite Johnston v Chief Constable of the Royal Ulster Constabulary* [1986] ECR 1651 . . . . . . . . . . . . . . . . . . 25
Case 314/85 *Foto-Frost v Hauptzollampt Lübeck-Ost* [1987] ECR 4199. . . . . . . . . . . . . . . . . . . . . . . . . . . . . . 28, 209–10
Case 203/86 *Spain v Council* [1988] ECR 4563. . . . . . . . . . . . . . . . . . 309
Cases 302/86 *Commission v Denmark* [1988] ECR 4607 . . . . . . . . . . . . . . . . . . . . . . . . . . 305, 307, 310
Cases 305/86 and 160/87 *Neotype Techmashexport v Commission and Council* [1990] ECR I-2945 . . . . . . . . . . . . . . . . . . . . . . . . . . 21
Case 70/87 *Fediol v Commission* [1989] ECR 1781. . . . . . . 332, 340, 342
Case 302/87 *European Parlia8ment v Council* [1988] ECR 5615 . . . . . 20
Case C-379/87 *Groener v Minister for Education and City of Dublin Vocational Education Committee* [1989] ECR 3967 . . . . . . 247
Case 5/88 *Wachauf v Federal Republic of Germany* [1989] ECR 2609 . . . . . . . . . . . . . . . . . . . . . . . . . . . . . . . . . . 100
Case 70/88 *European Parliament v Council* [1990] ECR I-2041 . . . . . . . . . . . . . . . . . . . . . . . . . . . . . . . . 19, 20
Case 152/88 *Sofrimport v Commission* [1990] ECR I-2477. . . . . . . . . . . 22
Case 177/88 *Dekker v Stichting Vormingscentrum voor Jong Volwassenen* [1990] ECR I-3941 . . . . . . . . . . . . . . . . . . . . . . . 241, 253
Case 361/88 *Commission v Germany* [1991] ECR I-2567 . . . . . . . . . . 238

Case C-69/89 *Nakajima v Council* [1991] ECR I-2069 .... 340, 340, 342
Case C-169/89 *Gourmetterie van den Burg* [1990] ECR 2143....... 314
Case C-188/89 *Foster v British Gas* [1990] ECR I-3313 ........ 23, 245
Case C-213/89 *The Queen v Secretary of State for Transport ex parte Factortame* [1990] ECR I-2433 ....... 33, 35, 240
Case C-260/89 *ERT* [1991] ECR I-2925 .................... 100, 139
Case C-298/89 *Gibraltar v Council* [1993] ECR I-3605............. 22
Case C-300/89 *Commission v Council* [1991] ECR I-2867 .......... 58
Case C-309/89 *Codorniu v Council* [1994] ECR I-1853 .................... 22, 43, 52, 111, 121, 211
Case C-358/89 *Extramet Industrie v Council* [1991] ECR I-2501 ............................... 21, 22, 341
Case C-2/90 *Commission v Belgium (Belgian Waste)* [1992] ECR I-4431 ............................... 305, 307–8
Cases C-6/90 and C-9/90 *Francovich and Bonifaci v Italy* [1991] ECR I-5357 ....... 5, 35, 37, 225, 226, 239, 242–44, 246–57
Case C-56/90 *Commission v United Kingdom* [1993] ECR I-4109 ................................. 231–32
Case C-62/90 *Commission v Germany* [1992] ECR I-2575 ......... 136
Case C-159/90 *SPUC v Grogan* [1991] ECR I-4685 .............. 100
Case C-208/90 *Emmott v Minister for Social Welfare and Attorney General* [1991] ECR I-4269................................ 36
Case C-355/90 *Commission v Spain* [1993] ECR I-4221 ........ 229–30
Case C-370/90 *Singh* [1992] ECR I-4265....................... 352
Case C-97/91 *Oleificio Borelli SpA v Commission* [1992] ECR I-6313 ..................................... 217
Case C-155/91 *Commission v Council* [1993] ECR I-939 ........... 58
Case C-271/91 *Marshall v Southampton and South West Hampshire Areas Health Authority (Marshall II)* [1993] ECR I-4367 ..................................... 245
Case C-11/92 *The Queen v Secretary of State for Health ex parte Gallaher* [1993] ECR I-3545 .............................. 352
Case C-91/92 *Faccini Dori v Recreb Srl* [1994] ECR I-3325 .... 225, 255
Case C-128/92 *H J Banks & Co Ltd v British Coal Corporation* [1994] ECR I-1209 ......................... 224, 252–53, 255
Case C-188/92 *TWD Textilwerke Deggendorf v Germany* [1994] ECR I-833 ................................ 21, 220
Case C-236/92 *Comitato di Coordinamento per la Difesa della Cava and others v Regione Lombardia and others* [1994] ECR I-483 ................................. 227–28
Cases C-46/93 and C-48/93 *Brasserie du Pêcheur v Bundesrepublik Deutschland and the Queen v Secretary of State for Transport, ex parte Factortame* [1996] ECR I-1029 ................ 35, 241, 243–44, 246, 249–50

Case C-392/93 *The Queen v H M Treasury ex parte British Telecommunications plc* [1996] ECR I-1631 . . . . . . . . . . . . . . . 241, 250
Joined Cases C-430/93 and C-431/93 *Van Schijndel and Van Veen* [1995] I-4705. . . . . . . . . . . . . . . . . . . . . . . . . . . . . . . . . . 36
Case C-2/94 *Denkavit International BV v Kamer van Koophandel en Fabrieken voor Midden-Gelderland and Others* [1996] ECR I-2827 . . . . . . . . . . . . . . . . . . . . . . . . . . . . . . . . . . 243
Case C-5/94 *The Queen v Ministry of Agriculture, Fisheries and Food, ex parte Hedley Lomas* [1996] ECR I-2553 . . . . . . . . . . . . . . . . . . . . . . 241, 243, 245, 249–50
Case C-25/94 *Commission v Council (Re FAO)* [1996] ECR I-1469 . . . . . . . . . . . . . . . . . . . . . . . . . . . . . . . . . . 329
Case C-58/94 *Netherlands v Council* [1996] ECR I-2169 . . . . . . . . . . . 45
Case C-61/94 *Commission v Federal Republic of Germany* [1996] ECR I-3989 . . . . . . . . . . . . . . . . . . . . . . . . . . . . . . . . . . 335
Case C-84/94 *United Kingdom v Council* [1996] ECR I-5755 . . . . . . . 168
Case C-90/94 *Haahr Petroleum v Abenra Havn* [1997] ECR I-4085 . . . . . . . . . . . . . . . . . . . . . . . . . . . . . . . . . . 243
Cases C-178, C-179, and C-188 to C-190/94 *Dillenkofer v Bundesrepublik Deutschland* [1996] ECR I-4845 . . . . . . . 241, 249–50
Case C-212/94 *FMC v Intervention Board for Agricultural Produce and Ministry of Agriculture Fisheries and Food* [1996] ECR I-389 . . . . . . . . . . . . . . . . . . . . . . . . . . . 220, 240–41
Cases C-283/94 and 291–92/94 *Denkavit International v Bundesamt für Finanzen* [1996] ECR I-5063. . . . . . . . . . . . . . . . . . 249
Case C-44/95 *R v Secretary of State for the Environment, ex parte Royal Society for the Protection of Birds* [1996] ECR I-3805 . . . . . . . . . . . . . . . . . . . . . . . . . . . . . . . 229–30
Case C-52/95 *Commission v France* [1995] ECR I-4443 . . . . . . . . . . . 138
Case C-66/95 *The Queen v Secretary of State for Social Security ex parte Sutton* [1997] ECR I-2163 . . . . . . . . . . . . . . . . . . . . 242, 248
Case C-72/95 *Kraaijeveld v Gedeputeerde Staten van Zuid-Holland* [1996] ECR I-5403 . . . . . . . . . 36, 226–27, 229, 231–32
Case C-87/95 P *CNPAAP v Council* [1996] ECR I-2003 . . . . . . . . . . . . . . . . . . . . . . . . . . . . . . . 23, 28
Cases C-94 and C-95/95 *Bonifaci and Berto v INPS* [1997] ECR I-3969 . . . . . . . . . . . . . . . . . . . . . . . . . . . . . . 245, 249
Case C-107/95 P *Bundesverband der Bilanzbuchhalter v Commission* [1997] ECR I-947 . . . . . . . . . . . . . . . . . . . . . . . . . . . . . . . . . . . 48
Case C-127/95 *Norbrook Laboratories v Ministry of Agriculture, Fisheries and Food* [1998] ECR I-1531 . . . . . . . . . . . . . . . . . 244, 249
Case C-142/95 P *Associazione agricoltori della provincia di Rovigo and others v Commission* [1996] ECR I-6669 . . . . . . . . . . . . 21
Case C-171/95 *Tetik v Land Berlin* [1997] ECR I-329. . . . . . . . . . . . . 352

Case C-180/95 *Draehmpaehl v Urania Immobilienservice* [1997] ECR I-2195 . . . . . . . . . . . . . . . . . . . . . . . . . . . . . . 241, 247
Case C-188/95 *Fantask v Industrministeriet* [1997] ECR I-6783 . . . . . . . . . . . . . . . . . . . . . . . . . . 36, 240–41, 243
Cases C-192 to C-218/95 *Comateb and Others v Directeur générales des douanes et droits indirects* [1997] ECR I-165 . . . . 241–42
Case C-242/95 *GT-Link v de Danske Statsbaner* [1997] ECR I-4449 . . . . . . . . . . . . . . . . . . . . . . . . . . . . . . . . . . 244
Case C-265/95 *Commission v France* [1997] ECR I-6959 . . . . . . . 136–38
Case C-321/95 *UEAPME v Council* [1998] II ECR 2335 . . . . . . . . . . 212
Case C-368/95 *Familiapress v Bauer Verlag* [1997] ECR I-3689 . . . . . . . . . . . . . . . . . . . . . . . . . . . . . . . 100, 139
Case C-373/95 *Maso and Others v INPS* [1997] ECR I-4051 . . . . . . . 245
Case C-1/96 *The Queen v Minister of Agriculture, Fisheries and Food, ex parte Compassion in World Farming* [1998] ECR I-1251 . . . . . . . . . . . . . . . . . . . . . . . . . . . . . . . . . . 352
Case C-3/96 *Commission v Netherlands* [1998] ECR I-3031 . . . . . . . . 233
Case C-15/96 *Schöning-Kougebetopoulou v Freie und Hansestadt Hamburg* [1998] ECR I-47 . . . . . . . . . . . . . . . . . . . . 247
Case C-53/96 *Hermès International v FHT Marketing Choice BV* [1998] ECR I-3603 . . . . . . . . . . . . . . . . . . . . . . . . . . 343
Case C-54/96 *Dorsch Consul Ingenieursgesellschaft v Bundesbaugesellschaft Berlin* [1997] ECR I-4961 . . . . . . . . . . . . . . 242
Joined Cases C-64/96 and 65/96 *Land Nordrhein-Westfalen v Uecker and Jacquet* [1997] ECR I-3171. . . . . . . . . . . . . . . . . . . . . . 352
Case C-90/96 *Petrie and Others v Università degli studi di Verona and Bettoni* [1997] ECR I-6527. . . . . . . . . . . . . . . . . . . . . . 247
Case C-149/96 *Portugal v Council* [1999] ECR I-8395 . . . . . . . . 336, 340
Case C-231/96 *Edis v Ministero delle Finanze* [1998] ECR I-4951 . . . . . . . . . . . . . . . . . . . . . . . . . . . . . . . . . . 248
Case C-225/96 *Commission v Italy* [1997] ECR I-6887. . . . . . . . . . . . 234
Case C-319/96 *Brinkmann Tabakfabriken v Skatteministeriet* [1998] ECR I-5255 . . . . . . . . . . . . . . . . . . . . . . . . . . . . . . 244, 250
Case C-392/96 *Commission v Ireland* [1999] ECR I-5901. . . . . . . . . . 231
Case C-403/96 P *Glencore Grain Ltd v Commission* [1998] ECR I-2405 . . . . . . . . . . . . . . . . . . . . . . . . . . . . . . . . . . 121
Case C-67/97 *Criminal Proceedings Against Ditlev Bluhme (Danish Bees)* [1998] ECR I-8033 . . . . . . . . . . . . . . . . . . 305, 317–18
Case C-73/97 P *Comafrica and others v Commission* [1999] ECR I-185 . . . . . . . . . . . . . . . . . . . . . . . . . . . . . . . . . . . 211
Case C-120/97 *Upjohn Ltd v The Licensing Authority established by the Medicines Act 1968* [1999] ECR I-223 . . . . . . . . 236
Case C-131/97 *Carbonari v Università degli Studi di Bologna* [1999] ECR I-1103 . . . . . . . . . . . . . . . . . . . . . . . . . . . . . . 224, 240

Case C-140/97 *Rechberger and Greindl v Republic of Austria* [1999] ECR I-3499 . . . . . . . . . . 244, 250
Case C-185/97 *Coote v Granada Hospitality* [1998] ECR I-5199 . . . . . . . . . . 251
Case C-293/97 *R v Secretary of State for the Environment and Ministry of Agriculture, Fisheries and Food, ex parte Standley* [1999] ECR I-2603 . . . . . . . . . . 235
Case C-302/97 *Konle v Republic of Austria* [1999] ECR I-3099 . . . . . . . . . . 244, 250
Case C-346/97 *Braathens Sverige AB v Riksskatteverket* [1999] ECR I-3419 . . . . . . . . . . 225
Case C-365/97 *Commission v Italy* [1999] ECR I-7773 . . . . . 227–28, 233
Case C-371/97 *Gozza and Others* [2000] ECR I-7881 . . . . . . . . . . 244
Case C-387/97 *Commission v Greece* [2000] ECR I-5047 . . . . . . 126, 228
Case C-424/97 *Haim v Kassenzahnärztliche Vereinigung Nordrhein* [2000] ECR I-5123 . . . . . . . . . . 250, 252–53
Case C-435/97 *WWF v Autonome Provinz Bozen* [1999] ECR I-5613 . . . . . . . . . . 226–27
Case C-281/98 *Angonese* [2000] I-4139 . . . . . . . . . . 247
Case C-287/98 *Grand Duchy of Luxemburg v Berthe Linster* [2000] ECR I-6917 . . . . . . . . . . 226
Case C-303/98 *Sindicato de Medicos de Asistencia Publica (Simap) v Conselleria de Sanidad y Consumo de la Generalidad Valenciana* [2000] ECR I-7963 . . . . . . . . . . 225
C-352/98 P *Laboratoires Pharmaceutiques Bergaderm and Goupil v Commission* [2000] ECR I-05291 . . . . . . . . . . 250
Case C-371/98 *R v Secretary of State for the Environment, Transport and the Regions, ex parte First Corporate Shipping Ltd* [2000] ECR I-9235 . . . . . . . . . . 230
Case C-376/98 *Germany v Parliament and Council (Tobacco case)* [2000] ECR I-8419 . . . . . 23, 73, 134–5, 163, 168, 238
Case C-379/98 *PreussenElektra AG v Schleswag AG* [2001] ECR I-2099 . . . . . . . . . . 305, 307–10, 317–19
Cases C-397 and 410/98 *Metallgesellschaft v Commissioners of Inland Revenue and HM Attorney General* [2001] ECR I-1727 . . . . . . . . . . 243
Cases C-441 and 442/98 *Kapniki Mikhailidis v IKA* [2000] ECR I-7145 . . . . . . . . . . 241
Case C-449/98 P *IECC v Commission* [2001] ECR I-3875 . . . . . . . . . . 48
Case C-467/98 *Commission v Denmark* (open skies) [2002] ECR I-9519 . . . . . . . . . . 265
Cases 63/99 *R v Secretary of State for the Home Department, ex parte Gloszczuk and Gloszczuk* [2001] ECR I-6369 . . . . . . . . . . 381
Case C-67/99 *Commission v Ireland* [2001] ECR I-5757 . . . . . . . . . . 234

Case C-74/99 *The Queen v Secretary of State for Health ex parte Imperial Tobacco Ltd* [2000] ECR I-8599 . . . . . . . . . . . . . . . . . . . . . 23
Joined Cases C-122/99 P and C-125/99 P *D and Kingdom of Sweden v Council of the European Union* [2001] ECR I-4319 . . . . . . . . . . . . . . . . . . . . . . . . . . . . . . . . 444
Case C-150/99 *Svenska Staten v Stockholm Lindöpark* [2001] ECR I-493 . . . . . . . . . . . . . . . . . . . . . . . . . . . . . . . . . . 243, 249
Case C-173/99 *The Queen v Secretary of State for Trade and Industry ex parte BECTU* [2001] ECR I-4881. . . . . . . . . . . . . . . . . 440
Case C-235/99 *R v Secretary of State for the Home Department, ex parte Kondova* [2001] ECR I-6427 . . . . . . . . . . . . 381
Case C-257/99 *R v Secretary of State for the Home Department, ex parte Barkoci and Malik* [2001] ECR I-6557 . . . . . 381
Case C-317/99 *Kloosterboer Rotterdam BV v Minister van Landbouw, Natuurbeheer en Visserij* [2001] ECR I-9863 . . . . . . . . 342
Case C-353/99 P *Council v Hautala* [2001] ECR I-9565 . . . . . 44, 46, 440
Case C-453/99 *Courage v Crehan* [2001] ECR I-6297. . . . . . . . . 242, 254
Case C-459/99 *MRAX* [2002] ECR I-6591 . . . . . . . . . . . . . . . . . . . . . 352
Case C-474/99 *Commission v Spain* [2002] ECR I-5293 . . . . . . . . . . . 231
Joined Cases C-20/00 and C-64/00 *Booker Aquaculture Ltd trading as Marine Harvest Mc Connell & Hydro Seafood GSP Ltd v The Scottish Ministers* [2003] ECR I-7411 . . . . . . . . . . . 440
Case C-50/00 P *Unión de Pequeños Agricultores v Council* [2002] ECR I-6677 . . . . . . . . . . . 21, 24, 25, 27, 28–29, 32, 33, 37, 38, 39, 40, 42, 63, 110, 120, 123, 124, 209, 214
Case C-60/00 *Carpenter v Secretary of State* [2002] ECR I-6279 . . . . . . . . . . . . . . . . . . . . . . . . 100, 136, 139, 352
Case C-62/00 *Marks & Spencer* [2002] ECR I-6325 . . . . . . . . . . . . . . 240
Case C-94/00 *Roquette Frères v Directeur général de la concurrence, de la consommation et de la répression des fraudes* [2002] ECR I-9011 . . . . . . . . . . . . . . . . . . . . . . . . . . . 100
Case C-112/00 *Schmidberger, Internationale Transporte und Planzüge v Austria* [2003] ECR I-5659 . . . 101, 113, 136, 137, 139–41, 250, 296, 305
Case C-118/00 *Larsy v Inasti* [2001] ECR I-5063 . . . . . . . . . 250, 252–53
Case C-129/00 *Commission v Italy*, Judgment of 9 December 2003. . . . . . . . . . . . . . . . . . . . . . . . . . . . . . . . . . . . . . . 36
Case C-142/00 P *Commission v Nederlandse Antillen* [2003] ECR I-3483 . . . . . . . . . . . . . . . . . . . . . . . . . . . . . . 22, 27, 39
Case C-258/00 *Commission v France* [2002] ECR I-5959 . . . . . . . 231–32
Case C-312/00 P *Commission v Camar and Tico* [2002] ECR I-0000 . . . . . . . . . . . . . . . . . . . . . . . . . . 39, 52, 63, 250
Case C-453/00 *Kühne & Heitz*, Judgment of 13 January 2004 . . . . . . 240

Case C-472/00 P *Commission v Fresh Marine* [2003] ECR I-7541 . . . . . 250
Case C-108/01 *Consorzio del Prosciutto di Parma* [2003] ECR I-5121 . . . . . 252
Case C-109/01 *Secretary of State for the Home Department v Akrich*, Judgment of 23 September 2003 . . . . . 352
Cases C-159/01–197/01 et al *Netherlands v EP and Council* (not yet decided) . . . . . 440
Case C-211/01 *Commission v Council (Road Transport Agreement)*, Judgment of 11 September 2003 . . . . . 297
Case C-224/01 *Köbler v Austria,* Judgment of 30 September 2003 . . . . . 35, 37
Case C-276/01 *Steffensen* [2003] ECR I-3735 . . . . . 100
Case C-281/01 *Commission v Council (Re Energy Star Agreement)* [2002] ECR I-12049 . . . . . 324
Case C-406/01 *Germany v European Parliament and Council* [2002] ECR I-4561 . . . . . 29
Case 486/01 P-R and 488/01 P-R *Front National and Martinez v European Parliament* [2002] ECR I-1843 . . . . . 59
Case C-488/01 P *Martinez v European Parliament*, Judgment of 11 November 2003 . . . . . 59
Case C-491/01 *The Queen v Secretary of State for Health ex parte British American Tobacco Ltd* [2002] ECR I-11453 . . . . . 29, 30, 41, 63, 124, 217
Cases C-93/02P and C-94/02P, *Biret International SA and Etablissements Biret et Cie SA v Council of the European Union*, Judgment of 30 September 2003 . . . . . 14, 343
Case C-141/02 P *Commission v Max.mobil Telekommunikation Service GmbH* [2002] . . . . . 47
Case C-162/02 P *Rothley and others v European Parliament* [2002] . . . . . 58
Case C-234/02 P *European Ombudsman v Lamberts*, Opinion of 3 July 2003 . . . . . 50
Case C-263/02 P *Commission v Jégo Quéré*, Opinion of 10 July 2003 . . . . . 27, 37, 40, 42–43
Case C-208/03 P-R *Le Pen v European Parliament*, Judgment of 31 July 2003 . . . . . 60

**Opinions**

Opinion 1/75 *Local Standard Cost* [1975] ECR 1355 . . . . . 326
Opinion 1/91 *EEA Agreement (No 1)* [1991] ECR I-6079 . . . . . 299
Opinion 2/91 *ILO* [1993] ECR I-1061 . . . . . 328
Opinion 1/94 *WTO*[1994] ECR I-5276 . . . . . 322–23, 325, 328–29, 338

Opinion 1/94 at I-5282 . . . . . . . . . . 327
Opinion 2/94 *Accession of the European Communities to the European Convention on Human Rights* [1996] ECR I-1759 . . . . . . . . . . 95, 105, 107, 299
Opinion 2/00 *Cartagena Protocol on Biosafety* [2001] ECR I-9713 . . . . . . . . . . 297

## European Court of First Instance

Case T-24/90 *Automec v Commission* [1992] ECR II-2223 . . . . . . . . . . 48
Joined Cases T-481/93 and T-484/93 *Exporteurs in Levende Varkens and Others v Commission* [1995] ECR II-2941 . . . . . . . . . . 52
Case T-489/93 *Unifruit Hellas v Commission* [1994] ECR II-1201 . . . . 22
Case T-585/93 *Greenpeace and Others v Commission* [1995] ECR II-2205 . . . . . . . . . . 52
Case T-174/95 *Svenska Journalistförbundet v Council* [1998] ECR II-2289 . . . . . . . . . . 44–45
Case T-95/96 *Gestevisíon Telecino v Commission* [1998] ECR II-3407 . . . . . . . . . . 48
Case T-135/96 *UEAPME v Council* [1998] ECR II-2335 . . . . . . 55–57, 63
Case T-14/98 *Hautala v Council* [1999] ECR II-2489 . . . . . . . . . . 44, 46
Case T-172/98, T-175/98 and T-177/98 *Salamander v European Parliament and Council* [2000] ECR II-2487 . . . . . . . . . . 22–23, 26, 28, 111, 217
Case T-173/98 *Unión de Pequeños Agricultores v Council* [1999] ECR II-3357 . . . . . . . . . . 23, 27, 28, 30–32
Case T-20/99 *Denkavit Nederland BV v Commission* [2000] ECR II-3011 . . . . . . . . . . 46
Case T-13/99 *Pfizer Animal Health SA v Council* [2002] ECR II-3305 . . . . . . . . . . 52–53
Case T-54/99 *Max.mobil Telekommunikation Service v Commission* [2002] ECR II-313 . . . . . . . . . . 25, 47, 48, 49, 440
Case T-103/99 *Associazione delle Cantine Sociali Venete v European Ombudsman and European Parliament* [2000] ECR II-4165 . . . . . . . . . . 50
Joined Cases T-222/99, T-327/99 and T-329/99 *Jean-Claude Martinez, Charles de Gaulle, Front national and Emma Bonino and Others v European Parliament* [2001] ECR II-2823 . . . . . . . . . . 58, 59, 62–63
Case T-17/00 *Rothley v European Parliament* [2002] ECR II-579 . . . . . . . . . . 58–59
Case T-17/00 R *Willy Rothley and Others v European Parliament* [2000] ECR II-2085 . . . . . . . . . . 58, 59

Case T-111/00 *British American Tobacco (Investments) Ltd v Commission* [2001] ECR II-2997 . . . . . . . . . . . . . . . . . . . . . . . . . . . 46
Case T-155/02 R *VVG International Handelsgesellschaft GmbH v Commission* [2002] ECR II-3239 . . . . . . . . . . . . . . . . . . . . 27
Case T-174/00 *Biret International SA v Council* [2002] ECR II-17 . . . . . . . . . . . . . . . . . . . . . . . . . . . . . . . . . . . . . . . . . . . 14
Case T-177/01 *Jégo-Quéré v Commission* [2002] ECR II-2365 . . . . . . . . . . . . . 24–27, 32, 111, 122–23, 214, 440
Case T-209/00 *Lamberts v European Ombudsman* [2002] ECR II-765 . . . . . . . . . . . . . . . . . . . . . . . . . . . . . . . . . . . . . . . . . . 50
Case T-209/00 *Lamberts v European Ombudsman* [2002] ECR II-2203 . . . . . . . . . . . . . . . . . . . . . . . . . . . . . . . . . . . 50–2, 63
Case T-210/00 *Etablissements Biret et Cie SA v Council* [2002] ECR II-47 . . . . . . . . . . . . . . . . . . . . . . . . . . . . . . . . . . . . . . . . . . . 14
Case T-211/00 *Kuijer v Council* [2002] ECR II-485 . . . . . . . . . . . . . . 44–5
Case T-212/00 *Nuove Industrie Molisane Srl v Commission*, Judgment of 30 January 2002 . . . . . . . . . . . . . . . . . . . . . . . . . . . . . 218
Case T-223/01 *Japan Tobacco JT International SA v European Parliament and Council* [2002] ECR II-3259 . . . . . . . . . . . . . . . 29, 213
Case T-295/01 *Nordmilch eG v Office for Harmonisation in the Internal Market (Trade Marks and Designs) (OHIM)*, Judgment of 15 October 2003 . . . . . . . . . . . . . . . . . . . . . . . . . . . . . . . . . . . . . 212
Case T-306/01 R *Aden v Council and Commission* [2002] ECR II-2387 . . . . . . . . . . . . . . . . . . . . . . . . . . . . . . . . . . . . . . . . . 64
Case T-311/00 *British American Tobacco (Investments) Ltd v Commission* [2002] ECR II-2781 . . . . . . . . . . . . . . . . . . . . . . . . . . 47
Case T-353/00 R *Jean-Marie Le Pen v European Parliament* [2001] ECR II-125 . . . . . . . . . . . . . . . . . . . . . . . . . . . . . . . . . . . . . 58, 60

*European Court of Human Rights*

*A v United Kingdom*, Application No 25599/94, 23 Sept 1998, Reports 1998 VI, 2692, 27 EHRR 611 . . . . . . . . . . . 372
*Ahmed v Austria*, Application No 25964/94, 17 Dec 1998, Reports 1996 VI, 2195, 24 EHRR 278 . . . . . . . . . . . . . . . . . . . . . . . 371
*Cantoni v France*, Application No 17862/91, 15 Nov 1996, Reports 1996 V . . . . . . . . . . . . . . . . . . . . . . . . . . . . . . . . . . . . . . . . 107
*Chahal v United Kingdom*, Application No 22414/93, 15 Nov 1996, Reports 1996 V, 1831, 23 EHRR 413. . . . . . . . . . . . 366
*Cruz Varas v Sweden*, Application No 15576/89, 20 March 1991, 14 EHRR 1 . . . . . . . . . . . . . . . . . . . . . . . . . . . . . 371
*Geouffre de la Pradelle v France*, Application No 12964/87, 16 Dec 1992, Series A Judgments and Decisions, Series A no 253-B (1993) . . . . . . . . . . . . . . . . . . . . . . . . . . . . . . . . . . . . 210

*Goodwin v United Kingdom*, Application No 28957/95, 11 July 2002, (2002) 35 EHRR 18 . . . . . . . . . . . . . . . . . . . . . . . . . . 96
*Handyside v United Kingdom*, 7 Dec 1996, Series A No 24, (1979–80) 1 EHRR 737. . . . . . . . . . . . . . . . . . . . . . . . . . . . . . . . 101
*Hatami v Sweden*, Application No 32448/96. . . . . . . . . . . . . . . . . . . . 366
*HLR v France,* Application No 24573/94 . . . . . . . . . . . . . . . . . . 366, 367
*Ireland v UK*, Application No 5310/71, 18 January 1978, 2 EHRR 25 . . . . . . . . . . . . . . . . . . . . . . . . . . . . . . . . . . . . . . 371
*Kudla v Poland* (2002) 35 EHRR 11 . . . . . . . . . . . . . . . . . . . . . . . . . . 101
*Matthews v United Kingdom* (1999) 28 EHRR 361. . . . . . . . . . . . . . . 107
*Nsona v The Netherlands*, Application No 23366/94 . . . . . . . . . . . . . 371
*Osman v United Kingdom*, Application No 23452/94, Reports 1998 VIII, 3124, 29 EHRR 245 . . . . . . . . . . . . . . 256, 371–72
*Posti and Rahko v Finland*, Application No 27824/95, 24 Sept 2002 . . . . . . . . . . . . . . . . . . . . . . . . 26, 31, 41, 43, 64, 111, 122
*Selcuk and Asker v Turkey*, Application No 23184/94, Reports 1998 II, 891, 26 EHRR 477 . . . . . . . . . . . . . . . . . . . . . . . . 367
*Selmouni v France,* Application No 25803/94, 28 July 1999 . . . . . . . . 371
*Smith and Grady*, 27 September 1999, (2000) 29 EHRR 493 . . . . . . . 238
*Soering v United Kingdom*, Application No 14038/88, 7 July 1989, 11 EHRR 439 . . . . . . . . . . . . . . . . . . . . . . . . . . . . . . . 366
*Vilvarajah v United Kingdom*, Application No 3163/87, 30 Oct 1991, 14 EHRR 248 . . . . . . . . . . . . . . . . . . . . . . . . . . . . 366, 367
*Z v United Kingdom,* 10 May 2001. . . . . . . . . . . . . . . . . . . . . . . . . . . . . 256

*WTO Dispute Settlement Body*

WT/DS8/AB/R, WT/DS10/AB/R, WT/DS11/AB/R *Japan — Alcoholic Beverages II*. . . . . . . . . . . . . . . . . . . . . . . . . . . . . 331
WT/DS16 *European Communities — Importation, distribution and sale of bananas (Complaint brought by Guatemala, Honduras, Mexico, US)* . . . . . . . . . . . . . . . . . . . . . . . . . . . . 339, 344
WT/DS26 *European Communities — Measures concerning meat and meat products (Hormones) (Complaint brought by US)* . . . . . . . . . . . . . . . . . . . . . . . . . . . . . . . . . . . . 14, 339, 344
WT/DS37 *Portugal — Patent protection under the Industrial Property Act (Complaint by the United States)* . . . . . . . . . . . . . 334–35
WT/DS48 *European Communities — Measures concerning meat and meat products (Hormones) (Complaint brought by Canada)* . . . . . . . . . . . . . . . . . . . . . . . . . . . . . . . . . . . . . . . . 14
WT/DS58/AB/R *WTO Appellate Body, United States — Import prohibition of certain shrimp and shrimp products* . . . . . . . . . . . . . 317
WT/DS62 *European Communities — Customs classification of certain computer equipment* . . . . . . . . . . . . . . . . . . . . . . . . . . . . 334

WT/DS67 *United Kingdom — Customs classification of certain computer equipment* . . . . . . . . . . . . . . . . . . . . . . . . . 333, 334
WT/DS68 *Ireland — Customs classification of certain computer equipment* . . . . . . . . . . . . . . . . . . . . . . . . . . . . . . . . . . . . . . . 334
WT/DS80 *Belgium — Measures affecting commercial telephone services (Complaint by the United States)* . . . . . . . . . . . . . . . . . . . . 334
WT/DS82 *Ireland — Measures affecting the grant of copyright and neighbouring rights (Complaint by the United States)* . . . . . . . . . . . 334
WT/DS83 *Denmark — Measures affecting the enforcement of intellectually property rights (Complaint by the United States)*. . . . . . . . . . . . . . . . . . . . . . . . . . . . . . . . . . . 334–35
WT/DS86 *Sweden — Measures affecting the enforcement of intellectual property rights (Complaint by the United States)*. . . . . . . . . . . . . . . . . . . . . . . . . . . . . . . . . . . 334–35
WT/DS108 *United States — Tax treatment of "Foreign Sales Corporations" (Complaint brought by the EC)* . . . . . . . . . . . . 331, 340
WT/DS114 *Canada — Patent protection of pharmaceutical products (Complaint by the EC and its Member States)* . . . . . . . . . . . . . . . . . 332
WT/DS124 *European Communities — Enforcement of intellectual property rights for motion pictures and television programmes (Complaint by the United States)* . . . . . . . . . . . . . . . . . . . . . . . . . . 334
WT/DS125 *Greece — Enforcement of intellectual property rights for motion pictures and television programmes (Complaint by the United States)* . . . . . . . . . . . . . . . . . . . . . . . . . . 334
WT/DS128 *Netherlands — Certain income tax measures constituting subsidies (Complaint by the United States)*. . . . . . . . . . 334
WT/DS129 *Greece — Certain income tax measures constituting subsidies (Complaint by the United States)* . . . . . . . . . . . . . . . . . . 334
WT/DS131 *France — Certain income tax measures constituting subsidies (Complaint by the United States)* . . . . . . . . . . . . . . . . . . 334
WT/DS135 *European Communities — Measures affecting asbestos and asbestos- containing products (Complaint by Canada)* . . . . . . . . . . . . . . . . . . . . . . . . . . 331, 335
WT/DS141 *European Communities — Anti-dumping measures on imports of cotton-type bed-linen from India* . . . . . . . . . . . . . . . . . . 341
WT/DS153 *European Communities — Patent protection for pharmaceutical and agricultural chemical products (Complaint by Canada)*. . . . . . . . . . . . . . . . . . . . . . . . . . . . . . . . . . . . . . . . . . . 335
WT/DS160 *United States — Section 110(5) of US Copyright Act* . . . . 332
WT/DS172 *European Communities — Measures relating to the development of a flight management system* . . . . . . . . . . . . . . . . . . 334
WT/DS173 *France — Measures relating to the development of a flight management system* . . . . . . . . . . . . . . . . . . . . . . . . . . . . . . 334

WT/DS186 *US Section 337 of the Tariff Act of 1930 and the amendments thereto (Complaint by the EC and its Member States)* . . . . 332
WT/DS210 *Belgium — Administration of measures establishing customs duties for rice (Complaint by the United States)* . . . . 333, 334
WT/DS246 *European Communities — Conditions for the granting of tariff preferences to developing countries (Complaint brought by India)* . . . . 340
WT/DS291, WT/DS292, WT/DS293 *European Communities — Measures affecting the approval and marketing of biotech products (Complaints brought by United States, Canada and Argentina respectively)* . . . . 340
WT/DS294 *United States — Laws, regulations and methodology for calculating dumping margins ("zeroing") (Complaint brought by the EC)* . . . . 342
WT/DS2/R, and AB-1996-1 WT/DS2/AB1R *Reformulated Gasoline, US Standards for Reformulated and Conventional Gasoline* . . . . 315
*Thailand — Restrictions of importation of and internal taxes on cigarettes*, Report of the Panel Adopted on 7 November 1990 (DS10/R-37S) (BISD 37S/200) . . . . 313
*Tuna-Dolphin I* BISD 40S/155 (DS21/R) (not adopted) Reproduced in (1991) 30 (ILM) 1594 . . . . 314, 315
*Tuna-Dolphin II* (1994) 33 ILM 839 . . . . 314, 315
*US Prohibition of Imports of Tuna Canada — Measures affecting exports of unprocessed herring and salmon* BISD 35 S (1988) 98 . . . . 313
*US Prohibition of Imports of Tuna and Tuna Products from Canada*, BISD 29S/81 Report Adopted 22/02/1982 . . . . 313

## *National Courts*

**Denmark**

*Hanne Norup Carlsen and Others v the Prime Minister* [1999] 3 CMLR 854 . . . . 141

**England**

*Associated Provincial Picture Houses v Wednesbury Corporation* [1948] 1 KB 223 . . . . 5, 237
*Barrett v Enfield LBC* [1999] 3 All ER 193 . . . . 256
*Clark v University of Lincolnshire and Humberside* [2000] 3 All ER 752 . . . . 256

*Kacaj v Secretary of State for the Home Department* [2002] Imm AR p 213 . . . . . . 365
*Horvath v Secretary of State for the Home Department* [2000] 3 WLR 391A . . . . . . 369
*Horvath v Secretary of State for the Home Department* [2000] 3 WLR 382G . . . . . . 370
*Horvath v Secretary of State for the Home Department* [2001] 1 AC 489 (HL), [2000] 3 WLR 379 . . . . . . 370, 372
*O'Reilly v Mackman* [1982] 3 All ER 1124 . . . . . . 256
*Phelps v Hillingdon LBC* [2001] 2 AC 619 . . . . . . 256
*R v Secretary of State for the Home Department, ex parte Sivakumaran* [1988] 1 All ER 365
*R v Secretary of State for the Environment, ex parte Kingston Upon Hull City Council and ex parte Bristol City Council and Woodspring District Council* [1996] Env LR 248 . . . . . . 230
*R v Secretary of State for the Home Department, ex p Adan* 37 ILM 1090 (1998) . . . . . . 366
*(Regina) Hoxha v Special Adjudicator* [2002] EWCA Civ 1403 . . . . . . 365, 369
*R v Secretary of State for Foreign and Commonwealth Affairs ex parte Lord Rees-Mogg* [1994] 1 All ER 457 [1993] 3 CMLR 101 . . . . . . 263
*R v Chief Constable of Sussex ex parte International Trader's Ferry Ltd* [1999] 2 AC 418 . . . . . . 136, 139
*Stovin v Wise* [1996] AC 923 . . . . . . 256
*X (Minors) v Bedfordshire CC* [1995] 2 AC 633 . . . . . . 256

**Germany**

*Brunner and Others*, Case 2 BvR 2134/92 & 2159/92, [1994] 1 CMLR 57 (German Constitutional Court, 12 Oct, 1993) . . . . . . 72, 91, 141, 175, 178, 192, 194, 263

# 1

# *Introduction*

TAKIS TRIDIMAS

THE CONTRIBUTIONS CONTAINED in this volume fall into two broad categories: Constitutional law of the EU, and external relations. These areas are key components of contemporary Union law and policy and give rise to some of the most important challenges that the Union currently faces.

At the beginning of the new millennium, the Union finds itself in constitutional turmoil. Over the last twenty five years, there have been eight major constitutional revisions, which include four waves of accession and four substantive revisions of the founding treaties. In addition, the draft Treaty establishing a Constitution for Europe spearheads further reforms. There is no nation state which has had its constitution revised so frequently in such a short period of time. This constant need for revisions and adjustments reflects the quest for optimal structures, procedures, and rules to make the project of European integration workable and sustainable, but also, equally importantly, the quest for Union legitimacy.

The draft Treaty establishing a Constitution for Europe was adopted by the European Convention in June 2003 and formally submitted to the European Council in Rome on 18 July 2003. It formed the basis of negotiations in the Intergovernmental Conference, which began under the Italian Presidency on 4 October 2003, but the European Council held in Brussels on 12 December 2003 failed to reach agreement on the final text. The major stumbling block proved to be the allocation of voting rights in the Council of Ministers. There appears to be firm political commitment to re-open negotiations and it is reasonable to expect that a compromise will be reached.

The proposed Constitution represents a veritable effort to respond to the Laeken agenda. Although its primary purpose is to clarify rather than to reform, it makes important changes to the institutional structure and revisits the vertical and horizontal division of powers, ie the division of competence between the Union and the Member States and the relations between the EU institutions. The main challenges faced by the constitution, which will ultimately determine its success, are functionality and legitimacy, ie to ensure that the EU can function as a political and economic Union of sovereign states and to engage the people of Europe with the organs of supra-national government bridging what is widely perceived to be a legitimacy gap.

The proposed constitution, however, is not the only challenge that the Union faces today. As from 1 May 2004, the Union comprises 25 States and its population increases from 375 million to 450 million, leading to the largest internal market in the world. This enlargement is unprecedented in terms of volume, diversity, and complexity. It has been hailed as a defining point in European history, ending centuries of divisions, and marks a new chapter in European integration. Linked to the enlargement and the constitutional debate are the external relations of the Union. In no other time since the establishment of the Communities has the EU been preoccupied so much with its position in the world. The Laeken Declaration itself identified the importance of the role that the Union should play in a globalised world as a force of peace, stability, economic development and democracy. The chapters contained in this volume identify and discuss key issues pertaining to constitutional law, enlargement, and the political and trade relations of the Union with the outside world.

## CONSTITUTIONAL LAW

In the field of constitutional law, the authors explore issues pertaining to the relations between the Union and the Member States, the relations between the institutions of the EU, the role of the European Court of Justice, the protection of human rights, and remedies. The draft Constitutional Treaty is a primary point of reference.

Snyder identifies three challenges that the development of a true EU Constitution faces. He calls those respectively the challenge of ordinary people, the challenge of empires, and the challenge of sites. By the challenge of ordinary people, he means that the Constitution must not engage only with the concerns of the elite but also meet the aspirations of the ordinary people and be perceived by them as their fundamental law. The second challenge refers to globalisation: In our era, sovereignty has acquired new forms embracing national and supra-national entities. The EU occupies its own place in the 'pyramid of global constitution' but how does the wider economic, political and social context affect its liberal post-war values? The third challenge refers to relations between sites of governance and raises the question of how the EU should manage rules originating from other sources of power, especially the WTO.

Lenaerts and Corthaut assess the contribution of judicial review to the development of European constitutionalism and examine, in wider terms, the role of the Community judicature in enhancing democracy and legitimacy. They provide a critical analysis of recent case law on the *locus standi* of individuals under Article 230(4) EC, and discuss the amendments proposed by the draft Constitutional Treaty. They argue in favour of a liberalisation of *locus standi*, a view which, notably, has recently been echoed by the House of Lords European Union Committee.

The division of powers between the Union and the Member States is central to the constitutional debate and closely related to the favourite themes of the Laeken declaration, namely, legitimacy, accountability, and legal certainty. Bermann assesses the provisions of the draft Constitution on competence. Their intention is primarily to explain and restate rather than to modify. The draft Constitution however enhances the role of subsidiarity and grants national parliaments political and judicial means to control the compatibility of Union law with that principle. Whatever the advantages or drawbacks of these provisions, the relative power of national governments and Union institutions cannot be assessed in isolation. It can only be evaluated by reference to the detailed provisions of Part III of the draft Constitution which serve as the bases of Union legislation and also, equally importantly, by reference to institutional, political and judicial practice. Surely, as Bermann points out, the devil is in the detail.

A criticism often levelled against the Community is that it lacks a coherent system of hierarchy of norms. The draft Constitutional Treaty takes steps to redress this by providing for new provisions on the legal acts of the Union. This is one of the most innovative parts of the draft Constitution. As Craig points out, the types of EU norm and the hierarchy between them have broader implications for the inter-institutional balance of powers within the EU and also for the vertical division of competence between the Union and the Member States. They are closely linked to the themes of legitimacy, democracy and separation of powers. The provisions of the draft Constitution may result in a shift of power in favour of the Parliament, which benefits through the extension of the co-decision procedure, and the Commission, which has ample regulatory discretion and is subject to relatively little control by the Council and the Parliament.

Arnull focuses on the protection of fundamental rights in Europe's new constitutional order. He hails the inclusion of the Charter in the draft Constitution as an important development but points out its drawbacks and limitations. There is some unnecessary or even harmful duplication between the provisions of the Charter and provisions included elsewhere in the Constitution. Arnull argues in favour of the accession of the Union to the European Convention for the Protection of Human Rights but, ultimately, the human rights culture matters as much as, if not more than, the legal instruments themselves. It is the way the government, the civil service, and the courts perceive and apply human rights that makes the difference.

Tridimas assesses the way the draft Constitution affects the function and jurisdiction of the European Court of Justice. Do its provisions owe more to a federal or to an inter-governmental model? There is no appetite for wholesale reform but the draft Constitution, countenanced by the Court's own case law on human rights, enhances its position as the Supreme Court of the Union.

Cuthbert and Willis place the role of the Commission in a historical context. They review proposals made for the reform of the Commission over the last twenty years and examine themes of democracy and good governance. Cygan reviews the role of national parliaments in the EU's constitutional order. He assesses their monitoring role over EU affairs as a form of substitute sovereignty and casts a critical eye on the Protocol on subsidiarity and proportionality which is included in the draft Constitutional Treaty. He concludes that national parliaments will have an important role to play in the EU not so much as legislators but as facilitators of democracy and accountability, ie by encouraging participation of civil society, promoting the accountability of EU institutions, and monitoring the effects of Union law at national level.

Ryan starts from the premise that, in the EU constitutional context, the Member States are the masters of the Treaties. Respect for democracy dictates that legitimacy of constitution-building at Union level lies first and foremost with the nation-states on whose consent the EU must be based. Inspired by a model based on Rawls's version of social contract, he understands consent in terms of the hypothetical outcome of idealised negotiations between Member States. Under his construct, Member States are expected to try and ensure the achievement of their common objectives whilst retaining as much of their discretion as possible. They seek to achieve this by placing limits on EU powers and ensuring that the EU does not violate their core constitutional attributes, such as respect for democracy and human rights.

Everson and Eisner view the constitutional processes of the EU from a more critical perspective. Based on empirical evidence provided by interviews with English judges and barristers, they suggest that the process of adjudication is based on a formalistic understanding of the origins and force of law which is divorced from the political processes and does not do justice to the proposed EU Constitution.

The remaining contributions in this part of the volume concentrate on remedies. Ward assesses the extent to which the draft Constitution resolves the problems associated with the effective protection of individuals before the Union courts, in particular, their capacity to challenge Union measures. Her main tenet is that *locus standi* of individuals should be linked to the procedure for the adoption of Community acts. Thus, legislative acts, owing to their democratic credentials, should remain immune from direct challenge by individuals. Regulatory acts, by contrast, should be open to challenge before the CFI. Ward goes further and argues that, provided that they can show an interest in the outcome of the proceedings, individuals should have *locus standi* to challenge before the CFI all non-legislative measures. National courts, by contrast, should remain the primary fora for initiating challenges by individuals against the validity of legislative acts.

Hilson examines the effects of directives as instruments of legality review, ie in circumstances where a directive is not sufficiently specific to grant a right but delimits Member State choices and thus permits judicial review of the way the national authorities have exercised their discretion. Such legality review can be carried out not only in the context of enforcement proceedings under Article 226 EC but also where individuals invoke directives before national courts. The intensity of review depends on the EU measure applicable. Hilson argues that, where the Court reviews the compatibility of national measures with environmental directives, it should not rely on a *Wednesbury* — type test of unreasonableness, ie whether Member States have manifestly exceeded their discretion, but apply a stricter degree of scrutiny in view of the importance of environmental protection.

Finally, Dougan invokes the public — private law distinction to ascertain the proper scope of the *Francovich* principle. He argues that state liability in damages should remain a remedy where an authority violates its public law duties. By contrast, where an authority breaches Community law acting in a private law capacity (eg as an employer), liability should be determined on the basis of the rules of Community law which are breached *per se* or according to the fault criteria suitable to the specific private law field in question.

## EXTERNAL RELATIONS

In the field of external relations, the contributions centre on the following themes: the development of the Union's common foreign, security, and defence policies, relations with the WTO, immigration and asylum policy, and the challenges of enlargement.

Denza reviews the provisions of the draft Constitutional Treaty on the common foreign and security policy and assesses the extent to which they mark a transition from the intergovernmental model to a more *communautaire* one. The draft Constitutional Treaty seems, at least in some respects, to honour the Union's aspirations of nationhood by strengthening its presence as an international actor but, in fact, the nature and effect of the Union's powers remain unclear. Those looking for a more precise delimitation of powers between the EU and the Member States as promised at Nice may find little comfort in the provisions of the draft Constitution. Denza thus questions whether this is a good basis to establish a new Treaty.

One of the main challenges that the Union faces in the external sphere is how to develop a meaningful Security and Defence Policy within the constitutional and institutional confines predicated by the Union's distinct nature and legal framework. Koutrakos argues against a maximalist approach. The constitutional constraints under which the EU operates and, most importantly, the lack of political support at Member State level, render the EU unsuitable to assume the role of a superpower. Instead of promoting a nation-state inspired model of security and defence policy, the EU should seek to assert its identity at international level by developing an inter-disciplinary approach to international issues recognising the interaction among foreign policy, development, trade, defence and international legal cooperation. Such an approach will enable the EU to utilise its existing legal panoply in diverse areas, exploit its comparative advantages, and turn its institutional weaknesses to a strength.

The issue of coherence of the various external policies of the EU is also discussed by Herrmann who reviews the challenges to governance posed by globalisation. One of the main problems in this context is the reconciliation of economic and non-economic interests. This theme is examined by Reid who compares the approach of the EC and the WTO. She concludes that the EU has made a veritable effort to reconcile economic and non-economic interests, in particular, free movement with environmental protection and human rights. She cautions however against the transposition of a strict proportionality test in assessing the compatibility of national measures with the rules of the WTO.

Antoniadis examines the provisions of the draft Constitutional Treaty on the common commercial policy and the problems surrounding the participation of the Community and the Member States in the WTO, especially their involvement as complainants or respondents in the Dispute Settlement System. The overriding duty of cooperation which governs participation in mixed agreements is not in itself sufficient to resolve the delicate issues that may arise. There may be scope for a Code of Conduct laying down a clearer division of responsibilities between the Community and the Member States within the WTO system.

One area where the draft Constitution increases significantly the powers of the EU is immigration and asylum law. Peers assesses whether the current EU law in those fields conforms to an internal market model or a human rights model. EU law seeks to achieve extensive harmonisation of the law concerning visa and border control. By contrast, with regard to asylum and immigration law, it aims to provide minimum standards allowing Member States to be more restrictive, although the appetite of the Community institutions for more comprehensive regulation should not be underestimated. But what does minimum harmonisation mean in this context? Peers suggests that whilst EU asylum legislation must always allow Member States to pursue a higher degree of protection for the individual, immigration measures may be interpreted as permitting more restrictions, or more protection, or full harmonisation. He argues for a human rights rather than a mutual recognition model in relation to asylum and immigration.

This theme is also taken on by Lambert who examines the proposed Qualifications Directive. This measure seeks to provide minimum standards for the protection of refugees bringing together the principles of the Geneva Convention and the practice of subsidiary protection under human rights law.

Phuong focuses on the impact of the EU immigration and asylum policy on the laws of the incoming Member States and the expectations placed upon them to control migration from the East in the enlarged Union. EU policy here pursues a twofold objective: it seeks to ensure that the new Member States do not become easy targets for asylum seekers and also that they improve their asylum systems so as to facilitate burden sharing with the current Member States. Issues, however, such as visa regulations, border controls, and asylum arrangements are far from unproblematic.

Cremona reviews the Union's policy initiatives concerning relations with its near neighbours and points out the similarities and differences between the new proximity policy and the pre-accession model which led, gloriously, to the last enlargement. The proximity policy differentiates between potential candidates (the Western Balkans) and countries for whom a new neighbourhood policy is proposed (Russia, the Western NIS and the Southern Mediterranean) taking into account different geo-political parameters and historical relations with Europe. Relations with the Western Balkans are governed by the Stabilisation and Association Process, which combines the Copenhagen criteria with a conditionality model specific to the Western Balkans region. Relations with Russia, the Western NIS and the Southern Mediterranean seek to build on existing bilateral agreements and envisage cooperation on migration issues, border management and the exportation of Union regulatory patterns. Closer relations with the Union and market access are seen as the *quid pro quo* of political and economic reform and adherence to the values of the Union. The Union's proximity policy is based on pre-accession structures and instruments but, crucially, pursues diverse and less specific goals and is not necessarily accompanied by the target of EU accession. The largest problems that the EU faces are how to engage its neighbours in a process of political and economic integration where, as Cremona puts it, they become participants rather than recipients of foreign policy, and how to draw the balance between inclusiveness and differentiation.

Velluti concentrates on the social aspects of enlargement. She examines the measures adopted by the new Member States to conform with the European Employment Strategy and assesses whether that Strategy, and its implementation through the open method of coordination, is a suitable policy instrument for the new Member States whose economies are still in the process of moving from a state-dominated to a functioning market system.

Finally, Czuczai explores the challenges posed by the Charter of Fundamental Rights to the acceding States and states aspiring to join the EU in the future. Notably, he identifies the implementation of Article 21, which contains an all-embracing prohibition of discrimination, as one of the most important problems that the new Member States are likely to face. He calls for further clarification of the concept of 'minority rights' which, in the constitutions of some Central and Eastern European countries, are addressed separately from human rights.

# 2

# *Three Challenges for European Constitutionalism in the 21st Century*

FRANCIS SNYDER

THE DEVELOPMENT OF a real constitution in the European Union (EU) in the 21st century faces numerous challenges. Three challenges are among the most important. We can call them 'the challenge of ordinary people', 'the challenge of empire' and 'the challenge of sites'.

## THE CHALLENGE OF ORDINARY PEOPLE

The first challenge is to put into practice an EU constitution that engages with the concerns not only of the elite, but also of ordinary people. In order to do this, we need a different constitutional practice, based on a conception of the EU constitution that diverges from those which are frequently used. An adequate conception of the EU constitution cannot be imagined only in legal terms; it requires systematic attention to the social, economic, political and cultural contexts. Our thinking of the EU constitution needs to take account systematically of the various contexts that produce EU law and shape its operation in practice.

EU constitutional scholarship would do well to focus on a single (if potentially all-embracing) theoretical problem: How does a 'constitution in the material sense' become also a 'constitution in the subjective sense'? By 'constitution in the subjective sense', I refer not necessarily to deliberation by the people, but rather to people's subjective orientation: that is, to use Weber's terms, whether people are subjectively oriented to the constitution in a substantive sense as if it were their fundamental legal act.

In turn, this requires us to refocus our constitutional lens. We need to go beyond rules, institutions and other structures. Four elementary hypotheses regarding the EU will make this more concrete. First, the EU is a social organisation. Second, 'social organization is a dynamic process'.[1] Third, 'social organization is the process of bringing order and meaning into human social life'.[2] Fourth, 'social organization is the process of merging social actors into ordered social relationships, which become infused with cultural ideas'.[3] In other words, we need to conceive of the EU constitution as a process.

From this perspective, we can distinguish three distinct but interrelated dimensions of the EU constitution. The first dimension refers to structures, namely constitutional principles. The second dimension concerns constitutionalising processes: those social processes which tend to transform (or block the transformation of) the EU constitution from a constitution in only a substantive sense to a constitution in both a substantive and a subjective sense. The third dimension consists of constitutional culture, a facet of legal culture. These three dimensions, in my view, constitute the basis for understanding the development of the EU constitution in the 21st century.

To illustrate this perspective, I focus briefly on constitutional culture. By 'constitutional culture' I mean a legal culture oriented to the legal framework of the EU as a set of fundamental norms. It is not concerned solely, or indeed primarily, with judicial review. Constitutional culture does not necessarily involve shared norms, based on common principles of justice and articulating an 'overlapping consensus'. Instead it may express conflicting moral ideas and different traditions of constitutional democracy.

The notion of a constitutional culture refers both to the actual provisions and the unwritten principles of the constitution. But it also involves the way in which the constitution is dealt with by the legislator, the administration, the judiciary and legal scholarship. My working hypotheses are two fold. On the one hand, a constitutional culture which is specific to the EU is now emerging and being created at the individual, organisational and societal levels. On the other hand, its main features are not all fixed, nor are they by any means entirely coherent and free from contradiction.

There are at least two different ways to read contemporary EU constitutional culture. One reading is historical. From this perspective, EU constitutional culture is a conjunction of two different strands. First, EU constitutional culture remains heavily influenced by the historical development of European regional integration since the 1950s. Of special importance is the fact that, until recently, European integration was oriented almost entirely toward the economy. A second strand is the historical (and continuing) legacy of the state. When thinking about the EU constitution, and trying to imagine how best to conceive of it and its future development, we find it

[1] ME Olsen *The Process of Social Organization* (New York, Holt, Rinehart and Winston, 1968) 2.
[2] *Ibid* at 2.
[3] *Ibid* at 3.

very difficult to escape the model of the state, particularly the historical model of the state in continental western Europe. While this poses a challenge to us as potential constitutional theorists, it nevertheless remains firmly anchored as a part of today's EU constitutional culture.

A second reading is based on social differentiation. There is a great divide between two domains of — or perspectives on — contemporary EU legal culture: elite or specific legal culture, and general or popular legal culture. As legal scholars or practising lawyers, we know a great deal about elite legal culture, albeit without always being conscious of it or without necessarily being able to analyse it. But we lawyers (and others) know very little about general EU legal culture. Its very existence is sometimes denied. This perception is seriously misleading, but nonetheless it indicates how little attention legal scholarship and studies of law in European society have paid to legal culture. To remedy this gap, we need the help of our colleagues in other disciplines. Only in this way can we achieve a serious understanding of EU legal culture, which in turn is essential for putting into practice an EU constitution which engages with the concerns of ordinary people. This is an indispensable element if we are to take seriously the idea of the EU constitution as a process.

## THE CHALLENGE OF EMPIRE

A second challenge is to come to grips, in theory and practice, with the role of the EU in the world today: its potential and its limits. Globalisation will help to shape the features of the EU constitution in the 21st century. It partly determines what kind of EU constitution is possible in the contemporary period. For present purposes, globalisation needs to be reformulated in geopolitical terms. Not long ago the *Financial Times* published a striking editorial, which was entitled 'We must get used to a world in which America makes the rules'.[4] How can we situate the European Union in this new world?

The concept of empire[5] provides a useful perspective. It takes account of two of the most significant features of the post-Cold War, post-9/11 world, the remarkable concentration of power and its notable fragmentation and dispersion. Hardt and Negri argue that the development of the global market and global circuits of production has been accompanied by the development of a 'new logic and structure of rule' or 'a new form of sovereignty'.[6] The basic hypothesis is that 'sovereignty has taken a new

[4] Philip Stephens, 'Learning to live in a world governed by American rules' (7 Feb 2003) *Financial Times* 11.
[5] Michael Hardt and Antonio Negri, *Empire* (Cambridge MA and London, Harvard University Press, 2000) (hereinafter *Empire*).
[6] *Empire*, p xi.

form, composed of a series of national and supranational organisms united under a single logic of rule. [7] This new sovereignty is empire, 'a decentered and deterritorializing apparatus of rule that progressively incorporates the entire global realm within its open, expanding frontiers.'[8] It is not an imperialist project, though the United States occupies a 'privileged position',[9] and even though '[t]he contemporary idea of Empire is born through the global expansion of the internal US constitutional project'.[10] Instead, 'empire' is a concept the basic characteristic of which is a lack of boundaries.'[11]

Hardt and Negri identify what they call the pyramid of global constitution. They write that 'When we analyse the configurations of global power in its various bodies and organizations, we can recognise a pyramidal structure that is composed of three progressively broader tiers, each of which contains several layers'.[12] At the top of the first, unified tier is the United States, the superpower with hegemony over the global use of force. This tier also contains on a second level 'a group of nation-states [which] control the primary global monetary instruments and thus have the ability to regulate international exchanges.'[13] In my view, this group includes the most powerful Member States of the European Union, and by a possibly permissible extension, the European Union itself.

What roles does the EU play in the context of empire, and what roles might it potentially play? So far, the EU has tried to preserve the shreds of embedded liberalism, the post-World War II compromise which tried to reconcile the operation of markets with the values of social community.[14] For the European Union and its institutions, a fundamental question must now be addressed: To what extent is it possible to preserve 'embedded liberalism' in today's world? Embedded liberalism was basically a projection of the US New Deal on an international scale.[15] The projection occurred in a bipolar international setting, in which the United States and the Soviet

[7] *Empire*, p xii.
[8] *Empire*, p xii.
[9] *Empire*, pp xiii–xiv.
[10] *Empire*, p 182. Hardt and Negri argue that the US constitution is imperial, not imperialist, because '(in contrast to imperialism's project always to subsume subject countries within its sovereignty) the US constitutional project is constructed on the model of rearticulating an open space and reinventing incessantly diverse and singular relations in networks across an unbounded terrain': *Empire*, p 182.
[11] *Empire*, pp xiv–xv.
[12] *Empire*, p 309.
[13] *Empire*, p 309.
[14] J Ruggie, '*International Regimes*, Transactions, and Change: Embedded Liberalism in the Post-War Economic Order', in S Krasner (ed) *International Regimes* (Ithaca, NY, Cornell University Press, 1983) 195–231.
[15] See A-M Slaughter-Burley 'Regulating the World: Multilateralism, International Law, and the Projection of the New Deal Regulatory State', in J Ruggie (ed) *Multilateralism Matters: The Theory and Praxis of an Institutional Form* (New York, Columbia University Press, 1993) 125–56.

Union were the dominant powers. However, this is no longer the case today. Now we live in a different historical period. The EU's political and legal strategies have to come to grips with this fact.

This will be a major challenge for EU constitutionalism during the 21st century. Empire places serious constraints on the elaboration of the EU constitution, while simultaneously it opens up new spaces for development. As scholars of EU law, it is important for us to analyse these constraints and opportunities. We need also to try to understand the preconditions which may help to determine whether alternative constitutional strategies are more likely to be successful or to fail.

## THE CHALLENGE OF SITES

A third constitutional challenge for the EU in the 21st century concerns relations between sites of governance. Today a multiplicity of sites of governance complement, supplement or compete with the State, even though the State remains powerful, if not predominant. The former is explicit in the concept of empire, while the latter is implicit in the concept's current empirical reference to the United States. The term 'global legal pluralism' refers to the totality of a multiplicity of sites of governance throughout the world. These sites can be situated in a pyramid in terms of political power, but in normative terms they are not necessarily arranged in a hierarchy. This raises the question as how the EU can and should manage rules originating from other sites, in other words how it can govern normative globalisation.

A pertinent example concerns relations between the EU and the World Trade Organisation (WT). They are two of the most significant sites governing economic globalisation today. Relations between them are always important and sometimes controversial. Article XVI of the Marrakech Agreement establishing the WTO requires each WTO Member to ensure the conformity of its laws, regulations and administrative procedures with its obligations as provided in the Uruguay Round agreements. What this means in practice in the EU has so far been determined by the gatekeepers, the European courts.[16]

Up to now the European courts have followed a strategy of promoting indirect effect rather than direct effect as a way of implementing WTO law in the EU legal order. However, this leaves important gaps. The clear reference exception applies only in limited and ill-defined circumstances. The transposition exception, though clear, is also limited in scope. The principle of consistent interpretation has well-known limitations. Most

[16] See F Snyder 'The Gatekeepers: The European Courts and WTO Law', (2003) 40 *CML Rev* 313–67.

importantly, there is a real problem about the implementation of adopted panel and AB reports.

These issues resurfaced recently in the *Biret* cases.[17] Two French companies brought actions against the Council, claiming compensation for damages allegedly suffered as a result of the EC's ban on imports of hormone-treated beef. They argued that the EC had failed to implement the ruling of the WTO Dispute Settlement body in *Hormones*[18] and therefore was in breach of its WTO obligations. The Court of First Instance rejected the applicants' claims. Biret appealed to the ECJ, and on 13 May 2003, Advocate General Alber delivered his Opinion.[19] He proposed that the Council had infringed a superior rule of law for the protection of the individual, and on which an individual could rely. He concluded that, consequently, Biret was entitled to compensation. In my view, the European Court of Justice (ECJ) is unlikely to accept this conclusion.[20]

Consider also recent legislation concerning the implementation of WTO law by the European Commission and the Council. In July 2001 the Council adopted Council Regulation (EC) No 1515/2001 of 23 July 2001 on the measures that may be taken by the Community following a report adopted by the WTO Dispute Settlement Body concerning anti-dumping and anti-subsidy matters (hereinafter the Enabling Regulation).[21] It provides that, whenever the DSB adopts a report concerning an EC measure taken pursuant to the basic EC anti-dumping regulation, the basic EC anti-subsidy regulation or the Enabling Regulation, the Council may repeal or amend the disputed measure or adopt any other special measures which are deemed to be appropriate in the circumstances.[22] It may also take any of these measures in order to take account of legal interpretations in a DSB report concerning a measure not in dispute, if it considers this appropriate.

[17] Case T-174/00 *Biret International SA v Council of the European Union* [2002] ECR II-17; Case T-210/00 *Etablissements Biret et Cie SA* [2002] ECR II-47; Case C-93/02P *Biret v Council*, Opinion of Advocate General Siegbert Alber of 15 May 2003. I am grateful to Candido Garcia Molyneux for this reference. See also 'Opinion of Advocate General Siegbert Alber in Cases C-93/02P and C-94/02P, *Biret International SA and Etablissements Biret et Cie. SA v Council of the European Union*', European Court of Justice, Press and Information Division, Press Release No 39/03, 15 May 2003.

[18] See DSB decision of 13 February 1998 adopting the Appellate Body Report of 16 January 1998 No WT/DS26/AB/R WT/DS48/AB/R.

[19] Opinion of the Advocate-General; see also Press Release, above n 17.

[20] See now the judgments of the ECJ in Cases C-93/02 P and C-94/02 P both delivered on 30 September 2003.

[21] OJ 26.7.2001 L201/10.

[22] The Council acts by a simple majority on a proposal from the Commission after consulting the appropriate Advisory Committee. It may take any of the measures which it considers appropriate.

The Enabling Regulation was designed to resolve a problem arising from a specific DSB ruling.[23] It was also intended to clarify the legal status of adopted WTO panel and AB reports in EC law, albeit only in specific fields. Whether it really resolves the latter, broader issue is open to question. However, one of its most interesting aspects concerns relations not between WTO and EC law, but rather between EC institutions. The underlying structure of the Enabling Regulation derives from judicially created exceptions to the (judicially created) EC law principle that WTO law cannot be used as a criterion for assessing the legality of EC law. But it goes further by allowing the legislator to adopt acts in order to take account of DSB interpretations on measures not in dispute. In both respects, it establishes a new normative role for the EC legislator in a domain which previously was left to the courts. At the same time, it preserves substantial legislative and administrative discretion.

Whether we consider the matter from the standpoint of the European courts or from that of the EU legislator, WTO law has only a relative, negotiated effectiveness in EU law. The implementation of WTO law in the EU is a form of negotiation involving relations between two sites, instead of a more or less automatic, top-down process. In this context, governance of normative globalisation is a kind of translation, by which the EU translates WTO law into its own language or vernacular. It renders a foreign text understandable, while simultaneously it serves to channel, control and preserve room for manoeuvre. The effect of WTO DSB recommendations (and perhaps WTO law more generally) in EU law is likely to remain problematic, but translation is an essential feature of relations between sites. This reinforces our conception of the EU constitution as a process.

## CONCLUSION

The challenge of ordinary people, the challenge of empire and the challenge of sites are likely to occupy the energies of EU constitutional lawyers and policy-makers for much of the 21st century. This is necessary, indeed inevitable, if the EU is to put into place a real constitution in the contemporary international context. These challenges deserves sustained attention from scholars and students of EU constitutional law.

[23] *European Communities: Anti-Dumping Duties on Imports of Cotton-Type Bed Linen from India*, Report of the Panel, 30 October 2000, WT/DS141/R, adopted 12 March 2001; Report of the Appellate Body, 1 March 2001, WT/DS141/AB/R, adopted 12 March 2001.

# 3

# *Judicial Review as a Contribution to the Development of European Constitutionalism*

KOEN LENAERTS AND TIM CORTHAUT*

## I. INTRODUCTION

THE COMMUNITY JUDICATURE definitely has a role to play in enhancing democracy and legitimacy of the EU institutions, by articulating norms of a constitutional nature. The case law of the ECJ and the CFI contains multiple instances where the judicature had to strike the balance between the institutions, or where it enhanced their transparency or accountability. Moreover, the Community Courts have an important role to play as protectors of fundamental rights in the EC legal order. However, before examining this body of case law, another fundamental issue must be settled: the question of access to the Community Courts. Indeed, it is logically only when institutions and individuals are able to bring their cases before the Community Courts that the latter can play their important role. It is precisely in this domain that we are currently witnessing a strong difference between the CFI and the ECJ, which forces the drafters of the Constitutional Treaty to make some tough choices. Therefore, this contribution will first review some of the latest developments in respect of the criteria for *locus standi* of individuals before the Community Courts. Next it will be demonstrated that when the Community Courts do have jurisdiction, they often make fundamental rulings on democracy, legitimacy, and transparency within the Community legal order.

* The first author is Judge of the Court of Justice of the European Communities; Professor of European Law, Leuven University. The second author is Assistant at the Institute for European Law, Leuven University. All opinions expressed are personal to the authors.

## II. CARVING OUT ITS OWN CONSTITUTIONAL POSITION: RULES ON STANDING

Access to the courts — and the restrictions thereon — is an important element in determining the checks and balances inherent in any constitutional system. This goes in particular for those systems where the judiciary has been given the power to review the legality of acts of not only the executive, but also the legislator. Such power has effectively been given to the Community Courts, and the way in which the ECJ defines its own jurisdiction thus greatly affects the subtle constitutional equilibrium between Member States and the Community institutions, both *vis-à-vis* one another and in their relationship with the citizens.

### A. Ensuring Checks and Balances Through *Locus Standi* ...

The importance and potential constitutional impact of granting access to judicial review before the Community Courts has never been played down by the ECJ. In its well-known judgment in *Les Verts* the ECJ did not hesitate to subject any act of the institutions to the control of the Courts and to stress its own pivotal role in upholding the rule of law by checking whether Community acts are in conformity with the *constitutional charter, the Treaty.*[1] The ECJ then went on to set out a coherent division of work between the ECJ and the national courts in order to guarantee this possibility of judicial review by referring individuals to the national courts unless they are challenging an act which is addressed to them or is of direct and individual concern to them.

All this was effectively done to open the way for the Court to hear a case brought by a political party against a decision taken by the European Parliament in respect of the division of money to political groups on the occasion of the 1984 elections. In this way the Court penetrated right into the heart of the constitutional organization of democratic life in the Community. However, in order to do so the Court had to clear several hurdles. It first had to establish the legal personality and capacity of the applicant to bring the action. Then the ECJ went on to include the European Parliament in the list of potential defendants in actions for annulment. This possibility now sounds very natural, but was not foreseen under the original Treaty.[2] The ECJ basically had to fill in the gaps in the Treaty in respect of

[1] Case 294/83 *Parti Ecologiste 'Les Verts' v European Parliament* [1986] ECR 1339, para 23.
[2] Compare the original version of the then Art 173 TEC with Art 230(1), *in fine* TEC. In doing so the Court went way beyond the text of the Treaty, which is all the more remarkable since a proposal by the Commission to add the acts of the European Parliament to the list of challengeable acts and the corresponding right for the European Parliament to act as

its own jurisdiction. It did so without much opposition from the Parliament itself, though the EP had asked for a *quid pro quo* in the form of a right of standing against the acts of other institutions[3] — on which the ECJ stayed silent.[4] It is clear that, if the European Economic Community is a 'community based on the rule of law, inasmuch as neither its Member States nor its institutions can avoid a review of the question whether the measures adopted by them are in conformity with the basic constitutional charter, the Treaty',[5] the European Parliament, too, cannot escape review of its acts.[6] Nonetheless, the ECJ still had to establish that this decision of the EP really produced legal effects and was of direct and individual concern to the applicants. Especially on the latter point, a classic reading of the *Plaumann* test[7] would have been disastrous for the applicants, since parties who had not been represented in the Parliament before 1984 formed a prime example of an 'open category' of applicants; namely, applicants who are clearly not affected by reason of certain attributes which are peculiar to them or by reason of circumstances in which they are differentiated from all other persons and which by virtue of these factors are distinguished individually, just as in the case of the person addressed. The Court realized it had to come up with a creative solution in the light of the seriousness of the alleged infringement. The organization and financing — with public funds — of the elections for the European Parliament go to the core of the legal order and denying the possibility of review of those acts would have strongly undermined the legitimacy of the Parliament. Therefore, the ECJ side-stepped the issue by stressing the unique situation in which the closed group of parties involved in drafting the contested system decided on both their own share of public funds and the share for the open category of political groups that were not yet represented in the Parliament in a potentially unequal way, without there otherwise being a way to redress this situation so critical for democracy in the Community.[8] The Court could then finally declare the action admissible and annul the contested acts, thus restoring the equal opportunities of the various political parties on the occasion of EP elections.

an applicant had not been acted upon by the Member States; see J-P Jacqué, '*Parti Ecologiste "Les Verts" c Parlement Européen* (Aff 294/83)' (1986) 22 RTDE 500 at 503.

[3] Case 294/83 *Parti Ecologiste 'Les Verts' v European Parliament* [1986] ECR 1339, para 22.
[4] See however later, Case 70/88 *European Parliament v Council* [1990] ECR I-2041 (below).
[5] Case 294/83 Parti Ecologiste '*Les Verts' v European Parliament* [1986] ECR 1339, para 23.
[6] In holding so, the ECJ followed the position defended by one of its prominent members on the occasion of the first elections for the European Parliament: see P Pescatore, 'Reconnaissance et contrôle judiciaire des actes du Parlement européen' (1978) 14 *RTDE* 581 at 585–89.
[7] Case 25/62 *Plaumann v Commission* [1963] ECR 95.
[8] Case 294/83 *Parti Ecologiste 'Les Verts' v European Parliament* [1986] ECR 1339, paras 33–35.

The ECJ, in the famous *Chernobyl* case, subsequently awarded *locus standi* to the EP in order to protect its own prerogatives through direct actions for annulment.[9] In this case again the importance of access to the Community Courts was not played down and the constitutional framework of the Community was adapted accordingly. The former Articles 173 EEC Treaty and 146 Euratom Treaty did not provide for *locus standi* for the European Parliament. The ECJ had first refused to act on this,[10] but later filled the gap in line with the increasingly important role played by the EP in the legislative procedure. In light of the present analysis, it is important to stress that the ECJ has not eschewed fundamentally redrawing the constitutional balance[11] through its case law on *locus standi*. It is equally important to notice that the Member States, as *Herren der Verträge*, subsequently consummated this fundamental change in the constitutional balance by taking over the formula devised by the Court in the text of the Treaties on the occasion of the following IGC. The position of the European Parliament has meanwhile been strengthened even further with the entry into force of the Nice Treaty, which makes the European Parliament a fully-fledged privileged applicant.[12]

### B. ... But Not for Individuals

Unsurprisingly, the Court's enthusiasm for expanding the *locus standi* of the European Parliament — and the willingness of the Member States to comply with this change — provoked further calls to alter the conditions for admissibility of individuals as well. Both in legal literature,[13] in

[9] Case 70/88 *European Parliament v Council* [1990] ECR I-2041.

[10] Case 302/87 *European Parliament v Council* [1988] ECR 5615.

[11] Though the ECJ itself rather considered that it was 'ensur[ing] that the provisions of the Treaties concerning the institutional balance are fully *applied* and to see to it that the Parliament's prerogatives, like those of the other institutions, cannot be breached without it having available a legal remedy': see Case 70/88 *European Parliament v Council* [1990] ECR I-2041, para 25.

[12] Art 230(2) TEC.

[13] Among others: A Arnull, 'Private Applicants and the Action for Annulment under Article 173 of the EC Treaty' (1995) 22 *CML Rev* 7 and 'Private Applicants and the Action for Annulment since *Codorníu*' (2001) 28 *CML Rev* 7; D Waelbroeck and A-M Verheyden, 'Les conditions de recevabilité des recours en annulation des particuliers contre les actes normatifs communautaires: À la lumière du droit comparé et de la Convention des droits de l'homme' (1995) 31 *CDE* 399; G Vandersanden, 'Pour un élargissement du droit des particuliers d'agir en annulation contre des actes autres que les décisions qui leur sont adressées' (1995) 31 *CDE* 535; L Allkemper, *Der Rechtsschutz des einzelnen nach dem EG-Vertrag: Möglichkeiten seiner Verbesserung* (Baden Baden, Nomos, 1995), 39–40; T Heukels, 'Collectief actierecht ex artikel 173 lid 4 EG: een beperkte actieradius voor grote belangen' (1999) 5 *NTER* 16.

Opinions of Advocates General before the ECJ,[14] and with the intervening creation of the CFI,[15] the Community Courts were asked to loosen the strict *Plaumann* test. As already noted above, the interpretation given by the ECJ to the requirements of Article 230(4) TEC is highly restrictive, in spite of the Court's own initial opinion that the words and the natural meaning of this Article justify the broadest interpretation, and that provisions of the Treaty regarding the right of interested parties to bring an action must not be interpreted restrictively.[16]

The Court's subsequent response has always been rather lukewarm.[17] The strict reading of the notion of individual concern has always been upheld, especially when individuals have attempted to challenge acts of general application such as regulations. However, several minor qualifications were added to the rule. In this way private actions for annulment were declared admissible in cases concerning competition,[18] state aid,[19] and anti-dumping[20] and

[14] Opinions of Advocate General Slynn in Case 246/81 *Bethell* [1982] ECR 2277, at 2299; and of Advocate SGeneral Jacobs in Case C-358/89 *Extramet Industrie* [1991] ECR I-2501, at paras 71–74, and Case C-188/92 *TWD Textilwerke Deggendorf* [1994] ECR I-833, at paras 20–23, and of Advocate General Ruiz-Jarabo Colomer in Case C-142/95 P *Associazione agricoltori della provincia di Rovigo and others* [1996] ECR I-6669, at paras 40 and 41.

[15] The CFI has the express task of improving the judicial protection of interests of individuals and allowing the ECJ to focus on the uniformity of the case law, through preliminary rulings and appeals limited to points of law against judgments of the CFI. See the recitals of Council Decision 88/591/ECSC, EEC, Euratom of 24 Oct 1988 establishing a Court of First Instance of the European Communities, [1988] OJ L319/1; Opinion of Advocate General F Jacobs in Case C-50/00 P *Unión de Pequeños Agricultores v Council* [2002] ECR I-6677, paras 91–96.

[16] Case 25/62 *Plaumann v Commission* [1963] ECR 95. The individual concern was defined as follows 'Persons other than those to whom a decision is addressed may only claim to be individually concerned if that decision affects them by reason of certain attributes which are peculiar to them or by reason of circumstances in which they are differentiated from all other persons and by virtue of these factors distinguishes them individually just as in the case of the person addressed.' This test is moreover applied very rigidly: 'In the present case the applicant is affected by the disputed decision as an importer of clementines, that is to say, by reason of a commercial activity which may at any time be practised by any person and is not therefore such as to distinguish the applicant in relation to the contested decision as in the case of the addressee.' See for a very critical analysis of the *Plaumann* test, P Craig and G De Búrca, *EU Law, Text, Cases and Materials* (Oxford, Oxford University Press, 2002), 488–91. As they rightly observe, it is precisely this application of the test that causes most of the difficulties: the fact that others in the future may also start with importing clementines does not prevent the present day importers from having 'certain attributes which are peculiar to them' and which distinguishes them from all other potential participants on the market, for they *effectively are* already importers of clementines and, therefore, are in this capacity also clearly affected by the measure — unlike the potential, virtual market entrant the ECJ uses as its point of reference.

[17] For an in-depth analysis of the action for annulment see K Lenaerts and D Arts, *Procedural Law of the European Union* (London, Sweet & Maxwell, 1999), 139–206; HG Schermers and DF Waelbroeck, *Judicial Protection in the European Union* (Kluwer Law International, The Hague/London/New York, 2001), 406–63, § 826–927.

[18] Case 26/76 *Metro v Commission* [1977] ECR 1875; Case 210/81 *Schmidt v Commission* [1983] ECR 3045; Case 75/84 *Metro v Commission* [1986] ECR 3021.

[19] Case 169/84 *Cofaz v Commission* [1986] ECR 391.

[20] Cases C-305/86 & C-160/87 *Neotype Techmashexport v Commission and Council* [1990] ECR I-2945, para 19.

when the institutions were under a duty to take the interests of the applicant into account while adopting the act.[21]

In very exceptional circumstances the ECJ has accepted that the factual situation — including the economic impact of an anti-dumping regulation on a particular importer — may be of such a nature as to distinguish the applicant from all other market participants.[22] The ECJ has, finally, accepted that there may be situations where a regulation can be considered to be a decision in respect of an applicant because of the exceptional attributes of that applicant, while continuing to be a normal regulation in respect of others.[23]

However, the majority of the cases were declared inadmissible and the applicants were referred to alternative routes for judicial review. The most coherent approach in this respect can be found in the judgment of the CFI in *Salamander*.[24] In that case, the applicants were companies with interests in tobacco activities (either because they had a monopoly on tobacco advertisement or because they produced all kinds of products, such as shoes and clothing, using the brand names of tobacco products) who sought annulment of a directive containing a ban on tobacco advertisement and sponsoring.[25] The applicants failed in their action because they were not directly concerned by the directive and thus did not fulfil the first requirement for standing in Article 230(4) TEC. As directives have to be transposed into national legislation first, individuals can, in principle, be affected directly only by the national implementing measure and not by the directive itself.[26] Nonetheless, the CFI correctly noted that the requirement of national implementation was not an absolute bar to the satisfaction of direct concern because there was still the possibility of the so-called vertical direct effect.[27] A directive indeed binds those 'public'

[21] Case 11/82 *Piraiki-Patraiki v Commission* [1985] ECR 207. As G van der Wal rightly noticed, this sometimes results in very bizarre situations where actions against very similar acts are alternately declared admissible or inadmissible depending on whether the institutions were under an obligation to take the applicant's interest into account: see 'Arrest Jégo-Quéré: een zwaluw die lente maakt?' (2002) 8 *NTER* 195 at 197. See also Case C-152/88 *Sofrimport v Commission* [1990] ECR I-2477, paras 11–13, and compare with Case T-489/93 *Unifruit Hellas v Commission* [1994] ECR II-1201, paras 18–29. In its very recent judgment of 10 Apr 2003, the ECJ seems to have severelly restricted this possibility: see Case C-142/00 P *Commission v Nederlandse Antillen* [2003] ECR I-3483. The ECJ now stresses that even if such an obligation to take the interest of the applicant into account exists, the applicant still has to demonstrate that he or she was affected by those regulations by reason of a factual situation which differentiates him or her from all other persons (at paras 71–76).

[22] Case C-358/89 *Extramet Industrie v Council* [1991] ECR I-2501.

[23] Case C-309/89 *Codorníu v Council* [1994] ECR I-1853, paras 19–22.

[24] Cases T-172/98, T-175/98, & T-177/98 *Salamander v European Parliament and Council* [2000] ECR II-2487, paras 52–71.

[25] Directive 98/43/EC of 6 July 1998 [1998] OJ L213/9.

[26] Cases T-172/98, T-175/98, & T-177/98 *Salamander v European Parliament and Council* [2000] ECR II-2487, paras 52–71.

[27] *Ibid*, paras 55–69. See earlier Case C-298/89 *Gibraltar v Council* [1993] ECR I-3605 and the accompanying Opinion of Advocate General Lenz.

bodies that meet the so-called *Foster* criteria,[28] even if there are no national implementing measures. Applicants that can prove that they are such bodies can argue that a directive may directly concern them after all. However, none of the applicants in *Salamander* was in that category and their respective applications were rightfully rejected. However, they had claimed that such a rejection would amount to a violation of their right to an effective remedy. Referring explicitly to its ruling in *Unión de Pequeños Agricultores*,[29] the CFI confirmed the classic position of the Court of Justice that the division of tasks between the Community Courts and the national courts as set out by the Treaties results in a coherent and complete system of judicial protection.[30] The CFI reiterated that the fact that particular Member States have failed to provide for sufficient legal remedies could not be a ground for departing from the system of legal remedies established by the Treaties.[31] Member States have an obligation under Article 10 TEC to help to ensure that the system of legal remedies and procedures established by the EC Treaty and designed to permit the Community judicature to review the lawfulness of acts of the Community institutions is comprehensive.[32] If Member States fail to fulfil their obligation to provide for efficient remedies, then the national system, rather than the rules on direct access to the CFI, must be adapted. Moreover, the CFI pointed out that alternative national remedies were available in some cases, *at least in certain Member States*. For example, while the *Salamander* case was being tried, another tobacco company had managed to go to the High Court of England and Wales, which had then asked the ECJ for a preliminary ruling on the validity of the same directive.[33] Yet, it may be extremely difficult in practice for companies, like the applicants in *Salamander*, that operate in other Member States — where no such court actions are possible — to convince their national courts to *create* a new national remedy which would allow them to challenge such a directive at an early stage as well. The CFI concluded its reasoning in *Salamander* with a reference to the action for damages.[34] By doing so, the

[28] Case C-188/89 *Foster* [1990] ECR I-3313, para 20.
[29] Case T-173/98 *Unión de Pequeños Agricultores v Council* [1999] ECR II-3357.
[30] Case 294/83 *Parti Ecologiste 'Les Verts' v European Parliament* [1986] ECR 1339, para 23.
[31] Case C-87/95 P *CNPAAP v Council* [1996] ECR I-2003, para 38.
[32] Case 294/83 *Parti Ecologiste 'Les Verts' v European Parliament* [1986] ECR 1339, para 23, and the order in Case T-173/98 *Unión de Pequeños Agricultores v Council* [1999] ECR II-3357, para 62.
[33] Cases T-172/98, T-175/98, & T-177/98 *Salamander v European Parliament and Council* [2000] ECR II-2487, para 76. See Case C-74/99 *Imperial Tobacco Ltd* [2000] ECR I-8599. However, the questions were not answered, because the ECJ had annulled the directive in its entirety at the request of Germany in a judgment of the same day: see Case C-376/98 *Germany v Council* [2000] ECR I-8419.
[34] Cases T-172/98, T-175/98, & T-177/98 *Salamander v European Parliament and Council* [2000] ECR II-2487, para 78.

CFI seemed to make of this procedure the tailpiece of the system of judicial protection, somehow suggesting that possible compensation for the damage caused by the act could be a valid alternative for annulment.

All this was called into question by the Court of First Instance in its judgment in *Jégo-Quéré*,[35] delivered shortly after[36] an opinion to similar effect given by Advocate General Jacobs.[37] The facts in *Jégo-Quéré* were simple. The Commission had enacted a regulation prohibiting the use of certain types of fishing nets in order to protect the stock of hake in certain Community waters.[38] A French fishing company, the only company that regularly catches hake in the waters south of Ireland while fishing for whiting, sought annulment of this regulation — which was basically an administrative measure significantly affecting the operating costs of the fishing company.

The CFI first applied the *Plaumann* test. Based on this test,[39] the Court found that the applicant was directly, but not individually, concerned by the regulation. The regulation was of general application and the Jégo-Quéré company was not able to differentiate itself from any other entity that might have been affected by the regulation.[40] The CFI was correct in holding that Jégo-Quéré ostensibly lacked individual concern since, at any given time, there might be someone else who wanted to fish in the designated areas and who would be equally prohibited from doing so.

[35] Case T-177/01 *Jégo-Quéré v Commission* [2002] ECR II-2365.

[36] Several authors have commented on the way the CFI expedited the procedure in *Jégo-Quéré*, noting that it looked as if the CFI wanted to make sure that its voice, too, was heard on such a sensitive issue by the ECJ before it rendered its judgment in Case C-50/00 P *Unión de Pequeños Agricultores v Council* [2002] ECR I-6677 and, ultimately, by the Convention on the Future of Europe. See in this sense: R Barents, 'Een midzomernachtdroom op de Kirchberg' (2003) 51 *SEW* 2 at 9; P Cassia, 'Continuité et rupture dans le contentieux de la recevabilité du recours en annulation des particuliers. A propos de l'arrêt *Jégo-Quéré* du 3 mai 2002 du Tribunal de première instance des Communautés européennes (Aff T-177/01)' (2002) 44 *RMCUE* 547 at 548; T Corthaut, 'Case CFI May 3, 2002, *Jégo-Quéré v Commission*, T-177/01 and C-50/00 P ECJ July 25, 2002, *Unión de Pequeños Agricultores v Council*' (2002) 9 *Columbia J of European L* 141 at 157; P Nihoul, 'Individus, entreprises et recours en annulation. Quelques soubresauts' (2002) 9 *JTDE* 199 at 200; L Parret, 'Zaak T-177/01, Jégo-Quéré et Cie SA/Commissie van de Europese Gemeenschappen' (2002) 50 *SEW* 296 at 296; G van der Wal, 'Arrest Unión de Pequeños Agricultores: de ontvankelijkheid van particulieren weer beperkt' (2002) 8 *NTER* 288 at 290 with several references to reports in *Agence Europe*. The present authors consider this case as a prime case of interaction between the CFI and the ECJ in the development of the law; for more on this see K Lenaerts, 'The European Court of First Instance: Ten Years of Interaction with the Court of Justice' in D O'Keeffe (ed), *Liber Amicorum in Honour of Lord Slynn of Hadley* (Kluwer Law International, The Hague/London/Boston, 2000), i, 97-116.

[37] Opinion of Advocate General F Jacobs in Case C-50/00 P *Unión de Pequeños Agricultores v Council* [2002] ECR I-6677.

[38] Commission Regulation (EC) No 1162/2001 of 14 June 2001 [2001] OJ L159/4.

[39] Case T-177/01 *Jégo-Quéré v Commission* [2002] ECR II-2365, paras 22–38.

[40] Case T-177/01 *Jégo-Quéré v Commission* [2002] ECR II-2365, paras 28–37.

In any other case this would have been the end of the matter. However, instead of issuing an order of the Court declaring the case manifestly inadmissible, the extended first chamber went on to consider the argument by the applicant that, were Jégo-Quéré's action dismissed as inadmissible, Jégo-Quéré would be denied a legal remedy enabling it to challenge the legality of the contested provisions. Since the regulation did not provide for the adoption of any implementing measures by the Member States, the applicant successfully maintained that, in the present case, it would have no right of action before the national courts unless it breached the regulation.[41] The CFI, referring to the Court's case law in *Les Verts*[42] and Articles 6 and 13 of the European Convention on Human Rights (ECHR) (as applied by the ECJ in *Johnston*[43]), recognized that access to the courts is one of the essential elements of a Community based on the rule of law and is guaranteed in the legal order based on the EC Treaty, inasmuch as the Treaty established a complete system of legal remedies and procedures designed to permit the Court of Justice to review the legality of acts of the institutions.[44] The CFI, moreover, also explicitly referred to Article 47 of the Charter of Fundamental Rights, which states that '[e]veryone whose rights and freedoms guaranteed by the law of the Union are violated has the right to an effective remedy before a tribunal in compliance with the conditions laid down in this Article'.[45]

The CFI then examined whether the indirect routes for challenging Community law were sufficient in light of this fundamental right to effective judicial protection. In respect of the preliminary rulings procedure, the CFI observed that the fishing regulation did not require national implementing measures that could be attacked before a national court.[46] Quoting Advocate General Jacobs' opinion, the CFI stressed that 'the fact that an individual affected by a Community measure may be able to bring its validity before the national courts by violating the rules it lays down and then asserting their illegality in subsequent judicial proceedings brought against him does not constitute an adequate means of judicial protection. Individuals cannot be required to breach the law in order to gain access to justice'.[47] This position has since been

[41] *Ibid*, para 39.
[42] Case 294/83 *Parti Ecologiste 'Les Verts' v European Parliament* [1986] ECR 1339, para 23.
[43] Case 222/84 *Johnston* [1986] ECR 1651, para 18.
[44] Case T-177/01 *Jégo-Quéré v Commission* [2002] ECR II-2365, para 41.
[45] *Ibid*, para 42. This is only the second time the CFI invoked the Charter of Fundamental Rights. The first time was in *max.mobil*, where the CFI used it as a decisive element in its reasoning: see Case T-54/99 *max.mobil Telekommunikation Service v Commission* [2002] ECR II-313, paras 48 and 57.
[46] Case T-177/01 *Jégo-Quéré v Commission* [2002] ECR II-2365, para 45.
[47] *Ibid*. See also the Opinion of Advocate General F Jacobs in Case C-50/00 P *Unión de Pequeños Agricultores v Council* [2002] ECR I-6677, para 43.

confirmed by the European Court of Human Rights in the case of *Posti and Rahko v Finland*.[48]

The action for damages, which the CFI in *Salamander* still considered to be a cornerstone of the Community system of judicial protection,[49] also did not offer an adequate alternative to the action for annulment.[50] The CFI correctly analysed that the conditions for admissibility of both actions differ considerably.[51] While any breach of a higher norm may result in the annulment of the act, an action for damages relating to an act of general application will be successful only if a sufficiently serious breach of a norm aimed at protecting the rights of the applicant is found to have occurred. The latter requirements are thus significantly more difficult to fulfil. Moreover, the action for damages does not result in the removal of the act from the EC legal order; it only results in compensation *post factum*.

Confronted with the conclusion that neither the reference procedure nor the action for damages suffices to fill the 'black hole' in judicial protection, the CFI considered it necessary to present a reinterpretation of the criteria for admissibility of Article 230(4) TEC in a way that was more in conformity with the fundamental right of access to the court.[52] The Court, still requiring that the condition of direct concern be satisfied,[53] presented a new definition of individual concern:

> ... A natural or legal person is to be regarded as individually concerned by a Community measure of general application that concerns him directly if the

[48] Judgment of the European Court of Human Rights of 24 Sept 2002, Application 27824/95 *Posti and Rahko v Finland*, para 64. In this way the European Court of Human Rights contradicts Barents, who only recently wondered 'Maar waarom zou dit juridisch kwestieus zijn?' ('But why should this [ie having to breach the law, before being able to obtain judicial review] be problematic from a legal point of view?'): see R Barents, 'Een midzomernachtdroom op de Kirchberg' (2003) 51 *SEW* 2 at 7. See also, below, n 82.

[49] Cases T-172/98, T-175/98, & T-177/98 *Salamander v European Parliament and Council* [2000] ECR II-2487, para 78.

[50] For a critical appraisal of the role of the action for damages in the Community system of judicial protection see F Schockweiler, 'L'accès à la justice dans l'ordre juridique communautaire' (1996) 4 *JTDE* 1 at 7; A Arnull, 'The Action for Annulment: A Case of Double Standards?' in D O'Keeffe (ed), *Liber Amicorum in Honour of Lord Slynn of Hadley* (Kluwer Law International, The Hague/London/Boston, 2000), i, 177 at 186–87.

[51] Case T-177/01 *Jégo-Quéré v Commission* [2002] ECR II-2365, para 46.

[52] *Ibid*, paras 47–50.

[53] This implies, moreover, that — except in the most exceptional circumstances involving private parties, which fulfil the *Foster* criteria and are thus to be regarded as a public body for the purpose of being bound by the directive — the test proposed by the CFI does not provide for the creation of a direct route for challenging directives, despite suggestions to the contrary in legal literature: see L Parret, 'Zaak T-177/01, Jégo-Quéré et Cie SA/Commissie van de Europese Gemeenschappen' (2002) 50 *SEW* 296 at 296; T Lübbig, 'EuG: Individuelle Betroffenheit durch EG-Verordnung' (2002) 13 *EuZW* 412 at 416. This implies that *Jégo-Queré* should not be regarded as overruling Cases T-172/98, T-175/98, & T-177/98 *Salamander v European Parliament and Council* [2000] ECR II-2487 in this respect.

measure in question affects his legal position, in a manner which is both definite and immediate, by restricting his rights or by imposing obligations on him.[54]

The Jégo-Quéré company satisfied the CFI's new criteria for individual concern and its action was thus held admissible.[55] The Commission has lodged an appeal against the ruling.[56] Judgment in that case is eagerly awaited, because it will force the ECJ to pronounce directly on the validity of the approach chosen by the CFI.

However, in its judgment in *Unión de Pequeños Agricultores v Council*[57] the ECJ already gave a clear hint of its position on the issue.[58] The Court of Justice is not won over at all. The case concerned an action for annulment by an interest group of Spanish farmers against a regulation[59] which abolished certain Community aid to olive farmers. Their application had been dismissed as manifestly inadmissible by an order of the CFI, which concisely set out the classic case law on admissibility and emphasized the role under Article 10 TEC for the legal orders of the Member States in ensuring the comprehensiveness of the system of judicial review.[60]

The applicants' core argument on appeal was interpreted by the Court to mean that in the absence of adequate national legal remedies it is up to

[54] Case T-177/01 *Jégo-Quéré v Commission* [2002] ECR II-2365, para 51.

[55] *Ibid*, paras 52–54.

[56] Case C-263/02 P *Commission v Jégo-Quéré* [2002] OJ C233/14.

[57] Case C-50/00 P *Unión de Pequeños Agricultores v Council* [2002] ECR I-6677.

[58] Most commentators inside and outside the Court would even consider the matter settled: see Case T-155/02 R *VVG International Handelsgesellschaft mbH v Commission* [2002] ECR II-3239, para 39 where the President of the CFI rejects the arguments of the applicants making express reference to the judgment of the ECJ in *Unión de Pequeños Agricultores v Council*; Opinion of Advocate General Léger in Case C-142/00 P *Commission v Nederlandse Antillen* [2003] ECR I-0000, para 8; F Berrod and F Mariatte, 'Le pourvoi dans l'affaire *Unión de Pequeños Agricultores c Conseil*: le retour de la procession d'Echternach' (Oct 2002) 12 Europe 7 at 10. See, however, N van den Broeck, 'A Long Hot Summer for Individual Concern? The European Court's Recent Case Law on Direct Actions by Private Parties … and a Plea for a Foreign Affairs Exception' (2003) 30 *LIEI* 61 at 72–4; T Corthaut, 'Case CFI May 3, 2002, *Jégo-Quéré v Commission*, T-177/01 and C-50/00 P ECJ July 25, 2002, *Unión de Pequeños Agricultores v Council*' (2002) 9 *Columbia J of European L* 141 at 164. Nonetheless, Advocate General Jacobs also acknowledged that the court had rejected both his own alternative and the approach of the CFI. In his opinion, in the appeals procedure against the *Jégo-Quéré* judgment he admitted that 'it clearly follows from the Court's judgement in *Unión de Pequeños Agricultores* that the traditional interpretation of individual concern, because it is understood to flow from the Treaty itself, must be applied regardless of its consequences for the right to an effective judicial remedy', even if he still considers this outcome unsatisfactory and continues to support a more liberal standing requirement in respect of individuals seeking to challenge generally applicable community measures: see Opinion of Advocate General Jacobs in Case C-263/02 P *Commission v Jégo-Quéré*, paras 46–47, available at *www.curia.eu.int*.

[59] Regulation (EC) No 1638/98 of 20 July 1998 amending Regulation No 136/66/EEC on the establishment of a common organization of the market in oils and fats [1998] OJ L210/32.

[60] Case T-173/98 *Unión de Pequeños Agricultores v Council* [1999] ECR II-3357.

the Court of Justice to hear a direct action for annulment, even if the applicant does not meet the requirements of direct and individual concern. Put in this way the argument by the applicant, the Unión de Pequeños Agricultores (UPA), sounds like an appeal to the Court to adopt a *contra legem* interpretation of the rules on admissibility. The ECJ, then, does not have any difficulty in dismissing the argument and thus the entire appeal by referring to the order in *CNPAAP v Council*.[61] It argues that if the conditions laid down by Article 230(4) TEC are not fulfilled a natural or legal person does not, under any circumstances, have standing to bring an action for annulment of a regulation.[62]

However, the ECJ then takes the opportunity to make several statements — technically by way of *obiter dicta* — on the coherence and the completeness of the Community system of judicial review of Community acts. It stresses that 'the European Community is a community based on the rule of law in which its institutions are subject to judicial review of the compatibility of their acts with the Treaty and with the general principles of law which include fundamental rights'.[63] But to reach this aim the Court explicitly turns to the Member States. The Treaties set out a coherent and complete system which in limited circumstances provides for direct routes to obtain judicial review of Community acts. These direct routes are complemented by the possibility for individuals to raise issues by way of plea of illegality before the Community Courts or the national courts. Those national courts in turn can — and sometimes must[64] — refer the issue to the ECJ. Thus, concludes the Court, 'it is for the Member States to establish a system of legal remedies and procedures which ensure respect for the right to effective judicial protection'.[65]

The ECJ basically joins in with the position advocated by the CFI in the contested order and in *Salamander*.[66] However, by stating that, 'in accordance with the principle of sincere cooperation laid down in Article 5 [now Article 10] of the Treaty, national courts are required, *so far as possible*, to interpret and apply national procedural rules governing the exercise of rights of action in a way that enables natural and legal persons to challenge before the courts the legality of any decision or other *national* measure relative to the application to them of a Community act of general application,

[61] Case C-87/95 P *CNPAAP v Council* [1996] ECR I-2003, para 38.
[62] Case C-50/00 P *Unión de Pequeños Agricultores v Council* [2002] ECR I-6677, para 37.
[63] *Ibid*, para 38.
[64] Case 314/85 *Foto-Frost* [1987] ECR 4199.
[65] Case C-50/00 P *Unión de Pequeños Agricultores v Council* [2002] ECR I-6677, para 41.
[66] Case T-173/98, *Unión de Pequeños Agricultores v Council* [1999] ECR II-3357, para 62; Cases T-172/98, T-175/98, & T-177/98, *Salamander v European Parliament and Council* [2000] ECR II-2487, para 74. See also F Berrod and F Mariatte, 'Le pourvoi dans l'affaire *Unión de Pequeños Agricultores c Conseil*: le retour de la procession d'Echternach' (Oct 2002) 12 *Europe* 7 at 9.

by pleading the invalidity of such an act',[67] the ECJ obviously leaves open at least two loopholes in the system. On the one hand, the degree of judicial protection available to an individual is made dependent on the ability and creativity of the national judge to provide such a remedy.[68] On the other hand, the Court provides no solution — unlike the CFI in *Jégo-Queré* — for those situations where no such national measures exist, despite the claim by the applicant that it was in precisely this kind of situation.

The approach taken by the Court thus needs refinement. The Court had a first chance to refine on the occasion of a request for a preliminary ruling on the validity of a tobacco directive[69] by the English High Court leading up to the ECJ case of *British American Tobacco*[70] where the applicants had brought an action against the Minister for Health in order to prevent him from implementing the contested directive. The Commission and France had argued that the question was inadmissible 'first, because the decision to make the reference was adopted before 30 September 2002, the date on which the time-limit set for implementation of the Directive expired and, second, because when the order for reference was made national legislation transposing the Directive in the United Kingdom had not yet been adopted. According to the French Government and the Commission, in such a situation it would be contrary to the nature of directives and to the system of judicial review of the lawfulness of Community acts if questions concerning the validity and interpretation of a directive could properly be referred to the Court'.[71]

The ECJ observed however that there was a genuine dispute before the High Court, where national procedural law effectively provides for this kind of preventive action. As to whether the applicants could be said to be circumventing the restrictions of Article 230(4) TEC,[72] the ECJ stated that 'the opportunity open to individuals to plead the invalidity of a Community act of general application before national courts is not conditional upon that act's actually having been the subject of implementing measures

[67] Case C-50/00 P *Unión de Pequeños Agricultores v Council* [2002] ECR I-6677, para 42 (emphasis added).

[68] F Berrod and F Mariatte, 'Le pourvoi dans l'affaire *Unión de Pequeños Agricultores c Conseil*: le retour de la procession d'Echternach' (Oct 2002) 12 *Europe* 7 at 11.

[69] Directive 2001/37/EC of the European Parliament and of the Council of 5 June 2001 on the approximation of the laws, regulations, and administrative provisions of the Member States concerning the manufacture, presentation, and sale of tobacco products [2001] OJ L194/26.

[70] Case C-491/01 *British American Tobacco (Investments) Ltd and Imperial Tobacco Ltd* [2002] ECR I-11453.

[71] *Ibid*, para 29.

[72] An attempt by Japan Tobacco to bring an action for annulment against the directive was moreover unsuccessful, because the applicants were not directly concerned: see Case T-223/01 *Japan Tobacco JT International SA v European Parliament and Council* [2002] ECR II-3259. A direct challenge by Germany was held to be manifestly inadmissible because it was lodged one day late: see Case C-406/01 *Germany v European Parliament and Council* [2002] ECR I-4561.

adopted pursuant to national law. In that respect, it is sufficient if the national court is called upon to hear a genuine dispute in which the question of the validity of such an act is raised indirectly.'[73]

Some have welcomed this approach.[74] One can arguably read the Court's judgments in *Unión de Pequeños Agricultores* and *British American Tobacco* as imposing on all national courts the obligation to provide for effective remedies enabling individuals to challenge Community acts in circumstances where a direct action for annulment does not appear to be available, either in the Community Courts or in the national courts.[75] This is particularly the case of acts that are of direct, but not of individual, concern to them and which do not require national implementing measures (yet). This approach is defended by pointing to the advantages for the Court of having national courts as a filter to avoid being inundated with manifestly unfounded actions and for the institutions not being 'interrupted' all the time by direct actions, other than those brought by privileged applicants. For reasons of equality between applicants across the Community and to avoid forum shopping this approach should be imposed also on Member States, whose legal systems currently do not know of such remedies. After all, at a more fundamental level, an effective remedy implies that an individual can challenge a Community act before national measures are adopted.[76] Moreover, since the Court has in the past often had recourse to Article 10 TEC to place restrictions on the autonomy of national procedural law, the ECJ is not doing anything exceptional.[77]

The present authors do not have the impression that the Court actually imposed such an obligation, which could then be seen as an alternative for loosening the conditions of admissibility under Article 230(4) TEC. The reasoning put forward in support of that obligation is in any event more coherent and effective than the judgment in *Unión de Pequeños Agricultores* taken at face value. It therefore deserves some closer scrutiny.

First, the argument derived from the workload for the Court seems questionable. As a matter of principle it is an admission of weakness to let the

[73] Case C-491/01 *British American Tobacco (Investments) Ltd and Imperial Tobacco Ltd* [2002] ECR I-11453, para 40.
[74] P Nihoul, 'Le recours des particuliers contres les actes communautaires de portée générale. Nouveaux développements dans la jurisprudence' (2003) 11 *JTDE* 38.
[75] *Ibid*, at 39. See also M Köngeter, 'Erweiterte Klageberechtigung bei Individualnichtigkeitsklagen gegen EG-Verordnungen?' (2002) 55 *NJW* 2216 at 2217; J Gundel, 'Die Tabakprodukt-Richtlinie vor dem EuGH: Zur Zulässigkeit der Nutzung doppelter Rechtsgrundlagen im Rechtssetzungsverfahren der Gemeinschaft' (2003) 38 *EuR* 100 at 100–1.
[76] P Nihoul, 'Le recours des particuliers contres les actes communautaires de portée générale. Nouveaux développements dans la jurisprudence' (2003) 11 *JTDE* 38 at 40–42.
[77] *Ibid*, at 42; M Köngeter, 'Erweiterte Klageberechtigung bei Individualnichtigkeitsklagen gegen EG-Verordnungen?' (2002) 55 *NJW* 2216 at 2217.

extent of judicial protection depend on the ECJ's perceived burden.[78] But also in practical terms the assessment is not that strong. An indirect route for judicial review basically is a cumbersome way to end up in Luxemburg after all, marred with all the procedural defects that have been convincingly summed up by Advocate General Jacobs.[79] Using the national courts as a filter could only discourage them from referring cases to the ECJ, especially in borderline cases. Yet, no one benefits from national courts that apply dubious Community laws instead. The only major shift rather seems to be a transfer of the legal protection of individuals from the CFI to the ECJ, contrary to the wishes of the Member States.[80]

Secondly, the argument derived from a possible disturbance of the functioning of the institutions is troublesome. Proponents of the ECJ's stance admit that there is a growing tendency to require an immediate and effective remedy but consider the solution devised by the Court to be a compromise between those who demand an effective remedy against Community acts and the classic jurisprudence, which does not allow for individuals directly to challenge acts of general application.[81] Yet, an indirect challenge can be as disruptive for the institutions — or even more so, since indirect challenges take place at a far later time when the institutions or Member States may already have taken hundreds of decisions on the basis of the contested act. Admittedly, the right to an effective remedy does not necessarily imply a right of access to a court with competence to invalidate or override a law enacted by the legislature.[82] However, two important points should be made in this respect.

[78] See also G van der Wal, 'Arrest Unión de Pequeños Agricultores: de ontvankelijkheid van particulieren weer beperkt' (2002) 8 *NTER* 288 at 292.

[79] Opinion of Advocate General F Jacobs in Case C-50/00 P *Unión de Pequeños Agricultores v Council* [2002] ECR I-6677, paras 38–44.

[80] See the recitals of Council Decision 88/591/ECSC, EEC, Euratom of 24 Oct 1988 establishing a Court of First Instance of the European Communities [1988] OJ L319/1; Opinion of Advocate General F Jacobs in Case C-50/00 P *Unión de Pequeños Agricultores v Council* [2002] ECR I-6677, paras 91–96. The role of the CFI is strengthened even further by the Nice Treaty: see in general D Ruiz-Jarabo Colomer, 'La réforme de la Cour de justice opérée par le traité de Nice et sa mise en oeuvre future' (2001) 37 *RTDE* 705; PJG Kapteyn, 'De rechterlijke organisatie van de Europese Unie en de Intergouvernementele Conferentie 2000' (2001) 76 *Nederlands Juristenblad* 1. See also B Vesterdorf, 'The Community Court System Ten Years from Now and Beyond: Challenges and Possibilites' (2003) 28 *EL Rev* 303.

[81] P Nihoul, 'Le recours des particuliers contres les actes communautaires de portée générale. Nouveaux développements dans la jurisprudence' (2003) 11 *JTDE* 38 at 41.

[82] A very interesting approach in this respect can be found in a judgment of the European Court of Human Rights of 24 Sept 2002: see para 52 of Case 27824/95 *Posti and Rahko v Finland*, available at the ECtHR website: *www.echr.coe.int/Eng/Judments.htm*. The ECtHR continues however with a bizarre mixture of elements derived from Art 6 ECHR and the case law of the ECJ on admissibility (most notably the unnamed *Plaumann* test and its exceptional application in *Extramet*, seemingly considered to be the normal application of the conditions on *locus standi*), in order to be able to apply the Convention on the situation of two Finnish fishermen whose rights had been curtailed by a Finnish decree they could not

First, as has been convincingly demonstrated,[83] Community law appears to be out of line with the law of the Member States. It appears that most Member States provide for far greater access to their courts, allowing their citizens to attack both administrative and (albeit sometimes to a lesser extent) legislative acts. Historically, a restrictive interpretation may have been defensible in the light of the differences in wording between the EC Treaty and the now expired ECSC Treaty,[84] though the founding fathers of the Community apparently did not have a clear idea on the way direct challenges by individuals against Community acts should be organized.[85] However, since then the administrative laws of the Member States — and in certain fields even the Courts' case law under the EC Treaty[86] — have evolved towards greater openness, and the coal and steel sectors have come to be governed by the EC Treaty. Therefore, there appears to be no reason not to bring the Community system of judicial protection back in line with the constitutional traditions of the Member States.

Secondly, the difficulties in obtaining judicial review are far from limited to acts of a democratically elected legislator. Often the contested acts emanating from the Council or the Commission, although of general application, are of an administrative nature. The *Jégo-Quéré* and *Unión de Pequeños Agricultores* cases serve as clear evidence in this respect. Advocate General Jacobs addressed those issues while defending his solution against the criticism that some systems of national law draw a distinction between legislation and administrative measures and allow only for judicial review

challenge directly. The ECtHR considered the Convention to be breached because the applicants were left without a remedy. On the facts the ECtHR considered at para 61 that it had not been demonstrated that the applicants could have expected with any reasonable degree of likelihood to obtain damages from the State on the basis of its liability for such mistakes or omissions in the use of public authority — even less so as the impugned decrees were undoubtedly based on formally correct statutory law, namely the Fishing Act. A similar problem seems to exist in respect of the action for damages under Community law, as was rightly recognized by the ECJ in *Jégo-Quéré*. Similarly, as remarked above, the idea that one could obtain judicial review by first breaching the contested acts was plainly rejected at para 64: 'no one can be required to breach the law so as to be able to have a "civil right" determined in accordance with Article 6 §1'.

[83] D Waelbroeck and A-M Verheyden, 'Les conditions de recevabilité des recours en annulation des particuliers contre les actes normatifs communautaires' (1995) 31 *CDE* 399. See also A Arnull, 'Private Applicants and the Action for Annulment under Article 173 of the EC Treaty' (1995) *CML Rev* 7 at 9–10; see also the Opinion of Advocate General F Jacobs in Case C-50/00 P *Unión de Pequeños Agricultores v Council* [2002] ECR I-6677, paras 85–90.
[84] Opinion of Advocate General M Lagrange in Cases 15/62 & 17/62 *Producteurs de Fruits v Council* [1962] ECR 449, though this thesis has always been contested: see F Schockweiler, 'L'accès à la justice dans l'ordre juridique communautaire' (1996) 4 *JTDE* 1 at 7; HG Schermers, 'De Groene Partij' (1986) 4 Ars Aequi 764 at 773.
[85] P Nihoul, 'Le recours des particuliers contres les actes communautaires de portée générale. Nouveaux développements dans la jurisprudence' (2003) 11 *JTDE* 38 at 41.
[86] Opinion of Advocate General F Jacobs in Case C-50/00 P *Unión de Pequeños Agricultores v Council* [2002] ECR I-6677, paras 83–84.

of administrative measures at the initiative of individuals.[87] In some Member States the possibility for judicial review of acts of the elected legislator is indeed rather limited. The argument goes that it is hard to see why the assessment of a judge should prevail over the opinion of a democratically elected parliament.[88] The critics' thesis is that since general Community measures are analogous in their effects to legislation, review at the instigation of individuals is not required.

Against this the Advocate General offers some very interesting thoughts on the role of the judiciary in enhancing the legitimacy of the Community system. First he makes the preliminary observation that the laws of the Member States do not in general *exclude* individuals from challenging legislation which violates constitutionally enshrined rights or fundamental principles of law, by actions either before constitutional courts or even ordinary judges. The Advocate General stresses that the restrictions on access to judicial review of legislation which exist in the Member States are moreover based on two essential premises: national laws generally establish a clear distinction between legislation and administrative measures and legislation is systematically adopted by more democratically legitimate procedures than administrative measures.[89] The Community system does not meet those criteria.

As to the first premise, it should be observed that the Community does not have a clear hierarchy of norms.[90] At the Community level, an ingenious institutional balance has replaced the normal division of powers, which is present in most nation states. As a result the Commission, the Council, and the European Parliament may all adopt measures that in a national legal order would be considered to be legislative as well as measures of an administrative nature. The distinction is, moreover, further blurred because of the lack of distinctive names for the various types of acts — this is precisely the reason individuals are allowed to bring an action against decisions taken 'in the form of regulation'.[91]

The second premise brings us to the still imperfect democratic legitimacy of the Community decision-making process. An important share of the legislation, also in economically sensitive fields, still results from a decision-making process with very limited input from democratically elected bodies. The ECJ once considered it necessary to let the UK courts abandon centuries-old constitutional traditions in order to improve judicial control over the conformity of UK law with EC law.[92] In this light

[87] *Ibid*, paras 87–90.
[88] HG Schermers, 'De Groene Partij' (1986) 4 *Ars Aequi* 764 at 772.
[89] Opinion of Advocate General F Jacobs in Case C-50/00 P *Unión de Pequeños Agricultores v Council* [2002] ECR I-6677, paras 89–90.
[90] *Ibid*, para 90.
[91] See in this respect also K Lenaerts and M Desomer, 'Bricks for a Constitutional Treaty of the European Union: Values, Objectives and Means' (2002) 27 *EL Rev* 377 at 397–406.
[92] See Case C-213/89 *Factortame* [1990] ECR I-2433.

there does not appear to be a sensible reason to shield Community legislation, which is often the result of far less transparent and legitimate decision-making procedures, from effective validity control. After all, judicial review of Community acts is not threatening to the Community. If an act is found to be invalid that proves only that the institutions themselves have violated higher rules of Community law, thus potentially endangering fundamental principles of the Community legal order. Whereas in the Member States this task of ensuring that the fundamental values of their legal order are not violated by unconstitutional legislation may sometimes solely be entrusted to the national parliaments, this cannot be so in the EC legal order. If sufficient democratic control does not exist at the moment an act is adopted, it is essential for a polity based on the rule of law, such as the Community,[93] that its citizens get at least the opportunity to obtain effective judicial review once the act affects them in their legal position.[94]

But there is more. At first sight the ECJ sets up a decentralized system of judicial review of Community acts, seemingly in accordance with the subsidiarity principle.[95] On a closer look a totally different picture appears, however, as the Court puts the responsibility for making that system work effectively with the Member States.

Hence, this approach significantly curtails national procedural autonomy.[96] Most Member States simply do not have the necessary remedies in place.[97] This means that national legislators and — pending legislative action — national judges must introduce entirely new procedures into their legal orders, or considerably alter internal procedural rules. This has, admittedly, been done before.[98] Notable examples are the introduction

[93] Case 294/83 *Parti Ecologiste 'Les Verts' v European Parliament* [1986] ECR 1339, para 23.

[94] D Waelbroeck and A-M Verheyden, 'Les conditions de recevabilité des recours en annulation des particuliers contre les actes normatifs communautaires' (1995) 31 *CDE* 399 at 436. See also F Ragolle, 'Access to Justice for Private Applicants in the Community Legal Order: Recent (R)evolutions' (2003) 40 *CML Rev* 90 at 101.

[95] This also seems to be the position of the ECJ as presented by its President, GG Rodríguez Iglesias, to the 'Discussion Circle' on the ECJ: see CONV 572/03, (1) 3.

[96] T Corthaut, 'Case CFI May 3, 2002, *Jégo-Quéré v Commission*, T-177/01 and C-50/00 P ECJ July 25, 2002, *Unión de Pequeños Agricultores v Council*' (2002) 9 *Columbia J of European L* 141 at 163.

[97] Currently similar remedies seem to exist only in the UK, Ireland, Portugal, and Germany. Even in Germany there seems to be disagreement in legal literature whether the current system is really sufficient if the ECJ is serious in putting the burden of creating remedies enabling a full review of Community law wholly on the Member States: compare D Dittert, 'Effectiver Rechtsschutz gegen EG-Verordnungen: Zwischen Fischfangnetzen, Olivenöl und kleinen Landwirten' (2002) 37 *EuR* 708 at 716–18 and H-P Schneider, 'Es gibt noch Richter in Luxemburg — Zum Individualrechtsschutz durch europäische Gerichte' (2002) 55 *NJW* 2927 at 2928.

[98] The national procedural autonomy is indeed qualified by way of exception by the principle of equivalence and the principle of effectiveness: see *inter alia* Case 811/79 *Ariete* [1980] ECR 2545, para 12.

of an action for damages against a Member State for breach of Community law[99] and the obligation to provide for a remedy enabling national judges to take provisional measures against any other branch of government in order to safeguard Community rights.[100]

However, those examples specifically demonstrate the intrusiveness of such incursion into the national procedural autonomy. Granting the same protection in other civil cases later mirrored the introduction of interim injunctive relief in civil proceedings involving EC law in the UK.[101] The introduction of the *Francovich* action has likewise created an ongoing debate in Belgium as to whether a general state liability regime for breach of higher norms by the legislator should be set in place.[102] It is only natural that the creation of an EC law remedy puts pressure on Member States to alter their laws on similar, but purely internal, situations — if only to avoid reverse discrimination.[103] In the cases at hand almost all Member States will have to loosen their national criteria on *locus standi* in order to make it possible to hear cases calling for the review of Community law in circumstances that before were not possible. It should be obvious that if the admissibility test an applicant must fulfil is considerably less strict in cases involving an element of EC law than in purely internal matters, a new reverse discrimination is created, which can be righted only by altering national procedural law in fields where Member States did not consent to be subjected to rules of EC law.

The ECJ has in the past proven to be sensitive to this problem. On the question whether national judges are under an obligation to raise issues of

[99] Cases C-6/90 & C-9/90 *Francovich and Bonifaci* [1991] ECR I-5357, para 45 and Cases C-46/93 & C-48/93 *Brasserie du Pêcheur and Factortame* [1996] ECR I-1029, para 74; J Temple Lang, 'The Principle of Effective Protection of Community Law Rights' in D O'Keeffe (ed), *Liber Amicorum in Honour of Lord Slynn of Hadley* (Kluwer Law International, The Hague/London/Boston, 2000), i, 235 at 242–49.

[100] Case C-213/89 *Factortame* [1990] ECR I-2433; J Temple Lang, 'The Principle of Effective Protection of Community Law Rights' in D O'Keeffe (ed), *Liber Amicorum in Honour of Lord Slynn of Hadley* (Kluwer Law International, The Hague/London/Boston, 2000), I, (235) 241–42.

[101] See C Harlow, 'A Common European Law of Remedies?' in C Kilpatrick, T Novitz, and P Skidmore (eds), *The Future of Remedies in Europe* (Oxford, Hart, 2000), 69 at 79–80.

[102] P Lewalle, *Contentieux administratif* (Brussels, Larcier, 2002), 329; M Mahieu and S van Drooghenbroeck, 'La Responsabilité de l'Etat Législateur' (1998) 117 *JT* 825; S van Drooghenbroeck, 'La responsabilité du fait de la fonction normative' (1997) 116 *JT* 105 at 110–11. See also the issue whether — contrary to national legislation — a Member State can be rendered liable for breach of Community law where that breach is committed by a supreme court: see Case C-224/01 *Köbler* [2003] ECR I-0000, in which the ECJ accepted the principle of state liability for sufficiently serious breaches by Member State courts of last instance in principle, but rejected the argument that in the case at hand the Austrian Supreme Court had made a manifest error so as to warrant liability in practice. In this way the ECJ did not entirely follow its Advocate General, who had argued that the Austrian courts had made an 'inexcusable' error: see Opinion of Advocate General Léger in Case C-224/01 *Köbler* [2003] ECR I-0000.

[103] C Harlow, 'A Common European Law of Remedies?' in C Kilpatrick, T Novitz, and P Skidmore (eds), *The Future of Remedies in Europe* (Oxford, Hart, 2000), 69 at 79–80.

Community law of their own motion, the ECJ ruled that in those Member States that allow for their judges to raise legal issues of their own motion, the judges are under an obligation to do so — however, in those national procedures that provide for strict passivity, no such powers for the national judge had to be introduced.[104] The ECJ is indeed willing to accept some degree of differentiation among the Member States and employs the requirement of 'effectiveness' only as an exception to the rule of national procedural autonomy which falls to be used with moderation.[105] If the same effectiveness can be obtained through less intrusive means, such as altering the *interpretation* of the wording of Article 230(4) TEC, this should be preferred from the perspective of subsidiarity.

A further difficulty in relying on the Member States for guaranteeing sufficient judicial protection is the enforcement of the system. In light of the division of competences the supervising authority should be the Commission.However, the Commission[106] had until recently never brought an action against a Member State for failure by the national judiciary to provide individuals with sufficient judicial protection.[107] The Commission has never used its powers under Article 226 EC, despite being perfectly entitled to do so, against a Member State because one of its courts of last instance had failed to ask for a preliminary ruling despite being under an obligation to do so.[108] There is no indication that the Commission would be more willing or able to monitor whether all

[104] Joined Cases C-430/93 & C-431/93 *Van Schijndel and Van Veen* [1995] ECR I-4705; Case C-72/95 *Kraaijeveld* [1996] ECR I-5403, paras 55–62; S Prechal, 'Community Law in National Courts: The Lessons from *Van Schijndel*' (1998) 35 *CML Rev* 681.

[105] A good example of this is the U-turn the ECJ has made in respect of the starting point for national time limits in cases involving a non-transposed directive. Originally the Court had ruled that such time limits could not run before the effective transposition of the directive. This simple but highly effective rule is however almost entirely eroded by the judgment in *Fantask*, which allows for reasonable time limits starting even before transposition to be applied and thus effectively barring cases such as that of the applicant in that case. Compare Case C-208/90 *Emmott* [1991] ECR I-4269 with Case C-188/95 *Fantask* [1997] ECR I-6783. See L Flynn, 'Whatever Happened to *Emmott*? The Perfecting of Community Rules on National Time Limits' in C Kilpatrick, T Novitz, and P Skidmore (eds), *The Future of Remedies in Europe* (Oxford, Hart, 2000), 51.

[106] J-D Braun and M Kettner, 'Die Absage des EuGH an eine richterrechtliche Reform des EGRechtsschutzsystems — "Plaumann" auf immer und ewig?' (2003) 56 *DöV* 58 at 66.

[107] See however the pending Case C-129/00 *Commission v Italy* [2000] OJ C129/00, where the Commission has taken legal action against the Italian Republic because of the excessive procedural burden the Corte Suprema di Cassazione imposes on taxpayers seeking reimbursment of taxes levied contrary to EC law. Advocate General LA Geelhoed delivered his opinion in the case on 4 June 2003, it is available at *www.curia.eu.int.*

[108] J Temple Lang, 'The Principle of Effective Protection of Community Law Rights' in D O'Keeffe (ed), *Liber Amicorum in Honour of Lord Slynn of Hadley* (Kluwer Law International, The Hague/London/Boston, 2000), i, 235 at 272–73. In Germany, however, the *Bundesverfassungsgericht* has classified such a refusal as a breach of the principle of the '*gesetzliche Richter*', which is enshrined in the German constitution: BVerfG 9 Jan 2001, 1 BvR 1036/99 (*www.bverfg.de*).

national legal systems ensure that individual are not left without a remedy allowing them to challenge the validity of Community acts without having to breach those acts first.

The only alternative enforcement mechanism would be a *Francovich* action for damages against a Member State because of its failure to provide the individual with an effective remedy.[109] Applied to a *Jégo-Quéré*-like situation this would result in a procedural nightmare. Instead of directly bringing a case before the CFI for annulment (and if necessary suspension) of the act, the company would first have to go through the national courts, presumably up to the highest level, only to find that no judge is willing to hear the case, and then start all over again in order to convince a court that it suffered damage because it did not have a chance of initially contesting the validity of the act. As this amounts to compensation for loss of an opportunity the national court thus addressed should then assess the likely success of the applicant's original application, provided that the court had been willing to hear the case, as it should have. This involves, then, an assessment of the probability that such a fictitious judge would have deemed it necessary to refer the case to the ECJ and ultimately of the probability that the ECJ would have declared the regulation invalid. Only the ECJ itself can clarify this issue, presumably by finally examining the validity of the act, if only it is requested to do so. Accordingly, sometime during this second procedure the ECJ will have to become involved after all. In the meantime the company will of course still be faced with the dilemma between compliance with a potentially invalid regulation and breaching that regulation with the risk of being prosecuted. Somehow it seems so much less trouble for everyone, if — at least in the *Jégo-Quéré* type of cases, where in the absence of any implementing measure no natural link with the national courts exists — the CFI would be allowed to deal with those cases directly.

So, what is wrong then with the option offered by the CFI to reinterpret the criteria for admissibility of actions for annulment brought by individuals? According to the ECJ[110] and some legal writing,[111] the new definitions by Advocate General Jacobs and the CFI are not mere interpretations of the EC Treaty, but outright amendments. The ECJ argues that the distinction between direct and individual concern is blurred to the extent that the CFI seems to erase the condition of individual concern. Yet, this is certainly not the case in respect of the *Jégo-Quéré* judgment, which was tailored to the special situation at hand, where no further implementation measures were required — and even then only for those applicants whose legal situation

[109] This was at stake in Case C-224/01 *Köbler* [2003] ECR I-0000. See also fn 102.
[110] Case C-50/00 P *Unión de Pequeños Agricultores v Council* [2002] ECR I-6677, para 44.
[111] R Barents, 'Een midzomernachtdroom op de Kirchberg' (2003) 51 SEW 2 at 2–9.

was effectively affected by the regulation. This definition of individual concern may seem to coincide with the requirement that the applicant has an interest in the annulment of the contested act.[112] This is however only really problematic if one considers it necessary that there is, in all cases, a difference between the interest in bringing the case and individual concern.[113] This distinction has indeed hitherto always been made, although it is not explicitly mentioned in Article 230(4) TEC. Therefore it is hard to see how blurring this distinction would amount to amending the Treaty as such — certainly not if compared to the adaptations the ECJ has made over the years to the other aspects of Article 230.[114]

In any event, it should be clear by now that at this stage the ECJ is set to hold on to its classic criteria as set out by it in *Plaumann*. Nonetheless, the ECJ makes two further overtures. First, the *Plaumann* test requires an important element of factual assessment. In this way the CFI, albeit under scrutiny of the ECJ, obtains some margin of appreciation in assessing the facts and deducing the relevant factors in determining whether an applicant is individually concerned. This has recently been reaffirmed in s*Camar*, where the ECJ ultimately annulled a judgment of the CFI declaring admissible an action for annulment brought by banana importers, but only after it recalled that '[c]learly, as the Court pointed out in paragraph 44 of the judgment in *Unión de Pequeños Agricultores v Council*, cited above, the condition that natural or legal persons may bring an action challenging a regulation only if they are concerned individually must be interpreted in the light of the principle of effective judicial protection *by taking account of the various circumstances that may distinguish an*

[112] R Barents, 'Een midzomernachtdroom op de Kirchberg' (2003) 51 *SEW* 2 at 2–9. See also P Cassia, 'Continuité et rupture dans le contentieux de la recevabilité du recours en annulation des particuliers. A propos de l'arrêt *Jégo-Quéré* du 3 mai 2002 du Tribunal de première instance des Communautés européennes (Aff T-177/01)' (2002) 44 *RMCUE* 547 at 557. The latter solves the puzzle by suggesting that the CFI should have kept the condition of interest in the annulment, and should have defined individual concern in terms of the factual situation that no other remedies are available.

[113] Though one could also argue that this distinction can be saved if the interest requirement is interpreted as meaning that the measure must have a potentially adverse effect on one's factual or legal situation. This then can be contrasted with the *Jégo-Quéré* definition of individual concern: 'if the measure in question affects his legal position, in a manner which is both definite and immediate, by restricting his rights or by imposing obligations on him'. In this way the condition of individual concern continues to serve as a limit to bringing an *actio popularis*. An example may clarify this distinction. Every consumer may have an interest in the annulment of a regulation imposing draconic emission standards on cars, making them so expensive that they are hardly affordable for the average household, yet only the car manufacturers who have to change their production methods and business model and who may be liable for sanctions if they violate this regulation will also be individually concerned. As argued above the distinction with direct concern is not an issue as *Jégo-Quéré* does not purport to change or limit the requirement of direct concern.

[114] See, above, section A of Part II, 18–20. See also A Arnull, 'Private Applicants and the Action for Annulment under Article 173 of the EC Treaty' (1995) 32 *CML Rev* 7 at 16–19.

*applicant individually*'.[115] A certain degree of leniency in the factual assessment whether the *Plaumann* criteria are fulfilled could indeed make a huge difference. As was rightly observed, it is its application, in particular, which makes the *Plaumann* test so rigid.[116]

The second way out is, of course, an intervention by the Member States by amending the Treaties. As the ECJ suggests, '[w]hile it is, admittedly, possible to envisage a system of judicial review of the legality of Community measures of general application different from that established by the founding Treaty and never amended as to its principles, it is for the Member States, if necessary, in accordance with Article 48 EU, to reform the system currently in force.'[117] The ECJ has in the past on the occasion of the Amsterdam IGC already made submissions in respect of Article 230 TEC itself.[118] However, the Member States never took up the issue. This time — and not at least due to the conflicting jurisprudence of the ECJ and CFI — the issue has landed high on the agenda of the Convention on the future of Europe.

The Convention was first confronted with the issue in the framework of the Working Group on the status of the Charter of Fundamental Rights. While inquiring into the possibilities for enforcing the Charter and offering a broad protection of fundamental rights, the Working Group was confronted with the recent diverging case law of the ECJ and CFI. At the start of its proceedings several options were presented to it by the Secretariat of the Convention.[119] The Secretariat noted that some advocated a special procedure to protect human rights, modelled on the Verfassungsbeschwerde or recurso de amparo[120] while others call for amendments to the criteria for standing in Article 230 TEC or considered the present situation to be sufficient, at least if Member States provide for national legal remedies. In its final report the Working Group had rejected the idea of a special procedure. However the Working Group noted that,

[115] Case C-312/00 P *Commission v Camar and Tico* [2002] ECR I-11355 (italics added). See also D Waelbroeck, 'Le droit au recours juridictionnel effectif du particulier trois pas en avant, deux pas en arrière' (2002) 38 *CDE* 3 at 7 and N van den Broeck, 'A Long Hot Summer for Individual Concern? The European Court's Recent Case Law on Direct Actions by Private Parties ... and a Plea for a Foreign Affairs Exception' (2003) 30 *LIEI* 61 at 73–74. However, read in combination with the recent judgment in Case C-142/00 P *Commission v Nederlandse Antillen* [2003] ECR I-3483, the room for manoeuvre by the CFI may turn out to be very limited.

[116] See above n 16, at 488–91.

[117] Case C-50/00 P *Unión de Pequeños Agricultores v Council* [2002] ECR I-6677, para 45.

[118] *Report of the Court of Justice on Certain Aspects of the Application of the Treaty on European Union* (Luxembourg, 1995), which may be consulted at *http://europa.eu.int/en/agenda/igchome/eu-doc/justice/cj_mp.html*.

[119] CONV 116/02, (1) 15–17.

[120] See also N van den Broeck, 'A Long Hot Summer for Individual Concern? The European Court's Recent Case Law on Direct Actions by Private Parties ... and a Plea for a Foreign Affairs Exception' (2003) 30 *LIEI* 61 at 75.

owing to the wording of Article 230(4) TEC, a certain lacuna in judicial protection might exist, especially in case of 'self-executing regulations'.[121] On the other hand a majority of its members seemed swayed by the arguments on the division of work between the national courts and the ECJ, with some even arguing to incorporate the formula used by the ECJ in *Unión de Pequeños Agricultores* to impose on the Member States the duty to provide for effective remedies.[122] It would not be the first time that the constitutionmaking powers copied a phrase by the Court while redrafting Article 230 TEC.[123] Ultimately, the Working Group decided to refrain from making any recommendations in respect of Article 230(4) TEC, because of its overall implications went way beyond the scope of the protection of fundamental rights.[124]

The matter of Article 230(4) TEC was later taken up again in the special Discussion Circle on the Court of Justice. The divergence of opinion among the Members remained. Both the President of the ECJ and the President of the CFI made contributions to the discussion on behalf of their courts, and again the divergence in preferences persisted, with ECJ President Rodríguez Iglesias[125] defending the current system on the basis of the principle of subsidiarity and CFI President Vesterdorf,[126] whilst recalling the judgment in *Jégo-Quéré* by the first extended chamber, expressing the division in his Court on the matter.

However, both Presidents did introduce an important element into the debate where they referred to the link of the reform of Article 230(4) TEC with the simplification of the normative instruments.[127] Working Group IX,[128] followed by the Praesidium[129] and the entire Convention,[130] has made bold proposals to reduce dramatically the number of instruments, to introduce a hierarchy of norms, and to make clear distinctions between legislative and executive measures. This has resulted in the proposed Articles I–32 to I–36 of the Draft Treaty establishing a Constitution for Europe.[131]

If the Convention proposals are accepted, the Union will in the future have two legislative acts, called European laws and European framework laws, which mirror the current (legislative) regulations and directives. These

[121] CONV 354/02 (1) 15–16.
[122] *Ibid*, 16.
[123] See above, p 20.
[124] CONV 352/02 (1) 16.
[125] CONV 572/03 (1) 3–5.
[126] CONV 575/03 (1) 4–5.
[127] The President of the ECJ in CONV 572/03 (1) 4, the President of the CFI in CONV 572/03 (1)5.
[128] CONV 424/02.
[129] CONV 571/03.
[130] CONV 630/03 (1) 2–5.
[131] [2003] OJ C169/1.

acts will be implemented at the Community — or better Union — level through implementing regulations, which will be executive acts of general scope and application, and implementing decisions, which will be of individual scope and application. Finally, the Convention introduces the delegated regulation through which the legislator can empower the Commission to supplement and amend non-essential provisions of its legislation.

As the basic procedure for adoption of legislative acts will in principle be the co-decision procedure, the possibility for individuals to challenge those acts directly could remain restricted. Indeed, one could argue that in those instances there is sufficient democratic control on the adoption of those acts.[132] It then suffices that the Member States[133] and the institutions involved in their adoption can challenge their validity directly. Individuals will still be able to challenge those acts indirectly through the national courts. This is self-evident for European framework laws, which in any event entail the adoption[134] of national measures,[135] and can also be justified for European laws containing basic choices of policy. Nonetheless, it should be noted that, at least in some Member States, individuals can also challenge general legislative acts, provided that they demonstrate a certain interest in the matter. Extending *locus standi* to

[132] S Prechal and L Parret, 'Zaak C-50/00 P Unión de Pequeños Agricultores t. Raad van de Europese Unie' (2003) 51 *SEW* 35 at 38; See also, pp 31–33 above on the basis of D Waelbroeck and A-M Verheyden, 'Les conditions de recevabilité des recours en annulation des particuliers contre les actes normatifs communautaires' (1995) 31 *CDE* 399 at 436.

[133] Note in this respect the creation of a course of action for national parliaments and the Committee of the Regions in order to enforce the principle of subsidiarity in the Draft Protocol on the application of the principles of subsidiarity and proportionality, CONV 820/03. For the commentary on this draft Protocol see CONV 579/03.

[134] Since the Nice Treaty, the European Parliament, the Council, and the Commission are on an equal footing as privileged applicants.

[135] In this respect one further nuance could be added. On one possible reading of the judgment of the European Court of Human Rights of 24 Sept 2002, in Application 27824/95 *Posti and Rahko v Finland*, available at the ECtHR website (see also, above, n 82) there should in practice always be a possibility of challenging legislation directly, despite the Court denying this at para 52. Yet, this may be the only way to avoid situations arising where people first have to violate the law before being able to obtain legal review. Current directives, or future framework laws, containing a prohibition are to be implemented through national legislation, which in turn imposes the prohibition on citizens in the national legal order concerned. However, as all Member States are party to the European Convention on Human Rights, the Member States in turn must then provide for an adequate procedure enabling individuals to challenge this national law without them having to breach the law first. This in turn may then result in early indirect challenges along the lines of Case C-491/01, *The Queen v Secretary of State for Health, ex parte British American Tobacco (Investments) Ltd and Imperial Tobacco Ltd* [2002] ECR I-11453, which can prove to be a valuable tool. The main drawback of this procedure remains, of course, that individuals must make a procedural detour through the national courts to obtain judicial review of the directive by the ECJ. This seems defensible, though, to the extent that in such situations there may often be some national law problems at issue as well, for which the national court is a convenient forum. The alternative evidently is to lower the criteria for direct access even further to allow direct actions against directives as well. Yet, in those instances it may be extremely difficult to avoid the introduction of an *actio popularis*.

similar Union acts would thus not be revolutionary, and it would avoid situations where individuals can obtain judicial review of the validity of directly applicable European laws, which require no further implementation by either the Union or the Member States, only by breaching them first. However, in accordance with the constitutional traditions of the Member States, no discussion should exist on whether implementing acts can be challenged by individuals. Furthermore, the *Jégo-Quéré* and *Unión de Pequeños Agricultores* cases show that there is a clear and legitimate demand for implementing acts of general application to be subject to challenge as well, though the ECJ does not see a possibility of hearing such cases under the current wording of Article 230(4) TEC. For implementing acts of general application the requirements should thus be rephrased in order to allow individuals to challenge them, in so far as they are of direct concern to them. The position of delegated regulations is open for debate. On the one hand, they do affect legislative provisions. On the other hand, they do not involve basic choices of policy. Delegated regulations are moreover not adopted according to a procedure involving full democratic scrutiny. Therefore it seems appropriate to allow individuals to bring challenges against such acts as well, provided that they are of direct concern to them. Apparently the wording of Article 230(4) TEC then needs to be altered. A promising suggestion was made in the final conclusions of the Discussion Circle on the Court of Justice: 'Any natural or legal person may, under the same conditions, institute proceedings against an act addressed to that person or which is of direct and individual concern to him, and against [an act of general application][a regulatory act] which is of direct concern to him without entailing implementing measures'.[136] In this way the Convention was left with two options. If the Convention were to choose the option of 'an act of general application', this would also include legislative acts. The notion 'regulatory acts' is more restrictive and would provide only for actions against implementing and (perhaps) delegated regulations. The addition 'without entailing implementing measures' is aimed to restrict *locus standi* to 'those (problematical) cases where the individual concerned must first infringe the law before he can have access to a court'.[137] Ultimately the Convention has decided to propose in Article III–270 of the Draft Treaty establishing a Constitution for Europe the restrictive solution excluding legislative acts.[138] Though this is undoubtedly

[136] CONV 636/03, (1) 7. This proposal moreover received the express backing of the Austrian representative, H Farnleiter, and the Belgian representative, L Michel, in a rare joint letter to the Members of the Convention: see CONV 716/03.

[137] CONV 636/03, (1) 7.

[138] [2003]OJ C169/01. Art III-270(4) reads: 'Any natural or legal person may, under the same conditions, institute proceedings against an act addressed to that person or which is of direct and individual concern to him or her, and against a regulatory act which is of direct concern to him or her and does not entail implementing measures'.

a major step forward, some problems still remain. First, the terminology is ill-chosen, as nowhere else in the Draft Treaty is the term 'regulatory act' defined; without the preparatory works one might even be tempted to think that legislative acts are actually included, while they are not. Secondly, the regime for legislative acts still seems hardly reconcilable with the *Posti and Rahko* judgment,[139] which also implies the possibility for direct review of legislative measures.[140] Thirdly, even for executive acts which require an implementing national measure — albeit a mechanical one, where the national authorities have no discretion at all — this national measure must be awaited and challenged in the national courts. In respect of those executive Community acts, the cumbersome preliminary rulings procedure will still be inevitable. Nonetheless, the Convention thus comes forward with a proposal, which is very close to the result intended by the judgment of the CFI in *Jégo-Quéré*. A new contribution of judicial review to European constitutionalism seems about to be consummated by the Member States.

## III. THE ROLE OF THE COMMUNITY COURTS IN ENHANCING DEMOCRACY AND LEGITIMACY

In this section we will demonstrate how the ECJ and the CFI[141] have been shaping the constitutional and administrative law of the Union in cases involving actions for annulment. Through judicial review the Community Courts have systematically enhanced the transparency, accountability, and democratic nature of the decision-making process in the EU. As an important number of the cited cases are currently under appeal, further developments in these fields are soon to be expected.

### A. Transparency

Transparency, as the President of the CFI rightly remarked, is not just a vogue word.[142] Ever since the rejection of the Maastricht Treaty in

[139] n 82 above.

[140] Nevertheless, in exceptional circumstances, admissible actions for annulment against legislative measures cannot be excluded. After all, it remains possible to demonstrate that a legislative act must be equated with a decision *vis-à-vis* certain individuals with exceptional attributes that distinguish them from all others, while at the same time continuing to be of a general nature *vis-à-vis* all other market participants: see Case C-309/89 *Codorniu v Council* [1994] ECR I-1853.

[141] See in this respect also P Mengozzi, 'The Protection of Individual Rights and the Court of First Instance of the European Communities' (1999–2000) 23 *FILJ* 707.

[142] B Vesterdorf, 'Transparency — Not Just a Vogue Word' (1998–99) 22 *FILJ* 902.

the Danish referendum (1992), the movement to lead the EU away from secrecy[143] has gained momentum. The Community Courts — and the Ombudsman — have played an important role in this respect through several broad rulings[144] concerning access to documents.[145]

Since the Treaty of Amsterdam the right of access to documents has been enshrined in Article 255 TEC. Moreover, Article 1 TEU stresses that in the European Union decisions are to be taken as openly as possible. From these provisions the ECJ and CFI have, often in the context of actions for annulment brought by citizens who were denied access to certain documents, developed a strong regime in respect of access to documents. The Courts have moreover from the outset accepted that this openness applies to any document in the possession of the institutions, even if they originate from the sphere of the second[146] or third[147] pillar of the Union. This, too, forms an example of a rule which was first formulated by the Courts, and then consummated by the Member States amending the EU Treaty accordingly.[148]

In *Kuijer v Council*[149] the CFI had the opportunity of nicely summarizing what has been achieved in this respect so far. The case concerned an application for the annulment of the decision of the Council denying Mr Kuijer access to certain documents from the Centre for Information, Discussion and Exchange on Asylum (CIREA).

The CFI first stresses the importance of access to documents. 'It is first necessary to point out that the principle of transparency is intended to secure a more significant role for citizens in the decision-making process and to ensure that the administration acts with greater propriety, efficiency and responsibility vis-à-vis the citizens in a democratic system. It helps to strengthen the principle of democracy and respect for fundamental rights.'[150]

[143] For an inside account of some of the worst practices see LJ Brinkhorst, 'Transparency in the European Union' (1998–99) 22 *FILJ* 129.

[144] For an overview and brief summary see the list maintained by the NGO Statewatch, itself a party to several complaints with the Ombudsman, at *www.statewatch.org/caselawobs.htm*.

[145] Bo Vesterdorf actually identifies at least 4 important principles deriving from the concept of transparency, all of which have been tackled by the CFI: (1) the right to a statement of reasons for a decision, (2) the right to be heard before a decision is taken, (3) a party's right of access to the file, and (4) the public's right of access to information: see 'Transparency — Not Just a Vogue Word' (1998–9) 22 FILJ 902 at 903. The present analysis will be focused on the fourth issue of access to documents.

[146] Case T-14/98 *Hautala v Council* [1999] ECR II-2489, confirmed by the ECJ on appeal in Case C-353/99 P *Council v Hautala* [2001] ECR I-9565.

[147] Case T-174/95 *Svenska Journalistförbundet v Council* [1998] ECR II-2289.

[148] Arts 28(1) and 41(1) TEU; HR Kranenborg, 'De Eurowob in de hand, de EU transparant? Het openbaarheidsregime in de communautaire rechtsorde: een stand van zaken' (2002) 50 *SEW* 447 at 449.

[149] Case T-211/00 *Kuijer v Council* [2002] ECR II-485.

[150] *Ibid*, para 52.

The link between democracy and the public's right of access to documents had been made from the outset by Advocate General Tesauro. It can be agreed that access to documents tends to secure better knowledge on the part of citizens of the acts and measures — even in the phase when they are being drawn up — adopted by those who have 'government functions'. The term 'government functions'[151] is very appropriate, because, as explained above, in Western democracies a lot of 'rule-making' is left to the administration, so access to documents should obviously not be limited to the legislator but also include the administration.[152] This is all the more so for the Community form of government which was characterized — provocatively — as involving members of the Council of Ministers confining themselves to 'rubber-stamping, in most cases behind closed doors, drafts prepared by an ambassadorial college (COREPER) and, at a lower level, by numberless, faceless and unaccountable committees of senior national experts'.[153]

Nonetheless, the right of access to documents is not absolute and the institutions do have a right to refuse access if the public interest may be undermined. In those circumstances the CFI is also correct in stressing the boundaries that must be set to judicial review. In most cases the CFI limits itself to verifying 'whether the procedural rules have been complied with, the decision at issue is properly reasoned and the facts have been accurately stated, and whether there has been a manifest error of assessment of the facts or a misuse of powers'.[154]

The reasoning for assessing whether a limit may be placed on access then goes as follows. First, the legal rule is that the public is to have access to the documents of the institutions and the power to refuse access is the exception.[155] Secondly, it is apparent from the case law[156] that the Council is obliged to consider in respect of each document requested whether, in the light of the information available to it, disclosure is in fact likely to undermine one of the public interests protected. It can refuse access only if this risk is reasonably foreseeable and not merely hypothetical.[157] Moreover, the exceptions must be interpreted in the light of the right to

[151] Opinion of Advocate General G Tesauro in Case C-58/94 *Netherlands v Council* [1996] ECR I-2169, para 14.
[152] M Broberg, 'Access to Documents: A General Principle of Community Law?' (2002) 27 *EL Rev* 194 at 204.
[153] G F Mancini, 'Europe: The Case for Statehood', in G F Mancini and JHH Weiler, 'Europe — The Case for Statehood ... and the Case Against, An Exchange', available at *www.jeanmonetprogram.org/papers/98/98-6-.html*, quoted with approval by U Öberg, 'Public Access to Documents After the Entry into Force of the Amsterdam Treaty: Much Ado about Nothing?', European Integration Online Papers, 1998–008, available at *http://eiop.or.at/eiop/texte/1998-008a.htm.*
[154] Case T-211/00 *Kuijer v Council* [2002] ECR II-485, para 53.
[155] *Ibid*, para 54.
[156] Case T-174/95 *Svenska Journalistförbundet v Council* [1998] ECR II-2289, para 112.
[157] Case T-211/00 *Kuijer v Council* [2002] ECR II-485, para 56.

information and the principle of proportionality; as a result the Council is under an obligation to examine for each document whether partial access could be granted.[158] The ECJ had in the *Hautala* case confirmed that the possibility of partial access must be examined, but it has so far declined to rule on the existence of a right to information.[159] Recognizing such a right, as the CFI has already done,[160] would further enhance transparency and could result in the duty of the institutions to make the necessary inquiries themselves in order to give as much information as possible, rather than demanding that applicants first identify the relevant documents. Moreover, it would bring the jurisprudence closer in line with the Member States' own aspirations in Declaration 17, attached to the Maastricht Treaty.

However, there seems to be an evolution in the Court's case law to a more profound review of the content of the documents itself.[161] The CFI now 'must, without substituting its own assessment for that of the Commission, ascertain whether the Commission has indeed struck a balance between the interests at stake without overstepping the boundaries of its power of assessment'.[162] The breakthrough in this respect has come with the introduction of a new rule in the Rules of Procedure of the CFI allowing for the Court to order the production of the contested documents to the Court (without the documents being communicated to the requesting party).[163]

[158] *Ibid*, para 57.
[159] Case C-353/99 P *Council v Hautala* [2001] ECR I-9565, para 31.
[160] Case T-14/98 *Hautala v Council* [1999] ECR II-2489, para 87. Admittedly, in legal literature there still is quite a debate on whether or not such a right to information exists. Moreover, even the status of the right of access to documents itself is still not settled. However, with the right of access to documents included in Art 42 of the Charter of Fundamental Rights, it seems difficult not to consider this to be a fundamental right. As far as access to information is concerned, as indicated, the debate is still open — though the CFI in *Hautala* has made the aforementioned interesting statement. For the debate see, *inter alia*, M Broberg, 'Access to Documents: A General Principle of Community Law?' (2002) 27 *EL Rev* 194; HR Kranenborg, 'De Eurowob in de hand, de EU transparant? Het openbaarheidsregime in de communautaire rechtsorde: een stand van zaken' (2002) 50 *SEW* 447 at 449; R Davis, 'The Court of Justice and the Right of Public Access to Community-held Documents' (2000) 25 *EL Rev* 303 at 306–9; B Vesterdorf, 'Transparency — Not Just a Vogue Word' (1998–9) 22 *FILJ* 902 at 920–22; Y Gauthier, 'Transparence' (2001) 128 *JDI* 591; P Leino, 'Case C-353/99 P *Council/Hautala*, judgment of the Full Court of 6 December 2001, nyr, appeal against the judgment of the Court of First Instance of 19 July 1999 in Case T-14/98 *Hautala v Council* [1999] ECR II-2489' (2002) 39 *CML Rev* 621 at 626–8 and U Öberg, 'Public Access to Documents after the Entry into Force of the Amsterdam Treaty: Much Ado About Nothing?', European Integration Online Papers, 1998–008, available at *http://eiop.or.at/eiop/texte/1998-008a.htm*, 2–5 and the many references therein at 3.
[161] HR Kranenborg, 'De Eurowob in de hand, de EU transparant? Het openbaarheidsregime in de communautaire rechtsorde: een stand van zaken' (2002) 50 *SEW* 447 at 452.
[162] Case T-111/00 *British American Tobacco (Investments) Ltd v Commission* [2001] ECR II-2997, para 41.
[163] See Art 67(6) of the Rules of Procedure of the CFI as amended by Amendments to the Rules of Procedure of the Court of First Instance of the European Communities [2000] OJ L322/4. This procedure was first used in Case T-20/99 *Denkavit Nederland BV v Commission* [2000]

Moreover, the mere fact that Court proceedings are started may result in a more flexible attitude of the institutions towards access to documents. A striking example of this is the recent case of *British American Tobacco (Investment) Ltd v Commission*.[164] In that case the tobacco company sought to obtain several documents in respect of scientific research and minutes of a cancer experts' committee that allegedly were in the possession of the Commission. Originally the Commission had denied their existence respectively the fact that those documents were in its possession. However, during the procedure, and especially when the CFI had decided of its own motion to summon witnesses to obtain more information on those documents, suddenly the Commission seemed able to release more documents. As a result the proceedings became more and more devoid of purpose, but costs were awarded against the Commission.

## B. Accountability

The Community Courts also greatly enhance the legitimacy of the institutions by making them answerable for their decisions. The institutions are often entrusted with a broad margin of discretion. However, such discretion should never be unlimited. The necessity of judicial review becomes apparent precisely in protecting this policy margin for the institutions, on the one hand, and ensuring that the institutions do not use this discretion beyond the purpose for which they have been entrusted with it, on the other. Three recent cases provide striking examples of the way the CFI strikes the balance between those interests.

In the *max.mobil* case[165] the applicants had complained to the Commission, seeking among other things a finding that the Republic of Austria had infringed the combined provisions of Articles 82 and 86(1) TEC, because of the difference in fees for operating a GSM mobile phone network it had to pay if compared to the fees asked of the incumbent state operator Mobilkom. The Commission had however not agreed with

ECR II-3011. It remains to be seen, however, whether the CFI can also order the institutions to produce sensitive documents. Reportedly, the legal service of the Council has indicated in an undisclosed opinion (document 7184/01 of 19 Mar 2001 on the treatment of sensitive documents), that the Council 'need not even comply with orders of the EU courts requiring "sensitive" documents to be furnished to the Court of First Instance during court proceedings': see S Peers, 'The New Regulation on Access to Documents: A Critical Analysis' (2001–2) 21 *YEL* 386 at 413.

[164] Case T-311/00 *British American Tobacco (Investments) Ltd v Commission* [2002] ECR II-2781.

[165] Case T-54/99 *max.mobil Telekommunikation Service GmbH v Commission* [2002] ECR II-313. This judgment is currently under appeal; for the pleas in law and main arguments see Case 141/02 P *Commission v max.mobil Telekommunikation Service GmbH* [2002] OJ C169/15.

the complainant and had thus refused to take a decision under Article 86(3) TEC. The applicant therefore asked for judicial review, through an action for annulment of this decision of refusal.

The Commission however questioned whether its decisions under Article 86(3) TEC were open for review, and it relied especially on the *Bilanzbuchhalter* case[166] to show that, in the past, such applications had been deemed inadmissible. Before the CFI addressed the issue of admissibility it presented some preliminary observations on the core issues at stake: the right to sound administration and the right to judicial review.

The right to sound administration is not unknown in the jurisprudence of the CFI and ECJ.[167] However, the CFI introduces a double justification for it. A first justification is found in the general principles that are observed in a State governed by the rule of law and are common to the constitutional traditions of the Member States as moreover confirmed in Article 41(1) of the Charter of Fundamental Rights which all provide that '[e]very person has the right to have his or her affairs handled impartially, fairly and within a reasonable time by the institutions and bodies of the Union'.[168] As a second justification the CFI identifies the obligation to undertake a diligent and impartial examination as an integral component of the general duty of supervision of the Commission under Article 211 TEC.[169] In this way the Court moreover manages to avoid treating a decision under Article 86(3) as any different from the obligations the Commission has under Articles 81 and 82 TEC or under Articles 87 and 88 TEC.[170]

However, this does not imply that the degree of judicial review should be the same in all cases. The CFI is to a large extent willing to protect the discretion of the Commission. It has no difficulty in recognizing that in the specific context of Article 86(3) TEC the Commission must not necessarily pursue its examination to the point of adopting a final decision or a directive addressed to one or more Member States.[171]

[166] Case C-107/95 P *Bundesverband der Bilanzbuchhalter v Commission* [1997] ECR I-947.

[167] Case T-24/90 *Automec v Commission* [1992] ECR II-2223; Case T-95/96 *Gestevisíon Telecino v Commission* [1998] ECR II-3407; Joined Cases 142/84 & 156/84 *BAT and Reynolds v Commission* [1987] ECR 4487; Case C-449/98 P *IECC v Commission* [2001] ECR I-3875; D Simon, 'Une théorie de l'intensité du contrôle juridictionnel est-elle possible? Brefs propos sur une tentative avortée du Tribunal de première instance' (Apr 2002) 12 *Europe* 3 at 4.

[168] Case T-54/99 *max.mobil Telekommunikation Service GmbH v Commission* [2002] ECR II-313, para 48. This was effectively the first time, moreover, that a chamber of the CFI ruled on the status of the Charter of Fundamental Rights.

[169] Case T-54/99 *max.mobil Telekommunikation Service GmbH v Commission* [2002] ECR II-313, para 52; D Simon, 'Une théorie de l'intensité du contrôle juridictionnel est-elle possible? Brefs propos sur une tentative avortée du Tribunal de première instance' (Apr 2002) 12 *Europe* 3 at 4.

[170] Case T-54/99 *max.mobil Telekommunikation Service GmbH v Commission* [2002] ECR II-313, paras 52–53.

[171] *Ibid*, paras 53–55.

Nonetheless, 'whilst emphasising that the Commission has no obligation to take action against Member States, that case-law does not however imply that the Commission is not under an obligation to undertake a diligent and impartial examination of complaints'.[172] In this respect, as this obligation needs enforcement, the CFI makes the link between this duty of diligent and impartial examination of complaints and its enforcement through judicial review.[173] Again the Charter of Fundamental Rights appears prominently in the reasoning.[174]

Even so, the CFI also recognizes that policy choices first of all have to be made by the Commission, so that it is not for the CFI to redo the entire exercise. Its judicial review will therefore be 'limited in scope and varied in depth. The material accuracy of the facts relied on must be thoroughly examined by the Court, whereas the prima facie appraisal of those facts and, more so, the decision whether it is necessary to take action are subject to limited review by the Court.'[175]

In the light of such an introduction, it is unsurprising that the CFI classified the refusal by the Commission as a challengeable decision addressed to the applicant, and therefore declared the action admissible.[176] As to the substance the CFI then, of course, followed the course of action it had announced in its preliminary observations.[177] Its judicial review was limited to the verification of the Commission's fulfilment of its duty to undertake a diligent and impartial examination of the complaints.[178] On carrying out such a review, the action proved unfounded, but the fact

[172] *Ibid*, para 55 *in fine*.
[173] *Ibid*, para 56.
[174] *Ibid*, para 57: 'Such judicial review is also one of the general principles that are observed in a State governed by the rule of law and are common to the constitutional traditions of the Member States, as is confirmed by Article 47 of the Charter of Fundamental Rights, under which any person whose rights guaranteed by the law of the Union are violated has the right to an effectiveremedy before a tribunal.'
[175] Case T-54/99 *max.mobil Telekommunikation Service GmbH v Commission* [2002] ECR II-313, para 59.
[176] *Ibid*, paras 61–72. Remarkably, the CFI, 'for the sake of completeness', also approaches the issue of admissibility from the perspective of a decision addressed to the Member State but which is of direct and individual concern to the applicant. This may be understandable from a desire to immunize the decision from criticism, but it makes the reasoning look rather ambivalent: see D Simon, 'Une théorie de l'intensité du contrôle juridictionnel est-elle possible? Brefs propos sur une tentative avortée du Tribunal de première instance' (Apr 2002) 12 *Europe* 3 at 5.
[177] Simon however considers that the way the CFI has exercised its review in practice hardly lives up to the solemn way it had introduced the concept of diligent and impartial examination ('On constate donc que l'obligation d'examen diligent et impartial si solennellement proclamée se réduit finalement à une exigence relativement limitée, le contrôle juridictionnel au fond se bornant à un "service minimum" '): see 'Une théorie de l'intensité du contrôle juridictionnel est-elle possible? Brefs propos sur une tentative avortée du Tribunal de première instance' (Apr 2002) 12 *Europe* 3 at 5.
[178] Case T-54/99 *max.mobil Telekommunikation Service GmbH v Commission* [2002] ECR II-313, para 73.

that the CFI reviewed the decision at stake has undoubtedly contributed to enhancing the accountability of the Commission — if only because the Commission should now realize that in dealing with complaints under Article 86(3) TEC it should also display due diligence as its assessment may be subject to scrutiny by the Community Courts.

An even more straightforward example of the judiciary limiting the way in which discretionary powers are being used is contained in the *Lamberts* judgment.[179] In this case the CFI was asked to rule on the non-contractual liability of the European Ombudsman. The European Ombudsman was created to enhance the transparency and legitimacy of the European Union by dealing with cases concerning misadministration. Ironically, the applicant, Mr Lamberts, was not very pleased with the way the Ombudsman dealt with his case, in particular because of the latter's refusal to seek a friendly settlement.

It was already established that the acts of the European Ombudsman could not be challenged by way of action for annulment, as they do not produce legal effects.[180] Neither can his acts be considered to constitute acts of the European Parliament.[181] However, in light of the autonomous nature of the action for damages, the question arose whether the European Ombudsman could be deemed liable for damage resulting from his handling of complaints. The stakes were high, as Mr Lamberts claimed about €2.5 million in damages because of the fact that he missed out on an appointment with the Commission and was unable to obtain any redress through the Ombudsman or through the Courts (as he did not realize that seeking a solution through the Ombudsman does not suspend the time limit for bringing an action for annulment). For all this he blamed the European Ombudsman.

The case is important for two reasons. The first is procedural. The Ombudsman had challenged the admissibility of the action for damages. However, the CFI is swift in establishing *locus standi*, given the autonomous

[179] Case T-209/00 *Lamberts v European Ombudsman* [2002] ECR II-2203. The European Ombudsman has lodged an appeal against this judgment: see Case C-234/02 P *European Ombudsman v Lamberts* [2002] OJ C180/19. On 3 July 2003 Advocate General LA Geelhoed opined that the constitutional objections of the European Ombudsman should be rejected. Making several references to the recent Opinion of Advocate General Léger in Case C-224/01 *Köbler*, available at *www.curia.eu.int*, he stresses that the independence of a Community organ does not exclude its liability; however — just like the CFI has done — in determining whether the violation is sufficiently serious one has to take into account the specificity of the organ. The result is again a judicial review, albeit limited in scope, of the acts of the Ombudsman: see Opinion of Advocate General LA Geelhoed in Case C-234/02 P *European Parliament v Lamberts*, para 85, available at *www.curia.eu.int*.

[180] Case T-103/99 *Associazione delle Cantine Sociali Venete v European Ombudsman and European Parliament* [2000] ECR II-4165; Case T-209/00 (Order of 22 Feb 2001) *Lamberts v European Ombudsman and European Parliament* [2001] ECR II-765.

[181] Case T-209/00 (Order of 22 Feb 2001) *Lamberts v European Ombudsman and European Parliament* [2001] ECR II-765.

nature of the action for damages, which is always addressed against the Community, but represented by the body that allegedly committed the fault.[182] The second one is the focus of our attention in this part: the limits placed by judicial review on the discretion of the European Ombudsman. Again the CFI stresses that the fact that a body enjoys a wide discretion does not make it immune from review. If Community law confers certain rights on individuals to have their cases studied in a proper manner, then the Court should at least be able to review whether the institutions have dealt with the complainant's case in a diligent manner. 'The Ombudsman has indeed, as he himself stressed, very wide discretion as regards the merits of complaints and the way in which he deals with them, and in so doing he is under no obligation as to the result to be achieved. However, even if review by the Community judicature must consequently be limited, it is possible that in very exceptional circumstances a citizen may be able to demonstrate that the Ombudsman has made a manifest error in the performance of his duties likely to cause damage to the citizen concerned.[183]

'As to the substance, the CFI then examines whether this is such an exceptional case in which the European Ombudsman has neglected his duties. It did not find any 'flagrant and manifest breach of his obligations'.[184] Nonetheless, this decision makes it clear that the Ombudsman is not above the law. The CFI does not hesitate to review, albeit in a very limited fashion, the acts of Community organs that are endowed by the Treaty with a very broad margin of appreciation. The limits of this review are perhaps best illustrated by the applicant's claim that he was not informed by the Ombudsman that seeking a friendly settlement could result in the loss of the chance to bring an action for annulment before the Court against the Commission under the Staff Regulations. The CFI almost takes on the role of an ombudsman itself in making recommendations for the better functioning of the office of the European Ombudsman. However, even if it does see room for improvement, as far as liability is concerned the CFI limits itself to its strict test: '[i]t may be in the interests of the proper performance of the task entrusted to him by the Treaty for the Ombudsman to routinely inform the citizen concerned of the measures to take in order to best serve his interests, including indicating to him the judicial remedies open to him and the fact that referring a complaint to the Ombudsman does not suspend the time-limit for pursuing such remedies. There is, however, no express provision requiring the Ombudsman to take such steps .... The Ombudsman cannot, therefore, be accused of having failed to draw the

[182] Case T-209/00 *Lamberts v European Ombudsman* [2002] ECR II-2203, paras 48–52.
[183] *Ibid*, para 57.
[184] *Ibid*, para 79.

applicant's attention to the fact that his complaint did not suspend the time limit for a direct action before the CFI and of not advising him to bring such an action before the Community Court. The Ombudsman did not, therefore, in this context commit a breach of administrative duty which could give rise to non-contractual liability on the part of the Community.'[185] Yet, the judgment has the effect of alerting the Ombudsman that his office, too, may be subject to scrutiny. Even if in practice no condemnation follows, the knowledge that their decisions are not totally beyond scrutiny should make the institutions far more prudent. In this way judicial review may also indirectly contribute to the protection of individuals.

The limits of this review are also demonstrated by the *Pfizer Animal Health* case,[186] which also addresses the question of the legitimacy of the role of expert groups. Apparently a Community expert committee, the Scientific Committee for Animal Nutrition (SCAN) had concluded that the use of virginiamycin as a growth promoter did not constitute a real immediate risk to public health. Nonetheless, the Commission and, on the latter's proposal, the Council decided not to follow that advice. The applicant thereupon sought the annulment of a regulation[187] that had the effect of further prohibiting the use of the antibiotic concerned.

The CFI, after declaring the action admissible in part,[188] found that the Commission and the Council were not bound by the advice of the expert group. However, it carefully draws the boundaries for exercising this discretion. 'To the extent to which the Community institution opts to disregard the opinion, it must provide specific reasons for its findings by comparison with those made in the opinion and its statement of reasons must explain why it is disregarding the latter. The statement of reasons must be of a scientific level at least commensurate with that of the opinion in question. In such a case, the institution may take as its basis either a supplementary opinion from the same committee of experts or other evidence, whose probative value is at least commensurate with that of the

[185] Case T-209/00 *Lamberts v European Ombudsman* [2002] ECR II-2203, paras 68–69.
[186] Case T-13/99 *Pfizer Animal Health SA v Council* [2002] ECR II-3305.
[187] Council Regulation (EC) No 2821/98 of 17 Dec 1998 amending, as regards withdrawal of the authorization of certain antibiotics, Directive 70/524/EEC concerning additives in feedingstuffs [1998] OJ L351/4.
[188] Case T-13/99 *Pfizer Animal Health SA v Council* [2002] ECR II-3305, paras 81–106. As this concerns a case involving a private applicant seeking the annulment of a Council regulation, it should be clear that in this case, too, admissibility was far from self-evident. The CFI, somewhat in the line of *Camar* (above), identified a mixture of facts, which it claims should be enough to differentiate the applicant from all other persons. The CFI supported this argument with references to cases like Case C-309/89 *Codorníu v Council* [1994] ECR I-1853; Case T-585/93 *Greenpeace and Others v Commission* [1995] ECR II-2205 and Joined Cases T-481/93 & T-484/93 *Exporteurs in Levende Varkens and Others v Commission* [1995] ECR II-2941.

opinion concerned. In the event that the Community institution disregards only part of the opinion, it may also avail itself of those parts of the scientific reasoning which it does not dispute.'[189]

The CFI offers a very fundamental argument for this by pointing to the link with the legitimacy of the decision-making process. In the end, the Treaties entrust the task of adopting legislation to bodies which are answerable to democratically elected institutions. This task entails more than simply applying the outcome of scientific research. Policy-making is also about taking into account broader fears and opinions that live in society. Therefore the Council could be allowed to take into account the precautionary principle and decide not to take the risk of allowing this product in feedingstuffs, even if at this time there is no scientific proof of a clear risk. The CFI clearly states in this respect '[t]hat finding can also be justified on grounds of principle relating to the political responsibilities and democratic legitimacy of the Commission. Whilst the Commission's exercise of public authority is rendered legitimate, pursuant to Article 155 of the EC Treaty (now Article 211 EC), by the European Parliament's political control, the members of SCAN, although they have scientific legitimacy, have neither democratic legitimacy nor political responsibilities. Scientific legitimacy is not a sufficient basis for the exercise of public authority.'[190] *In casu* the Court considered the approach taken by the Council, which had invoked both the SCAN opinion and conflicting evidence by other specialists in order to decide that departing from the SCAN opinion was in the interest of public health, to be within the margins set out.[191] Judicial review may place certain limits on the discretion of the institutions; it also helps to ensure that policy assessments are, in the end, made by those institutions that are accountable for them.

### C. Democracy

The *Pfizer* case leads us to some further cases in which the Court was to deal with the very essence of the workings of democracy. In some cases judicial review is necessary to ensure the correct balance between the institutions and the rights of their members. The CFI and the ECJ are increasingly called upon to rule on conflicts between the participants in the decision-making process in order to safeguard its representativeness and the prerogatives of, in particular, Members of the European Parliament. Those cases often offer the Courts a chance of recalling some

[189] Case T-13/99 *Pfizer Animal Health SA v Council* [2002] ECR II-3305, para 199.
[190] *Ibid*, para 201.
[191] *Ibid*, paras 203–5.

principles of political science and constitutional law, with an impact well beyond the case in hand.[192]

The most famous case where the ECJ ruled on the link between legitimacy and judicial control is undoubtedly *Les Verts*.[193] As set out above, the Court had to decide an action for annulment brought by the French Green Party, which participated in the 1984 elections for the European Parliament but was confronted on that occasion with a pre-decided system for dividing money among the political parties that participated in those elections. This scheme had been drawn up by the enlarged Bureau of the previous Parliament in which the applicant was not represented, and it was much more favourable for the incumbent parties than for new parties such as the applicant.

The ECJ proved willing to surmount the procedural barriers explained above in order to be able to review the acts of the European Parliament, because in a Community based on the rule of law no institutions could be shielded from judicial review.[194] In *Les Verts* the Court obviously had good reasons for going into the political thicket. A unique situation had arisen where the established parties stood accused of having given themselves a financial bonus ahead of the elections, as compared to their opponents, which were not represented in the European Parliament. In this way the equality of arms between the contestants to the elections could be distorted.[195] Moreover the Parliament had, in setting up a system for distribution of money that made it extremely difficult to differentiate between funds for legitimate information campaigns by the political parties on the European Parliament and campaign financing, breached the rules on competence between the Community and the Member States, who alone are competent to regulate campaign finances.[196]

Presumably the best way to prevent such discriminations is to ensure that all relevant actors are involved in the decision-making process. This principle has proven particularly difficult to put into effect in the specific context of framework agreements concluded by the social partners. Following the conclusion of the Social Policy Agreement (1992), it happens that legislation is the result of a framework agreement concluded among the social partners, without any involvement of the European

[192] In this sense see D Simon, 'Le recours "Martinez/de Gaulle/Bonino/Pannella" dans l'affaire de la constitution d' un "groupe technique" au Parlement est jugé recevable mais rejeté au fond' (Dec 2001) 11 *Europe* 9 at 10.

[193] Case 294/83 *Parti Ecologiste 'Les Verts' v European Parliament* [1986] ECR 1339.

[194] *Ibid*, para 23.

[195] As Jacqué rightly noticed, the Parliament stood accused of having done too much or too little: either it had done too much by changing the existing allocation model, or too little by changing it in a way that discriminated against the Green party: see J-P Jacqué, '*Parti Ecologiste "Les Verts" C Parlement Européen* (Aff 294/83)' (1986) 22 *RTDE* 500 at 503.

[196] Case 294/83 *Parti Ecologiste 'Les Verts' v European Parliament* [1986] ECR 1339, paras 39–55.

Parliament. This of course poses a whole new set of problems of democracy and legitimacy. The CFI has dealt with those issues in *UEAPME v Council*.[197] In that case the applicant, a representative body of small and medium-sized undertakings (SMUs), complained of the fact that it had been left out of the negotiations in respect of a framework agreement on parental leave, thus questioning the representativity of the parties to the framework agreement, and therefore the validity of the directive[198] adopted by the Council to make that agreement generally binding.

In deciding on the admissibility of the case the CFI already goes deep into this fundamental debate. Rarely has a single court case contributed so much to the constitutionalization of a major policy field such as social and labour policy. In its reasoning the CFI addressed three essential elements: the legitimacy of social dialogue agreements, the representativity of the parties to them, and the control by EU institutions of the social dialogue process.[199]

The democratic legitimacy of social dialogue agreements is not self-evident. Under the Social Policy Agreement, which, pursuant to the Amsterdam Treaty, has been incorporated in the EC Treaty, there are two procedures for adopting measures in the field of social policy. The measures under Article 2 of the Agreement, now Article 137 TEC, are adopted in accordance with the co-decision procedure. The Court recalls the importance of the participation of the European Parliament in the Community legislative process, which reflects at Community level the fundamental democratic principle that the people must share in the exercise of power through a representative assembly. It notes that the democratic legitimacy of measures adopted by the Council pursuant to Article 2 of the Agreement derives from the European Parliament's participation in that first procedure.[200] In contrast the directive at issue was adopted in accordance with the procedure referred to in Articles 3(4) and 4 of the Agreement, now Articles 138(4) and 139 TEC. This procedure does not provide for the participation of the European Parliament. This lack of democratic participation is however compensated for 'through the parties representative of management and labour who concluded the agreement which is endowed by the Council, acting on a qualified majority, on a proposal from the Commission, with a legislative foundation at Community level'.[201]

[197] Case T-135/96 *UEAPME v Council* [1998] ECR II-2335.
[198] Council Directive 96/34/EC of 3 June 1996 on the framework agreement on parental leave concluded by UNICE, CEEP and the ETUC [1996] OJ L145/4.
[199] B Bercusson, 'Democratic Legitimacy and European Labour Law' (1999) 28 *Industrial L J* 153 at 154.
[200] Case T-135/96 *UEAPME v Council* [1998] ECR II-2335, para 88.
[201] *Ibid*, para 89. This particular part of the reasoning of the CFI has provoked mixed reactions in legal literature. On the one hand it is challenged whether the representatives of

This implies of course that there are sufficient built-in guarantees that those parties are sufficiently representative. This is the case only if the parties to the framework agreement have 'sufficient collective representativity'.[202] The CFI requires that the social partners taken together have sufficient cumulative representativity in respect of the specific agreement to be concluded.[203] The criteria for this are not really examined by the Court.[204] The CFI limits itself to referring to a 1993 Commission Communication which defines representativity as implying European scope (cross-industry or sectoral),[205] comprising recognized bargaining organizations in the Member States, and being adequate to the task at EU level. The number of members represented by the organization seems hardly relevant.[206]

The CFI entrusts the task of monitoring this to the Commission and the Council.[207] In this way the CFI makes an important constitutional

management and labour, especially in the European context, can *überhaupt* provide democratic legitimacy to Community acts: see H-G Dederer, 'Durchführung von Vereinbarungen der europäischen Sozialpartner — Korporative Ausübung von Rechtsetzungsgewalt und ihr demokratisches Defizit' (2000) 53 *Recht der Arbeit* 216 and, implicitly, M-A Moreau, 'Sur la représentativité des partenaires sociaux européens' (1999) 62 *Droit Social* 53 at 55–59. On the other hand it is argued that the CFI, fails to take account of the fact that, even if the Council acts alone, it can still claim democratic legitimacy, albeit indirectly: see R Mehdi, 'Affaire T-135/96 *UEAPME c/ Conseil* soutenu par la Commission' (1999) 126 *JDI* 536 at 539. K Langenbucher effectively considers the legititmacy of the procedure of Art 139 TEC to lie solely in the role of the Council, rejecting any democratic legitimacy in the participation of the social partners: see 'Zur Zulässigkeit parlamentsersetzender Normgebungsverfahren im Europarecht' (2002) 10 *Zeitschrift für europäisches Privatrecht* 265 at 275–9. In this respect one could also argue that the justification of the participation of the social partners can be found in the absence of a Commission proposal, the widest possible participation of the social partners then helps to ensure that the measure conforms to general interests: see A Adinolfi, 'Admissibility of Action for Annulment by Social Partners and "Sufficient Representativity" of European Agreements' (2000) 25 *EL Rev* 165 at 175.

202 Case T-135/96 *UEAPME v Council* [1998] ECR II-2335, para 94. As Bercusson notes, a more appropriate translation of the original French '*une représentativité cumulée suffisante*' would be 'sufficient *cumulative* representativity': see 'Democratic Legitimacy and European Labour Law' (1999) 28 *Industrial L J* 153 at 156, n 13.

203 Case T-135/96 *UEAPME v Council* [1998] ECR II-2335, para 90 ff; on the challenges and opportunities resulting from this approach see B. Bercusson, 'Democratic Legitimacy and European Labour Law' (1999) 28 *Industrial L J* 153 at 165–70; M-A Moreau, 'Sur la représentativité des partenaires sociaux européens' (1999) 62 *Droit Social* 53 at 56–57; A Adinolfi, 'Admissibility of Action for Annulment by Social Partners and "Sufficient Representativity" of European Agreements' (2000) 25 *EL Rev* 165 at 176.

204 B Bercusson, 'Democratic Legitimacy and European Labour Law' (1999) 28 *Industrial L J* 153 at 155–59; M-A Moreau, 'Sur la représentativité des partenaires sociaux européens' (1999) 62 *Droit Social* 53 at 56.

205 COM(93) 600 final, para 24.

206 Case T-135/96 *UEAPME v Council* [1998] ECR II-2335, para 102. This has also been the subject of criticism: see B Bercusson, 'Democratic Legitimacy and European Labour Law' (1999) 28 *Industrial L J* 153 at 159; A Adinolfi, 'Admissibility of Action for Annulment by Social Partners and "Sufficient Representativity" of European Agreements' (2000) 25 *EL Rev* 165 at 176.

207 Case T-135/96 *UEAPME v Council* [1998] ECR II-2335, para 89.

choice,[208] as in doing so it greatly diminishes the autonomy of the social partners.[209] The CFI on the one hand confirms this autonomy by denying the existence for individual social organizations of a right to negotiate, allowing the social partners to choose among themselves with whom they conclude an agreement.[210] Yet, once this agreement must be enacted, both the Commission and the Council are required to verify whether the parties to the agreement were sufficiently representative.[211] All this is moreover done under control by the CFI, which reviews whether the institutions were justified in holding that the parties were sufficiently representative.[212] If this is not the case, the CFI is willing to declare admissible an action for annulment by an organization whose participation is essential for reaching a sufficient level of representativity. It was rightly observed that the CFI in this way confirms the existence of a Community constitution, which goes beyond the organization of the state powers but testifies to the belief that a Community based on the rule of law is not conceivable without sincere adherence to the political democracy and the socio-economic dimension thereof being taken into account.[213] In respect of the framework agreement on parental leave, the CFI did not consider the participation of UEAPME necessary and therefore declared its challenge inadmissible.[214]

However, in recent cases the applicants have been not outsiders who are being discriminated against or disowned social partners, but disgruntled MEPs bringing actions for annulment against acts relating to the internal organization of their own institution, which are moreover adopted with their involvement. In those cases the legitimacy of judicial review is sometimes called into question.[215] They all claimed that the rules of their body

[208] The Court admittedly equates the EU social dialogue with the EU legislative process; this results in a focus on representativity, autonomy, and legitimacy, but may overlook some of the peculiarities of industrial relations: see B. Bercusson, 'Democratic Legitimacy and European Labour Law' (1999) 28 *Industrial L J* 153 at 162–64.

[209] *Ibid*, 160–63. This is all the more true if the Commission also has the right or even obligation to review the content of the agreement, as convincingly suggested by A Adinolfi, 'Admissibility of Action for Annulment by Social Partners and "Sufficient Representativity" of European Agreements' (2000) 25 *EL Rev* 165 at 175.

[210] Case T-135/96 *UEAPME v Council* [1998] ECR II-2335, paras 77–80; B Bercusson, 'Democratic Legitimacy and European Labour Law' (1999) 28 *Industrial L J* 153 at 159; C Tobler, 'Artikel 173 EG-Verdrag: nietigheid van de richtlijn voor ouderschapsverlof?' (1999) 5 *NTER* 21 at 23–24.

[211] Case T-135/96 *UEAPME v Council* [1998] ECR II-2335, paras 90 ff; B Bercusson, 'Democratic Legitimacy and European Labour Law' (1999) 28 *Industrial L J* 153 at 160–63.

[212] Whether this is the most legitimate or appropriate forum to settle industrial relations is doubted in legal literature: see M-A Moreau, 'Sur la représentativité des partenaires sociaux européens' (1999) 62 *Droit Social* 53 at 58–9; B Bercusson, 'Democratic Legitimacy and European Labour Law' (1999) 28 *Industrial L J* 153 at 170.

[213] R Mehdi, 'Affaire T-135/96 *UEAPME c/ Conseil* soutenu par la Commission' (1999) 126 *JDI* 536 at 540.

[214] Case T-135/96 *UEAPME v Council* [1998] ECR II-2335, paras 111–12.

[215] D Simon, 'Le recours "Martinez/de Gaulle/Bonino/Pannella" dans l'affaire de la constitution d'un "groupe technique" au Parlement est jugé recevable mais rejeté au fond' (Dec 2001)

made it impossible for them to fulfil their mandate, thus endangering this fundamental principle that the people must share in the exercise of power through a representative assembly. In this way the CFI was confronted with high-profile political cases.

The classic case law on admissibility provides for ample escape routes for the CFI if it wants to avoid having to go into the political thicket. However, both the President of the CFI[216] and the CFI[217] itself seem to have adopted a rather flexible interpretation of the requirement that the acts should produce *legal* effects *vis-à-vis third parties*. Their approach can be justified by the stakes that are at issue in such cases for the overall institutional balance. Even if highly political, acts relating to the ambit of a parliamentary mandate do have spillover effects as they affect who can participate in the decisionmaking process and under which conditions, thus ultimately affecting the outcome of the decision-making process. The ECJ has repeatedly emphasized the important role of a democratically elected body in the Community framework,[218] but then its members must also be in a position to do their job properly. As one author rightly observes, this approach is moreover building further on the desire to ensure complete and effective judicial control over all acts of the institutions along the lines of the idea that the Community is a Community based on the rule of law, which implies a complete and coherent system of procedural routes to obtain review of any act of the institutions.[219]

In one case[220] about seventy MEPs sought the annulment of certain amendments to the Rules of Procedure of the European Parliament that would force them to co-operate with OLAF, the Commission body set up to combat fraud. Ironically, OLAF was established in the aftermath of the fall

11 *Europe* 9 at 9 and 'Du bon usage du référé' (Mar 2001) 11 *Europe* 10 at 10; P Cassia, 'Case T-353/00 R, *Jean-Marie Le Pen v European Parliament*, order of the President of the Court of First Instance of 26 Jan 2001, not yet reported' (2001) 38 *CML Rev* 1297 at 1299–304. The order is now reported at [2001] ECR II-125.

[216] Case T-353/00 R *Jean-Marie Le Pen v European Parliament* [2001] ECR II-125; Case T-17/00 R *Willy Rothley and Others v European Parliament* [2000] ECR II-2085; Case T-222/99 R *Jean-Claude Martinez and Charles de Gaulle v European Parliament* [1999] ECR II-3397.

[217] Joined Cases T-222/99, T-327/99, & T-329/99 *Jean-Claude Martinez, Charles de Gaulle, Front national and Emma Bonino and Others v European Parliament* [2001] ECR II-2823.

[218] Case C-300/89 *Commission v Council* [1991] ECR I-2867, para 20; Case 139/79 *Maizena v Council* [1980] ECR 3393, para 34. This bias towards legislative procedures with a strong parliamentary involvement can be misleading, though. If an act falls clearly within the sphere of a legal basis that does not provide for an important role for the Parliament; the Court does not hesitate to uphold this legal basis, to the detriment of the European Parliament: see Case C-155/91 *Commission v Council* [1993] ECR I-939.

[219] D Simon, 'Du bon usage du référé' (Mar 2001) 11 *Europe* 10 at 10.

[220] Case T-17/00 *Rothley v European Parliament* [2002] ECR II-579. This case is currently under appeal: see Case C-162/02 P *Rothley and Others v European Parliament* [2002] OJ C156/10.

of the *Santer* Commission, when a highly critical report was drafted at the request of the Parliament on the wheeling and dealing of the Commission.

The President of the CFI had accepted that the applicants had an arguable case in respect of admissibility.[221] He then considered that he could not exclude the possibility that the immunity of the applicants could be jeopardized. The most remarkable assessment can be found however in the balance of interests.[222] There the interest of the Community in effectively combating corruption and fraud is weighed against the Community's interest that the Members of the Parliament should be able to carry out their activities with the assurance that their independence will not be compromised; fully in line with the natural inclination of the Court to protect the prerogatives of the institutions and its members, the position of the MEPs was given precedence.[223] Ultimately the CFI dismissed this case as inadmissible for lack of individual concern. Nonetheless, the Court demonstrated, not to be blind to the consequences of the amendments, to the Rules of Procedure. The CFI admitted, 'the risk cannot be excluded a priori that, in conducting an investigation, the Office might perform an act prejudicial to the immunity enjoyed by every Member of the Parliament. However, if that were to occur, any Member of the Parliament faced with such an act could, if he considered it damaging to him, avail himself of the judicial protection and the legal remedies provided for by the Treaty.'[224] In this way the CFI continues to cast some doubt on the validity of the amendments, but seems satisfied that sufficient legal remedies will be open to address this problem if it ever were to become acute.

In the case of *Martinez v European Parliament*[225] the limitations on the rights of MEPs were far more intrusive,[226] so as to warrant real

[221] Case T-17/00 R *Rothley v European Parliament* [2000] ECR II-2085, paras 44–55. The President of the CFI had been of the opinion that it could not be excluded without making a full assessment of the case — which is a task for the CFI, not its President — that the measure produced legal effects on the Members of the Parliament outside the internal sphere. Therefore he had ruled that the applicants had an arguable case on direct and individual concern: see also D. Thym, 'Europaabgeordnete gegen Europaparlament — der erste Akt des Streits um OLAF' (2000) 35 *EuR* 990 at 992–93.

[222] Case T-17/00 R *Rothley v European Parliament* [2000] ECR II-2085, paras 85–87. For a critical assessment of the reasoning of the President see D Thym, 'Europaabgeordnete gegen Europaparlament — der erste Akt des Streits um OLAF' (2000) 35 *EuR* 990 at 993–98.

[223] Case T-17/00 R *Rothley v European Parliament* [2000] ECR II-2085, paras 112–15.

[224] Case T-17/00 *Rothley v European Parliament* [2002] ECR II-579, para 73.

[225] Joined Cases T-222/99, T-327/99, & T-329/99 *Martinez v European Parliament* [2001] ECR II-2823. Some of the applicants have lodged an appeal against this judgment: see Case 486/01 P *Front National v European Parliament* [2002] OJ C84/47 and Case 488/01 P *Martinez v European Parliament* [2002] OJ C84/48. Their request for suspension of the execution of the judgment has however been completely rejected: see Joined Cases 486/01 P-R & 488/01 P-R *Front National and Martinez v European Parliament* [2002] ECR I-1843. The main action on appeal is still pending.

[226] The most intrusive measure is of course putting an end to the mandate of an MEP. This has been the subject of a hard-fought case, too. The French MEP Le Pen had been involved in a

concern about soundness of the democratic representation. The problem resulted from the fact that the Rules of Procedure of the Parliament heavily favour the formation of political groups, by giving them important advantages which non-attached Members cannot obtain. These advantages are of a financial and administrative nature, but also directly affect the exercise of the mandate as such.[227] In order to avail themselves of

brawl during the election campaign, which ultimately had led to a criminal conviction limiting his political rights. As a result, as a matter of French law and the Act concerning the election of representatives to the European Parliament by direct universal suffrage, annexed to the Council Decision of 20 Sept 1976 ([1976] OJ L278/5; in its original version, 'the 1976 Act'), his mandate as an MEP had come to an end and the European Parliament was informed thereof. On 23 Oct 2000 the President of the European Parliament had taken note during the plenary session that no appeal procedures were left to Mr Le Pen and that his mandate accordingly was irreversibly terminated. Mr Le Pen then sought the annulment of this decision and, in a separate interim application, its suspension pending judgment in the main action. In Case T-353/00 R *Jean-Marie Le Pen v European Parliament* [2001] ECR II-125 the President of the CFI had again taken a liberal approach to standing and accepted that the applicant could have a case if the European Parliament still had any discretion in assessing whether the mandate had really been correctly terminated. Again he ruled in favour of the incumbent MEP over the interest of his successor and the interest of the Parliament. Simon argues, though, that allowing an ineligible MEP to continue to work is as irreparable for the Parliament, as it is for an elected MEP to be barred from participating in the debate pending procedures: see 'Du bon usage du référé' (Mar 2001) 11 *Europe* 10 at 11. Yet, on balance, it appears most defensible in cases of doubt to give precedence to the will of the electorate, until the termination of the mandate has become inevitable. Nonetheless, the CFI did not follow its President and held on 10 Apr 2003 that the European Parliament had no margin at all under the 1976 Act, so that there was no challengeable act and dismissed the case as inadmissible: see Case T-353/00 *Jean-Marie Le Pen v European Parliament* [2003] ECR II-1729. An appeal has been lodged against this judgment, but not yet published in the Official Journal: see Case C-208/03 P *Le Pen v European Parliament*. M. Le Pen has also sought the interim suspension of the effects of the CFI's judgment: see Case C-208/03 P-R.

[227] These include, *inter alia*:

- nominations for the positions of President, Vice-Presidents, and Quaestors (Rule 13);
- the opportunity to put questions to the Council or the Commission for an oral answer and to request that they be placed on the agenda of Parliament (Rule 42);
- tabling a proposal for a recommendation to the Council concerning subjects under Titles V and VI of the Treaty on European Union, or where Parliament has not been consulted on an international agreement within the scope of Rule 97 or Rule 98 (Rule 49);
- debates on topical and urgent subjects of major importance (Rule 50);
- renewed referral to Parliament under Rule 71(3);
- tabling a proposal to reject the Council's common position (Rule 79);
- tabling amendments to the Council's common position (Rule 80);
- proposals to request the Commission and the Council to take part in a debate before negotiations with an applicant State commence (Rule 96);
- proposals to request the Council not to authorise the opening of negotiations on the conclusion, renewal or amendment of an international agreement until Parliament has stated its position on the proposed negotiating mandate on the basis of a report from the responsible committee (Rule 97);
- tabling of amendments and recommendations drafted by the responsible committee within the framework of the common foreign and security policy (Rule 104);

those benefits, the applicants (of the far-right Front National (FN) and the rather left-wing Lista Bonino) had formed a political group as well, called the 'Groupe Technique des Députés Indépendants' (TDI). However, unlike other political groups, they expressly stated that their members had absolutely no political affiliation with each other. Upon notification of the constitution of this group the Committee on Constitutional Affairs proposed an interpretation of the rules on the formation of political groups to clarify that a political group can be constituted correctly only if its members seem to have minimal political affiliation. This interpretation was adopted by the plenum of the European Parliament. As a result the TDI was considered to be non-existent *ex tunc*, and by the same vote its members were reduced to non-attached members with limited rights. The applicants then sought the annulment of this act before the CFI.

Having declared the action admissible, the CFI tackled the substance of the case. It came to the conclusion that Article 29 of the Rules of Procedure indeed requires some political affinity, and therefore the Parliament was, in light of the statements by the TDI, correct in making the assessment that this condition was not fulfilled. To reach this conclusion the CFI had to make a very extensive analysis of the notion of political affinity. Simon questions in this respect the intensity of judicial review, where the CFI is subjecting the sovereign assessment of the Parliament based on, by definition, rather subjective criteria to very close scrutiny.[228] One could turn the issue round, though, and consider that in light of the consequences at stake for the functioning of directly elected MEPs, the burden of proof of the absence of any political affinity was on the Parliament, so the CFI had to establish that there basically was hardly a shred of evidence pointing to the contrary. Admittedly, the decisive factor after all appeared to be the applicants' own admission that no such affinity existed, yet even then the Court's assessment was not pointless. After all, one can argue that affiliating despite having no political affinity may be the expression of a very particular, albeit negative, affinity and, thus, result in some sort of political affiliation.

- proposals to amend the draft agenda of Parliament (Rule 111);
- proposals for urgent debate (Rule 112);
- requests for a split vote (Rule 131);
- requests for voting by roll call (Rule 134);
- tabling amendments for consideration in plenary session (Rule 139);
- requests for referral back to committee (Rule 144);
- requests for closure of a debate (Rule 145);
- requests for adjournment of a debate (Rule 146);
- requests for suspension or closure of the sitting (Rule 147);
- contesting an interpretation of the Rules of Procedure by the responsible committee (Rule 180).

[228] D Simon, 'Le recours "Martinez/de Gaulle/Bonino/Pannella" dans l'affaire de la constitution d' un "groupe technique" au Parlement est jugé recevable mais rejeté au fond' (Dec 2001) 11 *Europe* 9 at 10.

Subsequently, the CFI had to deal with the arguments that as a result the TDI and its members were discriminated against and basically reduced to second-class MEPs with only limited rights. Crucial in this respect is the analysis by the CFI of the role of political groups in the workings of the Parliament. The CFI demonstrates the necessity of political groups in order to meet a number of legitimate objectives dictated by the social and political circumstances peculiar to parliamentary democracy at the level of the European Union, by its specific features compared with those of national parliaments, and by the functions and responsibilities conferred on it by the Treaty.[229]

The Court first points to the diversity in the European Parliament. 'In fact, the formation of the Parliament in political groups comprising Members from more than one Member State and sharing political affinities appears, first, to be a measure consonant with the efficient organisation of the work and procedures of the institution in order in particular to allow the joint expression of political wills and the emergence of compromises, the latter being particularly necessary owing to the very high number of Members of the Parliament, the exceptional diversity of cultures, nationalities, languages and national political movements represented in it, the great diversity of the Parliament's activities and the fact that, unlike national parliaments, the Parliament does not have the traditional dichotomy between majority and opposition.'[230] A second reason is found in the practical organization of the legislative procedure. Especially when a co-decision procedure reaches the conciliation stage, it is necessary for a delegation to be made up reflecting the political composition of the European Parliament — with representatives of the various political groups.[231] Thirdly, the dual requirement for the organization of Members into political groups, namely that the members of a political group must share political affinities and come from more than one Member State, enables local political particularities to be transcended and promotes European integration as sought by Article 191 TEC.[232]

Even if the formation of political groups within the Parliament is a necessity, the question still arises whether this special role of the Parliament warrants all cases in which non-affiliated Members are treated differently. However, in this respect the CFI did not manage to make a definite statement, since the parties had only formally challenged, through an objection of illegality, the validity of the rules on formation of political groups[233] and

[229] Joined Cases T-222/99, T-327/99, & T-329/99 *Martinez v European Parliament* [2001] ECR II-2823, para 145.
[230] *Ibid*, para 146.
[231] *Ibid*, para 147.
[232] *Ibid*, para 148.
[233] Arts 29 and 30 of the Rules on Procedure of the European Parliament.

not the various potentially discriminatory rules.[234] Nonetheless, it becomes apparent from the judgment that the CFI is concerned about those possible discriminations.[235]

This technique of giving warnings to the institutions, which we also saw in *Lamberts*,[236] may not be an aim of judicial review in itself, but it is an interesting spin-off. From the perspective of enhancing the legitimacy of the institutions, it may indeed result in the institutions voluntarily adopting better rules. Moreover, in this way the institutions are given the opportunity to resolve potential conflicts themselves, making their own assessment of what is necessary and proportionate in a given situation, without the Court being required to come in to spell out the rules itself. The contribution of judicial review to the constitutionalization of the Union should not always be in setting new rules, but also in creating a climate in which the institutions and the Member States can themselves work out the institutional balance. Yet, at the same time, it is made clear that judicial protection will be available in those instances where the institutions or Member States do not assume this exercise in self-critique.

## IV. CONCLUSION

The foregoing considerations aim to contribute to the debate on the enlargement of the criteria for *locus standi* under Article 230 TEC, by arguing that the adaptations which the ECJ has made in respect of the institutions should be matched by a similar liberal approach in respect of the *locus standi* of individuals. As the present case law of the ECJ, even if *British American Tobacco*[237] and *Camar*[238] offer some nuances on the *UPA*[239] judgment, still offers insufficient protection, we turn to the European Convention on Human Rights (ECHR) for modernization of the rules on access to the Community Courts. Expanding the possibility for judicial review is warranted in the light of the principle of effective judicial protection, which forms part of the constitutional tradition of the Member States, which is confirmed in Article 47 of the Charter of Fundamental Rights and

[234] For an overview see n 227.

[235] Joined Cases T-222/99, T-327/99, & T-329/99 *Martinez v European Parliament* [2001] ECR II-2823, para 157. See also paras 200–2 with reference to the principle of democracy as set out in Case T-135/96 *UEAPME v Council* [1998] ECR II-2335.

[236] Case T-209/00 *Lamberts v European Ombudsman* [2002] ECR II-2203.

[237] Case C-491/01 *Britsh American Tobacco (Investments) Ltd and Imperial Tobacco Ltd* [2002] ECR I-11453.

[238] Case C-312/00 P *Commission v Camar and Tico* [2002] ECR I-11355.

[239] Case C-50/00 P *Unión de Pequeños Agricultores v Council* [2002] ECR I-6677.

Articles 6 and 13 ECHR, as recently confirmed in the judgment in *Posti and Rahko v Finland*.[240]

Such an expansion is moreover justified because both the ECJ and the CFI have in the past demonstrated that, through direct actions against the institutions, they can both make valuable contributions to the constitutionalization of the European Union, in respect of transparency, accountability, and democracy. Admittedly, the examples given did not always involve acts of general scope and were mostly derived from the administrative law of the Community. However, opening up the scope of judicial review will also give the opportunity of addressing new issues. The recent *Aden*[241] case — in which the President of the CFI had to review, at the request of affected individuals, the legality of a sanctions regulation of the Community taken in the war on terrorism — offers a prime example of the way ahead. Expansion of the rules on standing will offer the Union courts the opportunity to contribute in a crosspillar context to uphold the institutional balance, transparency, accountability, and democracy, as well as to protect fundamental rights through judicial review of all acts of the institutions. A Union based on the rule of law cannot afford anything less.

[240] Judgment of the European Court of Human Rights of 24 Sept 2002, Application 27824/95 *Posti and Rahko v Finland*.
[241] Case T-306/01 R *Aden v Council and Commission* [2002] ECR II-2387.

# 4

# *Competences of the Union*

GEORGE A BERMANN

IN THE CONTEXT of the Convention on the Future of Europe and the resulting draft constitutional Treaty,[1] the competences of the Union is one of those subjects which we cannot do without, but with which we seldom know what to do. We cannot do without this subject for the simple reason that it is inextricably linked to certain vital legitimacy issues that lie at the heart of the Convention and the constitutional Treaty; in any event, given the ongoing political preoccupation with where Union powers end and Member State powers begin, a draft constitutional Treaty would be unthinkable without it. On the other hand, we seldom know what to do with the subject because no treatment seems to make a contribution commensurate with the subject's importance.

The link between competences and legitimacy was recognized from the outset of the Convention enterprise. Both the Nice Treaty's Declaration on the Future of Europe[2] and the subsequent Laeken Declaration[3] underscored the importance of achieving a more precise delimitation of powers between the Union and the Member States. Moreover, both declarations emphasized the necessity of addressing that issue independently of the notion of subsidiarity.[4] While the notion of subsidiarity concerns the way in which Union powers, once granted, are exercised, the competences issue raises the prior question of who has what powers to begin with. Rhetoric in the runup to the Convention suggested that something more and better than subsidiarity by way of delimitation of competences — perhaps even a catalogue of competences — was needed and could be achieved.

[1] The European Convention, Draft Treaty establishing a Constitution for Europe, CONV 850/03 (18 July 2003) (hereinafter referred to as 'draft constitutional Treaty').
[2] Declaration 23 of the Treaty of Nice, OJ C80/1 (Mar 10, 2001).
[3] Annex I to Conclusions of the Presidency of the European Council meeting at Laeken, Dec 14–15, 2001, SN 300/1/01, rev 1.
[4] See A von Bogdandy and J Bast 'The European Union's Vertical Order of Competences: The Current Law and Proposals for its Reform' (2002) 39 *CML Rev* 227, 228 .

Belief in the feasibility of delineating Union and Member State competences was fueled by a conviction in certain quarters — including, notably, the German *Länder*[5] and broad segments of UK political scene[6] — that the Union's competences required not only clarification, but indeed change, in the form of a reversal of what had come to be called competence 'creep.' Under this view, the competences provisions of the prospective Constitution held the key not only to a sharper, but also to a healthier, line of jurisdictional demarcation.

## EXPECTATIONS AND RESULTS

Fast-forwarding to the Convention's results, we find that the high hopes for the competences dossier, particularly as regards containing and even reversing competence 'creep,' were disappointed, and not unpredictably. From the outset, commentators had warned against imagining that the competences provisions could produce real change;[7] even clarification would be 'a long shot.' Some went so far as to describe the hopes pinned on competences as having from the start been 'chimerical.'[8] As with the various constitutive treaties up to now, the devil continues to be in the details — and those details continue to be found not in Treaty articles denominated as 'competences,' but rather in the thick subject-by-subject treatment of EU law in the body of the Treaty, namely in Part Three,[9] where we find the crucial subject-specific provisions on how particular measures at EU level decisions are made, by whom, and subject to what procedural rules of the game. These are the provisions that continue to do 'the heavy lifting.' To this extent, the simplification to be achieved through artful drafting of Treaty articles on competences, as such, may be illusory.

Nor has subsidiarity, in the end, been sidelined. How could it have been? A constitutional Treaty which makes 'shared' competences the norm simply

[5] See I Pernice 'Rethinking the Methods of Dividing and Controlling the Competencies of the Union' in *Europe 2004: Le grand débat*: *Setting the Agenda and Outlining the Options* 96, 102–7 (European Commission, 2001); J Kokott, 'Federal States in Federal Europe: The German *Länder* and Problems of European Integration' (1997) *European Public Law* 607, 629.

[6] See M Dougan 'Some Comments on the Praesisium's "Draft Treaty Establishing a Constitution for Europe," in *Enlightening the Debate on Good Governance* (The Federal Trust for Education and Research, 2003) 5.

[7] See G de Búrca and B de Witte 'The Delimitation of Powers between the EU and its Member States' in A Arnull and D Wincott (eds), *Accountability and Legitimacy in the European Union* (Oxford, OUP, 2002) 3; S Weatherill 'Competence' (European University Institute-RSCAS/AEL, 2003) 46–47.

[8] AV Bausili 'Rethinking the Methods of Dividing and Exercising Powers in the EU: Reforming Subsidiarity and National Parliaments' *Jean Monnet Working Paper* 9/02 (New York University School of Law) 7.

[9] Draft constitutional Treaty, art 11, para 6: 'The scope of and arrangements for exercising the Union's competences shall be determined by the provisions specific to each area in Part III.'

cannot hope to segregate the 'who' questions from the 'how much' questions. The more that competences are shared, the less it makes sense to talk about simply 'delimiting' them. In the end, the much-maligned notion of subsidiarity has in fact resumed center stage, bringing with it once again the elements of uncertainty and unclarity for which it has come in for so much criticism over the years. I return to the role of subsidiarity in the draft constitutional Treaty further below.[10]

This pattern of results could be discerned early in the drafting process, and subsequent discussions in the Convention did little to alter that. The position was taken at an early point — and never departed from — that the Treaty articles on competences would be drafted in short and clear terms, and would distinguish among exclusive, shared and merely 'supporting' (or 'coordinating' or 'complementary') competences, with shared competences being the rule rather than the exception. The notion that talk about subsidiarity could be avoided was quickly abandoned. And no idea that might have been regarded as revolutionary from a competences point of view managed to gain substantial support in Convention circles.

## CATEGORIES — NOT CATALOGUES — OF COMPETENCE

The draft constitutional Treaty establishes three broad categories of competences: *exclusive* competences,[11] over which only the Union may legislate, except where the Union empowers the States to act for it; *shared* competences,[12] over which both the Union and the States may legislate, but the latter only to the extent that the Union has not exercised, or has ceased to exercise, its competence; and competence to *support, coordinate or supplement* Member State action,[13] short, however, of superseding it. Closely related to the latter category is the Union's express authorization to 'coordinate' the economic and employment policies of the Member States.[14]

Despite suggestions to add agriculture and the establishment of an area of freedom, security and justice to the list of exclusive EU competences, that list has not grown beyond the current exclusive competences, to wit, the common commercial policy and the customs union, competition policy within the internal market, monetary policy within the eurozone, conservation of marine biological resources, and the conclusion of international agreements where either provided for by a legislative act of the Union, needed to enable the Union to exercise an internal competence, or otherwise

[10] See notes 27–39 below and accompanying text.
[11] Draft constitutional Treaty, art 11, para 1.
[12] *Ibid*, para 2.
[13] *Ibid*, para 5.
[14] *Ibid*, para 3.

affecting an internal Union act.[15] Significantly, a proposal to declare free movement of goods, persons, services and capital an exclusive Union competence was defeated. Similarly, the list of areas for supporting, coordinating and supplementary actions contains no significant additions, and thus few surprises. It includes industry, health protection, education, vocational training, youth, sports, culture and 'civil protection.'[16]

While exclusive powers and areas of supporting measures are enumerated, shared powers are not, except by way of illustration. They include, among other things, the internal market, energy, transport, agriculture and fisheries (except for the conservation of marine biological resources), the environment, consumer protection, and the area of freedom, justice and security.[17] Significantly, from a subsidiarity point of view, it is shared rather than exclusive competence that becomes the residual category, in the sense that all competences referred to in the body of the constitutional Treaty are to be deemed shared unless they have been specifically designated in the competences section of the Treaty either as an exclusive competence or as one in which the Union may only act to support, coordinate or supplement Member State action.[18]

It would have been impossible for the common foreign and security policy (CFSP) to have passed unmentioned in the competences articles of the draft Treaty, although the drafters were understandably uncomfortable pigeon-holing it in any of the exclusive, shared or supporting measures categories. As if an autonomous authority, the Union's powers over CFSP are simply described as 'cover[ing] all areas of foreign and security policy, [possibly leading] to a common defense, while the Member States are enjoined to 'actively and unreservedly support' such policy and to comply with it.[19]

## SIMPLICITY

If, overall, the draft Treaty's articles on competence cannot be described as deeply innovative, they at least have the merit of turning back proposals that would have rendered them unnecessarily complex, thereby prejudicing the Convention's stated goal of simplification and transparency. The drafters thankfully rejected a distinction, within the shared competence category, between 'concurrent' and 'parallel' powers (with the former denoting that Member State competence lapses as soon as the EU has

[15] Draft constitutional Treaty, art 12.
[16] *Ibid*, art 16, para 2.
[17] *Ibid*, art 13, para 2.
[18] *Ibid*, para 1.
[19] *Ibid*, art 15.

acted, and the latter denoting that Member State competence continues even after the EU has acted, though subject of course to the supremacy of EU law).[20] They also turned back various other distinctions among competences, such as between those that denote functions and those that denote fields, or between those that are formal and those that are 'soft,' or between those that are 'market integrating' and those that are 'welfare enhancing.' Among rejected constructs should also be counted the distinction, championed by certain German *Länder*, between the competence to establish laws and a more restrictive competence merely to establish 'frameworks.'[21] Rejected, too, was any express recitation of matters 'excluded' from Union competence, in the sense of being expressly constitutionally reserved to the Member States.[22]

## THE SURVIVAL OF IMPLIED POWERS

Notable among the proposals that the Convention turned back was the elimination of the Union's implied powers authority (EC Treaty art 308),[23] now to be known as the Treaty's 'flexibility clause.' Notwithstanding pressures in that direction, the implied powers provision has been retained, along with the requirements of Commission proposal, parliamentary assent and unanimity in the Council for the adoption of implied powers measures.[24] Not only was the implied powers authority not abolished, but proposals for weakening it — such as subjecting its use to a favorable *ex ante* opinion by the Court of Justice or providing for the repeal of implied powers measures by a qualified majority vote — were beaten back. While keeping the Union's implied powers authority essentially intact may have struck some as a missed opportunity to curtail competence 'creep,' it was consistent with the Convention's basic preference for conservatism over change in regard to the Union's competences.

The drafters did not, however, miss the opportunity to give subsidiarity special consideration in the Union's exercise of implied powers. The Commission is specifically enjoined to solicit the views of national parliaments on the conformity with the subsidiarity principle of measures adopted pursuant to the Treaty's flexibility clause.[25] In doing so, the

[20] On the distinction between concurrent and parallel powers, see von Bogdandy and Bast, above note 4, 242–48; Weatherill, above note 7, 54.
[21] W Clement 'Europa gestalten-nicht verwalten', www.whi-berlin.de/clement.htm, paras 18–21 (2001), discussed in von Bogdandy and Bast, above note 4, 253.
[22] See Weatherill, above note 7, 52.
[23] Final report of Working Group V, CONV 375/1/02 REV 1 (Nov 4, 2002), 14–16.
[24] Draft constitutional Treaty, art 17, para 1.
[25] The draft Treaty also specifically precludes the use of implied powers authority to enact harmonization legislation where the Treaty otherwise excludes the harmonization of Member State laws or regulations. *Ibid*, para 3.

national parliaments will deploy the new subsidiarity monitoring procedures laid down in a separate Subsidiarity Protocol,[26] to which we now turn.

## SUBSIDIARITY IN THE COMPETENCES CONTEXT

The notion of subsidiarity remains, in the end, central to the competences discussion. The Treaty article on the 'fundamental principles' of competence highlights it,[27] and its definition is strengthened insofar as it is described as guaranteeing respect not only for the capabilities of the Member States, but also for those of regional and local governments.[28]

But the notion of subsidiarity also lurks behind much else that is to be found in the draft constitutional Treaty on the subject of competences. We read, unsurprisingly, that all competences not specifically granted to the Union are expressly reserved to the Member States.[29] Moreover, rather than describe EU powers as,'enumerated,' the draft describes them as having been 'conferred' and, to avoid any doubt, conferred '*by the Member States*.'[30] Then, too, 'supporting measures' themselves are defined in such a way as expressly to preclude harmonization in all matters subject to them.[31] Finally, while it is not apparent why the principle of primacy of Union law needed reiteration in the draft constitutional Treaty's section on competences in the first place, the final Treaty version reminds us that this principle comes into play only insofar as the Union stays within the limits of its competence.[32]

However, the most salient innovation with regard to subsidiarity is a distinctly operational one, found in a revised Protocol on the Application of the Principles of Subsidiarity and Proportionality,[33] which is itself attached to the draft constitutional Treaty, much as the current Subsidiarity Protocol was appended to the EC Treaty by the Treaty of Amsterdam. The Protocol's most innovative feature is an 'early warning' system which makes the national parliaments privileged participants in *pre-enactment* subsidiarity discussions with the Commission. Under the system, the Commission

[26] *Ibid*, para 2.
[27] 'The use of Union competences is governed by the principles of subsidiarity and proportionality.' *Ibid*, art 9, para 1.
[28] *Ibid*, para 3.
[29] *Ibid*, para 2.
[30] *Ibid*.
[31] Draft constitutional Treaty, art 16, para 3.
[32] *Ibid*, art 10: 'The Constitution, and law adopted by the Union's institutions *in exercising competences conferred on it*, shall have primacy over the law of the Member States' (emphasis added).
[33] The European Convention, CONV 850/03, p 229, expressly referred to in Article 9, para 3 of the draft constitutional Treaty. See also the separate Protocol on the Role of National Parliaments in the European Union. *Ibid*, 226.

is required to notify national parliaments promptly of any legislative proposals,[34] giving them six weeks in which to voice their subsidiarity concerns to the European Parliament, the Council and the Commission.[35] While in earlier drafts only the national parliaments could participate, the Protocol, as finally drafted, also empowers individual chambers of national parliaments to trigger the process.[36] (Accordingly, whereas, in the original proposal, one-third of the national parliaments would have had to call upon the Commission to reexamine a proposal in order for the Commission to be required to do so, in the final draft the figure has been changed to one-third *of national votes*, with the national parliament in each unicameral Member State having two votes and each chamber in bicameral Member States having a single vote, thereby preserving Member State equality.[37]) The Commission would then have to reexamine the proposal, stating its reasons for maintaining, modifying or withdrawing it. On the other hand, the final Treaty draft eliminates the provision found in an earlier draft which entitled the national parliaments to issue an opinion on a proposal's subsidiarity aspects whenever the measure should find itself before a conciliation committee empaneled as part of the parliamentary co-decision procedure.

The Protocol is more ambiguous about the national parliaments' *post-enactment* role in relation to subsidiarity. In early drafts, the national parliaments' role was, at most, to request their respective national governments to bring subsidiarity challenges to adopted measures in the Court of Justice under Article 230 of the EC Treaty (renumbered as Article III-270 in the draft constitutional Treaty). The final draft suggests, albeit only obliquely, that the national parliaments may hope for more. 'The Court of Justice shall have jurisdiction to hear actions on grounds of infringement of the principle of subsidiarity by a legislative act, brought in accordance with the rules laid down in Article III-270 of the Constitution by the Member States, or notified by them in accordance with their legal order on behalf of their national Parliament or a chamber of it.'[38] While this language could conceivably be read as extending to national parliaments (and even national parliamentary chambers) standing to challenge the conformity of a measure with the principle of subsidiarity in the Court of Justice, the more prudent reading would be that national parliaments (and their chambers) may only request the respective Member State government to bring such a challenge, and only insofar as Member State law allows them to do so. (The Protocol would also confer standing on the Committee of the Regions, but only as to

[34] Protocol on the Application of the Principles of Subsidiarity and Subsidiarity, above note 33, art 3.
[35] *Ibid*, art 5.
[36] *Ibid*.
[37] *Ibid*, art 6.
[38] *Ibid*, art 7.

conformity with the subsidiarity principle of measures on which that committee has the right to be consulted.[39])

In privileging the national parliaments within the early warning system, the drafters turned their back on various more adventurous alternative mechanisms under discussion in Convention circles, most of which entailed creating new subsidiarity-inspired institutions, such as a Commissioner for Subsidiarity, a subsidiarity ombudsperson, a European Parliament chamber composed of national parliamentarians, an *ad hoc* body to monitor respect for the subsidiarity principle, and even a competence court or constitutional council with final decisional authority on competence and/or subsidiarity questions. But any of these would have increased the Union's institutional complexity, while missing a valuable opportunity to empower the national parliaments, whose potential for helping to close the democratic deficit has never been fully exploited. Moreover, it is doubtful whether any such new creation would put competence or subsidiarity questions to rest unless they were to clearly vest *Kompetenz/Kompetenz* authority in the newly created institution — a step the Convention was unlikely, for reasons set out below, to take.

## UNANSWERED QUESTIONS

As implied just above, a large unanswered question in the drafting of the constitutional Treaty is the question of *Kompetenz/Kompetenz*. That this question remains unanswered in the constitutional text is hardly surprising, for however it might be answered, the discussion at this stage in the Union's evolution — given the divergent positions of the Court of Justice and various national courts,[40] not to mention divergences among popular sentiment — was bound to be deeply divisive, and possibly subversive of the entire enterprise. Even apart from that consideration, it would seem to be unwise to prevent the answer to that question from emerging in a more or less natural way from the Union's future evolution. It is instructive, by way of comparison, that, efforts in that direction notwithstanding, the US Constitution has never furnished a clear answer to the *Kompetenz/Kompetenz* question. It is also instructive that vesting *Kompetenz/Kompetenz* authority in the federal courts, as the US has done by dint of practice and custom, rather than textual edict, has by no means meant that the competence questions will

[39] *Ibid*. See further Tridimas, below Chapter Seven.

[40] Compare Case 6/64 *Costa v ENEL* [1964] ECR 585 (European Court of Justice), with, for example, *Brunner and Others*, Case 2 BvR 2134/92 & 2159/92, [1994] CMLR 57 (German Constitutional Court, Oct 12, 1993), and *Carlsen et al v Rasmussen*, Case I 361/1997 (1998), UfR 1998, p 800, para 9.6, [1999] 3 CMLR 854 (Danish Supreme Court, Apr 6, 1998).

invariably be resolved in the federal government's favor. Recent US Supreme Court case law clearly demonstrates the contrary.[41]

By posing the larger *Kompetenz/Kompetenz* question, I do not mean to imply that the scope or intensity of the Court of Justice's review of EU competence issues has itself been completely thought out or is well understood. While the *Tobacco advertising* judgment[42] assures us that the Court is prepared to face competence issues squarely, the Court's recent record of review on these issues furnishes us too thin a basis on which to gauge the level of review that it is likely to employ in the future. The unpredictability surrounding eventual judicial review of the Union's assertion of competences is not of course a reason to relax the search for clarity on issues of competence in the constitutional text. On the contrary, it provides an added reason for pursuing that search.

[41] See GA Bermann, 'The Role of Law in the Functioning of Federal Systems', in K Nicolaidis and R Howse (eds), *The Federal Vision* (Oxford, OUP, 2001) 191–212.
[42] Case C-376/98 *Germany v Council and Parliament* [2000] ECR I-8419.

# 5

# *The Hierarchy of Norms*

PAUL CRAIG

THERE HAS BEEN much comment and debate about many of the provisions in the EU Constitution. Relatively little attention has been given to the provisions concerning the hierarchy of norms, which is the focus of this chapter. The constitutional reforms concerning the types of EU norm, and the hierarchy between them, have often been regarded as a technical tidying up exercise, which has little implication for the balance of power between the EU institutions, or between those institutions and the Member States. This is mistaken. The constitutional provisions will have broader implications for the inter-institutional balance of power within the EU, and may give rise to tension between the EU and the Member States.

The analysis begins with consideration of the objectives underlying the reforms in this area. This will be followed by explication of the constitutional provisions. There will then be an evaluation of those provisions, the focus being on the implications for the horizontal balance of power between the EU institutions in the decision-making process. The discussion will then shift to the vertical dimension, through analysis of the supremacy clause that embodies a hierarchy between EU norms and Member State laws.

## SIMPLIFICATION, DEMOCRATIC LEGITIMACY, AND SEPARATION OF POWERS

It is necessary to have some criterion against which to judge the reforms to be considered below. The provisions in the Constitution on the hierarchy of norms followed, with some modifications, the recommendations of Working Group IX on Simplification.[1] It is instructive to note in this respect

[1] Final Report of Working Group IX on Simplification, CONV 424/02, Brussels 29 November 2002.

the cautionary warning of the group, that 'nothing is more complicated than simplification'.[2] It is clear nonetheless that the Working Group sought to attain a number of objectives.

*Simplification*, as the name of the group suggests, was a major concern, both in relation to the types of Union instrument and the legislative procedures for enactment.[3] This initial aim was to be secured while at the same time respecting *democratic legitimacy*. The Working Group proceeded on the assumption that the democratic legitimacy of the Union was based on the Member States and the people. Legislation must secure approval from both bodies, and acts that had the same nature and effect should be produced by the same procedure.[4] The *separation of powers* also informed the Working Group's thinking. The hierarchy of legislation was said to be 'the consequence of a better separation of powers',[5] the aim being not to pay tribute to Montesquieu, 'but out of concern for democracy'.[6] It is clear from reading the Working Group's report that separation of powers was regarded as the basis for a clearer delineation between matters that fall to the legislative arm of government and those that fall within the province of the executive. It recognised that the divide could not be as clear cut in the Union as in some national polities, but it felt that some advances could be made. This was the rationale for the new breed of delegated acts, whereby the Commission would be empowered to fill in the details of the legislative scheme, thereby avoiding excessive detail in the primary legislation.[7]

We shall consider in the course of this chapter whether these aims have been realised, the implications for the inter-institutional balance of power and the less obvious institutional consequences of these reforms.

## THE CONSTITUTIONAL PROVISIONS

The provisions concerning the hierarchy of norms are set out in Title V of Part I of the Constitution, entitled 'Exercise of Union Competence'.

The foundational provision is Article I-32(1). It provides that in exercising the competences conferred on it by the Constitution, the Union shall use as legal instruments, in accordance with the provisions of Part III, European laws, European framework laws, European regulations, European decisions, recommendations and opinions. Article I-37(1) stipulates that the choice as between these measures shall be in accordance with

[2] *Ibid*, 1.
[3] *Ibid*, 1.
[4] *Ibid*, 2.
[5] *Ibid*, 2.
[6] *Ibid*, 2.
[7] *Ibid*, 8.

the principle of proportionality, and Article I-37(2) imposes a duty to give reasons when making any of these Union acts.

*'Legislative Acts'*

The draft Constitution specifies two types of legislative act, European laws and European framework laws, Article I-32(1). The European Parliament and the Council are moreover instructed by Article I-32(2) to refrain from adopting legislative acts not provided for by Article I-32(1) in the area in question.

A *European law* is a legislative act of general application, which is binding in its entirety and directly applicable in all Member States. This corresponds to a regulation within the present system of norms.

A *European framework* law is a legislative act binding as to the result to be achieved on the Member States to which it is addressed, but leaving the national authorities entirely free to choose the form and means of achieving the result. A European framework law corresponds to an old-style directive. The definition in Article I-32(1) is however different from that of old-style directives in terms of the degree of discretion possessed by the Member States. The framework law is framed in terms of Member States being *entirely* free to choose the form and means of achieving the result. The intent is to emphasise the discretion possessed by the Member States. This discretion will nonetheless be bounded by the obligation to reach the result stipulated by the framework law, and it is therefore doubtful whether the addition of the word *entirely* will make much difference in this respect. The ECJ will continue to police the means-ends relationship in much the same way that it has done in the past.

Article I-33(1) specifies *the way in which legislation is made*. The general rule is that European laws and framework laws shall be adopted on the basis of a Commission proposal[8] jointly by the European Parliament and the Council, under what is now known as the ordinary legislative procedure, Article III-302, the old co-decision procedure. Where the two institutions cannot reach agreement the act is deemed not to be adopted. This reflects the centrality of the idea that the EP and the Council are the joint legislatures within the Union, which is a core element of the provisions on the institutions, Articles I-19(1) and I-22(1).

There is also provision in Article I-33(2) for specific cases provided by the Constitution in which European laws and framework laws are to be adopted by the European Parliament with the participation of the Council,

[8] The Commission monopoly over legislative initiation is qualified in the area of freedom, justice and security, in which the Member States can also exercise the right of initiative, Article III-165.

or by the Council with the participation of the European Parliament, in accordance with special legislative procedures.

### *'Non-Legislative Acts'*

Article I-32(1) also provides for what are termed non-legislative acts. A *European regulation* is a non-legislative act of general application for the implementation of legislative acts and certain specific provisions of the Constitution. It may either be binding in its entirety and directly applicable in all Member States, or be binding as regards the result to be achieved, on all the Member States to which it is addressed, but leaving the national authorities entirely free to choose the form and means of achieving that result. This provision therefore provides for secondary European laws, which are binding in their entirety and directly applicable in all Member States, and secondary European framework laws, which are binding as to result, but which leave the Member State discretion as to implementation.

Article I-32(1) also specifies a category of *European decisions*, which are non-legislative acts that are binding in their entirety. Where the decision specifies those to whom it is addressed it is binding only on them. This provision is helpful in capturing the duality in the meaning of decision. It is clear that many decisions are addressed to a specific person, and hence only binding on the addressee. It is however equally clear that some decisions set out more generally the applicable rules that operate in a particular area.

The other type of non-legislative act is the *recommendation or the opinion*, which do not have binding force.

Articles I-34–36 deal with *the way in which non-legislative acts are made*. Article I-34 stipulates that the Council and the Commission shall adopt European regulations and decisions in the cases referred to in Articles I-35 and 36 and in cases specifically laid down in the Constitution.[9] Article I-35 is an important new provision entitled 'Delegated Regulations', which gives significant power to the Commission. It provides, in Article I-35(1), that European laws and framework laws may delegate to the Commission the power to enact delegated regulations to 'supplement or amend certain non-essential elements of the European law or framework law'. The objectives, content, scope and duration of the delegation shall be explicitly defined in the laws and framework laws. The delegation may not cover the essential elements in the area, which shall be

[9] The European Central Bank can also make such norms when authorised to do so by the Constitution, Article I-34.

reserved for the law or framework law. Article I-35(2) specifies further that the conditions to which the delegation is subject *shall* be determined in the law or framework law, and that these *may* consist of the following possibilities: the European Parliament or the Council may decide to revoke the delegation; or the delegated regulation may enter into force only if no objection has been expressed by the European Parliament or the Council within a period set by the law or framework law.[10]

*'Implementing Acts'*

Although Article I-32(1) specifies the principal types of Union act it does not list all such measures. There is an important category of measure that is not mentioned in Article I-32(1), implementing acts, which is dealt with by Article I-36.

It imposes an obligation on Member States to adopt all measures of national law necessary to implement legally binding Union acts, Article I-36(1).

It also empowers the Commission. Implementing acts can take the form of European implementing regulations or European implementing decisions, Article I-36(4). Where uniform conditions are required for implementing binding Union acts, those acts may confer implementing powers on the Commission, or in specific cases concerned with common foreign and security policy, on the Council, Article I-36(2). The European laws shall lay down in advance rules and general principles for the mechanisms of control by Member States over implementing acts of the Union, Article I-36(3).

## THE HISERARCHY OF NORMS AND THE INTER-INSTITUTIONAL BALANCE OF POWER WITHIN THE EU

*Legislative Acts*

The decision to make a division between what may be termed primary legislative acts, European laws and European framework laws, and delegated acts is, in general terms to be welcomed. It is clearly right to preserve both species of legislative act, European laws, which correspond to old-style regulations and European framework laws, which correspond to old-style directives. The approach in the Constitution to the enactment of such

[10] The EP shall act by a majority of its members, and the Council by qualified majority, Art I-35(2).

legislation is also to be commended, and has built on the essentials of the institutional balance that has characterised the legislative process. The Commission has retained in general terms its gold standard, the right of legislative initiative, Article I-25(2). The EP and the Council are said to jointly enact legislation, Articles I-19(1) and I-22(1). The co-decision procedure under which such legislation is jointly enacted is now deemed to be the ordinary legislative procedure for the making of European laws and framework laws, Article I-33(1). The reach of the co-decision procedure has been extended to cover more areas than hitherto.

This treatment of legislative power in the Constitution is to be welcomed. It is generally accepted that the co-decision procedure has worked well. It allows input from the EP, representing directly the electorate, and from the Council, representing state interests. Article 251 (now III-302) provides a framework for a deliberative dialogue on the content of the legislation between the EP, Council and Commission. The extension of co-decision to cover new areas is a natural development, building on what has occurred in earlier Treaty reform. It enhances the legitimacy of Union legislation and its democratic credentials by enabling the EP to have input into the making of legislation in these areas.

### *'Non-legislative Acts': Delegated Regulations*

The provisions on 'non-legislative' acts contained in the Constitution are more contentious, and the implications for the inter-institutional balance of power between Council, EP and the Commission are likely to be more significant. It can be readily accepted that a modern polity should be able to create norms other than primary legislation. There are nonetheless a number of difficulties with the provisions in the Constitution.

The *depiction of European regulations in Article I-32(1) as being non-legislative acts is misleading*. These acts are only non-legislative in the formal sense that they are not primary laws: they are not European laws or European framework laws. This does not mean that they are not legislative in nature. They clearly are, and this conclusion is reinforced by the fact that they are said to be of general application, that they can supplement or amend certain elements of primary law, and because there is a separate provision dealing with administrative decisions. The reality is therefore that a European regulation will often be what would be regarded in domestic legal systems as secondary or delegated legislation. It is interesting to contrast the label attached to European regulations in the Constitution, with the Working Group's more honest depiction of these acts as a new category of legislation.[11]

[11] Final Report of Working Group IX, above note 1, 8.

The *Commission will therefore have significant power over what may be complex regulatory choices, with relatively little input from the Council and the EP*. The depiction of European Regulations as non-legislative acts serves, whether intentionally or not, to dispel fears that the Commission is making legislative choices of its own volition. The combination of greater use of less detailed primary laws, and increased Commission control over delegated norms, may significantly alter the institutional balance of power in the Community. It will reduce the power of the Council and EP, and increase that of the Commission. The category of European regulation will fill the 'space' presently occupied by norms made pursuant to the Comitology procedure. The Commission's desire to have greater autonomy over this area has been apparent for some time, and was an explicit feature of the White Paper on *European Governance*.[12] The key to the White Paper was the Commission's conception of the 'Community method',[13] with the Commission representing the general interest and the Council and the EP as the joint legislature, representing the Member States and national citizens respectively. This is in itself unexceptionable. It is the implications that the Commission drew from it that are contentious. It was, said the Commission, necessary to revitalize the Community method.[14] The Council and the EP should limit their involvement in primary Community legislation to defining the essential elements.[15] This legislation would define the conditions and limits within which the Commission performed its executive role. It would, in the Commission's view, make it possible to do away with the Comitology committees. There would instead be a simple legal mechanism allowing the Council and EP to control the actions of the Commission against the principles adopted in the legislation. The possibility of enhancing the Commission's control over European regulations by abolishing or amending the Comitology procedure was raised again by the Working Group on Simplification.[16] The reality is that the Comitology committees allow Member State oversight of what are often complex regulatory choices.[17] The fact that the matters are often complex and detailed does not alter this important fact. The committees were created precisely because the Member States sought greater regulatory input into the detail of delegated legislation than allowed for in the then existing Treaty provisions. Comitology-type committees were created as soon as the need to delegate

[12] COM(2001) 428 final. The White Paper provoked a variety of critical comment, see the *Symposium: Responses to the European Commission's White Paper on Governance*, http://www.jeanmonnetprogram.org/papers/01.
[13] COM(2001) 428 final, 8.
[14] *Ibid*, 29.
[15] *Ibid*, 20.
[16] Working Group IX, above note 1, 12.
[17] C Joerges and E Vos (eds), *EU Committees: Social Regulation, Law and Politics* (Oxford, Hart Publishing, 1999); M Andenas and A Turk (eds), *Delegated Legislation and the Role of Committees in the EC* ( The Hague, Kluwer Law International, 2000).

extensive powers to the Commission became a reality. They have been part of the institutional landscape for over thirty years. They were established to accord Member States an institutionalized method for input into the content of delegated legislation. These regulatory choices will not disappear. They will continue to be made through the new style European regulations, and these regulations will, so it is intended, be made against the background of less detailed primary European laws or framework laws. It is true that the Comitology structure has been criticised, primarily on grounds of transparency and access. The substantive results produced were nonetheless often good. The procedure moreover allowed input from Member State representatives, with increased possibility for involvement by the EP post 1999,[18] and with the ultimate possibility of legislative veto by the Council. The problems concerning transparency and access were in any event alleviated by the 1999 reforms.[19]

The *methods of control contained in Article I-35 will be difficult to monitor and enforce*. It might be argued that the fears expressed above are unwarranted because they ignore the controls over delegation stipulated in Article I-35(1). The delegated regulation can only amend or supplement 'certain non-essential elements of the European law or framework law', and cannot cover the 'essential elements of an area'. These must be reserved for the European law or framework law, which must also define the 'objectives, content, scope and duration of the delegation'. These limits are complemented by Article I-35(2). The conditions of application to which the delegation is subject 'shall' be determined in the law or framework law. These 'may' entail the possibility of revocation of the delegation by the EP or the Council, or a condition whereby the delegated regulation enters into force only if there is no objection expressed by the EP or the Council within a specified period of time.

These controls are important. We should however be mindful of the trade-off that is inherent in this schema for delegated regulation. In essence the pre-existing regime was based on *generalized ex ante input into the making and content of the delegated norms, with the possibility of formal recourse to the Council in accord with the Comitology procedures*. It allowed for regularised, general and detailed input into the content of such norms by Member State representatives, with some control exercised by the EP. We are switching to a system based on *ex ante specification of standards in the primary law, combined with the possibility of some control*

[18] *Agreement between the European Parliament and the Commission on Procedures for Implementing Council Decision 99/468*, [2000] OJ L256/19.

[19] *Council Decision laying down the Procedures for the Exercise of Implementing Powers Conferred on the Commission*, Dec 99/468, [1999] OJ L184/23; *Information from the Commission — List of Committees which Assist the Commission in the Exercise of its Implementing Powers*, [2000] OJ C225/2.

*ex post should the measure not be to the liking of the EP or Council, but this latter control will only operate where it is written into the primary law.* The efficacy of these controls is however questionable.

In terms of the controls set out in Article I-35(1), it will often be difficult for the Council and the EP to specify with any exactitude the criteria that should guide the exercise of delegated power by the Commission. The Council and the EP will often have neither the knowledge, nor the time to delineate in the primary European law precise parameters for the exercise of regulatory choices. The real issues about the assignment of regulatory risks and choice will often only be apparent when the matter is examined in detail. It was for these very reasons that the Comitology process was first created. It will therefore not be easy for the primary law to define with precision the 'objectives, content, scope and duration' of the delegation. If these requirements are to be taken seriously then there will have to be oversight by, *inter alia*, the Community courts. They will have to enforce a non-delegation doctrine, striking down delegations where the primary law was insufficiently precise about the 'objectives, content, scope and duration' of the delegation. Whether the Community courts would be willing to do this with vigour remains to be seen. Experience from other legal systems is mixed. The non-delegation doctrine in the USA has provided little by way of control of broad regulatory choices accorded to agencies,[20] although it, or its equivalent, has however been applied more often in some Continental legal systems.[21]

In terms of the controls set out in Article I-35(2), the possibility of revocation of the delegation by the EP or Council etc, it should be recognised that these are not mandatory. Article I-35(2) states that the conditions of application to which the delegation is subject *shall* be explicitly determined in the European laws or framework laws, and that they *may* consist of revocation of the delegation, and/or entry into force only if there is no objection from the Council or the EP. The wording of this provision was consciously altered to make it clear that 'these conditions do not constitute a mandatory element of such a law or framework law'.[22]

It should moreover be noted that the controls specified in Article I-35 are based on 'control from the top', through the specification of standards and the like in the enabling Union law. They do not embrace 'control from the bottom' through a legal regime for participation in the making of delegated regulation. It is true that the Commission consults widely before making such norms. It is equally true that it has been resistant to any formal legal regime equivalent to a US style Administrative Procedure Act 1946.

[20] AC Aman and WT Mayton, *Administrative Law* (St Paul, MN, West Group, 2001) Chap 1; JM Rogers, MP Healy, and RJ Krotoszynski, *Administrative Law* (New York, Aspen Publishers, 2003) 312–45.

[21] Such as Austria.

[22] CONV 724/03, Annex 2, 93.

There were hints a decade ago that such a regime might be developed for the Union,[23] but these have not been taken up through any formal legal regime. Such a legal regime may have disadvantages as well as advantages. If however we are concerned with the overall legitimacy of norms of a legislative nature made by the political organs of government, then we should be cognisant of all the options, whether control from the top or from the bottom. Thus the reluctance of the US courts to give real teeth to the non-delegation doctrine must be viewed against the system as a whole, an essential part being a notice and comment regime, which allows for participatory input into the content of secondary norms, this being monitored by the courts.[24] Having said this, there are welcome signs that the Commission is placing consultation and participation on a more regularised footing, albeit while not adopting a formal regime of participation rights.[25]

The *effect of the provisions on delegated regulations on the balance of power within the EU will ultimately depend on three factors*. It will be affected in part by the extent to which European laws and framework laws are drafted in more abstract, less detailed terms. The intent that this should be so was certainly a theme in the Convention's deliberations, and in the earlier Commission White Paper.[26] The more this becomes a reality, the more that will be done through delegated regulations, and hence the regime for the passage and control of such regulations will be all the more important. The balance of power will also be affected by the extent to which the controls on delegation set out in Article I-35 prove to be effective, combined with the extent to which the Community courts are willing to enforce them through a non-delegation doctrine. The final factor that will have an impact on the balance of power will be the fate of the Comitology procedures. We have seen that there has been talk of these procedures being abolished as a result of the new provisions on the hierarchy of norms. The Constitution itself does not however do so and any change in Comitology would have to be through repeal or amendment of the Comitology Decision. It remains to be seen whether the Member States in the Council are willing to do this. They might decide to retain such controls. They might decide to down grade them so as to abolish management and regulatory committees, while preserving the committees with a formal advisory status. If they did the latter, it would still be possible to give such committees some real 'bite'. Thus it would, for example, be possible for an adverse report from such a committee to operate as a warning signal to the Council or the EP, that they should consider using the powers in Article I-35(2).

[23] European Council's Inter-institutional Declaration on Democracy, Transparency, and Subsidiarity (1993).
[24] Aman and Mayton above note 20, chaps 2–4.
[25] COM (2002) 277 final.
[26] COM(2001) 428 final.

*'Non-legislative Acts': Implementing Acts*

Article I-36, which is concerned with implementing acts, also raises a number of important issues concerning the inter-institutional balance of power.

We should begin by making clear *the place of implementation in the overall hierarchy of norms*. The Working Group on Simplification spoke in terms of these acts as 'acts implementing legislative acts, delegated acts or acts provided for in the Treaty itself'.[27] The idea is that there should be a hierarchy with legislative acts at the top, then delegated acts which would flesh out the detail or amend certain elements of a legislative act, to be followed by implementing acts that would it seems put into effect the legislative or delegated act, but without thereby adding to the substance of what had already been decided. The combined effect of Articles I-34 and I-36(2) is that it is the Commission that generally[28] has the power to issue implementing acts, which are to take the form of European implementing regulations or European implementing decisions, Article I-36(4). The Commission's power is subject to Member State control as set out in Article I-36(3), which provides that the 'European laws shall lay down in advance rules and general principles for the mechanisms for control by Member States of Union implementing acts'. This Article clearly envisages some general Union laws that will establish the rules and principles for control by Member States over implementing acts of the Union.

It should however be recognised that *there is an important ambiguity as to the meaning of implementation that runs throughout the Convention documentation*. Implementation can bear the meaning that it has in Article 202 EC: delegated rulemaking or decision-making subject to conditions. Thus Article 202 is framed so as to allow the Council to delegate power to the Commission for the implementation of rules, subject to the Comitology procedure. Implementation can also mean the execution of other norms, whether Treaty provisions, primary legislation or delegated regulations. This latter sense of implementation is based on the premise that the norms will be taken as given, and they will be executed or applied: the existing rules in the primary law, or delegated regulation will not be substantively supplemented or amended. The consequence of this ambiguity is important. The Comitology procedure has hitherto applied to implementation in the first of these senses: it was the condition attached to delegated rulemaking or decision-making by the Commission. The discussion in the Convention documentation reveals an important shift in thought.

[27] Working Group IX, above note 1, 9

[28] The Council has power to issue such acts in specific circumstances covered by Article I-39, dealing with implementation of the CFSP.

The Constitution creates, as we have seen, a new category of delegated regulation. However the Comitology procedures were not considered to be of relevance directly to the making of this type of norm, even though this is the true analogy with the status quo ante. The Convention documentation considered the legitimacy of Comitology primarily in the context of implementing acts covered in Article I-36, where the emphasis is on implementation in its second sense, as execution or application. This is apparent in the literature from the Working Group.[29] It is apparent again in the Convention comments on Article I-36(3), which provision allows Member State control over implementing acts.[30] The Praesidium stated that several amendments were opposed to the *current* mechanisms for the committee procedure, and wished to delete this Article, while other comments proposed confining the control mechanisms to advisory committees alone. The Praesidium considered that this was a matter for secondary legislation and therefore did not amend the Article.

The *circumstances in which the Commission would be accorded the power in Article I-36(2) are not clear*. This Article provides that where uniform conditions for implementing binding Union acts are needed, those acts may confer implementing powers on the Commission.[31] It is therefore necessary for a binding Union act to confer implementing powers on the Commission. It is worth reflecting for a moment on the circumstances when this might operate, since they are not obvious.

Binding legislative acts take the form of European laws, or European framework laws. European laws are old style regulations. They are directly applicable within the Member States' legal systems, and are binding as to means as well as ends. They do not require adoption or transformation before they acquire legal force within those systems, and the ECJ has moreover held that they should not normally be cast into national legislation.[32] It is therefore difficult to see how the need for 'uniform conditions for implementing binding Union acts' would be of relevance in relation to European laws, given that they are directly applicable. It might be argued that such a power could still be relevant in relation to European laws for the following reason. Such laws may well be directly applicable, and bind as to means as well as ends. They might nonetheless require consequential changes in other areas of national law. It might then be contended that the power to impose uniform conditions contained in Article I-36(2) could be apposite in such circumstances. This will not readily withstand examination. Where consequential changes in national law are

[29] Working Group IX, above note 1, 9.
[30] CONV 724/03, Annex 2, 94.
[31] Or in specific cases covered by Art I-39 dealing with the CFSP on the Council.
[32] Case 34/73, *Variola v Amministrazione delle Finanze* [1973] ECR 981.

required as a consequence of a directly applicable European law, the nature of those required amendments are bound to differ as between the Member States, precisely because their previous laws in the area will often be very different. It will not therefore be possible to contemplate uniform changes to these other national legal provisions that could be stipulated by the Commission. The Member States would simply have the obligation, pursuant to Article I-36(1), to adopt all measures necessary to implement legally binding Union acts.

European framework laws seem at first sight to be more fertile ground within which to think of a need for the binding act to empower the Commission to impose uniform conditions for implementation. These are after all old style directives, which bind as to result, but leave the Member State with discretion as to the form and means of achieving it. A moment's reflection reveals however real tension in this respect. The very nature of a European framework law is meant to leave Member States with discretion as to means of implementation. That is its very raison d'etre. This has been further emphasized in the definition of such laws in Article I-32(1), which speaks of Member States being '*entirely* free to choose the form and methods of achieving the result'.[33] It would therefore be odd, to say the least, to enact a European framework law, but to empower the Commission to impose uniform conditions for implementation. The reality is that if the Commission's power to impose uniform conditions for implementation were to be used in relation to framework laws it would radically alter their nature. It would create a new hybrid species of primary legislative act, in which the means of implementation, normally left entirely to the discretion of the Member States, would be exercised instead by the Commission.

It might then be that the Commission's power over implementation dealt with in Article I-36(2) would apply in relation to regulations. The Working Party on Simplification considered that it would be possible for implementing acts to be made pursuant to delegated acts, as well as legislative acts.[34] It is clear also that this is possible in principle, given the language of Article I-36(2): a binding Union act can provide for the Commission to have implementing power, and a new style European regulation as defined in Article I-32(1) is such a binding act. While it is therefore possible in principle for Article I-36(2) to apply in relation to European regulations there are nonetheless two difficulties with this scenario.

There is, on the one hand, the fact that the problems discussed above concerning the application of Article I-36(2) to European laws and framework laws are equally applicable here. The reason is not hard to

[33] Emphasis added.
[34] Working Group IX, above note 1, 9–11.

discern. European regulations as defined in Article I-32(1) are in effect either secondary European laws, in the sense that they are binding in their entirety and directly applicable. Or they are in effect secondary European framework laws, binding as to the result to be achieved but leaving the national authorities entirely free as to choice of form and methods of implementation. The difficulties of finding 'space' for Commission implementing power analysed above in the context of European laws and European framework laws are therefore replicated in the context of the new style European regulation.

There is, on the other hand, a less obvious difficulty with attaching the Commission's power over implementation in Article I-36(2) to a binding Union act in the form of the new style European regulation. These new style regulations are made by the Commission pursuant to Articles I-35 and 36. The delegated regulation will be subject to the conditions discussed above. Subject to such conditions, the Commission then has autonomy over the passage of such norms. We have already seen that Article I-36(2) specifies that the Commission's implementing power can be conferred by a binding Union act, which includes a European regulation. It would therefore seem possible in principle for the Commission to enact a delegated regulation, for the Commission to decide that uniform implementing conditions are required, and for the Commission to then give itself the implementing power in the European regulation. This conclusion seems to follow from a reading of the Articles of the Constitution. Whether it is desirable in normative terms is far more contestable. It would, if used in this manner, certainly increase the Commission's degree of control over the legislative process taken as a whole. The only formal constraints on this happening would be the possibility for the Council or EP to object to the entry into force of such a delegated regulation pursuant to Article I-35(2), or through the provisions of laws that might be made pursuant to Article I-36(3), which accords Member States control over implementing acts.

## THE HIERARCHY OF NORMS: SECOND ORDER CONSEQUENCES FOR INTER-INSTITUTIONAL RELATIONSHIPS IN THE EU

It is axiomatic that particular Constitutional provisions cannot be considered in isolation. They necessarily react with other parts of the overall constitutional settlement. The inter-relationship between such provisions can therefore create what may be termed 'second order' consequences for the institutional balance of power within the overall Union legal order. There are important second order consequences flowing from the provisions on the hierarchy of norms and other parts of the Constitution.

*Constitutional Review*

The most significant such consequence is that the Constitution embodies constitutional review, whereby provisions of Union primary legislation can be invalidated for, *inter alia*, non-compliance with rights-based constraints and competence constraints contained in the Constitution itself.

It might of course be argued that the Community courts were exercising such power hitherto, and that therefore there has been no significant change in this respect. This would be however to underestimate the changes brought about by the Constitution. The assumption in the past was that the courts' power was justified because what was being reviewed was not primary legislation or equivalent thereto, and that there were democratic deficiencies in the way that such legislation was made. It was therefore felt that the normal 'problems' with constitutional review did not apply in the Community context.

The new Constitution weakens these assumptions. There is now a divide between primary and secondary Union norms. The norms are democratically made pursuant to the co-decision procedure, which is deemed to be the ordinary legislative procedure for union acts. The Council and the EP are said to share in the making of such provisions. The Charter of Rights is binding within Part I of the Constitution. The ECJ can review the legality of all Union norms for compliance, *inter alia*, with the Charter.

It might be argued that the EU legislative process embodied in the Constitution is still less democratic than that in national polities, and that therefore we need not be so concerned with the legitimacy of constitutional review. Space precludes analysis of this issue, and the complex literature surrounding it.

Suffice it to say for the present that the provisions on the hierarchy of norms, combined with those embodying competence constraints and the Charter in the Constitution, place the ECJ ever more squarely in the role of a constitutional court, with the power to invalidate primary legislation for breach of these constraints on governmental power.

*Standing and Legality Review*

Limits of space preclude detailed evaluation of the rules for individual standing to challenge the legality of EU action contained in Article III-270(4). Nor is that the purpose of this chapter. The object is rather to cast the spotlight on the implications that the provisions on the hierarchy of norms will have for the new rules of standing.

It is likely that individuals will find it very difficult to convince the Community courts that there is individual concern in relation to a European law or framework law. The very fact that these are cast as primary laws will reinforce judicial reluctance to allow direct challenge.

The individuals' difficulty in this regard will be exacerbated by the fact that there is nothing in the new rules of standing equivalent to the provision in Article 230(4), which expressly allowed the Community courts to look behind the form of an old style regulation and decide that it was in reality a decision that was of individual concern to the applicant. Article III-270(4) contains no analogous clause enabling the CFI or ECJ to decide that a norm cast as a European law is rather to be regarded as a new style regulation or decision. Even if the ECJ reads this possibility into Article III-270(4) it will be reluctant to come to such a conclusion, since this could well mean that the norm would be invalid, because it would not have been passed in accord with the requirements for a new style regulation or decision.

## THE HIERARCHY OF NORMS AND THE RELATIONSHIP BETWEEN EU AND MEMBER STATE LAW

The discussion thus far has focused on the hierarchy of norms and its impact on the balance of power between the EU institutions in the legislative process. The analysis has, in that sense, been essentially horizontal. There is however an important vertical dimension to this issue, because the Constitution contains an explicit primacy clause specifying the hierarchy between EU law and national law. The primacy of EU law over national law has not hitherto been enshrined in the Treaties. The supremacy doctrine has been developed by the ECJ, and has met with a mixed reception from Member States' courts.[35] The Constitution has now bitten this particular constitutional bullet: Article I-10(1) provides that the Constitution and law adopted by the Union's institutions in exercising competences conferred on it, shall have primacy over the law of the Member States. This is reinforced by Article I-10(2), which stipulates that Member States shall take all appropriate measures, general or particular, to ensure fulfilment of the obligations flowing from the Constitution or resulting from the Union Institutions' acts. So does this signal the death of one of the staple topics in EU law courses? Does it close the chapter on this part of EU scholarship? Not quite, for the following reasons.

The *wording of Article I-10 is ambiguous*. The phrase 'shall have primacy over the law of the Member States' could be interpreted to mean, following the jurisprudence of the ECJ,[36] that supremacy operates over

[35] P Craig and G de Búrca, *EU Law, Text, Cases and Materials* (Oxford, Oxford University Press, 3rd edn, 2002), Chap 7; P Craig, 'National Courts and Community Law', in J Hayward and A Menon (eds), *Governing Europe* (Oxford, Oxford University Press, 2003) Chap 2.
[36] Case 11/70, *Internationale Handelsgesellschaft mbH v Einfuhr- und Vorratstelle fur Getreide und Futtermittel* [1970] ECR 1125, para 3.

all national law, including provisions in a national constitution. It could alternatively be read so as to accord primacy to EU law over national law, but not the national constitution itself.

*It is doubtful whether some national constitutional courts will regard a supremacy clause that purports to trump national constitutional law as acceptable from the perspective of their own national constitutions.*[37] This is more especially so given that Article I-10 accords supremacy not just to the EU Constitution, but also to all law adopted by the Union institutions. This means that primary European laws and framework laws, delegated regulations, and implementing regulations would trump national law, including national constitutional norms as well as national legislation. The issue could come before national constitutional courts prior to ratification of the EU Constitution. The constitutional court would then have to decide whether its national constitution allowed ratification of an EU Constitution in such terms.[38] If the matter is not raised in this manner, it will come before the ECJ at some stage. It will then be for the ECJ to decide on the construction of Article I-10. If it sticks to its existing jurisprudence, and decides that supremacy operates even in relation to national constitutions, some national constitutional courts might not accept this, with a resultant constitutional crisis.

There is moreover the issue of the *conceptual foundation for EU supremacy*. Insofar as Article I-10(1) confers supremacy on Union law the conceptual foundation will almost certainly be treated by Member State courts as continuing to flow from their own constitutional provisions rather than the more *communautaire* reasoning of the ECJ. Supremacy of Union law will be held to exist because the Member States have agreed to this by their ratification of the Constitution. It will not necessarily be treated as inherent in the Community order.

There is *the problem of Kompetenz-Kompetenz*. Article I-10 only accords primacy to Union law 'in exercising competences conferred on it'. There is nothing within this wording that resolves the issue of *Kompetenz-Kompetenz*: who is to decide on the ultimate boundary of Union competences, the ECJ or the Member State courts. Nor is there anything in Article I-28 that resolves this issue. The wording of Article I-9, which is framed in terms of the Union acting within the limits of the competences conferred on it by the Member States, does nothing to bolster the claims of the EU to decide on the ultimate boundaries of competence. The wording and tenor of this Article point rather to the *Kompetenz-Kompetenz* residing with the Member States.

[37] A-M Slaughter, A Stone Sweet, and JHH Weiler (eds), *The European Court of Justice and National Courts: Doctrine and Jurisprudence* (Oxford, Hart Publishing, 1998); Craig, above note 35.

[38] *Brunner v The European Union Treaty* [1994] 1 CMLR 57.

The *problem of Kompetenz-Kompetenz might well be more significant under the Constitution than hitherto*. Boundary problems can arise either as a result of judicial or legislative action. An individual might argue before a national court that action is beyond the EU's competence because the ECJ has accorded an interpretation to certain articles of the Constitution that they cannot properly bear. An individual might in a similar vein contend that the EU legislature has enacted acts that go beyond those that could be based on the particular article in question. The very fact that Union competences have been divided into categories renders this type of challenge more likely than before. This is especially so in relation to the divide between shared competence, and competence that only allows supporting and co-ordinating action by the Union, or in relation to the divide between shared competence and the competence over economic and employment policy. The boundary lines between these heads of competence can be difficult to discern in certain instances.[39] The issue is who has the ultimate authority to decide on the breadth of the particular categories of competence listed in Article I-11. The ECJ will doubtless decide on such matters when they are raised before it. An individual might nonetheless argue before a national court that the ECJ's view is not final and conclusive, and that it should be for the national court to make the final determination of the boundaries of the categories of competence. The claimant might contend that the supremacy clause only becomes operative when the EU is 'exercising competences conferred on it'. Thus the EU may have harmonized laws on the assumption that the relevant area is within shared power, but the individual claims that the area falls within the category of supporting action, in which harmonization is not allowed. If the national court supports this view, and believes that it is the ultimate decider on competence, then the EU would have not in that sense be 'exercising competences conferred on it' and the supremacy clause would be irrelevant.

There is *a 'nice point' as to whether subsidiarity and proportionality serve to define the boundaries of Union competence*. Article I-10(1) accords primacy to the law made by Union institutions in '*exercising* competences conferred on it'.[40] There is clearly a distinction between the limits of competence, and the use of competence that has prima facie been accorded to the Union. This dichotomy is evident in Article I-9(1), which states that Union competences are governed by the principle of conferral, while the use of those competences is governed by subsidiarity and proportionality. Article I-10(1) conditions the primacy of Union law by insisting that it be made within the limits assigned to the Union, such that law can only be made within one of the designated areas, energy, consumer protection and

[39] P Craig, 'Competence: Clarity, Containment and Consideration', forthcoming.
[40] Emphasis added.

the like. The issue is whether the word *exercising* within Article I-10(1) also conditions the primacy of Union law in relation to the way in which conferred powers are used, with the consequence that if subsidiarity and proportionality are not complied with the resulting Union law does not have primacy over Member State law.

## CONCLUSION

It was undoubtedly correct for the Constitution to tackle the issue of EU decision-making instruments and the hierarchy between them. The range of instruments used from the inception of EEC had not altered. The instruments may have been suitable at that time, but things have moved on considerably since then. The very fact that the original instruments did not include anything termed 'laws' was reflective in part of the fact that the EP had such a small role in decision-making, and in part because of political sensibilities about openly according such power to regional institutions established by a Treaty. The terminology of regulations and directives can only be understood against this background.

Such terminology served however to conceal the distinction between primary norms and secondary norms. To be sure such a distinction has existed. There have always been regulations that were in effect secondary, in the sense that they were made pursuant to an earlier, hierarchically superior, 'parent' regulation. This could be discerned by the cognoscenti, but the distinction was not readily apparent from any difference in the label attached.

The constitutional strategy to distinguish between primary laws properly so called and other norms was therefore indubitably correct. The division of norms embodied in the Constitution, and most importantly the attribution of power over their making, is, as we have seen, not unproblematic. This is especially so in relation to delegated acts and implementing acts. The Working Group on Simplification may well have been correct to caution that 'nothing is more complicated than simplification'.[41] We might also add that there is 'no simplification without implications for the institutional balance of power'.

[41] Final Report of Working Group IX on Simplification, above note 1, 1.

# 6

# *Protecting Fundamental Rights in Europe's New Constitutional Order*

ANTHONY ARNULL*

## BACKGROUND

WHEN THE EUROPEAN Court of Justice held in 1996 that the European Community had no jurisdiction to accede to the European Convention on Human Rights (ECHR),[1] a degree of satisfaction must have been felt in the capitals of Member States which opposed accession. They had the power to block any proposal for a Treaty change to reverse the Court's ruling, a power they duly exercised at Amsterdam. Some of the States concerned perhaps experienced a frisson of concern at Cologne in June 1999, when the European Council was persuaded to agree to the drawing up a Charter of fundamental rights 'in order to make their overriding importance and relevance more visible to the Union's citizens.' None the less, that too was an initiative it might have seemed possible to contain. No decision was taken at Cologne on whether the proposed Charter should be integrated into the Treaties. Again that step could not be taken without the unanimous support of all the Member States.

In order not to pre-empt the decision of the Member States, the Charter Convention decided to proceed as if it had to submit a legally binding catalogue. That decision fanned the fires of the debate over the status of the Charter. At Nice in December 2000, opponents were able to ensure that the Charter was not made binding,[2] but it had soon been cited by all the

* I am grateful to my colleague, Jeremy McBride, and to participants at the WG Hart Workshop and the London-Leiden Meeting in June 2003 for their comments on some of the issues discussed in this chapter. An expanded version is published in the Winter 2003 issue of *Public Law* under the title 'From Charter to Constitution and Beyond: Fundamental Rights in the New European Union'.

[1] See Opinion 2/94 [1996] ECR I-1759. Opposition to accession was expressed in the course of the proceedings by France, Ireland, Portugal, Spain and the UK.

[2] It was instead 'solemnly proclaimed' by the European Parliament, the Council and the Commission: see [2000] OJ C364/1. The leading opponent of endowing the Charter with

Advocates General of the Court of Justice and by the Court of First Instance[3] as well as the European Court of Human Rights.[4] Moreover, the Nice Declaration on the Future of the Union made it clear that the Charter's status would be addressed in a process of reflection on enhancing the Union's accountability and legitimacy.

The stakes were raised further by a declaration adopted by the European Council at Laeken, Belgium, in December 2001, which set up a Convention on the Future of Europe to take forward the post-Nice agenda. Modelled on the Convention which drew up the Charter, the Convention on the Future of Europe[5] was asked to consider a range of questions concerning the Union's future development. These included:

— Whether the Union should be endowed with a constitutional text;
— If so, whether the Charter of Fundamental Rights should be included in that text;
— Whether the European Union should be authorised to accede to the ECHR.

The Convention's conclusions were to provide a starting point for an intergovernmental conference (IGC) which would gather after it had completed its work and where the final decisions would be taken. So there was now a real prospect, not just that the Charter of Fundamental Rights might be given constitutional status, but also that the Union would be authorised to accede to the ECHR.

The text ultimately agreed by the Convention, entitled 'Draft Treaty Establishing a Constitution for Europe', was submitted to the President of the European Council on 18 July 2003.[6] This chapter is concerned with the approach taken by its authors to the protection of fundamental rights

more than merely declaratory status was the United Kingdom, but its approach was shared by other Member States, including Ireland, the Netherlands and Sweden. See E Wicks, '"Declaratory of Existing Rights": The United Kingdom's Role in Drafting a European Bill of Rights, Mark II' [2001] *Public Law* 527, 530–31; Lord Goldsmith, 'A Charter of Rights, Freedoms and Principles' (2001) 38 *CML Rev* 1201, 1214; House of Lords Select Committee on the European Union (hereafter House of Lords EU Committee), 'EU Charter of Fundamental Rights', Session 1999–2000, 8th Report, HL Paper 67, esp pp 19–22.

[3] See further P Eeckhout, 'The EU Charter of Fundamental Rights and the Federal Question' (2002) 39 *CML Rev* 945, 946–52. The Court of Justice and the Court of First Instance are hereafter referred to collectively as the Union Courts.
[4] See *Goodwin v United Kingdom* (2002) 35 EHRR 18, paras 58 and 100.
[5] A great deal of information about the Convention is available on its web site: *http://european-convention.eu.int/default.asp?lang=EN*. The Convention documents referred to later in this chapter may all be found at this site.
[6] See CONV 850/03. The draft is divided into four Parts. The number of each article is prefaced by a roman numeral denoting the Part in which it is located.

in the new European Union they envisaged. Of particular relevance to the discussion is the final report, published in October 2002, of one of the working groups set up by the Convention in an early phase of its work, namely Working Group II on 'Incorporation of the Charter/accession to the ECHR'.[7]

## SHOULD THE CHARTER OF FUNDAMENTAL RIGHTS BE INCLUDED IN THE CONSTITUTION OF THE UNION?

The case for including the Charter in any constitution of the Union is straightforward. It would look extremely odd if a treaty intended to set out the basic values and organising principles of the Union did not include the Charter in some form. Most modern legal systems have catalogues of fundamental rights, usually in the constitution. It is widely felt that anyone drawing up a national constitution today would include such a catalogue. Although the EU is not, and does not aspire to become, a State, it has assumed powers previously exercised by States and ought to offer equivalent protection for the fundamental rights of citizens. For the EU to adopt a constitution which did not include a catalogue of fundamental rights would undermine the notion — currently expressed in Article 6(1) TEU and reiterated in Article I-2 of the draft Constitution — that respect for human rights is one of the values on which the Union is founded.

Although, as we have seen, the Charter was drawn up with a view to its being made legally binding, is it suitable as it stands for inclusion in a constitution or does it need to be revised first? Here Working Group II drew a distinction[8] between the substantive content of the Charter and the effect it is designed to have.

### Substantive Content

Attempting to renegotiate the substantive provisions of the Charter would have risked destroying the consensus so painstakingly constructed before it was proclaimed in Nice. Failure to find a consensus on a revised text would have dealt a hammer-blow to the Union's quest for greater transparency and legitimacy: it would effectively have disembowelled the Constitution at birth while at the same time undermining the existing text of the Charter. That text bears comparison with the ECHR and the catalogues of rights contained in many national constitutions. In any event, there could be no

[7] CONV 354/02.
[8] See CONV 354/02, pp 4–5.

guarantee that renegotiation, even if successful, would lead to any substantial improvement.[9]

It is true that the Charter contains provisions which the Union is perhaps unlikely to infringe.[10] However, the Union needs to be able to demonstrate that it recognises the fundamental rights it expects third countries to observe, notably in the context of the enlargement process[11] and its development cooperation activities.[12] There are other provisions of the Charter[13] which concern fields where the Union has no or only limited competence to legislate. Incorporation of the Charter would not change the position, because Article 51(2) says that the Charter does not affect the Union's powers or tasks. But provisions of this type are useful because they may affect the interpretation or even the validity of Union acts which are said to infringe the rights they lay down.[14]

Leaving aside the drafting changes needed to take account of the recasting of the Treaties which the Constitution would bring about, there are, however, two respects in which the text of the Charter might be thought to call for revision. These concern, first, what is sometimes called replication and, secondly, the so-called horizontal provisions.

## Replication

Because the Charter was originally conceived as a free-standing catalogue, certain rights were included in it in the interests of completeness even though they were also set out elsewhere in the Union Treaties. A striking example is the provisions on citizens' rights, which overlap with Part Two of the EC Treaty on citizenship of the Union.[15] That approach seems highly undesirable in a constitutional document which is intended to increase clarity. Some degree of replication might have been justified had there been a formal difference in the status of the different sub-divisions into which the draft Constitution is broken up. One indication of such a difference would

[9] See the evidence given by Professors Schermers and Lawson to the House of Lords EU Committee: 'The Future Status of the EU Charter of Fundamental Rights', Session 2002–03, 6th Report, HL Paper 48, p 94.
[10] *eg* Art 2(2) (prohibition of death penalty), Art 4 (prohibition of torture and inhuman or degrading treatment or punishment), Art 5 (prohibition of slavery and forced labour).
[11] See Art 49 TEU.
[12] See Art 49 TEU and Art 177(2) EC. *Cf* Arts I-3(4), I-56(1) and III-193 of the draft Constitution.
[13] *eg* Art 9 (right to marry and found a family) and Art 10 (freedom of thought, conscience and religion).
[14] For examples, see Goldsmith, above note 2, 1207; Schermers and Lawson, evidence to the House of Lords EU Committee, above note 9, 94.
[15] For a useful table of overlapping provisions, see G de Búrca, 'Fundamental Rights and Citizenship' in B de Witte (ed), *Ten Reflections on the Constitutional Treaty for Europe* (Robert Schuman Centre for Advanced Studies, 2003) 11, 29–44.

have been amendment procedures which varied in weight according to the status of the sub-division concerned. However, that idea was rejected by the Convention,[16] so the case for including the same rights in different sub-divisions of the Constitution seems weak.[17]

Avoiding replication offers a possible solution to an objection sometimes raised against the Charter,[18] that it is unacceptable for fundamental rights to be linked with the status of citizen of the Union, which is confined to nationals of the Member States. An incorporated Charter would not need to include provisions on citizenship if, as proposed in the draft, those provisions were inserted elsewhere in the Constitution.[19] In that event, removing them from the Charter would have no effect on the rights of Union citizens but would make it possible to extend the constitutional catalogue of fundamental rights to everyone present within the territory of the Union, regardless of nationality.

## Horizontal Provisions

Attention also focused on whether amendments should be made to the so-called horizontal provisions of the Charter. These govern its interpretation and application and are of great constitutional significance. Working Group II proposed several changes to them with a view to clarifying the scope and effect of the Charter[20] and these were adopted almost verbatim by the Convention.[21] Space precludes detailed examination of all the horizontal provisions and the proposed changes to them here.[22] Instead, the discussion will focus on a horizontal provision which the draft Constitution leaves essentially untouched but which goes to the heart of the Union's role in protecting fundamental rights.

Article 51(1) says that the Charter is 'addressed to the institutions and bodies of the Union ... and to the Member States only when they are implementing Union law ...' That provision confirms that the Charter was not

[16] See Art IV-7 and the commentary on para 2 in CONV 728/03, p 10.

[17] *cf* E Vranes, 'The Final Clauses of the Charter of Fundamental Rights — Stumbling Blocks for the First and Second Convention' (2003) 7 *European Integration Online Papers*, p 6, *http://eiop.or.at/eiop/*. If all replication were avoided, it would be possible to delete Art 52(2) of the Charter, which deals with the effect of Charter provisions which have counterparts elsewhere in the Treaties/Constitution. See K Lenaerts and E De Smijter, 'A "Bill of Rights" for the European Union' (2001) 38 *CML Rev* 273.

[18] See *eg* the evidence of Professor A Toth to the House of Lords EU Committee, above note 9, 110–11.

[19] See Art I-8 and Part III, Title II.

[20] See CONV 354/02, pp 5–8.

[21] See CONV 726/03, pp 2–4 ('Explanatory Note').

[22] See further de Búrca, above note 15, 20–25, and Vranes, above note 17. Note in particular the proposed new Art II-52(5), which purports to limit the effect of provisions containing 'principles' as opposed to 'rights'.

designed to convert the Union into a general human rights organisation, in other words, a polity one of whose main purposes is the protection and promotion of human rights.[23] Indeed, it is arguable that Article 51(1) makes the effect of the Charter on the Member States more limited than that of the general principle of respect for fundamental rights recognised by the Court of Justice for many years.[24] It has consistently been held that national rules falling 'within the scope of Community law' must be interpreted and applied in accordance with the fundamental rights upheld by the Court.[25] More specifically, the Court has made it clear that the general principle of respect for fundamental rights binds the Member States, not only when implementing Community law,[26] but also when relying on a derogation for which Community law provides.[27]

The former situation necessarily falls within the substantive scope of the Union Treaties. The Member State is effectively acting as the agent of the Community/Union and must therefore comply with the same standards as the Community/Union legislator, who cannot authorise the national authorities to depart from them. However, the latter situation is less clear cut: as Weiler puts it,[28] 'here we are dealing with a Member State measure in application of a Member State policy.' Provided a national restriction is invoked in good faith and in a proportionate and non-discriminatory manner, it is by no means clear that the question whether its application involves infringing fundamental rights should be treated as a question of Community/Union law.[29]

In practice, where Member States have sought to rely on a Community law derogation, the Court of Justice has encountered difficulty in offering national courts meaningful advice on the application of the general principle of respect for fundamental rights.[30] Recently, the Court emphasised the wide margin of discretion enjoyed by the national authorities in a case

[23] See Eeckhout, above note 3, 956–57.

[24] It would be for the Union Courts to work out the relationship between the general principle and an incorporated Charter. Art I-7(3) and Art 53 of the Charter suggest that the authority of the Union Courts to apply and refine the general principle would be preserved.

[25] Case C-94/00 *Roquette Frères v Directeur général de la concurrence, de la consommation et de la répression des fraudes* [2003] 4 CMLR 1, para 25. See also Case C-276/01 *Steffensen* [2003] 2 CMLR 13.

[26] See Case 5/88 *Wachauf v Federal Republic of Germany* [1989] ECR 2609, para 19.

[27] See Case C-260/89 *ERT* [1991] ECR I-2925, para 43.

[28] *The Constitution of Europe* (Cambridge, CUP, 1999) 126.

[29] FG Jacobs 'Human Rights in the European Union: the Role of the Court of Justice' (2001) 26 *EL Rev* 331, 335–39. *Cf* JHH Weiler and SC Fries, 'A Human Rights Policy for the European Community and Union: The Question of Competences' in P Alston, M Bustelo and J Heenan (eds), *The EU and Human Rights* (Oxford, OUP, 1999) Ch.5, 162–65; Eeckhout, above note 3, 977–79.

[30] See eg Case C-159/90 *SPUC v Grogan* [1991] ECR I-4685; *ERT*, above, n 27, paras 44–45; Case C-368/95 *Familiapress v Bauer Verlag* [1997] ECR I-3689, paras 24–33. *Cf* Case C-60/00 *Carpenter v Secretary of State* [2002] 2 CMLR 64, paras 40–46.

which involved balancing fundamental rights against the free movement of goods, a fundamental freedom guaranteed by the EC Treaty.[31] It therefore seems likely that the restricted formulation used in Article 51(1) of the Charter was chosen advisedly.[32]

The Charter Convention had no mandate to propose changes to the very character of the Union. Converting it into a general human rights body might have been suggested by the Convention on the Future of Europe and would be open to the IGC, but it is doubtful whether such a change would be desirable. It would entail a huge expansion in the competences of the Union, yet there is no compelling evidence that the Union would prove a more effective guardian of fundamental rights than the Member States and the European Court of Human Rights. That Court administers a system which is specially tailored to the protection of human rights. It is a system of minimum standards[33] applied principally by the national authorities,[34] who may enjoy a margin of appreciation. The ECHR regime is profoundly different from the so-called Community method,[35] designed originally to achieve mainly economic objectives, with its emphasis on uniformity and the strict enforcement of obligations.[36] The application of such a system in the human rights field outside the substantive scope of the Union Treaties/Constitution would risk undermining further the Union's accountability and legitimacy.[37]

It is true that there is now a mechanism for suspending the rights of any Member State found by the Council to be in 'serious and persistent breach' of the principle of respect for human rights and fundamental freedoms.[38] That mechanism is not limited by the scope of the Treaties and might be taken to imply that Member States' conduct should be monitored, so

[31] Case C-112/00 *Schmidberger v Austria*, judgment of 12 June 2003. The Court declined to interfere with the balance struck by the national authorities. For a discussion of the case, see T Tridimas, below, Chapter 7.

[32] See CONV 354/02, p 5; G de Búrca, 'The Drafting of the European Union Charter of Fundamental Rights' (2001) 26 *EL Rev* 126, 136–37. *Cf* Vranes, above note 17, 5.

[33] See Art 53 ECHR.

[34] See *eg Handyside v United Kingdom* (1979–80) 1 EHRR 737, para 48; *Kudla v Poland* (2002) 35 EHRR 11, para 152.

[35] Referred to in Art I-1(1) of the draft Constitution, which speaks of the Union exercising its competences 'in the Community way'.

[36] See the evidence of Judge Fischbach to the House of Lords EU Committee, above, note 9, Q 198. This remains the case notwithstanding the increasing prominence of the open method of coordination (OMC). Endorsed at the Lisbon European Council in March 2000, the OMC relies on non-coercive methods like peer review and benchmarking to achieve common goals. For discussion of the relationship between the OMC and the Charter of Fundamental Rights, see G de Búrca, 'The Constitutional Challenge of New Governance in the European Union' (2003) 28 *EL Rev* 814.

[37] See A von Bogdandy, 'The European Union as a Human Rights Organization? Human Rights and the Core of the European Union' (2000) 37 *CML Rev* 1307, 1317. *Cf* A Williams, 'EU Human Rights Policy and the Convention on the Future of Europe: a Failure of Design?' (2003) 28 *EL Rev* 794.

[38] See Art 7 TEU.

that breaches and potential breaches can be identified.[39] However, the mechanism for suspending States' rights applies only in extreme cases. It by no means implies that the Union's panoply of legislative and judicial procedures should be invoked to ensure respect by Member States for fundamental rights more generally. That does not mean that the Union should not adopt a more effective human rights policy, that is to say, mechanisms designed to ensure that, within the scope of the Treaties/Constitution, the Union's policy initiatives respect and promote human rights.[40] However, notwithstanding the strict (perhaps too strict) monitoring of the accession candidate countries by the Commission in the context of the enlargement process,[41] the case for giving the Union a more wide-ranging human rights role remains as yet unconvincing.

## How Should the Charter be Incorporated?

A preliminary draft Constitution published by the Convention Praesidium (or steering group) in October 2002[42] envisaged the inclusion in Part I of a provision on fundamental rights which either:

— Referred to the Charter;
— Stated the principle that the Charter was an integral part of the Constitution, the provisions of the Charter being set out in another part of the Constitution or in an annexed protocol; or
— Incorporated all the provisions of the Charter.

The majority view in Working Group II was that the text of the Charter should be included in the Constitution itself, although there was some support in the Convention for simply annexing the Charter to the Constitution as a protocol.[43] That would have the same legal effect as including the

[39] Following a resolution of the European Parliament of 5 July 2001, the Commission in September 2002 established a network of experts in fundamental rights with the task of preparing an annual report on the fundamental rights situation in the EU and assisting the Parliament and the Commission in developing EU policy on fundamental rights. The network's first report was published in May 2003: see *http://europa.eu.int/comm/justice_home/index_en.htm*.

[40] See P Alston and JHH Weiler, 'An "Ever Closer Union" in Need of a Human Rights Policy: the European Union and Human Rights' in P Alston, M Bustelo and J Heenan (eds) *The EU and Human Rights* (Oxford, OUP, 1999) Ch.1. There are already signs of the emergence of such a policy: see the report referred to in note 39 above.

[41] See A Williams, 'Enlargement of the Union and Human Rights Conditionality: A Policy of Distinction?' (2000) 25 *EL Rev* 601; C Hillion, 'Enlargement of the European Union: A Legal Analysis' in A Arnull and D Wincott (eds), *Accountability and Legitimacy in the European Union* (Oxford, OUP, 2002) Ch 23.

[42] CONV 369/02.

[43] See *eg* CONV 779/03, p 6.

Charter in the body of the Constitution[44] and might have been preferable if the Constitution itself had been relatively short.[45] But in a Constitution running to 465 articles, it would be undesirable to consign the 54 articles of the Charter to a protocol. The proliferation of protocols — many of them likely to be preserved[46] — is a major cause of the unwieldiness and complexity of the existing Treaties. It would be unwise to encumber the Constitution from the start with more than are absolutely necessary. Protocols should be reserved for questions of technical detail on which there is a wish to confer treaty status[47] or for regimes which derogate from the norm.[48] They are not suitable for fundamental principles of the constitutional order. Indeed, to relegate the Charter to a protocol might suggest that the rights of the very people with whom the Union needs to reconnect are being marginalised.

The Convention chose not to consign the Charter to a protocol. Instead, Article I-7(1) of the draft Constitution provides: 'The Union shall recognise the rights, freedoms and principles set out in the Charter of Fundamental Rights which constitutes Part II of the Constitution.' Part II is entitled 'The Charter of Fundamental Rights of the Union' and comprises the entire Charter, including its preamble. There are several reasons for regarding this solution to the problem of how to incorporate the Charter as unsatisfactory and inelegant.

First, the injunction to the Union in Article I-7(1) to 'recognise' the Charter does not make it clear precisely what its status is intended to be.[49] The preparatory documents suggest that the Union is intended to be bound by the Charter. However, as we have seen, the Charter is also addressed to the Member States. Is a reference to them in Article I-7(1) to be implied? If not, is the incorporation of the Charter devoid of legal effect as far as they are concerned? It might have been better simply to replace Article I-7(1) by the articles of the Charter (with the exception of those on citizens' rights).[50]

[44] See Art IV-6.

[45] See B De Witte, 'Simplification and Reorganization of the European Treaties' (2002) 39 *CML Rev* 1255, 1280.

[46] The Convention did not attempt to review the current protocols, a task which will fall to the IGC: see CONV 851/03, para 11.

[47] *eg* the Protocol on the Statute of the Court of Justice, currently annexed to the TEU, the EC and the EAEC Treaties, or the Protocol on the Statute of the European System of Central Banks and of the European Central Bank, currently annexed to the TEU and the EC Treaty.

[48] *eg* the protocols annexed to the EC Treaty at Maastricht on the participation of the United Kingdom and Denmark in the third stage of Economic and Monetary Union and those on the United Kingdom, Ireland and Denmark annexed at Amsterdam to the TEU and the EC Treaty

[49] See editorial by D Chalmers at (2003) 28 *EL Rev* 449, 450.

[50] It is argued above that the citizenship provisions of the Charter should be omitted, since they replicate provisions contained elsewhere in the draft Constitution: see text at n 19. Art I-7(2), on Union accession to the ECHR (see below), could be moved to Art III-229, on the Union's relations with international organisations, which refers expressly to the Council of Europe. Art I-7(3), on the general principle of respect for fundamental rights, could be added as a new horizontal provision at the end of the Charter.

Secondly, the insertion, at the beginning of Part II of the draft Constitution, of the Charter preamble renders it something of an excrescence. Much of the Charter preamble seems essentially rhetorical. Of its seven recitals, four[51] are not about the Charter in particular but about the Union more generally. If they are important, they should go in the preamble to the Constitution itself.[52] Two recitals[53] would be redundant if the Constitution were adopted in the form proposed. That leaves the fifth recital. In its original form, that recital listed the main sources from which the Charter was derived and referred to the case law of the Court of Justice and the European Court of Human Rights. In that form, it hardly seems worth preserving: in the last resort, the effect of the Charter will be determined by the Union Courts, which are fully aware of the sources on which it is based. As their case law develops, those sources are likely to decline in importance.

The Convention none the less decided, largely for political reasons,[54] to add to the fifth recital the following sentence: 'In this context the Charter will be interpreted by the courts of the Union and the Member States with due regard to the explanations prepared at the instigation of the Praesidium of the Convention which drafted the Charter.' The 'explanations' mentioned were originally published in October 2000.[55] They contain detailed accounts of the origins and purpose of individual provisions, but were not approved by the plenary of the Charter Convention. The importance of the 'explanations' was underlined by Working Group II, which asked that they be publicised more widely.[56] An updated and consolidated version was produced, under the authority of the Chairman of Working Group II and with the endorsement of the Praesidium, to take account in particular of the proposed changes to the horizontal provisions of the Charter.[57]

The proposed addition to the Charter preamble involves a certain sleight of hand. It represents an attempt to pre-empt decisions of the Union Courts on the effect of the incorporated Charter without reopening the text. The original version of the 'explanations' stated at the outset that they had 'no legal value'. The revised version states instead that, '[a]lthough they do not as such have the status of law, they are a valuable tool of interpretation

[51] The first three and the last. (In the version presented by the Convention to the European Council, the second recital was merged with the third. The present discussion is based on the original layout of the preamble.)

[52] The reference in the first recital of the Charter preamble to 'an ever closer union' among the peoples of Europe is not suitable for retention since such a reference was deliberately omitted from the preamble to the draft Constitution.

[53] The fourth and sixth.

[54] See CONV 814/03, para 9.

[55] See CHARTE 4473/00 CONVENT 49, available on the web site of the Council, *http://ue.eu.int/en/summ.htm*.

[56] See CONV 354/02, p 10.

[57] See CONV 828/03.

intended to clarify the provisions of the Charter.' If, as is claimed,[58] the 'explanations' played a role is securing consensus within the Charter Convention, the propriety of attempting to enhance their status in this way seems doubtful. If they did not play such a role, the case for mentioning them in the draft Constitution is weakened. In any event, the Charter preamble is not an appropriate place for a provision which purports to be binding. If the 'explanations' need to be publicised, it should be sufficient for this to be done by means of a declaration issued at the conclusion of the next IGC.

## ACCESSION BY THE EU TO THE ECHR

Opponents of Union accession to the ECHR sometimes say that it would undermine the autonomy of Community law and the role of the Court of Justice as the sole arbiter of that law.[59] That objection seems unconvincing. Indeed, incorporating the Charter in a Union constitution would reinforce the already strong case for Union accession to the ECHR.

### Avoiding Divergence between Luxembourg and Strasbourg

Incorporation of the Charter would clarify its legal effect and increase its profile. The result would probably be an increase in the number of challenges to the activities of the Union on fundamental rights grounds. Since many Charter rights are based on the ECHR, there would be a heightened risk that the case law of the Union Courts on the minimum standards compatible with those rights would diverge from the case law of the Strasbourg Court. That could result in the emergence of two competing regimes for the protection of fundamental rights in the EU, both based (at least in part) on the ECHR, with adverse consequences for consistency and legal certainty.[60]

The Charter itself contains a provision designed to reduce that risk. Article 52(3) provides:

> In so far as this Charter contains rights which correspond to rights guaranteed by the Convention for the Protection of Human Rights and Fundamental Freedoms [*ie* the ECHR], the meaning and scope of those rights shall be the same as those laid down by the said Convention. This provision shall not prevent Union law providing more extensive protection.

Ultimately, however, Article 52(3) does not offer complete protection against the risk of divergence between Luxembourg and Strasbourg over the applicable minimum standard. It may not be clear whether a Charter

[58] See CONV 726/03, p 4.
[59] See CONV 116/02, p 18; Opinion 2/94, above, n 1, p I-1781.
[60] See Resolution 1339 (2003) of the Parliamentary Assembly of the Council of Europe, para 5.

right 'corresponds' to a right laid down in the ECHR, particularly where a Charter right has more than one source or is worded differently to its ECHR counterpart.[61] It may not be clear what approach the Strasbourg Court would take to a given problem. A more secure way of guarding against such divergence would be for the Union to accede to the ECHR. That would enable someone who was unhappy with the way the Court of Justice had interpreted a Charter right based on the ECHR to challenge its decision in Strasbourg.

## Subjecting the Union to External Review

The general principle of respect for fundamental rights is inspired in part by the ECHR. As a result, the Court of Justice may already be required to rule on the effect of the ECHR. However, the lack of a formal mechanism[62] to enable its decisions to be scrutinised by the Strasbourg Court undermines the authority of the Court of Justice in fundamental rights cases and may lead to conflict with the national courts. Union accession to the ECHR would subject the Union to external review for compliance with its requirements by an authoritative, specialist arbiter in the form of the Strasbourg Court. If that Court concluded that Luxembourg had made a mistake, that would contribute to the protection of ECHR-based rights in the Union. However, there would inevitably be some cases where Strasbourg would say that Luxembourg had got it right, or that the outcome was within the limits of the Union's margin of appreciation. The effect of a ruling of that sort would be to enhance the authority of Luxembourg's pronouncements on ECHR-based rights. In both types of case, Strasbourg's involvement would help to ensure that the standards applied in the Union complied with those laid down in the ECHR. The result would be to strengthen the Union by helping to make its rhetorical commitment to fundamental rights a practical reality.

## Full EU Involvement in Strasbourg Proceedings

There are also procedural advantages to accession. At present, issues of Union or Community law may arise in cases brought against one of the EU's Member States. The issue has to be resolved by the Strasbourg Court on the basis of the arguments presented to it. Sometimes, the parties may be in agreement on controversial questions of EU law and the view they take

[61] The revised 'explanations' (above note 57, 50–51) contain an indicative list of Charter rights which may be regarded as corresponding to rights in the ECHR.

[62] But see *DSR Senator Lines v The Fifteen Member States of the EU*, App No 56672/00 (pending).

may play an important part in the reasoning of the Strasbourg Court.[63] If the EU were to accede, complainants would have to exhaust their domestic remedies[64] before going to Strasbourg. This would mean that the issues would be ventilated in the Union Courts first. An EU judge would sit whenever the EU was a party to a case[65] and the EU could expect to have the right to submit written comments and to take part in the hearing in any case brought by an EU citizen.[66] The Strasbourg Court would therefore be better informed about the position in EU law and consequently more likely to come to a decision which took into account the EU's special features.

## The Relationship between Luxembourg and Strasbourg

Union accession to the ECHR would be a major exercise. Article I-7(2) of the draft Constitution says that the Union 'shall seek accession',[67] but the apparent force of that provision is weakened by Article III-227, which provides that the Council, acting unanimously, must authorise the opening of negotiations and conclude any agreement reached.[68] Securing the unanimous agreement of the Council is unlikely to be straightforward. Even if the decision were taken to open negotiations, amendments to the ECHR itself would need to be agreed with all the Contracting States. In the process, difficult questions would be raised.[69]

One is the nature of the relationship between the Luxembourg and Strasbourg Courts. A major innovation which is sometimes mooted[70] in this connection is the introduction of a preliminary rulings mechanism to enable the Strasbourg and Luxembourg Courts to ask each other for guidance on the law for which each is the supreme authority. Theoretically, the suggestion has much to commend it. One advantage is that the Strasbourg Court would not have to deal with the thorny issue of the allocation of competences between the Union and its Member States. However, there are practical obstacles. On the Luxembourg side, one can see the utility of a procedure for referring questions to Strasbourg in direct actions, which

[63] See *eg Matthews v United Kingdom* (1999) 28 EHRR 361. *Cf Cantoni v France*, App No 17862/91, judgment of 15 November 1996, Reports of Judgments and Decisions 1996-V.
[64] See Art 35(1) ECHR.
[65] See Art 27(2) ECHR.
[66] *cf* Art 36(1) ECHR, which refers to 'nationals' of a High Contracting Party. The term 'citizens' might be added were the EU to accede as it does not have nationals.
[67] Art I-6 would give the Union legal personality.
[68] Art III-227(2) and (9). The consent of the European Parliament would also be required: Art III-227(7)(b). See the Report on the Convention by the Political Affairs Committee of the Parliamentary Assembly of the Council of Europe, Doc 9846, 24 June 2003 (Rapporteur: Mr Theodorus Pangalos), Explanatory Memorandum, paras 22–23.
[69] For a detailed analysis of the technical and legal issues that would need to be addressed on the Council of Europe side, see Working Group II, Working Document 8.
[70] See *eg* the observations submitted to the Court of Justice in Opinion 2/94, above note 1.

start and finish in the Union Courts. However, the utility of such a facility in cases which have originated in a *national* court may be more doubtful because of the long delay which would ensue. Moreover, if the Luxembourg Court were to be empowered to ask the Strasbourg Court for preliminary rulings, it might be hard to resist according the same right to national courts. That could cause difficulty in cases raising questions of both EU law and the scope of the ECHR. How could one ensure that references went to the right court? How could Luxembourg rule until Strasbourg had spoken and *vice versa*? In any event, it is doubtful whether the Strasbourg Court could at present cope with the further increase in its already heavy case load that a reference procedure would entail.[71]

As for the particular problem of determining the allocation of competences between the Union and its Member States in fundamental rights cases, a technical solution could probably be found. One suggestion, contained in a note to Working Group II from the Convention Secretariat,[72] would involve permitting the Union to attach itself to a Member State as a co-defendant (and *vice versa*), each co-defendant being jointly and severally liable. It would be made clear that the precise allocation of competence was an internal matter for the Union and its Member States. The competence issue could therefore be finessed in a way that would enable the Strasbourg Court to avoid having to confront it directly.[73] That would represent a considerable improvement on the present arrangements, under which the Strasbourg Court may be called upon to rule on the division of competences between the EU and its Member States[74] without the benefit of full EU involvement in the proceedings.

One possible drawback to accession is the possible effect of the domestic remedies rule on delay and costs, a matter raised by Lord Lester in the House of Lords EU Committee. He envisaged a case involving EU law with a human rights element. The case reaches the House of Lords without having been referred to Luxembourg. At that point, the domestic remedies rule would mean that the claimant would have to 'go through Luxembourg to get to Strasbourg — add another two or three years and a lot more legal costs.'[75] There are perhaps two responses to that objection.

First, the difficulty would only arise in litigation before the national courts where no reference is made until late in the proceedings and the

[71] See A Mowbray, 'Proposals for Reform of the European Court of Human Rights' [2002] *Public Law* 252, 260.
[72] CONV 116/02, p 22, n 2.
[73] Its importance should not in any event be exaggerated. See S Hyett, 'The Duty of Co-operation: a Flexible Concept' in A Dashwood and C Hillion (eds), *The General Law of EC External Relations* (London, Sweet and Maxwell 2000) Ch 16.
[74] *eg* where an application is made against a Member State on the basis of an EU act which cannot be reviewed before the Union Courts.
[75] Above note 9, Q 50.

ruling of the Luxembourg Court does not settle the issue in the claimant's favour. At that point, the applicant would be able, after accession, to go to Strasbourg. It is true that this would cost money and take time, but it will provide the claimant with a remedy he does not at present enjoy because the Union is not a party to the ECHR. The ruling of the Luxembourg Court would therefore settle the matter definitively. After accession, the claimant would have to decide whether the chances that Strasbourg might take a different view to Luxembourg justified the cost of taking the case there.

Secondly, where a domestic court of first instance made a reference to Luxembourg and an answer was given on an issue of Union law, including its fundamental rights implications, a claimant might be regarded as having exhausted his domestic remedy at that point, because it would not then be open to a higher domestic court to take a different view (at least, not without making a further reference). In this situation, the reference procedure might obviate the need for the claimant to take further proceedings in the domestic courts before going to Strasbourg, thus saving time and costs.

## REFORMING THE EU SYSTEM OF JUDICIAL REMEDIES

If the Charter is incorporated — and all the more so if the Union accedes to the ECHR — changes will be needed to the system of judicial remedies currently laid down in the Treaties. In particular, the Union's judicial system will need to comply with the requirements of the Charter and the ECHR concerning the right to an effective remedy and to a fair trial. These matters are dealt with in Article 47 of the Charter, which is based on Articles 6(1) and 13 ECHR. However, Article 47 of the Charter is broader in scope than both those provisions. Unlike Article 6(1), it is not limited to civil and criminal cases but applies to all 'rights and freedoms guaranteed by the law of the Union'.[76] Unlike Article 13 ECHR, Article 47 is not confined to cases involving ECHR-based rights, or even fundamental rights more generally. A further contrast with Article 13 is that Article 47 of the Charter grants a right to an effective remedy before a court: a non-judicial remedy would not be adequate.

The compatibility of the EU system of judicial remedies with these provisions is a large issue which cannot be discussed in detail here.[77] However, something should be said about the standing rules applicable to annulment proceedings before the Union Courts. At present, Article 230 EC

[76] See the account of the background to Art 47 in the revised 'explanations', above note 57, 41.

[77] See the evidence submitted by AG Jacobs to the House of Lords EU Committee, above note 9, 26–39.

distinguishes between three classes of applicant. Those who belong to the most favoured class (Member States, the European Parliament, the Council and the Commission, sometimes called 'privileged applicants') are not required to satisfy any standing requirements at all. By contrast, a member of the least favoured class (natural and legal persons, or 'non-privileged applicants') wishing to challenge the validity of a Community act (other than a decision addressed to him) must, under the fourth paragraph of Article 230, establish direct and individual concern.[78] The requirement of individual concern in particular has been interpreted very strictly by the Court of Justice, with the result that many challenges by non-privileged applicants are dismissed as inadmissible without any examination of their merits.

Although the validity of Community acts can sometimes be raised in the national courts, that is an unsatisfactory alternative for a variety of reasons.[79] In *UPA*,[80] Advocate General Jacobs therefore proposed that a non-privileged applicant should henceforward be regarded as individually concerned by a Community measure 'where, by reason of his particular circumstances, the measure has, or is liable to have, a substantial adverse effect on his interests.' In its judgment, however, the Court said that such a departure from the existing case law would require an amendment to the Treaty. The question whether the fourth paragraph of Article 230 EC should be amended was considered by a Discussion Circle on the Court of Justice set up within the Convention. The Circle was not asked to consider abolishing the distinction between privileged, semi-privileged and non-privileged applicants, notwithstanding the difficulty of reconciling that distinction with the principle of equality before the law enshrined in Article 20 of the Charter.

The Discussion Circle published its final report on 25 March 2003.[81] The Circle did not manage to achieve a consensus on changing Article 230, but the majority view was taken up by the Convention. Article III-270(4) would amend what is currently the fourth paragraph of Article 230 as follows:[82]

> Any natural or legal person may … institute proceedings against *an act addressed to that person or which is of direct and individual concern to him or her, and against a regulatory act which is of direct concern to him or her and does not entail implementing measures.*

[78] Members of the remaining category ('semi-privileged applicants') may bring proceedings where the purpose is to protect their prerogatives.
[79] See further AG Jacobs in Case C-50/00 P *UPA v Council* [2002] 3 CMLR 1, 17–20.
[80] *Ibid*, 38.
[81] CONV 636/03. For a detailed discussion, see Tridimas, above note 31.
[82] Proposed change in italics.

The proposed amendment involves two modifications to the present text of Article 230. The first reflects the case law of the Union Courts[83] by making it clear that a non-privileged applicant's right to bring proceedings is not confined to a single type of act (decisions under the EC Treaty). It is a matter for regret that the opportunity was not taken to abandon the notion of individual concern. It will admittedly remain possible for an applicant to challenge the validity of many Union acts in the national courts. Indeed, the second subparagraph of Article I-28(1) would give constitutional force to a duty imposed on national courts in *UPA* by providing: 'Member States shall provide rights of appeal sufficient to ensure effective legal protection in the field of Union law.' However, that duty is no substitute for ensuring that such protection is provided by the Union Courts themselves.[84]

There are some situations where it may be difficult to find a national cause of action which would enable the validity of the contested act to be raised in a domestic court. Examples are where the act concerned simply withdraws a benefit previously enjoyed by the claimant (the situation in *UPA*) or lays down a directly applicable prohibition.[85] It is this type of case which the second amendment is intended to address by providing that, in circumstances such as these, only direct concern need be established by an applicant seeking to bring annulment proceedings in Luxembourg.

Unfortunately, that more relaxed test of standing will apply only to so-called regulatory acts. Curiously, that category is not identified in the hierarchy of acts with which the Union would be equipped under Part I, Title V, Chapter I, of the draft Constitution. However, the Praesidium commentary[86] indicates that the term 'regulatory acts' means all acts other than legislative acts, a category which does feature in the proposed constitutional hierarchy.[87] The idea is that legislative acts should only be open to challenge by natural and legal persons where they can establish direct and individual concern.

Article III-270(4) therefore reflects the laws of those Member States which make it more difficult for individuals to challenge legislative measures

[83] See *eg* Case C-309/89 *Codorniu v Council* [1994] ECR I-1853; Joined Cases T-172/98 and T-175/98 to T-177/98 *Salamander and Others v Parliament and Council* [2000] ECR II-2487.

[84] As AG Jacobs has pointed out: see his evidence to the House of Lords EU Committee, above note 9, 30.

[85] See *eg* Case T-177/01 *Jégo-Quéré v Commission* [2002] 2 CMLR 44 (appeal dismissed: Case C-263/02 P, judgment of 1 April 2004). *Cf Posti and Rahko v Finland*, App No 27824/95, judgment of 24 September 2002, para 64 (ECtHR).

[86] CONV 734/03, p 20. See also the text of the oral intervention of the then President of the Court of Justice before the Discussion Circle, CONV 572/03, 4.

[87] The term 'non-legislative act' could not be used in Art III-270(4) because that is just one of the categories of act identified in the hierarchy which are not legislative: see Arts I-32 to I-36. The term 'regulatory' is also employed in Arts III-173 and III-217(5). See further P Craig, above Chapter 5.

than other types of measure.[88] As a result, it would remain very hard for natural and legal persons to seek the annulment of legislative acts which are of direct concern to them without the need for implementation. This is likely to lead to continuing pressure for relaxation of the test for individual concern, particularly where an applicant's fundamental rights are alleged to have been violated.[89] It may also make it difficult for a clear distinction to be maintained between legislative and regulatory acts.

## CONCLUSION

Equipping the Union with a constitution which makes it more transparent and responsive and demonstrates its capacity to change people's lives for the better may help dispel the feeling of alienation from its processes and activities which seems to have become so widespread. An essential element of such a constitution is a catalogue of the fundamental rights which the Union respects and promotes. But ultimately constitutions and catalogues of rights can only make a difference if their underlying ideals are given practical application by politicians, civil servants and judges. The challenge for the Union is a momentous one. Time will tell whether it is up to the task.

[88] See further the discussion by AG Jacobs in *UPA*, [2002] 3 CMLR 1, 32.
[89] The draft Constitution avoids any attempt to distinguish fundamental rights cases from others in this context. For discussion, see AG Jacobs (above note 9, 30), Judge Skouris of the Court of Justice (Working Group II, Working Document 19, 4–5) and the then President of the Court of Justice (CONV 572/03, 5).

# 7

# *The European Court of Justice and the Draft Constitution: A Supreme Court for the Union?*

TAKIS TRIDIMAS*

THE PURPOSE OF this chapter is twofold. First, it examines selectively the provisions of the draft Constitution pertaining to the Court of Justice and assesses the ways in which the draft Constitution is likely to affect the jurisdiction and the function of the Court. Secondly, it discusses the challenges faced by the Court in relation to the protection of human rights by reference to the recent judgment in *Schmidberger*.[1] Both aspects of the discussion serve to underlie that the Court is assuming the function of the Supreme Court of the Union whose jurisdiction is fundamentally constitutional in character. It has a central role to play not only in relation to matters of economic integration but also in deciding issues of political governance, defining democracy at European and national level, and contributing through the process of judicial harmonisation to the emergence of a European demos. This constitutional jurisdiction of the ECJ is not new but has acquired more importance in recent years and is set to be enhanced under the provisions of the new Constitution. The paper is divided as follows: The first section provides an overview of the way the new Constitution affects the ECJ. The subsequent sections examine respectively Article 28(1) of the draft Constitution, the appointment and tenure of the judiciary, *locus standi* for private individuals, sanctions against Member States, jurisdiction under the CFSP and the Chapter on freedom, security and justice, preliminary references, other provisions of the Constitution pertaining to the Court, the principle of subsidiarity, and the judgment in *Schmidberger*. The final section contains some concluding remarks.

* The author was senior legal adviser to the EU Presidency held by Greece (January–June 2003). All views expressed are personal.

[1] Case C-112/00 *Schmidberger Internationale Transporte und Planzüge v Austria*, judgment of 12 June 2003.

## THE DRAFT CONSTITUTION AND THE COURT

The role of the judiciary and the future of the ECJ did not feature prominently in the workings of the European Convention. It is indicative that, in outlining the responses of the Constitutional Convention to the Laeken declaration, the preface to Parts I and II of the draft Constitution states that the Constitution 'establishes the necessary measures to improve the structure and enhance the role of each of the Union's *three institutions,* taking account, in particular, of the consequences of enlargement'.[2] The reason for the absence of any reference to the Court is that the Laeken declaration identified themes and challenges which were *par excellence* political in nature and, consequently, focussed on the political institutions of the EU. Also, the workings of the ECJ and the future of the judicial architecture had received extensive consideration in the inter-governmental conference leading to the Treaty of Nice. It might have been thought, therefore, that it was not necessary to revisit issues of judicial architecture.

In February 2003, the Praesidium of the Convention set up a 'Discussion Circle' on the operation of the Court of Justice, with a view to examining possible changes to be made to the system of judicial protection as part of the new Constitution.[3] The Circle was asked to consider five specific questions: (a) the appointment of the members of the ECJ and the CFI; (b) the procedure for changing the rules of procedure of the ECJ and the CFI; (c) the names of the ECJ and the CFI; (d) *locus standi* for private individuals under Article 230(4); and (e) the penalties for non-compliance with judgments in enforcement proceedings. It is clear that, although some of these questions are of considerable constitutional importance, the mandate given to the Circle was in fact limited. It was not asked to rethink or recast the judicial architecture but rather to make limited proposals in well-circumscribed issues. It was not, for example, asked to look at the division of jurisdiction between the ECJ and the CFI or the future of the preliminary reference procedure. Even in relation to the questions that it was asked to examine, the Circle's role was not to promote a wide-ranging discussion but consider policy alternatives within a short period of time.[4]

The fact that the Court of Justice was not one of the central themes of the Convention does not mean that the draft Constitution leaves the ECJ unaffected. Far from it. Its provisions enhance the Court's jurisdiction

[2] See Draft Treaty establishing a Constitution for Europe as submitted to the President of the European Council in Rome on 18 July 2003, CONV 850/03 (emphasis added).

[3] For the terms of reference and the framework of proceedings of the Discussion Circle, see CONV 543/03, 7 February 2003. The Circle was chaired by Mr Antonio Vitorino.

[4] The Circle had its first meeting on 17 February and produced its final Report on 25 March 2003. See CONV 636/03. In addition to the work of the Circle, the jurisdiction of the Court was discussed in various contexts by the Praesidium and touched upon also by other working groups.

in a number of ways and lead it to acquire a central role in matters of governance. The ECJ will have a defining role to play in interpreting the new provisions of Part I of the draft Constitution and ascertaining, inter alia, the division of competence between the Union and the Member States, inter-institutional relations, and the application of the principle of subsidiarity. Furthermore, the incorporation of the Charter on Fundamental Rights into the Constitution will add a new parameter to the judicial enforcement of human rights at Union level. The Charter may be seen as a noble endeavour to provide an epigrammatic definition of European ideology but, as a product of political compromise, it contains principles and aspirations which are insufficiently concrete and suffers from drafting deficiencies. Title VII in particular, which contains provisions governing the interpretation and application of the Charter, is rife of uncertainties as to the scope of its application and even the enforceability of its provisions.[5] It will be left to the Court to untangle these problems and ultimately determine the relevance of the Charter.

Further, as Craig points out elsewhere in this volume,[6] the proposed Constitution enhances review of constitutionality of legislation. This is because it grants to the ECJ jurisdiction to annul legislative acts. Although the Court always had the power to annul measures of general application, such as regulations and directives, there is a qualitative difference in that the Constitution provides, for the first time, for a more cogent hierarchy of norms and draws an express distinction between legislative and non-legislative acts. Legislative acts remain subject to review by the ECJ despite the fact that the democratic input in their adoption is significantly increased through the co-decision procedure.[7]

The following sections discuss selectively provisions of the Constitution pertaining to the Court.

## ARTICLE 28(1)

A welcome change of the draft Constitution is that it provides for the essential features of the institutions in Part I. This contrasts with the

[5] Note that Arts II-51 and II-52 of the Constitution which correspond to Arts 51 and 52 of the Charter as it currently stands contain some important changes which appear to restrict the autonomous nature and enforceability of the Charter. See especially Art II-52(4)–(6). For a discussion of the current provisions of the Charter, see K Lenaerts and de Smijter, 'A "bill of rights" for the European Union' (2001) 38 *CMLRev* 273; P Eeckhout 'The EU Charter of Fundamental Rights and the Federal Question' (2002) 39 *CMLRev* 945. See further Arnull, Chapter 6, above.

[6] See above, Chapter 5.

[7] The co-decision procedure is extended to some new areas and elevated to the ordinary legislative procedure.

current Treaty arrangement in which, apart from a rudimentary reference in Article 7 EC, the powers of the institutions are found deep into the body of the Treaty. The Court of Justice is dealt with in Article 28 which provides for its function, composition and jurisdiction and is supplemented by the detailed provisions of Part III (Articles 258–89).

Article 28(1) formally recognises the emergence of a separate tier of Union courts, alongside the national judiciaries, by declaring that the Court of Justice 'shall include the European Court of Justice, the High Court and specialised courts'. Thus, the CFI is re-named 'High Court' and the judicial panels, whose introduction is envisaged by Article 225a EC, 'specialised courts'. The renaming of the CFI stems from the recognition that, with the introduction of judicial panels, the CFI will not always judge cases at first instance whilst in some cases it might act as the final court.[8] The name Court of First Instance would therefore be a misnomer.[9]

Article 28(1) states that the Court of Justice 'shall ensure respect for the law in the interpretation and application of the Constitution'. This provision is intended to replace Article 220 EC. Curiously, the English language text of Article 28(1) departs from the elegant formulation of Article 220 EC[10] whereas the French language text is identical.[11] This suggests that the variation in the English language text is a mistake in translation and should be rectified before the Constitution is adopted. As it currently stands, the English text appears to downgrade the importance of the ECJ. In terms of language, 'respect' for the law is weaker than the peremptory disposition of Article 220 that the law must be 'observed'.[12] The overall result is that the function of the ECJ is attributed by terms which are less imperative and less categoric. Article 220 is, arguably, the most important provision of the Treaty. Although seemingly innocuous, it lays down the rule of law and the principle of separation of powers as fundamental pillars. Its inclusion in the nascent European Economic Community back in 1957 facilitated

[8] So far, no panels have been set up but there are plans for the introduction of one panel to hear staff cases and another to hear disputes pertaining to European patents.

[9] The Circle had proposed the name 'Common Court of the European Union'. The term High Court is more elegant and succeeds in expressing the intention of the Circle which was to adopt a name that would accurately convey the future role of the CFI as the basic, general court of the Union.

[10] Art 220 EC, as amended by the Treaty of Nice states that 'The Court of Justice and the Court of First Instance, each within its jurisdiction, shall ensure that in the interpretation and application of this Treaty the law is observed'.

[11] The material terms of Art 220 EC and Art 28(1) of the Constitution in French are as follows: La Cour assure 'le respect du droit dans l'interprétation et l'application' de la Constitution.

[12] The linguistic difference is subtle but, nonetheless, important: the term 'observance' is stronger than 'respect'. It signifies the action or practice of adhering to a law or principle and is associated with following an ordinance, especially rules and regulations of a religious order. See *The Shorter Oxford English Dictionary*, 3rd edn (Oxford, OUP, 1993).

the transition from inter-governmentalism to supra-nationalism and enabled the ECJ to build the European law edifice. One could hardly think of a more fitting tribute to the *acquis communautaire* than preserving intact the original provision of Article 220 in the new Constitution.

Despite these criticisms, it is submitted that the current formulation of Article 28(1), in case that it survives the technical revision of the text, is not sufficiently different so as to mandate the Court to interpret it more restrictively than Article 220 EC or lead the Court to understand its own function differently.

Article 28(1), second sub-paragraph, states as follows:

'Member States shall provide rights of appeal sufficient to ensure effective legal protection in the field of Union law'.

This is a new provision whose inclusion in Article 28 appears, at first sight, odd. It imposes a substantive obligation on Member States whilst all other dispositions of Article 28 define the role and composition of the Court of Justice. The purpose of this provision is, in fact, twofold. It serves to underlie that national courts play an important part in the application and enforcement of Union rights. It also seeks to counter-balance the restrictive *locus standi* under Article 230(4). It mandates Member States to fill the remedial gap left by the strict interpretation of direct and individual concern. Whether this is a good alternative is a different matter. Suffice it to point out here that Article 28(1) formalises the pattern of de-centralised judicial review, favoured by the Commission and endorsed by the ECJ in its case law.[13]

It is submitted that the obligation imposed on Member States by Article 28(1) may be improved in two ways. First, as it currently stands, the provision appears to be concerned only with access to national courts. In its case law, the Court has laid down the principle of effectiveness which has a wider scope and means that national courts must provide full and effective protection of Community rights. Article 28(1) should reflect that principle and refer not only to rights of appeal but more broadly to the obligation of Member States to provide the judicial means, including remedies, which are sufficient to ensure effective protection of Community rights. This wider meaning is, arguably, already conveyed by the French text of Article 28(1).[14] It is further submitted that this provision should not be included in Article 28(1), where it currently stands, but as a new third paragraph of Article 10 of the Constitution. It will there complement the principles of primacy and loyal cooperation which provide the normative basis of the judge-made principle of effectiveness.

[13] See below p 120.

[14] The French text is as follows: 'Les États membres établissent les voies de recours nécessaires pour assurer une protection juridictionnelle effective dans le domaine du droit de l'Union'.

## THE UNION JUDICIARY: COMPOSITION AND TENURE

The draft Constitution maintains the strong prerogative powers of Member States in the appointment of members of the ECJ and the CFI, whilst introducing some timid steps to control their discretion. Thus, the principle of one judge per Member State is firmly retained in relation to the ECJ.[15] The members of the ECJ and the CFI continue to be appointed by common accord of the Member States, and there is no change in the terms of their tenure.[16] The European Parliament is also kept at safe distance. To counterbalance the nation-state's firm grip on the appointment of the judiciary, a new process safeguard is provided through the introduction of an advisory panel. The pattern that emerges owes more to the intergovernmental rather than the federalist model and is clearly different from that governing the appointment and tenure of the members of the US Supreme Court.

Article III-262 provides for the establishment of a Panel whose function is to give an opinion on candidates' suitability to perform the duties of Judge and Advocate General of the ECJ and the High Court before the governments of the Member States take the decision to make the appointment. The function of the Panel is to offer an opinion on whether a candidate fulfils the requirements of appointment on the basis of objective criteria relating to professional qualifications.[17] The Panel has a consultative role and its opinion is not binding on the Member States. It is however a process safeguard which is designed to influence the appointment in two ways: first, it has a preventive role in that Member States would be more reluctant to propose a candidate whom the panel might be less likely to find suitable. Secondly, an adverse opinion by the Panel on a candidate may lead Member States to refuse to give their common accord on his/her appointment.[18] Notably, the Circle took the view that the Panel should not hold any hearings and its deliberations should not be made public.[19] Article III-262 however remains silent on the issue of publicity. Clearly, the interests of the principle of transparency, which was one of the cardinal

[15] See Art 28(2).
[16] See Art 28(2), Art III-260 and Art III-261. Although the majority of the members of the Circle were in favour of maintaining the current system for the appointment of judges, ie common accord of the governments of the Member States, notably some members felt that appointment should be by act of the Council and several of those members considered that the Council should act by a qualified majority: See Final Report of the Discussion Circle on the Court of Justice, CONV 636/03, above n 4, para 5.
[17] See CONV 636/03, above n 4, para 6.
[18] It will be noted that, so far, on no occasion have Member States refused to give their accord to a candidate proposed by a national government. The preventive value of the panel was highlighted by the Circle which stated that the setting up of a Panel of this kind 'might make Member States more demanding in the choice of candidates put forward': *ibid*, para 6.
[19] *Ibid*, para 6.

themes of the Laeken declaration, and the preventive effect of the consultation requirement would be served much better if the recommendation of the Panel was reasoned and made available to the public.

Under Article III-262(2), the Panel comprises seven persons chosen from among former members of the ECJ and the High Court, members of national supreme courts and lawyers of recognised competence, one of whom must be appointed by the European Parliament.[20] It is notable that this provision finds for the first time a role for the European Parliament in the appointment of the judiciary although that role is so indirect as to be marginal. The reason why the Parliament has been kept at arm's length is a fear that, if Parliament was granted more input on the appointment process, that would risk the politicisation of the judiciary. There is also a cultural barrier. There is little tradition in the Member States of direct parliamentary participation in the selection of the judiciary.

Another issue that was addressed by the Circle was the length of the terms of office of the members of the ECJ and the CFI. Whilst the Circle considered that the existing system of appointing members for a renewable six year term should be retained for members of the CFI, it took the view that the term of office of members of the ECJ should be changed. A recommendation which gained ground was to prolong the term of office of ECJ members to a non-renewable twelve year term.[21] This proposal however was not adopted by the Convention which retained the current system of renewable six year term both for members of the ECJ and the CFI.

The perceived advantage of a non renewable term is that it enhances the independence of the judiciary. Since the possibility of re-appointment is excluded *a priori*, judges are not in a continuous agency relationship with the Member States who appointed them and the possibility is excluded that their judgments might be influenced by their wish to be re-appointed. Notably, the ECJ itself has seen a longer, non-renewable, term of office as

[20] Under Art III-262, the members of the Panel are appointed by the Council which also has the responsibility to establish the Panel's operating rules pursuant to a European decision adopted on a proposal from the President of the ECJ. The text of the provision suggests that the Panel will be appointed on an ad hoc basis each time the membership of the ECJ or the CFI falls to be renewed although the Council could reappoint the same Panel members. It also appears from Art III-262 that a Panel set up to provide an opinion for the appointment of members of the ECJ may comprise former members of the CFI.

[21] Note that the idea of appointing members for a longer non-renewable period is not new. It had been suggested, for example, by the European Parliament which in the Draft EU Treaty which it prepared in 1990 proposed appointment for a period of 12 years. In its Report of 6 July 1993, the Parliament's Committee on Institutional Affairs suggested a period of 9 years. The President of the ECJ and the President of the CFI, who gave evidence to the Circle, suggested a twelve rather than a nine year term for practical reasons. If the term of office was fixed at nine years, that would require the partial renewal of members every four and a half years which would give rise to major practical difficulties.

an added guarantee of independence.[22] This is not to say however that a fixed term tenure is without drawbacks. A fixed term tenure means that judges with a proven track record are not eligible for reappointment. Also, it is liable to break continuity and consistency more than the current system which allows renewal. Finally, proponents of a fixed term mandate may overestimate the extent to which members of a judicial body allow their decisions to be influenced by considerations of their re-appointment.

## *LOCUS STANDI* OF INDIVIDUALS BEFORE THE ECJ

The ECJ has persistently resisted calls to liberalise *locus standi* under Article 230(4). In its judgment in *UPA*,[23] it rejected the liberal test proposed by Advocate General Jacobs and reiterated the strict definition of individual concern applicable under the previous case law. In relation to *locus standi*, the Circle was divided into two groups. The first group was in favour of maintaining the classical 'decentralised model of justice' approach. It considered that the current wording of Article 230(4) complies with the essential requirements of providing effective judicial protection for private litigants since, in accordance with the principle of subsidiarity, it is mainly for national courts to protect their rights and make, where necessary, references to the ECJ.[24] A second group of the Circle considered that the conditions of admissibility were too restrictive and proposed various solutions to liberalise them. A majority of the members of that group were in favour of allowing individuals to challenge at least some acts which are of direct concern to them and which do not entail any implementing measures without the need to prove individual concern. This view prevailed.

Articled III-270(4) of the draft Constitution reads as follows:

> Any natural or legal person may … institute proceedings against an act addressed to that person or which is of direct and individual concern to him or her, and against a regulatory act which is of direct concern to him or her and does not entail implementing measures.

Thus, Article III-270(4) makes it clear, in line with the case law, that an individual may challenge a truly legislative act. In effect, it leaves unchanged the

[22] See Report of the Court of Justice on certain aspects of the application of the Treaty on European Union, Luxembourg, May 1995, reproduced in Court of Justice Annual Report 1995, pp 19–30 at 25.

[23] Case C-50/00 P *Unión de Pequeños Agricultores v Council* [2002] ECR I-6677.

[24] The members of that group considered that it would be appropriate for the Constitution to make express reference to the fact that the onus is on the national courts to interpret and apply, as far as possible, national procedural rules so as to enable individuals to assert their Community rights. This view appears to be reflected in Art 28(1) of the draft Constitution, see above, note 14.

current position on *locus standi* in relation to legislative acts and liberalises, to a limited extent, *locus standi* in relation to regulatory acts. In particular, it provides that an individual may challenge:

(a) both legislative and regulatory acts if he is able to prove direct and individual concern, and
(b) regulatory acts which require no further implementation if he is able to prove direct concern.

It follows that, in relation to legislative acts, the applicant has to overcome the high hurdle of proving individual concern. As reiterated recently in the Court's judgment in *UPA*[25], this will depend on the satisfaction of the strict criteria laid down in *Plaumann*[26] subject to the limited exception of *Codorniu*.[27]

Individual concern is no longer required where the following conditions are fulfilled:

(a) the contested measure is 'a regulatory act';
(b) it is of direct concern to the applicant; and
(c) it does not entail implementing measures.

The requirement of direct concern is defined by the existing case law and is relatively straightforward.[28] The other two conditions require further discussion.

The draft Constitution does not define the notion of a regulatory act. Title V of the first Part, which defines the legal acts of the Union, provides for legislative, non-legislative, and implementing acts.[29] It seems that a regulatory act is any binding measure which is not a legislative act within the meaning of Article 33.[30] This therefore encompasses European regulations as defined in Article 32 of the draft Constitution.[31] These include

[25] Above n 23.
[26] Case 25/62 *Plaumann* [1963] ECR 95.
[27] Case C-309/89 *Codorniu SA v Council* [1994] ECR I-1853.
[28] In general, direct concern is established where the addressee of the measure has no discretion on how to exercise it or where, even if the addressee has discretion, it is clear how it will apply it: see Case 62/70 *Bock v Commission* [1971] ECR 897; Case 11/82 *Piraiki-Patraiki v Commission* [1985] ECR 207; Case C-403/96 P *Glencore Grain Ltd v Commission* [1998] ECR I-2405. For a discussion, see A Arnull, 'Private Applicants and the Action for Annulment since *Codorniu*' (2001) 38 *CMLRev* 7.
[29] For a discussion, P Craig, Chapter 5 above.
[30] This is the interpretation given to the term by the Praesidium commentary: see CONV 734/03, p 20.
[31] Under Art 32(1), fourth sub-paragraph, a European regulation is a non-legislative act of general application for the implementation of legislative acts and of certain specific provisions of the Constitution. It can be binding in its entirety and directly applicable to the Member

delegated and other regulations adopted by the Council, the Commission, and the ECB under Articles 34 and 35. It also includes Union implementing regulations under Article 36(4). It further encompasses any form or administrative rule-making or subordinate legislation, ie any act of general application which is adopted by a Union institution or body and which is for the implementation, broadly understood, of other measures. Finally, it includes decisions. It may be thought that decisions should not be classified as regulatory acts since the latter term is better reserved to non-legislative acts of general application whereas decisions are individual in character. In the Community legal order, however, the term decision does not signify only acts addressed to specific persons but may also acts of wider application which lay down rules in a specific field. This is recognised by Article 32(1).[32]

Under Article III-270(4), a regulatory act can be challenged by an applicant without the need to prove individual concern, only where the act requires no further implementing measures. The aim of this proviso is to avoid a denial of justice in a *Jégo*-type situation[33], ie the case where a Community measure of general application is legally complete and affects adversely the legal position of an individual without the need for any implementing measures to be taken at national level. The classic example is a Commission regulation which prohibits fishing by the use of certain nets or in certain waters. In such a case, the application of the prohibition is not dependent on any prior measures by the Member States. As *Jégo* shows, the individual would be unable to prove individual concern and would also be unable to protect himself in the national courts since there is no implementing measure to challenge. The only way for the individual in such a case to have access to the court would be by violating the regulation and then asserting its illegality by way of defence in proceedings brought against him. This solution however would be unacceptable. As the CFI and the Strasbourg Court have stressed, individuals cannot be required to breach the law in order to gain access to justice.[34]

In some cases, it may not be clear whether a Union act requires implementing measures. The test, presumably, is whether the act is legally complete and leaves no discretion to the Member States. The issue whether an act requires further implementing measures is an issue to be determined

States or it can be binding only as to the result to be achieved leaving the national authorities free to choose the form and means of achieving the result.

[32] See Craig, above n 29. Art 32(1) states: 'A European decision shall be a non-legislative act, binding in its entirety. A decision which specifies those to whom it is addressed shall be binding only on them.' See also Art 36(4).

[33] Case T-177/01 *Jégo-Quéré v Commission* [2002] ECR II-2365.

[34] See *Jégo-Quéré, ibid*, para 45 and see the judgment of the ECtHR in *Posti and Rahko v Finland*, 24 September 2002, para 64.

by EU law and not by national law, ie it does not depend on national constitutional requirements. An interesting question is what happens if an act does not require any implementing measures but a Member State chooses to implement it. Would the national initiative in such a case deprive the individual from direct access to the ECJ? The answer should be in the negative. Insofar as a Union regulatory act does not require national implementing measures, the individual whose legal position is directly affected may challenge it before the CFI. If that solution was not accepted, the availability of an action before the CFI would depend on considerations of national law, an approach which the ECJ has consistently rejected.

## Critique

Consistently with the existing case law, Article III-270(4) views access of individuals to Luxembourg as exceptional. It endorses a decentralised model of access to justice under which, from the point of view of the individual, national courts remain the primary fora for challenging Community acts. The limited liberalisation of *locus standi* introduced by Article III-270(4) does not signal a desire to engage in wholesale reform but an attempt to redress some of the inequities of the case law as evinced, in particular, by *Jégo-Quéré*.

It is submitted that Article 230(4), as it currently stands, does not provide sufficient legal protection for the individual. The requirement of individual concern has been interpreted particularly restrictively by the ECJ and the CFI leading in some cases to injustice. Ideally, in accordance with the test proposed by Advocate General Jacobs in *UPA*, an individual should have *locus standi* to challenge the validity of a Community measure, whether legislative or administrative in nature, if he can establish that 'by reason of the particular circumstances, the measure has, or is liable to have, a substantial adverse effect on his interests'.[35] This view, however, has not prevailed. The arguments which are usually put forward against liberalisation of *locus standi* are the following:

1) The ECJ and the CFI are already overburdened by a heavy workload. If *locus standi* was liberalised, that would open the floodgates and the judicial system would be unable to cope. This is particularly so in view of the impending enlargement of the Union.

[35] See Case C-50/00 P, above n 23, at para 60 of the Advocate General's Opinion. Arnull in his contribution to this volume regrets that the drafters of the Constitution did not take the opportunity to abolish the requirement of individual concern, see Chapter 6 above.

2) A class of litigants which would benefit particularly from liberalisation of standing would be large corporations or associations of undertakings. These would be likely to challenge Community legislative measures which affected adversely their interests even if they had little chances of success on the merits, in an effort to delay the coming into affect of a measure.[36] This would still benefit them financially because it would postpone for a period the regulatory costs of compliance. This further stresses the danger of the proliferation of cases.
3) Apart from those arguments which are costs-based, there is a majoritarian argument. Community legislative measures tend to have a long period of gestation and be the product of painstaking negotiations conducted by political actors who are directly or indirectly accountable to their electorates. The jurisdiction of the courts to annul such measures at the instigation of individuals should therefore be restricted.
4) The limited standing of individuals to challenge legislative acts is in conformity with the constitutional traditions of most Member States.
5) Every system of law has mechanisms which seek to restrict undesirable litigation. Common law systems tend to have more liberal rules of standing but this is counter weighed by the fact that, traditionally, they exercise less rigorous review on the merits. In this light, a restrictive *locus standi* requirement can be seen as a *quid pro quo* for maintaining comparatively strict standards of substantive judicial review.
6) In any event, the system as it currently stands has its own internal economy and works satisfactorily. The right to judicial protection is safeguarded since individuals may challenge the validity of Community acts indirectly before national courts.

These arguments are potent but none of them is without a counter-argument. Suffice it to say here that arguments of costs appear particularly important and have weighed heavily in the general policy of the ECJ and the CFI not to liberalise standing for individuals.

The tide is clearly against broadening the rules of standing as suggested by Advocate General Jacobs in *UPA*. Still, one could propose a more limited liberalisation of *locus standi*.

It would be preferable if Article III-270(4) enabled an individual to challenge any act, whether legislative or regulatory in nature, which affects him

[36] For an example of a challenge before a national court, see Case C-491/01 *The Queen v Secretary of State for Health ex parte British American Tobacco Ltd* [2002] ECR I-11453.

directly and which does not require implementing measures. Such a rule has the following advantages. First, it is simpler and promotes legal certainty. It avoids, in particular, arguments as to whether an act is, or should be, regulatory rather than legislative in nature. As Article 270(4) currently stands, it encourages argument that an act which has been adopted in the form of a legislative act is, in fact, a regulatory one. The new formulation re-introduces uncertainties similar to those which marred the case law in the 1960s when the distinction between a legislative and administrative acts was perceived important for the purposes of *locus standi*.

Secondly, the proposed solution enhances access to justice and the protection of the individual. The fundamental right to judicial protection requires that *locus standi* should not depend on the nature of the contested measure but on whether it affects adversely the interests of the individual.

Before leaving *locus standi*, attention should be brought to the new provision of Article III-270(5) which states as follows: 'Acts setting up bodies and agencies of the Union may lay down specific conditions and arrangements concerning actions brought by natural or legal persons against acts of these bodies or agencies intended to produce legal effects.' This was included as an umbrella provision to cover the cases where means of redress are provided for by Union measures. Currently, EC measures which set up agencies or bodies may provide for one of the following:[37] They may grant to the ECJ jurisdiction to hear actions for judicial review against acts adopted by those agencies or bodies under the terms of Article 230(4).[38] They may provide that acts of such bodies are referable to the Commission for verification of their legality, in which case the Commission's decision can be challenged under Article 230(4).[39] Finally, they may be silent as to the possible means of redress.[40] Article 270(5) does not restrict those options. It makes it clear, however, that acts of such agencies or bodies which produce legal effects are amenable to judicial review in accordance with the fundamental principle of judicial protection provided for in Article 47 of the Charter. Two points may be made in relation to Article III-270(5). First, acts setting up agencies or bodies may specify the means of redress but, in any event, they cannot make access to justice subject to stricter conditions than those specified in Article III-270. Secondly, the provision does not necessarily apply to agencies or bodies established by Union acts adopted under the CFSP, since these have special characteristics.[41]

[37] See Circle, above n 4, para 24.
[38] See eg Council Regulation No 1035/97 establishing a European Monitoring Centre on Racism and Xenophobia, OJ 1997 L 151/1.
[39] See Council Regulation No 2062/94 establishing a European Agency for Safety and Health at Work, OJ 1994 L216/1.
[40] See Regulation No 1406/2002 of the European Parliament and the Council establishing a European Maritime Safety Agency, OJ 2002, L 208/1.
[41] See also here the comments of the Circle, above n 4, p 10.

## SANCTIONS AGAINST MEMBER STATES

Under Article 228 EC, where a Member State has failed to comply with a judgment delivered under Article 226, the Commission must initiate a second enforcement procedure in order to achieve the imposition of pecuniary sanctions. It must, in particular, give to the State concerned a formal notice and submit a reasoned opinion before being able to take the matter to the Court. This system, which was introduced by the Treaty of Maastricht, was clearly an improvement over the previous one which did not provide at all for penalties against recalcitrant Member States. The imposition of penalties was, obviously, a politically sensitive issue and the burdensome procedural safeguards of Article 228 were seen as a *quid pro quo* for Member States agreeing to be subjected to sanctions. Whilst, at the beginning, the Commission threatened the use of the Article 228 procedure only in the most blatant cases, in recent years it seems willing to have recourse to it more frequently.[42]

The sanctions procedure is inefficient and cumbersome. It may take several years from the time that an infringement has been committed until the ECJ imposes a sanction. The Circle considered three suggestions for improving the effectiveness of enforcement. The first suggestion was to simplify the machinery of Article 228 by abolishing the two administrative stages prior to referral to the ECJ, ie the stage of formal notice and the stage of reasoned opinion, or at least one of those stages. The granting of direct access to the Court would not be an innovation since this is already provided in relation to enforcement in other areas of the Treaty.[43] The second suggestion was to merge the procedures of Articles 226 and 228, ie empower the Commission to initiate before the ECJ in the same action both proceedings for failure to fulfil an obligation and for the imposition of sanctions. The third suggestion was to transpose to the EU the procedure provided for in Article 88 of the ECSC Treaty, namely empower the Commission to take a decision that a Member State has failed to fulfil its obligations after giving the State the opportunity to submit its observations. The State would then be able to seek annulment of the Commission's decision.

The Constitutional Convention opted for a combination of the first and the second solutions mentioned above, leading to a procedure which strengthens significantly the enforcement mechanism.

[42] So far, only one case has reached judgment in which the Court imposed penalties on Greece for failure to comply with obligations in the environmental field: Case C-387/97 *Commission v Greece* [2000] ECR I-5047. In recent years, however, the Commission has initiated the sanctions procedure in a number of cases in diverse areas of Community law, and demand for sanctions is no longer limited to the fields of environmental and social law as it was initially: see the Commission's Nineteenth Annual Report on Monitoring the Application of Community Law 2001 COM (2002) 324, p 6.
[43] See Art 88(2), Art 100(9), and Art 298 EC.

Article III-267(2) of the draft Constitution (currently Article 228(2) EC) states that, if the Commission considers that a Member State has not taken the necessary steps to comply with a judgment delivered in enforcement proceedings, it may bring the case before the ECJ 'after giving the State the opportunity to submit its observations.' The Commission must also specify the amount of lump sum or penalty payment which it considers appropriate in the circumstances. Thus, the new provision does away with the requirement to issue a reasoned opinion. The decision whether to impose a penalty continues to rest with the Court.

Further, the draft Constitution envisages an expedited procedure for the imposition of sanctions in cases of 'non-communication', namely where a Member State has not taken any measures to implement a Community directive. Article III-267(3) provides that, when the Commission brings an action under Article III-265 (currently 226 EC) on the ground that the State concerned has failed to fulfil its obligations to notify measures transposing a framework law,[44] the Commission may, if it deems appropriate, request that, in the course of the same proceedings, the Court impose the payment of a lump sum or penalty if the Court finds that there has been a failure. If the Court accepts the Commission's request, the payment in question takes effect within the time limit laid down in the judgment.

Thus, in cases of non-transposition, Article III-267(3) enables the Commission to merge the enforcement and the sanctions procedure. By contrast, in case where a Member State implements a directive but the Commission brings an enforcement action because it considers that the State has done so incorrectly, the Commission may not seek in the same procedure the imposition of penalties. In such a case, the dual safeguard of Articles 226 and 228 continue to operate as they do where the enforcement proceedings relate not to a State's failure to transpose a directive but to any other type of infringement.[45]

All in all, the provisions of Article III-267 make the imposition of sanctions more efficient and cost-effective. By strengthening the powers of the central authority to impose sanctions, they enhance the federal aspects of the enforcement procedure but are carefully crafted to accommodate national sensitivities and obtain political consensus. In practical terms, the most important and welcome innovation is the power of the Commission to seek immediately the imposition of penalties in the case of non-transposition of directives.

[44] Art 32(1) defines a framework law in terms similar to those of a directive.

[45] It may be thought paradoxical that the Commission may seek the immediate imposition of penalties in the case of non-transposition of a directive but not where a Member State acts in manifest breach of a fundamental Treaty provision. The two cases however can be distinguished on practical grounds. Complete failure to implement a directive is an easily definable class of breach. It constitutes a manifest violation which leaves virtually no margin of defence for the Member State concerned. It is therefore justifiable that penalties ensue automatically. By contrast, what is a flagrant violation of the Treaty may be more difficult to define.

## CFSP AND FREEDOM, SECURITY AND JUSTICE

The proposed Constitution abolishes the three pillar structure and brings under the same roof the EC and the EU. As a result, there is no equivalent provision to that of Article 46 TEU which imposes limitations on the jurisdiction of the ECJ in relation to matters covered by the TEU. The special preliminary reference procedures provided for by Article 68 EC for matters falling into Title IV and by Article 35 TEU for the Third Pillar are abolished, and the jurisdiction of the Court becomes unified. This is to be welcomed as the fragmentation of the preliminary reference procedure gives rise to problems and compromises the right to judicial protection.[46]

This is not to say that under the new Constitution the ECJ acquires full jurisdiction. Under Article III-282(1), the Court's jurisdiction continues to be excluded from matters concerning the CFSP.[47] The ECJ, however, is given competence in certain respects at the margins of foreign policy.

First, pursuant to Article III-282(2), it has jurisdiction to review the legality of restrictive measures adopted by the Council under Article III-224 against natural or legal persons.[48] Article III-224 is a new provision which expressly enables the Council to adopt economic sanctions against individuals and non-State groups where a measure adopted in accordance with CFSP provides for the interruption or reduction of economic and financial relations with a third country. Article III-282(2) safeguards the right to judicial protection in relation to 'restrictive measures'adopted under Article III-224. It does not provide for challenges against other CFSP measures which might impose non-economic sanctions on individuals (eg visa bans) . Also, it enables individuals to make a challenge by direct action under Article III-270(4). The possibility of an incidental challenge in preliminary reference proceedings is not expressly provided but that does not necessarily mean that it is excluded. Once it is accepted that such measures are subject to the jurisdiction of the Court, there is no reason why challenge should be restricted to a direct action.

The ECJ also retains jurisdiction to ensure that the implementation of the CFSP does not affect the other competences of the Union, in particular, its exclusive competences, the coordination of economic and employment policies, and the complementary policies.[49]

[46] For a discussion, see T Tridimas, 'Knocking on Heaven's Door: Fragmentation, Efficiency and Defiance in the Preliminary Reference Procedure' (2003) 40 *CMLRev* 9 at 14 *et seq*.
[47] Notably, as it currently stands, Art III-282(1) excludes from judicial control Arts I-39 and I-40 but not Art I-15. Thus, it could be argued that the Commission could bring an enforcement action against a Member State for failure to comply with the obligation of solidarity provided for in Art I-15(2).
[48] See Art III-282(2). Such proceedings may be brought under Art III-270(4).
[49] See Art III-209.

The Discussion Circle on the Court of Justice discussed the issue whether the jurisdiction of the Court to deliver opinions in relation to international agreements provided for in Article 300(6) EC[50] should be extended to cover also agreements falling within the sphere of the CFSP.[51] Most members of the Circle were in favour of that view.[52]Article III-204 does not provide a clear answer: It simply states that the Union may conclude agreements with third states or international organisations in the field of the CFSP 'in accordance with the procedure described in Article III-227'. It could be argued that 'procedure' should be strictly understood to include only the procedural steps for the conclusion of an international agreement stated in that article and does not include recourse to the Court under Article III-227(12). Where however an interested party, such as a Member State, has doubts about the compatibility of an agreement, referring the matter to the ECJ is also a procedural step. It is submitted that this broader interpretation should prevail.

The Constitution extends the presence of the ECJ in the field of freedom, security and justice. The jurisdictional restriction imposed by Article 68(2) EC in the fields of visas, asylum and immigration is not maintained.[53] By contrast in the areas of judicial cooperation in criminal matters and police cooperation, judicial powers are restricted. Article III-283 provides that, in those areas, the ECJ has no jurisdiction to review the validity or proportionality of operations carried out by the police or other law enforcement agencies of a Member State or the exercise of the responsibilities incumbent upon Member States with regard to the maintenance of law and order and the safeguarding of internal security, where such action is a matter of national law. Thus, Article III-283 maintains the restriction on the jurisdiction of the Court currently provided by Article 35(5) TEU in relation to Third Pillar matters.[54]

## PRELIMINARY REFERENCES

Article III-274 of the proposed Constitution corresponds to Article 234 EC and introduces some minor changes to the current system of preliminary references.

[50] The equivalent provision is contained in Art III-227 of the Constitution.
[51] See CONV 689/1/03, 16 April 2003.
[52] *Ibid*, p 3.
[53] Under Art 68(2), the ECJ does not have jurisdiction to rule on any measure or decision taken by the Council under Art 62 relating to the maintenance of law and order and the safeguarding of internal security.
[54] Note however that, under Art III-283, the jurisdiction of the ECJ on those matters is excluded only 'where such action is a matter of national law'. This is a rider which does not appear in Art 35(5) TEU.

Article 234, as it currently stands, grants to the Court of Justice jurisdiction to give preliminary rulings concerning (a) the interpretation of the Treaty; (b) the validity and interpretation of acts of the institutions of the Community and of the ECB and (c) the interpretation of the statutes of bodies established by an act of the Council, where those statutes so provide. Article III-274(1) states that the Court of Justice shall have jurisdiction to give preliminary references concerning:

(a) the interpretation of the Constitution;
(b) the validity and interpretation of acts of the Institutions of the Union.

The language of Article III-274(1) (b) may give rise to doubts as to whether acts of the ECB are included. This is because, under Article 18 of the draft Constitution, the ECB is not included as one of the 'Union's Institutions' although Article 29(3) proclaims that the ECB 'is an Institution which has legal personality'. It would be very odd, however, if Article III-274 intended to exclude the ECB from the preliminary reference procedure and thus restrict the scope of Article 234 EC. Such an exclusion would create a gap in the right to judicial protection and would be incompatible with Article 47 of the Charter. The absence of express reference to the ECB in Article III-274 may be owing to the fact that, in a previous draft of the Constitution, the ECB was included in the list of the Union Institutions in Article 18. It was later decided, however, to restrict the list of Union institutions and provide separately for the ECB and the Court of Auditors under the heading 'Other Institutions and Bodies'. The current formulation of Article III-274(1)(b) should be changed in the final text of the Constitution to make clear that the ECB is included.

Article III-274, however, does differ from Article 234 EC in that it does not contain a paragraph similar to paragraph (c) of Article 234. This omission, in fact, broadens the jurisdiction of the Court. This is because paragraph (c), as it currently stands, restricts the scope of paragraph (b). Under paragraph (c), the ECJ has jurisdiction to hear preliminary references in relation to the statutes of bodies established by an act of the Council only with regard to their interpretation, not with regard to their validity, and only where those statutes so provide. In the absence of paragraph (c), the jurisdiction of the ECJ in relation to such statutes is determined by paragraph (b) which applies to all acts of the institutions. This change is a tidying up exercise and is, in fact, of little practical importance.

Finally, Article III-274 contains a new paragraph four which states that where a preliminary reference is made 'in a case pending before a court or tribunal of a Member State with regard to a person in custody, the Court of Justice shall act with the minimum of delay'. This provision was included to take account of the fact that under the Constitution the ECJ will have much broader jurisdiction to hear preliminary references on issues which fall within the current Title IV of the EC Treaty. The provision is an illustration of the fundamental right to judicial protection and makes supreme sense. Where a reference is made in criminal proceedings and pertains to a person in custody, the Court should deliver its ruling with the minimum of delay since the freedom of the individual is at stake. The fact that this provision was included in the Constitution itself rather than the Statute of the Court or the Rules of Procedure illustrates that the Praesidium saw this guarantee as closely linked to the underlying themes of the Convention, ie liberty, democracy and justice.[55] Currently, the Rules of Procedure of the ECJ provide that in exceptional cases the ECJ may give priority to a preliminary reference and hear it under an accelerated procedure.[56] Presumably, when the Constitution is adopted, and in the absence of any new provision implementing Article III-274(4), the use of the accelerated procedure for such cases will be compulsory and no longer a matter in the Court's discretion.[57]

## OTHER PROVISIONS PERTAINING TO THE COURT

The draft Constitution amends Articles 225a and 229a EC. These concern respectively the setting up of judicial panels and the conferral on Union courts of jurisdiction to hear disputes pertaining to intellectual property rights created by EU acts. Under the existing articles, the Council may adopt the measures provided therein by unanimity whereas, under the draft Constitution, the measures must be adopted by the ordinary legislative procedure, namely jointly by the Council and the European Parliament, the former acting by qualified majority.[58] The draft Constitution also amends Article 245 which enables the Council, acting unanimously, to amend the Statute of the ECJ, save for Title I of the Statute which may be amended only by Treaty revision. Article III-289 enables the Statute to be amended by the ordinary legislative procedure, save for Title I and Article 64 of the Statute which provides for language arrangements. These provisions may be amended only by Treaty revision. This appears to be a regressive step with regard to language arrangements

[55] See V Skouris, 'Proposals for Reform of the System of Judicial Protection' (in Greek) (2003) *Nomiko Vima* (forthcoming).
[56] See Rules of Procedure of the ECJ, Art 104a. See also Art 62a and, for comments, Tridimas, above, n 46, at 20.
[57] See Skouris, above n 55.
[58] See Arts III-264(1) [existing Art 225a] and III-269 [existing Art 229a] in combination with Art I-33. Note also the special provision of Art III-302(15) which applies in relation to measures adopted at the request of the ECJ.

since, as it currently stands, Article 64 can arguably be amended by a unanimous Council decision and does not require Treaty revision.[59]

## SUBSIDIARITY

A novel feature of the draft Constitution is that it strengthens the role of national Parliaments in monitoring compliance with the principle of subsidiarity.[60] This accords with one of the key objectives of the Constitutional Convention which was to increase democracy by enhancing 'the contribution of national Parliaments to the legitimacy of the European design'.[61] The Protocol on the application of the principles of subsidiarity and proportionality annexed to the Constitution gives to national Parliaments both political and judicial means to challenge Commission legislative proposals.

Political control is exercised collectively by all national Parliaments acting through a novel voting system. Any national Parliament, or any Parliamentary chamber in the case of countries which have a bicameral system, may object to a Commission legislative proposal by submitting a reasoned opinion stating why it considers that the proposal does not comply with subsidiarity.[62] National Parliaments of Member States with unicameral parliamentary systems are allocated two votes whilst each of the chambers of a bicameral parliamentary system has one vote.[63] Where reasoned opinions against a Commission proposal represent at least one third of all the votes allocated to the Member States' national Parliaments and their chambers, the Commission is required to review its proposal.[64] After such review, the Commission may decide to maintain, amend or withdraw its proposal, giving reasons for its decision.[65]

[59] Note that Art 64 of the Statute does not make crystal clear the procedure by which it can be revised. Some members of the Circle suggested that the Court should change its current practice of not giving judgment in a case until the judgment has been translated into all languages and that it should, instead, deliver judgment in the language of the case, the other language versions being made available within a period of six months. This change would not require any amendment of the Treaty. See CONV 636/03, above n 4, para 11.

[60] See Article 9(3) of the draft Constitution. See also Bermann, Chapter 4 above.

[61] See the Preface to the Constitution.

[62] Protocol, para 5. Under the Protocol, the Commission must transmit all its legislative proposals to the national Parliaments at the same time as it transmits them to the Union legislator. National Parliaments may submit their reasoned opinions within six weeks from the date of transmission by sending them to the Presidents of the EP, the Council of Ministers and the Commission.

[63] Para 6.

[64] *Ibid.* The threshold of one third is lowered to a quarter in the case of a Commission proposal or an initiative emanating from a group of Member States under the provisions of Art III-165 of the Constitution on the area of freedom, security and justice.

[65] *Ibid.*

This system of political control works to the advantage of States with a bicameral system in that it gives them more chances to challenge Commission proposals. This may appear discriminatory but the authors of the Protocol would argue that the difference in treatment between Member States is justifiable because the system of political control does not seek to juxtapose the Member States *vis-à-vis* the Union institutions but to empower national representative assemblies to act independently of their national governments. The Protocol does not specify the way by which the national Parliaments may take the decision to object to a Commission proposal. The majority required is for the national laws to determine as is the involvement of regional assemblies. On the latter issue, the Protocol merely states that it is for each national Parliament or each chamber to consult, where appropriate, regional Parliaments with legislative powers.[66]

Judicial control is provided in paragraph 7 of the Protocol. This provision grants the Court jurisdiction to hear actions for judicial review on grounds of infringement of the principle of subsidiarity brought 'by Member States, or notified by them in accordance with their legal order on behalf of their national Parliament or a chamber if it.' Such actions can be brought against legislative acts of the Union in accordance with the rules of Article III-270 (currently Article 230). A similar right of action is also granted to the Committee of the Regions as regards legislative acts for the adoption of which it must be consulted.

Although the language of paragraph 7 does not make it clear, the intention of the provision is to require Member States to make available the right of action to national Parliaments and not simply to allow them to do so. The Preasidium notes attached to the Protocol suggest that the national Parliaments are given the right to challenge measures before the ECJ.[67] What is left to the Member States is to determine the arrangements for the exercise of that right, including the question whether it will be granted to each Parliamentary chamber in States with a bicameral system. These arrangements can be made by ordinary law and need not have the status of constitutional rules. [68]

Thus, it is for each Member State to decide the proportion of votes by which the Parliament needs to act to authorise the initiation of litigation before the ECJ. Many models are here conceivable. A Member State may, for example, require the Parliament to act by majority in which case the democratic value of the right of action is considerably reduced. Where the government controls the majority, it is unlikely that the Parliament will vote for the initiation of litigation if the government itself does not

[66] Protocol, para 5.
[67] CONV 724/1/03 REV 1, p 144
[68] *Ibid.*

consider it appropriate.[69] In such a case, the Parliament's right of action is tantamount to the right of action of Member States which is already granted under Article 230 EC. At the other extreme, national law may enable, say, a certain cross-party minority of parliamentarians to authorise litigation. Such an arrangement would enhance the power of the Parliament to question Union legislation, acting independently of the government's interests.

Granting to national Parliaments their own political and judicial means to monitor compliance with subsidiarity may be seen as an indication of respect to representative democracy. The Protocol seeks to promote national Parliaments as centres of political power with a say in the exercise of Community competence independently of their national governments. These newly founded rights may in some cases bring national Parliaments in a collision course with their respective governments. But they also juxtapose the national Parliaments with the European Parliament. Now that the latter is elevated, at least in most areas, to a co-legislator with the Council, an action on grounds of subsidiarity initiated by a national Parliament is as much a denial of Community competence as a refusal to heed to the supremacy of the European Parliament. These new provisions of the draft Constitution may be seen as enhancing dialogue, democracy, and decentralisation. They view Community competence not as a bi-polar exchange between the Union institutions, on the one hand, and the Member States, on the other hand, but as a pluralistic dialogue among various political actors at national and Union level. It should be noted however that these rights are very likely to have more impact in Member States with weak majorities or coalition governments where it is easier for parliamentarians to assert themselves as a political force independent from the government.

What is the likely impact of the Parliament's new right of action? So far, the impact of subsidiarity on judicial review has been benign and indirect. In no case has the Court annulled a measure on the ground that it contravenes the principle. Where the Court has annulled measures, it has preferred to do so on grounds of competence or proportionality rather than on grounds of subsidiarity even though the principle may have influenced the judgment.[70] By increasing the number of potential plaintiffs, the Protocol increases the justiciability of subsidiarity. Clearly the Protocol brings the Court of Justice closer to the political game. By transferring to the courtroom what are essentially political issues, it risks the politicisation of the judiciary, not in the sense of making the Court a partisan institution

[69] Unless the government allows the issue to be put in Parliament on a free vote or a sufficient majority of the ruling party considers the issue to be worth a rebellion.
[70] See eg C-376/98 *Germany v Parliament and Council (Tobacco case)* [2000] ECR I-8419.

but of involving it more directly in issues of European governance. Judicial control of subsidiarity is bound to become more complicated and possibly also more intense as the Court will have available at its disposal a lot more material from the Commission and national central and regional authorities on the basis of which to assess whether a measure meets the requisite test.[71]

A final point relates to the scope of the action. It appears that, where an application for judicial review is made pursuant to the Protocol, the only ground that can be invoked is breach of the principle of subsidiarity. A national Parliament may not ask its Member State to challenge a Community measure on any other ground. This may give rise to problems since, in practice, some grounds of review may be closely intertwined. In the *Tobacco Directive case*[72] the Court annulled the contested directive on ground of lack of competence and formally, at least, did not address the argument of the German Government based on subsidiarity. Would the Court have reached the same result if it examined the issue on the basis of subsidiarity? Also, since the existence of Community competence is a condition precedent to its valid exercise, and therefore to the application of the principle of subsidiarity, can the ECJ examine arguments based on competence in actions brought under the Protocol? Such problems will not arise where a Member State brings an action not only on behalf of its Parliament but also on its own behalf under Article III-270 of the Constitution, in which case all grounds of review are invokable.

## HUMAN RIGHTS VERSUS FUNDAMENTAL FREEDOMS

The tendency towards the constitutionalisation of the ECJ is not only brought forward by the new Constitution, but also reinforced by the ECJ itself through developments in the case law. This is particularly so in the area of human rights. A number of factors have contributed to the increase in the importance of human rights in the European Union. Fundamental rights have acquired greater prominence in all western societies. In an era where there is heightened zeal for the accountability of public authorities and the empowerment of the individual, respect for human rights is viewed not only as a *sine qua non* of legality but as the most important yardstick in assessing a polity's democratic credentials. In the EU, the observance of human rights by the Union institutions and by the Member States is part

[71] The Protocol views subsidiarity as a cost effectiveness exercise carried out on the basis of a detailed substantive and financial assessment of the Union-wide, national and regional implications of each proposal: see Protocol, para 4.

[72] Above n 70.

of the renewed calls for accountability, transparency and legitimacy. There is a shared belief that democracy is not exhausted in the majoritarian rule but encompasses respect for the individual, tolerance and pluralism.[73] There appears to be a consensus among the political elites that Europe is a society which elevates liberalism to its highest value, and where respect for human rights defines the limits of tolerance to political and cultural diversity. What challenges are there for the Court? At the danger of over-simplification, it can be said that the Court faces three challenges: its relationship with the Court of Human Rights, the interpretation of the Charter, and conflicts between human rights and fundamental freedoms. This paper concentrates on the third in the light of the recent judgment in *Schmidberger v Austria*.[74]

In most cases, respect for human rights and the fundamental freedoms guaranteed by the EC Treaty operate as complementary and converging forces. Thus, according to established case law, a national measure which restricts the free movement of goods or services cannot take advantage of an express derogation provided in the Treaty or a mandatory requirement unless it respects fundamental rights.[75] But in other cases, human rights and fundamental freedoms may find each other in a collision course. Although there are some examples in previous case law,[76] this conflict has never been so eminently illustrated as in the recent case of *Scmidberger v Austria*.[77] The Austrian authorities allowed an environmental group to organise a demonstration on the Brenner motorway, the effect of which was to close the motorway to traffic for almost 30 hours. The Brenner artery is the main transit route linking Germany to Italy. The applicant was an international transport undertaking based in Germany whose main activity was to transport goods to Italy. It brought an action seeking damages against the Austrian authorities claiming that their failure to prevent the motorway from being closed amounted to a restriction on the free movement of goods.

The Court started by pointing out that Article 28 EC applies both to acts and omissions. Referring to its previous judgment in *Commission v France*,[78] it held that Article 28 does not prohibit only measures emanating from the State which, in themselves, create restrictions on inter-state trade but applies also where a Member State abstains from adopting the measures

[73] Art 2 of the Constitution, headed 'The Union's values', refers to 'a society of pluralism, tolerance, justice, solidarity and non-discrimination'.
[74] Case C-112/00 *Schmidberger, Internationale Transporte und Planzüge v Austria*, judgment of 12 June 2003.
[75] For a recent confirmation, see Case C-60/00 *Carpenter v Secretary of State for the Home Department*, judgment of 11 July 2002, para 40.
[76] See eg Case C-62/90 *Commission v Germany* [1992] ECR I-2575. See also *R v Chief Constable of Sussex ex parte International Trader's Ferry Ltd* [1999] 2 AC 418.
[77] Above, n 74.
[78] Case C-265/95 *Commission v France* [1997] ECR I-6959.

required in order to deal with obstacles to the free movement of goods which are caused by private parties. Thus, the fact that the Austrian authorities had failed to ban the demonstration thereby resulting in the complete closure of a major transit route was a measure having equivalent effect to a quantitative restriction.[79] The Court then turned to examine whether the restriction was justified.

After pointing out that fundamental rights form an integral part of the general principles of Community law and referring to Article 6(2) TEU, the Court stated that the protection of fundamental rights 'is a legitimate interest which, in principle, justifies a restriction of the obligations imposed by Community law, even under a fundamental freedom guaranteed by the Treaty such as the free movement of goods'.[80] It then proceeded to examine how the conflicting principles should be reconciled.

The Court viewed the free movement of goods and the freedom of assembly and association as being of equal constitutional ranking. It pointed out that neither of the competing values was absolute. Under the EC Treaty, the free movement of goods may be subject to restrictions for the reasons laid down in Article 36 (now Article 30) or for overriding requirements relating to the public interest. Similarly, whilst freedom of association and freedom of assembly form fundamental pillars of a democratic society, it follows from Articles 10 and 11 of the ECHR that, unlike other fundamental rights enshrined in the Convention, they are subject to certain limitations justified by objectives in the public interest.

The Court then proceeded to weigh the interests involved in order to determine whether a fair balance was struck between them. It came to the conclusion that, having regard to their wide discretion, the Austrian authorities were reasonable in considering that the legitimate aim of the demonstration could not be achieved by less restrictive measures. The ECJ took into account the following considerations.[81]

First, it distinguished the case from *Commission v France*. In *Schmidberger*, the demonstration took place following a request for authorisation presented on the basis of national law and after the competent authorities had taken a decision not to ban it. Also, traffic by road was obstructed on a single route, on a single occasion, and during a period of almost 30 hours. The obstacle to the free movement was limited by comparison with both the geographic scale and the intrinsic seriousness of the disruption caused in *Commission v France*. The Court attributed particular importance to the fact that, in contrast to the latter case, the objective of the Austrian demonstrators was not to restrict trade in goods but to manifest in public their opinion.

[79] *Schmidberger*, above n 74, para 64.
[80] *Ibid*, para 74.
[81] Paras 84–93.

The Court also pointed out that the competent authorities had taken various administrative and supporting measures in order to limit as far as possible disruption. An extensive publicity campaign had been launched by the media and the motoring organisations in Austria and neighbouring countries and various alternative routes had been designed.

The Court then considered in some detail the argument of the less restrictive alternatives. It held that, taking account of the Member States' wide margin of discretion, the authorities were entitled to consider that an outright ban on the demonstration would have constituted unacceptable interference with their fundamental right to gather and express peacefully their opinion in public.[82] It also dismissed the argument that the authorities could have taken stricter measures to control the demonstration. In a statement revealing the way the Court prioritised the competing values, it held that the imposition of stricter conditions concerning both the site, for example requiring the demonstrators to stay by the side of the motorway, and the duration of the protest 'could have been perceived as an excessive restriction, depriving the action of a substantial part of its scope'.[83] It then continued: 'An action of that type usually entails inconvenience for non-participants, in particular as regards free movement, but the inconvenience may in principle be tolerated provided that the objective pursued is essentially the public and lawful demonstration of an opinion'.[84] The Court accepted the argument of the Austrian Government that, in any event, all the alternative solutions that could be countenanced could have risked reactions which would have been difficult to control and would have been liable to cause much more serious disruption to intra-Community trade and public order, such as unauthorised demonstrations, confrontation or acts of violence on the part of the demonstrators.

*Schmidberger* gives the clearer sign yet that the Court takes human rights seriously and conducts itself not as the Court of an economic union but as the Supreme Court of a constitutional order. The reasoning of the Court contrasts with that in previous cases where it readily gave the benefit of the doubt to free movement. In *Commission v Germany*[85] the Court had rejected the argument that respect for private life and the protection of medical confidentiality justified restrictions on the importation of medicinal products. Also, in previous cases,[86] it had dismissed the view that public disturbances and the risk of violence by protestors could justify protective measures. Although these cases can be distinguished on the facts, the

[82] Para 89.
[83] Para 90.
[84] Para 91.
[85] Above, n 76.
[86] See Case C-52/95 *Commission v France* [1995] ECR I-4443, para 38; *Commission v France*, above n 78, para 55; See also Case 231/83 *Cullet v Leclerc* [1985] ECR 305, para 35.

methodology followed by the Court in *Schmidberger* is clearly different. The Court attached as much importance to the freedoms of assembly and expression as to the free movement of goods viewing the two as being of equal ranking.

The ECJ attributed particular importance to the European Convention. It also paid homage to national laws. The judgment contains subtle but repeated references to the constitutional values of the Member States.[87] By acknowledging that fundamental freedoms are conditioned by human rights and giving priority to the latter, the ECJ honoured the constitutional expectations of the Members States. Seen in the background of rebellious judgments by national Supreme Courts, *Schmidberger* is a gesture of reconciliation, and an attempt to embrace the national constitutional courts. Notably, the ECJ went all the way offering a ready made solution to the national court rather than giving only general guidelines and leaving it to the latter to resolve the conflict.[88]

The ECJ declared in general terms that the protection of human rights may justify restrictions on free movement but did not place them in either of the established categories of limitations, ie it did not state whether they should be viewed as part of the express derogations of the Treaty (Article 30 EC) or as legitimate objectives in the public interest. The classification is important because, if human rights are viewed as part of the express derogations, they can justify even discriminatory restrictions on trade whilst if they are considered as mandatory requirements they can only justify indistinctly applicable restrictions. In principle, since human rights are viewed as being of equal ranking to the Treaty there is nothing to restrict them from justifying also discriminatory measures. This also follows from the fact that the protection of human rights may justify restrictions not only on the import but also on the export of goods which, if they fall within the scope of Article 29, are *ex hypothesi* discriminatory.[89]

Finally, a distinct feature of *Schmidberger* is that the Court applied a comparatively lax standard of proportionality. Traditionally, interference with the fundamental freedoms resulting from national measures is viewed by the Court as suspect and is subjected to rigorous scrutiny. In *Schmidberger*, the ECJ stressed that the competent authorities had wide discretion and made reference to the criterion of reasonableness, thus applying to national authorities a standard of scrutiny which is usually reserved to the Community institutions themselves.

[87] See eg paras 70, 71, 72, 74, 76 of the judgment.

[88] Preliminary rulings of the ECJ concerning the compatibility of national laws with the Treaty provisions on free movement and involving human rights are of varied specificity. See and contrast Case C-260/89 *ERT* [1991] ECR I-2925; Case C-368/95 *Familiapress* [1997] ECR I-3689; *Carpenter*, above n 75.

[89] See *Schmidberger*, *passim*, and also *R v Chief Constable of Sussex ex parte International Trader's Ferry Ltd*, above n 76.

## CONCLUSION

The draft Constitution enhances the position of the ECJ as the supreme court of the Union. The increase in the constitutional jurisdiction of the Court is the consequential effect of a number of developments. The Constitution provides for a clearer hierarchy of norms and grants to the ECJ jurisdiction to review the constitutionality of legislation. It formally incorporates the principle of primacy and contains a number of provisions which govern the division of competence between the Union and the Member States and the allocation of powers among the Union institutions. It is ultimately for the Court to interpret these provisions and determine their meaning. It brings the Court closer to the political game by encouraging judicial control of subsidiarity. The incorporation of the Charter of Fundamental Rights further increases the set of constitutional norms *vis-à-vis* which the Court may test the legality of Community action. Finally, the Constitution is imbued by a number of principles, such as democracy, transparency, subsidiarity, and equality, which can be expected to feature more prominently in judicial reasoning and assist in articulating standards of legality for Community and Member State action.

The draft Constitution contains both elements of the federalist model and of the inter-governmental model. Pro-federalist steps are measured and cautious. Thus, the system of sanctions against Member States for failing to comply with Union law is enhanced. Following the abolition of the pillar structure, the preliminary reference procedure becomes unified and the jurisdiction of the Court on Title IV matters is extended. The draft Constitution also provides for the setting up of a panel which must be consulted in relation to judicial appointments although Member States remain firmly in control.

*Locus standi* of individuals before the CFI is somewhat extended but, from the point of view of the individual, national courts remain firmly the primary venue for challenging Community acts. The proposed Article III-270(4) can be seen as an endorsement of the restrictive interpretation of individual concern given by the case law of the ECJ, which in turn has been prompted, first and foremost, by cost considerations.

The judgment in *Schmidberger* illustrates that, responding to the challenges of the times, the Court takes human rights seriously and assumes the position of the Supreme Court of the Union. What, then, are the main challenges that the Court is likely to face in the coming years? Although any attempt to look into the crystal ball is, by its nature, dangerous and marred by methodological difficulties, one could identify the following issues as being among those which are likely to give rise to problems or be of particular importance in the coming years.

First is what can be called the human rights challenge. As already stated, this includes the relationship between the ECJ and the ECtHR, the future interpretation of the Charter, and the resolution of conflicts between human rights and fundamental freedoms. As we saw in *Schmidberger*, the ECJ pre-empted Strasbourg by giving priority to human rights.

Secondly, there is the possibility of challenges to the primacy of Community law. The success of the ECJ in constructing the edifice of European law and attaining the constitutionalisation of the Treaties owes much to the approval, encouragement and cooperation of national courts. As the Maastricht decisions of the German Constitutional Court[90] and the Danish Supreme Court[91] show, however, such cooperation cannot be equated with submission. Primacy means different things to different courts.[92] The ECJ has the delicate task of embracing the national legal orders and addressing the sensitivities of the national supreme courts without endangering the fundamental principles of Union law.

A third area of concern is the division of competence between the Union and the Member States. The draft Constitution seeks to clarify the allocation of competences and enhance subsidiarity but, in terms of its practical application, the notion of competence remains elusive.

The assimilation of the acceding Member States poses a further challenge. The latest accession differs both in quantitative and qualitative terms from previous ones. It will fall upon the Court to interpret the myriads of derogations provided for in the Treaty of Accession but also, more importantly, to ensure respect for the *acquis communautaire* and forge a common set of pan-European constitutional values in the interpretation and application of the Treaty.

There is no doubt that the Court has acquired the role of the Supreme Court of the Union. The greatest challenge that will face in the coming years is how to ensure uniformity and functional adjustment of the *acquis communautaire* in an era where diversity is the prevailing pattern of integration.

[90] *Brunner* [1994] 1 CMLR 57.
[91] *Hanne Norup Carlsen and Others v the Prime Minister* [1999] 3 CMLR 854.
[92] For a detailed analysis, see Tridimas, above n 46 at 37 *et seq*.

# 8

# *The European Commission: Should it be at the Heart of the Future European Union?*

MIKE CUTHBERT AND SARAH WILLIS

THE FOUNDING TREATIES of the European Communities placed the European Commission at the very heart of the system of governance. Under the EC treaties it has exclusive rights of initiating legislation and contributes at all legislative stages. Article 211 EC defines the various roles of the Commission to include legislative, executive and legal guardian. Professor Walter Hallstein annoyed President de Gaulle of France by claiming in 1965 that as President of the Commission he could be regarded as a kind of European prime minister.[1] This 'presidential style' contributed to the breakdown of the functioning of the Community, only resolved by the Luxembourg Accord in 1966, but this was not the last time that there was friction between the President of the Commission and a Member State. As the areas of policy involvement grew over the decades, so the involvement of the European Commission has been expanded. With the growth in the use of experts via the system of comitology the influence of the Commission has been extended further. In its submission to the 2000 Intergovernmental Conference, the Commission described itself as 'the driving force behind European integration'.[2] This followed on from a decade of activist leadership under the Commission Presidency of Jacques Delors. However, from the early days of the European Communities the actual role and powers of the Commission were regular matters of discussion and proposals for reform. The forthcoming enlargement of the European

[1] D Urwin, *The Community of Europe: A History of European Integration Since 1945*, 2nd edn (Harlow, Longman 1995).

[2] 'Adapting the Institutions to Make a Success of Enlargement: Commission Opinion on the Calling of a Conference of Representatives of the Governments of MS to Amend the Treaties', Com (2000) 34 (26 January) Brussels.

Union has focused the minds of the Member States and the institutions on reform but many of the problems that they attempt to deal with are not new. A review of the history of these proposals may allow us a better view of the current proposals and directions for the future roles of the Commission within the EU.

In 1976 Leo Tindemans wrote to the European Council proposing that the European Commission should be given increased authority and cohesion. He proposed that:

(a) The President of the Commission will be appointed by the European Council;
(b) The President when appointed will have to appear before the Parliament to make a statement and have his appointment confirmed by vote.
(c) The President of the Commission will then appoint his colleagues in consultation with the Council and bearing in mind the number of Commissioners allocated to each country.[3]

Enlargement is not a new situation for the Commission to deal with, it is just the scale that has changed with ten new Member States joining in 2004. A Committee of Wise Men was established by the European Council meeting in Brussels in December 1978, with the brief to formulate 'specific proposals aimed at ensuring the proper operation of the Community on the basis of and in compliance with the Treaties, including their institutional arrangements, and progress towards European Union.[4] The Three Wise Men[5] recognised that the role and authority of the Commission had declined in the 1970's. It needed to be more effective in exercising its rights of initiative and guardian of the Treaties, 'together with its management and implementing tasks, need to be more effective and adapted to current circumstances'. With the number of Member States increasing to twelve they proposed that the number of Commissioners should be limited to one per Member State, with a corresponding reduction in the number of Directorates-General. 'The college of Commissioners should be more homogeneous and should act more as a collective body. Coordination between departments should be strengthened and the central services — budget, personnel, administration — grouped under the authority of the President. The President of the Commission's authority must be reinforced within the institution of which he is the head. He should be chosen by the European Council six months before the renewal of the Commission. He should be consulted by

[3] Leo Tindemans' Letter to his European Council Colleagues, Bulletin EC Supplement 1/76.
[4] Bulletin EC 11/1979 pp 25–28.
[5] Mr Barend Biersheuvel, Mr Edmund Dell and Mr Robert Marjolin.

the Governments on the selection of Members of the Commission, and should have the last word on the allocation of portfolios. '… The Council, for its part, must delegate more of the implementation of new policies to the Commission.'[6] The report by the committee on the internal workings of the Commission set up by Roy Jenkins when he became Commission President reported in 1979.[7] Many of its recommendations echoed those of the Tindemans report and followed the same fate of not being implemented. Perhaps the reforms put forward by Neil Kinnock would not have been required if some of these recommendations on the internal management of the Commission had been implemented!

When the EC grew to thirteen Member States there was a familiar theme when the Commission suggested that there should be only one national of each Member State. This was rejected because although it would lead to a marginal reduction in the number of Commissioners, certain practical problems would have been created by the fact that there was an increased burden of work in a wider Community.[8]

The decline in the 1970's of the political commitment of the Member States was identified by the Commission as the reason why there had been a strengthening of intergovernmental factors within the Community. This was reflected in the decision- making processes of the Council.[9] The Heads of State or Government had stated at the Paris Summit held in December 1974 that there were advantages in using Article 155 (4) EC (now Article 211 EC) to allow the Commission to deal with implementation measures, but 'then acted consistently otherwise'.[10] This resulted in a shift in the balance of powers from the Commission to the Council, resulting in the political power of the Commission being heavily compromised. This was at a time when the Commission was anxious to preserve its political function, by both its power to propose and its power to mediate.

The Commission recognised that there were shortcomings in the workings of all the institutions, including the Commission, but it wanted to move forward. If the Council could move away from unanimity, allowing the Commission to play its rightful role in the legislative process by allowing it to use its management powers to the full, the European Parliament could exercise the responsibilities conferred by the Treaties[11] and the balance would be restored!

[6] Bulletin EC 11/1979, p 27.

[7] D Spierenburg, 'Proposals for the Reform of the Commission of the European Communities and Its Services' (Brussels, European Commission, 1979).

[8] 'The Transitional Period and the Institutional Implications of Enlargement' April 1978, Bulletin Supplement 2/78, para 24.

[9] See 'The Institutional System of the Community — Restoring the Balance' Bulletin Supplement 3/82.

[10] See Sup. 3/82, 8.

[11] Namely to keep watch on the Commission and provide a democratic base for the Community's legislative process.

In 1985 the Commission produced a Draft Treaty establishing the European Union.[12] This was the most ambitious effort to achieve sweeping institutional and substantive reform of the European Communities. With three exceptions the proposed text confirmed the constitutional position under the EC Treaties. For the European Parliament it was proposed that it should approve the appointment of the Commission. Its President is to be appointed by the European Council; the President then selects the other members of the Commission. Finally the Commission obtains 'investiture' from Parliament. 'This procedure comes very close to the present selection system where Parliament has de facto no influence on the choice of members of the Commission, since the Governments are eager to preserve their prerogative in this respect'. 'Parliament's underlying assumption is that the President of the Commission, whose authority originates from the European Council, would seek an understanding with Parliament on the choice of his colleagues. This concept is likely to generate conflicts between the two rival institutions who both expect the Commission's loyalty. In any event it is at present difficult to imagine that a European Council would appoint somebody President of the Commission who has not before committed himself to a certain team'.[13]

In February 1984 the European Parliament adopted a Draft Treaty Establishing the EU.[14] Article 28 of this Draft Treaty lists the functions of the Commission:[15]

The Commission shall:

- define the guidelines for action by the Union in the Programme which it submits to the Parliament for its approval,
- introduce the measures required to initiate that action,
- have the right to propose draft laws and participate in the legislative procedure,
- issue the regulations needed to implement the laws and take the requisite implementing decisions,
- submit the draft budget,
- implement the budget,
- represent the Union in external relations in the instances laid down by this Treaty,
- ensure that this Treaty and the laws of the Union are applied, and
- exercise the other powers attributed to it by this Treaty.

[12] See R Bieber, J-P Jacqué, JHH Weiler, *An Ever Closer Union: A Critical Analysis of the Draft Treaty Establishing the EU* (European Communities, 1985).
[13] *Ibid*, 38.
[14] OJ 77/1984 p 33.
[15] Compare this list with those put forward in the Draft Constitution in 2003 and note the similarity.

In March 1985 the Dooge Committee produced a report for the European Council proposing a strengthening of the Commission.[16] The Commissions powers should be increased, 'in particular through greater delegation of executive responsibility in the context of Community policies'.

In an address to the European Parliament on 17 January 1990 Mr Jacques Delors, the then President of the Commission, posed three questions about the future Commission. These were (i) What kind of executive? (ii) What form of democratic control? (iii) What powers?[17] His answer to theses questions was that the Commission should be turned into a proper executive answerable for its actions to the democratic institution, namely the Parliament and 'the principle of subsidiarity will have to act as a constant counterweight to the natural tendency of the centre to accumulate power'.[18] The way to achieve this was seen to be by a strengthening of the powers of the European Parliament. Such views did not lend themselves to the agenda of the Member States or those who were concerned with the lack of a popular identification with the EU and the undemocratic structure of its institutions.[19]

Although this catalogue of reports and suggested reforms contains many discarded solutions to the problems of the Commission, there was no political will to take any firm action upon them at the time. The vision of Delors was given some practical realism by the problems encountered in getting the Maastricht Treaty (TEU) ratified in some Member States.[20] The Commission turned to other matters. 'Armed with its right of initiative, the Commission must remain a dynamic force for renewal, including in the new domains opened up by the Amsterdam Treaty'.[21] Human resources were recognised as being of crucial importance to the European public service. Therefore the Commission had introduced a far-reaching programme of reform that included the Sound and Efficient Management (SEM 2000) and Modernization of Administration and Personnel Policy (MAP 2000). As the Commission had had to take on a growing number of new tasks, it had not had time to give sufficient thought to the successive reorganisations which had been 'carried out hastily and without adequate preparation. The Commission decided that it needed to plan better and indicated that it intended to prepare for a reorganisation in time for the new Commission due to take office in 2000.

16 Ad Hoc Committee for Institutional Affairs Report to the European Council, March 1985.
17 Bulletin Supplement 1/90, 12.
18 *Ibid,* 13.
19 See 'Conceptualizing Legitimacy in a Contested Polity in T Banchoff and MP Smith, *Legitimacy and the EU: The Contested Polity* (London, Routledge, 1999).
20 For example the Danish and French referendum debates.
21 'Agenda 2000', Bulletin Supplement 5/97 pp 37 & 38.

However, things came to a head in the late 1990's when the Santer Commission resigned in 1999, six months before the scheduled end of its term of office. The low turnout of the electorate in European Parliamentary elections and the initial 'no vote' by the Irish to the Nice Treaty continued the pressure for reform. How was it to be achieved in time for the planned enlargement of the Union? The debate on the future of Europe provided an opportunity to deal with some of the recurring debates about how the EU was to be governed when it had twenty-five Member States.

In anticipation of the IGC at Nice in December 2000, the Commission decided to launch a debate on 'governance'.[22] What does this term mean? 'Governance means the rules, processes and behaviour that affect the way in which powers are exercised at European level, particularly as regards openness, participation, accountability, effectiveness and coherence'.[23] The White Paper went on to say that 'five principles underpin good governance and the changes proposed in this White Paper: openness, participation, accountability, effectiveness and coherence'.[24] Given the debates surrounding the Commission in the 1990's, the paragraph on 'accountability' seems very shallow by emphasising processes and the need for greater clarity and responsibility from Member States. What about the position of the Commission?

In 2000 the Commission launched a White Paper on Reforming the Commission.[25] 'A strong Europe needs a strong Commission.....Reform is, therefore, an essential pre-condition for realising our vision for Europe ...The Commission itself, therefore, needs to be independent, accountable, efficient and transparent, and guided by the highest standards of responsibility'.[26] How is this reform to be structured? 'In line with the tenets of good governance, the Reform is based on the following key principles: independence, responsibility, accountability, efficiency and transparency.'[27] Here the Commission clearly links its future with that of ensuring good governance within the EU. However, is it sufficient when the view of many is that the Commission is unaccountable in any democratic sense as the powers of the European Parliament remain weak in comparison with the Council? The paragraph on accountability states:

> Accountability goes hand in hand with the exercise of responsibility. The Commission is always accountable for its actions. This is expressed in different ways: for example, the Commission reports to the Council and the Parliament on its activities. But accountability goes further than that: exercising good stewardship of the variety of resources available to the Commission means

[22] 'European Governance — A White Paper' COM (2001) 428.
[23] *Ibid,* 8.
[24] *Ibid,* 10.
[25] 'Reforming the Commission, A White Paper — Part 1', COM (2000) 200.
[26] *Ibid,* 3.
[27] *Ibid,* 7.

> ensuring they are used efficiently and effectively. It applies within the Commission too, and relies on the culture of co-operation between staff and between departments which must be strengthened.[28]

This might be a clear statement but is it a little weak given the recent history of the Commission and the views expressed by the citizens of Europe? The report produced by the Commission on the responses to its White Paper on European Governance indicated that the public response was largely supportive.[29] But, 'Part of the public response regrets perceived limits to the White Paper's understanding of 'governance' which focuses predominantly on the effectiveness and efficiency of the EU decision-making system, while disregarding issues of democratic legitimacy and democratic deficit in European integration that are seen to be more important.[30] However, the main decisions were to be taken by the IGC and building upon the Laeken Declaration in December 2001, a Convention on the Future of Europe was established. This reported on 18 July 2003 by presenting a draft constitution to be considered by all the existing Member States and the ten who would join in May 2004. An IGC convened in October 2003 debated the constitution in order to come to an agreement in time for the European Parliamentary elections in May 2004. How do the proposals in the draft constitution affect the Commission? The main focus was on the size of the Commission and the role of the President. With more Member States there was a need to manage the number of Commissioners but also, as the reports dating from the 1970s mentioned above identified, their roles. All Member States were to be restricted to only one Commissioner but not all of these were to be 'active'!

A small college of fifteen European Commissioners are to form the Commission with voting rights but the remainder are to form a tier of non-voting Commissioners. The Commission is to be appointed so as to reflect satisfactorily the demographic and geographical range of all the Member States of the Union.[31] The President of the Commission powers are to be enhanced, following their election by the European Parliament. The Prodi expedient of getting the Commissioners to provide a letter undertaking to resign if requested to do so by the President of the Commission is no longer required as the draft constitution explicitly states that a European Commissioner or Commissioner shall resign if the President so requests. Does this mean that the suggested reforms chronicled above from the 1970s have been achieved? Are there any more reforms that can be made to the Commission?

[28] *Ibid*, 7and 8.
[29] Report from the Commission on European Governance, COM (2002) 705.
[30] Above note 25, 6. Emphasis added.
[31] When the High Authority was being established in the 1950's Monnet wanted a small group of five national representatives but the Benelux countries insisted that every member state should be represented. See N Nugent, *The European Commission* (London, Palgrave, 2001) 21.

However, the draft constitution also includes a more powerful President of the European Council, elected for a renewable term of two and a half years and whose roles include 'driving forward the work of the Council'. This did not please Romano Prodi, the President of the Commission. In a speech to the European Parliament he said that: 'Duplicating the executive would not bring the transparency and accountability EU citizens demand, and such an executive would escape Parliament's control'.[32] The views of the European Parliament Committee on Constitutional Affairs would seem to support this view when it reported that 'the role of the President (of the European Council) should be strictly limited to that of chair in order to avoid possible conflicts with the President of the Commission and not to endanger the latter's status'.[33] In another speech to the Parliament in September 2003, Prodi stated that a central problem is the future balance of powers between the Commission, the Council and the Parliament. 'The draft constitution proposes a Commission made up in a way that will ... make the institution representing the Unions' general interest less able to do its work effectively and credibly.[34] However, this ignores the accountability and legitimacy issues surrounding the Commission itself.[35] The accountability of the Commission to the European Parliament has not been strengthened, although that of individual European Commissioners to the President of the Commission has.

For Monnet and the authors of the founding treaties the legitimacy of the Community was to be secured through the outcomes of peace and prosperity. At that time democracy was a secondary consideration because it was felt that the best, or perhaps only, way of securing the desired peace and prosperity was by way of technocratic elite-led guidance.[36] Although it was acknowledging that without effective democratic control the legitimacy of the Community institutions would seem to be imperilled, this was secured because of the very gains which technology secured, notwithstanding the diminution which this could entail for the role or powers of elected bodies.[37] Those charged with the responsibility in the early 1950s to establish the High Authority, namely Monnet and the national governments, gave no thought to whether there should be a

[32] Ahead of the Thessaloniki European Council, speech to the European Parliament on 4 June 2003.
[33] See Draft EP Report 2003/0902 dated 5 August 2003.
[34] 'A Democratic Constitution for the European Union', speech by Romano Prodi to the EP on 3 September 2003.
[35] See the Committee of Independent Experts: First Report on Allegations of Fraud, Misman agement and Nepotism in the European Commission, 15 March 1999. See also TN Tomkins 'Responsibility and Resignation in the European Commission' (1999) *MLR* 744.
[36] P Craig and G De Búrca (eds), *The Evolution of EU Law* (Oxford, OUP, 1999) 7, 8.
[37] L Lindberg and S Scheingold, *Europe's Would-be Polity: Patterns of Change in the European Community* (London, Prentice-Hall, 1970) 268, 269.

democratic base for such an institution. The legitimacy of the High Authority was assumed to be derived from its establishment by democratic governments and the controls exerted by the Council of Ministers. Its position was to be as a non-partisan, technocratic, expert body.[38] The first President of the Commission, Professor Walter Hallstein, saw this as giving the wrong emphasis to the approach of the Commission — 'The members of the Commission are democrats, not technocrats'.[39]

But is it possible to have legitimacy by association? Can the Commission gain legitimacy through its relationship with the democratically elected European Parliament? The Commission is a complex 'multi-organisation',[40] but its views are based on the principle of 'governance' as against the government of the Union. The democratic system of government found in the Member States and familiar to their citizens, are absent from the White Paper on European Governance.[41] The attempts to deal with the democratic deficit of the EU has centred on increased powers to the European Parliament. At the same time the European Council President's role is to be strengthened. Where does this leave the Commission? Will it revert to its 'technocratic' model planned by Jean Monnet? The Commission's checklist for good governance did not include legitimacy. Was this because the Commission knew that they could not directly attain this? The responses to its White Paper on European Governance indicated the strong feelings that in a democratic Union, legitimacy was a very important factor. The role of the Commission in the development of the Union has been very great. 'Its achievements (the Commission's) have been substantial, providing much needed vision in the move towards a European integration which serves the interests of the Union and meets the aspirations of its citizens'.[42] But has its success in developing the Union diminished its future role?[43] Is it that the power of the Commission will in future be squeezed by the pressures from the President of the European Council, taking an intergovernmental perspective and a more demanding European Parliament that is looking for a Commission that reflects its own political profile. It maybe that new alliances will have to be made by the Commission, not so much with the European Parliament but with those small Member States who feel

[38] N Nugent, *The European Commission* (Palgrave, London, 2001) 21.

[39] See statement by Walter Hallstein to the European Parliament on 17 October 1962 reproduced in F von Geusau (ed), *European Unification in the Twentieth Century: A Treasury of Readings* (Tilburg, Vidya Publishers, 1998).

[40] L Cram, 'The European Commission as a Multi-Organization: Social Policy and IT Policy in the EU' (1994) (1:2) *Journal of European Public Policy* 195–217.

[41] 'Taking Governance Seriously: Response to the Commission White Paper on European Governance' by the LSE Study Group on European Administrative Law, March 2002.

[42] 'Reforming the Commission' A White Paper- Part 1, COM (2000) 200, 5.

[43] See the discussion by P Ludlow, *A Commentary on the EU: 2004 and Beyond* (CEPS, 2001).

that the Union of the future will be one where the large states will seek to dominate. The draft constitution produced by the Convention on the Future of Europe will ensure that the Commission will remain centre stage, but it is a stage that is becoming more crowded.

# 9

# *The Role of National Parliaments in the EU's New Constitutional Order*

ADAM CYGAN

## INTRODUCTION

THERE IS A degree of irony with national parliaments being given prominence within the work of the Convention. Working Group IV[1] examined how to integrate national institutions formally in to the EU decision-making process. Cynics could argue that national governments have suddenly woken up to the fact that domestic legislative chambers, from which they themselves are drawn, have a distinct role to play in an enlarged EU. It is politically expedient for incumbent governments to demonstrate domestically that national parliaments will not be irrelevant in an EU of twenty-five Member States. Accordingly, a role that they wish to assign to national parliaments is to bridge the democracy gap between the citizen and the EU Institutions. The irony in this arises from the fact that national parliaments with their traditions and principles of democratic scrutiny and accountability have remained a constant throughout a period when the supranational EU was developing in a less than democratic fashion. In this context why should domestic legislatures now be considered as integral to future EU integration?

At a time when the EU consisted of six, or even twelve Member States, and when their influence and contribution could arguably have been greater, national parliaments were viewed as peripheral to the development of European integration and their democratic features were largely ignored. Yet when the EU expands to twenty-five Member States, national parliaments are expected to contribute to spreading the message of a more

[1] Examining the role of National Parliaments in the EU. Proceedings are available at *http://european-convention.eu.int/doc_register.asp?lang=EN&Content=WGIV.*

democratic, accountable and transparent EU. Despite this expectation, national parliaments, such as the United Kingdom Parliament, have recognised they have a limited role in EU policy and decision-making and have tended to focus on two specific tasks.[2] This is recognition that within the EU context, Parliament fulfils a different role from the traditional one of supreme legislator.[3] Consequently the European Scrutiny Committees in the House of Commons and House of Lords ensure that firstly, effective scrutiny of executive action in the Council of Ministers occurs and that secondly, the application of the subsidiarity principle is subjected to stringent monitoring.

For those who have championed the cause of national parliaments the Convention outcomes may be considered a positive step. However, several practical issues still remain unresolved, and perhaps most importantly, whether national parliaments can actually bridge the feeling of disconnection that many citizens feel towards the EU?

## DEMOCRACY AND NATIONAL PARLIAMENTS IN THE EU

The two main sources of democratic legitimacy in the EU[4] are national parliaments and the directly elected European Parliament. For the overwhelming majority of EU citizens it is the executive, accountable to their national parliament that is the central element of democratic legitimacy. Yet this view does not correspond with the supranational character of the EU and the practical difficulties that exist when seeking effective accountability of ministers who take decisions in the Council of Ministers. Within a purely domestic context, a new legislative proposal will undergo rigorous review and require the assent of the national parliament. In contrast at EU level, government ministers act in a capacity without most of the procedural safeguards of a parliamentary democracy. Though the consent of the European Parliament is required under certain legislative procedures[5] the Council of Ministers may act independently when agreeing some legislative proposals. This Council autonomy is compounded by the lack of transparency and secrecy of Council proceedings.[6] While the Council is not collectively accountable, in a political rather than legislative sense to any other Institution, Council members remain, in theory at least, individually

[2] See HC 152 xxxiii-I (2001–02) *Democracy and Accountability in the EU and the Role of National Parliaments*.
[3] See A Cygan, *The United Kingdom Parliament and European Union Legislation*, (The Hague, Kluwer Law International, 1998), and A Cygan, *National Parliaments in an Integrated Europe: An Anglo-German Perspective* (The Hague, Kluwer Law International, 2001).
[4] Often referred to as the 'double democratic mandate'.
[5] Specifically under the co-decision procedure of Article 251 EC.
[6] HC 152-xxxiii-I, 2001–02, 18, para 20.

politically accountable to domestic legislatures. In practice, sufficient control over individual Council members remains difficult, given the lack of transparency and the collective nature of decision-making in Council.[7] Occasions have therefore arisen when it is impossible for a national parliament to know how, or why, their minister voted in the Council.

Direct accountability of the Council to the European Parliament is identified as the most appropriate way to remedy this deficit. In some respects, for example through the exercise of its veto over legislation introduced via the co-decision procedure, the European Parliament has more power than national parliaments. The ability to formally block legislation goes beyond the scope of what national parliaments can do. If we take the example of the House of Commons, then under existing arrangements, the European Scrutiny Committee merely scrutinises the Council's agreed common position on a legislative proposal, which occurs at an early stage of the co-decision procedure. This scrutiny will not automatically take in to account any amendments introduced by the European Parliament.[8] Furthermore, such scrutiny would not guarantee that the views of the House of Commons are represented in the final legislation, as other Member States may reject the view of the United Kingdom with regard to the amendments. With the use of qualified majority voting and restriction of the national veto through co-decision, the only effective control over legislation made via the co-decision procedure lies in the hands of the European Parliament.

Despite this pivotal position, there remains little popular support for the European Parliament amongst EU citizens. Turnout at elections is low by comparison with national parliamentary elections[9] and there is little knowledge of its activities among the electorate who tend to be motivated by national, rather than EU issues.[10] The effect of this is that political parties and individual MEPs are not held fully accountable for their actions and decisions at EU level.

Under existing Treaty arrangements national parliaments have no formal role in EU law making.[11] For the House of Commons, any contribution made via the scrutiny it conducts arises from domestic arrangements agreed with the government and established through parliamentary practice. In reality the European Scrutiny Committee is dependent upon the government to provide the necessary information and documentation required to carry out even this limited scrutiny. A failure to provide this

[7] Though a commitment to Transparency of the proceedings of the Institutions has been included in draft Art 36 of the Constitution and particularly with regard to access to documents.

[8] The second reading stage of the co-decision procedure.

[9] 49.8% at the 1999 elections, with the figure in the United Kingdom being 33%.

[10] HC 152-xxxiii-I, (2001–02) 16, para 15.

[11] Though national parliaments retain a major role in the implementation of EU legislation.

information ultimately prevents any effective review of the impact that the proposed legislation will have on the United Kingdom. The result therefore is a democratic deficit at the domestic level in addition to that which has already been identified at the EU level for many years.

## SCRUTINY AS SUBSTITUTE SOVEREIGNTY

For national parliaments the primary role is to scrutinise the activities of the government in the Council. Detailed and vigorous scrutiny of EU affairs can be considered as a cathartic exercise for national parliaments. Yet such scrutiny is no more than substitute sovereignty — the more scrutiny that occurs, the more this makes up for lost sovereignty and the less impotent national parliaments feel. In the House of Commons, the rigorous scrutiny process corresponds to the exacting scrutiny that occurs of domestic legislative proposals and may be viewed as the Chamber merely discharging its duty of ensuring executive accountability.

Despite its limitations, the requirement of executive scrutiny should not be understated. It is a crucial task, and remains the only direct control over the executive throughout the entire decision-making procedure. National parliaments do not want a new institution representing them at the EU level and performing this scrutiny function. It would also be inappropriate for any existing EU Institution to seek to influence or determine how national parliaments undertake their scrutiny activities. However, the difficulty for all domestic institutions lies in the fact that it is the progress of decision-making process itself that ultimately governs when, and to what extent, such scrutiny will occur. The present lack of co-ordination between the EU Institutions and domestic parliaments over issues such as the legislative timetable or providing sufficient time for effective scrutiny goes to the heart of the unease that exists in the relationship between them. For the House of Commons, these problems, with their roots firmly in the EU, must first be addressed before any progress can be made to resolve the wider problem of direct disconnection between the Institutions and EU citizens.[12]

Scrutiny is itself only effective if it is pre-legislative and based upon the *timely* provision of all available documentation. The primary means by which national parliaments seek to achieve this is through a scrutiny reserve that restrains the executive from voting on a legislative measure in Council, prior to completion of the scrutiny process. The objective of the scrutiny reserve, the precise scope and operation of which varies in the national parliamentary chambers, is to provide a minimum guarantee that some form of inquiry can take place prior to the final vote. The existence of such

[12] HC 63-xxiv, (2003–03) 7, para 8.

scrutiny reserves reinforces the argument that scrutiny procedures within domestic parliaments are substitute sovereignty. They seek to maximize executive accountability, they are primarily intended for domestic parliamentary consumption, and they operate independently of the Council timetable.

## GUARANTEEING EXECUTIVE ACCOUNTABILITY: THE IMPORTANCE OF THE SCRUTINY RESERVE

The two key issues for national parliaments when scrutinising EU legislative proposals are time and the prompt provision of the necessary information.[13] The overriding objective of the scrutiny process is to influence the minister *prior* to the Council adopting its definitive common position. A counter argument to affording more time to national parliaments for scrutiny is that this would slow down what is already a cumbersome and drawn out legislative process. Indeed, the reforms within the Treaty of Nice, together with statements in the Laeken Declaration[14] and the Commission's White Paper,[15] all seek to address the issue of how the co-decision procedure could be both simplified and hastened. By far the longest part of the decision-making process occurs when the Member States seek agreement on a common position towards a legislative proposal.[16] Under co-decision, the stages which follow the Council's adoption of a common position are clearly time limited.[17] Consequently, co-decision creates problems for scrutiny committees at both ends of the spectrum. First lengthy and complex political discussions are required by the Council to reach agreement. Secondly, there is a lack of the necessary time to conduct effective scrutiny when it most matters. The effect of this is the all too frequent agreement by the Council of badly drafted legislation.

Under current arrangements there are two mechanisms which seek to provide adequate time for scrutiny. These are the Protocol on the Role of National Parliaments in the EU[18] and the Scrutiny Reserve Resolution that operates within national legislatures.[19] The Scrutiny Reserve is the most

[13] HC 152-xxxiii-I, (2001–02), 22, para 33.
[14] Laeken Declaration on the Future of Europe, December 2001. Available at *http://www.europa.eu.int/futurum/documents/offtext/doc151201_en.htm*.
[15] COM(2001) 428, *European Governance — A White Paper*, 30.
[16] Recent examples of this difficulty include the seeking of agreement on proposals such as a Community patent, the Single European Sky, and gas and electricity liberalisation. All of these share the feature that they are of particular domestic importance and Member States were reluctant to relinquish total control to the EU.
[17] See Art 251 EC.
[18] Introduced by the Treaty of Amsterdam and replacing the Maastricht Treaty Declaration on National Parliaments.
[19] HC Debs, 17 November 1998 Col 779.

potent weapon in the armoury of the United Kingdom Scrutiny Committees because it can provide a brake on executive action. The inclusion of the Protocol on National Parliaments in the Amsterdam Treaty originated as a proposal from the House of Commons in 1995[20] and was pressed for very strongly by the UK government at the Amsterdam IGC. The objective of the Protocol is to provide specific time periods which are aimed at all actors involved in the legislative process, which, if followed, will provide national parliaments with adequate time to scrutinise legislative proposals. The Protocol provides the following:

> A six-week period shall elapse between a legislative proposal or a proposal for a measure to be adopted under Title VI of the Treaty on European Union being made available in all languages to the European Parliament and the Council by the Commission and the date when it is placed on the on a Council agenda for a decision .... *subject to exceptions on grounds of urgency* (emphasis added), the reasons for which shall be stated in the act or the common position.

There are a number of identifiable defects with the Protocol which undermine the ability of national parliaments to effectively influence the minister. First, the Protocol leaves the Council to decide which acts are of a legislative nature. As the Protocol only covers 'legislative proposals' it leaves discretion to the Council to apply nomenclature to a measure that can place it beyond the scope of the Protocol, yet the measure may still have a significant legal and political impact.

Second, the Protocol does not build in to the six week time period an additional (and probably shorter) period that can allow for scrutiny of a proposal which has been substantially revised by the European Parliament during second reading in the co-decision procedure. Third, the 'urgency' exceptions are vague and open to abuse because they only have to be justified *ex post*, by which stage it is too late for a national parliament to raise objections to the measure which has already been given approval. It is then only open to a Member State or EU Institution to challenge the measure before the Court. National parliaments cannot initiate such a challenge themselves.

National parliaments are most concerned with the fact that the Protocol does not apply to a measure which has been significantly amended in the course of co-decision, and particularly after the Council has agreed its common position. In the absence of any commitment in the Protocol, national parliaments will not automatically review an amended proposal. For the House of Commons with a long tradition of executive scrutiny, this is unacceptable. The revised measure could raise very specific questions of

[20] Known as the Select Committee on European Legislation. See HC 239, (1994–95), paras 65–68; HC 51-xxviii, (1995–6), paras 77–92; HC 36-xiii, (1996–97).

legal or political importance[21] which the original measure did not. Consequently, while the co-decision procedure seeks to remedy the democratic deficit at the EU level by giving the European Parliament an enhanced role, a democratic deficit in terms of ministerial accountability to parliament is created at the national level. The scrutiny of the original common position becomes irrelevant.

The Laeken Declaration stated that the European Union derives its legitimacy from the democratic values it projects, the aims and the powers and the instruments it possesses', but also that the 'European project derives its legitimacy from democratic, transparent and efficient institutions'. The Laeken Declaration further stated that 'national parliaments also contribute to the democratic legitimacy of the European project', a point repeated in the Declaration on the Future of Europe annexed to the Nice Treaty which stressed the need to examine their role in European integration.

These aspirations were the background to the establishment of Working Group IV. The Group's discussions fell into three distinct headings: the role of national parliaments in scrutinising governments; the role of national parliaments in monitoring the application of the subsidiarity principle; and the role and function of inter-parliamentary mechanisms and relations. A common feature of all three headings is the fact that for these tasks to be carried out successfully national parliaments require the timely provision of all relevant documentation. National parliaments rely on other actors, namely the Commission and their own governments to provide them with this information. A commitment to provide information promptly would therefore be an essential requirement of the new Protocol. These recommendations made by Working Group IV met with broad support from the Convention plenary in the debate on the final report.[22]

The implementation of Working Group IV's recommendations requires amendment of the Amsterdam Protocol. Given the defects with the Protocol outlined above this is a positive step. The amendments relate primarily to the provision of information intended for national parliaments concerning legislative proposals and other documents. In particular, Working Group IV recommended that 'Parliamentary scrutiny reserves should be given a clearer status in the Council's rules of procedure. Such reserves should furthermore have a specified time limit, so as not to unnecessarily block the decision procedure'.[23]

There are however problems with the inclusion of a specified time limit since the opportunity for scrutiny by national parliaments varies, depending

[21] Standing Order 119 which provides the Terms of Reference of the Committee requires it to consider the 'legal and political importance' of each document which is placed before the House of Commons.
[22] CONV 378/02.
[23] CONV 353/02, para 20.

on how promptly each government provides the necessary documentation which forms the basis of the scrutiny. The overriding problem is that amongst national parliaments there is no consistent approach as to how a scrutiny reserve should be used.[24] Different Member States have different political and legal priorities leading to the lack of a concerted approach to scrutiny of Council activities. Moreover some national parliaments make infrequent use of the scrutiny reserve, undermining the arguments of committees, such as that in the House of Commons, which have consistently tried to push the issue of the scrutiny reserve to the top of the IGC agenda.

For national parliaments, problems with effective scrutiny arise in three circumstances. Firstly when the minister votes in Council, prior to the completion of scrutiny by the appropriate committee, and secondly when the European Parliament proposes amendments. The third situation is when the Conciliation Committee agrees a joint text which is substantially different form the Council's common position.

Working Group IV considered the latter two issues very closely. The draft Protocol maintains the six-week period between Commission proposal and the document being placed on the agenda of the Council. However the European Scrutiny Committee in the House of Commons provided evidence to Working Group IV and noted that these first six weeks, are arguably the least important part of the legislative timetable.[25] The Conference of European Affairs Committees,[26] an informal body which comprises of all European affairs committees from parliaments in the Member States, proposed that there should be a minimum of 15 days between the final reading of the proposal by the Committee of Permanent Representatives (COREPER) and the Council formally taking a decision on it. This would be the minimum time required to allow for scrutiny of any amendments proposed by the European Parliament or arising out of the Conciliation Committee. In fact, the draft Protocol only provides for ten days.[27]

National scrutiny reserves do not operate in abstract from the political realities which govern decision-making in the Council. The reserves recognise that efficient decision-making will, on occasion, be required and the draft Protocol includes a clause allowing for decisions to be taken exceptionally on grounds of urgency.[28] In such circumstances the minister will breach the reserve but provide *ex post* justification of the decision to the national parliamentary chamber. In such circumstances,

[24] Of all 15 Member States, the United Kingdom, Denmark, Sweden and the Netherlands are the most frequent users of a scrutiny reserve, whereas Greece, Portugal and Spain apply a reserve most infrequently.
[25] HC 152-xxxiii-I, (2001–02) 24, para 38.
[26] This body is known by the acronym COSAC.
[27] Paragraph 4 of the draft Protocol on the Role of National Parliaments in the European Union.
[28] *Ibid*.

the House of Commons will be looking for a clear explanation of how the measure benefits the United Kingdom, and that any further delay, to its acquiescence, would fundamentally undermine the interests of the United Kingdom.[29]

What are the options for resolving these problems? Ideally the most comprehensive solution would be to include a form of scrutiny reserve within the Treaty to create a European Scrutiny Reserve and build national parliaments formally within the EU legislative system. This would provide a clear timetable and create a uniform set of deadlines which all Member States would adhere to. This solution however, is unlikely because it would be too prescriptive. Therefore, the Commission, Council, national governments and the national scrutiny committees must jointly develop practices and procedures to provide the necessary framework for a minimum standard of scrutiny within all Member States. The heightened awareness of the need to involve national parliaments more directly, ariseing out of the Convention and the draft Protocol may aid in this, particularly amongst the EU institutions and national governments. There are also several other developments which have the potential to improve both the frequency and quality of scrutiny within all national parliaments. These include[30] *inter alia*, greater transparency by providing a more accurate Council agenda within a minimum of fourteen days before the meeting, better planning of the legislative process to avoid 'log jams' through several complicated measures being presented to scrutiny committees simultaneously, and the delivery of prompt texts by the Commission. Perhaps the most controversial proposal requires an end to the current system of six-monthly Presidencies. On this point some progress has been made with a proposal for the appointment of a continuous President of the Council.

The current system of rotating Presidencies, though giving each Member State an opportunity to set the legislative agenda, is both inefficient and incompatible with the domestic parliamentary timetable. The Presidencies produce an artificial peak of activity towards the end of each six-month period as Presidencies apply political pressure to ensure agreement in priority policy areas. National scrutiny committees have identified this as regularly compromising the effective scrutiny of legislative proposals.

The most radical solution to these problems would be for the Council's rules to require that ministers had prior domestic parliamentary clearance before agreeing to a proposal. This would broadly mirror the rules of the

[29] This would include situations where the measure is one on which there is, in principle, unanimous agreement within the House of Commons and if the minister did not agree it could leave the United Kingdom as part of a blocking minority even though it supports the measure. Alternatively, applying the Reserve could lead to the minister not being excluded from any compromise agreement that is reached with the European Parliament with respect to any amendments proposed by that institution.

[30] HC 152-xxxiii-I, (2001–02) 25, para 41.

Danish *Folketing* where the minister is mandated to vote in a particular way which cannot be departed from without the prior consent of the European Committee. However, such a proposal is unlikely to ever be realised. Yet if parliamentary democracy remains a fundamental EU principle[31] a clear implication is that national parliaments should be able to scrutinise the activities of their ministers in the Council. The desirability of Treaty amendments to cement the position of national parliaments in EU affairs has already been alluded to. This would guarantee a legally enforceable role for domestic legislatures. However, such a move would not be without drawbacks. Most notably, there is the potential problem of delay arsing through waiting for all national legislatures to complete their scrutiny. Yet this may be preferable to the current system which marginalizes the voice of democratically elected legislatures.

One alternative solution could be to elevate the role of COSAC to create a forum for scrutiny at the European level through which Member States could articulate shared concerns with regard to a legislative proposal, for example relating to questions of subsidiarity.[32] This is unpopular among domestic scrutiny committees because it elevates what they consider to be a task for domestic legislatures to the European level. There is little appetite for the creation of a European scrutiny body which may be viewed as a form of EU revising chamber. This would not meet the primary concern of national committees, which remains effective ministerial accountability to their national parliament. This desire for effective domestic scrutiny does though lead to another specific and related issue. For effective scrutiny national parliaments need to know what they can actually influence, and crucially this requires an understanding of how the subsidiarity principle will operate, and what role domestic institutions will play to ensure that subsidiarity is observed.

## MONITORING THE APPLICATION OF THE SUBSIDIARITY PRINCIPLE: WHOSE ROLE IS IT ANYWAY?

Article 8 (3)[33] of the draft Constitution defines subsidiarity in the following way:

> … in areas which do not fall within its exclusive competence, the Union shall act only if and insofar as the objectives of the intended action cannot be sufficiently achieved by the Member States, but can rather, by reason of the scale or effects of the proposed action be better achieved at Union level.

[31] Art 6 TEU.
[32] The European Union Committee in the House of Lords considered such a forum during its inquiry in to the desirability of a second legislative chamber in the EU. See HL 48, 2001–02, *A Second Parliamentary Chamber for the EU: An Unreal Solution to Some Real Problems*.
[33] This comes within the Fundamental principles of the Union in the draft Constitution.

Article 8 (3) is explicit on the point that the principle of subsidiarity only applies 'in areas which do not fall within the Union's exclusive competence'. This is intended to address what some commentators have referred to as the 'creeping competences'[34] of the EU through use of soft law mechanisms, the open method of co-ordination, the extension of existing Treaty bases to justify action[35] or even Article 308 EC to justify action which appears to be legally questionable from a competence perspective.

Articles 9 (2) and (3) address the application of the subsidiarity principle. Article 9 (2) explicitly mentions that the Protocol[36] is intended to 'enable national parliaments to ensure compliance with the principle of subsidiarity'. This monitoring function provided for in the draft Constitution does raise one additional question. Should national parliaments be able to go beyond the political monitoring which the draft provides for and be able to challenge measures for compliance before the Court of Justice? This question will be returned to below.

The Convention recommended that national parliaments should take greater responsibility for monitoring the application of the subsidiarity principle. Working Group I[37] on Subsidiarity was established to complement the general discussion within the European Union on the delimitation of competence between the European Union and the Member States referred to in the Nice and Laeken Declarations on the future of the EU. Working Group I was therefore mandated to consider:[38]

— how compliance with the subsidiarity principle can be monitored in the most effective manner;
— whether a procedure for monitoring the application of the subsidiarity principle should be established;
— whether such a procedure should be of a political and/or legal nature; and
— the criteria established in the Protocol on the application of subsidiarity and proportionality needed to be extended to reflect its conclusions.

Monitoring of subsidiarity is undoubtedly a political concept and should be carried out by the institutions which participate in the European legislative process. The Amsterdam Protocol on subsidiarity requires Commission

[34] See D Hodson and I Maher, 'The Open Method as a New Mode of Governance: The Case of Economic Policy Coordination' (2001) 39 *Journal of Common Market Studies* 719.
[35] For example, Art 95 EC and Case C-376/98 *Germany v European Parliament and Council (Tobacco Advertising Directive)* [2000] ECR I-8419.
[36] Discussed in more detail below at p 166.
[37] CONV 71/02.
[38] *Ibid.*

justification of legislative proposals with regard to subsidiarity. The Commission is also under an annual obligation to submit to the Council a report on the application of the subsidiarity principle. Additionally national parliaments may provide political monitoring through their domestic scrutiny arrangements and the Court of Justice ultimately can conduct *ex post* review of the application of subsidiarity.

The conclusions of Working Group I suggest a shift in emphasis with regard to monitoring subsidiarity with the pendulum appearing to have swung in favour of national parliaments. The Working Group made three significant proposals with regard to monitoring subsidiarity. These were:

— reinforcing application of the principle during the legislative process
— establishing an early warning system for national parliaments to reinforce monitoring compliance
— broadening the right of referral to the Court of Justice to national parliaments and the Committee of the Regions.

Working Group I concluded that monitoring subsidiarity was a shared responsibility between the Commission, European Parliament and national parliaments.[39] However, the Report went further and singled out national parliaments as having 'an essential role to play'[40] which removed the need for establishing any specific committees at the EU level to monitor application of subsidiarity. The question which this raises is why are national parliaments placed at the centre of monitoring application of the subsidiarity principle?

There are three identifiable reasons for this conclusion. Firstly, EU institutions are not in practice keen on applying the subsidiarity principle. After all, the principle defines vertical power sharing and is used to determine how competences should be divided between different levels of governance. As conventionally understood, subsidiarity requires that decisions should be taken at the lowest level consistent with effective action. For integrationist EU institutions, a principle which acknowledges that national action may be preferable to EU regulation, could be perceived as undermining integration and accordingly have limited application to the decision-making process.

Secondly, national parliaments do not have an inherent institutional interest in transferring powers to the EU level. Thirdly, because they are generally considered closer to the people than any EU institution, national

[39] Working Group I Report, para 22.
[40] *Ibid*, para 23.

parliaments are more likely to reflect the views of the citizen on such matters.[41] Taken together these latter two reasons go to the heart of the concerns raised in the Commission's White Paper and Laeken Declaration that there is a feeling of disconnection which exists in the relationship between citizens and the EU. If national parliaments are to be placed in this pivotal position vis-à-vis monitoring subsidiarity, would this lead to a greater acceptance of EU action by citizens? After all, if national parliaments have accepted the legislation as being non-intrusive and not prescriptive, would it not follow that the citizens which they represent will adopt the same attitude? This is a big assumption to make and one which the conclusions of the Convention or the draft Treaty do not necessarily justify. Such an assumption fails to recognise that the feeling of disconnection and mistrust of decision-making institutions exists simultaneously with the political systems of several Member States. Effective monitoring of subsidiarity by national parliaments is undoubtedly part of the answer to addressing these problems. However what will in most cases be a mechanical and procedural exercise, cannot provide a comprehensive answer to the much wider issues of accountability of decision-makers and participation by citizens more directly in EU decision-making.

Working Group I recommended several amendments to the Subsidiarity Protocol that are designed to address the lack of national parliamentary involvement. The most significant proposal was for the creation of an 'early warning system' that would allow national parliaments to issue a reasoned opinion regarding the compliance of each proposal with subsidiarity in a theoretical rather than a substantial manner. Such reasoned opinions would be sent to the Presidents of the European Parliament, Council and Commission. In its final Report, Working Group I concluded that if negative opinions form one third of national parliaments are delivered, the Commission would re-examine the proposal with the options of maintaining, amending, or withdrawing it completely. The Commission would retain an ultimate discretion to override national parliamentary opinion by re-submitting the proposal. This procedure has been termed the 'yellow card',[42] and if the football analogy is maintained, then could the proposal be said to promote national parliaments to the Premier League of decision-making?

Such an early warning system could allow national parliaments greater involvement in the European legislative process without lengthening the process itself, as they would be obliged to provide any opinions within the existing six-week period between proposal and inclusion on the Council's agenda. This at least addresses an oft-cited justification for not bringing

[41] *Ibid*, para 24.
[42] Described so by Gisella Stuart MP to the House of Lords Select Committee on the European Union HL 70 (2002–03) *The Future of Europe: National Parliaments and Subsidiarity — The Proposed Protocols*, QQ 6–10.

national parliaments in to the decision-making loop — that any formal role for them would stagnate further an already lengthy decision-making process. But does this proposal go far enough?

## NATIONAL PARLIAMENTS IN THE EU'S NEW CONSTITUTION

The early warning mechanism described above has been included in the Praesidium's draft Protocol on the application of the principles of subsidiarity and proportionality. The draft provides that if one third of national parliaments send reasoned opinions to the Commission indicating that a legislative proposal does not comply with the principle of subsidiarity, the Commission shall review its proposal.[43] This is undoubtedly progress for national parliaments and is to be welcomed.

The proposed Protocol, however, is not to be considered as a panacea and there remain weaknesses with what has been proposed. Firstly, the Protocol does not cover the closely related principle of proportionality as the Praesidium was of the opinion that this is a legal rather than a political concept.[44] This is a rather narrow interpretation, as proportionality encompasses not only the idea of which legal instrument is to be used, but also concerns the extent of action taken by the Community.[45] Therefore, although the question of whether a legislative measure is proportionate or not is capable of analysis by the Court, it also has a substantial element of political judgment and should be brought within the early warning system.

Secondly, the draft is weak with regard to the duty placed on the Commission to give reasons to amend or maintain its proposals. The draft merely states[46] that in such circumstances 'the Commission is required to give reasons for its decision'. It would place the Commission under greater pressure not to abuse this power if it were required to give *detailed* reasons for why it had rejected the reasoned opinions of the national parliaments.

Thirdly, the draft does not provide for national parliaments to make reasoned opinions following the convening of a Conciliation Committee in respect of compliance of the Council's new common position, or the European Parliament's amendments, with the principles of subsidiarity and proportionality. It will be remembered that this lack of scrutiny by

[43] The threshold is proposed as one quarter in the case of proposals relating to the area of freedom, security and justice under Art III-160.
[44] CONV 724/03, annex 2, 145.
[45] The Amsterdam Protocol on Proportionality states that 'any action by the Community shall not go beyond what is necessary to achieve the objectives of the Treaty'.
[46] Para 6 of the draft Protocol.

national parliaments after the Conciliation Committee has agreed a joint text was highlighted as a weakness of the current scrutiny arrangements. It is also evident that this inability to review the measure has more substantive implications with regard to benchmarking the amended proposal against the principles of subsidiarity and proportionality. Scrutiny arrangements in national parliaments and the task of monitoring the application of the subsidiarity principle by national parliaments are two sides of the same coin. They are inextricably linked, implying that a weakness in the execution of one task will inevitably lead to a weakness in the execution of the other.

Finally, the draft leaves a presumption of power in the hands of the Commission. In addition to the yellow card mechanism a 'red card' mechanism was proposed to Working Group I. This proposed that if two-thirds of national parliaments present reasoned opinions which object to a legislative proposal on grounds of subsidiarity, then the Commission will be obliged to withdraw the proposal.[47] Though unlikely to be used regularly (simply because of the inability to obtain agreement amongst two-thirds of national parliaments) such a proposal could have important symbolic value that national parliaments are really at the heart of the decision-making process. Furthermore, if we remember the Laeken Declaration and the need to bridge the gap with the citizen then such a proposal would be an ideal starting point. Withdrawal by the Commission of a proposal which national parliaments have rejected on behalf of their electorate, would, perhaps, be the most explicit way in which the Commission directly engages with EU citizens. However, the exclusion of the red card mechanism from the draft leads to a conclusion that the Commission will remain the final political arbiter of which legislation is compatible with subsidiarity principles and whether to continue with the proposal. Herein lies the weakness of the draft for national parliaments. It recognises, as did the Working Group, that subsidiarity is a political principle, but concedes implicitly that further integration requires EU institutions to have supremacy of political decision-making in the same way that the draft Constitution states that EU law is supreme over national legislation.[48]

Should there be an additional mechanism for monitoring subsidiarity available to national parliaments? It was submitted to Working Group I that any national parliament should be allowed to refer a matter to the Court of Justice for violation of the subsidiarity Principle.[49] The draft Protocol however does not reflect this. The proposed Protocol instead provides that 'the Court of Justice shall have jurisdiction to hear actions brought by the Member States on the grounds of infringement of the principle of

[47] CONV 540/03.
[48] Art 9 (1) draft Constitution.
[49] CONV 540/03.

subsidiarity, where appropriate at the request of their national parliaments in accordance with their respective constitutional rules'. At first sight this looks impressive but in fact the provision represents no substantive development from existing procedures. The Court does not require any additional jurisdiction to rule on subsidiarity questions at the behest of a Member State. The Court is competent to hear such actions and has done so on at least one occasion.[50] Furthermore, there is nothing to stop a Member State having an arrangement whereby it will bring an action before the Court where its parliament requests it to do so. This could occur in situations where the national parliament believes that the Treaty does not give competence to legislate on the subject matter.[51]

The objective of granting national parliaments the opportunity to refer alleged violations of subsidiarity to the Court should be viewed as enabling those with legitimate interests to influence and hold to account the EU's legislative institutions. Any action would come at an early stage of the legislative procedure and therefore should not unduly delay the legislative process. As national parliaments would have six weeks to issue their reasoned opinions any action would be likely to commence within this period. Giving national parliaments such a voice at this early stage of the legislative process enhances the democratic legitimacy of the procedure. In addition to giving a reasoned opinion that a proposal is not compatible with subsidiarity, national parliaments would be able to challenge the Commission's view if it ultimately chooses to ignore such a reasoned opinion.

If the early warning system is to be effective then there must be real judicial enforcement of subsidiarity. However, the Protocol provides that any challenge may only be initiated by the Member State which will require that the executive commence the action. This will not always be possible as the executive which is being asked to commence the action is also a member of the Council. Consequently it may not share the concerns of legality which are held by the national parliament.[52] If national parliaments are to be brought directly within the legislative loop, it is essential that the influence and participation is real and complete requiring that both political and judicial involvement in monitoring subsidiarity are available to them.

## CONCLUSION

The discussion demonstrates that domestic legislatures have a central role to play within the supranational EU, though not as legislators. Rather than

[50] Case C-84/94 *United Kingdom v Council* [1996] ECR I-5755.
[51] This is what occurred in the *Tobacco Advertising* Case.
[52] For example, if the German *Bundestag* and government had disagreed about the legality of the Tobacco Advertising Directive, then under the draft Protocol, the *Bundestag* would not be able to initiate the judicial proceedings.

competing with EU institutions for political power, which they are unlikely to attain under the Treaty, their primary contribution should be to embed in the EU the principles of democracy and accountability upon which domestic legislatures are built. Theses include, promoting political accountability of the Institutions especially with regard to the subsidiarity principle, encouraging participation by civil society in the EU policy process and monitoring the effects of EU legislative action.

As has been suggested, there is a view that national parliaments can also bridge the disconnection gap that many citizens feel with the EU. In the short term at least this task is for the EU Institutions. Though in time national parliaments may wish to take on this role more directly, for the present their focus should remain on utilising domestic scrutiny procedures to ensure effective political accountability of the Council of Ministers. Practically, the Constitution will require changes to internal parliamentary procedures, perhaps with national parliaments adopting an additional role more akin to a lobbyist in EU affairs. Ultimately national parliaments will have little influence over the final Constitution, and perhaps all they can hope for is that this Constitution will provide the impetus for EU institutions to adopt their principles of accountability and democracy to address the residual feeling of disconnection.

# 10

# *For Substantive Constitutionalism in the European Union*

BERNARD RYAN*

## INTRODUCTION

THE RECONCILIATION OF constitutional with substantive considerations is among the peculiar challenges thrown up by the field of EU law. One question is whether thinking about substantive law can accept the legitimacy of constitutional limits to substantive action, even when those limits imply something other than the replication at the EU level of the law in a given field in the Member States. Constitutionalist thought too is faced with new questions in the EU context. If the pursuit at the EU level of substantive policies in a range of fields defies traditional constitutional concepts — organised around the separateness of sovereign states — can those concepts then suffice for analysis of the EU level?

This paper sets out to argue for the integration of substantive and constitutional considerations in the EU context. More specifically, it outlines a perspective on EU constitutionalism which starts from the fact that the Member States have established the EU for the achievement of certain substantive purposes. That starting-point makes it possible both to recognise that the Member States are basic to normative analysis concerning the EU, but yet to move away from taking the treaties as the last word on the EU constitutional order. Instead, it is argued that EU constitutional thinking can proceed from speculation as to the outcomes of idealised negotiations between potential Member States, in which they are imagined to seek a rational consensus as to the EU's constitutional design. This approach is offered as a framework for addressing 'metaconstitutional'

* I would like to thank Anneli Albi, John Fitzpatrick, Harm Schepel and Neil Walker for their comments on the paper in draft. They should not however be thought implicated in the argument developed in the paper.

questions concerning the EU: how are propositions as to the constitutional design of the EU to be evaluated?[1]

The argument of the paper is developed as follows. The first section defends the claim that, as things stand, the Member States ought to be treated as having normative priority over the EU level on grounds of authorship and/or democracy. If the Member States have priority, then a key implication is that the EU constitutional order ought to be justifiable in terms of the consent of the Member States. The second section therefore considers the most obvious means for the identification of the states' consent, which is the explicit mandate which they have given the EU through the treaties. It is argued that an exclusive focus on the treaty texts is problematic, however, both because of the difficulty in dealing with detail within the treaties, and because of the constraining effects of the requirement of unanimity upon treaty outcomes. For that reason, a third section outlines an alternative approach, which proceeds from member state consent to the EU's underlying purposes and which looks to the hypothetical outcomes of negotiations between potential Member States. In the final section, the possible outcomes of such idealised negotiations are considered, both in general terms and by reference to examples drawn from controversies within EU constitutionalism.

## THE NORMATIVE CLAIMS OF THE MEMBER STATES

The claim that the EU's tasks and activities should be integrated into normative thinking about its constitutional framework can be justified in a number of ways. One straightforward route would be to develop the idea that the EU is a multi-level polity, within which the EU level has a significant degree of autonomy from the Member States.[2] The result has been characterised by MacCormick as a situation of 'post-sovereignty', with 'no longer absolutely sovereign states interacting with and through a Community with an independent legal order of its own.'[3] That

[1] The term 'metaconstitutional' is taken from N Walker, 'Flexibility within a Metaconstitutional Frame: Reflections on the Future of Legal Authority in Europe' in G de Búrca and J Scott (eds), *Constitutional Change in the EU: From Uniformity to Flexibility?* (Oxford, Hart, 2000). In his account, 'metaconstitutional rules — or norms or axioms — are rules about constitutional rules' (p 15). Walker borrowed the term from L Alexander, 'Introduction' to L Alexander (ed), *Constitutionalism: Philosophical Foundations* (Cambridge, CUP, 1998), for whom it means 'agreed-upon norms' about the constitution (p 2). The term is used more loosely here to refer to principles by which constitutional rules are evaluated, without having to be rules, or to have been agreed upon.

[2] See G Marks, L Hooghe and K Blank, 'European Integration from the 1980s: State-Centric v Multi-Level Governance' (1996) 34 *Journal of Common Market Studies* 341.

[3] N MacCormick, 'Democracy and Subsidiarity in the European Commonwealth', Ch 9 of *Questioning Sovereignty: Law, State and Nation in the European Commonwealth* (Oxford, OUP, 1999), p 142.

interpretation of the EU system might be thought especially apt to sustain the view that the EU constitutional order should play close attention to the substance of EU's tasks and activities. If the EU level is to a significant extent autonomous of its Member States, then its autonomy is likely to consist above all in the pursuit of certain tasks and activities. It might be thought to follow that its constitutional order should be concerned above all with the manner in which those tasks and activities are realised.

This paper charts a different course, however. Its premise is that the Member States continue to be central to normative inquiry within the EU. The implication of that premise is that the EU constitutional order ought to be justifiable in terms of the Member States themselves. This approach is potentially more restrictive than one which assumes the autonomy of the EU from its Member States. Nevertheless, the paper as a whole seeks to show that, even with a starting-point of respect for the Member States, the conclusion that the EU's purposes should be central to its constitutional order can be sustained.

A focus on authorship offers one basis for insisting upon the normative priority of the Member States. On that view, the EU system is the common project of the Member States, and in practice remains dominated by them.[4] The EU has in particular been established and maintained by various actions of the Member States, including the negotiation of EU treaties, the making of budgetary contributions, the giving effect to EU obligations at the national level, and the defence of EU membership and actions in the domestic political arena. In constitutional terms, the EU is to be understood as the recipient of a transfer of sovereign powers from the Member States. That transfer of sovereignty is moreover a continuing one, in that the states remain free both to modify the extent of the powers which have been transferred, and to leave the EU altogether.

Respect for democracy offers an alternative route to the justification of the normative priority of states. Concern for democracy can support an analysis based on authorship. On that view, it is because the states' decisions to establish and maintain the EU are democratically rooted that their authorship of the EU commands respect. In addition — whatever view one takes of the relevance of authorship — it is hard to dispute that decision-making at the member state level has significantly greater democratic legitimacy than decision-making at the EU level. This greater democratic legitimacy of the state level is partly due to the much stronger

[4] For a classic interpretation of the EU in terms of intergovernmentalism see A Moravcsik, *The Choice for Europe* (Ithaca, Cornell UP, 1998), or the earlier A Moravcsik, 'Preferences and Power in the European Community: A Liberal Intergovernmentalist Approach' (1993) 31 *Journal of Common Market Studies* 473.

political culture there. To quote from a report written for the Commission in preparation for its 2001 White Paper on Governance,

> Despite well-established supranational political institutions, citizens have little in the way of a European political consciousness and are not given much encouragement nor facility to engage in a consistent public dialogue with these institutions. This is a critical weakness in our system of governance. Democracy is synonymous with dialogue, debate and belonging to a political community ... Our Member States' communities have developed over centuries rather than decades and are characterised by a shared political culture that shapes the way opinions are formed, expressed and debated.[5]

At the same time, the populations of the EU Member States continue to identify themselves with their Member States first and the EU level either second, or not at all.[6] The implication is that there is insufficient public identification with the EU to permit decision-making at that level to be favoured.

To claim that the member state level is to be preferred on democratic grounds is not to suggest that there is 'no demos' in the sense of a complete *absence* of identification between EU citizens, or by the EU population with decision-making at the EU level. Still less is it to argue that identification among the EU population or with the EU level cannot develop further over time. Indeed, the analysis here is consistent with proposals for the strengthening of the public sphere at the EU level, whether through international media, transnational political organisation, etc. It can also provide a basis for supporting a version of 'constitutional patriotism' within the EU — that an explicit constitutional order for the EU, embodied in a constitutional text, is desirable because it might itself promote identification.[7] If decisions anyway come to be taken at the EU level, measures which enhance public participation in EU-level decision-making, and identification with the EU level, are desirable on democratic grounds. But the acceptance of such initiatives does not affect the original conclusion: that, as things stand, concern for democratic legitimacy implies a clear preference for action at the member state level.

[5] European Commission, *Report of Working Group on Broadening and Enriching the Public Debate on European Matters* (2001), p 7. The report can be found at: *http://europa.eu.int/comm/governance/areas/group1/report_en.pdf*.

[6] See P Kraus, 'Cultural Pluralism and European Polity-Building' (2003) 41 *Journal of Common Market Studies* 665, pp 681–82.

[7] On the potential 'catalytic effect of a constitution', see J Habermas, 'Why Europe Needs a Constitution' (2001) 11 *New Left Review* 5, pp 16–17. In his assessment, this effect is bound up with a Europe-wide referendum, as that would provide 'a unique opportunity of transnational communication.' While such a referendum would be inconsistent with the preference for state-level decision-making argued for here, an EU constitutional text arguably has 'catalytic' potential even in its absence.

Once it is accepted that states are entitled to priority on democratic grounds — whether because of respect for state authorship, or independently of it — the relationship between the Member States and the EU becomes the critical question of EU constitutionalism. One implication of respect for Member States is that the *content* of the EU constitutional framework should favour state-level decision-making over EU-level decision-making where there is a choice between them. But the greater democratic claims of the Member States also imply a more fundamental proposition — that the constitutional framework should itself be justifiable in terms of the *consent* of the Member States. That follows readily from the proposition that the states are the EU's authors: if the EU is understood to be the common project of the Member States, then its constitutional arrangements ought to be justifiable in terms of the decisions of those states. But concern for the consent of Member States is also consistent with the line of argument which says that the state level is to be preferred solely on grounds of democratic legitimacy. If one assumes that the EU constitutional order must have democratic approval, then the greater legitimacy of the state level implies that it is there that such approval should be sought.

## THE INADEQUACY OF THE TREATIES

If the EU constitutional framework must be referable to the consent of the Member States, then the most straightforward way to apply that requirement is to conceive of consent in a formal manner. That was the approach adopted for example by the German Constitutional Court in its Maastricht decision, when it spoke of the EU as 'a federation of States, the common authority of which is derived from the member-States', and of the Member States as the '"Masters of the Treaties."'[8] Hartley too has relied on this approach in criticising the activism of the Court of Justice. In his assessment, 'the argument is that when the Member States signed the Treaties they agreed to transfer only certain powers to the Community; if the Court ... takes additional powers for itself or for the Community in general, it could be regarded as taking more from the Member States than they agreed to give, a justifiable cause for complaint.'[9]

The essence of a formal approach to consent is that the text of the treaties which the Member States have actually entered into is the only valid source of the rules governing their co-operation. The EU and its institutions

[8] This is the English translation in *Brunner* [1994] 1 CMLR 57, para 55. The original is at BVerfG 89, 155, 190.
[9] T Hartley, *Constitutional Problems of the European Union* (Oxford, Hart, 1999), pp 43–44.

are understood to be recipients of a mandate from the Member States through the EU treaties. The treaties provide for the powers of the EU, for the method of their exercise, and for any procedural or substantive limits to those powers. Where the treaties have provided for a given arrangement, the states are presumed to have consented to it. Conversely, when the treaties are silent on a given matter, then the Member States are taken *not* to have approved of it.

The result of a formal approach to state consent is, however, a kind of anti-metaconstitutionalism. That is because there is no obvious role within such an approach for criticism of the actual constitutional order. It is plainly possible to imagine criticism of the outcomes of their treaties on various grounds, including a lack of democracy or transparency, a failure to respect fundamental rights, ineffectiveness, etc. A formal approach can permit such critiques only as alternative perspectives on how the EU framework *might be*. But, within such an approach, it is essentially incoherent to argue that the Member States *ought to have* entered into the EU treaties on these different terms. There is no higher standard than the decisions actually taken by the treaty authors themselves.

It is critical therefore that there are grounds for criticism of the treaty-making mechanism which do not fail to give priority to the Member States. One such criticism concerns the inadequacy of intergovernmental conferences as a mechanism for dealing with questions of treaty detail. If proof were needed, it is to be found in the manifest failings in the agreements reached in the last two rounds of treaty amendment. After the Amsterdam summit in 1997, the Member States were faced 'on several points' with the 'delicate (and occasionally acrimonious) task of reaching subsequent agreement on what the European Council had actually agreed.'[10] Chief among these was the question of whether British and Irish participation in the Schengen *acquis* would require the unanimous approval of the other states — on which there were 'genuinely held differences of interpretation of what had been agreed.'[11] Then, the Nice summit produced a treaty which provided for greater representation in the European Parliament for Belgium, Greece and Portugal than for the Czech Republic and Hungary, despite their equivalent populations.[12] The point of these examples is though much broader than the examples themselves: that the

[10] B McDonagh, *Original Sin in a Brave New World: An Account of the Negotiation of the Treaty of Amsterdam* (Dublin, Institute of European Affairs, 1998), p 194.
[11] *Ibid*, 195. The Treaty of Amsterdam eventually required the unanimous approval of the other states: see Art 4 of the Schengen Protocol.
[12] See Art 2 of the Protocol on Enlargement and Table 1 of Declaration 20 on Enlargement in the official text of the Treaty of Nice, OJ 2001 C 80/1. The discrepancy was removed by Art 11 of the 2003 Act of Accession (OJ 2003 L 236/33), which allocated 24 seats to each of the five states.

participants in an intergovernmental conference simply cannot be said to have arrived at a considered view of the many matters of detail with which they are confronted.

A second, more fundamental, difficulty with the EU treaty-making mechanism is the need for unanimous agreement of the Member States to treaty changes. What is problematic in this regard is not so much that the EU system requires that the states which wish to participate in a *given* EU treaty must agree to it: that is a straightforward method of ensuring state consent to their international obligations. Rather, the difficulty with unanimity lies in the cumulative effects of the requirement that all the existing Member States must agree to all future amendments. The history of the EU shows that over time the preferences of the Member States, and the objective circumstances in which they find themselves, have undergone profound change. But, over time, the effect of the strong requirement of unanimity within the EU is to make it difficult to amend the treaties in order to adapt to those changes. Many Member States might have come to prefer that their co-operation be organised in a quite different manner to that provided for by the treaties. They might even have been able to agree to such co-operation among themselves had they now been negotiating afresh on the terms of their co-operation. Yet, faced with the requirement of securing the consent of all existing Member States, they may be unable to reach anything like the kind of settlement they would have obtained if given a free hand.

It might be thought that responses to these criticisms are possible within a formal approach. One such counter-argument is that it is open to the Member States to address these problems concerning detail and unanimity by agreeing to a different set of rules as regards treaty amendment. The convention method which was used to prepare the text of the draft EU constitutional treaty was certainly an improvement as regards the management of detail,[13] and there is for example a proposal in the draft EU Constitution for a legal requirement that a convention be convened in future in order to draft treaty amendments.[14] It would be possible to go further and adopt one of the recent proposals which would permit less-than-unanimous approval of amendments to the provisions of an EU Constitution.[15]

This line of response is firstly open to objection on practical grounds: states which anticipate that their concerns will be inadequately taken into

[13] On the merits of the convention method, see B de Witte, 'Entry into Force and Revision' in *Ten Reflections on the Constitutional Treaty for Europe* (Florence, Robert Schuman Centre, 2003), pp 215–16.

[14] Art IV-7(2) of the Draft Treaty Establishing a Constitution for Europe.

[15] See de Witte, above, n 13, pp 216–19, and European Commission, *A Constitution for the Union*, COM (2003) 548, pp 8–9.

account in a convention, or which anticipate being in a minority at an intergovernmental conference, may be thought unlikely to agree to modifications. But there is also a more fundamental, conceptual problem with the notion that the states can adjust the process of treaty amendment. While it may be possible for the states to curtail the role of the intergovernmental conference in deciding on the text of treaties, the logic of a formal approach to state consent appears to preclude a departure from the requirement of unanimity. This can be seen from the analysis of the requirements of state-level democracy in the German Constitutional Court's Maastricht decision. Its view was that the notion of respect for democracy, which it derived from Article 38 of the German Basic Law, would not be respected if EU law were to fail to 'establish with sufficient certainty the powers which are transferred and the intended programme of integration'. For the same reason, it went on to insist that, were what is now Article 308 EC to 'have effects that are equivalent to an extension of the Treaty ... such an interpretation ... would not produce any binding effects for Germany.'[16] The general point is that a formal approach to state consent has *some* substance. From a formal standpoint, the Member States must *each* agree to any significant change to the EU mandate. The objections of the German Constitutional Court to uncertain or open-ended legislative powers are equally applicable to a system of amendment which does not require unanimity. A formal approach to the EU mandate therefore appears positively to require the unanimous approval of treaty amendments.

A second counter-argument from within a formal approach would cast doubt on the possibility of criticism of the treaty-making procedure in terms of outcomes. It is one thing to say that outcomes would be different under a different set of procedures. But it is quite another to conclude that those other outcomes and procedures are preferable. In order to claim that the actual treaty-making process is inadequate because of the outcomes it gives rise to, it is necessary to have an external standard against which the adequacy of outcomes can be evaluated. In other words, some further justification is necessary.

This second counter-argument can be met by insisting that there is indeed a deeper level to member state decisions concerning the EU. The EU can be understood in general terms as a reflection of the incapacity of state-level systems of government to adequately meet the states' needs and objectives. The various pressures of globalisation mean that the reasons for co-operation between them have become even more compelling. Habermas has emphasised this transition in the European context: 'The globalization of commerce and communication, of economic production

[16] *Brunner*, above n 8, paras 48 and 99.

and finance, of the spread of technology and weapons, and above all of ecological and military risks, poses problems that can no longer be solved within the framework of nation-states or by the traditional method of agreements between sovereign states.'[17] Once member state co-operation is understood in this more basic way, it becomes possible to suggest an external standard against which the rules governing treaty amendment ought to be judged: their *rationality* in terms of the EU venture itself.

Ultimately, the criticism of the treaty-making process rests upon the claim that those processes may fail to ensure that treaty outcomes reflect the fact of member state co-operation within the EU. If that is correct, then it is no longer sufficient to base the EU constitutional order *solely* upon the formal mandate given to the EU by the Member States. Instead, allowance must *also* be made for the underlying fact that the Member States have established and participated in the EU in order to achieve certain substantive purposes. The task which remains is to operationalise the notion that the Member States have consented to the EU at a deeper level than the treaties themselves. It is to that question that the paper now turns.

## IDEALISED NEGOTIATIONS

In considering possible alternatives to the actual treaties in the interpretation of member state consent, an initial question is whether the treaties can nevertheless be taken as the starting-point. In other words, can the treaties be taken as the minimum agreement possible between the Member States, so that the Member States are presumed to have consented to at least that degree of displacement of their decision-making. The answer is that problems with detail and with unanimity-over-time suggest that the outcomes in the treaties cannot necessarily be taken as a minimum starting-point in attempting to interpret member state consent. Actual treaty outcomes can be taken as the starting-point for analysis, but it would be inconsistent with the analysis so far to limit the kinds of departure from the actual treaties which may arise.

In speculating about departures from the text of the treaties, one possibility would be to adopt an explicitly majoritarian approach. On that method, where it was necessary to judge between different possible outcomes, that which was thought likely to command the support of a large majority of states would be preferred. Such an approach would certainly

[17] J Habermas, 'The European Nation-State: On the Past and Future of Sovereignty and Citizenship', Ch 4 of his *The Inclusion of the Other* (Oxford, Blackwell, 1999, originally published in German in 1996), 106. See too J Habermas, 'The European Nation-State and the Pressures of Globalization'(1999) 235 *New Left Review* 46.

overcome the obstacle posed by the requirement of unanimity in the actual treaty-making process. But it would come up against the requirement of respect for the state level on democratic grounds. That which is attractive to even a large majority of states may be contrary to the interests and political preferences of the minority. The mere fact that an arrangement is rejected by only a minority of states is not in itself sufficient to justify overriding their objections to it.

Instead, a preferable solution is to think of state consent in terms of the hypothetical outcome of idealised negotiations between potential Member States. For that, one method would be to adapt Rawls's version of the social contract. On that approach, the Member States would be imagined to negotiate in an original position, in which they had to decide upon the EU constitutional order behind a veil of ignorance as to their own actual position. As in other contexts, a difficulty with the construction of an original position is to decide which of their characteristics the participants should be allowed to have knowledge of within these hypothetical negotiations. Rawls's model itself places significant limits on this kind of knowledge:

> First of all, no-one knows his place in society, his class position or social status; nor does he know his fortune in the distribution of natural assets and abilities, his intelligence and strength, and the like. Nor, again, does anyone know his conception of the good, the particulars of his rational plan of life, of even the special features of his psychology such as his aversion to risk or liability to optimism or pessimism. More than this, I assume that the parties do not know the particular circumstances of their own society. That is, they do not know its economic or political situation, or the level of civilization and culture it has been able to achieve.[18]

All the parties are allowed to know is 'general facts about human society,' including 'political affairs and the principles of economic theory; they know the basis of social organization and the laws of human psychology.'[19]

The severity of Rawls's assumptions might be thought to mean that his approach to the construction of an original position is unhelpful in the EU context. If applied rigorously, it would mean that the negotiators would be assumed not to know the geography, history, political outlook, economic development, etc, of their own states. Neither would they know the level of economic development and the cultural characteristics of the EU as a whole. Such 'ignorance' would be problematic for the stability of the EU system, since there could be no guarantee that the constitutional order which emerged would be one that real states would be willing to be

[18] J Rawls, *A Theory of Justice* (Oxford, OUP, 1999 revised edition, originally published in 1971) 118.
[19] *Ibid*, 119.

governed by. It is therefore important to understand the particular role of Rawls's restrictive assumptions within his overall theory.[20] In part, the severe constraints upon the participants served to remove unmanageable complexity. Without those assumptions, his analysis would have faced the impossible task of speculation about agreement between an infinite number of hypothetical negotiators with different characteristics. The same necessity does not however arise in the EU context, where the number of hypothetical negotiators is small. In addition, the restrictive assumptions were necessary for Rawls because he sought to justify a precise set of propositions as to the meaning of justice. The ambition of the argument here is the more modest one of outlining a way of thinking about EU constitutionalism. For that, it is unnecessary to make restrictive assumptions in order to generate a determinate outcome. Again, the implication is that a more relaxed approach to the characterisation of the original position is possible.

The notion of an original position can therefore be retained for our purposes without having to go as far as Rawls in denying relevant knowledge to the negotiators. Probably the most plausible modification would be to imagine the negotiators knowing the characteristics of the Member States, but being assumed not to know which of those states they actually represented. This modification would remain true to the notion of a veil of ignorance, but would at the same time have more chance of ensuring stability. Since the actual characteristics of states would be known, the parties to the hypothetical negotiations could be expected to design the EU framework so as to avoid the resignation of a Member States whose participation was desired. The prospect of ensuring stability would moreover be enhanced by a refinement which allowed negotiations within the original position to accommodate changes over time. The constitutional order could be imagined to be capable of revision in the light of updated information as to the characteristics of the Member States, or the circumstances in which they found themselves.

Models of deliberative democracy offer a second approach to the idealisation of negotiations. Deliberative models involve an ideal procedure within which participants aim to reach consensus on the basis of reasoned argument. In Habermas's terminology, one can think of an ideal discourse situation, where 'those principles are valid that meet with uncoerced intersubjective recognition under conditions of rational discourse.'[21] Similarly, in Cohen's account, the 'ideal deliberative procedure' is one which 'aims to arrive at a rationally motivated consensus — to find reasons that are persuasive to all who are committed to acting on the results of a free and reasoned assessment of alternatives by equals.' The key aspect of a deliberative

[20] Discussed *ibid*, 121–22.
[21] J Habermas, 'Reconciliation through the Public Use of Reason: Remarks on John Rawls's Political Liberalism' (1995) 92 *Journal of Philosophy* 109, 127.

model is that parties seek to resolve their disagreements by persuasive arguments, rather than through the deployment of power: 'they give reasons with the expectation that those reasons (and not, for example, their power) will settle the fact of their proposal.'[22]

Deliberative models are usually developed in order to specify an ideal for the democratic process itself.[23] They can also be thought to imply certain fundamental rights as preconditions, if the absence of those rights would compromise deliberative decision-making.[24] The suggestion here is that a deliberative approach might in addition provide a plausible basis for the thought-experiment of hypothetical treaty negotiations. At a given point in time, Member States would be assumed to search for a constitutional framework which was generally persuasive to the participating states as a whole. Here too, in the interests of stability, the hypothetical deliberations could be imagined to continue over time, so as to reflect changes in the circumstances of the states and EU.

It is unnecessary to the argument here that a choice be made between the original position and deliberative version of idealised negotiations. It makes little difference whether the negotiators are assumed not to know which state they are, or whether they are assumed to know which state they are, but to seek a rational consensus. Either approach can suffice for speculation as to the normatively persuasive rules for member state co-operation within the EU. By contrast with a majoritarian model, these approaches to hypothetical negotiation have the merit that they respect the need for consensus among the relevant states. At the same time, the hypothetical approaches permit the analysis of the constitutional order to overcome any deficiencies in the actual treaty-making procedure, by organising speculation as to the rational constitutional framework for the EU.

Within any hypothetical negotiations, the most plausible assumption is that the Member States will seek to advance their distinct interests. An assumption of this kind is open to criticism if one imagines a social contract for human society, given that individuals in human society may identify with one another's interests, or indeed conceive of common interests.[25] In the EU context, however, Member States cannot be assumed to be concerned for a putative common good which is distinct from their own separate interests. This is because the greater legitimacy of decision-making

[22] J Cohen, 'Deliberation and Democratic Legitimacy', in A Hamlin and P Pettit (eds), *The Good Polity* (Oxford, Blackwell, 1989) 22–23. Cohen's account does not require that decisions be arrived at by consensus, but that aspect of his model is inappropriate in the argument developed here.

[23] As in Cohen, *ibid*.

[24] See J Habermas, 'On the Internal Relation between the Rule of Law and Democracy,' Ch 10 of Habermas, above n 17.

[25] For this criticism of *A Theory of Justice*, see M Sandel, *Liberalism and the Limits of Justice* (Cambridge, CUP, 1982) 59–65.

at the state level implies the difficulty of pursuing policies with redistributive implications at the EU level. As Scharpf has put it in the EU context, only a '"thick" collective identity ... can be relied upon to legitimize measures of interpersonal and interregional redistribution.'[26] While hypothetical constitutional negotiations may well have distributive implications, the absence of a 'thick' common identity means that — as things stand — it is implausible to imagine states seeking to advance a common interest in such negotiations.

The objectives which the states can be imagined to express through our hypothetical negotiations will necessarily vary among them, given the differences in their circumstances and political cultures, and given the range of domestic opinions and interests which the states themselves express. From what we know of the EU, it is plain that economic calculations are a significant part of the overall motivation of states. But there need be no expectation that states will approach the EU solely with economic objectives. Security too — whether as between Member States, or vis-à-vis others — is clearly an important factor in the actual practice of the EU. Recognition must also be given to the achievement of regulatory and redistributive objectives; as the earlier quote from Habermas illustrates, these too may be among the states' motivations in negotiations. Finally, states will have certain state-specific objectives — with, for example, religious or historical components — which they will seek to express in negotiations.[27] While this variety of objectives makes any analysis of the hypothetical outcomes complex, it need not be thought fatal to an approach which does not seek definitive answers, but instead to set out a framework for the analysis of constitutional problems.

If Member States are seeking to advance their distinct interests, they can be expected to co-operate at the EU level so long as the net benefit to each of them exceed any costs to be borne by each of them. Negotiators can be assumed to wish to identify positive-sum constitutional outcomes. More specifically, they will seek to identify the set of constitutional provisions which imply the *greatest* advantage to the states, taken together. Moravcsik has offered just such an interpretation of the actual negotiations which have taken place between the Member States:

> we may usefully treat treaty-amending negotiations as bargaining games over the precise terms of mutually beneficial co-operation ... Generally there are numerous such agreements extending out to and along a Pareto frontier of efficient bargains, in which all possible joint gains have been exploited.[28]

[26] F Scharpf, *Governing in Europe: Effective and Democratic?* (Oxford, OUP, 1999) 8–9.
[27] The suggestions in this paragraph may be contrasted with the approach taken in Moravcsik, above, n 4. His analysis is essentially confined to the choice between economic and geopolitical explanations of European integration, and favours the latter on empirical grounds.
[28] *Ibid*, 51.

Within such a negotiation states can be imagined to bargain for side-payments or special arrangements which are made or contemplated in order to secure agreement. What is at issue is the net advantage to each state — taking into account the various elements. It is that which individual states can be expected to seek to maximise.

A final general observation is to underline that the participants in the hypothetical negotiations and agreement need not precisely correspond to the actual EU Member States. The hypothetical negotiations should initially be imagined to occur between all *potential* members of the EU. If the matter is understood in positive-sum terms, then the outcome which maximises joint benefits may exclude some actual EU Member States, and include some actual non-members. In general terms, the EU system would be designed to ensure that overall EU membership was advantageous for those states which it was desired should participate, and only for them. For the others, it would be desired that they either did not join the system of co-operation at the outset, or — later on — that they should resign from it.

## IMAGINING OUTCOMES

The suggestion that idealised negotiations be imagined between potential Member States is not intended to provide a determinate answer to normative questions concerning the EU constitutional order. Rather, its potential is in providing a framework for speculation about actual constitutional questions within the EU. Speculation of that kind permits a rationalisation of existing constitutional arrangements, whether explicit within the treaties themselves, or arrived at through judicial decision. Such speculation also provides a basis for criticism of the existing arrangements. The essential question in any case is the same: would the constitutional proposition in issue have been agreed in idealised negotiations between potential Member States, in which they sought to maximise the joint benefits of their co-operation? In cases where the constitutional proposition at issue is not explicit in the treaties, a further question may also be addressed: why have the actual Member States not amended the treaties to provide for that result? It is only if that can plausibly be explained that there is a convincing reason to critique the existing EU constitutional order.

The content of a hypothetical constitutional agreement between EU Member States is likely to have two broad characteristics. The first is that the Member States can be expected to try to ensure the effective realisation of their common objectives. This general proposition permits an explanation for example for the existence and powers of institutions at the EU level. As Moravcsik has shown in his intergovernmentalist account of European integration, the Member States can rationally agree to give up powers to central institutions in order to ensure the credibility of their commitments to one another. The Member States also have an interest in institutions which effectively govern their co-operation over time, because of the difficulty of specifying precise rules in advance on many matters. It is therefore rational both for the Member States to agree to empower central institutions to take decisions for them, and for them to allow non-unanimous decision-making among themselves.[29]

A concern for effectiveness within idealised negotiations also permits an explanation of the attempts by the Court of Justice to strengthen the effectiveness of EU law through the principles of supremacy, direct effect and state liability, and through the requirements as to the adequacy of remedies at the national level. These doctrines have on occasion been the subject of criticism. One line of argument has been the formal one that, since the treaties do not provide for these principles, the Court of Justice ought not to have developed them.[30] To that, it may be replied that the principles are consistent with the effective realisation of the common activities of the Member States. A second line of argument is that these principles concerning the effectiveness of EC law are anyway unnecessarily invasive at the national level.[31] That view is however open to doubt: the achievement of the purposes of the EU may indeed be consistent with extensive attempts to ensure effective and equal enforcement of EU law principles throughout the Member States.[32] In either case, the difficulty in the way of treaty amendment may be thought to lie both in the obstructiveness of Member States which anticipate being in breach of EC law, and in the technical nature of the questions in issue. The benefits of effective enforcement of EC law to the substantive activities of the EU, together with the difficulties of treaty amendment, offer a possible justification for judicial creativity in this field.

Speculation as to the pursuit of effectiveness within hypothetical negotiations also provides a basis for criticism of the limits to the EU's powers and of the restrictiveness of its legislative decision rules. A key issue in this respect is whether the EU has sufficient institutional capacity to regulate national public policy decisions which may affect the single market. The denial of competence over matters such as social security systems and

[29] *Ibid*, 67–68, 73–77.

[30] See for example Hartley's criticism of the doctrine of direct effect (Hartley, above, n 9, 24–26). In his view, the Court of Justice ought to have followed the traditional doctrine that the status of international law was a matter for the law of each state, even if that had undesirable consequences in practice.

[31] See for example, C Harlow, 'Francovich and the Problem of the Disobedient State' (1996) 2 *European Law Journal* 199 and 'A Common European Law of Remedies?' in C Kilpatrick, T Novitz and P Skidmore (eds), *The Future of Remedies in Europe* (Oxford, Hart, 2000).

[32] For an argument along these lines in relation to labour law, see B Ryan, 'The Private Enforcement of EU Labour Laws', in Kilpatrick, Novitz and Skidmore (eds), above, n 31.

core aspects of labour law is one problem in that respect.[33] Another is the retention of a requirement of unanimous decision-making in relation to member state tax policies which confer a competitive advantage upon economic activity within that state.[34] It is difficult to imagine that potential Member States in idealised negotiations would agree to allow one another to obtain competitive advantages in the EU market through significant differences in aspects of public policy which potentially impose significant costs upon market participants. Nevertheless, differences in actual state interests may mean that certain states will be reluctant to agree to an expansion of competence, or a relaxation of the legislative decision-rule, in actual treaty negotiations.

The second broad characteristic which may be anticipated in idealised negotiations between potential Member States is the placing of limits upon the EU itself. It can be expected for example that the Member States would seek to maintain their freedom of action unless there was a reason based on mutual advantage for giving it up. Decisions on the details of the constitutional order would therefore involve the reconciliation of respect for Member States with the requirements of co-operation through the EU. For many questions, the implication will be a balance between state and EU level action — with only some decisions taken at EU level, the reservation of certain areas of action to the Member States, the possibility of derogations, etc. In effect, the suggestion here is that a hypothetical constitutional agreement would apply the notion of subsidiarity to the EU constitutional order as a whole, and not just — as in Article 5 EC — to the question of the exercise of competence.

Rational states should also seek to ensure that the EU system did not violate their own core characteristics. It is for example implausible that the Member States in idealised negotiations would agree to a system of co-operation whose institutions or actions violated basic requirements of democracy. Speculation about ideal negotiations therefore provides a rationalisation for the gradual empowerment of the European Parliament,

[33] See Art 137(4) and 137(5) EC. For criticism of what is now Art 137(5), see B Ryan, 'Pay, Trade Union Rights and European Community Law,' (1997) 13 *International Journal of Comparative Labour Law and Industrial Relations* 305.

[34] See Art 93(4) EC. The final report of the European Convention's Working Group on Economic Governance proposed the extension of qualified majority voting so as to 'provide for sufficient approximation of rates, minimum standards and tax bases in the area of indirect and company taxation to ensure that the proper functioning of the single market is not affected by harmful tax competition or serious internal trade distortion.' (CONV 357/02, 21 October 2002, 6). The French and German foreign ministers expressed similar sentiments in their joint contribution on Economic Governance (CONV 470/02, 22 December 2002, 4). The draft Constitution for Europe has however retained a requirement of unanimity in areas which might concern tax competition: see Art III-62 of the Draft Treaty Establishing a Constitution for Europe.

including the provision for direct elections and the conferral of legislative and supervisory powers upon it. If decisions are to occur at the EU level which cannot fully be controlled by the democratic processes of the Member States, then it makes sense for liberal democratic states to ensure democratic input at the EU level. A similar argument can be developed to rationalise the controversial decision in *Les Verts*.[35] There, the Court of Justice ignored the absence in what is now Article 230 EC of provision for actions for annulment against acts of the European Parliament. It did so in order to permit a challenge to a decision which was likely to favour incumbent political groupings in elections to the European Parliament. While undoubtedly an example of judicial creativity, the decision makes sense from the perspective of ideal negotiations. It is implausible that the potential Member States, as liberal democracies, would have ceded power to an EU within which there is no remedy against anti-democratic decisions of a parliamentary body. The fact that the principle was subsequently written into the treaties shows the logic from the Member States' point of view of the Court of Justice's decision.

Much the same analysis can be applied to the protection of fundamental rights within the EU legal order. Since respect for fundamental rights is the norm among Member States themselves, it is implausible to imagine that they would have agreed in hypothetical negotiations to transfer tasks to the EU level if it was free of such control. This perspective therefore permits a defence of the Court of Justice's case-law since 1969–70 in which it has insisted that EU law must respect generally agreed fundamental rights norms, and that those norms can be used in the interpretation of EU law.[36] It also explains the subsequent endorsement of that approach by the Member States through treaty amendment and the adoption of the Charter of Fundamental Rights.[37] It follows however that a sharp distinction is to be drawn between the upholding of fundamental rights against the EU — which is effectively done on behalf of the Member States — and the upholding of fundamental rights against the Member States. If the latter is justified, that must be for other reasons, such as that the EU's legitimacy would be compromised if its Member States frequently violated fundamental rights norms. The likely conclusion is that fundamental rights scrutiny of

[35] Case 294/83 *Parti Ecologiste 'Les Verts'* v *European Parliament* [1986] ECR 339. For criticism of the judgment, see Hartley, above, n 9, 35–36.

[36] Case 29/69 *Stauder* [1969] ECR 419 and Case 11/ 70 *Internationale Handelsgesellschaft* [1970] ECR 1125.

[37] The combination of Arts 6(2) and 46(d) EU provides for the application of fundamental rights standards to acts of the EU institutions. Art 51(1) of the Charter of Fundamental Rights of the European Union provides for the application of the rights which the Charter sets out to the institutions and bodies of the EU, and also to the Member States when they are implementing EU law. This latter provision has also been included as Art II-51 of the Draft Treaty Establishing a Constitution for Europe.

EU decision-making should be more thoroughgoing than that of Member States' actions.[38]

## CONCLUSION

The argument of this paper is that a normative approach which takes the Member States as its starting-point is not inconsistent with a developed constitutional framework for the EU. It is possible to start with member state decision-making, and yet finish by justifying various aspects of the EU constitutional order which seek to ensure the effective realisation of the EU's purposes. An analysis which starts with the Member States also permits a rationalisation of various limits to EU action, including those which maintain state-level decision-making and those which ensure respect for democracy and fundamental rights standards at the EU level. Each of these two dimensions follows from an approach to EU constitutionalism which characterises the EU as having been established by the Member States for the achievement of certain substantive purposes.

The discussion has shown that the notion of an idealised negotiation between Member States can be used to account for key features of the constitutional framework provided for in the treaties themselves. The notion of an idealised negotiation also provides a plausible defence for judicial creativity in circumstances where treaty amendment may be thought difficult to achieve. That said, the 'metaconstitutional' approach set out here is no less applicable to the political sphere. There, it implies a political culture which is not focused solely on the immediate interests of the individual Member States, but which also has regard to the overall system of co-operation between the Member States through the EU. Such a political culture is of course difficult to imagine in some Member States. But it would have the merit that it would be truer to the fact of the Member States' participation in the EU than an exclusive orientation to the formal treaties or the uncritical defence of member state-level decision-making.

[38] For a developed argument along similar lines, which highlights the different roles of fundamental rights standards and rejects the notion that the EU and Member States should be subject to the same fundamental rights standards within the EU, see A von Bogdandy, 'The European Union as a Human Rights Organization? Human Rights and the Core of the European Union' (2000) 37 *Common Market Law Review* 1307.

# 11

# *Forgetting Law in the European Convention? Europe's 'Hidden' Constitution-Building and its Legitimation*

MICHELLE EVERSON AND JULIA EISNER

## INTRODUCTION

THIS CHAPTER ADDRESSES an age-old paradox in heightened modern form: constitutions are the product and source of law, but consideration of the nature of 'law' is often absent from political constitution-building processes. Critical lawyers construe law as playing a 'thick' role within constitution-making, not only giving 'normative force' to the constitution, but also adapting it to social reality. Where, however, constitution-building processes are seen as political moments, law is assigned a 'thin' role, acting as object rather than catalyst of constitutional change: politics 'makes' the constitution, law 'adjudicates'. Critical doubts about legal 'passivity', however, are intensified with regard to the EU, where law has traditionally played an elemental role in the constitutionalisation of an emergent and socially complex Europe. Revealing that European law has been assigned a subsidiary role within the European convention, where forces of non-law play the major role in setting the constitutional agenda, the paper argues that the convention's inattention to 'thick' law-lead constitution-building detracts from its claim to be initiating informed constitutive debate. In common with its famous Philadelphian counterpart, the convention has missed a prescient opportunity to publicise the more complex role that law plays in open-ended processes of constitution-building. More particularly, it has failed to address the creative forces that lie behind formalist narratives of constitutional adjudication and legitimate Europe's 'hidden constitution-building', or legal efforts to adapt normative constructions to a complex 'real-world' Europe.

## LAW AND NON-LAW IN CONSTITUTION-BUILDING PROCESSES

For Alexander Hamilton, one thing was very clear: the constitution was antecedent to politics and law. This dual pre-political and pre-legal constitutional character was manifest in the right of constitutional judges to overturn legislation, not since one might 'suppose a superiority of the judicial to the legislative power', but since '..[.]..the power of the people is superior to both'. In so far as judges remained true to 'fundamental' laws and did not, '..[.]..on the pretence of repugnancy..[.].., substitute their own pleasure to the constitutional intention of the legislature' they were giving voice to the original constitutive voice of the people.[1]

The fruits of the constitutional moment were elevated beyond the realm of human bargaining and institutional operation, whilst the bundle of compromises, obscurities and equivocations that Madison felt marked constitutional legislation[2] were lent a retroactive air of normative infallibility as the constitutive will of the people was formed within the Philadelphia convention and given force by the US Constitution.

The retrospective attribution of a normative circle-squaring function to the constitution-building process may readily be identified as a device to lend axiomatic 'theoretical propriety'[3] to a constructed and necessarily idealised scheme of human government that nonetheless claims primacy over daily legal or political relations. Less apparent within this process, however, is the manner in which a desire for normative perfection may also colour perceptions of the workings of 'real-world' institutions of human government, and more particularly of law. The reification of the convention process above the mundane reality of political compromise, social re-alignment and judicial pronouncement can lead to a paradox whereby the act of the creation of the primary legal instrument and source of law (constitution) is largely divorced, not only from all consideration of the internal character of legal operation, but also from careful analysis of the relationship of 'post-constitutional' law to the constituted society it regulates.

In the setting of US constitutional founding, such paradox is manifest in the 'thin' conception of the law that drew force from and gave force to the US Constitution, as Madison's stated concerns about the inevitable indeterminacy of language within the Constitution[4] were countered by Hamilton's simple conviction that political conflict on constitutional meaning could be

[1] A Hamilton, *Federalist Papers* (New York, Mentor, 1961) 468–69.
[2] *Ibid*, 229.
[3] *Ibid*, 230.
[4] *Ibid*, 229.

settled with recourse to an original constituted will of the people as directly represented by the doctrinal 'JUGDMENT' of 'independent' federal judges.[5]

This touching if naïve recourse to formalist perceptions of the law and adjudication and concomitant lack of consideration for the reality of adjudicative process finds its modern echo in a European convention process which, whilst seeking to delineate clearly the individual competences of Union and member states, pays little attention to the primary judicial mechanism of practical competence apportionment and adjudication, the decisional functions exercised within the preliminary reference procedure. Instead, the convention concentrates its few 'legal process' efforts upon the securing of the independence of the Justices of the European Courts.[6]

As such, the convention might be argued to reproduce traditionally reductionist perceptions of the role of legal process within the evolution of the EU found both within law itself and within political science. On the one hand, although the President of the ECJ's assertion to the convention[7] that 'the Court's case law..[.]..has (already) begun' to confer a 'constitutional character on the Community's legal system' might be seen as a highly political statement, it can, in contrast, be argued to be wholly indicative of a formalist legal account of the development of European law, which equates the ECJ's doctrinal pursuit of 'direct effect' and 'supremacy' with a *de facto* higher legal legitimacy for the European legal order as a whole.[8] By the same token, the convention's unwillingness to address directly the substantive process of adjudication within European and national courts might also be suggested to be reflective of a realist strand within political science which has long argued that European judicial process is merely a political 'tool'.[9]

Law as simple authoritative given versus law as chimera, or law and its courts as a force independent from but 'neutrally' governing of the social and the political versus law as servitor and protector of an individual

[5] *Ibid*, 469.
[6] 'Final report of the discussion circle of the Court of Justice', CONV 636/03. A limited discussion excluding the major concern of the judges of the European courts, the necessity of maintaining the unity of the Community law system by means of the preliminary reference procedure, cf., The Future Judicial System of the European Union (proposals and reflection), submission of the ECJ to the Nice IGC.
[7] Presentation by M Gil Carlos Rodríguez Iglesias to the 'discussion circle' on the Court of Justice on 17 February 2002, CONV 572/03.
8 E Stein, 'Lawyers, Judges and the Making of a Transnational Constitution' (1981) 75 *American Journal of International Law* 1.
[9] A-M Burley & W Mattli, 'Europe Before the Court: A Political Theory of Legal Integration', (1993) 47 *International Organization* 41, 72.

political agenda.[10] These are the two prevailing views of law-making and/or adjudication within Europe. They are both, however, wholly divorced from the reality of European legal process. Between facts and norms, each legal and political view of 'law and lawyers' in the evolution of the EU has betrayed an inability to bridge the gap between idealised pre-political normative orders of government and the reality of governance in a complex world. The non-settlement of Europe notwithstanding, formalist legal commentary has eschewed meaningful investigation of the real-world conflicts inherent to governance in a sphere of on-going integration. Complacently, it has remained trapped within a paradigm of hierarchical legal norms that has facilitated its 'declaration' of the supremacy of the European legal order over those of the member states. By the same token, political science has betrayed a realist inability to afford analytical value to 'the factual power of the normative', busying itself instead with an exposure of the political substance within legal pronouncements, but not looking further to identify the normative constraints and constructive impulses that law itself embodies and perpetuates.

Within the 'real-world' integration process, rude challenges to the supremacy of European law,[11] together with clear indications of the power of legal constructions such as the *acquis communautaire*[12] to determine the governing *telos* of Europe have clearly underlined the inadequacy of existing characterisations of legal and political operation within Europe. Within the convention, the apparent reproduction of reductionist perceptions of European legal process, likewise raises the spectre of renewed analytical ossification. With the European normative circle squared through a semantic claim to 'the constituting of Europe', and 'theoretical propriety' likewise established by means of an idealised constitutional antecedent to daily politics and law, the constitutionally-significant daily response of European legal processes to the yawning chasm which continues to exist between our state-derived constitutional orders and governance in a Europe marked by the breakdown of traditional polities may now be further masked by convenient assumptions that law's 'JUDGMENT' is a simple expression of Europe's constitutive will.

[10] A general conflict, having an effect far beyond the realm of European law, and bemoaned by Habermas as presenting a fatal weakness within many attempts to fashion governance orders that are both effective and moral, J Habermas, 'Über den internen Zusammenhang von Rechstaat und Demokratie', in UK Preuß (ed), *Zum Begriff der Verfassung* (Frankfurt am Main, Fischer, 1994). Within this analysis, however, the notion of 'legalism' replaces the more pejorative term 'formalism', paying due homage to the underlying commitment of lawyers, such as Stein, to dedicate doctrinal analysis to the service of the democratic norms of the constitutional legal state.

[11] *Brunner v European Union Treaty* [1994] 1 CMLR 57.

[12] Applying as a pre-condition for membership within the Union.

## THE REFERENCE PROCEDURE AND THE MAKING OF THE EUROPEAN CONSTITUTION

With the convention's overall mandate to specify more clearly the individual competences of Union and member states, its explicit efforts to identify the supremacy of European Law (Article I-10)[13] and incorporate the ECHR within EU norms, the claim that debate on the future constitution of Europe is characterised by its 'thin' conception of law may initially appear a strange one. Nonetheless, set in the evolutionary context of a European integration process driven by the early declaration of European legal specificity, the judicial integration of the 1980s, as well as the consequent unforeseen unravelling of national complexes of social, economic and cultural regulation, it may be argued that law's force within Europe derives not simply from the declaratory content of treaties but from a complex process of differentiated normative legal response to the 'real-world' requirements of a demanding integration *telos*.

Most importantly, however, such legal process must be clearly distinguished from conventional understandings of constitutional adjudication. As famously noted,[14] Article 234, the cornerstone of the European legal system, is embedded within a mutual relationship between the ECJ and national courts, which at an initial functional level, furnishes uniformity of legal interpretation throughout Europe. At a deeper level, however, the relationship between national and European judges also builds the legitimating fulcrum for a European law, which famously derives its formal normative power from the member states and their constitutional settlements (*Herren der Verträge*), and yet, with each and every competence unravelling adjudicative operation, potentially undermines those selfsame national frameworks and, by association, its own normatively coherent existence.[15]

Seen in this light, European legal process necessarily embodies intra-constitutional dialogue and adjustment, whereby the demands of competing normative legal orders are measured and weighed up against one another in an endeavour to identify overall equilibrium. On isolated

[13] Surely a redundant move given the recognition of European legal supremacy by all national legal orders? Nonetheless, it is tempting to conclude that the convention is concerned to see an end to the efforts of Courts such as the *Bundesverfassungsgericht* to set the limits to EU jurisdiction. However, this particular aim can only be seen as a failed one. Formally speaking, the proposed constitution simply does not solve the dilemma of the lack of a European *Kompetenz-Kompetenz*. European Law remains supreme only within the sphere of its own competences. National constitutional courts, still supreme within their own competences, can continue to challenge the breadth of European Law. Vitally, competition between normative orders with equally legitimate claims to supremacy has yet to be ended.

[14] JHH Weiler, 'The Transformation of Europe' (1991) 100 *Yale Law Journal*, 2403.

[15] M Everson, 'A Court between a Rock and a Hard Place: Social Pluralism and the European Court of Justice' (2003) *Journal of Legislative Studies*.

occasions, such legal processes are explicit and their constitutional and constitution-making consequences readily apparent as national constitutions and the breadth of jurisdiction of European law are amended, expanded or restricted in their scope by means of high profile jurisprudence.[16] More usually, however, constitutional significance must be teased out of the daily business of a treadmill of national referral to the ECJ.[17]

Identified by the ECJ as a vital guarantor of the 'rule of law' within the Union,[18] the reference procedure and process of dialogue between European and national courts, might thus be identified as a complex matrix of material response to the real-world demands made of the European legal system, together with normative re-adjustment between distinct legal orders, as the simple facts of integration strain, not only the norms of European treaties, but also national constitutional settlements, and ultimately the organic unity of normative legal governance within Europe as a whole.

Within this complex matrix, concerns must necessarily arise as to the appropriateness of thin perceptions of the legal process that maintains the European order. Quite apart from commonplace modern critical legal doubts about the ability of judges, or the 'living oracles of law',[19] to embody the people's original constitutive via 'JUDGMENT', the dual challenges of multiple competing claims to normative loyalty and necessary normative adjustment to factual circumstances, immediately indicate that, although the independence of judges might yet play its part, the source of the force of Europe's organically whole law must surely educe from a more complex well-spring than a simple legal formalism deduced from a single pre-legal constitutive will. In a very real sense, national and European judges are 'making' Europe's constitution on a daily basis. What then are the sources of Europe's 'hidden' constitution-making?

## JUDGES, LAWYERS AND THE SOURCE OF THE FORCE OF LAW

This current effort to build a 'thick' conception of the law to better reflect its role in European constitution-building is founded in empirical study of the existing reference procedure and internal-legal perceptions of 'political' constitution-building, more particularly, the narratives of UK judges and

[16] Exemplary, the German Constitutional Court's demand that creeping judicial Europeanisation be curbed (*Brunner*, above n 11), together with the ECJ's responsive restriction in the jurisdiction of Article 28 Consolidated Treaty (*Criminal proceedings against Keck & Mithouard*, [1993] ECR I 6097, [1995] 1 CMLR 101).

[17] With reference to the unforeseen unravelling of national social policy in the social insurance cases, see above n 16.

[18] See above, n 2.

[19] In the words of William Blackstone, S Katz, *Commentaries on the Laws of England* (Chicago, Chicago University Press, 1979), at I.69.

barristers in relation to their individual experience within the courtroom and to legal participation, or the lack thereof, within the current European convention process.

Based upon 44 questionnaire replies and ten semi-structured interviews with London barristers and Judges of the English High Court, Court of Appeal and House of Lords, the study is necessarily limited in scope, tackling only one of the many individual national orders that go to make up Europe's 'legal' arena of constitutional dialogue. Nonetheless, in seeking to differentiate and analyse constitutional dialogue, the particular methodology chosen by the study represents a useful first attempt to reach beyond the veil of formalist legal narratives in order to identify the legitimating sources for 'hidden' European constitution-making.

Empirical instruments were designed in line with an assumption that lawyers would adopt a formalist idiom when narrating their experiences within European law. Accordingly, whilst direct questions were asked on the constitutional character of European law, various indicators were developed to identify potentially constitutionally-significant shifts within legal process and to assess the quality and provenance of 'non-formalist' legal debate:

1) Changes in the language and instruments of legal argument: marked courtroom shifts to rights-based and principle-based legal argument being indicative of distinct constitutional argument, and providing a yardstick against which determining constitutional ideologies (rights-based vs procedural) might be measured.
2) Changes in the forms of evidence presented to the court: greater use of non-legal material within legal processes being indicative of 'the limits to formalist argument', more particularly, the search by law for sources of legitimation beyond normative legal frameworks.
3) Changes in the style of legal argumentation: varying degrees of informality between courts and marked shifts in legal argumentation being indicative of a move beyond formal reasoning within coherent normative orders to non-formalist adjustment between normative orders.

[IE], denotes interviewee, [IR] denotes interviewer.

## LAWYERS, (SELF)-ILLUSION AND THE MAKING OF THE CONSTITUTION

Perhaps the most striking of responses gathered was that of a Court of Appeal Judge to the question of whether the reference procedure entails constitutional consequences. Even in relation to *Factortame*,[20] a case of unparalleled constitutional significance in the UK and EU, legal self-narrative is wholly abrogating of law-driven constitutional consequence:

> IR: Did you not have any kind of greater constitutional sense of your role at that moment?
> IE: No, I don't think I did in the sense that I saw what it involved, but my approach was well that's what you've signed up to. And it's rather like getting married. It is, of course, a huge commitment, but once you've done it well then you say well is this or is not part of the deal? [laughs].

The humour is indicative; the legislative process may lead us where we would not wish to go, but what can the poor lawyer do? In the legal world, norms are self-fulfilling. The constitutive will expressed by European treaties is pre-legal and self-fulfilling by virtue of impartial and independent 'JUDGMENT' in the courts. The possibility that laughter might also mask a judicial *choice* not to draw the domestic constitutional line in the sand *à la Brunner Bundesverfassungsgericht*, is rejected.

Nonetheless, the interview and questionnaire data gathered reinforces a suspicion of the existence of a layered process of legal (self)-illusion, whereby a professional formalist narrative on occasions gives way to constitutional re-alignment processes that reflect the need to re-adjust normative constructs to the demands of the real world. Finally, however, formalist legal narrative is again underpinned by personal narratives of 'service' to law, rather than 'agency' in legal or constitutional change.

## THE FORMALIST NARRATIVE OF EUROPEAN CONSTITUTION-BUILDING

At the heart of a dominant formalist narrative of European law, lies a strange paradox. When asked whether the European legal system *already* comprised a 'constitutional order', a large majority of respondents, answered 'yes', overwhelmingly justifying this in formalist legal terms:

> 'As the supreme law within the sphere of its application overriding legislation'; 'It contains a hierarchy of legal norms which result in the disapplication of other rules where the latter are inconsistent'; 'It is concerned with the allocation of power to different sources of law'; '[It] provides a written document giving individuals enforceable rights and freedoms and overrides other inconsistent law'.

[20] [1996] 2 WLR 506.

Consistent with a formalist analysis, the mechanisms of 'constitutional recognition' are legal-internal in character, determining that where the boxes of 'supremacy', 'norm-hierarchy', 'division of powers' and 'enforceable rights' can be ticked, the European legal system might be elevated to constitutional status without reference to social, cultural or political influences, or indeed the convention. And yet, an inconsistency immediately arises to the extent that formalist paradigms of law remain, in their purest Kelsen-led manifestation, dependent upon the identification of the 'pre-legal' and 'pre-political' constitutive moment and 'source of law' (*Grundnorm*).

Within a European legal order educed from treaties rather than founding moments, the establishment of a hierarchical legal order replete with individual rights and a division of powers can be argued to be more a matter of factual re-adjustment to the integration *telos* rather than one of normative deduction. And indeed, two responses hint at a wholly political origin for constitutionality as national and European sovereignties are re-aligned in an on-going waltz of legislative contestation. Europe thus builds a constitutional order '[I]n the sense the sense that it can override parliamentary sovereignty' and to the degree that '[T]he abeyance of UK parliamentary sovereignty plainly has constitutional significance'. Further, one response emphasises the vital importance of a practical post-constitutive process of 'acceptance' of the constitutionality of the European order, not within national societies, but within the legal systems of the member states:

> The seminal case law of the ECJ, *which has been accepted by the Member States Courts including the UK Courts*, established the EC Treaty as a fundamental (and supreme) part of national law.

Potential embarrassment over the limits to formalist narrative is spared, however, as unwillingness unreservedly to admit that a formalist claim to constitutionality rests solely upon an acceptance of practical political and legal processes of the erosion of national sovereignty, is given more constructive form in the narrative's re-assertion of the 'conditional' nature of European legal supremacy. In an English legal formulation, constitutionality remains wholly dependent upon the continued vigour of the enabling 1972 European Communities Act: 'It constrains the UK legislative and judicial bodies' freedom of action so long as the 1972 Act subsists'. Meanwhile, in an interesting case of borrowing between legal orders, the formulations of the *Bundesverfassungsgericht* are reproduced within the assertion that European constitutionality is to be found within national *Grundnorms*: 'It is not an autonomous order because from the national perspective at least the member states remain Masters of the Treaties'.

In short then, all uncertainty as to the provenance of the existing 'constitutional' order notwithstanding, a formalist narrative of the European constitution is constructed. The advocacy and adjudicative actions of lawyers and judges are legitimated as a presumption of constitutionality and 'theoretical propriety' within European law raises courtroom pronouncement to the status of socially and political neutral 'JUDGMENT'.

Legal perceptions or non-perceptions of the convention process further reinforce this vital neutrality of the law, its self-contained status as servitor of the constitutional moment. With the vast majority of respondents professing no interest in the convention whatsoever, the cocooning attributes of a formalist narrative of the status of European law are supplemented by an account of the profession of law which adds force to the assertion that the constitutive act is a pre-legal moment, dealing with issues of non-law, such as '[P]olitical process of rationalisation of fundamental principles of EC law', in which lawyers, mere handmaiden to the constitutive will, have and should have no interest whatsoever. Judicial opinion is adamant:

> IR: Have you been following the debate around the European Convention?
> IE: [.]..I don't regard that as part of my job and I don't regard myself as having sufficient spare time to want to devote that time to that particular thing.

The logics of formalism and professional conduct further dictate that even where lawyers do become a part of the convention, furnishing expert legal advice to its members, the driving impression remains one of a constitutive process which is to be seen as 'non-law' and is to be forcefully shielded from contamination by the legal issues of 'daily practice':

> A member of the Euro team in these chambers, Professor Takis Tridimas, is in fact the chairman of the group of 15 legal experts who is drafting the Treat of Accession with the ten new States…[.]…And I think that we are all sort of deliberately standing a little bit away because, you know, we wouldn't wish to put him in a position as we discuss other things with him; *cases we're working*. We don't want to make it difficult for him (emphasis added).

In brief conclusion then, a dominant formalist account of European legal process reinforces traditional impressions of a stark distinction between constitution-making and the process of constitutional adjudication. The convention lies in a realm of 'non-law'. Legal process, by contrast, is neutral in character: educed from a circle squaring constitutional settlement, law regulates its social environment with reference to its *own* socially and politically neutral values.

## ARGUMENTATION, EVIDENCE, PROBLEM-SOLVING AND STRAINS IN THE FORMALIST NARRATIVE

Weaknesses in a formalist European legal narrative can nonetheless be distilled from the accounts of daily practice within national courts at the interface between national European normative orders. In particular, Barristers, engines of legal argumentation within English courts, when asked whether they feel themselves to be a part of a process of European constitution-building (rather than adjudication) are clear in their immediate response: '[U]nquestionably'.

Certainly, such responses may be caste in formalist terms:

> [.]...I accept that for example EU law is supreme over national law and so on. But you find that that concept is not as familiar to some lawyers, to some judges. Or at least, it's not as acceptable...[.]...you feel part of it when you're making arguments to prove in court that, well, ok, domestic law might say this but it can't stand...[..]

In other words, the act of constitution building lies in educating the domestic legal system upon the concrete mechanisms of an existing European constitution rather than in a 'consensual' act of the re-adjustment of the sovereign reach of the domestic legal order.

The contradiction within this account of 'acceptance', however, becomes apparent as the legal narrative admits of non-legal elements within its educational crusade:

> IR: Do you feel that your job is part of a European legal order that is itself the foundation of a European constitution?
> IE: And foundation of having a Europe that doesn't tear itself to pieces yet again as it's done three times over.

This contradiction becomes ever more evident in a partial judicial confirmation of a constitutional role:

> IR: So you don't see your role in the courtroom...[.]...you don't feel that is part of the constitution.
> IE: Well it clearly is to some extent. It depends

Whilst out judge does not feel that he is involved directly in cases establishing, say, a balance of powers between Council and Commission, he does feel he is part of a European constitutional arena since national and European judicial operations are organically entwined:

> IR: I want to talk more generally about the EU Constitution. Do you feel the same loyalty to European law that you feel to national law?

> IE: [.]...the answer is yes, totally. *But I don't accept the premise that they are distinct* (emphasis added).

In short, the matrix of normative and factual re-adjustment within the reference procedure necessarily remains the focus of a constitution-building process which must search far further in its search for its legitimating norms than the theoretical propriety of a pre-legal constitutive will.

**Judicial Dialogue: The Basis for Normative Re-Alignment?**

The measure of an alternative non-formalist source of constitution-building is not, however, to be found within the intensity of judicial dialogue between ECJ and national courts. Instead, legal narrative reveals various factors that militate against constant interchange between the distinct normative orders forming the European legal system. At a political level, the underlying reluctance of national governments to submit their actions to European judicial oversight, taken together with the general observation that the parties to a case (or rather their advocates) play the central role in determining whether an ECJ reference will be requested, determines that much potential national-European judicial dialogue is rudely cut off at domestic source: 'I didn't realise how easy it was to oppose a reference...[.]...Usually the government doesn't want a reference. Usually the government says it's perfectly clear'.

Equally, internal legal politics, for example, the desire of a lower Court to reach its own judgement, may discourage individual judges from engaging directly with the ECJ. Instead, a yardstick for the presence of non-formalist constitution-building within the reference procedure may be found in the 'quality' of discourse. Such quality is manifest not simply since '[.]..there's no's spiritual reluctance to refer at all'. Neither is it to wholly be deduced from a surprising, if occasional, lack of formality in this '..[.]..obviously very new and a one off' relationship:

> [.]..I don't ring up an ECJ judge saying I've got this problem. The nearest I've got to that...[.]...is when I've had a case to which the answer seems to me to be obvious, that I have rung acquaintances there...[.]...and said we are currently minded to say that this is *Acte Claire* and there is no problem here. Can you see a problem in us doing that?

Rather, it can be found in the general preparedness of national judges to consider and incorporate the norms, mores and principles of Community law within their own legal systems:

> [.]..I think English judges on the whole are appropriately willing to make references. It would be quite wrong, I think, to equate the making of frequent

> references with being a good European. It's not like that at all. Judges have a number of considerations to balance, one of which is giving judgements within a reasonable time..[.]..I think what one sees in England is that judges are becoming much more confident in applying Community law for themselves. I don't mean that they tend to apply it in a little Englander or xenophobic sort of way. I think on the whole they bend over backwards to be fair. The cases that are referred on the whole are cases that should be referred because the answer is going to be important for other member states as well.

**Legal Language and Constitution Building**

The integration of Community law within national legal systems might of itself be argued to reflect a process of constitution-building. Further, however, marked shifts in the modes and tools of legal argumentation across the member states can also clearly illustrate a new understanding of the constitutional nature of the national polity or 'European polity in waiting'. Within the UK context, for example, the introduction of community 'rights' to a polity more accustomed to a negative regime of freedoms, has contributed to a judicial evolution of a new understanding of the 'rule of law' measured in terms of the equality of rights:

> But I think one of the principal factors at work was the feeling of the English judges that if citizens from other community states could obtain these injunctions by relying on Community law, then surely British people should be allowed to obtain them as well…[.]…*incidentally the case wasn't followed in Scotland.*
>
> (comments on *Factortame*)

That the process of integration of Community law into national legal systems has not been one of the simple joint adoption of a single constitutional (rights-based or otherwise) understanding, however, is immediately confirmed by distinctions between the 'non-legal' perceptions of the UK polity exhibited by Scottish and English judges (see emphasis). Instead, the complexities of a constitution-building process rooted, not in the pursuit of a single constitutive will, but in the process of re-alignment between multiple normative orders is readily apparent in the choice of different courts within the Community legal order to lay a different emphasis upon particular instruments of European law as befits the individual 'non-legal' conditions pertaining within the forum:

> I think there are ways of presenting EU law in Luxembourg which differ from the ways in which you might present it in the United Kingdom. You raised earlier the example of subsidiarity which is a very good one. Mention the word to an English judge and most of them will nod briskly and say they understand what that means and they understand its importance.

> You mention it in Luxembourg and you get a tired smile as if to say well we know that had to go into the treaty....[but].

Once beyond the formalist veil, the peculiarities of European legal constitution-building discourse become apparent as lawyers themselves note that the major shifts within the grammar and semantics of the European legal system have centred not, as might have been expected, around increased incidence of material legal concepts such as rights, but within a marked shift to European principles of interpretation, such as purposive reasoning,[21] as well as, and most often cited by our respondents, 'proportionality'.

A long-standing and powerful instrument of Community law, supplying the yardstick of constitutionality within the ECJ's efforts to distinguish between national and European competences, proportionality is likewise confirmed within the current data-set as a vital instrument of judicial self-justification, furnishing the courts with a precision proceduralist tool with which to assess the competing political claims of different sources of authority. Judicial opinion concedes that European legal language has entered the UK courtroom. More importantly, however, it has also begun to contribute to the restructuring of UK law:

> Because concepts of which the European Court of Justice and also quite often the European Court of Human Rights have made use, such as the German concept of proportionality [have proved useful]. *Those as one can easily see have gradually been discovered by the judges as being useful intellectual tools for tackling problems which are common to any political system [in] which judges and politicians [operate]* (emphasis added).

The notion of judicial 'discovery' is pivotal. The formalist paradigm of neutral 'JUDGMENT' is swept away as courts struggle to adjust their judicial role to a reality of uncertain normative authority and competing claims to authority. Proportionality, a practical procedural test of whether political means are suited to social ends, furnishes courts with a neutrally-flavoured instrument of adjudication that no longer directly relies on the expression of constitutive will, but at the same time affords the courts a measure of protection from the realist political claim that they are substituting 'their own pleasure to the constitutional intention of the legislature'.

With this, the contours of alternate constitutive authorities within the European legal system begin to emerge. Within the legal system itself, theoretical propriety is redirected away from constitutive voice to a 'legal

[21] A concept that has extended beyond the European legal system to 'pollute' purely domestic reasoning: 'Well yes. I think there are so many examples now of courts reading statutes in a [purposive] way. Not only statutes I might add, but contracts'.

constitutionalism' or what has been termed a process of 'justif(y)-ication',[22] whereby law seeks, in each and every adjudicative act, a renewed normative force in its ability to ground 'JUDGMENT' not in ancient precedent, but in the proceduralised weighing up of immediate fact.

Equally, however, law's complementary constitutive force, or its normative ability to structure fact through procedural adjudication is also hinted at as counsel consider the effects of proportionality upon their own clients:

> [C]oming back to proportionality, if you are on the government side of the case and therefore you are trying to explain that a particular response was proportionate, you're usually involved in quite a difficult exercise because you are trying to look at what seemed to be a reasonable thing to do at the time and then to explain, expose why it was proportional. Now it may indeed be proportional. This is not..[.]...necessarily...[.]...an exercise in falsification. That's not what I'm suggesting. But the problem is likely to be that intellectually it wasn't initially approached as is the [decision] proportionate? It was approached as, given various policy constraints, and different political objectives, this is the right thing to do. Now that probably gets you out to something that more or less was proportionate, but you have to rethink it almost in order to present it as proportional.

If a modern measure of political legitimacy is to be found in the process of communicative self-reflection whereby political debate is shorn of 'irrational' self-interest,[23] then 'justif(y)-ication', a necessary discovery process of legal self-legitimation, becomes, by the same token, a socially-constitutive norm as policy-making, policy constraints and governing interests are subject to reformulation and review within a paradigm of factual appraisal.

## Evidence and Constitution-Building

The particular difficulties which law faces when it moves beyond its own normative narrative, however, are similarly manifest in relation to further noted changes within the (UK) courtrooms of the European legal system, more particularly in a greater reliance upon 'scientific' representations of real-world conditions. A necessary factual compliment to 'discovered' principles of normative re-adjustment, such as proportionality, renewed European recourse to economic or cultural studies of conditions pertaining in 'real' markets might thus be argued to mirror historical constitutional

[22] R Wiethölter, 'Recht-Fertigungen eines Gesellschafts-Rechts', in C Joerges and G Teubner (eds), *Festschrift für Rudolf Wiethölter* (2003).
[23] J Habermas, *Between Facts and Norms* (Cambridge, Mass, MIT Press, 1992).

moments, such as early 20th-century social constitutional re-alignment within the US, whereby law departed from 'JUDGMENT' to instead ground its decisions in scientific studies of prevailing social conditions.[24]

Although it is perhaps lacking in the immediate upheaval of necessary constitutional response to potentially revolutionary social inequality under conditions of rapid industrialisation ('there have been a whole series of cases on the beer trade...[.]...and whether it's easy to persuade a bitter drinker to move to lager'), the appearance of 'non-legal' material in European courtrooms is nonetheless a further indication of the limits to formalist reasoning.

However, the effort to 'socialise' law, releasing it from pre-conceived formalist paradigms and bringing it closer to the realities of an emerging European society, continues to suffer from the selfsame inconstancies that plagued earlier efforts to re-found law as a sociological discipline.[25] A claim might thus be made that law can re-invent itself and its authority within a 'scientific' paradigm that is no longer marked by 'imagined' normativism, but is instead underpinned by the truth-claims of analytical methodologies rooted within social reality rather than reconstruction. Nonetheless, the endeavour to shatter axiom and unveil reality appears itself to be illusory as 'scientific discipline' not only reveals that it is also a 'constructed reality', but also proves to be difficult to translate neutrally into existing structures of normative law:

> You could certainly find yourself presenting [economic material]. You would quite often find that you were trying to commission economic material. And then you have the usual fun interface between law and economics where you have the lawyers trying to explain to the economists what they want. And the economists saying but I don't understand at all. I build my model like this...[.]...Again it's a matter of either looking for material which is already there and finding a way of packaging it so that it fits within the framework of what you need to run the argument as...[.]...That is of course usually then subject to the objection that you went out looking for material.

## 'Functionality' and Constitution-Building

If the image of lawyers as 'scientifically-legitimated law-givers for Europe' fails immediately to convince, however, the increased use of material evidence within the courtrooms of the European legal system still contains its own constitution-building and constitutionally-legitimating potential if

[24] See, *The Brandeis Brief*, 208 US 412 (1908).

[25] H Rotthleuthner, 'Three Legal Sociologies: Eugen Ehrlich, Hugo Sinzheimer, Max Weber' (1988) *EYSEL*, 227–59.

seen in conjunction with a marked degree of what can provisionally be termed 'functionality' within the self-perception of European lawyers.

Ostensibly a description of purposive reasoning within European law, a young lawyer's statement that '[I]ts trying to make it work rather than interpret exactly what it is', thus furnishes a final key to an understanding of the constitutive impulses that guide and legitimate legal constitution-building processes within Europe. In other words, the need to *find solutions* within a complex interlocking series of normative orders that must also adapt themselves to an evolving European reality entails a rationality pressure which forces the legal system to rise above any easily accepted normative or practical self-interest in the search for mechanisms to guide the development of European law. Within this framework, although scientific evidence may be flawed, it is nonetheless an aid in the effort to circumnavigate political interests and normative constraints in order to furnish judgments that ease rather than hinder the integration *telos*.

In many ways an accidental rationalising force that is reproduced across European institutions for a variety of reasons,[26] the effort to 'make Europe and its legal system work' is not only to be identified as a non-formalist constitutional building task, but may also be argued to be a self-legitimating legal mechanism: the challenge of meeting *telos* replaces illusionary axiom to provide the vital link between law and the society by which it is constituted and which it in turn constitutes.

## SERVANTS TO OR AGENTS OF THE CONSTITUTION-BUILDING PROCESS?

A final twist in the (self) illusionary presentation of law is, however, provided by the descriptions by lawyers of their courtroom role, and more particularly, of their relationship with clients. At one level, the narratives of such lawyersconfirm the existence of an obscured non-formalist account of constitution-building within the European legal system. Counsel are the convinced European engines of a legal evolution which seeks to meet the demands of the integration process. Judges, to a large part remaining true to their national normative orders, must be inveigled into acceptance of the European order and dissuaded from turning away from 'funny foreign law'. And yet, such clear intimations of agency in a European constitution-building process are also immediately suppressed. The prevailing logic is of 'service' to the law; a self-contained professionalism which derives initially from the

[26] The rationalising effects of multi-lingualism were also confirmed: 'You are addressing a multilingual court in one of the languages of the Community. You have to plead in the way that expressly recognises that fact'.

duty to serve the client: 'Clearly as barristers we're essentially sort of mouthpieces for our clients and so it may be that in particular cases I would be arguing that EU law doesn't apply here', or, '[T]here's no magic about EU law. It's another weapon in the armoury'.

Translating such professionalism into service to the law then, the act of judicial persuasion is simply a neutral and didactic process of professional legal education:

> [I]f it is a judge who has never really looked at the case law of the European Court before, you'll be trying to explain that it won't read the same way as an English case reads..[.]..And you'll be saying, of course, you know, I'm showing you a case where the facts are slightly different from the present case, but the statement of principle is to be found here. I'm going to show you another three cases where you will find the same statement of principle. I'm therefore going to invite you to be prepared to accept that the statement of principle probably is a general statement of principle.

With this, the circle of (self)-illusion is complete. Even where the logic of the formalist paradigm appears strained, the new paths of courtroom legal evolution followed retain their 'neutral' character; a neutrality prompted and necessitated by the lawyer's professional duty to client and law.

## THICK LAW: FROM ADJUDICATION TO CONSTITUTION-BUILDING?

Politics is politics, law is law and never the twain shall meet; but neither shall they pollute the constitutive moment. For us, the most pressing paradox is the fact that our traditional understanding of constitution-building processes has long weaved a close relationship between 'law' and 'politics', and yet, has founded this relationship upon a disembodied view of both 'law' and 'politics'. Constitutional conventions of course, cannot but be marked by political disputation. Nonetheless, the constitutive moment is emptied of all contestation as the constitution is created and the gulf between facts and norms established as an equally neutered law adopts the mantle of the living oracle of the constitutive will, shielded from its own potentially disruptive influence by formalism.

Facts are facts and norms are norms and the never the twain shall meet: the most surprising conclusion of this survey is the continued narrative power of formalist accounts of the origins and the force of law, not only in the light of a century of critical legal scepticism,[27] but in the face of a

[27] D Kennedy, 'Freedom and Constraint in Adjudication: A Critical Phenomenology' (1986) 36 *Journal of Legal Education*.

political-legal entity, the EU, which has time and again demonstrated the redundancy of axiomatic constructions of society. Eschewing even the Habermasian effort to re-found norms in fact by means of the constituting and re-constituting of the rights-bearing political citizen, legal narrative withdraws beneath its formalist cloak refusing to play any but the most technical of roles in a realm of 'non-law'. By the same token, the convention, with a realist belief in the power of politics to direct law, dabbles briefly in an exercise of judicial restraint, restating the primacy of European for the benefit of recalcitrant national judiciaries, but likewise places renewed faith in the age-old mechanism of judicial independence to effect its constitution.

And yet, the survey also re-confirms various of the underlying reasons for a 'noble' legal endeavour to retain its formalist character. Formalist fiction retains its power to convince:[28] to depart from the axiom of *once* constituted governance is to place the origins of law in doubt and to risk the relativist dead-ends of critical jurisprudence or to court, as did a 'free' law movement, the implication of law in transient societal trends or 'science'. By this token, the pejoratively-flavoured appellation of legal narrative as a '(self)-illusion' is wholly unfair: a profession of law works with imperfect formalist means, but still shields itself from the follies of academic endeavour to found legal origin in ever more elusive realities.

Such potential unfairness is likewise heightened by the simple fact that narratives of (self)-illusion, once unravelled, reveal the extraordinary creativity of a legal system which has reacted sensitively both to normative *lacunae* and to factual demands, not only responding to the integration *telos* but also compensating, through problem-solving, to lacking political settlement.

Nevertheless, there is that within the re-invigorated proceduralism within the European legal order (proportionality) that still prompts a desire for the development of a more differentiated understanding of constitution-building processes within and beyond the convention. More specifically, justif(y)-ication and the imposition of rationality standards upon external political debate seem to represent a process of legal self-constitution and concomitant societal constitution which forcefully springs the constitution-building/constitutional adjudication paradigm. Given the inherent radicality of the European project, the analytical subtlety to date applied to the norms and institutions which guide it, as well as the potential inspirational power of legal constitutionalism, the time may now be ripe to openly assess the on-going presence of law within constitution-building processes.

[28] F Schauer, 'Formalism' (1988) 97 *Yale Law Journal* 509.

# 12

# *The Draft EU Constitution and Private Party Access to Judicial Review of EU Measures*

ANGELA WARD*

## INTRODUCTION

THIS CHAPTER ASSESSES the extent to which the draft Constitution of the European Union resolves access to justice problems for private parties wishing to challenge the legality of EU measures. The nature of these difficulties has been well rehearsed elsewhere.[1] The issues that will be considered here are as follows:

(i) the desirability of the change proposed by draft Article 270(4) to *locus standi* rules for non-privileged applicants in nullity proceedings;

(ii) the absence of an automatic right of reference to the Court of Justice when the validity of an EU measure is questioned before a national court. This barrier is important, given that national courts themselves have no authority to declare an EU rule invalid.[2] Failure to persuade a national court of the necessity of a reference means that a measure cannot be substantively reviewed for validity;

(iii) the absence of constitutional provisions addressing the sanctions that national courts are empowered to issue, and the maintenance of an inadequate remedial provision, namely

* Thanks to the Arts and Humanities Research Board for supporting this research. I would like to thank my colleague Steve Peers for commenting on an earlier draft. The usual disclaimer applies.

[1] See most notably AG Jacobs in Case 50/00P *UPA v Council*, judgment of 25 July 2002.

[2] Case 314/85 *Foto-Frost* [1987] ECR 4199.

> Article 231, with respect to the Court of Justice and the Court of First Instance. This, I would argue, forms part of a more general failure to regulate, at constitutional level, the relationship between the Court of Justice and the Court of First Instance.[3]

It will be contended here that, while the draft Constitution goes some way toward dismantling obstacles to judicial review of EU executive measures, many barriers remain. The most welcome development lies in the attempt to bring greater delineation in the hierarchy of norms; a problem which, as I have argued elsewhere, has hampered the crafting of a coherent test for standing under Article 230(4).[4] That aside, the redrafting of Article 230(4) suggested in the Constitution may still fall short of the desirable minimum to render the provision compliant with common European standards on access to justice. This requires, according to the European Court of Human Rights, the availability of a 'practical, effective right of access' to courts.[5] Further, problems (ii) and (iii), mentioned above, were wholly unaddressed in the draft Constitution, even though they clearly constitute significant impediments to judicial review of the legality of EU rules.

## ACCESS TO THE COURT OF FIRST INSTANCE UNDER ARTICLE 230(4)

### Legal Instruments Amenable to Review

The general principles on the types of EU instruments amenable to judicial review, under the draft Constitution, are laid out in draft Article 270(1). Pursuant to that provision, the Court of Justice is empowered to review the legality of 'European laws and framework laws' along with 'acts' of the Council of Ministers, the Commission, the European Central Bank, and the European Parliament 'intended to produce legal effects vis-à-vis third parties.' Thus, aside from the insertion of reference to new legal instruments, namely, 'European laws and European framework laws', the first sentence of Article 270(1) matches the text of Article 230(1) in its current form.

[3] *Foto-Frost ibid* being a prime example of case-based initiatives aimed at achieving such regulation.
[4] 'Locus Standi Under Art 230(4) of the EC Treaty: crafting a coherent test for a "wobbly polity"' (2003) *Yearbook of European Law* (forthcoming). This chapter builds on the themes explored in the *Yearbook* article.
[5] *de Geouffre de la Pradelle v France* judgment of the Court of Human Rights of 24 November 1992, Series A Judgments and Decisions, vol 253 (1993) para 35.

The test proposed for *locus standi* rights of private parties is laid out in Article 270(4).

> Any natural or legal person may ... institute proceedings against an act addressed to that person or which is of direct and individual concern to him or her, and against a regulatory act which is of direct concern to him or her and does not entail implementing measures.[6]

This is to be compared with Article 230(4) of the EC Treaty. It provides as follows:

> Any natural or legal person may .... institute proceedings against a decision addressed to that person or against a decision which, although in the form of a regulation or a decision addressed to another person, is of direct and individual concern to the former.

The first important change proposed by Article 270(4) relates to clarification of the types of instruments which non-privileged applicants are able to challenge. Article 230(4) refers only to 'regulations' and 'decisions' which, subject to certain conditions, are susceptible to challenge. Article 270 (4) is somewhat broader. It refers to challenge to an 'act' or 'regulatory act', again reviewable subject to additional requirements (considered further below).

Removal of reference to 'regulations' and 'decisions' from the wording of Article 230(4) would be a welcome development. It would render nugatory the protracted argument as to whether an individual must prove that the measure impugned in reality amounted to a 'decision' before it can be challenged under Article 230(4). Such doubts have, in the past, created difficulties for those wishing to challenge Regulations and Directives, with the case law sometimes suggesting that, in addition to satisfying the requirements of 'direct and individual' concern, the applicant must also show that the measure impugned is a disguised decision.[7] The Article 270(4) amendment would also cure the unsatisfactory implication, inherent in the wording of Article 230(4), that only regulations and decisions are amenable to

[6] For a similar proposal and discussion see paras 20 to 21 of the Final Report on the Discussion Circle of the Court of Justice CONV 636/03 Cercle I 13, Brussels, 25 March 2003. Note that the Naples Ministerial Conclave, Italian Presidency Proposal (CIG 52/1/03 Rev 1), proposes adding acts of the European Council, intended to have legal effects, to the range of measures amenable to judicial review. For the text of the proposed amendment see CIG 52/03 ADD 1, Annex 7.

[7] Eg Compare the approach in Case 64/69 *Compagnie Francaise Commercial e et Financière v Commission* [1970] ECR 221 with the approach in Case 100/74 *CAM v Commission* [1975] ECR 1393; compare Case C-309/89 *Codorniu v Council* [1994] ECR I-1853 with Case C-73/97 P *French Republic v Comafrica SpA and others* [1999] ECR I-185. For a recent discussion of this issue, see TC Hartley *The Foundations of European Community Law* 5th edn (Oxford, OUP, 2003) 356–62.

judicial review, even though the Court of Justice has ruled that other legally binding measures, such as Directives, can be impugned.[8] Reference to only two types of instruments in the text of EC Treaty Article 230(4) is misleading.

Specific reference, in the text of Article 230(4), to challenge the legality of EC Directives was particularly warranted after it was established that unimplemented Directives could have direct effect, and could be used as an aid to interpretation with respect to national measures falling within their scope.[9] An amendment, then, reflecting the law as developed by the Court of Justice is therefore well overdue. Draft Article 270(4), with its emphasis on the generic term 'act', brings greater transparency to the types of measures susceptible to challenge.

Article 270(1) goes on to supply a new mandate for review by the Community judicature. The Court is empowered to examine 'the legality of acts of bodies or agencies of the Union'.' Article 230(1) of the EC Treaty makes no specific reference to 'acts of bodies or agencies', and thus far there powers of review of such bodies has been limited, with a notable exception lying in decisions of the Office for the Harmonisation of the Internal Market (Trade Marks and Designs).[10] This represents a welcome step forward, and one foreshadowed by the discussion circle on the European Court of Justice, held during the Constitutional Convention.[11]

## 'Individual Concern' and Challenge to a 'Regulatory Act'

The second important development in Article 270(4) lies in removal of the requirement that private parties prove 'individual concern' if they wish to challenge a 'regulatory act'. This would mean that applicants challenging such measures would no longer have to show that they are differentiated from all others affected by the impugned measure, such that they stand in the shoes of an addressee, in order to sue before the Court of First Instance.[12] Provided that the test for 'direct concern' is satisfied, and the

[8] Eg Case T-135/96 *UEAPME v Council* [1998] II ECR 2335.

[9] A Arnull 'Private Applicants and the Action for Annulment under Art 173 of the EC Treaty' (1995) 32 *CML Rev* 7; 'Private Applicants and the Action for Annulment since Cordoniu' (2001) 38 *CMLRev* 7.

[10] For a recent example of challenge to a decision refusing registration see Case T-295/01 *Nordmilch eG v Office for Harmonisation in the Internal Market (Trade Marks and Designs) (OHIM)*, judgment of the Court of First Instance of 15 October 2003.

[11] Final Report on the Discussion Circle of the Court of Justice, above n 6, paras 24 to 26.

[12] For the classic exposition of this test see Case 25/62 *Plaumann v Commission* [1963] ECR 95, 107. For a recent detailed discussion of the operation of this test, and its exceptions, see Hartley above n 7 at 356–84.

regulatory act in question 'does not entail implementing measures', then *locus standi* requirements will be fulfilled.

This provision is unsatisfactory for a number of reasons. At the outset, it would seem that the phrase 'does not entail implementing measures', is tautologous. The test for direct concern entails proving that those entrusted with the impugned measure's implementation are left with 'no discretion ..... that being a purely automatic matter flowing solely from the Community legislation without the application of other intermediate rules'.[13] It is thus difficult to see what is added by words 'does not entail implementing measures'.

Even less satisfactory is the absence of a definition, in the draft Constitution, of the term 'regulatory act'. There are, I would argue, two possibilities, the former of which is preferable, but even then not optimal. First, the term 'regulatory act' may refer to delegated or executive legislation. These are designated, under the draft constitution, as 'non-legislative' acts, and take the form of regulations and decisions (Article 32(1)). On this interpretation, non-privileged applicants will be afforded *locus standi* before the Court of First Instance if they are able to prove that (i) they are challenging a regulation or decision (that is, an executive or administrative measure) and (ii) the measure impugned is of direct concern to them, which includes proof that it 'does not entail implementing measures'. The only executive measures that non-privileged applicants would be prevented from challenging, before the Court of First Instance would be those that *are* subject to further implementing rules. Legal challenge to such implementing rules would then have to be launched before the national courts. Further, on this interpretation, legislative acts, namely European laws and European Framework laws, as measures promulgated with ample participation of the European Parliament, would be precluded from Article 230(4) nullity review by non-privileged applicants. The route to Luxembourg for challenge to these measures would be Article 234 validity review.

The second possibility is somewhat broader. The term 'regulatory act' could be interpreted as extending to certain primary EU legislation, while still encompassing delegated and executive legislation. On this interpretation, the hierarchy of norms would be a less important guide to the development of *locus standi* rules. The touchstone would become the *opportunities for challenging* the measure concerned. Even a primary legislative act of direct concern to a private party would be reviewable by the Court of First Instance. Provided that the applicant could prove that (i) the impugned measure formed some sort of 'regulatory' function

[13] Case T-223/01 *Japan Tobacco Inc and JT International SA v European Parliament and Council*, judgment of 10 September 2002, at paras 45 and 46.

and (ii) the measure impugned is of direct concern to the applicant (which includes proof that it 'does not entail implementing measures') then *locus standi* will be satisfied. European framework laws would still be precluded from nullity review, because they, by definition, require implementing measures (see Article 32(1)). However, European laws, are cast in the Constitution, as legislative acts 'of general application ... binding in [their] entirety and directly applicable in all Member States.' These primary measures could thus pass all of the hurdles set by Article 270(4).

On this interpretation, crafters of Article 270(4) may have drawn inspiration from concerns expressed by the Court of First Instance in *Jégo-Quéré and Cie SA v Commission*.[14] That is, if there are no 'acts of implementation' then all an actor affected may be able to do is 'bring its validity before the national courts by violating the rules it lays down'. This, for the Court of First Instance 'does not constitute an adequate means of judicial protection. Individuals cannot be required to breach the law in order to gain access to justice.'[15] The Court of First Instance recalled that 'access to the courts' was 'one of the essential elements of a community based on the rule of law'[16] This was reflected in both Articles 6 and 13 of the ECHR[17], and Article 47 of the EU Charter of Fundamental Rights.[18]

The first of these two interpretations is preferable for a number of reasons.[19] Principle among these is that draft Constitution laudably introduces a much clearer delineation of the hierarchy of norms 'shaking the layers of law into place.'[20]Indexing, therefore, *locus standi* to the primary or secondary nature of the measure impugned would both compliment this improved coherency, and reflect the legal traditions of the Member States. As I have argued elsewhere, courts have traditionally played a diminished role in testing primary measures for compliance with the rule of law, on the logic that democratically elected national parliaments have played the principle role in assessing competing interests, and formulating policy. There is less guarantee, however, of adequate 'voice' for private citizens and undertakings with respect to secondary measures, in which national parliaments have played, at best, a supervisory role.[21]

[14] Case T-177/01, judgment of 3 May 2002.
[15] Para 45 *Jego-Quere ibid*, citing with approval point 43 of the Opinion of Advocate General Jacobs delivered on 21 March 2002 in Case C-50/00 P *Unión de Pequeños Agricultores v Council*.
[16] *Ibid* para 41.
[17] *Ibid*.
[18] *Ibid* at para 42.
[19] See also the Discussion Circle on the Court of Justice above n 6 at para 22.
[20] H Hofmann 'A Critical Analysis of the New Typology of Acts in the Draft Treaty Establishing a Constitution for Europe' *EIOP*, 30.09.03, 26.
[21] Ward, above n 4.

A study of the legal instruments proposed by the Constitution, and the procedures through which they are promulgated, provide the key starting point in illustrating improvement in the delineation of the hierarchy of norms which the Constitution prescribes.[22]

A distinction is made between what are termed 'legislative' and 'non-legislative' acts. European laws and European framework laws fall into the former category (Article 32 (1)), and European regulations and European decisions fall into the latter (Article 32(1). Pursuant to Article 33, European Union laws and European Union framework laws, are legislative acts are to be adopted either (i) on the basis of proposals from the Commission by the European Parliament and the Council of Ministers under the ordinary legislative procedure as set out in Article III-302; or (ii) in cases specifically provided for in Article III-165 (namely, judicial cooperation in criminal matters and police cooperation) there is an option, at the initiative of a group of Member States, in accordance with Article III-302; or (iii) in specific cases provided by the Constitution, legislative acts can be adopted by the European Parliament with the participation of the Council of Ministers, or by the Council of Ministers with the participation of the European Parliament, in accordance with special legislative procedures.

The 'executive' nature of regulations and decisions promulgated by the Council of Ministers and the Commission is indicated by draft Articles 35 and 36. Pursuant to Article 35 (1) 'delegated regulations' are to be the exclusive province of the Commission. The delegation, pursuant to that provision, is to be made in a European law or a European framework law (that is, via one of the legislative measures) 'to supplement or amend certain non-essential elements of the European law or framework law'. Moreover, Article 35(1) further provides that 'the essential elements of an area' are to be reserved to the European law or European framework law, and cannot be housed in a delegated measure. Article 35 (1) goes on to provide a guarantee that any delegation is tightly defined, and provides that the 'objectives, content, scope and duration of the delegation shall be explicitly defined in the European laws and framework laws

Article 36 (4) provides for the promulgation of European implementing regulations and European implementing decisions. Under Article 36(2) such measures are to be passed where 'uniform conditions for implementing binding Union acts are needed'. Implementing powers are generally to be conferred on the Commission. However, with respect to implementation of the common foreign and security policy, implementing acts are to be passed by the Council (s 39 (3)). Indeed, Article 39(7) expressly excludes European laws and framework laws from the range of measures that can be passed in implementing the common foreign and security policy. However, it is

[22] For a detailed discussion of attempts in this regard see Hofmann above n 20.

important to note that the draft Constitution retains the TEU Article 46 prohibition on Court of Justice jurisdiction over the common foreign and security policy (see draft Article III-282), save for review on the legality of restrictive measures against natural or legal persons adopted by the Council under Article 224, brought in accordance with Article 270(4) (see Article 282, second para). Article 224 provides for the procedures and voting rules on 'the interruption or reduction, in part or completely, of economic and financial relations with one or more third countries'. This means that Council decisions pertaining to CFSP, aside from those falling within the Article 224 exception, will not be subject to nullity review.[23]

The political institutions are bound by a duty to adhere to the hierarchial architecture supplied by the draft Treaty. Article 37 (1) provides that unless 'the Constitution contains a specific stipulation, the Institutions shall decide, in compliance with the procedures applicable, the type of act to be adopted in each case, in accordance with the principle of proportionality set out in Article 9.'

Further evidence of the importance of strict adherence to the hierarchy of legal norms can be found in the substantive chapters of the Constitution. The EC Treaty, in its present form, presents a rather chequered set of obligations when it comes to the type of instrument to be deployed in implementing specific policies. For example, title XIX on the environment makes no reference to the types of instruments to be deployed in elaborating this policy, and nor does Title XX on Development cooperation. Other areas of regulation are specific about the type of instruments to be used. For example, Article 94 expressly stipulates that the institutions shall issue 'directives' for the establishment or functioning of the common market.

The Draft Constitution is infinitely more rigorous, with various substantive areas of regulation expressly stipulating the types of measures to be deployed. So, for example, draft Article III-130 (1) states that 'European laws or framework laws', adopted after consultation with of the Committee of the Regions and the Economic and Social Committee, shall establish what action is to be taken to achieve the objectives of environment policy,[24] while draft Article III 130(3) provides that general actions programmes shall be enacted by way of 'European laws'. Development policy is to be implemented, under Draft Article III-219, by 'European laws or framework laws'.

Given, then, the attention to the hierarchy of norms present in the remainder of the draft Constitution, it might be logical to interpret the term

[23] See also "Supplementary report on the question of judicial control relating to the common foreign and security policy" Conv 689/1/03 Rev 1, Circle I 16, 16 April 2003.

[24] See, however draft Article III-130(2) for the exceptional procedure contained therein.

'regulatory act' in Article 270(4) as synonymous with 'non-legislative' measures. That is, with respect to that class of European regulations and decisions that do not 'entail implementing measures', non-privileged applicants would only be bound to prove direct concern before obtain nullity review before the Court of First Instance. However, if this were so, it might be asked why the framers of Article 270(4) did not craft the provision by recourse to the term 'non-legislative' which is used in Article 32(1), instead of 'regulatory act'.

The failure of the framers to do so is perhaps the most powerful argument in favour of extending Article 270(4) review to all measures not entailing further implementation, whether they be legislative or executive in nature. As mentioned above, such an interpretation would fill the void, which troubled by the Court of First Instance in *Jégo Quéré*, that emerges when there is no national implementing act on which to peg challenge to the validity of a 'parent' EC measure.

I would argue, however, that such an interpretation of Article 270(4) would be undesirable. First, the sharpening in the delineation of the hierarchy of norms presents an opportunity to develop parallel coherency in the test for *locus standi* for private parties in nullity proceedings. Indexing the test by reference to the legislative of executive nature of the measure impugned, and thus the procedure through which it was promulgated, is the best way forward to achieve this end,[25] and the solution most in keeping with the legal traditions of the Member States.

Moreover, the problem isolated by the Court of First Instance in *Jégo Quéré*, pertaining to how judicial review can be secured with respect to general Community measures that are not subject to implementing rules, can be cured in another way. As the Court of Justice held as far back as 1992 in the *Borelli* case, national courts must do their utmost to provide those seeking to challenge the validity of an EC measure with an effective national remedy; even if none existed prior to the commencement of the challenge.[26] More recently in *The Queen v Secretary for Health ex parte British American Tobacco Limited*[27] the Court of Justice accepted a reference from an English Court on the validity of a Directive which had not yet entered into force, and had not been the subject of implementing measures. There the Court observed that 'in the complete system of legal remedies and procedures established by the EC Treaty with a view to ensuring

[25] See further Ward above n 4.

[26] Case C-97/91 *Oleificio Borelli SpA v Commission* [1993] ECR I-6313. For a discussion see Garcia de Enterria 'The Extension of the Jurisdiction of National Administrative Courts by Community Law: the Judgment of the Court of Justice in *Borelli*' and Article 5 of the EC Treaty (1993) 13 *Yearbook of European Law* 19. See also the judgment of the Court of First Instance Joined Cases T-172/98 and T-175/98 *Salamander and Others v Parliament* [2000] ECR II-2487, para 74.

[27] Judgment of 10 December 2002.

judicial review of the legality of the acts of the institutions, where natural or legal persons cannot, by reason of the conditions for admissibility laid down in the fourth paragraph of that article directly challenge Community measures of general application, they are able, depending on the case, either indirectly to pleas the invalidity of such acts before the Community judicature under Article 241 EC or to do so before the national courts and ask them .... to make a reference to the Court of Justice'.[28] There would seem to be no reason, then, to take this a step further, and bind Member State courts, pursuant to their EC Treaty Article 10 duties, to receive challenges to the validity of primary EC rules, absent even domestic implementing principles. Such a step would also be supported by Article I-28 of the Constitution. It states that 'Member States shall provide rights of appeal sufficient to ensure effective legal protection in the field of Union law.' The European Parliament has interpreted this provision as obliging the Member States 'to establish a system of legal remedies and procedures which ensure respect for the right to effective judicial protection.'[29]

The abandonment, then, of the requirement to prove 'individual concern' with respect to a 'regulatory act' represents a welcome step toward more coherence in the test for standing under EC Article 230(4). Article 270(4), accompanied as it is by the introduction of a traditional 'hierarchy' of legislation has in some way dealt with the very heart of 'access to justice' problems for private parties seeking to challenge the validity of EC measures.

Yet, I would argue, that Article 270(4) does not go far enough. The best way of bringing coherency to the judicial architecture, would be to afford non-privileged applicants *locus standi* before the Court of First Instance with respect to challenge to *all* non-legislative measures, provided that they can show a legal interest in so doing,[30] rather than imposing a requirement, that is currently proposed, of proving that a measure is a 'regulatory act' of direct concern. It would then be for such litigants merely to comply with the two-month time-limit for bringing proceedings, and other procedural rules. Such a step would leave Article 234 validity review as the primary means for reviewing legislative acts that have been promulgated via the European Parliament. This solution would be in keeping with the legal traditions of the Member States, would reflect the clearer delineation of the hierarchy of norms supplied by the draft Constitution, and bring much needed clarity to the law.

[28] *Ibid* at para 39.

[29] Report on the Draft Treaty establishing a Constitution for Europe and the European Parliament's Opinion on the Convening of the Inter-Governmental Conference' FINAL A5/0299/2003, 10 September 2003, page 43. The Parliament says that this should be made clear in an explanatory protocol when the Treaty is adopted.

[30] Eg Case T-212/00 *Nuove Industrie Molisane Srl v Commission* [2002] II-ECR 347, para 45.

## SUBSISTING DIFFICULTIES AND CONSTITUTIONAL SILENCE

There are number of important issues which remain unaddressed in the Constitution. Indeed, aside from the reform, discussed above, reflected in Article 270(4), the provisions on the Court of Justice and the Court of First Instance remain largely unaltered, save for the change of name of the latter to the High Court.

Key issues that remain unaddressed pertain to the efficacy of the remedies that attach to challenge to the legality of EC measures. First, and perhaps primarily, no attempt has been made to remove the authority of national courts to issue interim orders in the event of challenge to the validity of a Union measure, and place it in the hands of the Court of First Instance. Such a change in the law is essential, so that an applicant who is able to convince a Member State judge to refer a question on validity has an opportunity to seek a *Union wide* interim order. As the law presently stands, such an applicant is bound to seek an interim order in all Member State courts, in order to ensure that the measure impugned is temporarily suspended. This is hardly practical, and may fail to meet 'access to justice' standards imposed by the ECHR.[31]

This problem could be easily solved by institution of a fast-track reference on interim relief to the Court of First Instance. It could then decide, pending the final outcome of proceedings, whether the measure impugned should be suspended *across the Union*. Given that the Court of First Instance currently carries jurisdiction to grant interim relief in Article 230(4) nullity proceedings, it would seem to make sense for it to have the same jurisdiction in validity proceedings.[32] It is noteworthy, however, that draft Article III-287 reflects the wording of EC Treaty Article 243, which states that 'The Court of Justice may in any cases before it prescribe any necessary interim measures.' It would have been preferable if this had been re-worded to refer to the Court of First Instance.

The absence of a right of reference to the Community judicature, with respect to validity proceedings, remains disturbing when there has been insufficient improvement in Article 230(4) rights of access to a court. The obligation to persuade a national judge of the necessity of a reference, even when the measure impugned in non-legislative (or executive) in nature, is undesirable, when there remain so many barriers to access to justice. On the other hand, if the reforms proposed in the section above entitled '"Individual Concern" and Challenge to a "Regulatory Act"' above were adopted, vesting national judges with a discretion to refer, when questioning the validity of EU basic acts, would be less problematic. Indeed, it could provide a useful filter against unmeritorious claims.

[31] Above.

[32] The draft Treaty includes the changes made at Nice that allows for references to be made to the Court of First Instance from national courts.

The draft Constitution is also disappointingly silent on the types of remedies that the Union courts are empowered to issue. Here too the letter of the law remains unchanged. In Article 230(4) nullity proceedings, the powers of the Court of First Instance and the Court of Justice would remain limited to declaring an act 'void' (draft Article 271, currently Article 231), leaving the Institution, body, or agency whose act has been declared void 'required to take the necessary measures to comply with the judgment of the Court of Justice' (draft Article III-267, currently Article 233). Thus, once a non-privileged applicant has made out their case for nullity, they will remain unable to ask the Court of First Instance for a particularised order that would remedy the wrong found to exist.

Equally, there are no guidelines written into the draft Constitution, and for the benefit of Member State judges, on the types of sanctions they are empowered to issue, in either the context of successful validity challenge, or when a litigant has been able to prove that national law is incompatible with a (lawful) EU rule. Given the growing complexity of Court of Justice case law on 'effective remedies', the foundation rules governing it merited codification in the primary Constitutional document. This could take the form of a clause referring to the principles of effectiveness and non-discrimination,[33] and attaching them to both claims for interpretation and validity.[34]

The draft Constitution also did little to pare back the TWD rule. Under this principle, litigants are prevented from activating the Article 234 validity route if they 'without any doubt' could have brought proceedings before the Court of First Instance.[35] This is a wholly unreasonable requirement, given the quagmire of difficult rules on *locus standi* confronted by non-privileged applicants. It's removal by express constitutional amendment would also be desirable, if it is unachievable through reinterpretation of the case law.[36]

One important step forward, however, is found in the proposal removal of Article 68 EC, which places limitations on references from national courts with respect to Title IV on visa, asylum and immigration policy. Article 68(1) confined the entitlement to refer to courts and tribunals 'against whose decisions there is no judicial remedy' under national law. Such measures, under the Draft Constitution, would become subject to the Article 234 reference procedure, leaving courts of all levels at liberty to refer questions on interpretation and validity to the Court of Justice.

[33] See, classically Case 199/82 *Amministrazione dello Stato v San Giorgio* [1982] ECR 3595.
[34] Case C-212/94 *FMC v IBAP and Ministry for Agriculture, Fisheries and Food* [1996] ECR I-389. Further discussed in Ward above n 4.
[35] Case C-188/92 *TWD v Germany* [1994] ECR I-833.
[36] See further Ward, above n 4.

## CONCLUSION

As can be seen from the above discussion, many key 'access to justice' problems were wholly unaddressed in the draft Constitution. These included some of the most well known, and widely analysed shortcomings in the judicial architecture. Progress, where it is proposed, has been confined to relatively minor issues, such as clarification of the types of legal instruments that are amenable to judicial review, and establishment of a right to challenge acts of bodies and agencies of the Union before the Union judicature. A further substantial improvement is found in the suggestion for removal of the requirement on private parties to prove 'individual concern' with respect to 'regulatory' acts challenged in nullity proceedings. Yet, this innovation is marred by the failure to provide a definition for 'regulatory act', adding to the confusion on whether a national court or the Court of First Instance is the correct venue for challenge to the legality of EU measures is in issue.

By far the most helpful development lies in the clearer differentiation proposed between primary and secondary law, cast as they are in the draft constitution, as 'legislative' and 'non-legislative' measures. Unfortunately, this enhanced 'structural clarity'[37] has not been directly indexed to the rules pertaining to *locus standi* under Article 230(4). Resort is yet to be made to the legislative or executive nature of a measure as a reference point for designating which court, national or Union, should be the first port-of-call to challenge to the legality of EU measures by non-privileged applicants. This, I would argue, could well hold the key to curing the 'access to justice' problems remaining in the EU judicial architecture.

[37] Hofmann, above n 20 at 5.

# 13

# *Legality Review of Member State Discretion Under Directives*

CHRIS HILSON

## INTRODUCTION

IN RECENT YEARS, in the context of directives, the Court of Justice has developed an enforcement doctrine which some have termed 'legality review'[1] of Member State discretion. The doctrine arose because the existence of discretion classically precludes the operation of direct effect and yet the Court was keen to allow individuals to enforce the discretionary provisions of the relevant directives in their national courts. This alternative doctrine is likely to be of increasing importance in certain policy areas such as the environment, where there is an increasing number of directives which leave considerable discretion in the hands of Member States. But more generally, given the historic centrality of the doctrine of direct effect to the Community's legal order, it is crucial that the precise contours, limitations and potential for development of this alternative are fully appreciated.

The chapter will begin by examining the role of discretion in the traditional direct effect case law and will proceed to examine the Court's development of legality review. While others have analysed this material,[2] they have tended to stop short of a thorough examination of the Court's case law on judicial review of Member State discretion under directives. Conducting such an examination is the principal aim of this chapter. As we shall see, while some guiding principles are discernible from the case law, there is a real need for the Court to systematise these into a workable and transparent formula.

[1] S Prechal, 'Does Direct Effect Still Matter?' (2000) 37 *CML Rev* 1047.
[2] Notably, Prechal, *ibid*.

## DISCRETION, DIRECT EFFECT AND LEGALITY REVIEW

Discretion has long been a feature of the Court's case law on direct effect. The classic preconditions for the direct effect of a Community provision are, rather confusingly, expressed by the Court of Justice in a variety of different ways. In some cases, the Court states that the relevant provisions should be unconditional and sufficiently precise.[3] In others, a provision is said to produce direct effect if it is clear and unconditional and not contingent on any discretionary implementing measure.[4] In practice, this variation in wording makes little difference for two reasons. First, because unconditionality is, in any case, itself definable in terms of the absence of discretion.[5] And secondly because, as Advocate General Van Gerven effectively stated in the *Banks* case, one should not get too hung up on the wording of the test for direct effect when what really matters is its purpose in identifying provisions which are justiciable[6]:

> The clarity, precision, unconditional nature, completeness or perfection of the rule and its lack of dependence on discretionary implementing measures are in that respect merely aspects of one and the same characteristic feature which that rule must exhibit, namely it must be capable of being applied by a court to a specific case.[7]

The fact that, under Article 249 EC, directives, as a source of law, leave Member States with a general discretion as to form and methods in their implementation is not, in itself, sufficient to make them fall at the unconditional/discretion hurdle. The authority for this lies in all of the many cases over the years — starting with the *Van Duyn* case[8] — in which the Court has held provisions from directives to be directly effective. Equally, as long as it is potentially severable, the direct effect of a provision of a directive will not be precluded just because other provisions of the directive are not unconditional (or indeed sufficiently precise). As the Court observed in *Becker*:

> Whilst the sixth directive undoubtedly confers upon the member states varying degrees of discretion as regards implementing certain of its provisions,

[3] Case 8/81 *Becker v Finanzamt Munster-Innenstadt* [1982] ECR 53, para 25.
[4] See eg Case 44/84 *Hurd v Jones* [1986] ECR 29, para 47. *Cf* to similar effect, Case 271/82 *Auer v Ministère Public* [1983] ECR 2727 (para 16), which speaks of the need for 'clear, complete, precise and unconditional obligations which exclude the possibility of discretionary assessments'.
[5] Case C-131/97 *Carbonari v Universita degli studi di Bologna* [1999] ECR I-1103, paras 46–47. TC Hartley, *The Foundations of European Community Law*, 5th edn (Oxford, OUP, 2003) 199.
[6] On direct effect and justiciability, see P Pescatore, 'The Doctrine of Direct Effect: An Infant Disease of Community Law' [1983] *EL Rev* 155 at 176.
[7] Case C-128/92 *H J Banks & Co Ltd v British Coal Corporation* [1994] ECR I-1209, para 27.
[8] Case 41/74 *Van Duyn v Home Office* [1974] ECR 1337.

individuals may not for that reason be denied the right to rely on any provisions which owing to their particular subject-matter are capable of being severed from the general body of provisions and applied separately.[9]

Furthermore, even if the relevant provision itself confers discretion on the Member State, that will not prevent its direct effect so long as it clearly grants a minimum right or floor. Thus, in *Faccini Dori* for example, although the relevant articles of the directive provided Member States with a degree of latitude or discretion in determining time-limits for cancellation, this was subject to a long-stop that cancellation had to be notified within a period of not less than seven days.[10]

Nevertheless, if the relevant provision of the directive is properly regarded as conditional in that it leaves Member States with discretion, the conditions for direct effect will not be satisfied. Thus, in *Von Colson*, for example, the Court held that Directive 75/207/EEC did not include any unconditional and sufficiently precise obligation regarding sanctions for discrimination that individuals could rely on to obtain specific compensation under the Directive.[11] And similarly in *Francovich*, the fact that the relevant directive granted the Member States a broad discretion in the organisation, operation and financing of the guarantee institutions, led the Court to conclude that it could not have direct effect.[12] Of course, in both of these cases, the conditional nature of the relevant obligation did not preclude other mechanisms of enforcement in the national courts — viz the doctrines of sympathetic interpretation and state liability respectively.[13]

There are, however, cases where, despite the relevant provision not satisfying the unconditionality requirement for direct effect, the Court has nevertheless allowed individuals to rely on it in a manner akin to direct effect, using what Prechal has termed 'legality review'.[14] Although there

[9] Above n 3, para 29. See also Case C-346/97 *Braathens Sverige AB v Riksskatteverket* [1999] ECR I-3419, para 30.

[10] Case C-91/92 *Faccini Dori v Recreb Srl* [1994] ECR I-03325, para 17. See also Case C-303/98 *Sindicato de Medicos de Asistencia Publica (Simap) v Conselleria de Sanidad y Consumo de la Generalidad Valenciana* [2000] ECR I-7963, para 68. In *Dori* of course, although successful in terms of satisfying the conditions for direct effect, the applicant failed because she was attempting to enforce the directive horizontally against another private individual.

[11] Case 14/83 *Von Colson and Kamann v Land Nordrhein-Westfalen* [1984] ECR 1891, para 27.

[12] Cases C-6/90 and C-9/90 *Francovich and Bonifaci v Italian Republic* [1991] ECR I-5357, paras 25–27.

[13] As Prechal rightly notes, the fact that individuals can rely on these other doctrines in their national courts should lead to caution in describing direct effect in terms of the ability of individuals to enforce Community law in their national courts (above, n1, p 1050).

[14] Above, n 1. Whether or not legality review should be considered a form of direct effect has been debated. See eg D Edward, 'Direct Effect, The Separation of Powers and the Judicial Enforcement of Obligations', in *Scritti in Onore di Giuseppe Federico Mancini*, Vol II

are some early cases of this nature,[15] it is only really recently, with the decisions in *Kraaijeveld*[16] and *Bozen*[17] that this situation has come to the fore. In *Kraaijeveld*, the Netherlands and the UK had argued that the discretion enjoyed by the Member States under Article 4(2) of the Environmental Impact Assessment (EIA) Directive meant that Article 2(1) was not sufficiently unconditional to have direct effect.[18] However the Court did not specifically address this question of the conditions for direct effect, contenting itself with the observation that the fact that Member States have a discretion under Articles 2(1) and 4(2) of the Directive did not preclude judicial review of the question whether the national authorities had exceeded their discretion.[19]

How then does one explain the differing effect that the presence of discretion has as between the two sets of cases? Why, in *Von Colson* and *Francovich* did discretion preclude the operation of direct effect and yet, in *Kraaijeveld* and *Bozen*, something very similar — in the form of legality review — was allowed. Prechal, based on the Opinion of Advocate General Léger in *Linster*,[20] answers to the effect that the legality review cases involve an 'exclusionary' effect whereas the 'no direct effect' cases would have involved a 'substitution' effect.[21] Ultimately, it boils down to a question of justiciability again: in a case where an individual is asking for something positive (as in, for example, *Francovich* and the creation of payment institutions) 'discretion will block the application. The court cannot make the choice, which is up to the legislature or executive';[22] however, where someone is merely seeking to have the relevant national

(Milan, Giuffè, 1998) 423 at 424 and 442. Although somewhat ambivalent, Edward seems to come down slightly in favour of a separate term, given that, on one view, direct effect is bound up with rights and the legality review cases do not involve rights. *Cf* Prechal (above n 1), who questions the worth of the classical conditions for direct effect and also the role of rights in the direct effect case-law and is thus more categorically of the view that legality review is a form of direct effect. Although I share Prechal's views on the utility of the conditions for direct effect, so long as the Court continues to use the conditions, my view is that clarity favours keeping legality review and direct effect separate.

[15] Eg Case 51–76 *Verbond* [1977] ECR 133.
[16] Case C-72/95 *Kraaijeveld v Gedeputeerde Staten van Zuid-Holland* [1996] ECR I-5403.
[17] Case C-435/97 *WWF v Autonome Provinz Bozen* [1999] ECR I-5613.
[18] Para 47.
[19] Para 59.
[20] Case C-287/98, [2000] ECR I-6917.
[21] This distinction has also been put forward as an explanation for the Court's so-called incidental horizontal direct effect case law in the case of directives — the argument being that the Court allows horizontal direct effect where there is merely an exclusionary effect but denies it where the effect would be substitutionary (see eg P Craig and G de Burca, *EU Law*, 3rd edn (Oxford, OUP, 2002) 220–27). While its use in that context has been contested (see eg M Dougan (2001) 38 *CML Rev* 1503 and (2003) 40 *CML Rev* 193), it is submitted that the distinction maintains its explanatory force here, in the context of judicial review.
[22] Prechal, above n 1, p 1062.

law excluded or disapplied (as in *Kraaijeveld* and *Bozen*), then 'discretion will not block the possibility of review.'[23]

Drawing on the above distinction, Prechal goes on to take issue with the Court of Justice's ruling in *Comitato*.[24] In that case, the Court ruled that, since Article 4 of the Waste Directive[25] merely defines the framework for the action to be taken by the Member States regarding the treatment of waste and does not require, in itself, the adoption of specific measures or a particular method of waste disposal, it was neither unconditional nor sufficiently precise and thus lacked direct effect.[26] However, just because Article 4 provides Member States with discretion — preventing the unconditionality requirement for direct effect from being satisfied — does not mean that legality review should not be available. Indeed, Prechal points to an Article 226 case — the *San Rocco* waste case[27] — where the Court was indeed prepared to review the limits of a Member State's discretion under Article 4 in the context of Article 226, public enforcement proceedings. If this is possible under Article 226 EC, then why not in a private action brought by an individual in national courts? Which is not of course to say that the *Comitato* case was wrongly decided. On the facts, the applicants in the national courts were seeking to challenge the decision to site a landfill site for the disposal of waste in their region and the national court was concerned about the compatibility of national law — with its almost exclusive reliance on landfill — with the Directive, which emphasises the importance of other methods of waste management such as recycling. However, the reference from the national court specifically inquired only about the direct effect of Article 4, which requires Member States to avoid harm to human health and the environment in its waste disposal operations.[28] To have ruled that Article 4 was directly effective in the context of this referral, the Court would have been ruling that this landfill site, *which had not yet been built* (and by implication therefore *any* landfill site) was necessarily polluting and hence

[23] *Ibid.*

[24] Case C-236/92 *Comitato di Coordinamento per la Difesa della Cava and others v Regione Lombardia and others* [1994] ECR I-483. See also C Boch, '*The Iroquois at the Kirchberg*; Or Some Naïve Remarks on the Status and Relevance of Direct Effect', in J Usher (ed), *The State of the European Union* (Harlow, Longman, 2000) 21 at 36.

[25] Directive 75/442/EEC, [1975] OJ L194/39. Art 4 at the time stated that: 'Member States shall take the necessary measures to ensure that waste is disposed of without endangering human health and without harming the environment, and in particular: without risk to water, air, soil and plants and animals, without causing a nuisance through noise or odours, without adversely affecting the countryside or places of special interest.' Art 4 has since been amended (by Council Directive 91/156/EEC of 18 March 1991, OJ [1991] L 78/32), adding a second paragraph, which further requires Member States to take the necessary measures to prohibit the abandonment, tipping or uncontrolled disposal of waste.

[26] Para 14.

[27] Case C-365/97 *Commission v Italy* [1999] ECR I-7773.

[28] See n 25 above.

in breach of Article 4.[29] This would have involved the Court replacing its opinion on suitable waste management options for that of the Community's political institutions, which had not completely ruled out the use of landfill. In other words, it looks decidedly like a non-justiciable, positive substitution request (the substitution here being the waste management option), which the Court was rightly keen to avoid.

The facts of the *San Rocco* case were different.[30] There, the subject-matter of the case involved Italy's failure to take appropriate measures to prevent pollution from the unlicensed tipping of, *inter alia*, biological and chemical materials from the local general hospital. In this case, the Court was not being invited to express a positive preference for a particular type of waste management option over another, or indeed for a particular waste disposal site location; it was simply ruling, in a negative, exclusionary-type manner, on the compatability of the existing Italian practice with Article 4. The Court held that Italy had a margin of discretion under Article 4, the limits of which were, nevertheless, reviewable by the Court. Although the Court seems to rule it out,[31] it is submitted that a similar legality review of discretion ought to be available to individuals in national courts in this type of situation. That *San Rocco* happened to be an Article 226 case, ought, in other words, to make no difference.

## CASE LAW ON MEMBER STATE DISCRETION

What Prechal is effectively arguing in relation to the *Comitato* and *San Rocco* cases considered above, is that there should be a degree of congruence between the Court's Article 226 case-law and its case-law on actions in national courts stemming from Article 234 references. This is surely true. After all, both types of proceeding can be seen as involving judicial review of Member State discretion.[32] The Court's approach to discretion ought therefore to be the same in both instances so that a coherent body of principles relating to the judicial review of discretion can be developed.

The aim of the remainder of the chapter is to examine the substance of the Court's case law on Member State discretion under directives, across both 226 and national court proceedings, to ascertain precisely when a Member State will be held by the Court to have exceeded the limits of its

[29] For a useful analysis of the Art 4 objectives and the associated Member State discretion, see further Bell (2003) 15 *Journal of Environmental Law* 59.
[30] For a very similar case to *San Rocco* (involving the first ever imposition of a fine under Art 228 EC), where the Court explicitly cites the discretion wording of that case, see also Case C-387/97 *Commission v Greece* [2000] ECR I-5047.
[31] Paras 62–63.
[32] To similar effect, see Boch, above n 24.

discretion. Many of the relevant cases, from which the relevant principles can be gleaned, involve the environment.

## Error of Law

The cases fall into two categories. First, there are those where the Member State is held to have exceeded the margins of its discretion because it has, effectively, committed an error of law. Examples here include a number of the cases involving the EIA Directive and also a number on designation of relevant areas under the Birds, Habitat and Urban Waste Water Treatment (UWWT) Directives. Article 4(2) of the EIA Directive states that:

> Projects of the classes listed in Annex II shall be made subject to an assessment, in accordance with Articles 5 to 10, where Member States consider that their characteristics so require. To this end Member States may inter alia specify certain types of projects as being subject to an assessment or may establish the criteria and/or thresholds necessary to determine which of the projects of the classes listed in Annex II are to be subject to an assessment in accordance with Articles 5 to 10.

In *Kraaijeveld*, the Court, though acknowledging that the second paragraph of Article 4(2) above confers a measure of discretion on Member States, ruled that 'the limits of that discretion are to be found in the obligation set out in Article 2(1) that projects likely, by virtue *inter alia* of their nature, size or location, to have significant effects on the environment are to be subject to an impact assessment.'[33] In other words, if a Member State had exercised its discretion — for example in drawing up size-based thresholds for certain types of development — which ended up in excluding smaller developments of that type which were nevertheless in, for example, a sensitive location and which could still therefore have a significant effect on the environment, then this discretionary decision would fall foul of the clear requirements of the wording of the Directive. A very similar approach is taken in the case of the Birds Directive in, for example, the *Santona Marshes* case[34] and, more emphatically, in the *Lappel Bank* case.[35] Article 2 of the Birds Directive requires Member States to take requisite measures in relation to naturally occurring wild birds, 'while taking account of economic and recreational requirements'. Article 3, which deals with *general* conservation measures, explicitly provides for account to be taken of these economic and social requirements in Article 2. Article 4, on the

[33] Para 50.
[34] Case C-355/90 *Commission v Spain* [1993] ECR I-4221.
[35] Case C-44/95 *R v Secretary of State for the Environment, ex parte Royal Society for the Protection of Birds* [1996] ECR I-3805.

other hand — which involves *special* conservation measures — contains no such explicit reference. Under Article 4, Member States are required to designate Special Protection Areas (SPAs) and a number of them had taken economic requirements into account in deciding which areas to designate. In the *Lappel Bank* case, for example, the UK did not wish to designate Lappel Bank, despite its importance as a habitat for wild birds, because the intention was to develop the land as part of the expansion plans for the Port of Sheerness. In both that case and the *Santona Marshes* case, the Court ruled that Member States are not authorized to take account of economic requirements mentioned in Article 2 when designating a SPA and defining its boundaries.

A similar approach can be seen in the *First Corporate Shipping* (*FCS*) case[36] and — in a decision by a UK domestic court — in the *Hull Estuary* case,[37] though in these cases, the limits of the Member State's discretion were less obviously defined by the language of the relevant directives. For that reason, they therefore take on more of the shade of what, in English administrative law, would be irrelevant considerations cases. In *FCS*, the Court stated that, in relation to Stage 1 of the procedure for classifying sites as Special Areas of Conservation (SACs) laid down by Article 4(1) of the Habitats Directive, the criteria for selecting sites are defined exclusively in terms of nature conservation.[38] The Member State's argument that Article 2(3) of the Directive (which states that '(m)easures taken pursuant to this Directive shall take account of economic, social and cultural requirements and regional and local characteristics'), meant that they could take economic, social and cultural requirements into account in making their initial designation of SACs under Article 4(1) could not be sustained.[39] The reason the Court gave for this was that it would frustrate the Directive's objective of achieving a coherent, European ecological network. A Member State would not be aware of the situation of habitats in other Member States and how its own habitats were, or were not, interconnected with these and the Commission would not end up with the complete picture.[40]

The *Hull Estuary* case[41] involved the exercise of the UK Secretary of State for the Environment's discretion in establishing the outer limits of estuarine waters under the UWWT Directive. In essence, the Directive requires expensive, secondary sewage treatment for agglomerations of a given size discharging into less sensitive areas (LSAs) in estuarine waters

[36] Case C-371/98 *R v Secretary of State for the Environment, Transport and the Regions, ex parte First Corporate Shipping Ltd* [2000] ECR I-9235.
[37] *R v Secretary of State for the Environment, ex parte Kingston Upon Hull City Council and ex parte Bristol City Council and Woodspring District Council* [1996] Env LR 248.
[38] Para 15.
[39] Para 25.
[40] Paras 23–24.
[41] Above, n 37.

and cheaper, primary treatment if the discharge is to a LSA in coastal waters. The Secretary of State had drawn the outer limits of the Humber and Severn estuaries quite far inland, at the relevant major road bridges, rather than further towards the sea. The consequence of establishing the outer limits of the estuaries in this way was that sewage from the relevant cities of Hull and Bristol discharged into coastal rather than estuarine waters, thus requiring only cheaper, primary treatment. Article 2(12) of the Directive defines an estuary as 'the transitional area at the mouth of a river between fresh-water and coastal waters' and requires Member States to establish the outer (seaward) limits of estuaries. Harrison J. observed that, since the Article does not specify any criteria which a Member State has to apply when establishing an outer estuarine limit, Member States therefore have a discretion in this regard.[42] While that discretion is not limited to considerations of salinity or topography in the absence of any provision in the Directive to that effect, its breadth does not however 'embrace consideration of the cost of treatment because it is not relevant to a genuine and rational assessment of what actually constitutes an estuary'.[43] Cost was, in other words, an irrelevant consideration.[44] He therefore effectively held that the UK had exceeded the limits of its discretion here because this irrelevant consideration had played a major role in its decision.

A number of error of law cases — including some of those mentioned above — involve the situation where a Member State has issued guidance of some kind in order to structure the exercise of its relevant discretion. In a number of the EIA cases,[45] for example, the guidance comes in the shape of, for example, thresholds, so that administrators are not obliged to consider every single development on its merits. Similarly, in the *French Nitrates* case,[46] the French government had issued guidance on implementation of the Nitrates Directive in the form of a circular, which stated that phosphorous and not nitrogen was the problem factor in the case of estuaries and hard freshwaters. And in the *UK Blackpool Bathing Water* case,[47] the UK government had originally issued guidance — again in the form of a circular — containing thresholds in terms of the number of bathers, which were to be used to determine whether a stretch of water should be classified as 'bathing water' for the purposes of the Bathing Water Directive.

In all of the above cases, one of the key reasons underlying the Court's finding that the Member State had exceeded the limits of their discretion was that the guidance excluded matters which properly fell within the scope

[42] *Ibid*, p 261.
[43] *Ibid*, p 262.
[44] *Ibid*.
[45] *Kraaijeveld*, above n 16. See also Case C-474/99 *Commission v Spain* [2002] ECR I-5293, and Case C-392/96 *Commission v Ireland* [1999] ECR I-5901.
[46] Case C-258/00 *Commission v France* [2002] ECR I-5959.
[47] Case C-56/90 *Commission v United Kingdom* [1993] ECR I-4109.

of the relevant directive. Hence, in *Kraaijeveld*, for example, the Court ruled:

> Thus a Member State which established criteria or thresholds at a level such that, in practice, all projects relating to dykes would be exempted in advance from the requirement of an impact assessment would exceed the limits of its discretion under Articles 2(1) and 4(2) of the directive unless all projects excluded could, when viewed as a whole, be regarded as not being likely to have significant effects on the environment.[48]

Similarly, in the *French Nitrates* case,[49] the Court held that although it may be true that phosphorous and not nitrogen plays the principal role in eutrophication of estuarine and hard waters, that was not to say that such waters could never be suffering from nitrate pollution, where nitrogen may be producing some polluting effect worthy of control under the Nitrates Directive.[50] With this in mind, it ruled that:

> The possibility that major classes of waters would never be designated as eutrophic, even though there was in fact pollution by nitrates from agricultural sources or a real risk of such pollution, would clearly be incompatible with the Directive, which requires Member States to identify polluted waters or those which could be so affected in order to take certain measures to reduce water pollution caused or induced by nitrates from agricultural sources and to prevent further such pollution ... [I]t is incompatible with the logic and objective of the Directive to exclude a priori from its scope major classes of waters, such as those mentioned in that circular. Notwithstanding the role that phosphorus may play in eutrophication, plant species whose growth is accelerated by nitrogen may appear in such waters, giving rise to a disturbance of the balance between the different organisms which are present there.[51]

Finally, in the *UK Bathing Water* case,[52] the Court stated that the objectives of the Bathing Water Directive in terms of the protection of the environment and public health would be frustrated if the UK's numerical thresholds were accepted. The Directive defines 'bathing water' in Article 1(2)(a) as all running or still fresh waters, or parts thereof, and sea water in which bathing is not prohibited and is traditionally practised by a large number of bathers. The problem with the UK's thresholds was that they potentially excluded from protection, areas where bathing could still be said to be practised by large numbers, based on other criteria:

> Those objectives would not be attained if the waters of bathing resorts equipped with facilities such as changing huts, toilets, markers indicating

[48] Para 53. See also the cases listed in n 45 above.
[49] Above, n 46.
[50] Paras 45–46.
[51] Paras 48 and 50.
[52] Above n 47.

bathing areas, and supervised by lifeguards, could be excluded from the scope of the directive solely because the number of bathers was below a certain threshold. Such facilities and the presence of lifeguards constitute evidence that the bathing area is frequented by a large number of bathers whose health must be protected ... The bathing areas of Blackpool and of Southport have for a long time been bathing resorts meeting the criteria mentioned above. Accordingly, as from the notification of the directive they should have been considered bathing areas within the meaning of the directive.[53]

## Manifest Error

In other cases, the Court has ruled that Member States have exceeded the limits of their discretion because of the manifest nature of the breach. The *San Rocco* waste case considered earlier,[54] falls into this category, with the Court ruling as follows:

From the fact that a situation is not in conformity with the objectives laid down in the first paragraph of Article 4 of the amended directive, then, the direct inference may not in principle be drawn that the Member State concerned has necessarily failed to fulfil its obligation under that provision to take the requisite measures to ensure that waste is disposed of without endangering human health and without harming the environment. *However, if that situation persists and leads in particular to a significant deterioration in the environment over a protracted period without any action being taken by the competent authorities, it may be an indication that the Member States have exceeded the discretion conferred on them by that provision.*[55]

Equally, with a number of cases involving designation of protected areas under the Birds and Habitat Directives, the Court has ruled that the relevant Member State is in breach of its obligations because of the manifest nature of the breach of discretion. Thus, in *Commission v Netherlands*,[56] the Court effectively agreed with the Commission's submission that the obligation to designate SPAs under the Birds Directive is infringed if a Member State manifestly disregards the number and area of the territories listed in what is known as IBA 89[57]:

Thus where it appears that a Member State has classified as SPAs sites the number and total area of which are manifestly less than the number and total area of the sites considered to be the most suitable for conservation of the

[53] Paras 34–35.
[54] Above n 27.
[55] Para 68, emphasis added.
[56] Case 3/96 [1998] ECR I-3031.
[57] An inventory of areas of great importance for the conservation of wild birds in the Community prepared for the competent directorate-general of the Commission by the Eurogroup for the Conservation of Birds and Habitats in conjunction with the International Council of Bird Preservation and in cooperation with Commission experts (see *ibid*, para 68).

> species in question, it will be possible to find that that Member State has failed to fulfil its obligation under Article 4(1) of the Directive.[58]

Given that the Netherlands had classified as SPAs territories whose number and total area were 'clearly smaller'[59] than those suitable for classification as SPAs under IBA 89, the Court ruled that it was in breach of its obligations under the Directive.[60]

A similar approach can be seen in *Commission v Ireland*,[61] in relation to designation of SACs under the Habitats Directive. Whilst noting that Member States have a margin of discretion when making their site proposals under Article 4(1) of the Directive,[62] the Court nevertheless ruled that the content of the Irish national list of sites sent to the Commission 'was manifestly inadequate, going well beyond the margin of discretion available to Member States for the purpose of drawing up the list of sites'[63] and that Ireland was therefore in breach of its obligations under the Directive.[64]

However, the *Italian Shellfish* case[65] is a little more ambiguous. There, the Commission contended that only 11 of Italy's 20 regions had made an initial designation of shellfish waters under the Shellfish Waters Directive and that the waters designated and notified therefore represented little more than 50% of the national territory.[66] In response, Italy argued that only regions with access to the sea could designate shellfish waters and that of the 15 such regions, designations had been made by 12. In its view, the fact that three regions had not yet made designations was insufficient to constitute failure to fulfil its obligation to designate shellfish waters under Article 4 of the Directive.[67] After observing that Member States do have a certain discretion in deciding on which waters require protection or improvement in order to support shellfish,[68] the Court nevertheless ruled that waters had to be designated if the relevant conditions (the need for protection or improvement) obtained.[69] There was, according to the Court, 'nothing in the wording of the directive to support an interpretation which would allow Member States not to designate all shellfish waters'.[70] The approach taken by the Court here could be said to turn on

[58] Para 63.
[59] Less than half — see the Commission's submission at para 44.
[60] Paras 72–73.
[61] Case C-67/99 [2001] ECR I-5757.
[62] Para 33.
[63] Para 37.
[64] Para 38.
[65] Case C-225/96 *Commission v Italy* [1997] ECR I-6887.
[66] Para 22.
[67] Paras 21 and 23.
[68] Para 25.
[69] Para 26.
[70] *Ibid.*

which of the factual submissions it has accepted (which, unfortunately, is not clear from its judgment). If it preferred the Commission's account, then 11 out of 20 looks rather like a manifest breach in any event. However, if it ruled as it did despite accepting Italy's account of 12 out of 15, then the ruling cannot easily be placed in the manifest exceeding of discretion category along with the other cases considered above. Alternatively, and more plausibly, one could argue that this was a case where Italy mistakenly believed it had a discretion not to designate in the sense of not actually getting around to making the decision to designate in the 3 regions concerned. In that sense, it is not on all fours with the previous cases which involved conscious, timely, non-designation decisions. It may well be therefore that the Court will be strict with the former type of case — there is effectively no discretion not to get around to the designation issue[71] — but more forgiving of the scientific discretion in the latter cases, where a manifest breach approach will be taken. In the shellfish case, had Italy's three regions taken their decisions and the Commission simply disagreed with some of the areas that had been excluded, then the case would have fallen into the latter category.

Of course, all of the above cases involved proceedings under Article 226, where one might expect the relevant breach to be manifest. After all, the Commission, in exercising its own enforcement discretion, tends to select cases where the breach is of this kind.[72] However, would the Court adopt the same approach in relation to actions in national courts, where relatively minor breaches could very well be litigated by less forgiving individuals? What if, for example, a Member State omitted to designate one small area in its list of SACs sent to the Commission under the Habitats Directive (and it had not taken into account irrelevant, economic, social or cultural considerations in doing so). Would it be regarded as in breach? The Commission may decide not to bring 226 proceedings in such a case, but if we are to have a coherent law on judicial review of discretion, the question is relevant for actions that may be brought by individuals in their national courts.

In fact, we do have a fairly clear indication from the Court that its approach is much the same in relation to national court actions. In *ex parte Standley*,[73] the Court was again concerned with the designation of nitrate vulnerable zones under the Nitrates Directive. The applicants in the case were farmers, who were seeking the annulment of the UK Government's decision to designate land draining into their local rivers and tributaries as nitrate vulnerable zones, because of the restrictions this would impose on

[71] In this sense, there are parallels with the state liability case law here where *Francovich*-type non-transposition of a directive has been regarded as automatically sufficiently serious (or, here, manifest).

[72] I am grateful to Donald McGillivray for this observation.

[73] Case C-293/97 *R v Secretary of State for the Environment and Ministry of Agriculture, Fisheries and Food, ex parte Standley* [1999] ECR I-2603.

their farming practices. The designation process under the Directive essentially falls into two parts. First, Member States are required, under Article 3(1), to identify '(w)aters affected by pollution and waters which could be affected by pollution if action ... is not taken.' Under Article 3(2), they are then obliged to 'designate as vulnerable zones all known areas of land in their territories which drain into the waters identified according to paragraph 1 and which contribute to pollution'. The main aspect of the ruling, which relates to the question of how one identifies 'waters affected by pollution' need not detain us here.[74] What is interesting, for present purposes, are the Court's comments on how national courts should approach Member State discretion under Article 3(1):

> When national courts review the legality of measures identifying waters affected by pollution in accordance with Article 3(1) of the Directive, as interpreted in this judgment, they must take account of the wide discretion enjoyed by the Member States which is inherent in the complexity of the assessments required of them in that context.[75]

The implicit suggestion is therefore, that, in reviewing the exercise of the discretion inherent in the initial part of the designation process, national courts ought to adopt a manifest error-type approach.

A more explicit statement regarding intensity of review can be found in the (pharmaceutical) *Upjohn* case,[76] although this statement was made in the context of a national court action involving traditional direct effect and the effectiveness of national procedural remedies rather than legality review as such. In *Upjohn*, the Court draws attention to the low-intensity review adopted in relation to complex assessments by the EC institutions and suggests that, where Member States are involved in similarly complex assessments, low-intensity review should also be adopted:

> According to the Court's case-law, where a Community authority is called upon, in the performance of its duties, to make complex assessments, it enjoys a wide measure of discretion, the exercise of which is subject to a limited judicial review in the course of which the Community judicature may not substitute its assessment of the facts for the assessment made by the authority concerned. Thus, in such cases, the Community judicature must restrict itself to examining the accuracy of the findings of fact and law made by the authority concerned and to verifying, in particular, that the action taken by that authority is not vitiated by a manifest error or a

[74] See para 40.
[75] Para 37. See also para 39.
[76] Case C-120/97 *Upjohn Ltd v The Licensing Authority established by the Medicines Act 1968* [1999] ECR I-223. Given the age of the *Upjohn* ruling, it is perhaps surprising that the Court did not refer to it in any of the other cases described in this section.

> misuse of powers and that it did not clearly exceed the bounds of its discretion ... Consequently, Community law does not require the Member States to establish a procedure for judicial review of national decisions revoking marketing authorisations, taken pursuant to Directive 65/65 and in the exercise of complex assessments, which involves a more extensive review than that carried out by the Court in similar cases.[77]

It appears therefore that, where complex assessments are concerned — be they pharmaceutical licensing decisions or environmental designation decisions — the Court does adopt a similar, manifest error approach as between Article 226 and actions in national courts. Whether the Court should be taking such an approach will be discussed below in the concluding section.

## CONCLUSION

What then can we conclude from an examination of the cases in the previous section? Several observations are in order. First, the law on Member State discretion is currently rather undeveloped and incoherent, although it is hoped that the discussion above may help, in a small way, to address this problem. What is needed is an organising statement by the Court of Justice along the lines of that of Lord Greene in the famous English *Wednesbury* case involving judicial review of discretion, where he held that a public body must exercise its discretion according to the terms of its powers, must not base its decision on irrelevant considerations and must not come to a decision that is manifestly unreasonable.[78] This statement seems to encapsulate exactly how the Court of Justice approaches the issue of Member State discretion and could do with being spelled out by the Court in an explicit formula.

Secondly, as noted at the start of the chapter, the case law on discretion is of particular relevance for the enforcement of EC environmental law. An increasing number of new environmental directives have moved away from the old, limit value approach to provide Member States with much more discretion.[79] Unlike the old-style directives — where the key obligations imposed on Member States easily satisfied the classic requirements for direct effect — the key provisions of the new measures are unlikely to be of direct effect in the classic sense because of their conditionality. That leaves

[77] Paras 34–35.

[78] *Associated Provincial Picture Houses v Wednesbury Corporation* [1948] 1 KB 223 at 228–29. This reading of the ruling is based on D Galligan, *Discretionary Powers: A Legal Study of Official Discretion* (Oxford, Clarendon, 1990) 227.

[79] See eg the Water Framework Directive 2000/60/EC and the IPPC Directive 96/61/EC.

legality review of the relevant Member State discretion. And it will worry many environmentalists if, other than in cases involving an error of law, the Court's approach to legality review is to interfere only where the Member State has manifestly exceeded its discretion. In enforcement terms, that is a very hands-off approach — much more so than with classic direct effect.

However, as with so many of the Court's doctrines, things tend not to stay still. With legality review, the Court may yet develop it in such a way that we move away from a manifest breach-type approach. Just as doubt has been cast by the European Court of Human Rights on low-intensity *Wednesbury*[80] review in fundamental rights cases,[81] it is submitted that the Court of Justice ought not to adopt a manifest-breach type approach in cases involving fundamental rights. Advocate General Fennelly specifically argued in the context of proportionality review of the Tobacco Advertising Directive that the standard of review should be more intensive because of the fundamental, personal right involved (freedom of expression).[82] So there is some precedent for such an argument at Community level, albeit that the Court did not consider it. Although not fundamental rights as such, one might argue that, where Community environmental rights are in play, the Court ought similarly to adopt a more intensive manner of review than a manifest-breach approach. Such rights have been said by the Court to exist where the relevant environmental directive is intended to protect human health.[83] Given that the Shellfish Waters Directive is just such a directive, the decision in the *Italian Shellfish* case considered above could therefore be regarded as correct even if the relevant Italian regions had decided against designating on scientific grounds rather than simply on the basis of delay.

[80] Above n 78.

[81] *Smith and Grady v UK* (2000) 29 EHRR 493.

[82] Cases C-376/98 and C-74/99 *Germany v European Parliament and Council* and *R v Secretary of State for Health and Others, ex parte Imperial Tobacco Ltd* [2000] ECR I-8419, para 157.

[83] As in eg Case C-361/88 *Commission v Germany* [1991] ECR I-2567. See further C Hilson, 'Community Rights in Environmental Law: Rhetoric or Reality?' in J Holder (ed), *The Impact of EC Environmental Law in the United Kingdom* (Chichester, Wiley, 1997).

# 14

# *What is the Point of* Francovich?

MICHAEL DOUGAN*

THIS CHAPTER WILL explore the basic legal functions performed by the *Francovich* principle of Member State liability to make reparation for losses caused through a breach of Community law, and its relationship with the broader case law on the effective judicial protection of rights derived from the Treaty system.[1] In particular, we will seek to provide an answer to the following question: under what circumstances should a *Francovich* action be available against a national authority which commits a purely operational breach of Community law (for example, by misapplying domestic rules on the levying of taxes, or which prohibit discrimination in employment)? It will be argued that the Court should develop a clearer distinction, as regards the requirements of effective judicial protection, not just between vertical and horizontal disputes, but also as regards public law and private law situations. In particular, *Francovich* should be concerned *only* with the public law liabilities of the Member State, *not* with its private law liabilities. Otherwise, the Court risks making as much of a mess of its jurisprudence on national remedies, as it has already done with its case law on the direct effect of directives.

## GENERAL PRINCIPLES GOVERNING THE LIABILITY OF PUBLIC AUTHORITIES UNDER COMMUNITY LAW

The Court's disparate case law concerning national remedies and procedural rules, which we know collectively as the principles of effective judicial protection, is capable of creating legal effects as regards any enforceable breach of Community law perpetrated by a public authority.[2] For these purposes,

* I am grateful to participants at the WG Hart Workshop 2003 for their comments. Many thanks to Eleanor Spaventa for her invaluable suggestions.

[1] Cases C-6 and 9/90 *Francovich* [1991] ECR I-5357.

[2] Present analysis does not require us to explore the full meaning of 'any enforceable breach of Community law'. Suffice to observe that it covers not only directly effective rights

it seems widely accepted that, whereas the presumption of domestic autonomy (subject to the principles of equivalence and effectiveness) applies to determine the modalities under which Treaty rights are exercised before the national courts,[3] the very existence of a right under Community law falls to be defined directly by the Court of Justice.[4] Since the conditions giving rise to liability to make reparation for an enforceable breach of the Treaty are so closely linked to the existence and nature of the substantive Community right itself, it has also been argued that competence over those conditions vests, as a matter of principle, in Community (not domestic) law.[5]

Let's accept the latter proposition to be correct, at least to the extent that the Community institutions and the Court are prepared, as a matter of practice, to define the conditions under which infringement of one's Treaty rights will lead to the imposition of liability to make reparation. It is then settled law that, in certain situations, effective judicial protection requires that the claimant be entitled to a remedy simply on the basis of the public authority's enforceable breach of Community law (without further requirements as to fault). However, it is equally clear that, in other situations, the claimant is only entitled to a remedy on the basis of an infringement of Community law which is considered sufficiently culpable. How do we tell these situations apart? Why in some cases does Community law prescribe a remedy without requirements as to fault; whereas in other cases fault-based criteria seem essential before the claimant can obtain relief? One of the basic submissions underpinning this analysis is that the answer lies partly in the division between the public law and private law liabilities of national authorities — a division which is, in fact, rarely articulated either by the Court, or in the academic literature.

In the case of *public law*, effective judicial protection may demand that relief be provided for a mere breach of the relevant Treaty right. Consider, for example, the reimbursement by Member States of taxes and other charges levied contrary to Community law. The Court in judgments such as *FMC* and *Fantask* made clear that liability to repay is imposed upon the defaulting Member State on the basis of illegality *per se*, without the need for the claimant to prove fault or unreasonableness on the part of the relevant

(eg Case C-213/89 *Factortame* [1990] ECR I-2433); but also certain non-directly effective rights (eg Case C-131/97 *Carbonari* [1999] ECR I-1103); and provisions of Community law which are correctly transposed into the national legal order as a matter of substance, yet still lack sufficiently effective levels of judicial protection (eg Case C-62/00 *Marks & Spencer* [2002] ECR I-6325).

[3] Such as limitation periods, evidential restrictions, heads of recoverable damages, the payment of interest etc.
[4] See, eg AG Léger in Case C-453/00 *Kühne & Heitz* (Opinion of 17 June 2003; Judgment of 13 January 2004).
[5] See, eg W van Gerven 'Of Rights, Remedies and Procedures' (2000) 37 *CML Rev* 501.

public authorities.[6] In fact, the only defence available to the Member State is to argue that the quantum due for reimbursement should be reduced to the extent that the claimant would otherwise be unjustly enriched, having already passed on a proportion of the charge to his/her customers.[7] However, in appropriate circumstances, effective judicial protection may instead permit relief to be made conditional upon the claimant satisfying certain additional considerations, aimed at balancing the individual interest in obtaining redress against the general interest in protecting public authorities in the efficient performance of their functions. This is the natural home of the *Francovich* case law and applies, for example, to the Member State's failure to transpose directives on time or correctly under Article 249 EC;[8] or a breach of the rules on the free movement of goods under Articles 28–30 EC.[9] In such situations, it is legitimate to take into account factors such as the degree of legislative or administrative discretion enjoyed by the Member State in discharging its public functions, and the relative clarity or ambiguity of the relevant Treaty legislation, before transforming a simple infringement of Community law into a breach which is sufficiently serious to warrant imposing liability to make reparation.

In the case of *private law*, effective judicial protection may again require that relief be provided for a mere breach of the claimant's Treaty rights. Sometimes the relevant Community legislation will say so explicitly. For example, the Product Liability Directive provides that producers shall be liable for damage caused by defects in their products; and that such liability shall not, in relation to the injured person, be limited or excluded by any other provisions.[10] In other cases, the Court will construe the relevant Community legislation to achieve the same effect. For example, discrimination against women (or men) as regards their terms and conditions of employment, contrary to the Equal Treatment Directive, of itself gives rise to liability on the part of the defaulting employer.[11] The Court held in *Dekker* and *Draehmpaehl* that national law may not curtail the scope of the consequent duty to make adequate reparation, by imposing additional fault-based requirements, even where these would, in practice, be very easy for the claimant to satisfy.[12] Again, however, in appropriate circumstances,

[6] Case C-212/94 *FMC* [1996] ECR I-389; Case C-188/95 *Fantask* [1997] ECR I-6783.

[7] And even then, successful reliance upon this defence is subject to strict conditions concerning, *inter alia*, the allocation of the burden of proof, eg Case 199/82 *San Giorgio* [1983] ECR 3595; Cases C-192-218/95 *Comateb* [1997] ECR I-165; Cases C-441 and 442/98 *Mikhailidis* [2000] ECR I-7145.

[8] Cases C-178-179 and 188-190/94 *Dillenkofer* [1996] ECR I-4845; Case C-392/93 *ex parte British Telecommunications* [1996] ECR I-1631.

[9] Cases C-46 and 48/93 *Brasserie du Pêcheur and Factortame III* [1996] ECR I-1029; Case C-5/94 *Hedley Lomas* [1996] ECR I-2553.

[10] Dir 85/374, OJ 1985 L 210/29.

[11] Dir 76/207, OJ 1976 L 39/40.

[12] Case C-177/88 *Dekker* [1990] ECR I-3941; Case C-180/95 *Draehmpaehl* [1997] ECR I-2195.

effective judicial protection may instead permit relief to be made conditional upon the claimant complying with additional criteria pertinent to the particular policy sphere at issue in the relevant dispute. Consider the judgment in *Courage v Crehan* (bearing in mind that this case involved a horizontal dispute, not the actions of a public authority). Breach of Article 81 EC should, in principle, give rise to an action for compensation in respect of losses incurred through the relevant anti-competitive practice. But this need not necessarily be the case — as, for example, where the claimant was itself party to the unlawful agreement. In such situations, national courts may take into account factors such as the relative bargaining power enjoyed by the claimant and the defendant, and thus their relative degrees of culpability, in determining whether compensation should be recoverable in practice.[13]

## *FRANCOVICH* AND PARALLEL REMEDIES

So, what is the point of *Francovich*? Based on these preliminary observations, the answer seems to be that *Francovich* contributes to the system of principles governing the administrative law responsibilities of public authorities under the Treaty. In particular, it establishes a threshold of culpability designed to balance the private interest in obtaining reparation against the public interest in limiting liability.[14]

However, the situation becomes confused because the Court says that *Francovich* runs parallel to the direct effect of *any* provision of Community law intended to confer rights on the individual.[15] This creates the possibility of double remedies, through the cumulative application of *Francovich* liability and any other action deriving directly from the relevant Community right. In this regard, one should distinguish between two separate situations: public law situations which carry parallel public law actions; and private law situations which carry parallel but mixed private and public law actions.

[13] Albeit phrased in terms of preventing unjust enrichment and not profiting from one's own wrong: Case C-453/99 *Courage v Crehan* [2001] ECR I-6297. For a good example of Community legislation which would create both strict and fault-based liability, consider the Commission's proposal for an Environmental Liability Directive: COM(2002) 17 Final; cf COM(2000) 66 Final.

[14] It is through this primary purpose that *Francovich* also performs certain secondary functions under Community law, eg acting as a surrogate for the horizontal direct effect of directives; and for more intrusive forms of intervention in national remedial autonomy (as in Cases C-192–218/95 *Comateb* [1997] ECR I-165; Case C-66/95 *Sutton* [1997] ECR I-2163; Case C-54/96 *Dorsch Consult* [1997] ECR I-4961). Further: M Dougan 'The *Francovich* Right to Reparation: Reshaping the Contours of Community Remedial Competence' (2000) 6 *European Public Law* 103.

[15] As well as applying to provisions of Community law which are insufficiently clear, precise and unconditional to have direct effect but are intended to confer rights on individuals nevertheless.

In *public law* situations (for example, where the claimant has a restitutionary action in respect of an unlawfully levied charge, but could also bring a *Francovich* claim against the defaulting Member State), the possibility of parallelism is resolved in practice by reference to rules on the exhaustion of alternative remedies. The case law gives divergent guidance about the correct scope of application of these principles. The Court in *Brasserie* certainly recognised that national rules requiring claimants to mitigate their losses by first pursuing alternative remedies were acceptable under Community law, albeit qualified in the *Metallgesellschaft* case with the inevitable proviso that such alternative remedies must in any case be adequate in nature.[16] Otherwise, the Court in both *Lindöpark* and *Metallgesellschaft* seemed to assume that claimants are entitled to bring *Francovich* claims, even if restitutionary actions are available in respect of exactly the same losses.[17] This idea was criticised by Advocate General Jacobs in *Denkavit*, who believed that *Francovich* could thereby be abused so as to avoid the stricter procedural requirements (such as shorter time limits) applicable to restitutionary, as compared to compensatory, claims.[18] But the Advocate General's views on this issue have since evolved. In *Fantask*, he observed that the claimant's ability to use *Francovich* as a means of evading the shorter time limit for restitutionary actions could perhaps be justified by the fact that the Member State had committed not just a breach, but a sufficiently serious breach of its Treaty obligations, warranting a reappraisal of the relationship between the individual interest in obtaining redress and the collective interest in preserving legal certainty.[19] The point is that, although the case law here may be confused (or at least underdeveloped), it reflects differing views about the appropriate balance to be struck between competing public interest requirements, as embodied in different types of public law action. *Francovich* is merely struggling to find its rightful place in the Community's evolving system of administrative law.

However, the possibility of parallelism is more difficult to understand in *private law* situations which carry mixed private and public law remedies.

[16] Cases C-46 and 48/93 *Brasserie du Pêcheur and Factortame III* [1996] ECR I-1029; Cases C-397 and 410/98 *Metallgesellschaft* [2001] ECR I-1727.
[17] Case C-150/99 *Stockholm Lindöpark* [2001] ECR I-493; Cases C-397 and 410/98 *Metallgesellschaft* [2001] ECR I-1727. Cf AG Léger in Case C-5/94 *Hedley Lomas* [1996] ECR I-2553. Cf AG Jacobs in Case C-90/94 *Haahr Petroleum* [1997] ECR I-4085.
[18] Case C-2/94 *Denkavit* [1996] ECR I-2827. Cf P Oliver 'State Liability in Damages Following *Factortame III*: A Remedy Seen in Context' in J Beatson and T Tridimas (eds), *New Directions in European Public Law* (Oxford, Hart Publishing, 1998).
[19] Case C-188/95 *Fantask* [1997] ECR I-6783. Cf P Eeckhout 'Liability of Member States in Damages and the Community System of Remedies' in J Beatson and T Tridimas (eds), *New Directions in European Public Law* (Oxford, Hart Publishing, 1998). Further: A Anagnostaras 'State Liability and Alternative Courses of Action: How Independent Can an Autonomous Remedy Be?' (2002) 21 *Yearbook of European Law* 355.

There are two questions here: does parallelism actually apply to private law situations; and if so, how should one react to it?

As for the first question, the Court has not offered much by way of explicit guidance. *Francovich* cases have so far always involved what we would probably think of as 'public law obligations': failing to transpose directives correctly or on time;[20] enacting or maintaining legislation incompatible with the Treaty itself;[21] or taking individual administrative decisions within a general regulatory framework which fail to comply with Community law.[22] Moreover, the Court in *Brasserie* alluded to the existence of a distinction between the general duty to make reparation for one's legal defaults, and the particular situation of imposing liability upon public authorities performing public functions.[23] However, the basic principles remain framed so broadly as to be capable of catching public authorities, not only when acting as legislators or regulators, but also as employers or contractors: *any* breach of a Community norm which is intended to confer rights on the individual is capable of activating the *Francovich* right to reparation against the wrongdoing Member State.[24]

The academic debate is similarly unclear. Pre-*Brasserie*, some observers saw *Francovich* as conferring a general right to reparation based on unlawful conduct by the Member State, without further reference to any requirement of culpability, and thus applicable to the realms of both public and private law;[25] whereas other commentators speculated that the Court would soon introduce fault-based criteria more appropriate to an administrative law context, and thus implied that *Francovich* was best considered a form of public law action.[26] Post-*Brasserie*, many writers recognised the administrative law provenance of the substantive liability conditions borrowed by the Court from its case law under Article 288(2) EC;[27] but some commentators still interpreted *Francovich* as providing a general right to reparation against the defaulting Member State, without drawing any further distinction between the different public and private law contexts in

[20] Eg Case C-140/97 *Rechberger* [1999] ECR I-3499; Case C-371/97 *Gozza* [2000] ECR I-7881.
[21] Eg Case C-242/95 *GT-Link* [1997] ECR I-4449; Case C-302/97 *Konle* [1999] ECR I-3099.
[22] Eg Case C-127/95 *Norbrook* [1998] ECR I-1531; Case C-319/96 *Brinkmann* [1998] ECR I-5255.
[23] Eg contrast paras 20–23 with paras 43–45. Also: AG Tesauro, paras 12 and 67–68 Opinion. Consider also: Case C-261/95 *Palmisani* [1997] ECR I-4025, para 38.
[24] Eg *Brasserie*, para 51. More recently, eg Case C-224/01 *Köbler* (Judgment of 30 September 2003), paras 30–31.
[25] Consider, eg C Lewis and S Moore 'Duties, Directives and Damages in European Community Law' [1993] *Public Law* 151.
[26] Eg P Craig '*Francovich*, Remedies and the Scope of Damages Liability' (1993) 109 *LQR* 595. Cf J Steiner 'From Direct Effects to *Francovich*: Shifting Means of Enforcement of Community Law' (1993) 18 *EL Rev* 3.
[27] Eg P Craig 'Once More Unto the Breach: The Community, the State and Damages Liability' (1997) 113 *LQR* 67.

which public authorities might operate.[28] Indeed, Advocate General Léger in *Hedley Lomas* seemed happy to use the benefit of hindsight to recategorise *Foster v British Gas* as a *Francovich*-style case. Yet *Foster* clearly involved a purely operational breach of Community law by an emanation of the state,[29] which had arisen within a private law context, and as regards which the claimant already had access to effective private law remedies.[30] For the most part, however, the issue of whether *Francovich* applies to vertical-yet-private-law disputes appears simply to have gone unnoticed, or at least unaddressed.[31]

If the tacit indications in the case law and the assumptions in certain of the academic literature are correct, then this leads to our second question: how should one react to the possibility of parallelism in the private law sphere? To help illustrate the potential difficulties, imagine the discriminatory dismissal of a female employee by her employer, which just happens to be a public authority (another purely operational breach of Community law). The Equal Treatment Directive requires reparation without further proof of fault; and (if the Member State chooses to make reparation by way of compensation) insists upon the payment of full damages.[32] By contrast, *Francovich* requires the Member State to make reparation only upon proof of a sufficiently serious breach; and (though the case law can hardly be considered entirely clear) insists upon the payment of merely adequate damages.[33] The traditional view is that, although it would be theoretically possible, the claimant will usually have no practical interest in bringing a *Francovich* action in this type of situation. Indeed, *Francovich* looks like a useless overlap — unless (of course) it provides a second bite at the remedial cherry, for those who have missed the shorter time limit applicable to actions under domestic legislation implementing the Equal Treatment Directive. In that case, we simply come back to the question of whether *Francovich* should be available as a means of overcoming the procedural restrictions imposed upon

[28] Eg N Emiliou 'State Liability Under Community Law: Shedding More Light on the *Francovich* Principle?' (1996) 21 *EL Rev* 399; though note the query raised by E Deards 'Curiouser and Curiouser? The Development of Member State Liability in the Court of Justice' (1997) 3 *European Public Law* 117.

[29] Actionable as such through the vertical direct effect of the Equal Treatment Directive; and triggered, of course, by the transpositional breach committed by the Member State itself.

[30] Case C-5/94 *Hedley Lomas* [1996] ECR I-2553; Case C-188/89 *Foster v British Gas* [1990] ECR I-3313. Also: W van Gerven 'Non-Contractual Liability of Member States, Community Institutions and Individuals for Breaches of Community Law with a View to a Common Law for Europe' (1994) 1 *Maastricht Journal* 6.

[31] All three of the main English language textbooks are basically silent on this issue: S Weatherill and P Beaumont *EU Law* (London, Penguin Books, 1999); A Arnull, A Dashwood, M Ross and D Wyatt *Wyatt and Dashwood's European Union Law* (London, Sweet & Maxwell, 2000); P Craig and G de Búrca, *EU Law: Text, Cases, & Materials* (Oxford, OUP, 2002).

[32] Eg Case 14/83 *von Colson* [1984] ECR 1891; Case C-271/91 *Marshall II* [1993] ECR I-4367.

[33] Eg Cases C-94–5/95 *Bonifaci* [1997] ECR I-3969; Case C-373/95 *Maso* [1997] ECR I-4051.

the claimant's primary means of relief (and to the Court's still-adolescent case law on exhausting adequate alternative remedies).

However, one should question more fundamentally the underlying possibility of parallelism in such situations. In particular, one might argue that the Court should not permit *Francovich* to be available in private law situations *at all*. The objection here is not that parallelism is unfair to those claimants who now have a choice of remedies under Community law. After all, from their point of view, parallelism means *more* effective judicial protection. Rather, the problem is that to have parallel remedies in private law situations seems conceptually inappropriate. The substantive liability conditions established in *Brasserie* serve no useful purpose, since the public authority is not acting in the general interest; and we have no expectation that a sufficiently serious breach of Community law, judged according to those conditions, should furnish a gateway to reparation under the Treaty, as compared to either liability *per se* or some more appropriate framework of culpability. Moreover, accepting the possibility of dual remedies in (vertical) private law cases would mean unfairly discriminating between the levels of effective judicial protection offered to citizens in entirely comparable (horizontal) situations. Individuals who cross private law swords with a public authority may find that they have two remedies at their disposal (in private law, *and* under *Francovich*); whereas those who have exactly the same type of dispute with another private individual would have only a single remedy (in private law, *not* under *Francovich*). This has nothing to do with the debate over the vertical and horizontal direct effect of directives — after all, there is nothing like the text of Article 249 EC here to distort artificially the proper scope of the principle of effective judicial protection. It is simply the result of an attitude which sees *Francovich* as being linked to Community law rights enforceable against the Member States, rather than to public law situations recognised and given special status as such within the framework of Community law.

## *FRANCOVICH* AND REMEDY BLINDSPOTS

The potential problems do not rest there. It should be recalled that those situations in which the legislature or the Court have actually exercised their assumed competence to clarify the relationship between the breach by a public authority of a given provision of Community law, and the appropriate basis upon which reparation should be made to the individual right-holder, are surprisingly few and far between. In many cases, we have little or no direct guidance about whether the claimant who invokes rights under Community law is entitled to a remedy for a breach of those rights *per se*, or is able to claim relief only on the basis of some fault criterion. We are left instead to draw what seem like appropriate analogies with the available case law. And so here, it is more difficult to repine against the possibility of parallelism through the cumulative application of *Francovich* and whatever other forms of relief might exist by virtue of the Treaty — precisely because we do not know which other actions (if any) Community law might provide. But these gaps in our current legal knowledge pose dangers of their own.

Consider, by way of illustration, three scenarios involving the free movement of workers under Article 39 EC. First, imagine that a Member State enacts legislation imposing a language requirement for certain categories of employment, creating indirect discrimination against foreign workers which cannot be objectively justified by an imperative requirement of the public interest.[34] Besides insisting that foreign workers be restored to a situation of equality with domestic nationals by setting aside the incompatible domestic legislation,[35] the claimant seeks damages against the Member State for losses suffered through his/her failure to obtain employment. Traditional analysis would tell us that this is a vertical relationship, and therefore *Francovich* applies to determine the conditions under which the claimant's action for reparation can proceed. Our alternative analysis would tell us instead that this is a public law situation, concerned with the regulatory competence of the national legislature, and therefore *Francovich* applies to help balance the individual against the general interest. Different reasoning, same result.[36]

Secondly, imagine that a private employer imposes of its own volition an unjustified language requirement for a specific post.[37] Again, the claimant relies upon Community law to claim damages for any losses incurred through the employer's refusal to consider his/her application. Traditional analysis would now tell us that this is a horizontal situation, and therefore *Francovich* cannot be available. Our new analysis would say that this is a private law situation, concerned with the mandatory obligations applicable to prospective employment relationships, and therefore *Francovich* should not apply. But beyond this, it is difficult to identify with any certainty the proper basis upon which liability to make reparation should be incurred (ie *per se* or fault-based). By analogy with the case law under the Equal Treatment Directive, the Court might well insist that the mere breach of Article 39 EC is in itself sufficient to warrant relief — even if one still recognises that recoverable damages may nevertheless be limited under domestic law, for example, where the claimant would have failed to obtain employment in any case for objective reasons related to his / her qualifications and experience.[38]

[34] Consider, eg Case C-379/87 *Groener* [1989] ECR 3967.
[35] Consider, eg Case C-15/96 *Schöning* [1998] ECR I-47.
[36] Consider, eg Case C-90/96 *Petrie* [1997] ECR I-6527.
[37] Consider, eg Case C-281/98 *Angonese* [2000] I-4139.
[38] Consider, eg Case C-180/95 *Draehmpaehl* [1997] ECR I-2195.

Thirdly, imagine that a public authority imposes of its own volition the same unjustified language requirement for a given job (another purely operational breach of Article 39 EC). When it comes to the claimant's action for damages, the available case law again offers us little concrete guidance about the appropriate criteria for imposing liability. Which model should the Court opt for? Traditional analysis would suggest that, since a vertical situation is involved, *Francovich* may now legitimately apply. However, it is difficult to see here why the simple factor of institutional identity should be crucial in determining liability: this dispute does not involve any special responsibility for administering the public interest (making it less like situation one), and can basically be equated to a private law relationship between public body and individual citizen (making it more like situation two). As with cases of parallelism between private and public law remedies in private law situations, it again seems conceptually inappropriate to invoke *Francovich* — albeit *this time* to patch-up our existing remedy blindspot with a single course of redress. And again, traditional analysis could well result in two essentially comparable situations being treated differently — *but here*, to the detriment of the claimant in a vertical situation (who now finds that his / her only means of relief depends upon the existence of a sufficiently serious breach in accordance with the *Francovich* case law), as compared to the claimant in a horizontal situation (whose remedy would likely be provided for the breach *per se*, and at worst reduced in value on the basis of some more suitable criteria of 'culpability').[39]

There is therefore a risk that, as regards those Community provisions for which the abstract principles of effective judicial protection as yet supply little firm indication about the specific rules for transforming 'breach' into 'remedy', a viewpoint which equates *Francovich* with vertical relationships would result in less favourable conditions for individual enforcement than an approach which stresses the public or private law nature of a given situation — especially as compared to the liability principles which one would expect the Court to apply in identical disputes which happen to arise within a horizontal relationship.[40] Our new analysis would therefore lead us to argue that the public authority guilty of perpetrating a purely operational

[39] Note that the principle of equivalence would not necessarily help to resolve this problem. The Court accepts that horizontal and vertical cases may be treated differently for the purposes of the principle of equivalence, eg Case C-231/96 *Edis* [1998] ECR I-4951, though this probably assumes the existence of objective distinctions between the two situations. More importantly, the relevant discrimination would not have not arisen between comparable rights deriving from Community and national law, through choices attributable to the Member State; but rather between two Treaty claims, due to factors deriving from Community law itself.

[40] It is hardly idle speculation to fear the emergence in the Court's case law of arbitrary distinctions between the standards of judicial protection available in vertical and horizontal situations. Consider, eg the recovery of interest. Within the context of a non-compensatory action brought against the defaulting Member State, the Court in Case C-66/95 *Sutton* [1997] ECR I-2163 held that the claimant's proper means of redress was to bring a *Francovich* action

breach of Article 39 EC, by imposing an unjustified language requirement, should not be treated any differently from an ordinary private employer. We would anticipate that liability to make reparation should be incurred through the breach of Article 39 EC *per se*, subject to any appropriate limitations on the value of the claimant's recoverable damages.

## PROBLEMS COMPOUNDED! THE COURT'S 'UNIFIED APPROACH' TO *FRANCOVICH* LIABILITY ...

Traditional analysis thus presents us with two major difficulties, which nevertheless stem from the same underlying attitude: private law situations where *Francovich* is made available in parallel with private law actions, and remedy blindspots which are filled by *Francovich* rather than some more suitable private law action, both simply because the relevant disputes are vertical in character. These difficulties are compounded yet further by recent developments in the case law, concerning the very substantive conditions for incurring *Francovich* liability, whereby the Court is now tending to adopt a new 'unified approach' to the sufficiently serious breach test.

The Court has clearly established that the sufficiently serious breach criterion applies to all *Francovich* actions, even though its application varies according to the circumstances of each case. But pinning down exactly what the sufficiently serious breach test consists of can be a surprisingly difficult task. It is, in fact, possible to identify two main approaches in the case law.

Older judgments (such as *Hedley Lomas* and *Dillenkofer*) suggested that a sufficiently serious breach could be established in one of two ways.[41] First, where the Member State had an appreciable degree of discretion in discharging its Treaty obligations, whether that discretion was legislative or administrative in nature, the claimant must demonstrate a manifest and grave disregard by the Member State of the limits of its powers.[42] For these purposes, the national court should take into account various factors as identified in *Brasserie*: the degree of the Member State's discretion, the clarity of the Community rule, the existence of good faith or bad faith, whether the

seeking damages for losses suffered through the effluxion of time. Within the context of a non-compensatory action brought instead against a defaulting private party, this reasoning could hardly apply: the private party is not directly susceptible to a *Francovich* action for recovery of the interest; and the Member State has not perpetrated any wrong capable of justifying the imposition of liability on its shoulders instead. The implication of such judgments is thus to create artificial cleavages in the standards of effective judicial protection applicable in vertical as compared to horizontal disputes.

[41] Case C-5/94 *Hedley Lomas* [1996] ECR I-2553; Cases C-178–179 and 188–190/94 *Dillenkofer* [1996] ECR I-4845. Also, eg AG Tesauro in Cases C-46 and 48/93 *Brasserie du Pêcheur and Factortame III* [1996] ECR I-1029; AG Cosmas in Cases C-94–5/95 *Bonifaci* [1997] ECR I-3969.

[42] Case C-127/95 *Norbrook* [1998] ECR I-1531; Case C-150/99 *Stockholm Lindöpark* [2001] ECR I-493. Cf Cases C-46 and 48/93 *Brasserie du Pêcheur and Factortame III* [1996]

Community institutions encouraged the Member State to believe it was in fact behaving lawfully etc. Secondly, where the Member State had no appreciable degree of discretion in discharging its Treaty obligations, the mere breach of Community law will be considered sufficiently serious to incur liability to make reparation — without the need to take into account any other factors.[43] Thus, in this line of case law, the existence of discretion is the overriding factor which determines the imposition of *Francovich* liability.[44]

However, more recent case law (such as *Haim* and *Larsy*) suggests an important change in the Court's approach.[45] Again, a sufficiently serious breach may be established in one of two ways. First, where the Member State had an appreciable degree of (legislative or executive) discretion, the claimant must demonstrate a manifest and grave disregard, taking into account the various factors listed in *Brasserie*. Secondly, where the Member State had no appreciable degree of discretion, the mere breach of Community law *may* be considered sufficiently serious — *but not necessarily so*. It is still necessary to take into account the various factors listed in *Brasserie*. In other words, this case law recognises that discretion is not the only factor involved in limiting the liabilities of public authorities performing functions in the general interest. There might well be an insufficiently serious breach, even though the Member State had no real discretion in discharging its Community law obligations.[46] The logic of this case law would be to dispense altogether with the bipartite approach to establishing the existence of a sufficiently serious breach, and adopt a genuinely unified approach to liability based on a global assessment of the *Brasserie* factors (discretion among them).[47]

ECR I-1029; Cases C-283/94 and 291–292/94 *Denkavit* [1996] ECR I-5063. Cf also Case C-392/93 *ex parte British Telecommunications* [1996] ECR I-1631; Case C-140/97 *Rechberger* [1999] ECR I-3499.

[43] Cases C-178–179 and 188–190/94 *Dillenkofer* [1996] ECR I-4845, para 27. Also, eg AG Jacobs in Case C-112/00 *Schmidberger* [2003] ECR I-5659.
[44] Consider also recent case law on Article 288 EC, eg Case C-352/98 P *Bergaderm* [2000] ECR I-5291; Case C-312/00 P *Camar* [2002] ECR I-11355; Case C-472/00 P *Fresh Marine* [2003] ECR I-7541. See further: A Ward, *Judicial Review and the Rights of Private Parties in EC Law* (Oxford, OUP, 2000); T Tridimas 'Liability for Breach of Community Law: Growing Up and Mellowing Down?' (2001) 38 *CML Rev* 301.
[45] Case C-424/97 *Haim* [2000] ECR I-5123; Case C-118/00 *Larsy* [2001] ECR I-5063. Also, eg Case C-319/96 *Brinkmann* [1998] ECR I-5255; AG Léger in Case C-5/94 *Hedley Lomas* [1996] ECR I-2553; AG Saggio in Case C-140/97 *Rechberger* [1999] ECR I-3499.
[46] Also, eg J Steiner 'The Limits of State Liability for Breach of European Community Law' (1998) 4 *European Public Law* 69. Cf R Van den Bergh and H-B Schäfer 'State Liability for Infringement of the EC Treaty: Economic Arguments in Support of a Rule of "Obvious Negligence"' (1998) 23 *EL Rev* 552.
[47] Consider, in this regard, eg AG Jacobs in Case C-319/96 *Brinkmann* [1998] ECR I-5255; AG La Pergola in Case C-302/97 *Konle* [1999] ECR I-3099. Also: AG Léger in Case C-224/01 *Köbler* (Opinion of 8 April 2003). Subject to the special treatment of national supreme courts by the ECJ in Case C-224/01 *Köbler* (Judgment of 30 September 2003). Cf the approach of the EFTA Court in Case E-9/97 *Sveinbjörnsdóttir* (Judgment of 10 December 1998); and of the House of Lords in *Factortame V* [2000] 1 AC 524.

This second line of case law has so far concerned (purely operational) breaches of public law obligations (misapplying the rules on free movement of persons when deciding whether to register dentists, or misapplying the rules on social security coordination when calculating pension entitlements) — so at least the sufficiently serious breach criterion is still being applied to cases in which national authorities are performing some sort of public function. However, the same approach could easily be transposed, according to a traditional analysis of the current case law focusing upon the mere existence of a vertical relationship, to equivalent (purely operational) infringements by the Member State of its ordinary private law obligations in realms such as employment law. This is true as regards both those cases involving the possibility of parallelism between *Francovich* and any other claim based on the direct effect of Community law; and those situations where *Francovich* might be invoked as a knee-jerk solution to the need to identify some basis for making reparation under the Treaty. Indeed, were these various lines of case law to coalesce, so that factors such as the clarity of the relevant legislation and the good faith of the defendant raised the threshold of culpability and exonerated public authorities of their wrongdoing even in the private law sphere, this would surely have the effect of distorting (or simply diluting) still further the principles of effective judicial protection, by introducing wholly inappropriate fault requirements without any general interest to justify them.[48]

Consider an example inspired by the ruling in *Coote*.[49] A public authority victimises one of its former employees for having brought a sex discrimination claim against it, by refusing to supply references to potential future employers. National law does not explicitly prohibit such victimisation, and nor on its face does the Equal Treatment Directive. However, the Court interprets the Directive in a fairly creative manner, so as to offer former employees protection against harassment in just such circumstances. That obligation becomes binding upon the public authority, if necessary even in the absence of correct national transposition, thanks to the principle of vertical direct effect. Under the current law, the claimant then seems to have two options. Either she can bring an action for compensation derived directly from the Directive, without having to prove any particular threshold of culpability over and above the simple infringement of Community law. Or alternatively, she can bring an action for damages under *Francovich*, based on the existence of a sufficiently serious breach, as regards the operational infringement committed by the public authority.[50] But in that event,

[48] Cf W van Gerven 'Bridging the Unbridgeable: Community and National Tort Laws After *Francovich* and *Brasserie*' (1996) 45 *ICLQ* 507.

[49] Case C-185/97 *Coote* [1998] ECR I-5199.

[50] Again, this *Francovich* action would *not* relate to shortcomings in transposition (if any) committed by the Member State itself.

the public authority might well escape liability because, even though it had no real discretion in complying with its directly effective Community law obligations, the relevant provisions of the Equal Treatment Directive were very obscure; and it acted in the genuine belief that it was under no Community obligation to provide the references. That is the logic of the principle of parallelism, read together with the judgments in *Haim* and *Larsy* — but it is difficult to divine any compelling reason why this logic should apply to purely private law disputes which just happen to involve a public authority. Clarity of legislative drafting may well be relevant in determining the Member State's liability as a matter of public law, and this may well be true even in the absence of any appreciable legislative or administrative discretion on the part of the public authority when discharging its obligations under the Treaty. But since when could clarity of legislative drafting exonerate any defendant from liability, in fields such as employment, as a matter of private law?[51]

## PROBLEMS RESOLVED? ANOTHER 'UNIFIED APPROACH' TO *FRANCOVICH* LIABILITY…

There is an argument — another 'unified approach' to the *Francovich* case law, based upon the opinion of Advocate General van Gerven in *Banks* — that all these problems are not insurmountable.[52] The argument runs as follows.

According to Article 288 EC, the conditions underpinning the non-contractual liability of the Community institutions and, since *Brasserie*, underpinning also the non-contractual liability of the national authorities, represent general principles derived from the common legal traditions of the Member States.[53] As such, they could readily extend across, and be tailored to, *every kind* of non-contractual liability — encompassing both public and private law situations, indeed whether those situations are vertical or horizontal in nature.[54] Thus, one might argue that the sufficiently serious breach criterion is flexible enough to catch private law disputes, including even cases where reparation should be made on the basis of illegality *per se*. For example, in *Banks* itself, Advocate General van Gerven submitted that, for the purposes of applying the general principles of non-contractual liability underlying Article 288 EC to infringements of Community competition law,

[51] Though note that considerations of legal certainty may, in exceptional circumstances, prevent enforcement of the otherwise valid provisions (say) of a Community regulation against private parties: eg Case C-108/01 *Consorzio del Prosciutto di Parma* [2003] ECR I-5121.
[52] Case C-128/92 *Banks* [1994] ECR I-1209.
[53] Eg *Brasserie*, paras 29 and 41.
[54] *Banks*, paras 49 and 50 Opinion.

there would be no question of permitting the relevant undertakings to benefit from rules developed specifically to evaluate the conduct of public authorities exercising broad discretionary powers. Referring to *Dekker* (a private law judgment), the Advocate General contended that liability to make reparation should instead be engaged, within the over-arching framework of the *Francovich* case law, on the basis of a breach of the Treaty *per se*.[55]

As a prescriptive model for the future development of the principles of effective judicial protection, this approach might well appear legally attractive for two main reasons.

First, the availability of *Francovich* actions (in parallel or by default) need not necessarily lead the Court to introduce inappropriate culpability criteria into private law disputes, because such criteria could readily be dispensed with in cases where they are not deemed suitable. On the other hand, such a 'unified approach' might seem so abstract as to be almost meaningless — more paying lip-service to the grand idea of constructing a macro-framework for dealing with non-contractual liability under Community law, than helping address the practical problems of identifying *why* and *when* liability to make reparation should be incurred on a *per se* basis or instead through fault criteria. Moreover, there is perhaps a risk that this argument over-estimates the ability of incremental case law developments to sustain coherent dividing-lines between the treatment of different categories of situation. Indeed, the very idea of a 'single test for non-contractual liability' might in itself make it more difficult to ensure that appropriate factors are taken into or left out of account in the various public and private, vertical and horizontal contexts which require judicial attention.

This would seem especially true in the light of case law such as *Haim* and *Larsy*. In terms of the historical reach of the Court's culpability criteria, the barrier between national authorities exercising wide discretionary powers in the general interest, and domestic authorities acting without any appreciable discretion in the public law sphere, was perhaps wider than the barrier still separating domestic authorities acting without any appreciable discretion in the public law sphere from national authorities operating in a purely private law capacity. If *Brasserie* factors such as drafting quality and good faith were able to jump across the former gulf, it may prove more difficult than one would imagine to contain them from seeping across the latter crevice. And so, the present author at least entertains doubts about whether a 'unified approach' to non-contractual liability could resist the momentum

[55] *Banks*, para 53 Opinion; Case C-177/88 *Dekker* [1990] ECR I-3941. See also: W van Gerven 'Non-Contractual Liability of Member States, Community Institutions and Individuals for Breaches of Community Law with a View to a Common Law for Europe' (1994) 1 *Maastricht Journal* 6; D Edward and W Robinson 'Is There a Place For Private Law Principles in Community Law?' in T Heukels and A McDonnell (eds), *The Action for Damages in Community Law* (The Hague, Kluwer Law, 1997); A Alvizou, 'Individual Tort Liability for Infringements of Community Law' (2002) 29 *Legal Issues of European Integration* 177;

of the current case law, without ultimately being forced to articulate exactly the same type of basic public-private distinction now being advocated by this paper.

Secondly, because the proposal for a 'unified approach' to non-contractual liability would apply as much to horizontal as to vertical relationships, it need not lead the Court to discriminate unfairly between claimants faced with public or private defendants. In particular, although this model would leave in place (as regards private law situations) the possibility of parallel relief under *Francovich* and other actions based directly on the relevant provisions of Community law, that possibility could apply against both public and private bodies — and would have to be resolved in the same way (through the duty to mitigate one's losses by exhausting alternative remedies) — thus ensuring that comparable situations are treated in like manner. Conversely, where *Francovich* is employed to fill existing remedy blindspots, the claimant in a vertical situation need not necessarily be any worse off than the claimant in a horizontal situation: both would be dealt with according to the same framework of principles, within which the sufficiently serious breach criterion could, if necessary, equate to reparation for the infringement *per se*. On the other hand, any real likelihood of the case law actually yielding these potential advantages has perhaps been weakened by the judgment in *Courage v Crehan*.[56]

Academic debate has yet to generate consensus about how best to interpret the Court's foray into the principles of private liability to make reparation under Articles 81 and 82 EC: for example, whether the Court intended to create a new right to seek compensation under the Treaty in respect of any breach of Community competition law; or sought only to ensure that Member States provided an effective remedy under national law, which (depending on the circumstances) might well be in restitution or through specific relief, rather than by compensatory damages.[57] But in any case, it is surely clear that *Courage* is neither simply an extension of *Francovich* to horizontal disputes, nor even an adaptation of the *Francovich* principles, in any meaningful form, so as also to cover the conduct of private parties.[58] This in itself undermines the idea that the sufficiently serious breach criterion

C Kremer 'Liability for Breach of European Community Law: An Analysis of the New Remedy in the Light of English and German Law' (2003) 22 *Yearbook of European Law* 203.

[56] Case C-453/99 *Courage v Crehan* [2001] ECR I-6297.

[57] Contrast, eg A Komninos 'New Prospects for Private Enforcement of EC Competition Law: *Courage v Crehan* and the Community Rights to Damages' (2002) 39 *CML Rev* 447; with O Odudu and J Edelman 'Compensatory Damages for Breach of Article 81' (2002) 27 *EL Rev* 327. Consider also, eg A Albors Llorens 'The Ruling in *Courage v Crehan*: Judicial Activism or Consistent Approach?' [2002] *CLJ* 38; A Jones and D Beard 'Co-Contractors, Damages and Article 81: the ECJ Finally Speaks' [2002] *ECLR* 247.

[58] See, eg M Dougan 'Enforcing the Single Market: The Judicial Harmonisation of National Remedies and Procedural Rules' in C Barnard and J Scott (eds), *The Law of the Single European*

is a general principle, derived from the common legal traditions of the Member States, ripe for catching private as well as public infractions of Community law, at anything other than the very highest level of abstraction. And this in turn suggests that the proposal for a 'unified approach' to non-contractual liability is incapable of reconciling itself entirely to the current law, whose logic of parallelism (or risk of blindspots) would still conspire to punish claimants merely for having picked their private law fight with another individual rather than a public authority (or vice versa).

For these reasons, rather than support the (over-)ambitious model suggested by Advocate General van Gerven in *Banks*, it would seem preferable to lobby for the Court simply to clarify that *Francovich* is confined to the sphere of public law — whilst private law liabilities (whether they arise in vertical or horizontal disputes) remain to be dealt with through a different legal framework.

## CONCLUSIONS

A mature system of effective judicial protection needs to reach beyond our enduring tendency to see the entire Community landscape in terms of the vertical and the horizontal, so as to incorporate also a more rigorous distinction between liabilities arising under public law and those governed by private law.

In particular, Community lawyers seem traditionally to think of *Francovich* in terms of effective judicial protection for Community rights against the actions of public authorities. But insofar as this leads us to treat *Francovich* as applicable to *all* directly effective Community actions in vertical situations: first, the Court risks obscuring the fundamental policy function of the sufficiently serious breach test, by applying inappropriate fault-based criteria to determine the liability of public authorities in purely private law situations; and secondly, the Court risks unfairly discriminating between the levels of effective judicial protection offered to citizens in entirely comparable situations, creating new and entirely unnecessary distinctions between vertical and horizontal disputes, which lack even the weak constitutional reasoning used to prop up the *Marshall* and *Dori* case law on the direct effect of directives.[59]

*Market: Unpacking the Premises* (Oxford, Hart Publishing, 2002). On the outer boundaries of the 'state' for *Francovich* purposes, consider: Case C-242/95 *GT Link* [1997] ECR I-4449; Case C-302/97 *Konle* [1999] ECR I-3099; Case C-424/97 *Haim* [2000] ECR I-5123.

[59] Case 152/84 *Marshall* [1986] ECR 723; Case C-91/92 *Faccini Dori* [1994] ECR I-3325.

It has been argued that we should move away from an institutional view of *Francovich* liability (based on whether or not there is a public authority), and more towards a functional view of *Francovich* liability (posing the question of whether or not the dispute is one of public law or private law). This means that the Court should not treat *Francovich* as running parallel to all directly effective Community actions. *Francovich* should only be available as a parallel action (if at all) where the dispute concerns the public law liabilities of public authorities, not where it concerns their private law obligations. The latter should be determined either on the basis of liability *per se*; or as liability judged according to fault criteria suited to the particular private law sphere at issue.

This is, in itself, hardly a very radical idea: after all, the Member States learned exactly the same sorts of lesson decades ago. For example, under French law, the early post-revolutionary notion that public law applied to all legal relations involving the state, whilst private law applied only to legal relations between individuals, gave way in the later nineteenth century to a more complex approach, based on the concept of 'the performance of a public service', by which the activities of public authorities may be subject to private law before the ordinary courts (say) when carrying out activities of a commercial or industrial character, and as regards other types of conduct which can be classified as essentially private in nature.[60] Conversely, the Diceyan ideal of the English constitution, whereby the rule of law requires public authorities to be subject to the same legal obligations as any private individual, has given way to the development of administrative legal principles imposing special duties upon bodies engaged in the performance of public functions; and also to extensive adaptations of ordinary tort law principles which make it more difficult to impose liability (say) in negligence, when a public authority is performing duties in the general interest.[61] In neither legal system can public authorities shelter behind simply their capacity *qua* public authorities, so as to evade the responsibilities which they would otherwise engage as a matter of private law.

It remains for the Court to make clear that the same elementary principles hold true for effective judicial protection under Community law. It is unfortunate that, in the context of the *Francovich* right to reparation, this would actually mean *reducing* the range of remedies which currently appear

[60] See, eg L Neville Brown and J Bell *French Administrative Law* (Oxford, Clarendon Press, 1998) Ch 6.

[61] Eg *X v Bedfordshire CC* [1995] 2 AC 633; *Stovin v Wise* [1996] AC 923. Note the impact of the ECHR here: *Osman v United Kingdom* (Judgment of ECtHR, 28 October 1998); *Barrett v Enfield LBC* [1999] 3 All ER 193; *Phelps v Hillingdon LBC* [2001] 2 AC 619; *Z v United Kingdom* (Judgment of ECtHR, 10 May 2001).

available to certain classes of individual. But this apparently ungenerous proposal ultimately seems justified in the interests of doctrinal coherence and practical consistency.[62]

[62] This is not to deny the inevitable difficulties which would themselves follow from any attempt to clarify when, for the purposes of Community law, public authorities act in the public or private law sphere. Consider the quandary experienced by the English courts in attempting to separate public from private law activities, for the purposes of the principle of procedural exclusivity related to the action for judicial review, in the case law from *O'Reilly v Mackman* [1982] 3 All ER 1124 to *Clark v University of Lincolnshire* [2000] 3 All ER 752.

Proposed Framework for Analysis: *Francovich* as a Public Law Remedy (Liability on a Culpability Basis)

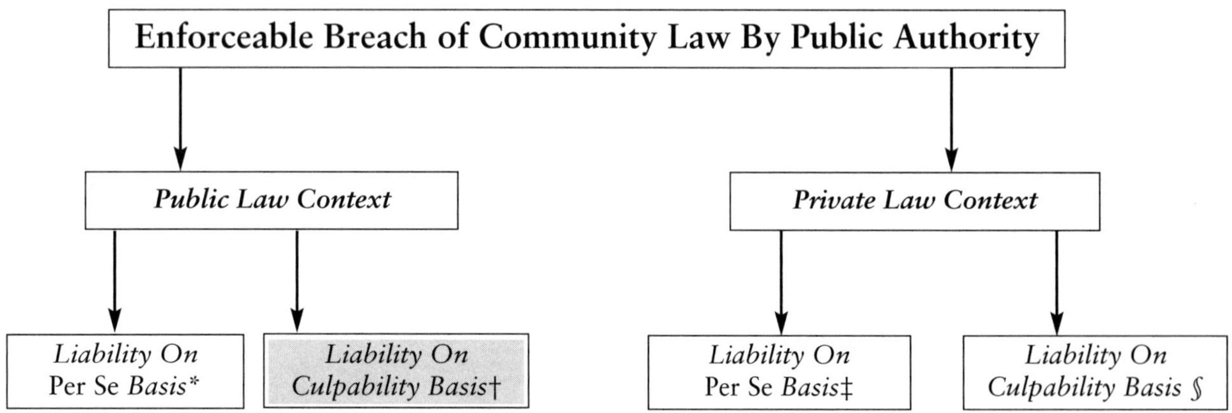


**As compared to framework for analysis which sees *Francovich* as a vertical remedy:**
* Possibility of mixed public law remedies (resolved through exhaustion of alternative remedy rules). Or alternatively, *Francovich* alone ends up filling remedy blindspot (bringing with it inappropriate culpability requirements)
† *Francovich* as the natural Community law action
‡ Possibility of mixed private and public law remedies (the latter introducing inappropriate culpability requirements; and better off than comparable horizontal situations, which have only one remedy). Or alternatively, *Francovich* alone ends up filling remedy blindspot (again introducing inappropriate culpability requirements; but worse off than comparable horizontal situations, which have liability on *per se* basis)
§ Possibility of mixed private and public law remedies (with potentially differing culpability requirements; and still better off than comparable horizontal situations). Or alternatively, *Francovich* alone ends up filling remedy blindspot (with potentially inappropriate culpability requirements; and now treated differently than comparable horizontal situations)

# 15

# *Lines in the Sand: Between Common Foreign Policy and Single Foreign Policy*

EILEEN DENZA

THE CONVENTION ON the Future of Europe, as was to be expected of a representative gathering of people who cared passionately about the development and the future structure of Europe, was deeply divided over the shape of that structure. For some, the true objective is that Europe should form a single federal State. Europe as a single State might not be attainable through the forthcoming Intergovernmental Conference, but a single political identity, a single legal personality embracing all areas where Europe has been given powers, should ideally cover itself with as many as possible with as many as possible of the visible signs of statehood. For others, the continued survival of the nation States is paramount. Further powers for the European Union must in their view be justified on grounds of functional need and must not call into question the separate nationhood of the Member States. The recently liberated States of Eastern Europe, forming a large majority of those joining the Union in 2004, have generally made clear that they have not regained full sovereign independence from Moscow in order to surrender it to Brussels.

An impartial study of the draft Constitution emerging from the Convention shows that each of these camps won some ground and lost some ground. The object of this paper is to identify certain provisions in the text which might if endorsed by treaty call into question the separate nation status of the Member States. The lines in the sand — given the importance of independence in the conduct of external relations in defining a sovereign State — are between a common foreign policy and a single foreign policy. States forming a confederation or a Union under which they retain their sovereign independence may under international law undertake commitments which substantially limit their freedom of action even on issues central to their survival. The United Nations and the North Atlantic Treaty

Organisation are striking examples. The fusion of separate foreign policies into a single foreign policy is however a sign of the fusion of sovereign States.

## THE TEST OF SOVEREIGN NATION STATUS

The general structure established by the Constitution is certainly one of a political Union among sovereign States. The Constitution will be established by a treaty requiring for its entry into force under Article IV-8 ratification by all Member States of the European Union. Under Article IV-7 it can be amended only after ratification by all Member States in accordance with their respective constitutional requirements. Another Convention would form part of the amending procedure, but is given no direct powers to change the Constitution. If four fifths of the Member States ratify the new Constitution while one or more Member States encounter difficulties, the matter is under Article IV-7.4 to be referred to the European Council (as happened following the first Danish referendum on the Treaty of Maastricht) but there is no power thereafter to override or modify the general rules of international law regarding treaty amendment.

Some language which might have cast doubt on the nature of the constitutional structure was removed at a late stage of the Convention negotiations. Article I-1 establishes 'the European Union' rather than the threatening (and also confusing) United States of Europe. The reference to exercising powers conferred on the Union 'on a federal basis' was also taken out of Article I-1. It would be the Member States who under the Constitution conferred competences on the Union to attain objectives they have in common. This wording implies that the powers of the Union derive ultimately from delegation by the sovereign States who set it up.

The form may be contrasted with that of the Constitution of the United States of America which — though entering into force on ratification by nine of the original thirteen States — was proclaimed by the people of the United States and begins:

> We the People of the United States, in order to form a more perfect Union, establish Justice, insure domestic Tranquillity, provide for the common defence, promote the general Welfare and secure the Blessings of Liberty to ourselves and our Posterity, do ordain and establish this Constitution for the United States of America.

Article I-5 of the draft Constitution for the European Union requires the Union to respect the national identities of the Member States, and also provides that:

> It shall respect their essential State functions, including those for ensuring the territorial integrity of the State, and for maintaining law and order and safeguarding internal security.

It is however notable that the 'essential State functions' listed do **not** include the independent conduct of their external relations.

In public international law, a sovereign State is defined by four criteria — territory, population, a government able to exercise effective control of that territory and independence in the conduct of its external relations. In Oppenheim's International Law, this fourth element of statehood is described in these terms:

> There must, fourth and last, be a *sovereign* government. Sovereignty is supreme authority, which on the international plane means not legal authority over all other states but rather legal authority which is not in law dependent on any other earthly authority. Sovereignty in the strict and narrowest sense of the term implies, therefore, independence all round, within and without the borders of the country.[1]

Warbrick says of the fourth element of international sovereignty that

> .... the capacity referred to indicates a legal authority to do so — legal independence which permits the government to make the arrangements it wishes with foreign States and to give effect to them domestically where that is necessary.[2]

When States, whether by agreement or otherwise, become independent, the visible sign of this is that they are accepted as having capacity to conclude and to succeed to treaties, to send and receive diplomatic and consular missions, to join international organizations and to defend themselves, with or without the assistance or support of other independent States, from external attack. Conversely, the fusion of States, for example Scotland and England, Texas and the United States of America, North and South Vietnam, East and West Germany, is marked by the disappearance of separate embassies and ambassadors, of separate treaty relations and of separate membership of international organisations. The new sovereign entity takes over the totality of relations with other States and begins to conduct a single foreign policy.

## THE IMPLICATIONS FOR THE STRUCTURE OF THE EUROPEAN UNION

From 1969, when political cooperation on foreign affairs among the Member States of the European Economic Community began, the foreign

[1] R Jennings and A Watts, *Oppenheim's International Law,* 9th edn (Harlow, Longman, 1996)Vol I, 122. See also UK statement of criteria for recognition of a State, Hansard HC Debs vol 55 col 226, Written Answers, 29 February 1984; E Denza, *The Intergovernmental Pillars of the European Union* (Oxford, OUP, 2002) 33–35; R Gardiner, *International Law* (Harlow, Longman, 2003) chap 5, *States*.

[2] C Warbrick 'States and Recognition in International Law', in M Evans (ed), *International Law* (Oxford, OUP, 2003) 229–30.

ministers and diplomats who practised it were fully conscious of the need for legal as well as for political reasons to distance it from the European Community method. Political cooperation meetings took place not in Brussels but in the capital of whichever Member States held the Presidency, the Commission and the Council Secretariat were excluded unless discussions touched on some area of Community competence, political consensus was reflected not in legally binding instruments but in press releases and joint statements. It was generally understood that certain features of the Community method were inconsistent with ultimate independence in the conduct of foreign relations. These features were in part institutional — for example the near monopoly of the Commission's power to propose and the role of the European Court of Justice — and in part related to the nature of Community legal obligations — for example direct effect, primacy and consequential loss of national power to legislate and to conclude separate treaties. The disadvantage of this loose form of cooperation was that foreign ministers might arrive at understandings — common positions — and fail to carry them out. In 1980, for example, European Foreign Ministers came to the collective position that sanctions should be imposed by the Member States against Iran on a retroactive basis in response to the breach of its obligations towards the United States diplomats held hostage in Teheran. Lord Carrington, then United Kingdom Foreign Secretary, failed to persuade the British House of Commons to implement such sanctions on a retroactive basis. This was embarrassing for Lord Carrington, but the United Kingdom was not in breach of any legal obligation towards the other Member States.

In 1986, the Single European Act for the first time placed political cooperation on a treaty basis, while carefully separating it from the European Community Treaty structure and indeed stopping short of imposing hard legal obligations. The Member States were to 'endeavour jointly to formulate and implement a European foreign policy' and the institutions of the Community — even the Council — were given no formal role. The Commission had only the right to be 'fully associated' — mainly to ensure consistency between the external policies of the Community and policies agreed by the Member States within political cooperation.

In 1992 the Treaty of Maastricht formalised this dichotomy between intergovernmental cooperation and the European Community by establishing the new European Union under a three pillar structure. Although the new Common Foreign and Security Policy (CFSP) for the first time placed the Member States under legal obligations, these were treaty obligations under public international law and not European Community law obligations. The Council was for the first time given power to adopt instruments imposing further specific legal obligations on Member States — but these CFSP instruments would not have primacy in the strong form elaborated by the European Court of Justice over potentially conflicting national laws, they would not entail direct effect and they would not entail loss of national power to act even in the limited areas 'occupied' by CFSP commitments. The Member States would be legally bound to support agreed joint actions and common positions, but their ultimate independence in foreign policy matters was not further compromised. They were further protected by a general requirement of unanimous voting in the Council when policies were being agreed and by the comprehensive exclusion of the jurisdiction of the European Court of Justice.[3]

The importance of the intergovernmental character of the Second (CFSP) Pillar in safeguarding the sovereign status of the individual Member States was emphasised in judgments testing the Treaty of Maastricht in the English High Court and in the German Federal Constitutional Court.[4] The German Court emphasized that under the new Treaty there could be no supranational action on foreign and security policy, so that Germany would remain a sovereign State in its own right and retain the status of sovereign equality with other States.

In the period of nearly ten years since the entry into force of the Treaty of Maastricht, the institutions have become increasingly skilled at implementing broad political and practical objectives of external policy by the use of instruments from First, Second and Third Pillars in a coherent and consistent manner. Obvious defects in the Common Foreign and Security Policy relating in particular to the resources available to it, both civilian and military, and to its financing, have been remedied by the entry into force in 1999 of the Treaty of Amsterdam. There has been an increasing degree of understanding (setting aside the special case of Iraq in 2003), sharing of information and practical collaboration among diplomatic and consular services. The structure itself, with its guarantees of ultimate national power to conduct independent foreign policy, has however not been challenged.

The Convention was given no mandate by treaty or by Heads of State and Government to revise the structure of the Union. But apparently on grounds of simplification or 'tidying up' it has abandoned the three-pillar structure which clearly differentiated between activities carried out within the Community legal order and those carried out on an intergovernmental basis and subject to public international law. This was not a necessary or inevitable consequence either of the decision to merge the Treaty on European Union with the Treaty establishing the European Community or of the merger of the European Union with the European Community. Given

[3] See I Macleod, I Hendry and S Hyett, *The External Relations of the European Communities* (Oxford, OUP, 1996) 412: 'But the process remains intergovernmental, subject to international law, not Community law. Its product is instruments governed by international law, not Community legislation.'

[4] *R v Secretary of State for Foreign and Commonwealth Affairs ex parte Lord Rees-Mogg* [1994] 1 All ER 457 [1993] 3 CMLR 101; *Brunner v European Union Treaty* [1994] 1 CMLR 57; Denza, above note 1, 57–61.

that the conduct of common foreign and security policy under the distinct framework of international law has been regarded as a safeguard of ultimate national independence in the conduct of foreign policy, it has now become essential to analyse those features of the draft text which appear to call this distinction into question.

## ASPECTS OF THE INTERGOVERNMENTAL METHOD WHICH ARE PRESERVED

There has been an attempt in the draft Constitution to preserve some characteristic features of the Second Pillar. These are, generally speaking, the institutional features. The European Court of Justice remains excluded from supervising the common foreign and security policy.[5] The European Parliament will continue to have only rights to be generally consulted and informed (again with the exception of external agreements where its powers will increase).[6] Qualified majority voting in the Council will continue to be possible only in very limited circumstances.[7] These features are presentationally and politically important, but they are not specially characteristic of the international legal method, nor are they the essential safeguards of ultimate national independence. Treaty obligations under international law are increasingly subject to judicial supervision, and majority voting is common in international organisations — in particular in the Security Council where only the Permanent Members have a veto.

## FEATURES OF THE DRAFT CONSTITUTION INCONSISTENT WITH ULTIMATE INDEPENDENCE

Article I-1.1 prescribes that

> The Union shall coordinate the policies by which the Member States aim to achieve these objectives, and shall exercise in the Community way the competences they confer on it.

The words 'in the Community way' carry the implication that the merger of the Community Pillar and the Intergovernmental Pillars would take the form of absorption of the intergovernmental elements of the Union into a single entity operating and making laws under the Community method. There is no provision authorising the Union to exercise some of its competences under

[5] Art III-282.
[6] Art III-227.7.
[7] Arts I-39 and III-201.

the more highly integrated Community legal order and others — notably the formation and conduct of common foreign policies — under the different legal order of public international law.[8]

Article 6 provides that:

> The Union shall have legal personality.

This implies a merger of the full international legal personality of the European Community with that of the European Union. At present the Union has express treaty-making capacity, and has exercised it on a few occasions, though it may still be argued that the separate ultimate responsibility of the Member States for the discharge or indeed the breach of commitments has not been eliminated. The draft Constitution however is silent as to whether international agreements to be concluded by the Union on CFSP matters will carry implications for loss of concurrent national legislative and treaty-making powers. The position has been carefully considered and clarified by the European Court of Justice in the context of external agreements of the European Community[9], but the fusion of legal personalities proposed would leave it uncertain to what extent the jurisprudence of the Court should be extended to agreements concluded under Article III-225 and relating exclusively or principally to the common foreign and security policy. Article III-228.4 provides that

> Without prejudice to Union competence and agreements as regards economic and monetary union, Member States may negotiate in international bodies and conclude international agreements.

While this makes clear that Member States are not to lose their own international legal personality, it does not resolve the problem of the effects of 'Union competence' on the treaty-making capacity of Member States in the area of foreign and defence policy.

The European Court of Justice will have no jurisdiction over external Union agreements on CFSP matters, but this cannot be regarded as an adequate

[8] For a list of the differences between the legal orders see E Denza, 'Two Legal Orders: Divergent or Convergent?' (1999) *ICLQ* 257; Denza above note 1, chap 1; Piris, 'Does the European Union have a Constitution? Does it Need One?' (1999) *EL Rev* 557, 559–61; A von Bogdandy, 'The Legal Case for Unity: the European Union as a Single Organisation with a Single Legal System' (1999) *CML Rev* 887; AG Tizzano, 'The Foreign Relations Law of the EU: Between Supranationality and Intergovernmental Model' chap 7 in Cannizarro (ed), *The European Union as an Actor in International Relations* (Kluwer Law International, 2000).

[9] Most recently, in the Open Skies cases brought by the European Commission against Denmark (Case C-467/98), Sweden, Finland, Belgium, Luxembourg, Austria, Germany and the United Kingdom. See Holdgaard, 'The European Community's Implied External Competence after the Open Skies Cases' (2003) *European Foreign Affairs Review* 366. House of Lords Select Committee on the European Union, 17th Report 2002–03, HL Paper 92, *'Open Skies' or Open Markets*.

justification for leaving the position obscure. If the position is not clarified, the result is likely to be that Member States will try to resolve it by means of declarations — thus undermining the simplicity of a single self-contained text which is a fundamental objective of this proposed Treaty revision. External agreements based on CFSP powers will certainly become more numerous and more significant, and it should not be left to academic writers to determine the implications for national treaty-making.

## COMPETENCE

In Articles I-9 to I-17 the Union's competences are ascribed and defined. If Union action on foreign policy matters is to be distinguished clearly from its action in other areas it is here that it must be done. Article I-11 distinguishes clearly between the various categories of competence and defines them in terms deriving from the jurisprudence of the European Court of Justice. Exclusive competence, shared competence and competence 'to support, coordinate or supplement the actions of the Member States without thereby superseding their competence in these areas' are three kinds of competence familiar to Community lawyers. To clarify them as has been done fulfils the mandate given 'to establish and monitor a more precise delimitation of powers between the European Union and the Member States'.[10] Article 12 then lists the areas of exclusive competence, Article 13 lists the areas of shared competence while Article 16 lists areas of supporting, coordinating or complementary action.

At this point, however, the Convention appears to have lost its nerve. In the middle of these clearly defined competences there appears Article 15 which says simply:

> 1. The Union's competence in matters of common foreign and security policy shall cover all areas of foreign policy and all questions relating to the Union's security, including the progressive framing of a common defence policy which might lead to a common defence.
> 2. Member States shall actively and unreservedly support the Union's common foreign and security policy in a spirit of loyalty and mutual solidarity and shall comply with the acts adopted by the Union in this area. They shall refrain from action contrary to the Union's interests or likely to impair its effectiveness.'

[10] Declaration 23 on the Future of the Union, adopted by the Intergovernmental Conference at Nice, February 2001.

The substance of Article 15 does not alter the position established under earlier Treaties and is not in itself open to objection. But taken in context, the effect is that the nature and effects of Union powers over foreign policy, and of the instruments to be adopted under these powers is left entirely unclear. It is not provided that CFSP powers and instruments will be governed by the rules of international law. When these Articles are taken together with Article 1, providing that the Union 'shall exercise in the Community way the competences [the Member States] confer on it', they suggest that 'the Community way' of law-making comprises three kinds of competence and that foreign and security policy (as well as coordination of economic and employment policies — Article I-14) must fall within one or other of these three. Given the remit from the Nice Conference to clarify competences, it would be highly unsatisfactory if this uncertainty were not resolved by the forthcoming Intergovernmental Conference.

The Member States have established and developed a common foreign and security policy since the entry into force in 1993 of the Treaty of Maastricht within the framework of international law. Given the mandate from the Nice Conference that there should be 'a simplification of the Treaties with a view to making them better understood without changing their meaning' there is no reason why this position should be changed. There are strong arguments in terms of the continuing sovereign independence of the Member States for preserving the status quo. If the intention is — as has been stated by United Kingdom Ministers[11] — that foreign policy will continue to operate on an intergovernmental basis, under the rules of public international law, this must be made clear in Articles 11 and 15.

## PRIMACY

Article I-10 of the draft Constitution, entitled Union law, provides that

> 1. The Constitution, and law adopted by the Union's institutions in exercising competences conferred on it, shall have primacy over the law of the Member States.

This provision, like the Articles on competences, must be taken together with Article I-1 requiring the Union to exercise 'in the Community way' the competences conferred on it. The implication is that the strong form of

[11] For example, the UK Foreign Secretary, speaking in the House of Commons on 11.6.2003 said '... the UK firmly believes that the process must remain intergovernmental, recognising that national governments have to be accountable for their decisions on foreign, security and defence policy to their own parliaments....we have resolutely opposed proposals in the Convention to 'communitise' CFSP. We will continue to do so in the IGC.'

primacy established by the European Court in *Costa v Enel*[12] would apply to all kinds of Union law, including obligations under the common foreign and security policy.

International law does regard itself as hierarchically superior to national laws, and prior or subsequent conflicting national laws can never justify a failure to comply with an international law obligation. But it looks only to result, and does not prescribe the method whereby compliance is achieved in national legal orders. National legal orders vary greatly in how they give effect to international law, and national legislators and courts treat the relationship as a constitutional matter. The position is explained thus by Cassese:

> A survey of national systems shows a conspicuous lack of uniformity. This anarchic state of affairs can be easily accounted for. States consider that the translation of international commands into domestic legal standards is part and parcel of their sovereignty and are unwilling to surrender it to international control. National self-interest stands in the way of a sensible regulation of this crucial area. As a consequence each State decides, on its own, how to make international law binding on State agencies and individuals and what status and rank to assign to it in the hierarchy of municipal sources of law.[13]

Under European Community law, supremacy is a very much more intrusive doctrine than under international law. The position has been described in these terms:

> For the national legislator, it implies a prohibition to adopt laws that are inconsistent with binding rules of Community law. For national courts, the primary focus of analysis here, respecting the principle of supremacy means that, when an EC rule applies in a given case, any conflicting national norm should immediately be set aside. This is often called a duty to disapply national law.[14]

The Community rules on supremacy, as well as those on direct applicability and direct effect, made it necessary in the European Communities Act 1972 which paved the way for United Kingdom accession to the European Communities to make special provision for European Community rights and obligations. These special provisions have never been applied by United Kingdom law to any other treaty and they have never been applied to the intergovernmental pillars of the European Union. Extension of the strong

[12] Case 6/64 [1964] ECR 585.

[13] International Law, at p 168. See also Gardiner, *International Law* above n 1, ch 4, 'International Law and National Laws'; E Denza, 'The Relationship between International and National Law' in M Evans (ed), *International Law* (OUP, 2003) 415.

[14] P Craig and G de Burca (eds), *The Evolution of EU Law* (Oxford, OUP, 1999) 189–90.

Community form of primacy to the areas now covered by intergovernmental cooperation, and in particular to foreign and security policy, would be a significant shift in the balance of power between the Union and the Member States. In the case of foreign policy it would call into question the ultimate autonomy of the Member States which is an essential element in their independent sovereign status.

## CONSTRAINTS ON INDEPENDENT ACTION

Article I-39.5 of the draft Constitution contains a new requirement framed in remarkably broad terms:

> .... Before undertaking any action on the international scene or any commitment which could affect the Union's interests, each Member State shall consult the others within the European Union or the Council of Ministers....

Given that that the Union's competence in matters of common foreign and security policy 'shall cover all areas of foreign policy and all questions relating to the Union's security' this is a constraint on independent national action which is very difficult to reconcile with ultimate independence. It is very much wider than the constraints imposed, for example, by membership of the United Nations or of NATO. As drafted it is wide enough to preclude even action in self-defence in the face of an armed attack, where the UN Charter permits exercise of the inherent right of self-defence until the Security Council has taken measures necessary to maintain international peace and security, provided that such measures are immediately reported to the Security Council.[15]

This undertaking in Article I-39.5 cannot be reconciled with independent nation status which implies the inherent right to defend the State and to take external actions provided that these are not in conflict with binding international obligations. If it intended that the constraint should be more limited, this must in the context of a Constitution intended to clarify the relations between the Union and its Member States, be precisely spelt out.

Article I-40.2 moreover provides that

> The common security and defence policy shall include the progressive framing of a common Union defence policy. This will lead to a common defence, when the European Council, acting unanimously, so decides. It shall in that case recommend to the Member States the adoption of such a decision in accordance with their respective constitutional requirements.

[15] Article 51 of the Charter.

The second sentence of this provision is inconsistent with Article I-15.1 which, in line with existing commitments, says that the progressive framing of a common defence policy 'might lead to a common defence'. The firm prediction in Article I-40.2 of a common defence also implies that national parliaments — apparently given a discretion in accordance with their respective constitutional requirements to accept or reject a common defence — will in fact be required to endorse any decision by the European Council to move to a common defence. This inconsistency may be no more than a drafting oversight, but the provisions should be aligned in such a way as to leave Member States and their national parliaments, ultimate choice over the possibility of moving to a common defence.

## THE UNION MINISTER FOR FOREIGN AFFAIRS

Article I-27.1 creates a new post of Union Minister for Foreign Affairs to be appointed by the European Council with the agreement of the President of the Commission. The Minister for Foreign Affairs would be given power 'to conduct the Union's common foreign and security policy'. The proposed title would be a novelty for an individual working within and representing an international organisation. Although 'Minister' is a diplomatic rank, Ministers within State embassies are not given the title of 'Minister for Foreign Affairs'. This proposed title clearly implies ultimate aspirations of statehood for the European Union, given that only States now have Ministers for Foreign Affairs.

At present, the High Representative for the common foreign and security policy assists the Presidency in the representation of the Union,[16] and he assists the Council in the formation and implementation of policy decisions.[17] The draft Constitution would radically shift the balance of power between the Council and its chief agent in foreign policy matters, giving the proposed Minister a greater authority — even if his responsibilities are to be carried out ' as mandated by the Council of Ministers'.

Paragraph 3 of Article I-27 would give the Minister the status of Vice-President of the Commission, thus widening his executive authority. The replacement of the existing close and constructive cooperation between the High Representative for the CFSP (Javier Solana) and the Commissioner

[16] TEU, as amended, Article 18.3.

[17] TEU Article 26: 'The Secretary-General of the Council, High Representative for the common foreign and security policy, shall assist the Council in matters coming within the scope of the common foreign and security policy, in particular through contributing to the formulation, preparation and implementation of policy decisions, and, when appropriate and acting on behalf of the Council at the request of the Presidency, through conducting political dialogue with third parties'.

for External Affairs (Christopher Patten) by a fusion of their responsibilities would be inconsistent with the separation of powers between Council and Commission. It would inevitably lead to impossible conflicts of interest — most obviously when Council and Commission resolve important legal disputes over external matters by submitting them to the European Court of Justice.

## CONCLUSION

The original mandate given by the Intergovernmental Conference at Nice in 2001 called for a deeper and wider debate about the future of the European Union which should address four questions. Two of these are of particular relevance to the provisions on external relations:

> — how to establish and monitor a more precise delimitation of powers between the European Union and the Member States, reflecting the principle of subsidiarity;

and

> — a simplification of the Treaties with a view to making them clearer and better understood without changing their meaning;[18]

Heads of State and Government at Laeken in 2001, in their Declaration on the future of the European Union, set out grander and more extensive aspirations in convening the Convention. They asked whether Europe's role was

> that of a power able both to play a stabilising role worldwide and to point the way ahead for many countries and peoples?

But on the following page, more modestly, they noted that their citizens expected

> .... more results, better responses to practical issues and not a European superstate or European institutions inveigling their way into every nook and cranny of life.

It seems probable that a new Constitution which corresponds to the mandates given at Nice and at Laeken is most likely to command general support among the national parliaments and the peoples of Europe who must endorse it if it is

[18] Declaration 23 on the Future of the Union.

to enter into force. A very large part of the draft Constitution does faithfully carry out these elements of the mandate. The text codifies and clarifies doctrines on the division of powers between the Union and its Member States which have been developed by the European Court of Justice. It does simplify the Treaties, and many of the changes it proposes reflect emerging practice or progressive development which can be justified on grounds of effectiveness.

It seems however that the importance of national independence in the conduct of external relations as a criterion of sovereign statehood has been given little attention. Whether this reflects strategy, stealth or inadvertence is difficult for an outsider to determine. There has sometimes been a tendency for writers to take the position that the Treaties can be developed on the basis that the European Union is *sui generis* in its institutional structure and that little attention need be paid to the world-wide rules of international law within which it operates.

A new Constitutional Treaty for the European Union should not be established on such a basis. To introduce into the Treaties uncertainties over primacy in the conduct of foreign affairs, over the nature of Union competence to establish and conduct foreign policy and over whether the Member States retain any power of independent action in foreign affairs would call into question the separate nation status of the Member States. The changes are not necessary in order to create or develop an effective common foreign policy and they would radically alter the balance of power between the Union and its Member States. It is to be hoped that the forthcoming Intergovernmental Conference will accept the need for changes to the draft text which would consistently preserve the sovereign status of the Member States under the rules of international law.

# 16

# *Which Policy for Which Europe? The Emerging Security and Defence Policy of the European Union*

PANOS KOUTRAKOS*

## INTRODUCTION

SINCE 1 MARCH 2002, the European Union has been engaged in an extraordinary process of group therapy within the European Convention. This culminated to the submission of the Draft Treaty establishing a Constitution for Europe to the President of the European Council on 18 July 2003.[1] One of the areas examined by the Convention was the European Security and Defence Policy (ESDP). In political terms, in shaping its security dimension, the European Union is called upon to define its role within the new European security architecture. In legal terms, the development of a credible security and defence policy might require reliance upon a variety of instruments, ultimately entailing more transfer of sovereign powers from the Member States to the European Union. In constitutional terms, the character of the emerging policy raises fundamental questions about the identity of the European Union. The objective of this essay is to reflect on how the European Union may meet these challenges in a manner which would enable it to assert its identity on the new international security arena whilst taking into account the constitutional particularities of its legal order.

## THE POLITICAL BACKGROUND

The constituent parts of the tripartite structure upon which the European Union has been based since its inception were devised as legally distinct,

* A long version of this essay is published in (2003) 10 *Columbia Journal of European Law*.
[1] CONV 850/03 (*http://european-convention.eu.int/docs/Treaty/cv00850.en03.pdf*).

albeit interrelated, sets of rules. In contrast to the supranational features which have shaped the institutional and constitutional development of the EC legal order, foreign policy has always been conducted by the Member States on the basis of intergovernmental procedures and structures formalised in the set of rules entitled Common Foreign and Security Policy. The main objective of that framework is to enable the European Union to 'assert its identity on the international scene'.[2]

An elaborate analysis of the development and structures of the CSFP is not only beyond the scope of this essay[3] but may also become soon relatively outdated in the light of the incoming Intergovernmental Conference. For the purposes of this essay, suffice it to stress the central role retained by the Member States both in institutional and procedural terms as consolidated by recent TEU amendments[4] and drawn upon by the Draft Constitution. It is within this intergovernmental framework that the EU has sought to shape its international presence over the years. In doing so, two interrelated factors were taken into account. The first one was subjective in nature and consisted of the expectations of third parties for the EU to flex a political muscle commensurate to its economic power. The second factor was objective and was defined by the progress achieved within the EC framework: the establishment of the single market and the introduction of a common currency had a spill-over effect on the political arena. However, in taking these two factors into account, the European Union had to strike a balance between the deeply entrenched rights of the Member States to define and protect their individual security interests and the effectiveness of the CFSP which required a degree of convergence.

This has not been an easy balance to strike. It has been pointed out that 'foreign policy making in Western Europe is still the foreign policy of 15 nation-states rather than the foreign policy of one supranational state'.[5] This conclusion has often been expressed with regret, if not thinly disguised contempt for what is perceived to be a rather unhealthy obsession of the Member States for their right to determine their policies as fully sovereign subjects of international law. Following the success of the internal market project, security and defence have been seen as the next challenge for European integration. To that effect, a number of voices have expressed the need for a grand design which, if properly implemented, would ensure the position of the European Union at the very centre of the

[2] Art 2 TEU.

[3] See E Denza, *The Intergovernmental Pillars of the European Union* (Oxford, OUP, 2002).

[4] See A Dashwood, 'External Relations Provisions of the Amsterdam Treaty' (1998) 35 *CMLRev* 1019 and I Oesterdahl, 'The EU and its Member States, Other States, and International Organisations — The Common European Security and Defence Policy after Nice' (2001) 70 *Nordic Journal of International Law* 341.

[5] B Soetendorp, *Foreign Policy in the European Union* (London, Longman, 1999) 147.

world stage: in the Laeken Declaration on the Future of European Union, the European Council wonders: '[d]oes Europe not, now that it is finally unified, have a leading role to play in a new world order, that of a stabilising role worldwide and to point the way ahead for many countries and peoples?'; in his speech in Warsaw in October 2000, British Prime Minister Blair, whilst dismissing the idea of a European 'super-state', called for a European 'superpower'.[6] It was even suggested that George W Bush's close victory at the last USA presidential election would enable the EU to take centre stage and exercise a role akin to that of a world power.[7]

The debate about how the European Union may fill in the perceived post-Cold War security vacuum has acquired momentum following the recent war in Iraq. The failure of the European Union to agree on a single view as to how to deal with the regime of Saddam Hussein and the tensions between Great Britain, France and Germany at the UN Security Council have been seen as leaving the Union's credibility in tatters. The support for the American policies offered by eight European leaders in writing and without any prior consultation with the other Member States was seen as 'a guided missile' to the heart of Europe.[8] In a statement on the first day of the war, President Prodi argued that '[w]hatever the outcome of the war, there can be no denying this is a bad time for the Common Foreign and Security Policy, for the European Union as a whole' and pointed out that 'it is not in our interest to continue relying on others when it comes to defending our values militarily'.[9] However, it should not be inferred from the above that the CFSP has failed. The crisis in Iraq and the way it has been handled by the international community have not only challenged all the structures of international cooperation which dominate the post-World War II arena but have also provoked very considerable reactions within individual States. The painful negotiations within NATO, the questions about the role of the United Nations, the opposition of public opinion in Continental Europe, the parliamentary disquiet in Great Britain, the refusal of Turkey to cooperate as required by United States, all highlight the unique nature and profound implications of this conflict. Therefore, the Iraqi crisis revealed the inherent limitations of all institutionalised forms of international cooperation within the current unique geopolitical environment. To expect the European Union to succeed where the United Nations and the Western powers individually and collectively failed demonstrates considerable lack of realism. Equally, to mourn for the missed opportunity of strengthening the EU foreign policy is not only unduly pessimistic but also unwise. After all, the aftermath of the Iraqi crisis has seen the debate about the future of

[6] See *http://www.scotlandeuropa.com/DOWNLOAD/SPEECH%20PM.doc.*
[7] *European Voice*, 5–11/4/2001 at 11–13.
[8] *La Liberation*, 31/1/03.
[9] IP/03/419.

the EU security and defence policy acquire considerable momentum. This may be viewed, perversely, as a positive outcome of the Iraqi crisis.[10]

The apparent consensus on the inabilities of the current legal framework and the readiness of the EU actors, at least in rhetorical terms, to reform it radically so as to enable the EU to take its place at the very centre of the international scene appears to be yet another version of a debate which was popular within academic circles in the 1990s, that is 'the capabilities — expectations gap' characterising the effectiveness of CFSP.[11] However, the debate currently taking place as to how to remedy that gap has two unique features: it is underpinned by remarkable intensity and momentum and it is focused on security and defence. Indeed, the ESDP is deemed to be intrinsically linked to the EU external posture to such an extent that, according to one commentator, 'it is abundantly clear that the credibility of the second pillar is on the line'.[12]

## LAW AND HIGH POLITICS

In the light of the above, the question is whether the European Union may assume the role of a superpower on the international scene and, if so, to what extent could it achieve this by defence integration. In order to address this question, it is essential to consider the main characteristics of the development of the framework within which the Member States have sought to present a common stance in the international arena. To a certain extent, the distinct intergovernmental features of that framework were determined, albeit by default, prior to the establishment of the European Economic Community, that is in the early 1950s when the attempt to create a European Defence Community failed.[13] The ensuing common foreign policy and security framework, irrespective of its formal status, has developed on the basis of three interweaving threads.

The first one is incrementalism which became apparent even prior to the incorporation of European Political Cooperation in the Treaty structure by the Single European Act in mid-1980s. That policy had developed on the basis of three Reports presented by the Ministers of Foreign Affairs of the Member States to the Heads of State and Government.[14] These developed various

[10] President Giscard d'Estaing stated that 'a common European consciousness is emerging': *Financial Times*, 16/4/2003 at p 19.

[11] See C Hill, 'The Capabilities-Expectations Gap, or Conceptualising the European International Role' (1993) 31 *JCMS* 305.

[12] S Duke, 'CESDP: Nice's Overtrumped Success?' (2001) 6 *European Foreign Affairs Review* 155, 174.

[13] See E Furdson, *The European Defence Community: A History* (London, Macmillan, 1980).

[14] These were the Luxembourg, Copenhagen and London Reports; for their text, see *European Political Co-operation (EPC)* (Bonn: Press and Information Office of the Federal Government, 5th edn, 1988).

informal arrangements whose accumulation constituted the core of what was to become the foreign affairs system of the Union. The most important illustration of the incremental evolution of the EU foreign and security policy is the development of its legal machinery, both in substantive and procedural terms.[15]

The second characteristic of the developing legal framework has been its immense focus on the procedural aspects of foreign policy-making: the effectiveness of the EU foreign policy has been viewed as directly associated with the establishment or reform of various procedural mechanisms. This was clearly the case within the context of EPC and remained so within the EU framework. Indeed, an external observer of all recent Intergovernmental Conferences would be under the impression that the only obstacle to the European Union taking its well-deserved place at the very centre of the international arena was raised by the cumbersome procedures laid down in the TEU.[16]

The third main characteristic of the development of the CFSP has been its dynamic and *sui generis* nature. Policies have been formulated and positions expressed often beyond the mechanisms laid down in legal rules. Whilst this phenomenon may be understandable in the light of the very specific external and internal factors instrumental to the development of a common foreign policy, the dynamic nature of the CFSP is also indicative of the pathology of its legal framework. An illustration of this is the role of *ad hoc* national alliances in the development of policies either in parallel to formalised institutional mechanisms or even beyond them.[17] As a result, the foreign policy pursued by the Member States within the formal structures established incrementally over the years has been of a *sui generis* nature.[18]

## THE PARADOX

In order to fully appreciate the repercussions of the above characteristics of the EU foreign policy, two points need to be made. On the one hand, the

[15] See, for instance, the gradual introduction of majority voting from Art J.3(2) of the Maastricht Treaty to the three exceptions under Arts 23(1) sub 2 and 23(2) of the Amsterdam Treaty to the introduction of flexibility under the Nice Treaty.

[16] Even following the Iraqi crisis, in the informal Athens summit of April 16, 2003 considerable attention was drawn to whether the post of a single 'Foreign Affairs Secretary' ought to be established: *Financial Times,* 17/4/2003 at p 16.

[17] See, for instance, the bi-annual meeting that the leaders of the five big EU States used to have with the Turkish Prime Minister. Another example is the meetings between the President of the Commission and the German Chancellor decided to take place prior to each European Council summit: see Written Question P-0891/02, [2002] OJ C 229E/156.

[18] See, for instance, the assumption of the administration of Mostar as one of the most successful interventions by the EU in the war in ex-Yugoslavia: see J Monar, 'Mostar: Three Lessons for the European Union' (1997) 2 *European Foreign Affairs Review* 1.

material scope of that policy was unlimited, both within the EPC[19] and CFSP frameworks.[20] The absence of a criterion which would confine the scope of common intervention by the Member States made it clear that foreign policy was understood in identical terms, irrespective of whether it would be carried out by the Member States individually or determined and expressed collectively through the established political and legal procedures. In other words, it was the national model of foreign policy which was adjusted within the political, constitutional and legal constraints existing at the time. On the other hand, the national concerns over the exercise of their sovereignty and the concomitant intense proceduralisation of the common foreign policy framework enabled Member States to claim that they retained control over its conduct.

What emerges is a paradox: a state-centred and inspired policy formulated pursuant to elaborate procedural rules and carried out by Member States eager to stress both its limits and their status as fully sovereign subjects of international law. In legal terms, this paradox was bound to give rise to acts whose significance and repercussions could not be defined easily on the basis of our traditional legal vocabulary. The extraordinary instrumentalisation of legal recognition by the EC and the Member States in the process of the disintegration of Yugoslavia in the early 1990s brings this point home.[21] The emergence of this paradox is not a coincidence: it has not arisen merely in response to political circumstances, just as the incremental development of the ensuing policies cannot be explained merely on the basis of the practical need of the EU to develop a political role commensurate with its economic power. The idiosyncrasies of CFSP have been too consistent and their intensity too noticeable across a wide range of actions to be explained merely in terms of the prevailing political circumstances.

Instead, the paradox of the EU foreign and security policy may be explained in the light of the constitutional structure within which the Member States have chosen to pursue integration, that is one based on various legal frameworks which are distinct and yet interrelated and which ensure integration in a wide range of areas, albeit at a different pace and on the basis of differing methods. It is this unique legal phenomenon[22] whose development has given rise to the paradox illustrated by the policies the EU

[19] See Art IV of the Luxembourg Report.
[20] See Art 11 TEU. For the range of areas in which the Member States deemed it necessary to intervene, see W Wessels, 'EC-Europe: An Actor *Sui Generis* in the International System' in B Nelson, D Roberts and W Weit (eds), *The European Community in the 1990s: Economics, Politics, Defence* (Oxford, Berg Publishers, 1992) 161.
[21] See DH Bearce, 'Institutional Breakdown and International Cooperation: the European Agreement to Recognize Croatia and Slovenia' (2002) 8 *European Journal of International Relations* 471.
[22] From the abundance of literature seeking to define the EC and the EU, the definition of the former as 'a constitutional order of States' is noteworthy: see A Dashwood (ed), *Reviewing Maastricht: Issues for the 1996 IGC* (London, Sweet and Maxwell, 1996) 1.

is expected to carry out on the international arena. What is noteworthy is that the incremental development of a *sui-generis* and dynamic policy heavily focused on the elaboration of procedural rules is not confined to the development of the CFSP — it has also defined the development of the security and defence policy of the EU.

## THE EUROPEAN SECURITY AND DEFENCE POLICY

The development of the ESDP has been described often and in detail.[23] For the purpose of this analysis, suffice it to point out that it has exhibited the same characteristics that have shaped the development of CFSP. Under Article 17(1) TEU, the CFSP 'shall include all questions relating to the security of the Union, including the progressive framing of a common defence policy, which might lead to a common defence, should the European Council so decide'. The Draft Constitution states that the progressive framing of a common defence policy 'will lead to a common defence, when the European Council, acting unanimously, so decides'.[24] According to Article 2 TEU as amended at Amsterdam, the objective of the EU to assert its identity on the international scene is to be achieved 'through the implementation of a common foreign and security policy including the progressive framing of a common defence policy which might lead to a common defence'.

As the starting point for the development of the ESDP was the Blair-Chirac initiative at St Malo in December 1998, what is to become the core of the EU security presence does not have its genesis within the EU framework. Instead, the ESDP is the product of a dynamic development whose political character remained informal until the Treaty of Nice. The objective of this policy was defined quite early on in terms of the ability of the Member States to deploy and sustain forces capable of humanitarian and rescue tasks, peacekeeping and tasks of combat forces in crisis management, including peacekeeping, in operations of up to 50,000–60,000 persons. The Member States should be able to sustain such deployment for at least a year and provide support with the necessary command, control and intelligence capabilities, logistics, other combat support services and, as appropriate, air and naval elements.[25]

In establishing the new ESDP structures, both the Member States and the EU institutions have been acutely aware of the balance between national sovereignty and the development of an assertive EU security presence. To that effect, they have been tireless to stress what the EU armed force

[23] See, for instance, S Duke, *The Elusive Quest for European Security: From EDC to CFSP* (Basingstoke, MacMillan, 2000).
[24] Art 40(2).
[25] Progress Report by the Finnish Presidency on Strengthening the Common European Policy on Security and Defence, submitted to the Helsinki European Council in December 1999 and annexed to the Presidency Conclusions.

in-the-making is not to be, namely a European army.[26] It is interesting that in all documents setting out improved structures and new arrangements for the ESDP, the European Council was at pains to stress their intergovernmental nature and acknowledge emphatically the powers retained by the Member States. What is intrinsically linked to that is the acknowledgement of the limited scope of the new policy. This was expressed in a twofold way: on the one hand, it was positively stated that the ESDP would be confined to the so-called Petersberg tasks; on the other hand, the new armed force would in no way affect the right of the Member States to protect their sovereignty when they deem it to be in danger. In a Declaration annexed to the Presidency Conclusions, the Seville European Council 'acknowledges that the Treaty on European Union does not impose any binding mutual defence commitment'[27] and 'confirms that the situation ... would be unchanged by the entry into force of the Treaty on Nice'.[28]

In addition to its dynamic and incremental character, the development of the ESDP has been underpinned by a distinct emphasis on procedural rules, clearly illustrated by the painfully protracted process of reaching agreement as to the conditions under which the ESDP could rely upon NATO intelligence. The Helsinki European Council stated that 'modalities will be developed for full consultation, cooperation and transparency between the EU and NATO, taking into account the needs of all EU Member States'.[29] According to the Feira European Council, the interaction between NATO and EU ought to cover four areas, namely security issues, capabilities goals, the modalities of EU access to NATO assets and the definition of permanent consultation arrangements.[30]

It follows that both ESDP and CFSP have been defined by similar principles. Incrementally developed and of a dynamic nature, they have been carried out on the basis of *sui generis* arrangements heavily focused on procedural aspects; as for their intergovernmental character, it has only varied in intensity.[31] It was argued above that these characteristics, along with the paradox of the policy to which they have given rise, reflect the inherent limitations of the international posture of the EU and may be explained in the light of the constitutional idiosyncrasies of the Union. Their inherent nature may be illustrated by the examination of two issues central both the

[26] See *Declaration on the operational capability of the Common European Security and Defence Policy*, annexed to Presidency Conclusions of Laeken European Council (December 2001). In addition, see *Declaration by the European Council* annexed to the Presidency Conclusions of Seville European Council (June 2002), Annex IV at para 4.
[27] Annex IV to the Presidency Conclusions, para 4.
[28] Ibid, para 5.
[29] Presidency Conclusions, para 28.
[30] Presidency Conclusions, Feira European Council (June 2000), para 9.
[31] For an analysis of the increasing reliance upon legal mechanisms in the area of foreign policy, see ME Smith, 'Diplomacy by Decree: The Legalization of EU Foreign Policy' (2001) 39 *JCMS* 79.

CFSP and the emerging ESDP, namely the issue of territorial protection of the Member States and the management of EU-NATO relations.

## TWO ILLUSTRATIONS OF THE PARADOX

According to Article 11(1) TEU, as amended by the Amsterdam Treaty, one of the CFSP objectives is 'to safeguard [amongst others] the integrity of the Union in conformity with the principles of the United Nations Chapter'. This begs the question whether it refers to the territorial integrity of the European Union. In the past, this was answered in the affirmative.[32] Had this been the case, it would have been an encouraging response to a past episode which found the EU embarrassingly unable to express, within the CFSP framework, a common stance towards a claim by one of its Member States that its territorial integrity was threatened by a non-Member State.[33] At that time, war was avoided due to American intervention, a fact that was publicly acknowledged by the Greek Prime Minister. However, this incident was not merely symptomatic of the times, as a similar one occurred in the Spanish islet Leila as recently as the summer of 2002. At that time, the EU did seek to react, only to demonstrate its limits in an embarrassingly public manner: following the incident on 11 July, it took the Danish Presidency two days to issue a two-sentence long statement with no reference whatever to a potential EU reaction, whereas four days later the Political Committee failed to reach agreement as to what statement to produce. In the meantime, the Commission sought to assert its role: President Prodi held talks over the telephone with the Moroccan Prime Minister[34] and issued a forceful statement of support for Spain[35] whilst his spokesman referred to the incident as a threat to EU territory. This caused dissatisfaction in various European capitals,[36] which in turn made the Commission retreat and offer its services 'in order to facilitate … the restoration of friendly relations between the two countries in any way that would be helpful', only later to make it clear that that 'would not suggest … any mediation'.[37] The whole incident was resolved following the intervention of the American Secretary of State Colin Powell.[38]

[32] See J Monar, 'The European Union's Foreign Affairs System After the Treaty of Amsterdam: A "Strengthened Capacity for External Action"?' (1997) 2 *European Foreign Affairs Review* 413, 415.

[33] When Turkey claimed that Greek islets in the Aegean Sea were of disputed sovereignty and invaded one of them, causing a particularly serious escalation in the Greek-Turkish relations, Richard Holbrooke, the then US Undersecretary of State, pointed out that the EU 'was sleeping through the night' (*Financial Times*, 1/4/1998, p 18).

[34] IP/02/1064.

[35] Statement of 16/7/2002.

[36] See *Financial Times*, 19/7/2002, p 7.

[37] Statement of 17/7/2002 (IP/02/1090).

[38] *Financial Times*, 22/7/2002, p 8.

This is a stark illustration of the inherent limitations of the security role that the EU can assume.[39] First, more than six years following the Imia incident and pending a considerable process of developing the Union's military capacity, solidarity, both in words and practice, is not to be taken for granted in cases where Member States feel that the core of their sovereignty is under external threat. Second, the reluctance of Member States to act within the CFSP framework in a way which would deviate from their individual relations with third countries inevitably force non-State actors, in that case the Commission, to fill in the political vacuum; this development in itself illustrates, yet again, the dynamic nature of the CFSP, hence making it clear that legal rules constitute merely one part of foreign and security policy-making. Third, whilst the supranational EU actors might have grown to be sufficiently self-confident and, hence, daring in the foreign policy arena, their impact is directly related to the degree of their acceptance by the intergovernmental EU actors, namely the Member States. In the absence of such acceptance, the reactions of the Commission would merely highlight even further the diversity of interests prevailing in the CFSP arena. Finally, the existence of elaborate procedural requirements has proved to be entirely irrelevant in the absence of political will of the Member States to rely upon them.

This is a gloomy reading of the ability of EU to assume the role of a security superpower. As it is incapable of adopting a common stance, let alone deciding a positive action, when one of its Members feels under threat, the EU is incapable of becoming a defence superpower. This is not attributable to the intergovernmental nature of the existing procedures; nor would the outcome be likely to be any different were more powerful figures in control of national policies. It is because the successful assumption of this function by the EU would be tantamount to assuming a role well beyond its constitutional identity and inherent limitations.

Another illustration of these tensions is provided by the management of EU access to NATO assets. What became a protracted exercise in delicate diplomacy was due to the relationship between an EU Member State with a non-EU European Member of NATO, namely Greece and Turkey respectively. What made this dispute all the more controversial was the significance of its subject matter: the avoidance of duplication of resources was sought both by the EU and NATO,[40] hence rendering the whole issue 'essential for the ESDP [as it would] substantially increase the Union's available capabilities'.[41] It is recalled

[39] See the excellent comment in J Monar, 'The CFSP and the Leila/Perejil Island Incident: The Nemesis of Solidarity and Leadership' (2002) 7 *European Foreign Affairs Review* 251. See also T Garton-Ash, 'The Price of Parsley', *The Guardian*, 25/7/2002, who wonders 'what credibility has Europe as critic and partner if it cannot even resolve such a piffling little dispute on our own front doorstep?' before concluding 'so much for the great peacemaker and bridgebuilder'.
[40] See the statement by the then US Defence Secretary Cohen to that effect: *Financial Times*, 7/12/2000 at p 2.
[41] Declaration on the operational capability of the Common European Security and Defence Policy, annexed to the Presidency Conclusions of the Laeken European Council.

that Turkey had made it clear that it could only agree to such an arrangement on condition of guaranteed participation in policy-making, a request to which Greece objected. In yet another illustration of the dynamic character of the emerging policy which was not confined to the institutional arrangements formally set out, an agreement was brokered by the US and British governments and accepted by Turkey (the so-called 'Ankara Agreement'), only to be rejected by Greece. Finally, the European Union set out the framework within which the EU-NATO interaction could be managed at the Brussels European Council in October 2002. Whereas no agreement had been reached with Turkey, the Presidency Conclusions expressly provided that any decisions reached between EU and NATO, along with their implementation, would be in compliance with the TEU and that no action would be undertaken that would violate the principles of the United Nations Charter.[42] The importance attached to this rather self-evident formulation by the Greek Government becomes all the more apparent with the express reference to the integrity of the Union and peaceful settlement of disputes and the duty to refrain from the threat or use of force. This was deemed to assuage fears that Turkey's participation, either direct or indirect, in the decision-making and implementation of ESDP might endanger Greek security.

Following elaborate statements in Annex II to the Presidency Conclusions about cooperation between Member States and non-EU allies and various assurances for respect of the principles of the UN Charter, an EU-NATO agreement was reached in December 2002. In a Council Declaration annexed to the Presidency Conclusions of the Copenhagen European Council, the following compromise was reached: on the one hand, EU Member States which are neither NATO members nor parties to the 'Partnership for Peace' would not be involved in ESDP operations; on the other hand, they would still participate fully in defining and implementing CFSP as defined under the TEU.[43] The effect of this arrangement is to exclude Cyprus from the implementation of ESDP operations when the latter has recourse to NATO assets. This paved the way to an 'EU-NATO declaration on ESDP' adopted on 16 December 2002.[44]

Whilst hardly a novelty within the context of CFSP and ESDP, the focus on procedure underlying the above negotiations has been criticised as indicative of 'excessive legalism' which should be avoided.[45] This comment signifies a failure to appreciate the underlying dynamics of the development of ESDP. It ignores not only the limited scope, at least originally, of the emerging policy but also the concomitant absence of a defence mechanism

[42] See paras 19 and 20 of the Presidency Conclusions.

[43] See Annex II to Presidency Conclusions at paras 1 and 2.

[44] The EU-NATO Agreement on the Security of Information has now been concluded: [2003] OJ L 80/36.

[45] J Cloos, 'L'Union a-t-elle besoin d'une politique européenne de securité?' (2001) 452 *Revue du marché commun et de l'Union européenne* 581, 584 who goes on to point out that '[d]ans le domaine de la politique étrangère, les bases legales ne valent pas, hélas, les bases navales'.

which would protect the very core of national sovereignty. Furthermore, it underestimates the duty of the Member States to protect their people and territory and their right, as fully sovereign subjects of international law, to decide how to do so effectively. National concerns regarding territorial integrity need to be addressed: in the absence of a defence mechanism within the ESDP, it is by no means surprising that the latter's emerging structures ought to take those concerns into account. In the light of the above, the exclusion of Cyprus, the assurance that no NATO crisis operation will be carried out against an EU Member State, the limited role of Turkey, albeit broadly defined, within the ESDP framework, all agreed upon following two years of negotiations, point out the following: at this juncture, due to inherent limitations, constitutional constraints and national considerations, the EU is fundamentally unsuited to assume the role of a 'superpower' advocated in many quarters.

## MANAGING THE PARADOX: WHICH WAY FORWARD?

It follows from the above that, in developing its security and defence policy, the European Union has found itself caught between a rock and a hard place: on the one hand, it is expected to develop a security role not only commensurate with its economic power and emerging political identity, but also capable of responding to the challenges raised in the current post-modern geopolitical environment;[46] on the other hand, it cannot ignore the constitutional idiosyncrasies of its structure and the integration of its policies at a different pace and pursuant to different methods, account being taken of the central role of States. Against this background and in so far as they promote a state-centred model of security and defence policy, the popular calls for the European Union to assume the role of an international security superpower are as maximalistic as they are unwise. They also have an old-fashioned feel about them as they appear to construe 'power' and 'security' within an exclusively state-oriented international environment. However, the fall of the Cold War and the dominant role of international financial institutions and trade structures on the political arena, along with the remarkable development of European integration, have given rise to a geopolitical framework in which 'a new multi-dimensional configuration of authority' is prevalent.[47] In such an environment, trade, foreign policy and defence interact continuously and in very subtle ways. Viewed from this

[46] See R Cooper, 'The Post-Modern State' in M Leonard (ed), *Re-Ordering the World* (London, Foreign Policy Centre, 2002) 11.

[47] N Walker, 'The EU and the WTO: Constitutionalism in a New Key' in G de Burca and J Scott (eds), *The EU and the WTO: Legal and Constitutional Issues* (Oxford, Hart Publishing, 2001) 31, 36.

angle, the European Union *is* a major security power and the imminent enlargement constitutes a security act of profound significance.

It is in the light of these parameters that the EU should seek to assert its identity on the international scene and, hence, respond to the political imperative of assuming a security and defence function without challenging its constitutional identity. Far from being an obstacle to the assumption of a meaningful security role, the constitutional idiosyncrasies of the EU may become the foundation of a lasting and effective defence function. Indeed, the great strength of the EU is its ability to act in a wide range of areas, albeit pursuant to different methods. Increasing reliance upon this ability may provide an imaginative alternative to that of a state-centred defence superpower.

A recent example of this approach is offered by the EU response to the terrorist attack of 11 September 2001. When the crisis actually occurred, there was no doubt as to the solidarity expressed by the EU institutions. The European Council met in extraordinary session and stated that it was 'totally supportive of the American people', made it clear that 'it will cooperate with the United States in bringing to justice and punishing the perpetrators, and accomplices of such barbaric acts' and 'called for the broadest possible coalition against terrorism'.[48] The Seville European Council in June 2002 expressed its 'determin[ation] to reinforce the role of the European Union in combating terrorism and recognis[ed] the importance of the contribution of the CFSP, including the ESDP, to that end'.[49]

For the purpose of this analysis, suffice it to focus on the framework within which the EU has undertaken to respond to international terrorism as originally set out by the European Council. This was conceived as 'a coordinated and inter-disciplinary approach embracing all Union policies'.[50] Indeed, the Presidency Conclusions set out broad guidelines for EU action within the areas of police and judicial cooperation, international conventions and organisations, regulation against any form of financing terrorism, air security, political relations with third countries, participation in the security environment in regions with instabilities, bilateral and multilateral economic relations. In setting out this broad framework, the European Council referred to various EU institutions, namely the Commission, the Council in a variety of formations (Justice and Home Affairs, ECOFIN, Transport, General Affairs) and the European Central Bank and the actions these were envisaged to take. Therefore, the European Council provided a

[48] Conclusions and Plan Action of the Brussels Extraordinary European Council Meeting on 21 September 2001, part 1.

[49] Para 11 of the Presidency Conclusions. For a more detailed analysis of the EU response, see, amongst others, S Duke, 'CESDP and the EU Response to 11 September: Identifying the Weakest Link' (2002) 7 *European Foreign Affairs Review* 153.

[50] *Ibid.*

most clear example of what Article 4 TEU envisages when referring to its role as 'provid[ing] the Union with the necessary impetus for its development and … defin[ing] the general political guidelines thereof'.

Reference to 'a coordinated and inter-disciplinary approach enhancing all Union policies, including development of the Common Foreign and Security Policy … and making the European Security and Defence Policy … operational' was subsequently made by the Seville European Council.[51] In the area of judicial and police cooperation, measures against combating terrorism were adopted[52] and a European arrest warrant established.[53] In the area of CFSP, specific measures were taken in order to combat terrorism[54] and the direct and indirect supply of arms to terrorism was prohibited.[55] Within the EC framework, measures have been taken freezing funds, financial assets and economic resources of persons associated with terrorist activities.[56] In referring to the global approach adopted by the EU, the Seville European Council 'welcomes the progress achieved since 11 September on incorporating the fight against terrorism into all aspects of the Union's external relations policy'.[57] The examples referred to therein include strengthening EU instruments for long-term prevention, focusing political dialogue with third countries on the fight against terrorism as well as on non-proliferation and arms-control, providing assistance to third countries in order to reinforce their capacity to respond effectively to the international threat of terrorism, including anti-terrorism clauses in EU agreements with third countries, re-evaluating relations with third countries in the light of their attitudes towards terrorism and taking appropriate measures accordingly and implementing specific measures in the fight against terrorism in accordance with UN Security Council Resolution 1373.[58]

The multidisciplinary nature of the EU response is indicative of the strengths that its *sui generis* structure enjoys in terms of its international posture. The policies outlined above include measures of mid/long term effect which draw upon the web of legal frameworks under the EU umbrella rather than the expression of military might. In other words, the legal reflexes of the European Union have given rise to a policy response which transcends the limits of traditional security powers. It is noteworthy that

[51] Declaration by the European Council on the Contribution of the Common Foreign and Security Policy, including the Security and Defence Policy, to the fight against terrorism, Annex V to Presidency Conclusions, Seville European Council, para 1.
[52] Council Framework Decision 2002/475/JHA [2002] OJ 164/3.
[53] Council Framework Decision 2002/584/JHA [2002] OJ L190/1.
[54] Common Position 2001/931 [2002] OJ L 344/93, updated by Common Position 2002/847/CFSP, [2002] OJ L 295/1.
[55] Common Position 2002/402/CFSP [2002] OJ L 139/4.
[56] Reg 2580/2001 [2001] OJ L 344/70.
[57] *Supra* note 51, para 4.
[58] *Ibid.*

the most remarkable progress has been achieved within the framework of the third pillar. Even those areas within CFSP and ESDP which were considered to be of a priority were of a 'soft defence' nature.[59] All in all, the EU response impliedly acknowledged that it was recourse to inter-pillar legal measures which would make its security policies have teeth rather than conventionally understood defence mechanisms.

The less pronounced role of the ESDP in the EU overall response has been viewed as a weakness.[60] However, a more positive reading is justified. On the one hand, the less pronounced role of the ESDP is indicative of political maturity: in order to address a present challenge efficiently, the EU utilised its existing legal panoply whose potential had been tested against years of legal ingenuity and practice. In doing so, its legal reflexes worked successfully. On the other hand, the ability of the EU to articulate its reliance upon a cross-pillar set of rules is a sign of constitutional maturity. In historical terms, it was the economic growth of the EC and the intensity of its integration that rendered the development of a foreign policy framework conceivable and, then, feasible. Most importantly, in legal terms, the economic aspects of European integration have been central to the conduct of EU external relations. This has been the case both directly and indirectly, as illustrated by the regulation of economic sanctions against third countries.[61]

In the light of the above, the post-11 September legal experience has an important message to send: the EU external posture may be strengthened and, hence, the CFSP become assertive, not by confining itself to the high politics framework but by increasing reliance upon the array of instruments of varied legal intensity offered across the existing pillars. This conclusion is not altered by the abolition of the pillar structure recommended in the Draft Constitution as the role of the State would still be central to the conduct of the EU external policies. As to the efforts to strengthen the EU security role, the current debate is heavily focused on maximalistic positions. In doing so, it has ignored the development of the means in which the Union may actually build a credible and efficient ESDP, as indicated by the failure of the Member States to address the problematic state of their defence industries. As this development has been addressed elsewhere,[62] suffice it to recall that the major problems of national defence industries and their

[59] Ibid at para 7, where reference to strengthening arrangements for sharing intelligence and 'exploring further how military or civilian capabilities could be used to help protect civilian populations against the effects of terrorist attacks'.

[60] See Duke, above n 49 at 164 *et seq*.

[61] See P Koutrakos, 'Trade, Foreign Policy and Defence' in *EU Constitutional Law* (Oxford, Hart, 2001) chs 3 and 4.

[62] See P Koutrakos, 'Inter-pillar Approaches to the European Security and Defence Policy: The Economic Aspects of Security' in von Kronenberger (ed), *The European Union and the International Legal Order: Discord or Harmony?* (The Hague, TMC Asser Institute, 2001) 435.

highly fragmented treatment have been subject to considerable analysis by the Commission. Having made the case for their rationalisation,[63] it put forward an integrated approach to the development of a European armaments policy which would consist of a combination of EC and CFSP instruments adopted in areas such as public procurement, defence and technological development, standardisation and technical harmonisation, competition policy, structural funds, export policies and import duties on military equipment.[64] It is noteworthy that that approach advocated by the Commission is not confined to measures adopted within the EU framework but would comprise instruments adopted following close coordination between EU and other international organisations.

Following the launch of the ESDP, the Member States have failed to respond to the Commission proposals effectively. It is regrettable that the approach to the economic aspects of security should be, at best, fragmented and, at worst, at the margin of the development of ESDP. The reluctance of the Member States to engage in the restructuring of their defence industries signifies their failure to construe a credible security policy. It is the concomitant failure to deal with the management of that policy that makes the pronouncements about the role of the EU as a 'superpower' hollow and renders the, otherwise justifiable, focus on procedural arrangements, pathological.

## CONCLUSION

This analysis sought to set out the canvass against which the EU seeks to define its security role on the international arena. A maximalistic approach was rejected as unsustainable in practical terms and inappropriate in legal terms. Instead, the Union should seek to develop its security and defence policy by relying upon its constitutional idiosyncrasies. The fact that it may do so successfully was illustrated by its legal response to the 9/11 crisis. However, it need not confine itself to the legal response to terrorism. Indeed, the 'multi-disciplinary' approach advocated by the European Council and adopted by the EU institutions is similar to the 'inter-pillar' approach to the rationalisation of national defence industries put forward by the Commission seven years ago. In conceptual terms, both acknowledge the need for new challenges to be addressed on the basis of a variety of legal instruments which would transcend traditional legal categorisations and whose combined effect would enhance the stature of the EU. Therefore, the economic aspects of security should be brought at the centre of the ESDP

[63] See COM(96) 10 final.
[64] See COM(97) 583 final.

and be dealt with as a matter of priority on the basis of the sophisticated multi-layered approach advocated by the Commission. In addressing these issues, the EU would be able to implement the ESDP in an efficient manner. It is not inconceivable that the issue of the rationalisation of the defence industries of the Member States may become prominent in the near future. In March 2003, the Commission reiterated the need for a coherent cross-pillar approach to the regulation of defence[65] whereas the Draft Constitution states that a European Armaments, Research and Military Capabilities Agency shall be established'.[65] This is not an opportunity to be missed.

This practical step, whilst essential to the development of the ESDP, would require that a fundamental choice about the EU international posture be made. This would acknowledge that the EU cannot — and should not- assume a maximalistic role; instead, it would carry out a security function on the basis of the multilayered legal and political instruments at its disposal. Its approach to the stabilization process in West Balkans provides an illustration of how, by relying upon its strengths, the EU may act as an important security actor, albeit not of a nature traditionally assumed by superpowers. In other words, it is suggested that the EU render its constitutional idiosyncrasies the cornerstone of its role in the new international security architecture. This is a legally feasible and politically sensible alternative to the various calls for a grand design. Whilst appearing to be *de rigueur* in the current open-ended debate about the future of Europe, the calls for a European super-power are misguided in both historical and legal terms, as they ignore the development of the framework within which the EU has conducted its foreign and security policy and they trivialise its constitutional idiosyncrasies. Most importantly, such claims have the effect of trivialising the specific ways in which the European Union makes a difference on the international scene: whilst they might appear technical in character and very specific in detail, they represent the true power of the European Union.

[65] COM(2003) 113 final.
[66] Art 40(3) subpara 2.

# 17

# *Gripping Global Governance: The External Relations of the EU Between the Treaty of Nice and the Convention on the Future of Europe*

CHRISTOPH HERRMANN

## INTRODUCTION

BEYOND DOUBT, A far reaching consensus exists in Europe, that today's world faces problems or is at least likely to face them in the years to come that make new forms of governance beyond the nation state indispensable. Not solving issues like international migration, environmental degradation, terrorism, health, nutrition and over-population might very well indeed risk the future, the very existence of the world and mankind as such. Globalization, however difficult and disputed the concept,[1] induces a spill-over of problems from one nation state to the other. The ever freer flow of goods, services, capital and human beings around the globe makes it easier for individuals and Transnational Enterprises to circumvent restricting regulation. Many fear a 'race to the bottom' with a view to regulatory intervention pursuing non-economic aims.

In the view of neo-liberal institutionalism as a way of looking at international relations in general, global governance is the most promising answer to the aforementioned threats, the Utopia to strive for if you like[2]. I will not

[1] See eg D Held, A McGrew, D Goldblatt, and J Perraton, *Global Transformations: Politics, Economics and Culture* (Cambridge, Polity, 1999).
[2] See eg R Gilpin *Global Political Economy: Understanding the International Economic Order* (Princeton UP, 2001) 379 *et seq*.

indulge into the difficult discussion about what exactly global governance means in terms of international relations theory. As a lawyer I do not exactly feel prepared to make a helpful contribution to that side of the discussion anyway. However, I will try to sketch out briefly the reading of the concept that underlies my elaboration on the legal dimension.

Globalization is partially due to the abolition of discriminatory restrictions for the sake of economic welfare: restrictions on the free flow of goods, services and capital as well as people[3]. However, even in market-oriented open economies the need for non-discriminatory regulation that serves a 'common good' which may not be delivered by the market otherwise is widely accepted. Defining this common good is one of the main tasks of global governance. It relates to the balancing of economic and non-economic interests and must in the long-run lead to a hierarchization of principles and standards. The legitimacy of this process is one of the biggest questions. To what extent is, eg the protection of public health more important than the protection of a patent right holder's intellectual property? And who should decide such a question?

The instruments of global governance are international standardization and value-building in international organizations and multilateral *fora* as well as bilateral and plurilateral agreements and a consequential reduction of state sovereignty.

I will take this (admittedly somewhat superficial) reading of global governance as a starting point for an analysis of the changes global governance would mean for public international law and which external relations law the EU would need to avail itself of, if it wished to make a significant contribution to these changes. Against this backdrop, I will try to assess the changes to the external constitution of the EU introduced by the Treaty of Nice as well as those proposed by the Draft Treaty establishing a Constitution for Europe (DTCE)[4].

## GLOBAL GOVERNANCE AS A CHALLENGE FOR PUBLIC INTERNATIONAL LAW

Much has been written about the impact of globalization on Public International Law[5]. The changes to Public International Law which are

[3] The second driving power of globalization is the technological quantum leap that has occurred in the second half of the last century and which has made interaction and communication significantly easier.

[4] *European Convention*, Draft Treaty Establishing a Constitution for Europe of 18 July 2003, OJ 2003 C 169/1.

[5] See eg A Coleman and J Maogoto, 'After the Party, is there a Cure for the Hangover? The Challenges of the Global Economy to Westphalian Sovereignty' (2003) 30 *Legal Issues of Economic Integration* 35–60; J Delbrück, 'Structural Changes in the International System and

constituted most commonly are an extension of the so far *numerus clausus* of its subjects (NGOs, TNEs, Individuals), a change to the creation and effect of its rules (customary law, erga omnes effects) and a relaxation of rules on standing before international tribunals. However, this is only a description of a process that takes place or is likely to take place in the years to come. Global Governance as a reaction to globalization of all kinds of economic and non-economic activities bears also a normative notion, ie it embraces changes that *would be necessary* whether likely or not at the moment.

If Global Governance means primarily a constitutional balancing and hierarchization of universal values, a first challenge to the international legal order will be to work out the relationship between its multiple more or less self-contained regimes pursuing a great deal of different and sometimes conflicting economic (free trade, free movement of capital and payments) and non-economic (environmental protection, sustainable development, human rights etc) goals.[6] Current developments in Public International Law, particularly in relation to the WTO, present different reactions to this task. Forms of cooperation between international organizations which lead to a reciprocal integration into the other organization's tasks present new forms of coordinated *governance of equals*.[7] The agreements of the WTO with organizations such as WIPO or the IMF point in that direction. They build on the acceptance that no organization has the necessary — normative and pragmatic — capacity to deal with every aspect of governance that may be affected by its rules. They may also offer the

its Legal Order: International Law in the Era of Globalization' (2001) *Swiss Review of International and European Law*, 1–36; S Hobe, 'Die Zukunft des Völkerrechts im Zeitalter der Globalisierung — Perspektiven der Völkerrechtsentwicklung im 21. Jahrhundert', (1999) 37 *Archiv des Völkerrechts* 253–82; C Schreuer 'The Waning of the Sovereign State: Towards a New Paradigm for International Law' (1993) 4 *European Journal of International Law* 447–71; G Seidel, 'Die Völkerrechtsordnung an der Schwelle zum 21. Jahrhundert (2000) 38 *Archiv des Völkerrechts* 23–47; P Zumbaansen 'Die vergangene Zukunft des Völkerrechts' (2001) 34 *Kritische Justiz* 46–68.

6 On that specific problem see J Neumann, *Die Koordination des WTO-Rechts mit anderen völkerrechtlichen Ordnungen. Konflikte des materiellen Rechts und Konkurrenzen der Streitbeilegung* (Berlin, 2002); G Marceau, 'Conflict of Norms and Conflict of Jurisdictions' (2001) 35 *Journal of World Trade* 1081–31; J Pauwelyn *Conflict of Norms in Public International Law: How WTO Law Relates to Other Rules of International Law* (Cambridge, CUP, 2003).

7 On the importance of inter-agency cooperation for global governance in general see C Tietje, 'Global Governance and Inter-Agency Co-operation in International Economic Law', (2002) 36 *Journal of World Trade* Vol 3, 501–15; on the problem of delimitation of competences between different International Organizations see M Ruffert, 'Zuständigkeitsgrenzen internationaler Organisationen im institutionellen Rahmen der internationalen Gemeinschaft', (2000) 38 *Archiv des Völkerrechts* 129–68; on the problems with regard to membership of International Organizations in other International Organizations see C Herrmann, 'Rechtsprobleme der parallelen Mitgliedschaft von Völkerrechtssubjekten in Internationalen Organisationen', in Bauschke et al (eds), *Pluralität des Rechts — Regulierung im Spannungsfeld der Rechtsebenen* (Stuttgart, 2003) 139–61.

opportunity to integrate the foreign organization as the *advocate of the common good* into the balancing of the conflicting interests of its Members. Again, the WTO provides an example with the IMF's judgment as to whether balance of payments problems in fact exist being binding for the application of Art XII GATT.[8] The earlier EC proposal to involve the WHO into the question if a certain pandemic in a developing or least developed country justifies a compulsory license for a patent was underpinned by similar considerations.[9]

However, the WTO is also at the focal point of the debate about the more stressful relationship between different international legal orders, in particular between WTO/GATT rules and MEAs.[10] The WTO legal system is already partially open to rules of a different source. International standards are referred to in the SPS and TBT-Agreements[11] and some notions of WTO norms may be interpreted in the light of environmental treaties such as the Washington Convention (CITES).[12] Nevertheless, the WTO agreements — inspired by the goal of free trade — are potentially at odds with other international treaties, such as the Cartagena Protocol[13] or the UNCLOS, as already demonstrated by the *Swordfish* case.[14] The negotiations under the Doha Development Agenda are dealing with this problem, but only limited to situations in which all parties to a conflict have signed an international agreement.[15] Rights and obligations of non-signatories must explicitly not be altered by the solution still to be found. The increased 'risk' or 'chance' of spill-overs from one into another international regime has already led to great carefulness in the negotiation of clauses dealing with the relationship of a new treaty — the Cartagena Protocol — with other legal systems,[16] making them difficult to interpret at the least.

[8] See D Ahn, 'Linkages between International Financial and Trade Institutions' (2000) 34 *Journal of World Trade* 1–35; D Siegel, 'Legal Aspects of the IMW/WTO Relationship: The Fund's Articles of Agreement and the WTO Agreements' (2002) (3) 96 *American Journal of International Law* 561–99.

[9] See Commission Press release: 'EU seeks to break the current deadlock on WTO access to medicines: A multilateral solution is needed', Brussels, 9 January 2003.

[10] See above n 6.

[11] See W Weiß and C Herrmann, *Welthandelsrecht (*Munich, 2003), paras 540 *et seq*; M Matsushita, T Schoenbaum and P Mavroidis, *The World Trade Organization* (Oxford, OUP, 2003) 485 *et seq*; M Trebilcock and R Howse, *The Regulation of International Trade*, 2nd edn (London and New York, 1999) 142 *et seq.*

[12] See *WTO Appellate Body*, United States — Import Prohibition of Certain Shrimp and Shrimp Products, WT/DS58/AB/R, paras 130 *et seq.*

[13] *Cartagena Protocol on Biosafety* of 29 January 2000, ILM 39 (2000), pp 1027 *et seq*=OJ 2002 L 201/50.

[14] See M Orellana, 'The Swordfish Dispute Between the EU and Chile at the ITLOS and the WTO' (2002) (1) 71 *Nordic Journal of International Law* 55–81.

[15] *Doha Ministerial Declaration* of 14 November 2001, WT/MIN(01)/DEC/1, para 31 (i).

[16] See Preamble of the *Cartagena Protocol* (footnote 13 above); see also P Phillips and W Kerr 'Alternative paradigms: The WTO versus the Biosafety Protokol for Trade in Genetically

The issue of hierarchization and balancing is closely related to the lack of an international organization with overarching competence and a centralized constitutional juridical body, whose main task would be to integrate conflicting values laid down in international law. The legitimacy of such body would of course be a significant problem. Right now, not even a formalized way exists, in which a situation like the one in the *Swordfish* case with two international dispute settlement systems being involved — and possibly delivering conflicting rulings — could be solved. A 'preliminary reference procedure' among international dispute settlement bodies may be an answer to this procedural problem,[17] however certainly not a conclusive one. Problems of jurisdiction, forum shopping and balancing would persist.

Similar balancing issues arise with regard to IMF conditionality or the Worldbank's Comprehensive Development Framework (CDF).

If such described balancing exercise failed, international judges could be tempted to fill the existing *lacuna* by giving a more precise interpretation to imprecise provisions such as the chapeau of Art XX GATT. The constitutional consequences of judges assessing eg the proportionality of sovereign nation states' measures without a clear legal basis can hardly be exaggerated.[18] To demonstrate judicial self-restraint in that regard would only constitute a different way of agreeing to disagree, that could hamper the liberalization achieved hitherto significantly.

If, however, the balancing succeeded and led to a coherent international normative order, there would be much less an argument against the justiciability of constitutional value-based questions in the international realm. As soon as we arrived at an international legal order of that kind, governments should not be allowed to opt-out unilaterally from that system anymore. The most effective way to prevent such opt-out — as we have been taught be the ECJ — is direct effect complemented by the doctrine of consistent interpretation and state liability for damages suffered. Giving private individuals standing before international tribunals whose *lex fori* is made up from rules of Public International Law could produce a theoretically similar, even though by no means equally effective outcome.

Modified Organisms' (2000) (4) *Journal of World Trade* 63 *et seq*; A Qureshi, 'The Cartagena Protocol on Biosafety and the WTO — co-existence or incoherence?' (2000) (4) 49 *International and Comparative Law Quarterly* 835 *et seq*.

[17] See J Neumann, *Die Koordination des WTO-Rechts mit anderen völkerrechtlichen Ordnungen* (Diss, Berlin, 2002) 600 *et seq*.

[18] See J Neumann and E Turk, 'Necessity Revisited: Proportionality in World Trade Organization Law After *Korea — Beef*, *EC — Asbestos* and *EC — Sardines*' (2003) (1) 37 *Journal of World Trade* 199–233.

**Changing Public International Law and European External Relations Law: Repercussions and Prerequisites**

The EU is the best example of governance beyond the nation state, a kind of 'regional governance' if you like, that fulfils the criteria defined above. The whole process of the internal market legislation devoted to harmonization is a question of value-building, the *Cassis* case-law is the juridical recognition of legitimate government intervention and a number of provisions of the Treaties explicitly call for balancing and coherence (eg Art 6, 95 (3) and most recently the new Art 133 (3) (1) (2) EC Treaty, Art 3 (2) EU Treaty). The recent *Schmidberger* judgment of the ECJ marks the latest example of such balancing of economic and non-economic interests.[19] Community law is directly applicable in national proceedings and private individuals have standing before the Court of Justice. It has become conventional thinking to stress the responsibility the EU bears for the development of public international law and relations due to its exemplary character.[20]

The early EEC only had a very limited external dimension. Association of third countries and international organizations (ex-Art 310 EEC) and the common commercial policy (ex-Art 113 EEC) were the only areas in which the conclusion of international agreements was explicitly foreseen with provisions on the relations with international organizations except for membership (ex-Arts 229–31 EEC) complementing them. Accordingly, except for the goals stated in ex-Art 111 EEC (harmonious development of world trade, progressive abolition of restrictions on international trade and the lowering of customs barriers), the EEC lacked a clear policy aim for its external action. Even the EC Treaty as amended by the Treaty of Nice does scarcely define external policy goals of the EC. The preamble only mentions international trade and the solidarity with overseas countries; Art 2 EC Treaty is focused exclusively on the internal sphere and Art 3 EC Treaty only mentions common commercial policy, development cooperation and the association of overseas countries and territories. However, the new Art 181a (1) (2) EC Treaty refers to the development and consolidation of democracy, the rule of law, human rights and fundamental freedoms, but is limited to development cooperation and supplementary measures.

It was only following the *AETR* case-law of the ECJ, that the goals of the internal policies could also be pursued through external action, insofar

[19] ECJ, C–112/00, *Eugen Schmidberger, Internationale Transporte und Planzüge v Austria*, [2003] ECR I–5659.

[20] See only S Dillon, *International Trade and Economic Law and the European Union* (Oxford, Hart, 2002) 14 *et seq*, and 384 *et seq*.

as external action was necessary for the achievement of internal policy aims.[21] They did not, however, become external goals as such. The EU Treaty for the first time introduced a vision of international relations in its preamble, where the promotion of peace, security and progress in Europe *and in the world* is explicitly laid down. This is further elaborated in Art 11 EU Treaty.

Many of the problems of EU external relations law that occurred over the years are maybe attributable to this lack of guidance as to what the EC/EU stands for in the world. The exclusive competence in the traditional field of common commercial policy, exercised by qualified majority voting and aimed a free trade, was confronted with non-exclusive and hence at least practically unanimity-requiring competences in the fields of the environment, public health etc. Coherence among the different policies, including the CFSP has been one of the key questions throughout the last couple of years and gets more and more pressing with the ever increasing area in which the EC/EU becomes externally competent. Coherence is particularly troublesome because of the integrative process in the sphere of Public International Law described above. If the different legal systems of the international legal order are growing more and more together, the choice of the appropriate legal basis becomes a more and more difficult task and the ECJ's 'primary objective test'[22] is poorly suited to deal with it. This would not be of great significance, if the question had not such important consequences as exclusiveness, voting requirements and parliamentary participation. Incoherent procedural rules are likely to deliver an incoherent substantial outcome. The repercussions of the increased interaction and interconnectedness of topics dealt with in separate legal systems of public international law is eg reflected in the dispute about the legal basis for the *Cartagena Protocol* which is one the more recent examples of an effort to balance trade and environment.[23] A further dismantling of the scope of the CCP seems to be almost unavoidable in times where the focus of International Economic Law has shifted from tariff to non-tariff barriers to trade that lie much closer to the core questions of governance. A further increase of 'mixity' and the consequential unanimity would be the outcome.

Lacking explicit external policy goals other than free trade, the key purpose of the external action of the EU in all policy areas over the years has become the exportation and protection of the balance between the

[21] ECJ, Case 22/70, *Commission v Council (AETR)* [1971] ECR 263. See M Cremona, 'External Relations and External Competence: The Emergence of an Integrated Policy', in P Craig and G de Búrca (eds), *The Evolution of EU Law* (Oxford OUP, 1999) 137–75 for a general survey of the development of the EC's external powers.

[22] See most recently ECJ, C–211/01, *Commission v Council (Road Transport Agreement)*, judgment of 11 September 2003, not yet officially published, paras 38 *et seq*.

[23] ECJ, Opinion 2/00, *Cartagena Protocol on Biosafety* [2001] ECR I-9713.

economic and non-economic values struck internally, the exportation of the 'European social model'. One may as well call it 'parallelism in content', as *Marise Cremona* has done in one of her writings.[24] One can see this export also as a way to subjugate the free trade paradigm in Art 131 EC to the non-economic values of the other Treaty provisions. Exportation is the most effective way of protecting the values Europe claims to stand for and rebut allegations of a 'fortress Europe' at the same time: The recognition of EU legislation on food safety at Codex level not only makes food imported into the EU safer, but also safes EU food legislation from challenge under the WTO SPS and TBT agreements. At the same time, it alleviates the EU from the legally extremely difficult question of the relationship between Arts I, III and XXIV GATT, ie to what extent preferences relating to topics mentioned in Art III:4 GATT do not have to be granted to third countries under Art XXIV GATT.

Shaping global governance is hence in the very self-interest of the EU. The new Art 133 (3) (1) (2) EC Treaty, according to which '*the Council and the Commission shall be responsible for ensuring that the agreements negotiated [within the framework of the CCP] are compatible with internal community policies and rules'*, is another example of the silent hierarchy of values that has sneaked into the EU external relations. *Marise Cremona* already correctly described this provision as the maybe most significant of the changes made to Art 133 EC by the Treaty of Nice, in '*direct[ing] trade policy makers to internal Community policies and rules*'.[25] That trade liberalization has become a second-tier objective for the EC is also made visible by the statement of France before the ECJ in the case of the Cartagena Protocol, in which the French government made clear relatively bluntly, that the Cartagena Protocol was aimed at preventing trade and hence likely to be in conflict with WTO rules.

The question of values seems also to be relevant for the ECJ when it comes to the issue of direct effect of international agreements as well their interpretation insofar as they are literally identical with provisions of the EC Treaty. *Sara Dillon*, in her 'International Trade and Economic Law and the European Union'[26] drew the conclusion that WTO law must not be held to have direct effect, since it is not sufficiently open to non-economic concerns, or not balanced enough if you like.[27] Somewhat comparable, the ECJ has approached the interpretation of international agreements' wording with a view to the respective treaty's objectives and context. On this basis, the Court has been considerably more willing to

[24] M Cremona, above n 21, 148.
[25] M Cremona, 'A Policy of Bits and Pieces? The Common Commercial Policy after Nice', (2001) *Cambridge Yearbook of European Legal Studies*, 61–91 at 76.
[26] See above n 20.
[27] *Ibid*, 1 *et seq* and 384 *et seq*.

grant direct effect the more the respective provisions constituted an export of the Community *acquis* and the more the ECJ was in the position of the ultimate interpreter of these provisions, since the respective agreements did not provide for a separate jurisdiction of a different court. To accept the direct effect of WTO/GATT rules on the other hand would dismantle the ECJ of much of its constitutional power, ie its competence to ultimately decide the constitutional questions of the Union, including in particular the balancing between economic and non-economic values. The reluctance of the Court to recognize a superior judicial body is also reflected by the Courts approach in the *EEA I* opinion[28] and may also have been underlying its reasoning in Opinion 2/94.[29] In general, the Court has not demonstrated great willingness to accept a true transfer of sovereign rights from the EC to other international organizations if the autonomy of the EC legal order in the pursuit of its aims could be impaired thereby. Insofar, the ECJ does not behave much different from national courts vis-à-vis EC law in the past. This approach may have been justified from the perception of the EU as the regional alternative answer to globalization. However, participation of the EU in global governance does require a somewhat more outward looking perspective, ie the understanding that the EU needs to be willing to compromise in ways similar to those expected from the Member States internally. The EU will not be able to influence multilateral negotiations substantially, if it always struggles for an internal compromise first that is subsequently offered to the international community on a take-it-or-leave-it basis as we witness right now in the area of agriculture again.

## THE EU RESPONSE: EXTERNAL RELATIONS PROVISIONS OF THE TRETY OF NICE AND THE DRAFT CONSTITUTION

A reform of the external relations regime of the EU/EC has been on the Agenda for a long time. However, the Treaty of Nice once more failed to address the relevant questions, not to speak of solving any of them. Only moderate changes to the EU and EC Treaty were made. The European Parliament was granted the right to request an Opinion under Art 300 (6) EC, an additional provision on economic, financial and technical co-operation was introduced as Art 181a and Art 133 EC Treaty underwent awful changes with regard to the competence for international agreements

[28] ECJ, Opinion 1/91, *EEA Agreement (No 1)*, [1991] ECR I-6079.
[29] ECJ, Opinion 2/94, *Accession of the European Communities to the European Convention on Human Rights*, [1996] ECR I-1759.

concerning trade in services and commercial aspects of intellectual property rights.[30] However, the amendments are in a way indicating an ongoing change of perspective of the Union that focuses more strongly on the policy dimension of external relations of the EU.

One of the main driving forces towards the Convention of the Future of Europe and one of its main tasks has been to give an answer to the '*weakening of Europe's position in the world*'.[31] '*Europe's new role in a globalised world*' is one of the core themes of the Laeken Declaration and the Convention has devoted a separate working group to the External Action of the Union. The Draft Treaty establishing a Constitution for Europe (DTCE), according to the conclusions of the Thessaloniki European Council '*[enhances the] Union's ability to act as a coherent and unified force in the international system and to deal effectively with the challenges globalisation and interdependence create.*' It is of course too early to really assess the external relations regime contained in theDTCE; however, I will try to make some very preliminary remarks on some of the provisions which I find the most remarkable.[32]

For the first time, the Union would have a complete set of goals for its external action. The key aim as laid down in Art 3 (4) and III-193 DTCE reflects the process described before. According to Art 3 (4) (1) DTCE '*in its relations with the wider world, the Union shall uphold and promote its values and interests*'. Pursuant Art III-193 (1) (1) DTCE, the '*Union's action on the international scene shall be guided by, and designed to advance in the wider world, the principles which have inspired its own creation, development and enlargement*'. Also in Art III-193 (2) DTCE, to '*safeguard the common values, fundamental interests, security, independence and integrity of the Union*' is on top of the list of goals to be pursued in the field of international relations. It's at the end of the list of Art III-193 (2) DTCE that the promotion of '*an international system based on stronger multilateral cooperation and good global governance*' is explicitly stated as one of the external aims of the EU. Interestingly, Art 3 (4) DTCE refers not only to free, but also to fair trade, a notion that is conceptually difficult to grasp. Art III-216 DTCE, dealing with the goals of the CCP does, however, not replicate this wording. Instead, Art III-217 (1) DTCE (ie the current Art 133 ECT), strengthens the link between the CCP and the other external policies of the Union. It reads: '*The common commercial policy shall be conducted in the context of the principles and objectives of the Union's external action, as set out in Article 1 of this Title.*' Art III-193 (3) DTCE calls for an integration of the

[30] See C Herrmann, 'Common Commercial Policy after Nice: Sisyphus would have done a better job', (2002) (1) 39 *Common Market Law Review*, 7–29.

[31] *Laeken Declaration* of 15 December 2001.

[32] See also M Cremona, 'The Draft Constitutional Treaty: External Relations and External Action' (2003) 40(6) *Common Market Law Review* 1347–66.

aims into all policies of the Union and for coherence among them. However, the dualism of and the division between the High Politics of the CFSP and the down-to-earth external policies of the EC[33] will persist. Another significant change to the external relations regime of the Union might be contained in Art 12 (2) DTCE, according to which '*The Union shall have exclusive competence for the conclusion of an international agreement when its conclusion is provided for in a legislative act of the Union, is necessary to enable the Union to exercise its competence internally, or affects an internal Union act.*' This provision becomes particularly interesting read in comparison with Art III-225 (1) DTCE, which regulates the general capacity of the Union to enter into international agreements with third countries or international organisations. Such capacity shall be given, '*where the Constitution so provides or where the conclusion of an agreement is necessary in order to achieve one of the Union's objectives, where there is provision for it in a binding Union legislative act or where it affects one of the Union's internal acts.*' It is clear that these provisions are meant to codify the *AETR*-case-law in the DTCE's provisions.[34] However, as the provisions are worded and in the context of the other changes their silent power may be much greater than was envisaged in the first place. Troublesome are in particular the phrases '*when it affects one of the Union's internal acts*', justifying exclusive external competence, and '*necessary in order to achieve one of the Union's objectives*', given the far-reaching objectives the Union will pursue in its international relations in the future. In terms of procedural requirements, it is noteworthy, that the specialties of the CCP will probably come to an end; this may make the choice of a legal basis much easier in the future.

## CONCLUSION

As the European Union itself, its external relations regime has developed substantially over the decades. From a mere free-trade oriented system of a customs union to a more or less fully fledged international identity of a Union, based on fundamental rights and actively pursuing a broad range of non-economic aims in its international relations. Different procedural requirements and conflicting policy aims applying have made this process a thorny one that mirrors the ongoing process of integration and hierarchization in public international law.

[33] See J Monar, 'The European Union's Foreign Affairs System after the Treaty of Amsterdam: A "Strengthened Capacity for External Action"?' (1997) (4) 2 *European Foreign Affairs Review* 413–36 at 435.
[34] See *European Convention, Working Group VII — External Action*, Final Report, CONV 459/02, p 4.

The DTCE reflects the international role that the EU already plays and ends the inward-looking self-occupied orientation of the EU on the level of primary Union law. With the DTCE, the Union would make 'good global governance' one of its explicit goals. It does also put the Union into a better position to strive for that goal, even though some of the problems of the past are not sufficiently solved by the DTCE (eg the transfer of sovereignty by the Union to other International Organizations). '*Gripping* Global Governance' is hence the title for the external action of the Union in the years to come. It describes the process of 'getting a grip' rather than an 'already tight hold' and it is capable of 'arousing and holding the attention' of the Union alike.

# 18

# *Squaring the Circle for Tomorrow's World: A Comparative Analysis of the EC and WTO Approaches to Balancing Economic and Non-economic Interests in International Trade*

EMILY REID*

## INTRODUCTION

THE POTENTIAL RECONCILIATION of economic and non-economic interests in the context of international trade is an issue of great importance, since in this context a conflict is exposed between some of the most celebrated causes of our time: on the one hand trade liberalization, and on the other non-economic interests such as environmental and human rights protection. Yet while these interests can, and do conflict on occasions, they are also, in the long term, mutually dependent. Evidence of this long term mutual dependency may be observed in the definition and recognition of the principle of sustainable development.[1]

Although the definition of sustainable development remains controversial[2] there can be no doubt as to its significance on the

* I am grateful to Malcolm Ross and Nick Hopkins for their comments on earlier drafts of this paper.

[1] The most commonly accepted definition of the concept was articulated in the 'Brundtland Report' (the report of the World Commission on Environment and Development 'Our Common Future' (1987)).

[2] See Wetlesen, 'A Global Ethic of Sustainability?' in Lafferty and Langhelle (eds), *Towards Sustainable Development: On the Development and Conditions of Sustainablity*; P Sands, 'Sustainable Development: Treaty, Custom and Cross Fertilisation of International Law' in

international stage.[3] The Brundtland definition is 'development that meets the needs of the present without compromising the ability of future generations to meet their own needs'.[4] This concept clearly embraces the needs of both the environment and humans, yet it should be noted that while promoting the consideration of environmental and human rights issues, sustainable development does not prioritise these *over* economic development: rather it promotes each of these *in relation to* development. Sustainable development embraces the notion that 'development' must comprise a balance of each of these factors, thus suggesting that pure 'economic development', with no benefits for other interests, is not sustainable.

This paper compares the approaches of the European Community (Community) and the World Trade Organisation (WTO) to the balance between the protection of economic and non-economic interests, focusing in particular upon the relationship between free trade and environmental protection.[5] This reflects both the significance of environmental protection as one of the most celebrated non-economic interests, and also the fact that both the WTO Dispute Settlement Body and the European Court of Justice (ECJ) have ruled upon this specific issue on several occasions.[6]

The reason for drawing this comparison between the EC and WTO approaches is threefold: firstly, the European Community is an economically and politically influential organisation, which is seeking to export its own values in its relations with third states,[7] thus the global significance of its stance should not be underestimated. Secondly, the Community constitutes 15 members of the WTO, and is itself a member. In that respect it is not only an influential organisation within, but its actions are constrained by, the WTO — it may even be suggested that theirs is a symbiotic relationship. Thirdly, since the 1970s the European

A Boyle and D Freestone (eds), *International Law and Sustainable Development* (Oxford, OUP, 1999) ; AV Lowe, 'Sustainable Development and Unsustainable Arguments' in Boyle and Freestone; Lee, 'Global Sustainable Development: Its Intellectual and Historical Roots' in Lee, Holland and McNeill (eds), *Global Sustainable Development in the 21st Century*; Holland, 'Sustainable Development: The Contested Vision' in Lee, Holland and McNeill.

[3] This is demonstrated by the United Nations Convention on Sustainable Development (Johannesburg, 2002) as well as in the fact that it has been adopted by the European Community (Art 6 EC, Art 3, Draft Constitution) and is now included as fundamental to the Community's relations with certain third states (including its relations with the ACP states).

[4] The Brundtland Report, 43.

[5] This paper does not seek to provide a comprehensive account of the issues arising from this comparison, but rather to raise questions to be more fully explored in another context.

[6] Below. The issues raised in this context apply also in relation to other non-economic issues but the focus in the present analysis is limited primarily (due to constraints of space) to environmental protection.

[7] Note inclusion of sustainable development in EC Agreements with third states, as in Art 9, Cotonou Agreement, at: *http://www.europa.eu.int/comm/development/development_old/cotonou/agreement_en.htm*; see also COM (2002) 82 final, *Towards a global partnership for sustainable development.*

Community has grappled with the issue of how to balance the realisation of the single market with the pursuit of non-economic interests, including, *inter alia*, environmental protection and human rights. There have been many instances over the last thirty years in which measures pursuing environmental protection and concerning the enjoyment of fundamental rights have come into conflict with the removal of barriers to trade.[8] This issue has recently intensified as the European Union has increased the priority given to both environmental protection[9] and human rights[10], and adopted the principle of sustainable development.[11] It is, consequently, interesting to establish what, if anything, the international community can learn from the European Community experience for its pursuit of both economic and non-economic interests.

There can be little doubt that a strong, consistent stance by the European Community may be crucial in determining the direction pursued by the international community (including the WTO) in the process by which economic and non-economic interests may be reconciled. At the least, any evidence that the Community has achieved *some* reconciliation of these interests, can serve to illustrate how these interests may be reconciled.[12]

The significance of the WTO approach to the reconciliation of economic and non-economic interests is clear. The WTO is *the* global trading organisation, its dispute settlement is binding upon its members and its rulings are potentially normative. This significance is increased in view of the fact that there is no alternative forum within which to consider the balance to be drawn between free trade and the protection of non-economic issues. The implications of this are profound, not least that it is imperative that WTO rulings are legitimate, and that they reflect the intentions of its members, rather than determining the direction of the international community.

The first section of this paper examines the approach of the European Community to environmental protection, focusing in particular upon a few of the leading ECJ cases concerning the relationship between free

[8] See inter alia, Case 302/86 *Commission v Denmark* (*Danish Bottles*) [1988] ECR 4067; Case C-2/90 *Commission v Belgium* (*Belgian Waste*) [1992] ECR I-4431, Case C-379/98 *PreussenElektra AG v Schleswag AG* [2001] ECR I-2099; Case C-67/97 *Criminal Proceedings Against Ditlev Bluhme* (*Danish Bees*) [1998] ECR I-8033; Case C-112/00 *Eugen Schmidberger Internationale Transporte Planzuge v Republik Österreich*, judgment of 12 June 2003.

[9] Duty of Integration, Art 6 EC; see also the proposed status of environmental protection under the Draft Constitution Art II-37.

[10] See for example Art 6 and 7 TEU, and note the Proclamation of the Charter of Fundamental Rights.

[11] See Art 6 EC, Art 3 Draft Constitution. Note also the development of the Community's Sustainable Development strategy: COM (2001) 264 final, *A sustainable Europe for a better world: A European Union strategy for all*; COM (2002) 82 final, above n 7.

[12] Although not necessarily to the same effect as within the Community.

movement of goods and environmental protection. The second section explores provision for the protection of non-economic interests in the WTO, and introduces the tests applied to the exceptions by the GATT/WTO dispute settlement panels in relation to environmental protection. The third section compares the approaches and tests adopted and applied in each context, and finally some conclusions are drawn as to the implications for both the EC and the global community.

## ENVIRONMENTAL PROTECTION IN THE EUROPEAN COMMUNITY

Environmental protection itself has long been recognised as a justification for derogation from the EC rules on free movement of goods, despite the fact that it was not mentioned in the Treaty of Rome. The contribution of the Court of Justice to this development was considerable. In 1985, it ruled that environmental protection was 'one of the Community's essential objectives'[13], despite there being no basis for this in the Treaty. This appears, *prima facie*, to be an example of judicial activism. The Member States, however, had made a clear commitment to environmental protection through the 1970s and 1980s[14] and, arguably, any failure by the Court to recognise this development would have constituted a greater act of judicial activism. In the Single European Act the Member States laid out the principles of Community Environmental Policy. This already effectively existed in Community Action Programs, but now had the authority provided by a clear legal base. Notably, in the requirement that environmental consequences be considered in the development of other Community policies,[15] the groundwork was laid for the subsequent development of the requirement of environmental integration.[16]

### Free Movement of Goods v Environmental Protection: The Influence of the ECJ

In 1986 the Court ruled that 'the protection of the environment is now a mandatory requirement which may limit the application of Article 30

[13] Case 240/83 *Procureur de la République v Association de Défence des Bruleurs de l'Huiles Usagées* [1985] ECR 531 at para 13.
[14] See for example the Declaration of Heads of State and Government of 19/20 October 1972 at the Paris summit on collaboration in environmental policy, Environmental Action Programmes [1973] OJ C112/1; [1977] OJ C139/1; [1983] OJ C46/1.
[15] Art 130r(2) SEA
[16] Art 6 EC 'Environmental protection requirements must be integrated into the definition and implementation of the Community policies and activities referred to in Art 3 ... ' (emphasis added).

[now 28] of the Treaty'.[17] In this ruling, the Court implicitly recognised that environmental protection may take precedence over economic objectives, but held that a proportionality test would be applied to this: that the measure implemented constituted the 'least restrictive' possible measure.[18] The Court consolidated this approach in the *Belgian Waste* case[19] when it declared that the principle that 'environmental waste should as a priority be rectified at source'[20] could be invoked to limit the free movement of waste for its disposal.[21] This was particularly significant as the measure in question was *prima facie* discriminatory (banning the import of waste into a particular area). Yet the Court held that the particular nature of 'waste' was such that it should be disposed of locally, and each area should deal with its own waste. Consequently, the Court held that despite its *prima facie* appearance, the measure was not in fact discriminatory. This reasoning has been the subject of substantial criticism, notably from Advocate General Jacobs in *PreussenElektra*.[22]

Perhaps disappointingly, the Member States have not yet addressed the issue of the relationship between environmental protection and free trade,[23] despite this question having arisen before the Court in the past.[24] The Court recently revisited this question in *PreussenElektra*,[25] which concerned a German scheme that supported the purchase of electricity from renewable energy sources. Significantly, the scheme favoured German suppliers, and thus inhibited the operation of the single electricity market. This raised the question of whether a discriminatory scheme such as this could be justified, since it appeared to breach Article 28 EC. Advocate-General Jacobs, having refused to follow the approach of the Court in *Belgian Waste*,[26] submitted that this measure was a discriminatory quantitative restriction and that even if it were possible to justify a discriminatory measure this one would fail the proportionality test.[27]

Despite having traditionally, formally, held that mandatory requirements are not available to justify a discriminatory measure, the Court has not, in fact, applied this consistently in relation to measures pursuing

[17] Case 302/86 *Commission v Denmark*, above n 8.
[18] The difficulties surrounding the application of this test will be returned to below.
[19] Above n 8.
[20] Art 130r (now 174) EC.
[21] Above n 8, at para 34.
[22] Above n 8 at para 225.
[23] The duty of environmental integration (above n 16) notwithstanding.
[24] *Commission v Denmark* (*Danish Bottles*) above n 8; *Belgian Waste*, above n 8.
[25] Above n 8. See S Poli, 'National Regulatory Schemes Supporting the Use of Electricity Produced from Renewable Energy Sources and the Community Legal Framework' (2002) *Journal of Environmental Law* 209.
[26] Above n 22.
[27] There was a less restrictive means (certification of origin) which could have been applied to promote the use of renewable energy, without automatically favouring German sources.

environmental protection, as is evident from the *Belgian Waste* case.[28] In *PreussenElektra* the Court simply held that the measure did not breach Article 28, without assessing whether it was distinctly applicable.[29] This appears rather remiss given that the measure inhibits the purchase of electricity from sources outside Germany. In effect the Court used 'environmental protection' to support the compatibility of the measure with Article 28, rather than permitting environmental protection to be used to justify a derogation. Yet, to permit environmental protection to be used to justify a derogation from Article 28 would have been difficult, in view of the fact that environmental protection is not included in Article 30, and the mandatory requirements have only traditionally been available with respect to indistinctly applicable measures.[30] Consideration of the proportionality of the measure was notable by its absence, but this is a logical consequence of the fact that the measure was not deemed to be a derogation, and thus was not restrained by the requirement of proportionality.

## THE IMPLICATIONS OF *PREUSSENELEKTRA*

The potential effect of the decision in *PreussenElektra*[31] is that segregation of the market will be permitted within the Community, where that segregation is in the name of environmental protection. The implications of this for the single market are potentially enormous. The very substantial achievements in the liberalisation of the Community market may well be compromised in the pursuit of environmental protection, or for protectionism in the name of environmental protection.

If *PreussenElektra* were followed this would indicate a change in the direction of the Community. This has significant implications, raising the question of how this decision could have been reached. The answer must lie in the deepening of the commitment to environmental protection within the Community: rather than being simply an adjunct to the single market, environmental protection is now, meaningfully, an objective in its own right. This reflects a policy choice by the Member States to fully integrate and pursue environmental protection.[32] Such a policy choice would not have been possible without *consensus* as to its value.

Yet it is questionable whether the decision in *PreussenElektra* does indeed reflect the wishes of the Member States. Is it, in fact, a step too

[28] Above n 8, para 236.
[29] Above n 8.
[30] For further comment see Poli, above n 25.
[31] Above n 8.
[32] Above n 9.

far? It would arguably have been better in the long term, for both environmental protection and economic integration, if the Court had recognised environmental protection as a legitimate derogation from Art 28 (a mandatory requirement), but held that the particular measure failed the proportionality test, as AG Jacobs argued. This would have required that the Court recognise that mandatory requirements may apply also to discriminatory measures, but this would arguably have been a shorter step than the leap which it actually took. The doubts surrounding *PreussenElektra* suggest that it will remain an aberration, but the decision is rendered particularly surprising since, on the facts, there were means by which the Court could have given effect to environmental protection, without permitting the segregation of the market on national lines, thus without compromising the 'conflicting' objective of market integration. That being so this was surely a case in which the application of the proportionality test would have been particularly apt.

Arguably, the introduction of the duty of integration[33] could mean that environmental protection now overrides all other areas of policy. This, however, would be a very static view of the relationship between environmental and other interests, and would give no consideration to issues of proportionality in how and where a balance should be drawn in the pursuit of these potentially conflicting interests.

## BALANCING CONFLICTING OBJECTIVES: LESSONS FROM OTHER FIELDS

In relation to the Common Agricultural Policy the ECJ has been explicit that where a conflict arises between different objectives, the Institutions must not give effect to one to the exclusion of pursuit of the other,[34] although it may give temporary priority to one where circumstances require it.[35] Extrapolating from this, as a model, it appears unlikely that the Court will give absolute priority to environmental over all other concerns. A further indication as to how this may be dealt with can be seen in *Schmidberger*,[36] in which Austria invoked fundamental rights as a reason for derogation from Art 28 EC. The Court, having noted that the particular fundamental rights at issue (freedom of assembly and the right to protest) were not 'absolute', stated that these may be restricted, as long as this did not, 'taking account

[33] Above n 16.
[34] Case 197/80 *Ludwigshafener Walzmuhle Erling KG v Community* [1981] ECR 3211 at para 41.
[35] Case 203/86 *Spain v Council* [1988] ECR 4563 at para 10; Case 29/77 *Roquette Freres v France* [1977] ECR 1835.
[36] Above n 8.

of the aim of the restrictions, constitute disproportionate interference, impairing the very substance of the rights guaranteed.'[37] While permitting a proportionate restriction on the enjoyment of fundamental rights, the Court also required that any restriction on free movement of goods must be proportionate.[38] Thus, fundamental rights and free movement of goods must be balanced against each other, with each being subject to the other according to circumstances. In one sense this is nothing new, derogations to free movement have always, formally, been subject to the test of proportionality,[39] yet the two-way nature of that test is, perhaps, a development. It would not be unreasonable however (particularly in view of the spirit of sustainable development) to assume that this may also be the case with environmental protection and the free movement of goods.

It seems *likely* therefore, particularly in view of developments in other contexts,[40] that the Court will maintain its use of a proportionality test. What is *certain*, however, is that the Community, and the Court of Justice in particular, has found a means by which (more or less effectively) to balance economic and non-economic interests.

The development of environmental protection in the European Community was, like that of other non-economic interests, initially driven by economic interests. Yet, despite its origins, environmental protection can now be seen to be an objective in its own right[41] which is central to the governance of the EC.[42] This development reflects an underlying consensus as to values (and objectives) to be pursued, and in turn reflects the developing polity that is the European Union.[43] As such, the EU is a unique international organisation, yet it does not operate in isolation, it interacts with other states and organisations, including the WTO to which attention now turns.

[37] *Ibid* at para 80.
[38] *Ibid* at para 82.
[39] This was applied to environmental protection in *Huiles Usagees* above n 13, and was defined in *Danish Bottles* above n 8, (*PreussenElektra*, above n 8, notwithstanding).
[40] Both in relation to fundamental rights in *Schmidberger*, above n 8 and in relation to the CAP, above text accompanying n 34.
[41] Rightly or wrongly this was particularly clearly demonstrated by the Court's decision in *PreussenElektra*, above n 8, which would not have been possible without this development in the status of environmental protection.
[42] This can clearly be seen in the prominence given to the Duty of Environmental Integration contained in Art 6 EC following Amsterdam, rather than as previously in Art 130r(2) EC (in the Title on Environment).
[43] It is also noteworthy that environmental protection is now typically referred to in the EC's agreements with third states, see for example the Cotonou Agreement (above n 7) in which environmental issues are included in the 'thematic of cross-cutting themes' to be taken into account in all areas of cooperation, Art 20(2), and respect for human rights has become an essential element of the Community's Agreements with third states, see inter alia M Cremona, 'Human Rights and Democracy Clauses in the EC's Trade Agreements', in N Emiliou and D O'Keefe (eds), *The European Union and World Trade Law after the Uruguay Round* (Chichester, Wiley, 1993).

NON-ECONOMIC INTERESTS BEFORE THE WTO

**The Significance of Binding Dispute Settlement**

The principal objective of the WTO is trade liberalisation. Consequently, the WTO only impinges upon non-economic interests in respect of their relations with trade. Yet in this respect, the effect of the WTO rules, and its dispute settlement body's rulings, could be profound. The WTO dispute settlement system is notable for the fact that it is binding, and has proved controversial for the effect that this may have upon the sovereignty of its members.[44] The impact of binding dispute settlement on national policy choices, including in relation to environmental protection and human rights, is potentially significant, particularly if there is no mechanism by which to balance such issues. This immediately raises the question of whether the WTO is an appropriate body to be carrying out such a balancing act, and whether it should be considering such issues at all.

**Liberal Trade: A Means to an End**

In any consideration of the relationship between economic and non-economic interests in the WTO it is worth first recalling that liberal trade was originally seen as a tool towards the enhancement of both international relations and (primarily economic) welfare gains. If, therefore, liberal trade has developed as a tool, the status it has earned in that role should not necessarily mean that it is now seen as an end in itself. Consequently, if one major objective of liberal trade is welfare gain (even primarily economic), then free trade should not be pursued to the exclusion of all other welfare interests. Where the policies or priorities of the international community change, trade policy should evolve to reflect this.

**Provision for Non-economic Interests in the GATT[45]**

The key provision concerning non-economic interests in the GATT is Article XX which provides for general (public policy related) exceptions from the GATT rules. When the GATT was negotiated the environment was not an issue of global concern. It is consequently unsurprising that Article XX does not explicitly refer to 'environmental protection' (despite environmental protection and sustainable development both being referred

[44] See J Jackson, *The World Trade Organisation: Constitution and Jurisprudence* (London Thomson, 1998) Chapter 4.

[45] For reasons of space, this paper focuses upon the provisions of, and jurisprudence arising under, the General Agreement on Tariffs and Trade (GATT) and does not in any detail consider the provisions under the other WTO agreements.

to in the preamble to the WTO).[46] The grounds of exception are, however, capable of encompassing environmental protection — these include measures: (b) necessary to protect human, animal or plant life or health; and (g) relating to the conservation of exhaustible natural resources. As a result Article XX has been central to the environment-related disputes that have come before the dispute settlement procedure, both under the GATT and the WTO. This provides direct comparison with the original EC treaty, in which the exceptions to the prohibition on restrictions to free movement of goods provisions include 'the protection of health and life of humans, animals or plants'.[47] Similarly, the Services (GATS) and Intellectual Property (TRIPS) agreements provide for exceptions relating to the protection of human, animal or plant life,[48] while the Technical Barriers to Trade (TBT) and Sanitary and Phyto-Sanitary (SPS) Agreements provide explicit provisions relating to environmental protection.[49] The Article XX exceptions are subject to an additional requirement (the 'chapeau'): that excepted measures do not constitute 'a means of arbitrary or unjustifiable discrimination between countries where the same conditions prevail, or a disguised restriction on international trade'.

Article XX clearly recognises that the attainment of the objective of free trade may legitimately be restricted by the regulation, and protection, of other common public interests.

## TRADE-ENVIRONMENT DISPUTES BEFORE THE GATT PANEL

Unlike the ECJ, the GATT panel did not take a leading role in developing environmental protection. This is inevitable given the different means by which these organisations have pursued trade liberalisation (positive integration in the Community, as opposed to the WTO's negative integration) and their resultant, very different, natures. The framework nature of the EEC treaty, and the consequent interpretative role of the ECJ are clearly significant here, as there is no such role, or interpretative room, for the Dispute Settlement Panel or Appellate Body in the WTO. This demonstrates a fundamental difference, even in the early stages, in what each organisation was seeking to create, and in what can now be expected of each.

[46] Environmental protection is, however, specifically referred to in other WTO agreements below.

[47] Art 30 (ex 36) EC. (This is unsurprising since the EC measure was modelled upon the GATT provision.)

[48] GATS Art 14, TRIPS Art 27.

[49] In the SPS Agreement, Art 5.2 permits consideration of the environment in the assessment of risk. In the TBT Agreement the environment is referred to in the Preamble and also in Art 2.2, in which it is included as a legitimate objective of technical regulation.

### *Interpreting Article XX*

The first environmental dispute to come before the GATT raised the question of *the required relationship* between the measure at issue, and the objective of conservation of natural resources in the Article XX(g) exception for measures '*relating to* the conservation of exhaustible natural resources'.[50] The panel avoided addressing this question directly, however, and thus avoided addressing what the exception in fact means. This dispute did serve to demonstrate, however, what was to be a recurring difficulty facing the GATT and WTO; that is distinguishing genuine environmentally inspired measures from disguised trade protectionist measures.

The question of the interpretation of the requirement that the measure 'relate to' conservation of natural resources was revisited in the *Herring and Salmon* Dispute,[51] in which the Panel was unambiguous that 'relate to' meant that the measure must be '*primarily aimed at*' conservation, which it held was rather less than the Article XX(b) requirement of 'necessity'. To establish the primary intention of the measure the panel considered the 'least restrictive means' available to the restricting state.

## THE ECJ AND WTO TESTS COMPARED

In terms of reasoning *Herring and Salmon* can be compared with the EC case *Commission v UK*[52] in which the UK sought to impose an import ban on UHT milk, on grounds of public health. The ECJ, having considered the ban and its objective, concluded that the ban breached Article 30 (now 28), and could not be justified by Article 36 (now 30), as there were less restrictive means by which the public health objective could be achieved. Consequently the ban was held not to be 'necessary.' This is interesting because the Panel in the *Herring and Salmon* dispute held that the requirement that the measure 'relate' to conservation, was not as strong as the requirement of necessity, yet, in finding that the measure related to conservation, the Panel applied what in the EC would be a proportionality or even 'necessity' test.

The 'least restrictive means' test applied by the panel in the *Herring and Salmon* dispute was followed in the *Thai Cigarettes* Panel report in relation to public health.[53] This dispute arose from a complaint by the US that Thai

[50] *US Prohibition of Imports of Tuna and Tuna Products from Canada*, BISD 29S/91 Report Adopted 22/02/1982.
[51] *Canada — Measures affecting Exports of Unprocessed Herring and Salmon* BISD 35 S (1988) 98.
[52] Case 124/81 *Commission v UK* [1983] ECR 203.
[53] *Thailand — Restrictions of Importation of and Internal Taxes on Cigarettes*, Report of the Panel Adopted on 7 November 1990 (DS10/R - 37S) (BISD 37S/200).

provisions prohibited the import of cigarettes and other tobacco products, while permitting the sale of domestic cigarettes. The panel accepted the objective of the measures but found them discriminatory, and found that a less restrictive means was available to achieve the public health objective, which the Thai Government could reasonably have been expected to apply. In contrast to the GATT panels' tests of 'least trade restrictiveness' and 'necessity', both the SPS and TBT Agreements make provision for consideration of both necessity and some degree of proportionality.[54]

## THE MERITS OF THE PROPORTIONALITY TEST

The relative value of the proportionality test can be seen by looking at the ECJ's decision in *Red Grouse*[55], which concerned a ban imposed by the Netherlands on offering wild birds for sale. This constituted an import ban, including of Red Grouse — the species in question. The Court was requested to give a ruling on whether this ban was a legitimate measure under Article 36 (now 30) EC, to promote the protection of health and life of animals.

To answer this question the ECJ looked at the Council Directive on Wild Birds, which it found did not prohibit the hunting of Red Grouse. As Red Grouse are legitimately hunted in the UK, are not native to the Netherlands, and do not occur within the Netherlands, the Court found there was no direct Netherlands interest in the conservation of Red Grouse, and held the ban to be unlawful.

This is arguably a rather convoluted way of arriving at this conclusion, and indeed AG Van Gerven demonstrated that the question could simply be addressed through the application of the proportionality test (which the ban failed).[56] The advantage of the proportionality test is that it dealt with the issue on the basis of the particular facts, without generalising in a manner which could be problematical in future cases. The difficulty encountered by the ECJ in dealing with measures of extra-territorial effect[57] is also evident in the rulings of the GATT and WTO dispute settlement panels.[58] Yet, while the proportionality test is a useful tool in

[54] Art 2.2 TB and Arts 2.1 and 5.1 SPS read together. See Desmedt 'Proportionality in WTO Law' (2001) *Journal of International Economic Law* 441–80 for discussion of proportionality under the SPS and TBT Agreements.

[55] Case C-169/89 *Gourmetterie van den Burg* [1990] ECR 2143.

[56] At para 10 of his Opinion.

[57] Measures imposed by one state but impacting upon behaviour in other states, eg the Netherlands ban on sale of Wild Birds.

[58] See *Tuna — Dolphin* I BISD 40S/155 (DS21/R) (not adopted) Reproduced in (1991) 30 (ILM) 1594; *Tuna — Dolphin* II at (1994) 33 *ILM* 839 and *United States — Import Prohibition of Certain Shrimp and Shrimp Products* and Report of the Appellate Body both

the EC context, questions arise concerning the legitimacy of the WTO applying a proportionality test.[59] Since the creation of the WTO, the panels have attempted to avoid such controversy by adopting what is ostensibly a more literal, and legal, approach.[60]

## ANALYSIS OF THE TESTS

It is evident that the test applied in different contexts to the interface between economic and non-economic interests is of crucial importance. It is, therefore, surprising how little clarity there has been on this matter.

The GATT/WTO 'necessity' test[61] requires both a causal link between the measure and the objective pursued under Article XX, and that no reasonably available less restrictive, alternative measure existed. The extent to which the Panel is competent to judge upon the 'reasonable availability' of alternatives is, however, questionable.

It appears from the 'least-restrictive means' test that the fundamental aim is to remove trade restrictions, or at least minimise their effect, and it has been argued that this test avoids the concerns, which may apply to a proportionality test, about the legitimacy of a trade panel carrying out cost-benefit analyses, or 'second-guessing' the objectives of a state in implementing a trade restricting provision.[62]

Yet the least restrictive means test itself ultimately requires a trade panel to weigh up the available resources and the objectives, and could be subject to the same concerns and criticisms as are applied to a trade panel deciding on 'proportionality', dependent on the evidence made available to the panel. Essentially, whether a panel is deciding upon the availability of resources, or balancing objectives, there is still a judgment being made. Such a judgment may, in some circumstances, require very little discretion on the part of the panel, but in others could conceivably require the panel to consider (or not) national policy choices and priorities. In this sense the decision on the availability of natural resources can also involve an element of subjectivity. There appears to be no strong reason why similar

available at *http://www.wto.org*. See J Scott, 'On Kith and Kine (and Crustaceans): Trade and Environment in the EU and WTO' in JHH Weiler (ed), *The EU, the WTO and the NAFTA: Towards a Common Law of International Trade* (Oxford, OUP, 2000).

[59] See Desmedt, above n 54.

[60] See, inter alia R Howse, 'Adjudicative Legitimacy and Treaty Interpretation in International Trade Law: The Early Years of WTO Jurisprudence' in Weiler, above n 58.

[61] *Thai Cigarettes*, above n 53, see also *Tuna — Dolphin* above n 58 and *Reformulated Gasoline, US Standards for Reformulated and Conventional Gasoline* WT/DS2/R, and AB-1996-1 WT/DS2/AB1R.

[62] M Trebilcock and R Howse, *The Regulation of International Trade*, 2nd edn (London, Routledge, 1998) 338–39.

evidence to that made available for the panel to rule on the availability of resources, could not be made available to a panel ruling on the basis of 'proportionality' of the measure. Thus the argument against the WTO ruling upon the proportionality of a measure is weakened if it is deemed to be legitimate that it rules upon the availability of resources.

The introduction of the principle of 'proportionality', however, brings its own problems (notwithstanding its strengths) not least of which is what the concept entails. As seen already, in *Danish Bottles*[63] the ECJ defined the test of proportionality as being that of whether the measure implemented constituted the 'least restrictive' possible measure. Thus the test was drawn within substantially the same ambit as the requirements of the GATT's 'necessity' test. Yet, as seen above, in its application of the test the Court appeared to go beyond 'least restrictiveness' and weigh up the trade restriction as against the environmental benefit,[64] introducing what Notaro has described as proportionality *strictu sensu.*[65]

This disparity between the expressed definition of proportionality and its application has led to inconsistency of application of the test by the ECJ.[66]

Van Gerven AG in *Red Grouse*[67] defined *'necessity'* as requiring firstly, a causal link between the objective and the measure and secondly, that there is no less restrictive measure available. Up to this point his test mirrors the approach of the GATT as regards 'necessity' but the approaches diverge in his recognition of a further element, '*proportionality*'. Under his analysis proportionality clearly *requires consideration of the relationship, and balance to be drawn, between the objective pursued (ie environmental protection) and the restriction upon free trade.*

Despite the lack of clarity as to the test to be applied in ruling upon the legitimacy of an environment regulatory measure, it can be seen that the critical element of either the proportionality test, or the 'least restrictive means' test is that both move the decision away from being one based purely, or predominantly, upon trade-restricting (or liberalising) considerations. This approach, however described, is consistent with the approaches of the Advocates-General of the ECJ, as well as the practical application of the test by the ECJ. Since the conclusion of the WTO the dispute settlement panels have applied the rhetoric of greater consideration of the competing interests and objectives at stake, yet have continued, consistently, to reach results which give precedence to trade liberalisation.[68]

[63] Above n 8.
[64] At para 21.
[65] N Notaro, 'The New Generation Case Law on Trade and Environment', (2000) 25 *ELRev* 467–91.
[66] See inter alia, *Danish Bottles*, above n 8; *Danish Bees*, above n 8.
[67] Above n 55.
[68] In itself this is not inherently a matter for criticism as it arguably reflects the nature of the complaints brought to the WTO, and sheds little light on the cases in which complaints are not brought, as a direct consequence of recognition of the applicability of an exception. It also

The dangers which exist where proportionality is abandoned are clearly demonstrated by the Court's decision in *PreussenElektra,*[69] in which the Court appeared to prioritise one interest over another, in a manner which perhaps did not reflect the wishes of the Member States, and which was certainly not necessary.

## COMPARISON OF THE APPLICATION OF THE TESTS

In view of the contrasting approaches of the ECJ and WTO panels, it is interesting to compare what might have been the outcome before the WTO, of two of the more recent ECJ cases: *Ditlev Bluhme,*[70] and *PreussenElektra* itself.[71]

### *Ditlev Bluhme*

This case concerned a Danish prohibition on keeping a certain species of bee within a particular territory, for the purpose of protecting the indigenous species of bee, which would otherwise die out. If this measure were challenged in the WTO how would it be treated? The first issue is that this creates an obstacle to trade which breaches GATT Article XI, raising the question of whether this is a discriminatory measure. Since the measure also applies to Danish beekeepers wishing to sell to that particular territory, it does not breach Article III. In this respect it may be distinguished from the *Tuna and Tuna Products* ruling,[72] in which a total import ban was rejected because there was no internal regulation. The next question is whether the ban may be justified under Article XX? The ECJ dealt with the measure as a matter concerning 'animal health' but it did not have the option of 'conservation of natural resources' as a possible exception. There has been little objection to Article XX(g) being used in principle for the protection of endangered species,[73] therefore the measure would come within its scope. Thus the question arises as to whether the measure is 'primarily aimed at' conservation, which appears to be the case. This in turn raises the question of 'necessity'. It seems likely that Denmark would have to provide evidence of risk, and prove the rational relationship

reflects the primary objective of the WTO, and the consequent constraints upon its Dispute Settlement panels.

[69] Above n 8.
[70] *Ibid.*
[71] *Ibid.*
[72] Above n 50.
[73] *Tuna — Dolphin* above n 58. See also *Shrimp — Turtle*, Panel Report, *United States — Import Prohibition of Certain Shrimp and Shrimp Products*, WT/DS58/R (98-1710) Appellate Body Report AB-1998-4 WT/DS58/R (98-0000), 12 October 1998 (1998) ILM 121.

between the risk and the measure, as this would seem relevant to determining whether there is a less restrictive measure available. On the facts, given the nature of the species and the risk, a less restrictive measure appears unlikely to be available. The final question is whether the fact that this is a unilateral measure is relevant,[74] again on the facts this seems unlikely: the nature of the species and the particular conservation issue renders it a specifically Danish issue and the protection is directed towards Danish territory. Consequently, it appears that this case would be one in which an environmental measure would be successful before the WTO. This is unsurprising, the measure is a genuinely environmentally inspired one, and it raises no problematic issues of extra-territoriality, thus there is no reason why it should not satisfy the Article XX exception.

### *Preussen Elektra*

Turning now to *PreussenElektra,*[75] there can be little doubt that before the WTO, the outcome would have been different. This was a scheme which would breach Article XI and Article III, raising the question of whether it came within the Article XX exceptions. It was a measure primarily aimed at conservation of natural resources, so could come within paragraph(g). However, there is no doubt that a less restrictive means was available. The scheme would, therefore, fail the least restrictive means test. In the interests of economic integration of markets there is no doubt that this is the correct outcome,[76] since the ECJ decision invites segregation of the market.

### Lessons from the Comparison

What these comparisons demonstrate is the difference in objectives of the WTO and EC. The WTO seeks liberalisation of markets, and to remove obstacles to trade, while recognising the legitimacy of certain exceptions. In this its objectives and rules coincide with those of the EC, leading to a similar outcome in cases such as *Ditlev Bluhme.*[77]

The EC, however, has gone a step further. While originally EC environmental protection was seen only in terms of its relationship with free movement, this has changed. Although *PreussenElektra* is subject to criticism,

[74] See *Shrimp — Turtle, ibid* in which the AB expressed a preference for multi-lateral measures.
[75] Above n 8. Arguably, had the ECJ decided *PreussenElektra* 'correctly', the outcome would also have been different. The significance of *PreussenElektra*, for present purposes, lies in the evident confusion arising from the developing integration of environmental protection within the Community, without the necessary clarity in how it is to be treated where it impinges upon the achievement of the Community's other objectives.
[76] This outcome would also have been consistent with earlier ECJ jurisprudence.
[77] Supra note 8.

and probably an aberration, the decision demonstrates that environmental protection has moved to a new level. It is now an element of a discernable polity. The EC's system of governance is developing: it is clearly distinguishable from the WTO perspective, and indeed from its own original position. Without such a shift the Court could not have reached this decision. At the same time *PreussenElektra* demonstrates the inherent dangers where there is no clearly established mechanism by which to address the 'problem' of 'conflicting' objectives.

## CONCLUSION: TURNING A CORNER — THE CIRCLE MADE OVAL?

It is apparent from the EC experience that pursuit of both economic and non-economic interests may be reconciled. It is also apparent, however, that it is necessary to have a consensus to achieve this, and that there is some mechanism by which this balance may truly be achieved, without automatically prioritising one interest over the other. Without this, the very positive steps taken by the EC in this context may be compromised. The application of the proportionality test therefore appears to be of crucial importance.

It is also clear, however, that despite certain similarities in outcome in individual cases, the EC experience is not directly transferable to the WTO. This is because the EC's legal system, positive integration and development of governance (beyond simply negative integration) are fundamental to the direction in which it has developed.

The WTO does not currently have, in the context of the GATT, a mandate to do, with any legitimacy, what the EC has done: either in developing the significance of environmental protection in its own context, or in applying the proportionality test. Although the WTO has applied a test which effectively resembles 'proportionality', and notwithstanding the flexibility inherent in the wording of the Agreement which permits this, there can be little doubt that the WTO's primary function, trade liberalisation, raises questions as to the appropriateness of it doing so, and even concerning its ability to do so in more problematic cases. There are instances in which the lack of an objective, genuinely balancing mechanism may cause difficulties. There can be no doubt that this is an issue which the members of the WTO must address: the WTO, as a classic contract-based organisation cannot reform itself.

Yet in other branches of international law, outside the trade context, there has been a shift, not only with the acceptance of sustainable development: international environmental law, and also branches of human rights law are evolving. This suggests that some consensus is possible in the international context, harnessing that into the WTO context, however, and reaching a consensus on priorities, is unlikely to be easy. Yet if the WTO does not move forward it risks marginalisation, a loss of credibility and constant conflict with other branches of international law. The challenge for the EC will be in using its experience, strength and force as one actor to influence this development.

# 19

# *The Participation of the European Community in the World Trade Organisation: An External Look at European Union Constitution-Building*

ANTONIS ANTONIADIS*

## INTRODUCTION

SINCE ITS INCEPTION in 1995, the WTO has developed into a key player in the global economic system and an institutional mechanism of undoubted importance for global governance.[1] Within the European Union, the model of governance for managing globalisation on a regional scale,[2] the ongoing constitutional process seems to be reaching some sort of *finalité* and the proposed changes to its founding treaties have now been vested with the grandeur of the term 'Constitution'. The two systems interact and since their competences significantly overlap they eventually cross-fertilize in a number of ways.[3] This process is not always easy as despite the foundation of both systems on essentially the same basic political philosophy and economics theories, the European Union, serving its integrationist objectives, has demonstrated increased sensitivity

* I am indebted to the Alexander S Onassis Public Benefit Foundation for their financial support and to Professor Anthony Arnull and Olympia Bekou for useful comments on a previous draft. Responsibility for all errors remains mine alone.

[1] M Matsushita, TJ Schoenbaum, and PC Mavroidis, *The World Trade Organization: Law, Practice, and Policy*, (Oxford, OUP, 2003) 14.

[2] See the insightful analysis by F Snyder, 'The Gatekeepers: The European Courts and WTO Law' (2003) 40 *CMLRev* 313.

[3] G de Búrca, and J Scott, 'The Impact of the WTO on EU Decision-making' in G de Búrca and J Scott (eds), *The EU and the WTO: Legal and Constitutional Issues* (Oxford, Hart Publishing, 2001) 1.

to the treatment of non-trade concerns such as public health, the protection of the environment, and social policy.[4] It is therefore unavoidable that constitutional conflicts at the elusive quest for the ideal model of global governance will emerge.

The Dispute Settlement mechanism of the WTO represents the forum where the policy choices of the European Union have been met with unprecedented rigour. In this process, not only the substantive policy choices of the European Union are tested but also its ability to unite divergent views of twenty-five Member States. This is a fundamental problem for the Union constitutional order and, surprisingly, the procedural norms for its resolution, partly because of the GATT inheritance,[5] have developed *de facto*. This contribution aims to analyse the division of competences between the European Union and its Member States enshrined in the draft Constitutional Treaty in the field of external trade. It will then analyse the practice in the WTO Dispute Settlement to date and demonstrate how the issue of competences may undermine the Union's ability to protect its policy-making autonomy on the international plane. Finally, it will make proposals for the procedural and substantive insulation of the European Union Constitution. In the present analysis, the latest version of the draft Constitutional Treaty shall be taken into account.[6]

## DIVISION OF POWERS BETWEEN THE UNION AND ITS MEMBER STATES IN EXTERNAL TRADE

### The Common Commercial Policy and the Draft Constitutional Treaty

The EC and its Member States joined the WTO in 1995 as founding members on the basis of a division of competences prescribed in the infamous *Opinion 1/94*.[7] It is clear from *Opinion 1/94* that the content of the WTO Agreement and the annexed agreements is broader than the EC Common Commercial Policy enshrined in Article 133 EC Treaty. This necessitated resort to several Articles of the Treaty at the conclusion of the WTO Agreement with regard to trade in services and intellectual property rights falling outside the CCP.[8] The competence flowing from those Articles is non-exclusive and the WTO Agreement was concluded

[4] S Dillon, *International Trade and Economic Law and the European Union* (Oxford, Hart Publishing, 2002) p 11.
[5] E-U Petersmann, 'The dispute settlement system of the WTO and the evolution of the GATT dispute settlement system since 1948' (1994) 31 *CMLRev* 1157.
[6] CONV850/03, Brussels, 18 July 2003.
[7] Opinion 1/94 [1994] ECR I-5276.
[8] Articles 43, 54, 57, 66, 75, 84(2), 99, 100, 100a and 235 (new Articles 37, 44, 47, 55, 71, 80(2), 93, 94, 95, 308) EC Treaty.

as mixed.[9] The subsequent Treaty amendments in Amsterdam and Nice enhanced the scope of the Common Commercial Policy and established it as the basic conduit for the conduct of external trade policy. At the same time, the Treaty of Nice amendments intruded the formerly exclusive Community competence *par excellence*, and transformed part of this 'new generation' Common Commercial Policy into shared competence.[10]

The draft Constitutional Treaty marks a significant development of this constitutional construction.[11] It aims to address the concerns caused by the post-Nice CCP by further enhancing the scope of the CCP to include all, broadly defined, commercial policy objectives and by restoring the CCP as exclusive Union competence.[12] More importantly, it sets the CCP within the framework of the broader objectives of the Union's external action.[13] In doing so it adds three safeguard clauses: first, Article III-217(4) subparagraph 1 requires unanimity in the Council for the conclusion of all agreements involving either the provision of services that require movement of persons or the commercial aspects of intellectual property rights insofar as unanimity is required for the adoption of internal rules. Regarding the adoption of internal measures, it was convincingly argued in the literature on post-Amsterdam and Nice CCP that the adoption of internal measures should be based on the internal legal bases and not on Article 133 EC Treaty.[14] By contrast, it has been argued that the new Article III-217 could serve as the legal basis for the adoption of internal measures concerning external trade in services, intellectual property and direct investment.[15] If this interpretation is correct, this subparagraph would be redundant. If not, its usefulness in practice would still be questioned since hardly any Constitutional provision which could serve as the legal basis for the adoption of internal measures in services, IP and direct investment requires unanimity.[16] The issue is also relevant

[9] Opinion 1/94 paras 98 and 105. For a comprehensive analysis of mixed agreements see, A Rosas, 'The European Union and Mixed Agreements' in A Dashwood and C Hillion (eds), *The General Law of EC External Relations* (London, Sweet & Maxwell, 2000) 200.

[10] For further criticism see, C Herrmann, 'Common Commercial Policy after Nice: Sisyphus would have done a better job' (2002) 39 *CMLRev* 7; HG Krenzler, and C Pitschas, 'Progress or Stagnation? The Common Commercial Policy after Nice' (2001) 6 *European Foreign Affairs Review* 291.

[11] Article III-217 draft Constitutional Treaty.

[12] Article I-12(1) draft Constitutional Treaty.

[13] Article III-193 draft Constitutional Treaty.

[14] M Cremona, 'A Policy of Bits and Pieces? The Common Commercial Policy After Nice' (2001) 4 *CYELS* 61 at 72–73; M Cremona, 'The External Dimension of the Single Market: Building (on) the Foundations' in C Barnard and J Scott (eds), *The Law of the Single European Market: Unpacking the Premises*, (Oxford, Hart Publishing, 2002) 351 at 375.

[15] Statewatch & S Peers, *EU Constitutional Annotation No 2*, *www.statewatch.org/news/2003/aug/constitution-annotation2.pdf*.

[16] Article III-130(2) (fiscal, town planning aspects of environmental legislation), Article III-46(3) (restrictive measures on the free movement of capital), Articles III-62–63

when the adoption of internal measures with a commercial policy effect is not limited to traditionally controversial trade in services, IP rights and investment. For instance, the Court of Justice, in the Energy Star Agreement case,[17] declared that the correct legal basis for the Decision concluding the Agreement was Article 133 EC Treaty.[18] The legal basis for the Regulation intended to implement the Energy Star Agreement was Article 175(1) EC Treaty.[19] The same approach is expected in these cases also under the new Constitution as to the choice of legal basis. In any event however, the voting requirement in the Council will generally be qualified majority. This limits the practical significance of this subparagraph.

Second, Article III-217(4) subparagraph 2 provides for unanimity at the negotiation and conclusion of agreements in the field of trade in cultural and audiovisual services where 'these risk prejudicing the Union's cultural and linguistic diversity'.[20] The main problem with this insertion, not unknown in the tormented history of Article 133,[21] is the open-ended content of its terms. As most international agreements are likely to have broader subject matter than the provision of cultural or audiovisual services yet include provisions affecting those, a subjective determination by any Member State that an envisaged agreement risks prejudicing the cultural and linguistic diversity of the Union would suffice for unanimity to be requested. Such a request will result in a potential stalemate in the Council and jeopardise the effectiveness of the Commission to broker agreement within the Union as well as with the Union's international partners.

The first two clauses for safeguarding Member States' interests in the proposed CCP require unanimity in the Council. While as mentioned above the first one is of limited practical significance, it demonstrates an endorsement of the principle of procedural parallelism, namely the alignment between internal and external legislative procedures already present in the post-Nice CCP.[22] The second is of greater importance since, compared to the post-Nice CCP, it marks the substitution of mixity as a

(aspects of taxation), Article III-104(3) (aspects of social policy) are among the few remaining internal legal bases requiring unanimity in the Council.

[17] Case C-281/01 *Commission v Council (Re Energy Star Agreement)* [2002] ECR I-12049.
[18] *Ibid* at para 48.
[19] Regulation 2422/2001/EC of the European Parliament and of the Council of 6 November 2001 on a Community energy-efficiency labelling programme for office equipment, OJ L 332, 15.12.2001, p 1.
[20] Subparagraph 3 was also added to provide that the negotiation and conclusion of agreements in the field of transport is excluded from the scope of the CCP.
[21] This provision is known as *specificité culturelle* and was inserted into the Nice CCP at the insistence of the French representatives.
[22] For a fuller analysis see Cremona, above n 14 at 75. Also, Groux, 'Le parallélisme des compétences internes et externes de la Communauté économique européenne' (1978) 32 *CDE* 1.

method for safeguarding Member States' interests for unanimity in the Council in the field of cultural and audiovisual services. Constitutionally, this is an important step forward as it moves these important aspects of commercial policy into the exclusive competence of the Union. Procedurally, it is a breach of the principle of procedural parallelism since the possible internal legal bases for the regulation of trade in cultural and audiovisual services do not require unanimity.[23]

The third safeguard clause, enshrined in Article III-217(5), states that the exercise by the Union of its exclusive external trade competence shall not have any impact on the delimitation of internal competences and shall not lead to the harmonisation of legislative and regulatory provisions of Member States. This aims to address the concerns expressed within the context of *Opinion 1/94*[24] that if the EC achieves complete harmonisation externally, Member States' own competence would be prejudiced. It should be noted however, that this exception is limited to areas where the Constitution excludes such harmonisation. In the draft Constitutional Treaty the areas where harmonisation of the laws of the Member States is excluded are the so-called 'complementary competences'.[25] Those include industry, protection and improvement of human health, education, vocational training, youth, sport, culture, civil protection and administrative cooperation.[26] In the areas of shared competence, a combined reading of Article III-217(5) with Article I-11(2)[27] suggests that harmonisation of the laws of the Member States is possible by virtue of the Union's external action, except where the Constitution so precludes. Where the Union exercises its competence and exhaustively regulates the given field, Member States shall be precluded from exercising their competence.[28] Despite harmonisation Member States shall maintain their residual powers which may re-emerge if the EC seizes to exercise its competence on the matter.[29] The delimitation of internal competences shall not be affected as this, unlike the current Treaties, now requires a Constitutional amendment. It is, therefore, questionable whether Article III-217(5) adds something to the Constitutional system.

[23] Characteristically, new Article III-68 requires unanimity only on the language arrangements at the introduction of measures of uniform IP protection. Culture on the other hand (Article III–181) which required unanimity since its insertion into the current Treaties has been moved to qualified majority voting.

[24] At para 60.

[25] Article I–16 draft Constitutional Treaty.

[26] Among those sport and civil protection are new to the Constitution. Administrative co-operation is not listed in Article I–16(2) but it has been inserted as Article III–185.

[27] '... The Member States shall exercise their competence to the extent that the Union has not exercised, or has decided to cease exercising, its competence.'

[28] Case 22/70 *Commission v Council (Re AETR)* [1971] ECR 263.

[29] Article I–11(2).

From a broader systemic perspective, the CCP amendments affect the principle of parallelism both procedurally and substantively. Procedurally, the alignment of voting requirements in the Council was intended to remedy problems previously pointed out.[30] As mentioned above, this is not the case regarding agreements in the field of trade in cultural and audiovisual services. Substantively, the fact that the CCP became an exclusive Union competence while most internal competences remain shared marks a deviation from the principle of parallelism.[31] The designation of the CCP as an exclusive Union competence, a result of design rather than accident, was endorsed in order to enable the Union to protect its Constitution from external threats by guaranteeing its uniform representation externally and the promotion of its internal objectives.[32] The breadth of the scope of the CCP however, makes it increasingly likely that, irrespective of the choice of legal basis for the adoption of internal measures, external trade agreements will affect internal Union policies and vice versa. This may compromise the intentions of the authors of the draft Constitutional Treaty unless, as will be analysed below, complementary action is taken.

In sum, a nine year cycle of mixity in the EC external trade policy is closing by virtue of the new Common Commercial Policy, enshrined in the revamped Article III-217. It is made clear that the conclusion of the WTO Agreement by the EC and its Member States as a mixed agreement is a result of a historical accident. This came as a result of a minimalist understanding of the CCP's scope and nature which coincided with the most important development in the history of the world trading system, the foundation of the WTO. In the terms of the new CCP, a faithful reader of *Opinion 1/75* can recognise a CCP of 30 years ago which was characterised by its broad scope and which conferred exclusive competence on the Community.[33]

## Negotiation and Conclusion of Multilateral Trade Agreements and the Doha Development Round

The changes in the new CCP are expected to have a limited effect on the constitutional aspects of the Union and Member States' participation in multilateral trade negotiations conducted under the auspices of the WTO.

[30] Cremona, above note 14 at 73.
[31] Article I-13 draft Constitutional Treaty.
[32] In this sense, Dashwood and Heliskoski should feel vindicated for their disdain of the principle of parallelism and their preference towards the principle of complementarity. See, A Dashwood and J Heliskoski, 'The classic authorities revisited' in A Dashwood and C Hillion (eds), *The General Law of EC External Relations*, (London, Sweet & Maxwell, 2000) 3 at 11–17 and A Dashwood, 'The Attribution of External Relations Competence' in *idem*, 115 at 134–38.
[33] Opinion 1/75 *(Re Local Standard Cost)* [1975] ECR 1355.

In this respect, the ongoing round of Multilateral Trade Negotiations launched in Doha, Qatar on 14 November 2001 is scheduled to finish no later than 1 January 2005.[34] These negotiations, which are treated as a single undertaking, are conducted by the Commission on behalf of the EC and the Member States without prejudice of competence, in line with established practice.[35] Unless the Constitutional Treaty comes into force before the end of the negotiations, the package deal, should there be one, shall be concluded as a mixed agreement on the basis of the post-Nice Common Commercial Policy.[36] The Council Decision concluding the agreement on behalf of the EC shall have Article 133 as its sole substantive legal basis instead of the string of legal bases employed to conclude the WTO Agreement.[37] It has been pointed out that Article 57(2) EC Treaty should also be added should it be accepted that the movement of capital aspects of investment escape the scope of post-Nice CCP[38] and Article 71(1) EC Treaty should also be used to cover transport services.[39] In the event that the Constitutional Treaty comes into force before the conclusion of the Doha Development Round, the agreement shall be concluded as an EC agreement only, on the basis of Article III-217.[40] In line with the analysis of Article III-217(4) in the previous subsection, this may be concluded by unanimous vote in the Council.

## PARTICIPATION OF THE EC IN THE WTO

### Decision-Making Process

The WTO is equipped with a sophisticated institutional structure but does not generate much secondary legislation.[41] However, the participation of the EC in the operation of the Organisation on a daily basis raises issues of constitutional importance. The conferral of exclusive competence on the Union indicates that voting in the General Council and the other WTO

[34] Doha Declaration of 14 November 2001, paragraph 45. There is significant delay in the negotiations and this deadline will not, in all probability, be met. The collapse of the negotiations in Cancún, Mexico in September 2003 further strengthen this proposition.
[35] Opinion 1/94 at I-5282.
[36] J Heliskoski, 'The Nice Reform of Article 133 EC on the Common Commercial Policy' (2002) 1 *Journal of International Commercial Law* 1, 13.
[37] Council Decision 94/800/EC concerning the conclusion on behalf of the European Community, as regards matters within its competence, of the agreements reached in the Uruguay round multilateral negotiations (1986–94), OJ L 336, 23/12/1994, p 1.
[38] For a full analysis see, Cremona, above note 14, 72.
[39] Article 133(6) last sub-paragraph EC Treaty.
[40] Without prejudice to the addition of Article III-134 to cover transport services.
[41] P Holmes, 'The EU and the WTO: Some Constitutional Comparisons' in G de Búrca and J Scott (eds), *The EU and the WTO: Legal and Constitutional Issues*, (Oxford, Hart Publishing, 2001) 59, 66.

bodies shall be exercised by the Commission. The task of representing both the EC and the Member States has been delegated to the Commission without prejudice to the division of competences and reflects current practice. Having the Commission as the sole spokesperson proceduralises the mechanism of participation in the WTO and succeeds in internalising the problems of competence that may arise.[42] Consequently, if an issue of competence needs to be resolved, its resolution shall take place internally without affecting the procedure for participation in the WTO.

### *The Principle of Cooperation*

The principle of cooperation is the basic norm informing the proceduralised system of participation in mixed agreements and the WTO Agreement in particular.[43] While granting the Union's trade diplomacy broad room for manoeuvre, the principle of cooperation is not particularly helpful at addressing all challenges raised at the WTO level. The principle of cooperation flows from the requirement of unity in the international representation of the EC[44] and requires that the Member States take all the necessary measures when negotiating at an international organisation, in the process of ratification, and most importantly, in the implementation of the commitments arising from an international instrument.[45] The normative content of the principle can be analysed into two separate obligations. First, the Member States should strive to coordinate their policies and cooperate until a common position is reached and second, this common position should be expressed by a single voice.[46] The extent of the first obligation is rather nebulous as it is debatable whether the achievement of a common position is an inalienable element of the principle or whether the effort to achieve a common position in good faith is without prejudice to its outcome. Second, regarding the single voice requirement, in practice to date, the Commission represents the EC in international organisations and expresses its position in areas of exclusive Community competence while the Presidency expresses the common position in areas where competence is predominantly shared.[47] In the WTO, despite the designation of competences by virtue of

[42] For more see, J Heliskoski, *Mixed Agreements as a Technique for Organizing the International Relations of the European Community and its Member States*, (The Hague, Kluwer Law International, 2001) p 207.
[43] Opinion 1/94 cited above at paras 106–9. See also Article I-5(2) draft Constitutional Treaty.
[44] Opinion 1/94 cited above at para 108; Opinion 2/91 *(re ILO)* [1993] ECR I-1061 at para 36.
[45] Opinion 2/91 at para 38.
[46] I MacLeod, ID Hendry and S Hyett, *The External Relations of the European Communities* (Oxford, OUP, 1996) 148.
[47] *Ibid.*

*Opinion 1/94* as shared, practice has followed the GATT assumption that the Common Commercial Policy was an exclusive Community competence and developed accordingly. Consequently, the EC and Member States kept being represented by the Commission alone. The duty of cooperation is discharged in the meetings of the 133 Committee and with the Member States' representatives in Geneva.

The proposed CCP is an exclusive Community competence.[48] Currently, the consequence of exclusivity is that 'Member States no longer have the right to undertake obligations against third countries that affect common rules'[49] and 'measures of commercial policy of a national character are only permissible by virtue of specific authorisation by the EC'.[50] The case law is followed by the draft Constitution with two variations: first, only the Union may 'legislate and adopt legally binding acts' and second, the Member States can only do so if empowered by the Union or at the implementation of acts adopted by the Union.[51] The determination of whether voting in the political organs of the WTO is a legislative or a legally binding act as such is a matter of international law but the presumption is that international organisations do not generally have law-making powers.[52] Therefore, should WTO decision-making be deemed non-legislative, Member States could participate. Even if WTO decision-making is deemed legislative, Member States can still argue that they act at the 'implementation of acts adopted by the Union'.[53] Both interpretations should be resisted on two grounds: first, the principle of cooperation analysed above[54] and second, WTO law itself. Accordingly, since the EC and the Member States are both Members of the WTO, they could in principle vote separately should they fail to arrive at a common position. It is however assumed that where the EC exercises its right to vote the number of votes cast equals the number of its Member States.[55] It should be noted here that, in its proper interpretation, the provision 'where the European Communities exercise their right to vote' does not mean that the EC exercises its right to vote as alternative to the voting rights of its Member States; instead, it indicates that the exercise of voting is less preferable when compared with the established practice of arriving at decisions by consensus. It should be concluded that voting in the WTO should

[48] Article I-12(1) draft Constitutional Treaty.
[49] Case 22/70 cited above, para 17.
[50] Case 41/76 *Donckerwolcke and others v Procureur de la République* [1976] ECR 1921 para 32.
[51] Article I-11(1) of the Draft Constitutional Treaty.
[52] D Akande, 'International Organizations' in M Evans (ed), *International Law* (Oxford, OUP, 2003) 269, 282.
[53] Council Decision 94/800/EC, above note 37, is the obvious Union act to that effect.
[54] See also, Case C-25/94 *Commission v Council (Re FAO)* [1996] ECR I-1469.
[55] Article IX of the WTO Agreement along with the interpretative footnote.

be exercised by the Union and Member States could only be allowed to do so if empowered by the Union.[56]

## Participation of the EC and its Member States in the WTO Dispute Settlement Mechanism

Annex 2 to the WTO Agreement contains the Dispute Settlement Understanding which provides for a single uniform dispute settlement procedure for all covered agreements.[57] The main characteristics of this modern dispute resolution system are: automatic and compulsory jurisdiction, right of appeal before a standing Appellate Body on a point of law, tight deadlines and enforcement mechanisms that allow for compensation or suspension of concessions across the covered agreements. The participation of the EC in the WTO Dispute Settlement Understanding raises complex constitutional issues. Both as a complainant and as a respondent, the EC is set to meet several challenges under the current as well as the proposed CCP.

### *As a Complainant*

There are two routes available to the EC to launch a complaint in the WTO, Article 133 and the Trade Barriers Regulation.[58] The analysis of the Common Commercial Policy, its scope and nature are of fundamental importance for complaints launched on the basis of either since the legal basis of the TBR is Article 133. The main characteristic of the 133 route is that it is an informal means for initiating a complaint. The Commission may receive an informal complaint from the industry, a Member State or its own services. These cases shall be scrutinized by DG Trade in continuous cooperation with a dedicated Unit within the RELEX Team of the Commission's Legal Service. Other Commission Directorates-General may be involved depending on the nature of the dispute while the '133 Committee' is kept informed at all times.[59] After consulting all the above

[56] Wuorinen suggests that when the EC has not exercised its right to vote individual Member States could still exercise theirs in M Wuorinen, 'The Cross-Retaliation in the WTO Dispute Settlement System: Can the European Communities benefit from it?' (1997) VIII *Finnish Yearbook of International Law* 340.
[57] Subject to a limited number of derogations. For more, JH Jackson, *The World Trade Organization: Constitution and Jurisprudence* (London, RIIA, 1998) 73.
[58] Hereinafter, TBR. Council Regulation 3286/94 of 22 December 1994 laying down Community procedures in the field of the common commercial policy in order to ensure the exercise of the Community's rights under international trade rules, in particular those established under the auspices of the World Trade Organization OJ L 349, 31/12/1994, p 71.
[59] CG Molyneux, *Domestic Structures and International Trade* (Oxford, Hart Publishing, 2001) 194–201.

the Commission shall determine whether it is in the Community interest to pursue the dispute and take the first procedural step which is to request consultations.[60] From then on, the same pattern shall be followed with the experts of the Commission Legal Service handling the dispute before the Panels and Appellate Body of the WTO with the assistance of specialists from the Commission's DGs while always keeping the '133 Committee' informed.[61] Member States' trade diplomats usually attend the proceedings in Geneva but they hardly interfere. The disadvantage of this route is that it lacks transparency. None of the EC institutions are obliged to provide feedback on the progress of a dispute and, coupled with the confidentiality governing WTO Dispute Settlement, the public, along with those who have a direct interest in the outcome of the dispute, will only be able to find out how it develops by the DG Trade press releases or the documents circulated by the WTO Secretariat.

The TBR, on the other hand, provides a structured procedure for the initiation of a dispute. The foundation of the TBR on Article 133 is designed in such a fashion so as to take account of the dynamic character of the CCP, already at the time of its adoption. Cottier contends that the Trade Barriers Regulation is at odds with WTO as to the pertinent criteria for a complaining party to have a case.[62] Article 3 TBR requires the Community industry to prove that there is an obstacle to trade enacted by another WTO Member and injury caused to the Community industry as a result of this obstacle. In WTO law on the other hand, the crucial criterion is whether a measure has caused nullification or impairment of the benefits accruing from the covered Agreements. While the former is quantitative the latter, in accordance with established GATT and WTO jurisprudence, is qualitative. Consequently, it is not the trade flows whose interruption might trigger the WTO Dispute Settlement but the protection of the competitive relationship between like domestic and imported products in a given market.[63] From a critical point of view, it can be argued that the TBR and the WTO Dispute Settlement do not overlap but the former is a condition for the triggering of the latter. As provided in the preamble to the TBR, the injury to the domestic industry caused by an obstacle to trade shall trigger the reaction of the institutions provided that a right of action exists under the international

[60] Article 4 DSU.

[61] PJ Kuijper, 'The New WTO Dispute Settlement System: The Impact on the European Community' (1995) 29:6 *Journal of World Trade* 49, 54–55.

[62] T Cottier, 'Dispute Settlement in the World Trade Organization: Characteristics and Structural Implications for the European Union' (1998) 35 *CMLRev* 325, 361.

[63] WT/DS8/AB/R, WT/DS10/AB/R, WT/DS11/AB/R *Japan — Alcoholic Beverages II*, at 109–10, quoting from Panel Report, *United States — Section 337 of the Tariff Act of 1930*, adopted 7 November 1989, BISD 36S/345, para 5.10. Also, WT/DS135/AB/R *European Communities — Measures Affecting Asbestos and Asbestos-Containing Products* ('*EC — Asbestos*'), at para 97 and WT/DS108/AB/RW *United States — Tax Treatment For 'Foreign Sales Corporations'* (recourse to Article 21.5 of the DSU by The European Communities).

trade rules.[64] The 'obstacle to trade' therefore, should be determined with reference to the nullification or impairment of the benefits accruing from the covered Agreements. The judgement of the Commission at the determination of whether a foreign obstacle to trade is in violation of these rules may be reviewed by the Court of Justice at the request of the economic agents affected.[65] A successful invocation of the TBR is subject also to the existence of Community interest.[66] In its proper construction, injury to the Community industry satisfies the Community interest test.

The EC has initiated disputes in the WTO, under both the Article 133 and the TBR routes, over subject-matter which was broader than the EC's external trade competence. The level of difficulty at mustering support in the Council in areas falling within the shared competence of the EC varies. For instance, the complaint against the United States in *US-Section 110(5) of US Copyright Act*,[67] was launched by the EC alone under the TBR on the basis of a complaint initiated by the Community industry (IMRO).[68] This came as a result of the willingness of the Member States to allow a broad interpretation of the TBR to include IP rights with a view to removing foreign obstacles.[69] Practice is far from uniform in complaints launched under the informal 133 route. In *Canada — Patent Protection* the request for consultations and establishment of the Panel were submitted by both the EC and its Member States.[70] Similarly, in *US — Section 337* the request for consultations was launched by the EC and its Member States.[71] The inclusion of Member States in the proceedings is of nominal value with regard to the procedure to be followed. In terms of substance however, it is not a sensible move as it harbours problems of competence should the dispute reach the stage of retaliation or cross-retaliation. Member States may be tempted to retaliate in their own right against the majority intention in the Council.

When a Member State has a special interest in the removal of an obstacle to trade abroad and the Commission decides not to initiate proceedings, it is unclear whether the said Member State could in principle, initiate its own

[64] The Agreements annexed to the WTO Agreement including the DSU.

[65] Case 70/87 *Fediol v Commission* [1989] ECR 1781 at para 22.

[66] Last recital from the TBR Preamble.

[67] WT/DS160 *United States — Section 110(5) of US Copyright Act.*

[68] See, for instance, Commission Decision 98/731/EC of 11 December 1998 under the provisions of Council Regulation (EC) No 3286/94 concerning section 110(5) of the Copyright Act of the United States of America (notified under document number C(1998)4033), OJ L 346, 22/12/1998, p 60.

[69] Schuren and Luff, 'The Trade Barriers Regulation and Community's Market Access Policy' (1996) 1 *European Foreign Affairs Review*, 211, 217.

[70] WT/DS114 *Canada — Patent Protection of Pharmaceutical Products (complaint by the EC and its Member States)*. See documents WT/DS114/1 and WT/DS114/5. In the Article 21.3(c) DSU arbitration no mention was made of the Member States.

[71] WT/DS186 *US Section 337 of the Tariff Act of 1930 and the amendments thereto (complaint by the EC and its Member States).*

proceedings under the post-Nice CCP. In the light of the principle of cooperation analysed above, a negative answer should be given to the question. Equally, the question whether a Member State is entitled to retaliate in its own right against Canada or the US in the IP disputes mentioned above, where agreement in the Council cannot be reached for EC retaliation should be answered in the negative. In practice, retaliation and cross-retaliation is impossible under GATT, since Member States do not possess their own Schedules of Concessions,[72] as well as GATS because it would affect the EC's Schedules of Specific Commitments.[73] To date, despite the launch of several complaints against individual Member States, there has never been a complaint launched by an individual Member State under the WTO DSU. Neither has there been any autonomous retaliation.

*As a Respondent*

When the EC and/or the Member States are on the defensive, the procedure for handling the disputes to date has developed *de facto*. Several trading partners, the US more often than others, attempted to isolate Member States in disputes whose subject matter obviously fell within exclusive Community competence.[74] The practice of moving against individual Member States is of doubtful legality under WTO law. In principle, as both the EC and the Member States are Members of the WTO, all other WTO Members could avail themselves of the rigorous WTO Dispute Settlement system, if they consider that a measure nullifies or impairs their benefits accruing from the WTO Agreement. It can be argued that the trading partners are not obliged to know the internal constitutional relations between the EC and its Member States nor to make a complete study of the internal rules before choosing their rival. The main counterargument stems from GATT practice where the EC participated as a *sui generis* GATT Contracting Party substituting the Member States.[75] Since 1974, all trade disputes had been brought against the EEC, even when they challenged national trade restrictions.[76] According to Article XVI:1 of the WTO

[72] Article II GATT.
[73] Article XX GATS.
[74] See for instance, WT/DS67 *UK — Customs Classification of Certain Computer Equipment*, WT/DS68 *Ireland — Customs Classification of Certain Computer Equipment* and WT/DS210 *Belgium — Administration of Measures Establishing Customs Duties for Rice (complaint by the United States)*. For a broader discussion, Cottier, above note 62 and J Heliskoski, 'Joint Competence of the European Community and its Member States and the Dispute Settlement Practice of the World Trade Organization' (1999) 2 *CYELS* 61.
[75] Cases 21–4/72 *International Fruit Company NV and others v Produktschap voor Groenten en Fruit* [1972] ECR 1279.
[76] E-U Petersmann, 'The EEC as a GATT Member–Legal Conflicts between GATT Law and European Community Law' in M Hilf, F Jacobs, and E-U Petersmann, *The European Community and the GATT* (Kluwer Law and Taxation, 1986) 23, 47.

Agreement '... the WTO shall be guided by the decisions, procedures and **customary practices** followed by the CONTRACTING PARTIES to GATT 1947 and the bodies established in the framework of GATT 1947'.[77] Consequently, in WTO law, at least disputes relating to trade in goods should be brought against the EC.

In WTO practice to date, the decisive criterion for the determination of the respondent in a dispute is alien to the Union's esoteric constitutional considerations. In most cases, it is the source of the measure or practice under scrutiny that will determine the party to the dispute. Accordingly, where national measures were deemed to nullify or impair the benefits enjoyed under the covered agreements by a WTO member, a request for consultations was made against the Member State responsible for the measure or practice.[78] When the measure was a result of joint action, both the responsible Member State and the EC were joined in the request for consultations. For instance, the United States brought a complaint against both the EC and France, for subsidies granted by the French government, after approval by the Commission, to Sextant Avionique, a French company, in order to develop a flight management system.[79] In the *LAN* case, the EC was joined as a party in the proceedings.[80] In *European Communities* and *Greece — Audiovisual Piracy*,[81] the dispute was settled by virtue of a mutually agreed solution.[82] In this case, Greece's failure to comply with the TRIPS Agreement was healed partly because of its implementation of EC

[77] Emphasis added.

[78] WT/DS210 *Belgium — Administration of Measures Establishing Customs Duties for Rice (complaint by the United States);* WT/DS82 *Ireland — Measures Affecting the Grant of Copyright and Neighbouring Rights (complaint by the United States);* WT/DS86 *Sweden — Measures Affecting the Enforcement of Intellectual Property Rights (complaint by the United States);* WT/DS37 *Portugal — Patent Protection under the Industrial Property Act (complaint by the United States);* WT/DS128 *Netherlands — Certain Income Tax Measures Constituting Subsidies (complaint by the United States);* WT/DS83 *Denmark — Measures Affecting the Enforcement of Intellectually Property Rights (complaint by the United States);* WT/DS80 *Belgium — Measures Affecting Commercial Telephone Services (complaint by the United States);* WT/DS125 *Greece — Enforcement of Intellectual Property Rights for Motion Pictures and Television Programmes (complaint by the United States);* WT/DS129 *Greece — Certain Income Tax Measures Constituting Subsidies (complaint by the United States);* WT/DS131 *France — Certain Income Tax Measures Constituting Subsidies (complaint by the United States).*

[79] WT/DS172 *European Communities — Measures Relating to the Development of a Flight Management System*; WT/DS173 *France — Measures Relating to the Development of a Flight Management System.*

[80] WT/DS62 *European Communities — Customs Classification of Certain Computer Equipment*; WT/DS67 *United Kingdom — Customs Classification of Certain Computer Equipment*; WT/DS68 *Ireland — Customs Classification of Certain Computer Equipment.*

[81] WT/DS124 *European Communities — Enforcement of Intellectual Property Rights for Motion Pictures and Television Programs (complaint by the United States);* WT/DS125 *Greece — Enforcement of Intellectual Property Rights for Motion Pictures and Television Programs (complaint by the United States).*

[82] WT/DS125/2, 26 March 2001.

legislation on Copyright protection.[83] In other cases, while the EC was not joined as a party in the proceedings, it participated in the consultations and signed the mutually agreed solution that brought the dispute to its end.[84] It is questionable whether the participation of the EC in the mutually agreed solution is in conformity with Article 3.7 DSU, as it refers to the 'parties to the dispute'. In *Portugal — Patent Protection*, Portugal discharged the consultations alone and reached a mutually agreed solution with the United States.[85] This will not be feasible under the proposed CCP. When the source of the measure or practice is the EC, complaints have been initiated against it even in areas where there is still some competence vested in the Member States.[86]

Exceptionally, regarding Member State measures, the complaining party may decide to launch the complaint only against the EC, presumably in response to the latter's request. The only case in the WTO practice to date where this happened is the *Asbestos* dispute.[87] This case can serve to illustrate the constitutional questions common in most of the above mentioned disputes. In this case, France enforced a ban on several categories of chrysotile asbestos because of its carcinogenic qualities. This measure was in conformity with a relevant EC Directive whose deadline for implementation had not expired. Canada, a major asbestos exporter, made a complaint which was addressed to the EC and not the French Republic. The EC won the case on all grounds.[88]

It is interesting to explore what would happen in a case with similar facts in which the EC loses. In this eventuality, the EC would be required under WTO law to amend the challenged legislation so as to remedy the violation.[89] The measure is a national one however, and the *res judicata* does not extend to France *ratione personae*. Should France resist compliance, the Commission could initiate infringement proceedings. National legislation will be examined under WTO law,[90] as Snyder rightly points out, 'as part of the obligations of the Member States under EC law'.[91] While the violation of WTO law will be readily established, the situation is affected by the

[83] Bulletin Quotidien Europe No 7930, Saturday 24 March 2001, p 11.
[84] WT/DS86 *Sweden — Measures Affecting the Enforcement of Intellectual Property Rights (complaint by the United States)*; WT/DS83 *Denmark — Measures Affecting the Enforcement of Intellectually Property Rights (complaint by the United States)*.
[85] WT/DS37/2, 8 October 1996.
[86] WT/DS153 *European Communities — Patent Protection for Pharmaceutical and Agricultural Chemical Products (complaint by Canada)*.
[87] WT/DS135 *European Communities — Measures Affecting Asbestos and Asbestos-Containing Products (complaint by Canada)*.
[88] In order to win the point of principle it had to launch an appeal. See, A Antoniadis, 'Greening the WTO? The Appellate Body Report on the *EC-Asbestos* Case' (2002) 14 *ELM* 77.
[89] Article 3.7 DSU.
[90] Case C-61/94 *Commission v Federal Republic of Germany* [1996] ECR I-3989.
[91] Snyder, above note 2, 354.

existence of the EC Directive, which the French measure was designed to implement. As the French ban is in conformity with the relevant Directive, it is EC law which is *de facto* challenged as being contrary to WTO law. In accordance with established ECJ case law, WTO rules are not, in principle, among the rules in the light of which the Court is to review the legality of measures adopted by the EC institutions.[92] The Court in such a case would be faced with a prisoner's dilemma and it would be interesting to see whether it would accord priority to the Community legal order. The Commission, in full awareness of the existing possibilities, would take advantage of the wide discretion it enjoys at the initiation of infringement proceedings[93] and attempt to resolve the matter diplomatically. Until a satisfactory solution is found, the EC will be subject to retaliation by Canada.[94] Similar considerations apply if France conforms to the DSB reports and repeals the measure. In that case, infringement proceedings will have to wait until the deadline for implementation of the directive has passed.[95]

## PROBLEMS WITH MEMBER STATE PARTICIPATION IN THE WTO

It can be argued that a major problem, inherent in the system, is the fact that the Member States themselves are also members of the WTO and as such they can function independently therein, at least from a WTO perspective. In the current Treaty framework, Member States enjoy wide discretion at the adoption of internal rules with external trade dimensions. On the basis of the draft Constitutional Treaty, the law-making method appears to be shifting in favour of national legislative autonomy within the large bulk of shared legislative competence in two respects. First, the principles of proportionality and subsidiarity are granted a more rigorous understanding.[96] Second, the draft Constitutional Treaty provides that the Member States may take measures to implement binding Union acts.[97] This is in contrast with the Court's case law regarding regulations since national measures would conceal the nature of the EC regulations and this would jeopardize the simultaneous and uniform application of those regulations.[98] The existence of national measures in areas where the Union has legislated too, may open the Pandora's Box for the reception of

[92] Case C-149/96 *Portugal v Council* [1999] ECR I-8395 at para 47. See below.
[93] A Evans, 'The Enforcement Procedure of Article 169 EEC: Commission Discretion' (1979) 4 *ELRev* 442, 445.
[94] Article 22(2) DSU.
[95] In the ordinary interpretation of Article 249 EC Treaty.
[96] Article I-9(3) draft Constitutional Treaty and annexed Protocol on the Application of the Principles of Subsidiarity and Proportionality.
[97] Article I-36(1) draft Constitutional Treaty.
[98] Case 34/73 *Variola v Amministrazione delle Finanze* [1973] ECR 981 paras 10–11.

complaints either against the Member States or both the Union and its Member States. The resulting polynomy shall externalise the conflict which would have otherwise been resolved internally and make it subject to the WTO Dispute Settlement. The Union has achieved, to date, to proceduralise the internal disputes and conceal the internal divergences of legislation behind the EC protective veil. If law-making is shifted in favour of Member States, divergences shall be exposed and the veil lifted.

In view of this, the proposals brought forward by the Constitutional Convention do not resolve the problem. The designation of the CCP as an exclusive Union competence does not insulate the system from external threats. Consequently, the conferral of exclusivity on the Union regarding the CCP, in the absence of alignment of legislative exclusivity in policy areas capable of having an effect on international trade, perpetuates the constitutional conflicts described above. Similar considerations apply horizontally in Union legislation adopted under enhanced cooperation.[99] The problems may be accentuated in case of an international crisis, especially if the EC needs to retaliate or cross-retaliate on sensitive products or against an important trading partner.

## RESOLVING PROCEDURAL PROBLEMS: A CODE OF CONDUCT

It has been made clear that the vaguely formulated principle of cooperation is inadequate to ensure the viability of the system. There are several arguments that could be brought forward for the insulation of the EC legal order against the threats analysed above. One proposal would call for the withdrawal of the Member States from the WTO.[100] This proposal is politically unattainable and arguably not in the Union interest since the EC now holds twenty-five votes in the WTO.[101] Another proposal would be a Declaration of competences similar to that submitted upon accession to the UN Convention on the Law of the Sea.[102] This would appease the contention for certainty[103] but it would hamper the flexibility of the EC within the WTO. Assuming that the proposal in the draft Constitutional Treaty represents some sort of *finalité* regarding the nature of the CCP, the Union shall enjoy exclusive competence in external trade matters anyway.

[99] Article III-322 *et seq.*
[100] Article XV of the WTO Agreement.
[101] Article IX of the WTO Agreement.
[102] Declaration concerning the competence of the European Community with regard to matters governed by the United Nations Convention on the Law of the Sea of 10 December 1982 and the Agreement of 28 july 1994 relating to the implementation of Part XI of the Convention (Declaration made pursuant to Article 5(1) of Annex IX to the Convention and to Article 4(4) of the Agreement), OJ 1998, L 179, 23/6/98 p 129.
[103] Heliskoski, above note 42, Chapter 3.

The problem could be resolved on the basis of a uniform Code of Conduct of constitutional value drawing from existing WTO practice and containing clear and unequivocal rules. In addition, the necessary negotiations with the Union's international partners to accommodate its provisions on the international plane should be undertaken. The need for a Code of Conduct has been recognised in the aftermath of *Opinion 1/94*[104] and during the IGC-2000 several drafts were circulated.[105] While an analysis of those drafts goes beyond the confines of this contribution it must be submitted *in passim* that they provide a helpful insight into the considerations raised by the Member States. It is implicit in the IGC-2000 drafts that the extension of the scope of the CCP will make the adoption of the Code redundant.[106] This is not the case as elaborated above.

In the drafting of such a Code, in addition to the IGC-2000 drafts, account must be taken of the several existing internal arrangements for EC coordination in international fora.[107] The very complexities of the WTO and the breadth of its ambit should also be appropriately evaluated. The Union further needs to respond to the demands of the dispute settlement itself, as it has developed into a facts-intensive,[108] highly-complex exercise. In order to achieve this task it needs to draw on the institutional memory of the Commission which concentrates a high level of expertise and experience in dispute settlement and combine it with the active engagement of the Member States.[109] A final source of input into the unified Union front should be what can be described as the 'Community industry'.[110] When the

[104] Cremona, above note 14, 65. A Dashwood, 'External Relations Provisions of the Amsterdam Treaty' (1998) 35 *CMLRev* 1019, 1043.

[105] SN 2705/00 of 10 May 2000; CONFER 4753/00 of 3 July 2000, CONFER 4767/00 of 29 August 2000, CONFER 4770/00 of 14 September 2000, CONFER 4789/00 of 26 October 2000, CONFER 4790/00 of 3 November 2000, CONFER 4795/00 of 9 November 2000, CONFER 4800/00 of 16 November 2000 and CONFER 4810/00 of 23 November 2000.

[106] Cremona, above note 14, 65–67.

[107] See for instance, Internal Agreement between the representatives of the governments of the Member States, meeting within the Council, on measures to be taken and procedures to be followed for the implementation of the ACP-EC Partnership Agreement, OJ L 317, 15.12.2000, p 376. Also, the Arrangement regarding participation in FAO meetings, statements and voting, unpublished, available at R Frid, *The Relations Between the EC and International Organizations: Legal Theory and Practice*, (The Hague, Kluwer Law International, 1995), Annex VI. As Hyett convincingly points out, each organisation has its own characteristics and an arrangement devised for one may not be suitable for another. For more, see S Hyett, 'The Duty of Co-operation: A Flexible Concept' in Dashwood and Hillion (eds), *The General Law of EC External Relations* (London, Sweet and Maxwell, 2000) 248, 252–53.

[108] PJ Kuyper, 'The New WTO Dispute System: The Impact on the Community' in J Bourgeois, F Berrod, E Gippini Fournier (eds), *The Uruguay Round Results: A European Lawyer's Perspective*, (Brussels, European Interuniversity Press, 1995) 87, 99.

[109] Both within the 133 Committee in Brussels and *sur place* in Geneva.

[110] Article 2(5) of the Trade Barriers Regulation.

Community industry is faced with treatment abroad which is allegedly in violation of the WTO rules, the Commission undertakes to rectify the situation by making an investigation and by bringing a complaint. Since the Commission cannot afford having specialists on all aspects of trade it has to consult the specialists from the private sector and base itself on the data and guidance they provide it with.[111] The Commission has been active in involving the Community industry at several stages in the proceedings. In accordance with the TBR, it is obliged to keep the industry informed of the proceedings.[112] Importantly, when an authorisation for the suspension of concessions is granted by the DSB, it circulates a list of products on which it aims to impose retaliatory duties and asks the Community industry to submit their observations.[113]

In a nutshell, the Code of Conduct for participation of the Union in the WTO should

- be of constitutional value attached to the new Constitution;
- be acknowledged by the Union's trading partners in a decision by the WTO Ministerial Conference;
- build on the existing practice after clarifying and consolidating it;
- be custom-made for the WTO Dispute Settlement and provide procedures for all steps of the DSU;
- designate the Commission as the sole spokesperson for both the Union as of right and the Member States as their agent;
- provide a fast-track mechanism for the resolution of problems of constitutional nature;
- provide transparency into the workings of the system; and
- involve industry and civil society.

This solution is not alien to the EC practice in other international *fora*[114] and does not differ dramatically from a, broadly speaking, successful WTO practice to date. Judging from the outcome, nine years of practice on the basis of this arrangement have been successful for the EC. It managed to overcome the hard places of *Bananas*[115] and *Hormones*[116] without having to sacrifice its development and public health policy

[111] Article 8(2)(a) of the Trade Barriers Regulation.
[112] Articles 5(3) and 8(1)(a) of the Trade Barriers Regulation.
[113] Notice relating to the WTO Dispute Settlement proceeding concerning the United States tax treatment of Foreign Sales Corporations (FSC) — Invitation for comments on the list of products that could be subject to countermeasures OJ C 217, 13/09/2002, p 2.
[114] See above note 107.
[115] WT/DS16 *European Communities — Importation, distribution and sale of bananas (complaint brought by Guatemala, Honduras, Mexico, US).*
[116] WT/DS26 *European Communities — Measures concerning meat and meat products (hormones) (complaint brought by US)*; WT/DS48 *European Communities — Measures concerning meat and meat products (hormones) (complaint brought by Canada).*

choices. On the offensive, it achieved a number of significant victories culminating in the *FSC* case.[117] With crucial challenges ahead and fundamental policy choices under challenge in the *GSP*[118] and *GMOs*[119] cases, the major question is whether the Member States are prepared to delegate this responsibility wholeheartedly to the Commission or whether they will vitiate any arrangement with so many procedural safeguards that will make it impossible to operate.

## RESOLVING SUBSTANTIVE PROBLEMS: IMPROVING COMPLIANCE

There are two judicial approaches informing the implementation of WTO rules in the EC and Member States legal orders. The first denies individuals the right to invoke provisions of the WTO Agreement and annexed Agreements in national and EC courts (direct effect) and to assess the legality of EC law against the provisions of those Agreements.[120] The second represents the exception and accepts that an EC measure may be examined against these WTO norms which EC legislation has been adopted to implement or to which it explicitly refers.[121] This division is not based on an assessment of policy aims and objectives of the Union and their ranking in terms of importance. It may nevertheless, be connected with considerations of competence. This judicially induced categorisation has a significant impact on compliance with WTO law.

On the issue of compliance with WTO rulings, the second category of cases has recently provided important legislative developments. In these cases, after *Nakajima*,[122] individuals may invoke the WTO Anti-Dumping

[117] WT/DS108 *United States — Tax Treatment of 'Foreign Sales Corporations' (complaint brought by the EC).*

[118] WT/DS246 *European Communities — Conditions for the granting of tariff preferences to developing countries (complaint brought by India).*

[119] WT/DS291, WT/DS292, WT/DS293 *European Communities — Measures affecting the approval and marketing of biotech products (complaint brought by United States, Canada* and *Argentina* respectively*)*. Despite the amendment of the EC legislation on the matter the United States, Canada and Argentina made a request for the establishment of a Panel on 18 August 2003.

[120] Case C-149/96 *Portugal v Council* [1999] ECR I-8395 complemented by a plethora of judgments by the Court of Justice and CFI. For an insightful analysis see, Snyder, above note 2.

[121] Case C-69/89 *Nakajima v Council* [1991] ECR I-2069 and Case 70/87 *Fediol v Commission* [1989] ECR 1781. See also, P Eeckhout, 'The Domestic Legal Status of the WTO Agreement: Interconnecting Legal Systems' (1997) 34 *CMLRev* 11, 42–7. Snyder, above note 2, 342 where he calls the former 'transposition exception' and the latter 'clear reference exception'.

[122] Case C-69/89 *Nakajima v Council* [1991] ECR I-2069.

Agreement[123] in EC courts to challenge the legality of EC regulations imposing anti-dumping duties which affect their interests.[124] The same measures may also be challenged at intergovernmental level in the WTO Dispute Settlement. In response to adverse rulings in the latter, the Council adopted Regulation 1515/2001 laying down the measures to be taken by the EC so as to comply with the adverse Panel and Appellate Body Reports.[125] In accordance with the Enabling Regulation, the EC should either amend or repeal the disputed measures or adopt any special measures which are deemed to be appropriate in the circumstances.[126] The Council and the Commission may also review measures which are not the subject of the dispute if they are affected by the legal interpretations made in the Report adopted by the DSB.[127] For example, in *EC — Bedlinen*,[128] a case involving provisional anti-dumping duties imposed on bedlinen originating in India, the Appellate Body found that the practice of 'zeroing'[129] applied by the EC at the determination of dumping margins was incompatible with Article 2.4.2 ADA.[130] The Commission issued a Notice inviting all importers, not only of bedlinen, against whom the zeroing methodology had been applied at the determination of the anti-dumping duty imposed, to request a review of the anti-dumping duties on the basis of Article 2 of the Enabling Regulation in the light of the WTO Panel and Appellate Body interpretations.[131]

[123] Hereinafter, the ADA.
[124] *Cf* the relaxed rules of standing for private parties when challenging Anti-Dumping Regulations; Case 264/82 *Timex Corporation v Council and Commission* [1985] ECR 849; Case C-358/89 *Extramet Industrie SA v Council* [1991] ECR I-2501.
[125] Hereinafter, the Enabling Regulation. Council Regulation (EC) No 1515/2001 on the measures that maybe taken by the Community following a report adopted by the WTO Dispute Settlement Body concerning anti-dumping and anti-subsidies matters OJ L 201, 26/07/2001, p 10. See, G Zonnekeyn, 'The *Bed Linen* Case and its Aftermath: Some Comment of the European Community's "World Trade Organization Enabling Regulation" ' (2002) 36 *Journal of World Trade* 993; D Horowitz, 'A Regulated Scope for EU Compliance with WTO Rulings' (2001) 7 *International Trade Law Review* 153; N McNelis, 'What Obligations are Created by World Trade Organization Dispute Settlement Reports?' (2003) 37 *Journal of World Trade* 647.
[126] Article 1(1) Enabling Regulation.
[127] Article 2 Enabling Regulation.
[128] WT/DS141 *European Communities — Anti-dumping measures on imports of cotton-type bed-linen from India.*
[129] In the calculation of the dumping margin the Community applied the following methodology: First, it divided the Indian bedlinen into several categories. In some, the export price was lower than the normal price and in some it was higher, the later being called a 'negative dumping margin'. Then, it calculated the average dumping margin calculating the negative dumping margins as zero. Obviously, the 'zeroing' methodology resulted into a higher dumping margin.
[130] Paragraph 6.119 of the Panel Report upheld by the Appellate Body in Paragraph 86(1) of its Report.
[131] Notice regarding the anti-dumping measures in force following a ruling of the Dispute Settlement Body of the World Trade Organisation adopted on March 2001 OJ C 111, 08/05/2002, p 4.

Consequently, in the field of anti-dumping, individuals have two routes available to challenge anti-dumping duties against the same normative benchmark, the ADA. In this choice of forum it seems that the WTO Dispute Settlement System enjoys a significant comparative advantage. First, a WTO dispute would normally end more quickly than a challenge against an Anti-dumping Regulation in the ECJ.[132] Second, it is less expensive since the costs will be undertaken by the government acting on behalf of the traders in the WTO DSU. Third, owing to the Enabling Regulation, the decision of the WTO DSU has an *erga omnes* effect which means that even undertakings unrelated to the litigation are invited to have their anti-dumping duties reviewed.[133]

Once the EC clears its own backyard, it can utilize the WTO Dispute Settlement System in order to coerce other trading partners to comply with the same legal interpretations and establish a level playing field. For instance, on the issue of 'zeroing' methodology, as soon as the dispute with India ended, the EC initiated a dispute against the United States challenging the 'zeroing' methodology applied at the implementation of their anti-dumping legislation.[134] In this small category of cases the impact of WTO law on EC legislation can be intentionally dramatic.

Returning to the first category of cases, in which the Court denied direct effect to WTO law, it should be stated that compliance comes second to the preservation of the autonomy of the Union legal order. Besides the well-founded legal arguments of flexibility and reciprocity there is an additional reason in the light of the draft Constitutional Treaty for maintaining this position. Despite the CCP's designation as exclusive Union competence, the internal competences affected by WTO law are shared.[135] The crux of the argument is that, quite simply, the Court of Justice does not have jurisdiction to grant direct effect to WTO law as its subject-matter is broader than the internal Union competence. Such a step would pre-empt the regulatory autonomy of the Member States and encroach on their competence.[136] The limited jurisdiction of the Court of Justice also explains the current *jurisprudence constante* on direct effect. In areas where the Member States have given up their competence by adopting legislation, as for example in *Nakajima* and *Fediol*,[137] direct

[132] 12 as opposed to 23 months when the cases involve an appeal.

[133] Article 2 Enabling Regulation.

[134] WT/DS294 *United States — Laws, Regulations and Methodology for Calculating Dumping Margins ('Zeroing') (complaint brought by the EC)* on 19 June 2003.

[135] Article I-13(2) draft Constitutional Treaty.

[136] Less explicitly, Snyder, above note 2 at 352, 358–59. Also, P Eeckhout, 'Judicial Enforcement of WTO Law in the European Union — Some Further Reflections' (2002) 5 *Journal of International Economic Law* 91, 95.

[137] Also importantly, Case C-317/99 *Kloosterboer Rotterdam BV v Minister van Landbouw, Natuurbeheer en Visserij* [2001] ECR I-9863.

effect of WTO law becomes legally possible. In all other cases the standard is set at the consistent interpretation obligation.[138] The Court should add this argument to its armour and resist the calls from academic community and the Advocates General to broaden the scope of WTO law having direct effect in the EC and Member States legal orders.[139] More importantly it should resist appearing, as in the recent *Biret* case,[140] to gradually give in.

## CONCLUSION

The WTO represents both an opportunity and a threat for the Union. WTO law is perceived as both the cause and the consequence of globalisation.[141] From this eminent position, it determines the Union's agenda and is determined by it. The successful interaction is conditional upon the insulation of the Union's system with procedural safeguards so as to avert a real possibility of normative subordination. An important step is currently undertaken by the draft Constitutional Treaty with the enhancement of the scope of the CCP and its designation as an exclusive Union competence. There remains a further task which is twofold: on the one hand, it is up to the political institutions of the Union to devise a Code of Conduct for the participation of the Union in the WTO so as to maximise the benefits and minimise the risk from this exercise, whereas, on the other, it lies with the Court to maintain its case law denying direct effect to WTO law. The task is cumulative as failure on the one front would suffice for the autonomy of the Union legal order to be undermined. On the one hand, should Member States be effectively isolated in the WTO Dispute Settlement Mechanism and national measures affecting external trade challenged, the regulatory authority of the Union's institutions shall be jeopardised. On the other hand, should individuals be allowed to invoke WTO law and challenge Union acts against its provisions in national and Union courts, regulatory authority will shift from the political institutions to the courts. The consequences of this are not limited to a simple procedural anomaly but affect the substance of those norms. A challenge of Union legislation against the normative benchmark of WTO law is effectively a challenge of the Union's social, environmental and public health legislation. While there is a presumption that Union law is compatible with

[138] C-53/96 *Hermès International v FHT Marketing Choice BV* [1998] ECR I-3603.
[139] For a comprehensive review see Snyder, above note 2, 329–33.
[140] Case C-93/02P *Biret International SA v Council*, judgment of 30 September 2003, not yet reported, paras 51–66.
[141] Snyder, above note 2, 313.

WTO law,[142] the *Bananas* and *Hormones* cases offer evidence to the contrary. When the stakes are as high as the Union development and public health policies, action should be taken to protect them. The ongoing constitutional debate offers the appropriate forum. It is to be hoped that this issue will find a place on its agenda.

[142] *Ibid*, 316.

# 20

# *EU Immigration and Asylum Law: Internal Market Model or Human Rights Model?*

STEVE PEERS

## INTRODUCTION

THE PRINCIPLE OF mutual recognition has long been established as a core rule governing the development of the EU's internal market. Since the conclusions of the Tampere European Council in 1999, mutual recognition has also become the core principle of the EU's system for cooperation on civil and commercial law and now criminal law. But to what extent does the principle apply to the development of EU immigration and asylum law, which has links both to the development of the internal market and the criminal and policing law of the Union? And to what extent can the principle apply to immigration and asylum law in light of the EU's and Member States' human rights obligations?

As this Chapter will demonstrate, a 'pure' form of mutual recognition would be in breach of human rights obligations. A better framework for the development of the framework of EU immigration and asylum law would be a human rights model, which would posit the EU's competences in this area as a mechanism for ensuring the effective implementation of those human rights obligations. Moreover, such an analysis has implications for the exercise and extent of EU competence in this area, as the limitations of a 'pure' mutual recognition approach require the development of high minimum standards (and ultimately 'common' policies based on a high level of protection) in EC legislation.

More broadly, it is also useful to examine the extent of the EC's immigration and asylum competence by comparison with its internal market competence. To what extent does the EC have competence to harmonise immigration and asylum law at present? What are the implications of human rights obligations for the exercise of that competence?

## MUTUAL RECOGNITION AND MINIMUM STANDARDS: THE CURRENT AND FUTURE TREATY FRAMEWORK

Within internal market law, as is well known, the EC aimed initially at full harmonization of national law in order to allow free movement, but then ultimately developed a principle of mutual recognition. The purpose of this principle in internal market law is to facilitate free movement by preventing Member States from limiting free movement where another Member State has already regulated a person, product or service. Usually, the principle either requires a 'host' Member State to check to see whether a 'home' Member State has already imposed requirements that aim to achieve objectives comparable to that which the host Member State seeks to achieve by its further regulation, or requires mutual recognition of persons, products or services that have already been subjected to a Community standard of regulation. So, for example, doctors may circulate freely within the EC if they have qualified from an EC university, because their training has been harmonized by EC legislation. Either way, the usual approach is that mutual recognition can only function if there is some underlying similarity of national rules, whether this has occurred spontaneously or has been accomplished by the adoption of EC legislation.[1] The EC still has the power to harmonize national law fully to achieve the objectives of the internal market, but in practice it frequently instead aims to set minimum standards to facilitate or introduce the application of the mutual recognition principle in particular fields.[2] Even where the EC introduces full harmonization, Article 95 EC guarantees that Member States have the possibility to apply higher national standards under certain conditions.

In the field of immigration and asylum, at present, the EC Treaty framework specifies that the EC can only adopt 'minimum standards' as regards most aspects of asylum law (reception conditions, the definition of 'refugee', asylum procedures, temporary protection and subsidiary protection). However, this limitation does not apply to the issue of allocation of responsibility for asylum applications. As regards immigration law, Article 63 specifies that EC measures 'shall not prevent any Member State from maintaining or introducing in the areas concerned national provisions which are compatible with this Treaty and with international agreements.' Finally, as regards visas and borders, the Treaty refers to the adoption of measures on a 'uniform format' for visas and of 'rules on a uniform visa'.

Despite the limitations imposed by the Treaty, the Tampere European Council of 1999 appeared to call for a more far-reaching policy than the EC could adopt by means of its existing powers. A section of the

[1] K Armstrong, 'Mutual Recognition', in C Barnard and J Scott (eds) *The Law of the Single European Market: Unpacking the Premises* (Oxford, Hart, 2002), 225–67.
[2] See M Dougan, 'Minimum Harmonisation and the Internal Market' (2000) 37 *CMLRev* 853.

conclusions is entitled 'A COMMON EU ASYLUM AND MIGRATION POLICY' and there is a detailed call to adopt a 'Common European Asylum Policy', comprising 'in the short term' *inter alia*, 'common standards' on asylum procedures, 'common minimum conditions of reception of asylum seekers', and 'approximation of rules on the recognition and content of the refugee status'. 'In the longer term,' EC rules should establish 'a common asylum procedure and a uniform status for those who are granted asylum valid throughout the Union'. There should also be 'measures' on subsidiary protection. The reference to a 'common' migration policy is not repeated, but there is reference to the 'approximation' of national law on the admission and residence of third-country nationals and to the conferral of 'uniform' rights on long-term resident third-country nationals. Subsequently, the Treaty of Nice added a new Article 67(5) EC, which refers to curtailing the transitional period for decision-making rules on most asylum measures when the EC has adopted legislation 'defining the common rules and basic principles governing these issues'.

The framework for EC immigration and asylum law would change drastically if the draft EU Constitution is signed and ratified in the form agreed by the EU's constitutional Convention in July 2003.[3] In that event, the EU would have power to establish a 'common policy on asylum and temporary protection', including 'a common European asylum system, comprising' *inter alia* 'a uniform status of asylum ... valid throughout the Union', 'a uniform status of subsidiary protection', 'a common system of temporary protection', 'common procedures' for asylum and subsidiary protection, and 'standards' (rather than '*minimum* standards') for reception conditions. It would also have express power to develop a 'common immigration policy', although the relevant Article would preclude the EU from affecting Member States' right to control the initial admission of third-country nationals from outside the EU on economic grounds. There would also be powers concerning a 'common policy on visas and other short-stay residence permits' and the clause listing the objectives of the EU's 'area of freedom, security and justice' would refer to a 'common policy on external borders'.[4] Clearly the draft Constitution would effectively put into Treaty language the more ambitious approach to EC/EU competence set out in the Tampere conclusions. While the EU's powers over this area would expressly be a matter of shared competence,[5] this area would differ from several 'classic' areas of shared competence (such as environmental and social policy) because the EU would not be limited to adoption of minimum standards only.[6] In one sense,

[3] OJ 2003 C 169, Arts III-166 to 168.
[4] Art III-158(2).
[5] Art I-13(2).
[6] See also Art I-13(3) and (4), which specify that EU policies on research, technology and space and on development and humanitarian aid are parallel to Member States' policies in those areas, with the consequence that the EC is unable to pre-empt Member States' competence.

asylum and immigration policy would be unique: never before has an EC/EU competence been *upgraded* from the power to adopt 'minimum standards' only to the power to adopt a 'common policy'.

It is striking that there is no mention of 'mutual recognition' in the current or proposed future provisions governing immigration and asylum policy. This can be compared with the proposed provisions on criminal and civil law cooperation.[7] Then again, the internal market rules in the Treaty have never made extensive references to the principle, but that has not prevented it from becoming a central principle of internal market law.[8]

## MUTUAL RECOGNITION AND MINIMUM STANDARDS: THE CURRENT COMMUNITY PRACTICE

To what extent does the EC approach to immigration and asylum law to date resemble the internal market approach in practice? First, as noted above, the substantive rules on visas and border controls have a strong resemblance to the internal market rules concerning movement of goods in the context of the EC's customs union. These rules were inherited from the Schengen acquis and amended by EC measures following the entry into force of the Treaty of Amsterdam.[9] They provide for standard criteria for crossing the external border and for the issue of a uniform visa.[10] A person who does not meet the standard criteria *must* be refused entry or a visa into Schengen territory generally, although a Member State can grant purely national entry on humanitarian grounds or grounds of national interest or international obligations.[11] The standard criteria are supplemented by an obligation to check external borders in accordance with 'uniform principles' and to 'as far as possible harmonise the instructions' given to border guards.[12] As for visas, Member States undertook to 'adopt a common policy on the movement of persons and, in particular, on the arrangements for visas' and 'to pursue through common consent the harmonization of their policies on visas'.[13] This takes the specific form of a 'uniform visa valid for the entire territory' of the Member States.[14] The Schengen Executive

[7] Arts III-158(3) and (4), 170 and 171.

[8] Art 47 EC makes express reference to the principle in the context of diplomas and qualifications. Art 100b EC, inserted by the Single European Act, made reference to the principle but was deleted by the Treaty of Amsterdam. It could be argued that the principle is implicit in Art 49 EC on free movement of services.

[9] For more detail, see chaps 6–9 of Rogers and S Peers *EU Immigration and Asylum Law* (forthcoming, Martinus Nijhoff, 2004).

[10] Arts 5(1) and 16, 1990 Convention (OJ 2000 L 239).

[11] Arts 5(2) and 15(1), 1990 Convention.

[12] Arts 6 and 7, 1990 Convention. For the current Border Manual, see OJ 2002 C 313/97.

[13] Art 9(1), 1990 Convention; see possible derogation in Art 9(2). For the current Common Consular Instructions, see OJ 2003 C 310/1.

[14] Art 10, 1990 Convention; see possible derogation in Art 10(3).

Committee also had power to adopt 'common rules' on the examination of visa applications and also 'the principles governing the drawing up of a common list of [third-country nationals] for whom an alert has been issued for the purposes of drawing up entry'.[15] Furthermore, there were standard criteria on movement within the Schengen area for short periods for persons with a uniform visa or a national residence permit, or who did not require a visa to enter. In practice, the Schengen States were ultimately able to agree almost fully harmonized lists of which non-EU countries and territories would be subject to or exempt from a visa requirement, although this was subject to uncertainty as to whether the latter list was binding.[16]

Following entry into force of the Treaty of Amsterdam, the EC has fully harmonized the lists of non-EU countries or territories which are (or are not) subject to a visa requirement, and it is now beyond doubt that the 'white list' of countries whose nationals do not require a visa is binding.[17] The EU had already adopted a common format for the uniform visa (since amended),[18] and has now adopted a common format for documentation for persons whose territory of origin is not recognized.[19] It has also adopted implementing measures to ensure further harmonization of visa policy by establishing a standard form for visa applications, a standard fee for considering applications and harmonized rules for considering visa applications submitted by travel agents.[20] Furthermore, another category of persons has been added to those who enjoy the 'freedom to travel' throughout the (Schengen) Union,[21] and the Council has now adopted a standard form concerning refusal of entry at the external borders.[22]

Secondly, as regards asylum policy, the Dublin Convention, now replaced (except as regards Denmark) by a Regulation, sets out rules concerning responsibility for considering asylum applications.[23] In doing so, it implicitly establishes a system for mutual recognition of rejection of asylum applications, and thereby assumes that Member States are

[15] Art 17(1) and 17(2)(g), 1990 Convention. See further discussion of illegal immigration below.

[16] For an analysis of the Schengen visa and border rules, see R Cholewinski, 'No Right of Entry: The Legal Regime on Crossing the EU External Border' in E Guild, P Minderhoud and K Groenendijk (eds) *In Search of Europe's Borders* (The Hague, Kluwer, 2003).

[17] Reg 539/2001 (OJ 2001 L 81/1), as amended by Reg 2414/2001 (OJ 2001 L 327/1). Arguably it is still open to Member States to derogate from these arrangements pursuant to Art 9(2) of the 1990 Convention, but no Member State has ever done so.

[18] Reg 1683/1995 (OJ 1995 L 163/1), amended by Reg 334/2002 (OJ 2002 L 53/6). The Commission has proposed a further amendment (COM (2003) 558, 24 Sep. 2003).

[19] Reg 333/2002 (OJ 2002 L 53/4)

[20] See Decisions in OJ 2002 L 20/5, OJ 2002 L 123/50, OJ 2002 L 187/44 and OJ 2003 L 152/82.

[21] Reg 1091/2001 (OJ 2001 L 150/4).

[22] OJ 2004 L 157/136.

[23] OJ 1997 C 254/1 (Convention); OJ 2003 L 50/1 (Reg 343/2003).

entitled to have full confidence in each other's application of the Geneva Refugee Convention and the European Convention on Human Rights (ECHR).

As for other asylum legislation, the adopted Directive on temporary protection establishes a framework for an EC-wide temporary protection system that can be taken 'off the shelf' when its use is considered necessary.[24] So Member States' existing national temporary protection systems are left unaffected by the Directive. If the EC system is applied, Member States will be free to set higher standards for persons covered by the scheme and will be free to include other categories of persons within the scope of the scheme, although they cannot receive any of the EC funding connected with implementation of the scheme to cover the costs of the latter decision.

Next, the adopted Directive on minimum standards for reception conditions states that Member States are free to set more favourable conditions for asylum applicants or other close relatives.[25] However, it specifies that Member States 'shall determine a period of time … during which an applicant shall not have access to the labour market'.[26]

A similar approach can be found in the proposed Directive on asylum procedures, which has not yet been adopted by the Council at time of writing,[27] although the Council agreed on a general approach in April 2004.[28] The Council's agreed text specifies that Member States may establish more favourable provisions (Article 4). However, Article 9a (likely Article 11 in the final text) allows Member States to impose obligations upon applicants 'insofar as these obligations are necessary' for processing an asylum application, giving as examples obligations to report to the authorities, hand over documents, give information on their place of residence and to submit to searches, photography, and recording of oral statements. Moreover, Article 25 assumes Member States will consider an application inadmissible if another Member State was responsible pursuant to the 'Dublin' rules on responsibility for asylum applications. Also, rules on 'safe country of origin' were agreed at the JHA Council in October 2003. Article 30 and a new Annex will provide for a 'minimum common list' of non-EU States that all Member States must regard as 'safe countries of origin'. Member States would still be free to add *additional* states to purely national lists of such countries, subject to the criteria set out in

[24] Dir 2001/51 (OJ 2001 L 212/12).
[25] Art 4, Dir 2003/9 (OJ 2003 L 31/18).
[26] Art 11(1) *ibid.*
[27] For the initial proposal, see COM (2000) 578, 20 Sept 2000; for the amended proposal see COM (2002) 326, 18 June 2002.
[28] Council doc 8771/04, 30 April 2004. The text is still subject to national parliamentary reservations and reconsultation of the European Parliament.

Article 30a and Annex II, but could not remove a State from the common list unilaterally. A special procedure for removing names from the list would entail provisional suspension of a country from the list for all Member States (if the Council requests the Commission to propose changes to the list) or for individual Member States (if they request the Commission to propose changes), but the suspension would end if Council rejected the subsequent Commission proposal for suspension, or if a three-month period passes without a proposal from the Commission. According to Article 30b, Member States would be obliged to reject applications as unfounded if applicant came from a State on the common EC list, following an individual examination of the claim. In effect, the Directive would establish a 'minimum standard' on this issue only in the sense that Member States can be more *restrictive*, not more *generous*. However, the Council did not show any interest in discussing a parallel Austrian proposal for a Regulation on 'safe third states', which would establish a common list of fifteen countries (the twelve States which the EU has opened membership negotiations with, plus Norway, Iceland and Switzerland) to be regarded as 'safe' if an asylum-seeker passes through or comes from them.[29]

As for the definition and content of refugee status and subsidiary protection status, all Member States but Germany agreed the proposed Directive in the Council by June 2003, and after a compromise with Germany, the Council adopted the Directive with amendments in April 2004.[30] The Directive provides simply that Member States have the right to adopt more favourable provisions.[31]

Finally, as regards immigration policy, Community legislation on legal immigration has usually set minimum standards for the protection of the individual, while conversely, legislation on illegal migration has set minimum standards for Member State *control*. As examples of the first policy, the adopted family reunion Directive specifies that Member States can adopt 'more favourable provisions'.[32] So does the Directive on long-term residents. However, that Directive specifies that persons who qualify for purely national long-term residence status under national law will not be able to enjoy the free movement rights in other Member States provided for by the Directive.[33] This is comparable to the type of 'optional harmonization' seen in some EC internal market legislation, which provides that Member States can provide for higher standards of regulation than the minimum set out in Directives, on condition that these

[29] OJ 2003 C 17/6. This proposal lapsed on 1 May 2004.
[30] The agreed text is in Council doc 7944/04, 31 March 2004.
[31] Art 4 of the agreed text (likely final Art 3).
[32] Directive 2003/86 (OJ 2003 L 251/12), Art 3(6).
[33] Directive 2003/109 (OJ 2004 L 16/44), Art 13.

higher standards only take effect within its territory.[34] There is also an element of mutual recognition in the Directive: each Member State has to accept persons who have spent five years of legal residence in another Member State as long-term residents with the capacity to move within the Community, regardless of differences between national laws on initial entry of persons and possible subsequent regularization of legal status.[35]

Having said that, there are some common rules on the acquisition of EC long-term residence status, and several groups are excluded from the scope of the Directive altogether.[36] The exclusions include most notably refugees and persons with subsidiary protection status,[37] even though the Council had largely agreed on an EC-wide definition of these statuses (see above) and nominally the Geneva Refugee Convention has harmonized the definition of refugee already. Conversely, the beneficiaries of the Directive will largely not have been governed by EC rules before they qualify for EC long-term residence status, except for those persons covered by EC association agreements with Central/Eastern Europe and Turkey, third-country national family members of EC nationals; and those who are in future covered by the family reunion Directive. But the Europe Agreements with Central/Eastern Europe only cover admission of persons who seek to exercise a right of establishment, and in any event neither the Directive nor the Agreements will be applicable to nationals of countries once they have joined the Community; the EC-Turkey agreement does not cover the initial admission of Turkish workers and their family members, but only their status after admission;[38] EC free movement law only covers family members of EU citizens who have moved within the Community;[39] and as noted above, Member States are free to be more generous than the minimum standards set by the family reunion Directive. The initial entry and status of the beneficiaries of the long-term residence Directive will only be harmonized by EC law once EC legislation extensively harmonizes admissions on economic grounds and further harmonizes family reunion

[34] See Case C-1/96 *CWF* [1998] ECR I-1251 and Case C-11/92 *Gallaher* [1993] ECR I-3545.

[35] During negotiations on the Directive, the question of whether Member States might refuse to accept the result of other Member States' regularization was raised but then dropped. See chap 20 of Rogers and Peers, n 9 above.

[36] Art 3(2) of Directive 2003/109 (n 33 above).

[37] The JHA Council agreed in May 2003 to consider a Commission proposal to include these groups within the scope of the Directive, to be tabled within a year of the Directive's adoption. However, there is no guarantee that this future proposal will be adopted.

[38] See case law beginning with Case C-171/95 *Tetik* [1997] ECR I-329.

[39] See Joined Cases 35/82 and 36/82 *Morson and Jhanjan* [1982] ECR 3273; Case C-370/90 *Singh* [1992] ECR I-4265; Joined Cases C-64/96 and 65/96 *Uecker and Jacquet* [1997] ECR I-3171; Case C-60/00 *Carpenter* [2002] ECR I-6279; Case C-459/99 *MRAX* [2002] ECR I-6591; and judgment of 23 Sept 2003 in Case C-109/01 *Akrich*, not yet reported. For further discussion, see S Peers, 'Family Reunion and Community Law', in N Walker (ed) *Europe's Area of Freedom Security and Justice* (Oxford, OUP, 2004).

rules, including admission of all family members joining EU citizens. If we compare the long-term residence rules with the approach of internal market law, it is peculiar that those persons whose initial entry and status in the first Member State has been most fully harmonized by national (and soon Community) law are excluded from the application of the mutual recognition rules, while the persons who can benefit from those rules are largely not covered yet by EC rules concerning their admission.

Then again, perhaps Member States are not perturbed by the lack of harmonization of rules on initial entry and status of the beneficiaries of the long-term residents' Directive because it will allow them extensive possibilities of controlling long-term residents who seek to move from another Member State.[40] Moreover, the Directive provides that if a long-term resident wishes to bring his/her family from the first Member State to a second Member State, Member States are only obliged to admit 'core' family members as defined by the family reunion Directive, not those family members which each Member State has only an option to admit initially according to that Directive.[41] So on the issue of family reunion for long-term residents who move within the EC, mutual recognition has been made contingent upon the application of minimum standards.

As for the agreed Directive on third-country national students and volunteers, Member States may 'maintain or adopt more favourable provisions', even though the rules governing entry in the agreed Directive appear to be mandatory rules which the Member States must comply with if they wish to admit third-country students. It also appears that for a student to take advantage of the right to move to another Member State to continue studies or pick up a new course of studies, he or she must have been admitted to a first Member State pursuant to the minimum rules set out in the Directive.[42]

Finally, the proposed Directive on migration for employment and self-employment contains some provisions which would allow Member States to be more generous to the persons covered by the Directive, but also some provisions which would only allow Member States to be more *restrictive*.[43] In the former category, Member States would be permitted to apply more favourable treatment to an exhaustive list of certain categories of persons (in the absence of move favourable provisions of EC law).[44] Otherwise, Member States could only admit workers or self-employed persons if the criteria in the Directive are met.[45] However, some provisions give Member

[40] See particularly Arts 14 and 15 of the Directive.
[41] Art 16(1) and 16(2) of the Directive.
[42] Arts 4 and 7 of agreed text (Council doc 8013/04, 31 Mar 2004).
[43] COM (2001) 386, 11 July 2001.
[44] Art 3(4).
[45] Arts 4(1) and 17(1).

States an option to be more liberal than the standard rules,[46] or to be more restrictive,[47] and some place a 'ceiling' on the extent of possible liberality.[48]

In the area of illegal immigration, the principal application of the mutual recognition principle is Article 96 of the Schengen Convention, which provides for the creation of a list of persons to be denied entry into the Schengen area on the basis of national alerts issued in accordance with the procedures of 'national law'. Such decisions 'may be based on a threat to public policy or public security or national security', 'in particular' where a person has been convicted of an offence carrying a penalty of over one year, where there are 'serious grounds' for believing that a person has committed 'serious criminal offences' or where there is 'clear evidence of an intention to commit such offences' in the Schengen area. They 'may' also be based on an outstanding deportation order (or a comparable decision) entailing a prohibition on entry or residence, issued due to a breach of national immigration law. As noted above, the power for the Executive Committee (now the Council) to adopt standard rules on drawing up a list of banned persons banned from Schengen territory, which is presumably a reference to the list established pursuant to Article 96 of the Convention, has not been exercised.

The same criteria essentially apply to Directive 2001/40 on mutual recognition of expulsion decisions,[49] except here they appear to be exhaustive and the Directive only permits, not requires, Member States to expel a person pursuant to the mutual recognition mechanism it sets out. Furthermore, expulsion is effected according to the requested State's national law, and the requested State is obliged to offer the person concerned a remedy and to consider whether national law or relevant international instruments conflict with enforcing the expulsion decision.[50]

In practice, there have been disputes between Member States as to the correct interpretation of Article 96 of the Schengen Convention, and difficulties for individuals who sought a remedy against the operation of the Schengen rules.[51]

The Commission has called for moves towards an *obligation* for Member States to recognise each other's expulsion orders, subject to the adoption of minimum standards for expulsion proceedings.[52] In

[46] See Arts 5(1), 6(3), 6(4), 6(5), 11(1), 12(1), 19(2) and 19(3).
[47] See Arts 5(3)(e), 8, Art 11(2), 12(2), 18(3)(e), 21, 26 and 27.
[48] See Arts 7(1) and 20(1), which require Member States to issue an initial residence permit for up to three years; implicitly they cannot issue a permit for a longer period.
[49] OJ 2001 L 149/34.
[50] Arts 1(2), 4 and 6 of the Directive (*ibid*).
[51] See T Eicke, 'Paradise Lost? Exclusion and Expulsion from the EU' in Guild et al, n 16 above, 147 at 161–64 and Staples, 'Adjudicating the External Schengen Border', *idem*, 215 at 221–35.
[52] See Green Paper on return policy (COM (2002) 175, 10 Apr 2002), s 3.1; and see also Communication on follow-up to the Green Paper (COM (2002) 564, 14 Oct 2002), s 2.1 and s 2.3.

response, the Council's Action Plan on Returns gave a fairly half-hearted endorsement of these ideas,[53] and no further measure was yet forthcoming at time of writing, although the Commission still intends to propose a Directive on the issue.[54] However, the Council has taken forward the idea of mutual recognition in the context of transit for expulsion. At time of writing, it had adopted a Directive on assistance for transit by air and had adopted conclusions on the issue of assistance for transit via land.[55] These measures do not explicitly require each Member State to accede to another Member State's request for assistance, but that is obviously the underlying assumption. Since there is nothing in these measures that would expressly require or even permit a requested Member State to consider whether it would expel the relevant person under its own law, the application of the measures in practice would amount to a 'raw' form of mutual recognition, obliging one Member State to execute another's decisions even without any underlying harmonization.

There has also been further harmonization of Member States' carrier sanctions obligations and of the obligation to punish facilitation of illegal entry into any Member State,[56] in both cases building on the Schengen Convention rules. However, EU measures concerning substantive criminal law, including the parallel Framework Decision on trafficking in persons,[57] inherently only set minimum standards for the definition of crimes and related penalties.[58] But since the measures on facilitation of illegal entry require Member States to punish anyone who facilitates illegal entry in breach of *any* Member State's law,[59] they require each Member State to enforce other Member States' immigration laws, and so again implicitly impose a mutual recognition obligation without any underlying harmonization.

An early suggestion for a set of readmission rules between Member States, which would parallel the Dublin rules and therefore raise similar issues, did not attract interest in the Council.[60] The Commission subsequently tried to revive the idea,[61] but the Council's Action Plan on returns makes no mention of it.

[53] See Council doc 14673/02, Nov 2002, points 40–45 and 49–53.
[54] See Communication on external borders, illegal immigration and return plans (COM (2003) 323, 3 June 2003), p 9.
[55] See Directive 2003/110 (OJ 2003 L 321/26) and conclusions adopted by the Environment Council, 22 Dec 2003.
[56] On carrier sanctions, see Dir 2001/51 (OJ 2001 L 187/45); on facilitation of illegal entry, see Dir 2002/90 (OJ 2002 L 328/17) and connected Framework Decision (OJ 2002 L 328/1).
[57] OJ 2002 L 203/1.
[58] This results from the wording of Art 31(1)(e) TEU; the position would not change under the draft constitution (see Art III-172).
[59] See Art 1(1) of Dir 2002/90 (n 56 above).
[60] OJ 1999 C 353/6.
[61] See Green Paper on returns and follow-up Communication (n 52 above).

## ASSESSMENT

What type of competence does the EC currently have over immigration and asylum law, and what rules govern its exercise? First of all, the secondary law of the Schengen acquis and later EC measures shows clearly that the EC is aiming for fairly extensive harmonization of the law governing visa and borders, possibly even extending to full harmonization in some or all areas, although (in common with most areas of EC law) implementation is left to national authorities. It can also be argued that the principle of abolishing internal border checks (and the power to adopt related rules) and the internal freedom to travel of third-country nationals for a three-month period necessarily entails a considerable degree of harmonization of visa policy and rules on crossing external borders. The references to rules on 'uniform' visas support this. This interpretation is further strengthened by comparison with the EC's pre-existing framework for the movement of third-country goods across external EC borders and subsequent internal free circulation of those goods.[62] Therefore there can be no fundamental legal objection to the pursuit of full harmonization in this field (subject to the application of the principles of subsidiarity and proportionality).

The issue is not as clear-cut when it comes to asylum and immigration law. As regards asylum law, we have seen that the most of the competences set out in the Treaty are subject to a 'minimum standards' limitation, but that in several cases the Council is setting minimum standards from the point of view of restriction (Member States can be more restrictive), not of protection (Member States can be more generous). Furthermore, an opinion from the Council legal service on the proposed Directive on the definition and content of refugee and subsidiary protection status raises the question of whether the 'minimum standards' powers actually allow the Council to set *common* standards.[63] This argument is potentially crucially important to the issue of the extent of EC competence over all asylum matters. The Opinion argues that:

> The term 'minimum standards', which is used in Article 63(1)(b), (c) and (d) and in Article 63(2) (a) EC, indicates that the Council shall adopt measures aiming at a certain degree of harmonization establishing a common denominator which is binding on all Member States, without precluding Member States from maintaining or introducing standards which are more favourable for the persons falling under the scope of the acts in question. However, in order not to annihilate the objective of harmonization, this possibility cannot be unlimited. More favourable standards must remain within the limits laid down in those acts, as it is expressed by the phrase

[62] See Arts 23 and 24 EC and further analysis in S Peers, 'EU Borders and Globalisation', in E Guild et al above n 14, 45–66.
[63] Council doc 14348/02, 15 Nov 2002.

'insofar as those standards are compatible with this Directive' in Article 4 of the proposed directive.

In the view of the legal service, the compatibility of a 'particular Member State's law or regulation providing for more favourable standards' with the proposed directive could only be answered following a 'careful case-by-case analysis'. However, it offered 'some criteria in order to guide this analysis'. In particular, a number of key provisions in Chapters I to VI of the proposal would define 'the content of a number of notions which determine the scope *ratione personae* of the directive and which are fundamental not only for the directive in question, but also have a bearing on other areas, such as the notion of refugee status, which is pertinent also for the minimum standards on procedures for granting or withdrawing this status, to be adopted on the basis of Article 63(1)(d) EC. Hence, any deviation in national law from the definitions laid down in' a number of key provisions defining refugee and subsidiary protection status 'would be incompatible with the objective of harmonizing the content of those notions, unless the definition itself allows for the inclusion or exclusion of a certain group of persons as part of a wider category'.

So we have two questions here. Can minimum standards be set only as regards protection of individuals, or can they also be set as regards restriction by Member States? Secondly, notwithstanding the text of the Treaty, can the minimum standards powers actually be used to establish common standards?

Answering the second question first, the analysis of the Council legal service is, with great respect, surely incorrect. The very concept of 'minimum standards' inherently means that the legislation adopted pursuant to the relevant legal bases must always leave Member States free to establish rules going above and beyond the rules set out in the legislation. Treaty Articles clearly distinguish between cases in which the EC can only set minimum standards and cases in which the EC can or must fully harmonize a field. Possibly there might be cases where as an ancillary effect of minimum standards legislation, a certain matter is fully harmonized. But logically minimum standards legislation cannot have at its heart full harmonization of national law on a given matter.

The more difficult question is whether a 'minimum standards' system can also apply to restriction, as well as protection. On this point, the context and wording of the EC Treaty points to the conclusion that minimum standards can only apply as regards protection. First, the term 'minimum standards' has always been applied and understood in this sense in other areas of the Treaty: it has never been argued that the EC can set 'minimum standards' permitting Member States only to allow more, not less, pollution than a certain level, or to allow only lower employment standards, not higher standards. However, it must be admitted that Articles 137(4) and 176 are clearer on this point, by expressly allowing 'more stringent protective measures' as regards social and environmental law.

Secondly, there is a clear difference in wording between Article 63(1) and (2) on the one hand, and Article 63(3) and (4) on the other, with the latter powers governed not by the 'minimum standards' rule but by a rule that Member States can always adopt national provisions consistent with the EC Treaty and national commitments. This difference in wording suggests that the Treaty drafters intended a difference in interpretation of the rules governing the two powers. The most logical interpretation is surely that EC asylum legislation must always allow Member States to ensure greater protection for the individual, but that EC immigration legislation can allow more restriction *or* more protection *or* impose full harmonization, depending on the choice of the legislator. This interpretation of the immigration powers is logical in light of the subject-matter (since measures on both illegal and legal migration are covered by the proviso), and is consistent with both the pre-Amsterdam and post-Amsterdam practice of the institutions. The pre-Amsterdam soft law allowed only for more generous treatment in some areas and only for more stringent treatment in others,[64] and now the post-Amsterdam adopted or proposed rules take the same approach, as seen above.

Thirdly, this interpretation best respects the *chapeau* of Article 63(1) and the general Title IV obligations imposed upon the EC institutions by Article 61 EC. The former refers to acting in accordance with the Geneva Convention and other relevant treaties, which usually expressly set only minimum standards for the protection of the individual,[65] while the latter obliges the Council to adopt legislation 'safeguarding the rights' of third-country nationals.

It follows that the relevant legislation must either be interpreted to mean that Member States retain the power to set higher standards for the protection of individuals in all cases, or that in the alternative the relevant provisions are simply invalid.

As for powers over migration, it has already been argued above that Article 63(3) and (4) permit the EC legislator either to set minimum standards as regards restriction or protection or to impose full harmonization. While the closing words of Article 63 could be interpreted to permit Member States to adopt whatever immigration law provisions they wish regardless of EC immigration legislation, this interpretation must be rejected as absurd. What would be the point of providing for EC power to harmonize national law if it was not binding on Member States to any

[64] S Peers, 'Building Fortress Europe: the Development of EU Migration Law' (1998) 35 *CMLRev* 1235.
[65] For instance, see Art 53 ECHR.

extent? The closing words of Article 63 must instead mean that EC immigration competence is not *intrinsically* exclusive; that competence can only become exclusive once exercised, and to the extent of its exercise. This interpretation is also logical because it would make sense to provide for a possible greater degree of harmonization over long-term entry and residence into the EU in light of the powers to permit movement of third-country nationals between Member States and residence in additional Member States.

Finally, the case for interpreting the EC's competence consistently with human rights law is strengthened by the decision of the European Court of Human Rights in *TI v UK*[66] In this case, the Court decided on the admissibility of an application claiming that the UK would breach Article 3 of the ECHR by applying the Dublin Convention to a particular case to remove an asylum applicant to Germany, which would consider the asylum application. In the applicant's view, the ECHR would be breached because Germany would not allow a person in his situation to stay on the territory, and would therefore remove him to face a real risk of an Article 3 breach in another country, in breach of ECHR case law. The Court ruled that:

> ... indirect removal in this case to an intermediary country, which is also a Contracting State, does not affect the responsibility of the United Kingdom to ensure that the applicant is not, as a result of its decision to expel, exposed to treatment contrary to Article 3 of the Convention. Nor can the United Kingdom rely automatically in that context on the arrangements made in the Dublin Convention concerning the attribution of responsibility between European countries for deciding asylum claims. Where States establish international organisations, or *mutatis mutandis* international agreements, to pursue co-operation in certain fields of activities, there may be implications for the protection of fundamental rights. It would be incompatible with the purpose and object of the Convention if Contracting States were thereby absolved from their responsibility under the Convention in relation to the field of activity covered by such attribution....The Court has therefore examined below whether the United Kingdom have complied with their obligations to protect the applicant from the risk of torture and ill-treatment contrary to Article 3 of the Convention.

It is clear from this ruling that cooperation between EC Member States cannot be exempted from the international human rights obligations, whether carried out on an intergovernmental or Community basis. In particular, Member States cannot insist upon an automatic and unchallengeable presumption in favour of mutual recognition of other Member States' decisions. Since the Court clearly required an examination of the fate of the applicant in German hands, it follows that Member States cannot simply

[66] Decision of 7 Mar 2000, Reports of Judgments and Decisions 2000-III.

rely on each other as signatories of the ECHR (or presumably other human rights treaties) to uphold those treaties. And since the Court assumed that the UK would have responsibility for the fate of the applicant in Germany, it is not possible for Member States simply to transfer their ECHR obligations along with the transfer of an asylum applicant.

## CONCLUSION

A human rights model of EC immigration and asylum law gives us a very different approach to the issue than the Council has adopted to date. To ensure full compliance with the ECHR, and correspondingly to ease application of the mutual recognition principle in cases where human rights obligations are engaged, a human rights model would require that the Community's competence over immigration and asylum law must be exercised to set high minimum standards in this area, at the very least compliant with the standards set by ECHR case law. Community legislation allowing for or requiring mutual recognition without either setting minimum standards at least at ECHR levels or requiring each Member State to check the human rights standards of others would appear to violate the principles established in the *TI* decision. In particular, legislation which sets minimum standards below the level of the ECHR or other treaties would violate the requirement to 'respect' human rights as general principles of law, as set out in Article 6 EU. There is a strong argument that a number of provisions of the agreed asylum procedures Directive will violate this requirement.

It follows that the Council's application of a limited 'internal market' model is deeply flawed from the perspective of human rights, due to low or non-existent minimum standards upholding the mutual recognition principle, and cases of setting minimum standards from the point of view of restriction, not protection. In fact, the Council's approach is even questionable by comparison with the internal market model, due to selective application of the mutual recognition principle (in effect requiring mutual recognition of refusals of asylum applications, but not mutual recognition of successful applications, even limited to long-term residents), while claiming to have achieved full harmonization in other areas, in excess of the powers to set minimum standards only. One can only hope that if the EC's powers in this field are ultimately revised by the EU Constitution, the obligation to apply an approach to these powers in accordance with human rights principles will be clearly expressed and strengthened.

# 21

# *A Missed Opportunity? EU Law and Asylum in the 21st Century*

HÉLÈNE LAMBERT*

WHO WILL BE eligible for international protection in the European Union (EU) in the coming century? The new legal order in European asylum is being shaped by a key document — a proposal from the European Commission for a Directive on minimum standards for the qualification and status of third country nationals and stateless persons as refugees or as persons who otherwise need international protection (hereinafter the Qualification Directive).[1] International protection for individuals in the EU is currently provided under two mechanisms. First is the 1951 Geneva Convention Relating to the Status of Refugees as amended by the 1967 New York Protocol (hereinafter the Geneva Convention) which offers protection against *refoulement* and a legal status to individuals recognised as refugees under its definition. Second is the practice of subsidiary protection, which provides temporary protection against *refoulement* for individuals under human rights law.[2] The Qualification Directive promises to combine these two forms of protection under one umbrella, to institutionalise minimum standards for international protection whatever form it takes, ie, to codify a common definition of third country nationals in genuine need of international protection.[3] This is the

* I wish to thank Daphné Bouteillet-Paquet for her invaluable help.

1 COM (2001) 510 final. Another key document, which complements the Qualification Directive, is the amended Commission Proposal for a Council Directive on minimum standards on procedures in Member States for granting and withdrawing refugee status (COM (2002) 326 final).

2 'Temporary protection' in the even of mass influx of displaced persons is not a third form of protection but rather a temporary measure to avoid the asylum system clogging up.

3 Peers argues that the Qualification Directive does not in fact provide minimum standards but full harmonisation with the potential risk that harmonisation will be set at a level below the minimum standards of human rights law: S Peers, 'EU Immigration and Asylum Law: An Internal Market or Human Rights Model?' Paper presented at the W G Hart Legal Workshop (2003), published in this volume.

most ambitious attempt to combine refugee law and human rights law in this way. Moreover, given the status of this document, it will have profound implications for the future direction of international protection in Europe.

The proposal for a Qualification Directive was presented to the Council in October 2001. Following five Council meetings,[4] agreement was reached by the Member States (subject to one reservation) on the provisions relating to qualification for international protection. The rights to be granted to the beneficiaries of refugee status have also been agreed. However, the level of the rights to be granted to the beneficiaries of subsidiary protection status remains contested. Since then negotiations have been blocked by the veto of Germany and discussions have been postponed until September.[5]

In this chapter I compare the original Commission Proposal with the latest draft Directive as at 19 June 2003.[6] I am going to concentrate on the key question of who is eligible for international protection in the EU. The first section of this chapter examines the distinction between protection under the Geneva Convention (hereinafter Convention protection) and subsidiary protection. It finds significant similarities in the nature and necessity of protection afforded under refugee and human rights law, and this argues for the merging of these two bodies of law. In sections two and three I respectively examine two critical aspects in determining eligibility for international protection, the standard of proof and what constitutes persecution and serious harm. In each section I begin by examining provisions for each under refugee law and human rights law, before comparing these provisions with those specified in the Commission Proposal and draft Council Directive. I am particularly interested in how these two documents draw on and integrate refugee law and human rights law principles of international protection. One might hope to find progression in the merging of these two bodies of law. But, of course, given the drafting process, hope differs greatly from expectation. Is the EU missing a golden opportunity to have one common normative framework for asylum in Europe?

## INTERNATIONAL PROTECTION UNDER REFUGEE AND HUMAN RIGHTS LAW

The 'gold standard' in international protection is provided under the Geneva Convention. The definition of a refugee is central to the operation

[4] One on 15 October 2002, the second on 28 November 2002, the third on 27 February 2003, the fourth on 8 May 2003, and the fifth on 6 June 2003.

[5] It is still uncertain as to when the Council will reach political agreement on the Directive considering that article 67 TEC requires unanimity of the Member States.

[6] This is the latest draft available in the public domain (document 10576/03 ASILE 40).

of the Convention. A refugee is defined under article 1A(2) of the Geneva Convention as anyone who 'owing to a well-founded fear of being persecuted for reasons of race, religion, nationality, membership of a particular social group or political opinion, is outside the country of his nationality and is unable or … unwilling to avail himself of the protection of that country'. According to the Convention, anyone falling under the definition of a refugee is entitled to refugee status; the Convention is silent about those who do not fall under this definition.[7] The purpose of the Geneva Convention is to provide substitute protection and fair treatment in the absence or unavailability of national protection; protection under the Geneva Convention is only surrogate. But EU states practice over the last 50 years shows that asylum (understood as a permanent right to remain) is granted to anyone recognised as a refugee. Because the Convention is silent on how to interpret its article 1A(2), the UNHCR adopted guidelines to help the Member States apply the definition of a refugee. In spite of these guidelines, the practice of the Member States has come to vary enormously from one country to another. For example, the Member States adopted different interpretations of the words 'persecution' or 'membership of a particular social group'. This in turn has led to the non-recognition of refugee status to the majority of persons seeking refuge in the EU and to the creation of alternative forms of protection.

Subsidiary protection (also known as complementary protection)[8] has basically arisen to deal with those who require some form of protection but who do not qualify as a refugee under the Geneva Convention. It is a policy response by states where and when the test applied under article 1A(2) of the Geneva Convention is either too narrow or too strict or because the applicant clearly falls outside the ambit of the Geneva Convention. Subsidiary protection applies only once it has been determined that the person does not qualify for refugee status but that under human rights law, there still is a genuine need for international protection. Given its discretionary basis, subsidiary protection offers much weaker rights to its beneficiaries than the rights recognised to refugees under the Geneva Convention. In particular, protection against refoulement is normally only provided on a short-term basis and the right of family reunion is often denied.

[7] However, the 1951 Final Act of the Geneva Convention called for states parties to the Convention to consider according protection to individuals not covered by it.

[8] See, generally, D Bouteillet-Paquet, *Subsidiary Protection of Refugees in the EU: Complementing the Geneva Convention?* (Brussels, Bruylant, 2002) 800. Note that the use of the term 'complementary' or 'subsidiary' is an issue of disputes. For instance, the Commission Proposal for a Qualification Directive refers to 'subsidiary' protection whereas the European Council on Refugees and Exiles refers to 'complementary' protection on the ground that the term 'subsidiary' has too much of a 'secondary' connotation to it, as opposed to 'primary', ie, Convention protection. ECRE's comments on the Proposal, available at *http://www.ecre.org/statements/statuscomms.shtml*.

Thus, the Member States are treating these two forms of protection as separate solutions. Yet, there are strong reasons to argue for the merger of protection under refugee law with protection under human rights law. Firstly, both forms of protection are subject to the rule of law, in particular the principles of international refugee law and international human rights law. This is not the case for instance of applications made purely on compassionate grounds. Moreover, dealing with these two forms of protection as one solution would further contribute to the creation of a unifying normative framework whereby the Geneva Convention would remain the primary instrument of international protection but read in a strong human rights context. Secondly, Convention protection and subsidiary protection both rest on genuine need. Thus there is a strong ethical imperative for treating individuals in a consistent way under both forms of protection. Thirdly, unlike the treatment of persons in genuine need of protection under refugee law, the treatment of those in genuine need of protection under human rights law has so far been left to the discretion of national authorities. This has resulted in contradictory practice and legislation between states that needs ironing out. For instance, in the UK, family reunion is recognised to beneficiaries of subsidiary protection (ie, exceptional leave to remain) after four years. In France, this right is recognised on a case-by-case basis. In Belgium or Sweden, these persons are recognised their right of family reunion straight away.[9] Finally, the conceptual distinction between Convention protection and subsidiary protection is, in some respects, collapsing in practice. This is particularly evident with regard to the customary permanent status of refugees versus the temporary status of beneficiaries of subsidiary protection. In reality, those provided with 'temporary' protection under human rights law rarely return to their country of origin. For instance, in the UK most persons granted exceptional leave to remain have been allowed to remain permanently at the expiry of the four-year period. This situation is expected to continue in spite of current reform to revive the power to review such cases at the four-year stage.[10]

I am now going to discuss the extent to which the Commission Proposal for a Qualification Directive and the latest draft Council Directive reconcile this view that the two types of protection should merge. In doing so I will look at two key elements in deciding who will be eligible for international protection in the EU: standard of proof and the treatment feared.

[9] Replies to Questionnaire on Family Reunion, Council of Europe, CAHAR (99) 4.

[10] Letter from the Home Office, 27 February 2003. Note that since 31st March 2003, 'exceptional leave to remain' has been replaced by 'humanitarian protection' and 'discretionary leave'. See http://194.203.40.90/default.asp?PageId=2655 and 3791.

## STANDARD OF PROOF UNDER THE COMMISSION PROPOSAL AND THE DRAFT COUNCIL DIRECTIVE

To decide who will be eligible for international protection in the EU, two standards of proof may be applied: the 'well-founded fear' standard provided in refugee law or the 'real risk' standard to be found in human rights law, in particular the European Convention on Human Rights (hereinafter the ECHR). Although in some states practice, the two tests reflect the same standard of proof (eg, in the UK)[11], there is still one major difference between the two: the principle of the benefit of the doubt is applied more restrictively under the ECHR than under refugee law.

### Well-founded Fear under Refugee Law

The UNHCR Handbook requires that 'good reasons' be shown by the applicant that his or her fear be of a 'reasonable degree'.[12] UK courts have interpreted 'well-founded' to mean 'real and substantial danger' or 'reasonable likelihood' or 'real or substantial risk'.[13] It is a well-established principle of refugee law that while the burden of proof in principle lies on the applicant, the duty to ascertain and evaluate information on the human rights situation in the country of origin is shared between the applicant and the examiner.[14] Furthermore, applicants should always be given the benefit of the doubt in cases where there is no conclusive evidence of the facts.[15] Refugee law recognises the principle that 'that which happened in the past may happen in the future'.[16] But in the EU past persecution alone is not a sufficient basis for eligibility to international protection. This is because, as the UNHCR itself points out, 'the word 'fear' refers not only to persons who have actually been persecuted, but also to those who wish to avoid a situation entailing the risk of persecution'.[17] The situation is different in the United States for example where eligibility for refugee status can be

[11] In the UK, for instance, in considering whether a person would face a serious risk to life or person, the standard of proof that is being applied is that which applies in asylum cases or ECHR cases, ie, a reasonable degree of likelihood or a real risk. These two terms reflect the same standard of proof. See *Kacaj v Secretary of State for the Home Department* [2002] Imm AR 213 at paras10–12, referring to *R v Secretary of State for the Home Department, ex parte Sivakumaran* [1988] 1 All ER 193 at 201c.

[12] *UNHCR Handbook*, paras 42 and 45.

[13] *R v Secretary of State for the Home Department, ex parte Sivakumaran* [1988] 1 All ER 193, at 199 and 202 ('real and substantial danger'), at 197–98 ('reasonable likelihood') and at 201 ('real or substantial risk').

[14] *UNHCR Handbook*, para 196.

[15] *UNHCR Handbook*, paras 196–99 and paras 203–4.

[16] *UNHCR Handbook*, para 45.

[17] *UNHCR Handbook*, para 45. See also, in the UK, *(Regina) Hoxha v Special Adjudicator* [2002] EWCA Civ 1403.

established on the basis of past persecution *or* of a well-founded fear of persecution.[18] Finally, 'well-founded fear' has also been interpreted to mean that there must be a danger to the person individually.[19]

### Real Risk under Human Rights Law

Numerous human rights instruments are relevant to international protection. In this section I concentrate on the most important in Europe, namely the ECHR and case-law of the European Court of Human Rights. According to the European Court of Human Rights, a state party to the ECHR may not send a person to another state where 'substantial grounds' have been shown for believing that s/he would face a 'real risk' of being subjected to treatment contrary to article 3 ECHR if removed to that state.[20] The Court considers that 'substantial grounds' exist when there are reasonable grounds that expulsion is going to take place; mere possibility is not enough.[21] It is then up to the person concerned to come up with the first evidence of any real risk of maltreatment; the state can always produce counter-evidence thereafter.[22] Furthermore, a state party to the ECHR is only responsible for *foreseeable* risks, ie, for the *foreseeable* consequences of the state's decision to expel that the applicant will be subject to treatment contrary to article 3.[23] Thus, risks that cannot be verified or that are falsified do not generally lead to a violation of article 3 ECHR.[24] This is an important difference with the examination of asylum applications under refugee law where the principle of the benefit of the doubt has long been recognised. It is only recently that this principle has been endorsed in

[18] *In re Chen*, 20 I & N Dec at 18.
[19] *UNHCR Handbook*, para 45. *R v Secretary of State for the Home Department, ex p Adan* 37 ILM 1090 (1998), at 1099, the House of Lords found that the person must be able to show a differential impact, that is a fear of persecution over and above the ordinary risk that exists during a civil war. If however it can be established that there is a systematic pattern of state abuse and denial of the fundamental human rights of a class of people, then this will amount to persecution. It will not be necessary for the applicant to show that s/he has been targeted individually.
[20] *Soering v United Kingdom*, application No 14038/88, para 91. See also *Chahal v United Kingdom*, application No 22414/93, para 80.
[21] *Vilvarajah v United Kingdom*, application No 13163/87, para 111.
[22] The European Court of Human Rights is not a court of appeal and in most cases it will find the facts established by the national courts to be correct. For a case to the contrary, see *Hatami v Sweden*, application No 32448/96.
[23] *Vilvarajah v United Kingdom*, application No 13163/87.
[24] See the case of *Chahal v United Kingdom* where the defence team gathered an unprecedented amount of evidence and a violation of article 3 ECHR was found (application No 22141/93). In the similar case of *HLR v France*, where ill-treatment was similarly serious, the Court found that the concrete evidence of such a risk were much weaker than in Chahal and it found no violation of article 3 (application No 24573/94). H Lambert, 'Protection Against Refoulement from Europe: Human Rights Law Comes to the Rescue' (1999) 48 *International and Comparative Law Quarterly*, 535–43.

human rights law, and only in specific cases of contradictory and inconsistent testimonies due to traumatic experiences.[25] Consistent with refugee law, the European Court of Human Rights requires that the risk posed to the individual be specific to him/her.[26]

## Commission Proposal

Under article 5 of the Commission Proposal both refugees and persons eligible for subsidiary protection are eligible for international protection. Article 5(1) defines a refugee as 'any third country national who, owing to a *well-founded fear of being persecuted* for reasons of race, religion, nationality, political opinion or membership of a particular social group, is outside the country of nationality and is unable or, owing to such fear, is unwilling to avail himself or herself of the protection of that country' (my underline). Thus, the Commission Proposal is using the same wording as in the Geneva Convention, with the difference that it refers to he or she. Article 5(2) of the Commission Proposal then defines a beneficiary of subsidiary protection as 'any third country national or stateless person who does not qualify as a refugee ... or whose application for international protection was explicitly made on grounds that did not include the Geneva Convention, and who, owing to a *well-founded fear of suffering serious and unjustified harm* ... has been forced to flee ...' (my underline).[27] It follows from a reading of these two definitions that all applications under the Proposal are to be assessed by reference to the 'well-founded fear' test existing in refugee law. Significantly, the Commission chose to set aside the more restrictive test relied upon in human rights law even though the Explanatory Memorandum provides that, with regards to subsidiary protection, 'the ECHR and the case law of the European Court on Human Rights provide for a legally binding framework'.[28] This merging of the standard of proof in the Commission Proposal is to be welcome for at least two reasons. One, because it institutionalises in law the actual practice of states.[29] Two, because under refugee law, when assessing the well-founded

[25] *Alan v Switzerland*, communication No 21/1995 (Committee Against Torture) and *Selcuk and Asker v Turkey*, application No 23184/94 (European Court of Human Rights).

[26] *Vilvarajah v United Kingdom*, application No 13163/87, para 111. *HLR v France*, application No 24573/94, para 42.

[27] See also article 15 which provides the grounds for subsidiary protection, ie, torture or inhuman or degrading treatment or punishment, severe violation of a human right, or a threat to life, safety or freedom.

[28] Explanatory Memorandum, 5.

[29] G Goodwin-Gill and A Hurwitz, 'Draft Council Directive on minimum standards for the qualification and status of third country nationals and stateless persons as refugees or as persons who otherwise need international protection', submission to the House of Lords, April 2002, at p 1.

fear, applicants should always be given the benefit of the doubt in cases where there is no conclusive evidence of the facts. This is not the case under human rights law, as highlighted above.

Furthermore, in line with refugee law, the Proposal recognises that the fear is well-founded when there is a 'reasonable possibility' that the applicant will be persecuted or will suffer serious harm if returned to the country of origin (ie, 'real and substantial danger' or 'reasonable likelihood' or 'real or substantial risk'); it does not require 'a clear probability' but it requires more than 'the mere chance or remote possibility'.[30] It also endorses the principle of refugee law that past persecution strongly indicates a reasonable possibility of future persecution and extends this principle to other acts causing serious harm.[31] It further recognises that in assessing whether or not an applicant has a well-founded fear, it is immaterial whether the applicant is a victim of generalised violence;[32] this principle goes beyond the standard set in refugee law and human rights law. On the downside, the Commission Proposal says nothing about the burden of proof.[33]

**Draft Council Directive**

There is some re-ordering of content in the draft Council Directive. Article 5 of the Commission Proposal has been deleted and its content transferred to article 2 of the Directive concerned with 'definitions'. According to article 2(c), a refugee is still defined by reference to the '*well-founded fear of being persecuted* on grounds of race, religion, etc' (my emphasis). However, under article 2(e), eligibility for subsidiary protection is now reserved for those individuals 'in respect of whom substantial grounds have been shown for believing that the person concerned, if returned [...] would face a *real risk of suffering serious harm*' (my emphasis). It follows that the Member States decided to revert to the traditional distinction between the refugee law test (ie, the well-founded fear) and the human rights law test (ie, the real risk) when considering who will be eligible for international protection.

At first reading, the draft Directive is a real step backwards in terms of developing a common normative framework for asylum in Europe, because it applies different tests in determining eligibility for Convention protection

[30] Article 7(b) of the Qualification Directive and Explanatory Memorandum, 15.
[31] Article 7 ( c).
[32] Article 11(2)(c) and article 15(c).
[33] The Explanatory Memorandum (p 14) nevertheless acknowledges the principle of refugee law that the burden of proof lies in principle with the applicant but that the duty to ascertain and evaluate information on the human rights situation in the country of origin is shared between the applicant and the examiner. *UNHCR Handbook*, para 196.

and subsidiary protection. In contrast, the Commission Proposal not only promised a common test for both Convention protection and subsidiary protection, but also one which conformed to the higher standard of the Geneva Convention. Upon closer reading, it is evident that while the draft Directive maintains the two tests approach, it nonetheless applies the higher standard of refugee law by endorsing the key principle that applicants should *generally* be given the benefit of the doubt regardless of which test is applied.[34] This conforms to the practice of most Member States which have found it necessary *not* to be too restrictive in applying the 'real risk' test for subsidiary protection, which itself is suggestive of the ethical and policy desirability of institutionalising in law the less restrictive 'well-founded test' for all forms of international protection

## PERSECUTION AND SERIOUS HARM UNDER THE COMMISSION PROPOSAL AND THE DRAFT COUNCIL DIRECTIVE

Another critical aspect in determining eligibility for international protection is the existence of persecution or of other serious harm. Here I see it as important for the future of international protection in the EU that both concepts be defined by drawing upon both refugee law and human rights law.

### Persecution in Refugee Law

There exists no comprehensive definition of the word 'persecution' in international law. The UNHCR Handbook notes that 'a threat to life or freedom on account of race, religion, nationality, political opinion or membership of a particular social group is always persecution. Other serious violations of human rights — for the same reasons — would also constitute persecution'.[35] Hathaway in particular considers persecution to be the sustained or systemic denial of a basic human right.[36] Persecution has often been found to require a serious harm which is not limited to severe physical harm or threats to life or freedom, but which must be read in the context of the principle of non-discrimination.[37] UK courts have adopted this wider interpretation.[38] The UNHCR also recognises the cumulative effect of

[34] Article 7(5). It also endorses the principle that 'that which happened in the past may happen in the future' unless there are 'good reasons' to consider that such persecution or serious harm will not be repeated. See *(Regina) Hohxa v Special Adjudicator* [2002] EWCA Civ 1403.
[35] Para 51.
[36] J Hathaway, *The Law of Refugee Status* (Toronto, Butterworths, 1991) at 112.
[37] Hathaway above n 36 at 105. *UNHCR Handbook*, paras 53–55.
[38] Per Lord Lloyds of Berwick, *Horvath v Secretary of State for the Home Department* [2000] 3 WLR 391A.

certain measures which in themselves may not amount to persecution. Thus some forms of discrimination may amount to persecution if combined with other adverse factors, such as a general atmosphere of insecurity in the country of origin.[39] Furthermore, discrimination per se does not amount to persecution except in cases where it leads 'to consequences of a substantially prejudicial nature for the person concerned'.[40] The UNHCR even recognises that measures of discrimination which are not of a serious character 'may nevertheless give rise to a reasonable fear of persecution if they produce, in the mind of the person concerned, a feeling of apprehension and insecurity as regards his future existence'.[41] The above UNHCR guidelines have generally been well received by states. Finally, it is recognised that persecution although normally related to action by state's authorities, may also be committed by private individuals if they are knowingly tolerated by the authorities or if the authorities refuse, or prove unable, to offer effective protection.[42] The issue of what constitutes effective state protection against persecution in cases where the agent of persecution is not the State, is at the core of the definition of persecution in refugee law. It is generally accepted that effectiveness may be measures against two standards. The minimal standard is whether there exists in the country a system of criminal law which makes violent attacks by the persecutors punishable and a reasonable willingness to enforce that law on the part of the state. A more effective standard requires that the protection by the state to be such that it cannot be said that the person has a well-founded fear. At present, the House of Lords in the UK has opted for the former test, whereas the Refugee Status Appeals Authority in New Zealand has opted for the latter.[43]

## Serious Harm in Human Rights Law

In this section, again I concentrate on the most important human rights instrument in Europe, ie, the ECHR and case-law of the European Court of Human Rights. Although the words 'serious harm' have never actually been

[39] *UNHCR Handbook*, para 53.
[40] *UNHCR Handbook*, para 54. See also, *UNHCR Guidelines on International Protection: Gender-Related Persecution within the Context of Article 1A(2) of the 1951 Convention and/or 1967 Protocol relating to the Status of Refugees* (7 May 2002), para 14 (reproduced in (2002) 14 *International Journal of Refugee Law*, 457–70.
[41] *UNHCR Handbook*, para 55.
[42] *UNHCR Handbook*, para 65.
[43] As per Lord Hope of Craighead, *Horvath v Secretary of State for the Home Department* [2000] 3 WLR 382G. Refugee Appeal No 71427/99, decision of 16 August 2000, para 63. To read more on this issue, see H Lambert, 'The Conceptualisation of 'Persecution' by the House of Lords: *Horvath v Secretary of State for the Home Department*', (2001) 13 *International Journal of Refugee Law*, 16–31.

used by the European Court of Human Rights,[44] they refer to a well-known concept in human rights law, in the sense that ill-treatment (ie, harm) must attain a certain level of severity for it to fall under the scope of article 3 ECHR. What constitutes torture or inhuman or degrading treatment or punishment under article 3 ECHR is in the nature of things relative and it depends on the circumstances of each case.[45] Furthermore, the distinction between 'inhuman and degrading treatment' and 'torture' is not fixed because the European Court of Human Rights regards the ECHR as a living instrument. Thus acts which in the past may have been classified as 'inhuman and degrading' as opposed to 'torture' may in future be classified differently. This is due to 'the increasingly high standard being required in the area of the protection of human rights'.[46] Harm does not need to be physical to be considered unlawful. The European Commission of Human Rights, for instance, found that racial discrimination may constitute an interference with the applicants' human dignity and amount to 'degrading treatment' in the sense of article 3 ECHR.[47] Also the European Court of Human Rights recognises the application of article 3 ECHR from the cumulative effect of ill-treatment, which if taken individually would not reach the threshold of severity required by article 3.[48] When at the hand of non-state agent, the European Court of Human Rights recognises a risk of ill-treatment contrary to article 3 if state protection is found to be ineffective. The Court focuses on the risk and the elimination of that risk. It views the duty of state protection in terms of negative obligation (ie, the obligation to refrain from acts contrary to the ECHR) and positive obligation (ie, the obligation to act in order to safeguard the rights of those within its jurisdiction). According to the Court, the latter also implies 'a positive obligation on the authorities to take preventive operational measures to protect an individual whose life is at risk from the criminal acts of another individual'.[49] This led the Court to conclude that when faced with an alleged violation of a positive obligation, 'it is sufficient for an applicant to show that the authorities did not do all that could be reasonably expected of them to avoid a real and immediate risk to life of which they have or

[44] These words can only be found in the 'domestic law' part or the 'dissenting opinion' part of the Court's judgments. Eg, dissenting opinions in the case of *Cruz Varas v Sweden*, application No 15576/89 and in the case of *Nsona v The Netherlands*, application No 23366/94.

[45] *Ireland v UK*, application No 5310/71.

[46] *Selmouni v France*, application No 25803/94, para 101.

[47] *East Africans Asians v United Kingdom*, para 208.

[48] Eg, *Ahmed v Austria*, application No 25964/94, and *HLR v France*, application No 24573/94.

[49] Albeit in a reasonable way, that is, 'in a way which does not impose an impossible or disproportionate burden on the authorities'. *Osman v United Kingdom*, application No 23452/94, paras 115–16.

ought to have knowledge'.[50] This is a higher standard than the one used in the UK in refugee law cases.

## Commission Proposal

There is no evidence in the definition of persecution in the Commission Proposal of the use of human rights law as basic standards for determining the existing of persecution. The definition of a refugee in article 5(1) of the Commission Proposal refers to the well-known notion in refugee law of 'being persecuted' on five grounds which incorporates the issue of the sufficiency of state protection as an inherent element in the inquiry.[51] The Proposal is satisfied that effective state protection exists where 'the State takes reasonable steps to prevent the persecution or infliction of harm', and where 'the applicant has reasonable access to such protection. There must be in place a system of domestic protection and machinery for the detection, prosecution and punishment of actions which constitute persecution or other serious and unjustified harm'.[52] According to this standard, the effectiveness of state protection is measured against the availability of a system of protection for the citizen and a reasonable willingness to operate that system. As noted above, this is a standard based on states practice, in particular the UK;[53] it is not one applied by the European Court of Human Rights.[54]

More specifically, article 11(1) of the Proposal defines 'persecution' by reference to four situations summarised as follows: the act in question must be sufficiently serious by its nature or repetition to prevent return to the country of origin, the act in question may take the form of legal, administrative, police and/or judicial measures which are in themselves discriminatory or implemented in a discriminatory manner, or it may take the form of prosecution or punishment which is disproportionate or discriminatory or which may lead to a denial of judicial redress. In all these situations persecution has to be on one of five grounds: race, religion, nationality, political opinion or membership of a particular social group. This definition is clearly based on the Geneva Convention without actually using the same wording as in article 1A(2) thus potentially leading to the fragmentation of the concept of persecution.[55]

[50] *Osman v United Kingdom*, application No 23452/94, para 116. See also *A v United Kingdom*, application No 25599/94, para 22.
[51] See article 11(2)(a).
[52] Article 9(2).
[53] *Horvath v Secretary of State for the Home Department* [2001] 1 AC 489 (HL), [2000] 3 WLR 379.
[54] *Osman v United Kingdom*, application No 23452/94.
[55] J McAdam, 'The European Union proposal on subsidiary protection: An analysis and assessment', UNHCR Working Paper No 74 (2002), at p 10.

There is also a problem with the definition of harm in the Commission Proposal. For beneficiaries of subsidiary protection, article 5(2) refers to the notion of 'suffering serious and unjustified harm' which is unclear in human rights law. As mentioned above, the notion of 'serious harm' is well-known in human rights law only in the sense that ill-treatment must attain a certain threshold of severity for it to fall under article 3 ECHR. The notion of 'unjustified harm' however is alien to refugee law and human rights law, even though the word 'unjustified' is well-known to the European Court of Human Rights in the context of interference with, for instance, family life under article 8 ECHR. As pointed out by Goodwin-Gill and Hurwitz, reference to the notion of 'unjustified harm' is a matter of concern because it allows for situations in which a state may be justified in taking measures that would cause harm to individuals (eg, in cases of national emergency or national security), ignoring the fact that the prohibition under article 3 ECHR is absolute and that the norm prohibiting torture has acquired the status of *jus cogens*.[56] On the other hand, the Commission Proposal offers a broad definition of 'serious and unjustified harm' which in addition to torture, degrading treatment, etc, includes also 'severe' and 'generalised' violations of human rights. This generous definition has the potential of covering several articles of the ECHR, in particular articles 2, 3, 5, 6 or 8. Also the entitlement to protection in situations of generalised violence in both cases of persecution or of serious harm must be welcome for it is consistent with the standards set in other regions, in particular Africa and South America.[57]

### Draft Council Directive

There are both good and bad points with regard to the draft Council Directive. In terms of refugees, the definition of 'persecution' is firmly set in a human rights context. Thus, acts of persecution must 'be sufficiently serious by their nature or repetition as to constitute a severe violation of basic human rights'.[58] However, there is also a downside, in that the focus is only on those rights protected under the ECHR from which no derogation is allowed. Excluded therefore are broader civil and political rights, such as protection against arbitrary detention or protection for family life. It also excludes all economic, social and cultural rights protected by other

[56] G Goodwin-Gill and A Hurwitz, 'Draft Council Directive on minimum standards for the qualification and status of third country nationals and stateless persons as refugees or as persons who otherwise need international protection', submission to the House of Lords, April 2002, at 1–2.

[57] OAU Convention Governing the Specific Aspects of Refugee Problems in Africa (1969) and OAS Cartagena Declaration on Refugees (1984).

[58] Article 11(1)(a).

instruments of human rights law.[59] Another downside is that, like the Commission Proposal, the draft Council Directive rejects the standard of effective state protection applied by the European Court of Human Rights, in favour of the minimum standard based on states practice.[60]

As regards the form that these acts may take, the draft Council Directive includes all those listed in the Proposal. It also adds 'acts of physical or mental violence, including acts of sexual violence' and 'acts of a gender-specific or child-specific nature'.[61] This is a significant improvement from the original Proposal, where reference to gender-specific or child-specific persecution was only mentioned in the context of the assessment of applications for international protection. In this regard, the draft Directive goes beyond the principles of refugee law by expressly providing that persecution may be child-specific.[62]

As far as subsidiary protection is concerned, the Member States decisions to abandon reference to the unclear notion of 'unjustified harm' is to be welcome. However, the draft Directive definition of 'serious harm' has become more restrictive than in the original Proposal. Thus, there is no longer any reference to the general concept of severe violations of human rights as in the original Proposal; the draft Directive is now targeting two specific types of harm in the ECHR: death penalty under Protocol 6 and ill-treatment under article 3. This means that all other violations of human rights fall outside the scope of this Directive and remain in the discretionary domain of the Member States. In addition, 'generalised violence' is now conceived in terms of threats to individuals, a more narrow concept from the original Proposal and from existing states practice (with the exception of France).[63]

## CONCLUSION

In conclusion, I want to briefly consider three questions. First, to what extent are the Commission Proposal and draft Council Directive drawing on refugee and human rights law? Both areas of law inform the Commission Proposal and draft Directive. Predictably, refugee law impacts

[59] For example, Hathaway argues that in some extreme cases, the denial of the right to food, shelter or health care may be considered as persecution — Hathaway above n 36, 110–11.
[60] Article 9A.
[61] Article 11(2).
[62] For gender-related persecution, see UNHCR Guidelines (7 May 2002) IJRL 14 (2002). For child-specific persecution, see Summary Note on UNHCR's Strategy and Activities concerning Refugee Children (May 2002), available at *http://www.unhcr.ch*.
[63] D Bouteillet-Paquet, 'Quelle harmonisation européenne en matière d'asile après Tampere?' (121) *Revue du droit des étrangers* (n spécial) actes de colloque des 23 et 24 october (2002) 759–76.

most strongly on Convention protection and likewise human rights law on subsidiary protection. But there is some cross-fertilisation. Persecution is defined by reference to human rights law, and the refugee law principle of the benefit of the doubt is extended to subsidiary protection. Second, to what extent do the Commission Proposal and draft Directive suggest the merging of Convention protection and subsidiary protection? The Commission Proposal was promising on this score, in that it provided one standard of proof — the 'well-founded fear' test — for assessing eligibility for both Convention and subsidiary protection. Equally, the draft Directive is a step backwards because it reverts to the separate 'real risk' test for subsidiary protection. This is a curious move since, from the viewpoint of the applicant, there is little difference in how states apply the two tests. Third, and last question, will the final Council Directive raise the standard of international protection in the EU? As I've discussed, some good points in the Commission Proposal have survived the drafting of the Council Directive, and the draft Directive does improve on the Commission Proposal in its definition of persecution. Nevertheless, there is a missed opportunity here. By failing to pave the way for the merging of Convention and subsidiary protection, the draft Directive institutionalises the current two-tier system of protection in Europe. We've missed the opportunity, with this Directive at least, to develop a common normative system of international protection for the EU in the new century.[64]

[64] There remains an opportunity in the form of the proposal for a Directive on minimum standards on procedures in Member States for granting and withdrawing refugees status (COM (2002) 326 final).

# 22

# *Asylum and Immigration in the Context of Enlargement*

CATHERINE PHUONG[1]

THE FIFTH ENLARGEMENT of the European Union took place in May 2004. Ten countries, mainly from Central and Eastern Europe, have finally become members of the much sought-after club after a lengthy and complex pre-accession process.[2] The ten new Member States are Cyprus, the Czech Republic, Hungary, Malta, Poland, Slovakia, Slovenia and the three Baltic states (Estonia, Latvia and Lithuania). In about 2007, Bulgaria and Romania will probably also become Member States. Previous enlargements have taken place,[3] but there is no doubt that this new wave of enlargement is unprecedented not only in terms of scale, but also for its political significance: for the candidate states, EU membership signals European (re-)unification after decades of political isolation.

Much has already been written about the impact of eastward enlargement on the EU's institutional framework and current EU policies. This chapter deals with the impact of enlargement on the regulation of future intra-Community migration flows, as well as migration flows from outside the enlarged EU. It examines current Member States' response to anticipated migration movements from the new States and increasing migration from further East. The chapter argues that the restrictive logic currently followed by EU Member States is being imposed on candidate countries. In particular, it will demonstrate that recent changes in the asylum and immigration laws of candidate countries have been largely affected by current EU efforts to devise a common immigration policy

[1] I would like to thank Ann Sinclair for her research assistance. The author alone is responsible for the opinions expressed in this paper.

[2] For more detail on the pre-accession process, see M Maresceau, 'Pre-accession', in M Cremona (ed), *The Enlargement of the European Union* (Oxford, Oxford University Press, 2003), 9–42.

[3] Denmark, Ireland and the UK first joined in 1973, Greece in 1981, Spain and Portugal in 1986, and Austria, Finland and Sweden in 1995.

and a possible common asylum system. Instead of formulating their own response to migration, candidate countries are merely aligning their asylum and immigration laws and policies with EU practice and expectations.

Because of their geographical location, candidate countries will be responsible for policing the new eastern border of the EU and receiving asylum seekers and other migrants travelling from further East. Cyprus and Malta are thus excluded from the analysis which only examines the candidate countries from Central and Eastern Europe. Current Member States are very concerned about illegal immigration from further east and are putting considerable pressure on candidate countries to set up efficient asylum systems and, more importantly to them, strict border controls. Until recently, most of the academic literature had concentrated on the emergence of EU immigration and asylum laws under Title IV which was introduced at Amsterdam in 1998.[4] Little attention has so far been given to the impact of these developments on candidate countries.[5]

## RESTRICTING ASYLUM AND ECONOMIC MIGRATION FROM THE NEW MEMBER STATES

As far as current Member States are concerned, a crucial matter in the accession negotiations was to control future asylum and economic migration flows from the new Member States. Controlling asylum migration is relatively simple since there is already a mechanism in place which denies EU citizens access to asylum procedures in any Member State. Regulating economic migration from the new Member States has proved more problematic since freedom of movement of workers has been one of the most important principles established by the Treaty of Rome.

### Denying Access to Refugee Protection

The Protocol on asylum for nationals of Member States of the European Union, the so-called 'Aznar Protocol', was annexed to the Treaty of

[4] See for instance see E Guild and C Harlow (eds), *Implementing Amsterdam: immigration and asylum rights in EC law* (Oxford, Hart Publishing, 2001); K Hailbronner, 'European immigration and asylum law under the Amsterdam treaty' (1998) 35 *Common Market Law Review* 1047; D O'Keeffe, 'Can the leopard change its spots? Visas, immigration and asylum — following Amsterdam', in D O'Keeffe and P Twomey (eds), *Legal issues of the Treaty of Amsterdam* (Oxford, Hart Publishing, 1999), 271–88.

[5] For recent studies of asylum and immigration laws in candidate countries, see R Byrne, G Noll and J Vested-Hansen (eds), *New asylum countries? Migration control and refugee protection in an enlarged European Union* (The Hague, Kluwer Law International, 2002), and F Laczko et al (eds), *New challenges for migration policy in Central and Eastern Europe* (Geneva, IOM, ICPMD and TMC Asser Press, 2002).

Amsterdam in 1998. It establishes that no national from any EU country can be granted asylum in any other Member States. Such a rule is based on the clear presumption that all EU Member states are safe countries of origin: considering their human rights record, no one can possibly be subject to political persecution in any EU Member State. Any asylum application made by an EU national will be only be taken into consideration if the country of origin formally derogates from the European Convention on Human Rights,[6] or is determined under article 7 TEU to be a serious and persistent violator of human rights. Otherwise, each Member State can decide to examine an asylum application lodged by a national of another Member State, but it must inform the Council of such a decision. The Protocol was proposed by Spain which disapproved of France and Belgium refusing to extradite members of the Basque nationalist organisation ETA.[7] Not all Member States fully agreed with the Protocol and Belgium made a Declaration stating that it would still examine asylum applications from EU nationals.[8] The Protocol was also criticised by the UN refugee agency, UNHCR.[9]

The Protocol will automatically apply to the new Member States. It will not be a completely new policy for them. When Central and Eastern European countries became members of the Council of Europe in the early 1990s, EU Member States took the opportunity to declare them safe third countries, despite their unsatisfactory asylum legislation. If these countries were considered to be safe third countries, asylum seekers who had travelled to the EU via these countries could be returned there without their application being examined in substance in any EU Member State. Similarly, some Central and Eastern European countries were also declared safe countries of origin where there was a presumption of protection: no genuine asylum seeker could come from such countries.[10] In order to ensure returns to safe third countries and safe countries of origin in Central and Eastern Europe, EU Member States concluded a series of readmission agreements with most countries in the region. In effect, EU Member States have been using these agreements to transfer the 'asylum burden' to Central and Eastern European countries.

One would suggest that the general extension of the safe country of origin rule to all new Member States may not be justified. There are still a number of asylum seekers, mainly Romas, coming from candidate

[6] *European Convention for the Protection of Human Rights and Fundamental Freedoms*, 4 November 1950, 213 *UNTS* 221.

[7] See K Landgren, 'Deflecting international protection by treaty: bilateral and multilateral accords on extradition, readmission and the inadmissibility of asylum requests', *New issues in refugee research*, Working Paper No 10, June 1999, 33–34.

[8] *Ibid*, 16–17.

[9] *Ibid*, 12.

[10] See D Bouteillet-Paquet, *L'Europe et le droit d'asile* (Paris, L'Harmattan, 2001), 279–80.

countries. It appears that some of them may suffer real persecution by state authorities and/or the local population. These individuals should not be denied access to protection in other EU Member States. In 2001, there were more than 14,000 asylum applications lodged in Europe (EU and candidate countries) from Bulgaria, Romania, Slovakia and even Poland.[11] Very few are granted asylum, but a small minority are given some humanitarian status, eg exceptional leave to remain.[12] One can also challenge the validity of the safe country of origin rule since protection should in principle be awarded after an assessment of each individual situation.

## Postponing Economic Migration

Although migration from Central and Eastern Europe initially increased after the fall of the Iron Curtain, it has stabilised and even decreased since 1993.[13] Labour mobility within the reunified Germany has been substantial, but it must be noted that migrants were moving within the same country, ie to areas where the same language was spoken and where they may have relatives and/or friends.[14] There has been a fear, notably in Germany and Austria, of a mass influx of migrants from the East similar to that witnessed in the final months leading to the fall of the Berlin Wall in 1989.[15] Nevertheless, fears about migration from the East do not date from the 1990s: the long tradition of labour migration from countries like Poland goes back to the mid-19th century and coincides with the industrial revolution in Western Europe.

One of the main concerns of the general public with regard to the impending enlargement is the arrival of cheap labour from the new Member States. The entire EU *acquis* should normally apply to any new Member State of the Union and one would have expected that nationals of the new countries would benefit from the whole range of rights granted by EC law to all EC nationals upon accession. However, in response to

[11] See *UNHCR Statistical Yearbook 2001, Refugees, Asylum-seekers and Other Persons of Concern-Trends in Displacement. Protection and Solutions,* October 2002, Geneva, Annex C.7.

[12] See for instance *Asylum statistics United Kingdom 2002,* HOSB 8/03, tables 3.1 and 3.2, *http://www.homeoffice.gov.uk/rds/pdfs2/hosb803.pdf.*

[13] See Statement by Mr Jonas Widgren, Director of the International Centre for Migration Policy Development at the EU enlargement Seminar in Stockholm on 28 September 2000, 'The EU enlargement — migration and free movement of labour: threat or opportunity', *http://www.icmpd.org/uploadimg/EU%20EnlargmentMigration%20Stockholm%20Seminar%20280900.pdf.*

[14] See J Hunt, 'Lessons from East Germany on labor mobility', in B Funck and L Pizzati (eds), *Labor, employment, and social policies in the EU enlargement process: changing perspectives and policy options* (Washington DC, The World Bank, 2002), 197–206, at 202.

[15] See J Zielonka, 'How new enlarged borders will reshape the European Union' (2001) 39 *Journal of Common Market Studies* 507, at 520.

the public's concerns, the Commission suggested that free movement of labour may not be granted immediately and that several options were available for negotiation with candidate countries. These options ranged from full and immediate application of the *acquis*, to fixed quota systems and general non-application of the *acquis* for a limited period of time.[16] Member States opted for transitional arrangements which were presented to candidate countries at a fairly late date in the accession negotiations. Some candidate countries were initially reluctant to accept the deal.[17] Transitional agreements are usually concluded for the benefit of the acceding State which is given 'the chance to incrementally adapt their national regulations in some sectors to the Community law',[18] but this is not the case here.

Negotiations on transitional provisions for the free movement of workers have now been concluded. The transitional provisions establish that free movement can be delayed for up to seven years after accession.[19] For the first two years, EU Member States will apply national legislation to regulate the employment rights of nationals from the new Member States. For the next three years, they will be free to apply the EU *acquis* and remove obstacles to free movement of workers, or continue to apply national rules. This transitional period can be extended for a further two years in case of serious disturbances of the labour market or threat thereof. However, access to current Member States' labour markets cannot be restricted from the time of accession and during the whole transitional period (standstill clause). In addition, preference will be given to the nationals of the new Member States over third country nationals. One must also note that nationals from candidate countries already have a limited right of establishment (as self-employed persons and to set up and manage undertakings) under the Europe Agreements which were signed between the EU and each candidate country in the 1990s.[20]

[16] See European Commission Information Note, *The free movement of workers in the context of enlargement*, 6 March 2001.

[17] On the Polish reaction, see E Jileva, 'Visa and free movement of labour: the uneven imposition of the EU acquis on the accession states' (2002) 28 *Journal of Ethnic and Migration Studies* 683, at 696.

[18] See U Becker, 'EU-enlargements and limits to amendments of the EC Treaty', Jean Monnet Working Paper 15/01, 6.

[19] See Annexes V, VI, VIII, IX, X, XII, XIII, XIV to the Act of Accession.

[20] See Cases 63/99 *R v Secretary of State for the Home Department, ex parte Gloszczuk and Gloszczuk* [2001] 3 CMLR 46, *235/99; R v Secretary of State for the Home Department, ex parte Kondova* [2001] 3 CMLR 47, *257/99; R v Secretary of State for the Home Department, ex parte Barkoci and Malik* [2001] 3 CMLR 48. For comments, see B Bogusz, 'Regulating the right of establishment for accession state nationals: reinforcing the 'buffer zone' or improving labour market flexibility' (2002) 27 *European Law Review* 472 and A Pedain, ' "With or without me": the ECJ adopts a pose of studied neutrality towards EU enlargement' (2002) 51 *International and Comparative Law Quarterly* 981.

The negotiation of these transitional agreements has been based on inconclusive studies assessing possible migration pressure following enlargement. A detailed review of such studies is beyond the scope of this chapter.[21] Nevertheless, it should be noted that most studies predict that between 3 and 4% of the population in candidate countries will move to Western European countries. This amounts to about 2.5 million people. Among those, as many as half may return to their country of origin within ten years. However, there is disagreement on how long this migration flow will last. Simplistic surveys of reported intentions concluding that up to 40% of the population may come and seek employment in the current Member States do not give any clear indication of future migration flows:[22] when asked whether they would consider moving to Western Europe, most nationals of candidate countries respond in the affirmative, but this does not demonstrate that their intentions are serious. It is more likely that any immediate and substantial migration flow will decrease within a few years as economic conditions improve in the new States. Moreover, the overwhelming majority of migrants will go to border regions in Germany and Austria. It has been demonstrated that in the longer term, trade acts as a substitute for migration and economic integration should therefore reduce economically motivated migration.[23]

In the short term, a temporary influx of young and well-educated workers from the new Member States[24] may be a reasonable price to pay for less migration in the longer term. Some Western European countries, in particular Germany, may benefit from such an influx of workers to bring some dynamism to their ageing societies and slowing economies. Such countries which seek to attract highly skilled migrants forget that many workers from the new Member States would actually prefer to migrate to North America and Australasia.[25] The best qualified migrants might just do so if access to the Western European labour market is too restricted. More fundamentally, the transitional agreements create the impression that the nationals of the new States are 'second-class' citizens: the right to work in another Member State is one of the most well-recognised and relevant rights granted to EU citizens. It is thus regrettable that this right was not extended to the citizens of the new States. Whereas enlargement should be about inclusion, the differential legal treatment of two groups of EU citizens indicates that new forms of exclusion may appear within the EU.

[21] For a comparative analysis of the various surveys available, see H Fassmann and R Muenz, 'EU enlargement and future East-West migration', in F Laczko et al (eds), *New challenges for migration policy* (The Hague, Kluwer Law International, 2002), 59–86.

[22] See for instance F Laczko, 'Introduction', in F Laczko et al, *ibid* 1–9, at 5.

[23] See P Martin, *Economic integration and migration: the Mexico-US case,* WIDER discussion paper No 2003/35, April 2003, 9–12.

[24] See Fassmann and Muenz, above n 21, 72.

[25] See M Anderson, 'Border regimes and security in an enlarged European Community: implication of the entry into force of the Amsterdam Treaty', RSC paper 2000/8, 21.

When Greece joined the EC in 1981, and Spain and Portugal did the same in 1986, transitional agreements on free movement of labour were also concluded. As migration pressure did not appear to increase in the years following accession, the transitional periods were subsequently shortened. The granting of free movement rights did not produce marked increases in overall worker mobility within the EC.[26] One could argue that the wage differential between North Western European States and Southern European States was not as important as the wage differential between current Member States and candidate countries. Be that as it may, several Member States, including Denmark, Greece, Ireland, the Netherlands, Sweden and the UK, have already announced that they will grant workers from the new Member States full rights of free movement upon accession.[27] It thus appears that transitional provisions may have been negotiated almost exclusively for Germany and Austria. The problems that these two countries will face could be addressed through other less radical means. Allowing immediate freedom of movement of labour and calling for increased support for regional disturbances in certain border areas may be more appropriate than insisting on restrictions that will not discourage illegal labour migration. Finally, it is ironic that the Commission's position is to encourage the free movement of workers within the EU,[28] but when actually confronted with a significant potential movement of workers, Member States' inclination is to adopt the opposite stance.[29]

## HELPING THEM TO HELP US CONTROL MIGRATION INTO THE ENLARGED EU

Once the EU expands eastwards, current Member States will no longer be able to control entries at the new eastern border. Since the new Member States will eventually become part of the Schengen area in which internal border controls have been removed, it is crucial that they are able to police their eastern borders and deal with asylum seekers arriving from unstable areas further East. The effects of EU membership on the asylum and immigration laws of the candidate countries are already visible. I will identify here which changes have been and are still being implemented in candidate countries in order to fulfil the conditions of membership. These changes must be understood within the context of the emerging EU immigration and asylum regime.

[26] See C Dustmann, *The impact of EU enlargement on migration flows*, Home Office Online Report 25/03, 41–46.

[27] See 'EU: asylum, aid', *Migration News*, April 2003, vol 10, no 2, *http://migration.ucdavis.edu.*

[28] Only about 1.5% of EU nationals live and work in a Member State other than their state of nationality.

[29] See Jileva, above n 17, 696.

## Setting up 'Efficient' Asylum Systems

EU asylum policy is being transferred to candidate countries which are under considerable pressure to adopt 'efficient' asylum systems. These systems must be 'efficient' to the extent that they must provide adequate protection to asylum seekers, but also act as a deterrent to those who do not have a genuine need for protection. Consequently, candidate countries have to adopt restrictive measures such as applying the safe country of origin and the safe third countries concepts, implementing accelerated procedures, signing readmission agreements, etc. While it is true that candidate countries have recently witnessed an influx of asylum seekers and thus need the legal framework to deal with them, it is argued here that some of these changes may not be entirely appropriate for these countries which are in a different migration situation to current EU Member States.

During the Cold War, the countries examined here were mainly refugee-producing countries. The only country to have received some asylum seekers in the late 1980s was Hungary which took on refugees from neighbouring Romania.[30] In the early 1990s, it also received asylum seekers from the former Yugoslavia but most of these returned to their country of origin as soon as the security conditions had improved. Since the mid-1990s, most candidate countries have become transit countries for people wanting to seek asylum further west. The number of asylum applications has increased in most candidate countries but there are substantial differences between the countries. Indeed, the Baltic countries still receive a relatively low number of asylum applications whereas countries like the Czech Republic and Hungary have seen a dramatic increase in the number of asylum applications. Nevertheless, when compared to the numbers of asylum applications lodged in Western European countries, candidate countries clearly do not face the same pressures.

So far, most asylum seekers in candidate countries have not actually remained in these countries and have often attempted to move to Western Europe. Since border controls are still relatively strict between current EU Member States and candidate countries, these asylum seekers often remain 'trapped' in candidate countries which form a buffer zone between Western Europe and poorer and more unstable regions in Asia. The combination of migration pressure from the East following the disintegration of the Soviet Union and restrictive migration policies in the EU have led Central and Eastern European countries to become countries of destination. This phenomenon has been described as the 'closed sack' effect.[31] This situation

[30] See C Wallace, 'Opening and closing borders: migration and mobility in East-Central Europe' (2002) 28 *Journal of Ethnic and Migration Studies* 603, at 609.

[31] See R Byrne, G Noll and J Vested-Hansen, 'Western European asylum policies for export: the transfer of protection and deflection formulas to Central Europe and the Baltics', in Byrne et al, above n 5, 5–28, at 28.

will be confirmed with EU accession: more asylum seekers will target the new Member States as countries of destination. To anticipate this change and in order to gain EU membership, these countries have been encouraged to implement major changes to their asylum laws and policies.

**Numbers claiming asylum in candidate countries (1992–2001)**

| | 1992 | 1995 | 1998 | 2001 |
|---|---|---|---|---|
| Czech Republic | 817 | 1,413 | 4,082 | 18,087 |
| Estonia | - | - | 23 | 12 |
| Hungary | 458 | 130 | 7,097 | 9,554 |
| Latvia | - | - | 58 | 14 |
| Lithuania | - | - | 163 | 256 |
| Poland | 592 | 843 | 3,373 | 4,506 |
| Slovakia | 87 | 359 | 506 | 8,151 |
| Slovenia | | 499 | | 1,511 |

Source: *UNHCR Statistical Yearbook 2001, Refugees, Asylum-seekers and Other Persons of Concern-Trends in Displacement. Protection and Solutions,* October 2002, Geneva, Annex C.1.

Before the end of the Cold War, there were no procedures for determining refugee status in Central and Eastern European countries, and no provisions regulating the situation of asylum seekers and refugees, because there was just no need for asylum systems in the former Communist states. As the first asylum seekers arrived in these countries in the early 1990s, the first generation of asylum legislation was hurriedly adopted. At the same time, all Central and Eastern European countries became parties to the 1951 Geneva Convention on the Status of Refugees and its 1967 Protocol.[32] Nevertheless, the asylum systems initially set up in these countries raised some problems in terms of refugee protection standards.[33] This was to be expected since there was a lack of a tradition of asylum and/or a human rights culture. When the EU realised this, more attention was paid to asylum matters in the accession strategy.[34] Originally, candidate countries adopted relatively generous policies towards asylum seekers because they had not yet realised the impact of

[32] *Convention Relating to the Status of Refugees*, 28 July 1951, 189 UNTS 1950 and *Protocol Relating to the Status of Refugees*, 31 January 1967, 606 UNTS 267. See UNHCR, *State parties to the 1951 Convention relating to the Status of Refugees and the 1967 Protocol as of 1 June 2003*, at *http://www.unhcr.ch*. Hungary had already been a party to the 1951 Convention since 1989.

[33] See Bouteillet-Paquet, above n 10, 333.

[34] S Lavenex, 'Asylum, immigration, and Central-Eastern Europe: challenges to EU enlargement' (1998) 3 *European Foreign Affairs Review* 275, at 277.

future EU accession and also thought that the influx of asylum seekers was going to be temporary.[35] This attitude towards asylum seekers soon had to be modified as all candidate countries found themselves under obligation to adopt the EU asylum acquis and align their practices to the current restrictive EU policies. A second generation of asylum legislation was adopted in most candidate countries in the late 1990s in order to reflect these changes.[36] In addition, one project, funded by the Phare Programme, was implemented in April 1998 in order to help candidate countries adapt their asylum legislation. The Joint Support Program on the Application of the EU Acquis on Asylum and Related Standards and Practices in the Associated Countries of Central and Eastern Europe resulted from co-operation between the Commission, UNHCR and the German Federal Office for the Recognition of Refugees, with the assistance of six other Member States (Austria, Denmark, France, the Netherlands, Spain and Sweden).[37]

EU assistance to candidate countries in the field of asylum has two underlying objectives. Firstly, it is in the interest of current Member States, most notably Germany, to improve asylum systems in candidate countries. Indeed, if these countries implement refugee protection standards that are equivalent to those of Western European states, such states will have less difficulty justifying returns of asylum seekers because they will benefit from an equivalent level of protection in candidate countries. In other words, by improving protection capacities in candidate countries, Member States are preparing them to receive returned asylum seekers and hoping that they will be able to shift the 'asylum burden' eastwards.[38] Although the motivation of Member States can be seen as problematic, EU pressure to implement changes in the asylum systems of candidate countries has brought about some positive consequences. Asylum procedures have been adopted and/or improved, specialised administrative structures have been set up to deal with asylum seekers and refugees, support groups have been created, and so on. It must be noted, though, that significant differences remain between candidate countries, with the Czech Republic, Poland and Slovenia much ahead of the others. The second objective of EU efforts to modify asylum systems in candidate countries is to ensure that these countries do not become too attractive to asylum seekers: they must therefore also adopt deterrence measures similar to those in place in Western Europe.

[35] See Bouteillet-Paquet, above n 10, at 334.
[36] See for instance Czech Republic: Act No 325 of 11 November 1999 on Asylum, Estonia: Law on Refugees of 18 February 1997, Hungary: Act CXXXIX of 9 December 1997 on Asylum, Poland: Aliens Law of 25 June 1997, Slovenia: Law on Asylum of 30 July 1999.
[37] For more detail, see S Anagnost, 'Challenges facing asylum systems and asylum policy development in Europe: preliminary lessons learned from the Central European and Baltic states (CEBS)' (2000) 12 *International Journal of Refugee Law* 380.
[38] See Byrne et al, above n 5, at 17.

One can wonder whether restrictive EU standards currently being imposed on candidate countries are adapted to those countries' situation. A UNHCR officer has noted that 'some CEBS (Central Europe and Baltic states) have adopted notions they might not otherwise have contemplated introducing.'[39] For instance, accelerated procedures have been introduced in all candidate countries' asylum systems to deal with manifestly unfounded applications.[40] One may argue that in some cases, these procedures have been introduced without the necessary procedural safeguards. In any case, what candidate countries need in the first instance are adequate, rather than accelerated, procedures. Indeed, the usefulness of accelerated procedures can be doubted for countries such as Estonia or Latvia which receive less than 30 asylum seekers per year.[41] Candidate countries have also incorporated other well-established EU concepts such as 'safe third country'[42] and 'safe country of origin' whose conformity with international refugee protection standards may be in doubt.[43] As candidate countries are going through the transition from countries of transit where asylum seekers did not stop to lodge an application, to countries of destination, they must focus on establishing asylum procedures and reception conditions which are in full conformity with international human rights law and refugee law. They should not merely import EU policies which may not be adapted to their current asylum situation and/or administrative structures and practices.

One of the main problems encountered by candidate countries relates to the fact that the exact content of the EU asylum provisions, which they are to adopt, is currently under negotiation. There is thus uncertainty as to what norms must be implemented (the problem of the 'moving target').[44] European asylum law has emerged only in the last few years and is not yet very elaborate. At the moment, it is mainly composed of non-binding instruments adopted in the first half of the 1990s.[45] These non-binding

[39] M Petersen, 'Recent developments in Central Europe and the Baltic states in the asylum field: a view from UNHCR and the strategies of the High Commission for enhancing the asylum systems of the region', in Byrne et al, above n 5, 351–72, at 367.

[40] On accelerated procedures, see J van der Klaauw, 'Towards a common asylum procedure', in Guild and Harlow, above n 4, 165–93, at 180–83.

[41] On accelerated procedures, see for instance articles 43–47 of the amended Hungarian Act CXXXIX of 9 December 1997 on Asylum; article 14(2) of the amended Lithuanian Refugee Law of 29 June 2000, No VII–1784, No 56–1651; and section 19 of Latvian Asylum Law of 1 September 2002.

[42] On the adoption of the safe third country concept by candidate countries, see S Lavenex, ' "Passing the buck": European Union refugee policies towards Central and Eastern Europe' (1998) 11 *Journal of Refugee Studies* 126, at 138.

[43] See ECRE, *Position on the enlargement of the European Union in relation to asylum,* September 1998, *http://www.ecre.org/positions/eu.pdf.*

[44] See S Lavenex, 'EU enlargement and the challenge of policy transfer: the case of refugee policy' (2002) 28 *Journal of Ethnic and Migration Studies* 701, at 702–04.

[45] See for instance *Resolution on manifestly unfounded applications for asylum, Resolution on a harmonised approach to questions concerning host third countries, Conclusions on*

instruments were presented to candidate countries as binding and therefore to be implemented by them: there has thus been a 'hardening' of soft law which is a cause for concern.[46] These instruments have been supplemented by international conventions concluded outside the EU framework such as the Dublin Convention on asylum and the Schengen Implementation Agreement which contains some provisions dealing with asylum.[47] It was only in 1998 that asylum became an EC competence under article 63 EC, which envisaged the adoption of legally-binding instruments in a number of areas by April 2004. So far, some instruments have been adopted and are now clearly part of the EU asylum *acquis* to be adopted by candidate countries.[48] Nevertheless, the other proposed directives, which are also more important, remain under negotiation, and candidate countries can only speculate as to what their final content will be.[49] At this point, when adopting new asylum legislation, they can try to anticipate EU developments and, if in doubt, may choose the most restrictive standards in order to demonstrate that they can stem the influx of asylum seekers as well as can current Member States. What we are also witnessing is candidate countries amending their asylum and immigration legislation almost on a yearly basis in order to take into account recently adopted EU instruments: such frequent legislative changes create serious challenges to the stability and certainty of the law in candidate countries.

In terms of immigration, the emphasis has, not surprisingly, been on combating illegal immigration. Three strategies are being employed to

*countries in which there is generally no serious risk of persecution* (London, 30 November and 1 December 1992), and *Council Resolution of 20 June 1995 on minimum guarantees for asylum procedures*, OJ 1996 C 274/13.

[46] See for instance Anagnost, above n 37 at 386.

[47] *Convention determining the State responsible for examining applications for asylum lodged in one of the Member States of the European Communities*, 15 June 1990 (hereinafter the Dublin Convention) OJ 1997 C 254/1, and *Agreement on the Implementation of the Schengen Agreement of 14 June 1985 concerning the Gradual Abolition of Checks at their Common Borders*, 19 June 1990 (1991) 30 ILM 84. For more detail, see K Hailbronner and C Thiery, 'Schengen II and Dublin: responsibility for asylum applications in Europe' (1997) 34 *Common Market Law Review* 957.

[48] *Council directive No. 2001/55 of 20 July 2001 on minimum standards for giving temporary protection in the event of a mass influx of displaced persons and on measures promoting a balance of efforts between Member States in receiving such persons and bearing the consequences thereof*, OJ 2001 L 212/12, *Council directive No. 2003/9 of 27 January 2003 laying down minimum standards for the reception of asylum seekers*, OJ 2003 L 31/18, and *Council regulation No 343/2003 of 18 February 2003 establishing the criteria and mechanisms for determining the Member states responsible for examining an asylum application lodged in one of the Member States by a third-country national*, OJ 2003 L 50/1.

[49] *Proposal for a Council directive laying down minimum standards for the qualification and status of third country nationals and stateless persons as refugees, in accordance with the 1951 Convention relating to the status of refugees and the 1967 Protocol, or as persons who otherwise need international protection*, 12 September 2001, COM(2001) 510 final; *Proposal for a Council Directive on minimum standards on procedures in Member States for granting and withdrawing refugee status*, 18 June 2002, COM(2002) 326 final.

control future migration flows into the enlarged EU: restricting entries, preventing illegal entries and facilitating returns of illegal migrants and/or failed asylum seekers.

### Restricting Entries: New Visa Requirements

The EU's visa policy has become a central instrument of migration control. Candidate countries have to adopt this strict visa policy which requires nationals of a long list of countries to apply for a visa in order to gain entry to the EU.[50] Most candidate countries used to have open border policies with their eastern and southern neighbours, in particular with former Communist states. EU Member States are especially concerned about restricting the entry of nationals of the states created in the aftermath of the disintegration of the Soviet Union. With the exception of the Baltic states, these states are all included in the EU visa list. However, candidate countries are reluctant to impose visa requirements on their neighbours with whom they have often maintained close cultural, political and economic links.[51]

Although candidate countries have already terminated visa exemption agreements with a number of countries, mainly former Soviet Union Republics and other Communist states, the imposition of visa requirements on the nationals of neighbouring countries have raised some problems. For instance, some candidate countries want to allow national minorities living in neighbouring countries easy access to their territory. For instance, more than 3 millions ethnic Hungarians are living outside Hungary as a result of the 1920 Treaty of Trianon.[52] Some live in other candidate countries such as Slovenia, Slovakia and Romania, but others live in neighbouring countries such as Serbia, Croatia and Ukraine which are included in the EU visa list and for whom EU membership is a very distant prospect. There are also some Polish minorities living in Belarus (418,000) and Ukraine (220,000).[53] Such people want to retain access to the territories of candidate countries in order to visit their relatives. It must also be noted that some of the former Soviet Republics are still refugee-producing countries and that the imposition of strict visa requirements

[50] See *Regulation No 539/2001 of 15 March 2001 listing the third countries whose nationals must be in possession of visas when crossing the external borders and those whose nationals are exempt from this requirement,* amended by *Regulation No 2414/2001 of 7 December 2001* and Regulation No 453/2003 of 6 March 2003.

[51] See Jileva, above n 17, at 686–89.

[52] See J Zielonka, 'How new enlarged borders will reshape the European Union' (2001) 39 Journal of Common Market Studies 507, at 514, and H Grabbe, 'The sharp edges of Europe: Extending Schengen eastwards' (2000) 76 *International Affairs* 519, at 531.

[53] See IOM/ICPMD, *Migration in Central and Eastern Europe: 1999 review* (Geneva, IOM, 1999) 112.

would in effect contribute to denying persecuted individuals access to asylum procedures. It has been recommended that the EU should consider the long-standing relationships between the candidate countries and their neighbours, and envisage special visa arrangements such as fast-track, multiple-entry visas or single-country visas.[54] Hungary had also suggested special visa arrangements for ethnic Hungarians living abroad, but these proposals were abandoned.[55]

Some candidate countries are very reluctant to impose visa requirements on their immediate eastern neighbours. For instance, the introduction of visas for citizens of Belarus, Russia and especially Ukraine has posed a dilemma for Polish policy-makers who want to protect close historical, cultural and economic links with these countries. There is, for instance, a concern that the introduction of visas will pose a threat to economic activities in eastern areas:[56] such activities have been partly fuelled by 'shuttle migration' from Ukraine.[57] Moreover, successive Polish governments have pursued dynamic foreign policies towards their eastern neighbours, in particular Ukraine, in order to stabilise the region.[58] Measures introduced in 1998 to restrict entries from Belarus and Russia had already provoked strong protests from these countries.[59] This may explain why Poland tried to delay the introduction of visas for as long as possible. Visas were initially to be introduced in 2001 for Belarus and Russia and in 2002 for Ukraine,[60] but these dates were considered to be premature and visas were introduced on 1 October 2003 for all three countries.

The introduction of visas will contribute to a shift of responsibility for immigration control from border services to internal administrative services which will deal with an increased number of applications for residence permits (as migrants will use other means of entering and staying in the new Member States). More importantly, external embassies will have to deal with visa applications. The implementation of the new visa regime required by the EU will not be cost-free and embassies will have to be staffed and equipped in order to deal with high numbers of visa requests. It is also to be expected that some migrants will have to turn to illegal channels of migration as a result of the new visa requirements. In order to

[54] See House of Lords' Select Committee on European Union, Enlargement and EU external frontier controls, 24 October 2000, para 76.

[55] See Grabbe, above n 52, at 531.

[56] See Anderson, above n 25, at 21.

[57] See K Iglicka, 'Migration movements from and into Poland in the light of East-West European migration' (2001) 39 *International Migration* 3, at 8; and K Wolczuk, 'The Polish-Ukrainian border: on the receiving end of EU enlargement' (2002) 3 *Perspectives on European Politics and Society* 245.

[58] See K Wolczuk, 'Poland's relations with Ukraine in the context of EU enlargement', ESRC One Europe or Several Programme, Briefing note 4/01, April 2001.

[59] See Grabbe, above n 52, at 530.

[60] See Mikolajczyk, 'Poland', in Byrne et al above n 5, 48–77, at 60.

limit the negative impact of visas, it is crucial to ensure that the issuing of visas remains as easy and cheap as possible.[61] The Russian enclave of Kaliningrad raises some specific problems because it will soon be surrounded by EU Member States: Russians transiting EU territory by land between Kaliningrad and the rest of the Russian Federation will have to hold a special transit document.[62]

## Preventing Illegal Entries: Border Controls at the EU's Future Eastern Borders

During the 1990s, the EU's internal security agenda has been developing at a fast pace. One of the central elements of this agenda is external border controls which are becoming increasingly elaborate. Immigration to candidate countries has traditionally been negligible, hence the lack of immigration controls. Before 1989, there were a few, mainly Soviet, border guards on the eastern border, because most border controls took place on the western and southern borders. This lack of controls, particularly on the future eastern border of the enlarged EU, has been a major source of concern for current Member States because of the nature and location of this border. The border stretches along 3,000 kilometres and mainly runs through open country and mountains. It will be difficult to police and has traditionally been a relatively open border with many cross-border activities. This border will be shared with countries which are unlikely to join the EU in the near, or even distant, future and host criminal networks which will try to smuggle goods and people into the EU.

The improvement of border controls in candidate countries is seen as an essential condition for accession. Once candidate countries become EU Member States, and especially when internal border controls are abolished between current Schengen states and themselves, an increase in the number of attempts to enter the new Member States illegally is to be expected. Current Member States are thus extremely concerned that border controls must be set up and/or reinforced to prevent such illegal entries. Over the past few years, candidate countries such as Hungary, Poland, Slovakia and the three Baltic states have been under considerable pressure from the EU to adopt measures to establish and reinforce controls on their eastern borders.

Border controls are regulated by the Schengen framework which has been integrated into the EU *acquis* since Amsterdam.[63] In order to comply

[61] See IOM/ICPMD, *Migration in Central and Eastern Europe*, 115.
[62] See *Protocol No 5 on the transit of persons by land between the region of Kaliningrad and other parts of the Russian Federation*, AA2003/ACT/P5/en 4770.
[63] See *Protocol integrating the Schengen acquis into the framework of the European Union* (hereinafter Schengen Protocol).

with Schengen standards, the first challenge for candidate countries was to organise a complete overhaul of the border guard services. More crossing points have been established on the future eastern border, several thousand new staff were recruited and trained, equipment was purchased and so on. The Commission has been keen to stress the 'need to strengthen border management, most urgently at future EU external borders, and to prepare for the participation in the Schengen Information System.'[64] Each of its country reports, produced yearly, focuses on the need to improve border controls. This has thus become the main EU demand in the area of Justice and Home Affairs and a priority area for EU aid and assistance.

The EU, as well as individual Member States such as Germany and the UK,[65] have invested considerable resources in the export of EU border control technology and staff training. Many Phare projects on migration and border control have been funded in the last few years. It is estimated that candidate countries have received several hundred million euros of Phare funding to upgrade their eastern frontier controls.[66] Nevertheless, upgrading border controls to Schengen standards is proving extremely expensive and EU funding is still insufficient to implement all the required changes.[67] In particular, candidate countries will need elaborate technological frameworks to enter the Schengen Information System (SIS) which is a computerised system storing information on persons, and stolen vehicles and objects for the use of border control. The SIS also requires the setting up of effective data protection mechanisms. The current development of the second generation Schengen Information System (SIS II) which will be set up within the next few years will require even more elaborate technological adaptations from candidate countries. Moreover, border services need to invest in expensive surveillance equipment such as thermo/infrared cameras, x-ray units and police helicopters.[68] All in all, the adoption of the Schengen standards of border controls is not so much a problem of political will but of resources and is already proving to be extremely expensive for candidate countries. In order to ensure that Member States with the longest external borders, which include several new Member States, do not bear a disproportionate burden for policing these borders, the Commission has suggested the establishment of a financial burden-sharing mechanism leading to the progressive creation of a European Corps of Border Guards.[69]

[64] *Making a success of enlargement, strategy paper and report of the European Commission on the progress towards accession by each of the candidate countries*, 13 November 2001, 18.
[65] See House of Lords' Select Committee on European Union, *Enlargement and EU external frontier controls*, para 63.
[66] *Ibid*, para 61.
[67] *Ibid*, para 60.
[68] *Ibid*, para14.
[69] See *Towards integrated management of the external borders of the Member States of the European Union*, 7 May 2002, COM(2002) 233 final, para 45.

Apart from the funding problem, a fundamental change of attitude is also required from border guards who now have to 'keep foreigners out rather than keep citizens in'.[70] The complete overhaul of border control mechanisms in candidate countries thus requires a significant amount of human and financial resources, as well as training, and will not be achieved as promptly as Member States would wish. Nevertheless, no concessions are being granted and the Schengen *acquis* must be complied with in full,[71] even though it is well-known that some current Member States still do not comply with it.[72] In reality, there is doubt as to whether candidate countries will be able to implement the Schengen *acquis* in full by the time of accession.[73] If this is the case, the problem remains that candidate countries are uncertain what standards of border control, short of the Schengen standards, they are supposed to reach in order to gain accession.[74] Considering how costly upgrading border controls is, there is also uncertainty as to whether the borders with Bulgaria and Romania should also be 'sealed' to the same extent as the eastern borders: since these countries are to join the EU within the next few years, it would appear counterproductive to invest in expensive border control infrastructures which will then have to be dismantled. Because of the lack of funding, training border guards to deal with asylum seekers or to avoid racial stereotyping when operating controls on entry is, unfortunately, not a priority.

Even though candidate countries comply fully with the Schengen *acquis*, they will not immediately become fully part of the Schengen area when they become EU Member States. Consequently, internal border controls will continue to operate. It follows that candidate countries have to comply with the obligations arising from Schengen *before* benefiting from the advantages in terms of abolition of internal border controls and free movement of persons.[75] An assessment of the new Member States' implementation record will be made by existing Schengen members at some future date.[76] In other words, tougher border controls must first be applied on the eastern borders of the candidate countries before concessions are made on their western borders.[77]

[70] Grabbe, above n 52, at 529.
[71] See article 8 of Schengen Protocol.
[72] See House of Lords' Select Committee on European Union, *Enlargement and EU external frontier controls*, para 25.
[73] *Ibid*, para 52.
[74] *Ibid*, para 54.
[75] See *Towards the enlarged Union: strategy paper and report of the European Commission on the progress towards accession by each of the candidate countries*, 9 September 2002, COM(2002) 700 final, 28.
[76] See article 3(2) of the Act of Accession.
[77] See Grabbe, above n 52, at 527.

**Facilitating Returns: Re-admission Agreements**

There is no doubt that the most important obligation arising from the 1951 Convention to which all candidate countries are parties, is the obligation of *non-refoulement* (article 33): state parties shall not return a refugee to a country where he would face threats to his life or freedom. The scope of this obligation has been extended beyond the refugee context by the Convention against Torture (article 3)[78] and the ECHR case law on article 3.[79] EU Member States have concluded readmission agreements with a number of third countries. The aim of these agreements is to facilitate the return of illegal immigrants and some asylum seekers to their country of origin or a transit country. EU Member States have concluded such agreements with all candidate countries. Most famously, a readmission agreement was signed between Schengen states and Poland in 1991. Candidate countries are now adopting the same strategy as Schengen states in order to ensure that people cannot stay in Central and Eastern Europe: they have also started concluding re-admission agreements with their Eastern and Southern neighbours, as well as other countries further afield.[80]

When examining the text of some of these re-admission agreements, it appears that they may not contain sufficient guarantees against *non-refoulement*. One minimum prerequisite before signing a readmission agreement should be to ensure that the other party is at least a party to the 1951 Convention, which should guarantee that it is under the obligation of *non-refoulement*. However, it is worrying to note that a number of readmission agreements were signed with countries which were not parties to the 1951 Convention at the time of signature. Some agreements which cover asylum seekers do not contain any reference to the 1951 Convention, or even, in some cases, to any human rights instrument. For instance, the readmission agreement concluded between Poland and Lithuania in 1998, which is undoubtedly one of the most important in that both countries are on one of the main migrant routes to Western Europe, contains no reference to the 1951 Convention, nor does it guarantee access to asylum procedures.[81] There is also a concern that some candidate countries have signed or are about to conclude readmission agreements with countries which are still refugee-producing.

[78] *Convention against Torture and Other Cruel, Inhuman or Degrading Treatment or Punishment*, 10 December 1984, 23 *ILM* 1027 and 24 *ILM* 535.
[79] See H Lambert, 'Protection against *refoulement* from Europe: human rights law comes to the rescue' (1999) 48 *International and Comparative Law Quarterly* 515.
[80] See the full list of agreements concluded by candidate countries, see Lavenex, above n 44, 708.
[81] See the number of asylum applications lodged in Lithuania upon readmission from Poland, in Sesickas et al, 'Lithuania', in Byrne et al, above n 5, 226–66, at 238.

It appears that some of the readmission agreements signed by candidate countries with their neighbours do not contain enough guarantees that asylum seekers are not removed by these states to yet another third country which may not be safe and/or may even be the country of origin. To some extent, candidate countries are replicating the German strategy which has been to sign readmission agreements with all its eastern neighbours.[82] Nevertheless, Germany has also attempted to engage in bilateral cooperation with these countries to reinforce their protection capacities: candidate countries cannot offer the same level of support to their eastern neighbours as Germany has to its neighbours.[83]

## CONCLUSION

The recent eastward enlargement has already prompted a number of changes in the asylum and immigration regimes of the EU and the candidate countries. These changes do not always correspond to rational decisions about future migration flows, but reflect the fears of the general public in the old Member States. Two types of concerns have been expressed: fear of an influx of cheap labour from the new Member States and an even greater fear of uncontrolled and illegal migration movements from further East.[84] In order to address these concerns, transitional agreements for the free movement of workers have been negotiated and dramatic changes in the asylum and immigration laws and policies of candidate countries are taking place. Despite EU pressure, candidate countries must not forget that they have international obligations not to return people to situations where their lives or security would be at risk. This shows that EU demands are inconsistent to the extent that candidate countries must demonstrate their commitment to democracy and human rights whilst adopting restrictive asylum and immigration policies towards foreigners. Candidate countries' adherence to international human rights law and refugee law is thus being tested, and it is crucial that domestic developments in the areas of immigration and asylum continue to be scrutinised.

Earlier EU developments in the field of immigration and asylum already demonstrated the prioritisation of security concerns over humanitarian concerns and followed a strong logic of inclusion/exclusion as illustrated by strict border controls. Current efforts to align candidate countries on EU policies follow the same logic. Recent developments, especially in the

[82] See list of agreements concluded by Germany, see Lavenex, above n 42, at 133.
[83] Interview with Christian Mahr, London, 29 September 2001.
[84] See L Baan, *Creating a Europe 'whole and free'? Migration, freedom of movement and border issues in Central and Eastern Europe in the context of enlargement*, July 2002, *http://www.euractiv.com/ndbtext/enlarge/Migration_gronuni.rtf*.

area of visa policy, also show the prioritisation of security concerns over legitimate economic or foreign policy concerns. It is striking that the formulation of asylum and immigration policies in candidate countries is mainly dictated by older EU Member States' security concerns, rather than by the new Members' own concerns. So far, these countries have been so keen to gain EU membership that they have agreed to adopt most measures, but they may already be starting to regret it. Not surprisingly, candidate countries are becoming increasingly nervous about accession as they have realised that 'asylum and immigration are being instrumentalised by EU Member States in order to establish a filter or buffer zone between them and the countries of emigration'.[85] With EU accession, the responsibility for ensuring border controls, tackling illegal immigration and dealing with asylum seekers will fall disproportionately on candidate countries which do not have the same financial and human resources as older Member States.

This new heavy responsibility that is being imposed on candidate countries is not the only consequence of EU accession. The recent reinforcement of controls on the future eastern border of the enlarged EU has some disturbing historical connotations. Although the Iron Curtain fell almost fifteen years ago, recent measures to change the asylum and immigration regimes in candidate countries are contributing to the establishment of a new dividing line between the enlarged EU and poorer countries further East.

[85] Lavenex, above n 34, at 290.

# 23

# *Enlargement: A Successful Instrument of Foreign Policy?*

MARISE CREMONA

## INTRODUCTION

> Enlargement ... the most successful act of foreign policy that the EU has ever made.
>
> Wim Kok, *Enlarging the European Union: Achievements and Challenges*, Report to the European Commission, EUI, 19 March 2003

> Over the past decade, the Union's most successful foreign policy instrument has undoubtedly been the promise of EU membership.
>
> Commissioner Patten, 11 March 2003

MY INTENTION IN this chapter is to examine the claim that enlargement is the most successful ever instrument of EU foreign policy, and to explore the implications of that success for the future of that policy. Of course, enlargement has been successful in that there has been a good deal of it, and there is likely to be more. The Union has moved from being a Community of six states with a population of 183 million, to a Union of fifteen with a population of 375 million, and from 1 May 2004 became a Union of 25 with a population of 450 million. The fifth enlargement is the biggest and will change the face of Europe in ways we cannot yet predict. It is in fact no small success to have completed the process at all, given the scale of the project. However Patten and Kok were not talking about numbers, nor were they merely recording the successful completion of a major endeavour.

Nor is enlargement just a case of creating a larger Union with more clout and a stronger voice in pursuing its external economic and foreign policy.[1] What is claimed, rather, is that enlargement as an instrument has enabled

[1] M Cremona, 'The Impact of Enlargement: External Policy and External Relations' in M Cremona (ed), *The Enlargement of the European Union* (Collected Courses of the Academy of European Law, OUP, 2003).

the EU to achieve (at least some of) its foreign policy objectives. How is enlargement an *instrument* of foreign policy? As an 'act' or an 'instrument', enlargement is not merely a reaction to pressure from outside, a result of foreign policy; nor does it simply influence the future development of foreign policy, although it does do both these things. The Union is actively seeking to achieve specific objectives by means of enlargement. Enlargement in this sense includes the pre-accession process as well as the end result.

The following sections of this chapter will first outline the foreign policy objectives which might be said to be served by the process of enlargement and the key component of enlargement as a foreign policy instrument: the use of conditionality to structure relations with candidate and potential candidate countries (section 2). The chapter then turns to the implications of that success (section 3), in particular in terms of the EU's relations with its near neighbours including the 'potential candidates' in the western Balkans and its southern and eastern neighbours including Russia and Ukraine (sections 4 and 5). In a concluding section, the continued effectiveness of conditionality based on a pre-accession model but in the absence of accession as an ultimate incentive is questioned. The key to continued success, it is argued, will be the development of shared objectives and shared goals.

## THE OBJECTIVES OF EU FOREIGN POLICY THAT MAY BE SERVED BY ENLARGEMENT

Foreign policy may be justified in terms other than the straightforwardly utilitarian (that is, in terms of achieving specified objectives). It may be judged with reference to its appropriateness in terms of collective or common values, and/or in terms of a moral justification based on universally-acknowledged rights.[2] Enlargement could therefore be regarded as a success — or not — in these terms as well as, or alternatively to, its utilitarian effectiveness. At this stage we will focus on identifying objectives; however the identification and promotion of common values is, as we shall see, an important aspect of the way the Union defines itself in its relations with the outside world.

The objectives of the Union's common foreign and security policy (CFSP) are defined very broadly in Article 11 TEU, and it is not difficult to see a link between those objectives and the reunification of Europe symbolised by this enlargement: the preservation of peace, strengthening international security and the security of the Union, safeguarding the common

[2] Sjursen and Smith, 'Justifying EU Foreign Policy: The Logics Underpinning EU Enlargement', Arena Working Papers, No.01/1; *http://www.arena.uio.no/*.

values, fundamental interests, independence and integrity of the Union, the promotion of international cooperation and the development and consolidation of democracy, the rule of law and respect for fundamental rights. The same might be said of the Union's objectives as set out in the draft Constitutional Treaty (Article I-3), which refer to the promotion of peace and security, as well as the more specific external policy objectives in Article III-193.[3]

The EU has presented itself as a model for overcoming conflict, in promoting its own values of security, stability and economic prosperity across the continent as a whole.[4] Javier Solana, for example, has proposed as a strategic objective for the EU, 'a particular contribution to stability and good governance in our immediate neighbourhood.'[5] Article I-56 of the draft Constitutional Treaty reflects this concern by highlighting the Union's relations with its neighbouring States, setting as its objective the establishment of 'an area of prosperity and good neighbourliness, founded on the values of the Union and characterised by close and peaceful relations based on cooperation.'[6] More concretely, these objectives include, as well as political stability and stable borders, good governance, migration policy, and combating international crime.

Of course, enlargement is not just an aspect of the CFSP but rather of the EU's foreign policy taken generally. Just as it impacts on the whole spectrum of internal EU law and policy, other aspects of external policy — including economic and trade policy — may also be served by enlargement. One thinks of trade liberalisation, regional integration and the desire of the EU to demonstrate leadership in global regulatory policy-making. But it is certainly within its immediate neighbourhood that enlargement has had the most impact, and it is here that the challenges arising out of that success present themselves most acutely.

[3] Art III-193 states that the Union shall seek to develop relations and build partnerships with countries and regional or global organisations which share its values and principles; 'principles which have inspired its own creation, development and enlargement'. These include democracy, the rule of law, the universality and indivisibility of human rights and fundamental freedoms, respect for human dignity, equality and solidarity, and for international law. The Union's external policy objectives will include (inter alia) safeguarding the common values, fundamental interests, security, independence and integrity of the Union; preserving peace, preventing conflicts and strengthening international security, in conformity with the principles of the UN Charter. EDNV 850/03

[4] 'The EU is itself a model for overcoming conflict and promoting reconciliation through close co-operation to achieve common goals, while respecting national sovereignty and territorial integrity. States aspiring to closer relations with the EU should behave in a similar manner ...' Commission Communication to the Council and European Parliament on the Stabilisation and Association process for countries of South-Eastern Europe, 26 May 1999, COM (1999) 235.

[5] J Solana, 'A Secure Europe in a Better World', paper for the European Council, Thessaloniki, 19–20 June 2003, SO 138/03.

[6] See further section 5.

The mechanism by which it is argued that enlargement has been instrumental in achieving at least some of these objectives is conditionality. The pre-accession process, with the Copenhagen criteria, Commission Opinions, National Programmes for the Adoption of the Acquis, annual Accession Partnerships and Regular Reports, is entirely structured around the progressive meeting of conditions. Progress towards membership, indeed the negotiating process itself, has been measured in terms of compliance. Membership (in the words of Wim Kok) is a 'powerful incentive for progress and reform' and a 'catalyst for change.'[7] And these membership conditions are themselves linked to the foreign policy objectives already identified, such as good neighbourliness, settlement of border disputes, economic reform, and the strengthening of democratic institutions.

How successful has this aspect of enlargement policy been? In general, it has been successful for the ten central and eastern European candidate states (the eight who joined in May 2004[8] and Romania and Bulgaria who aim to join in 2007) for whom it was specifically designed. The acceptance of the *acquis* involves, by definition, alignment with the EU's current policy goals (be they defined in trade instruments or CFSP common positions) and in that sense the pre-accession process has resulted in an exporting of those goals to a wider group of states. Beyond these shared objectives, convergence of policy and the fulfilment of the political and economic membership criteria have resulted in an increased level of political and economic stability in the accession States, thereby contributing to achieving the EU's policy goals. Commission President Prodi argues that 'the current enlargement is the greatest contribution to sustainable stability and security on the European continent that the EU has ever made'.[9] In October 2002, the Commission summarised this positive view:

> Both the existing Member States and the prospective members benefit from political stability. Stable democracies have emerged in Central and Eastern Europe. The credit for this success belongs mainly to the people of those countries themselves. The political stability in the Central and East European candidate countries is rooted in common European values: democracy, the rule of law, respect for human rights and the protection of minorities. Causes of conflict, such as minority issues and border problems, are removed. A stable political framework is a precondition for lasting peace and neighbourly co-existence, as well as for a successful economy.[10]

[7] W Kok, *Enlarging the European Union: Achievements and Challenges*, Report to the European Commission (EUI, 19 March 2003) 14.

[8] Czech Republic, Estonia, Hungary, Latvia, Lithuania, Poland, Slovakia and Slovenia.

[9] R Prodi, 'A Wider Europe — A Proximity Policy as the key to stability', speech to the Sixth ECSA-World Conference, Brussels, 5–6 December 2002, SPEECH/02/619.

[10] Towards the Enlarged Union, Strategy Paper and Report of the European Commission on the progress towards accession by each of the candidate countries, 9 October 2002, COM(2002) 700, at p 5.

The success is less obvious with respect to Cyprus and Turkey, and even the pressure to reach a settlement before the Treaty of Accession was signed in April 2003 has not yet produced definitive results. However, we will not here enter into the question of the accuracy of the Union's generally positive assessment of the political stability of the candidate states, though no doubt things are much improved since 1989 in terms both of internal security and relations with neighbouring states. Rather, we will turn to the position of those neighbours following enlargement. What of stability and security beyond the immediate candidate states?

## THE MAGNET EFFECT

In spite of the criticisms that may be made of the conditionality mechanisms and the pre-accession process generally,[11] one measure of its success is the degree to which EU membership has become a goal for a widening group of countries. However, it is just this magnet effect which poses new challenges for EU foreign policy, and may threaten the increased security and stability within Europe that the current enlargement has helped to achieve.

The Union is seeking to replicate the success of what one might term the 'enlargement effect' with its neighbouring states, thus raising the question of the sustainability of the process. When applying conditionality to its relations with South-East Europe the Union has found itself engaged in an inherently dynamic or progressive process. This is not just a question of bigger and better carrots being required in order to get results. It is more a question of the level of commitment that the EU is prepared to offer, with the result that the nature of the relationship changes. In proposing the Stabilisation and Association Process (SAP) in 1999 the Commission recognised 'the failure of the countries to adequately respond to the incentives already offered (notably as regards the need to cooperate on a bilateral, multilateral or regional level)'.[12] The SAP was designed to respond to that failure by, among other things, proposing a new type of close relationship with the EU, one which has seen the Western Balkan States categorised as 'potential candidates' for EU membership.[13] Conditionality in practice

[11] C Hillion, 'Enlargement of the European Union: A Legal Analysis' in A Arnull and D Wincott (eds), *Accountability and Legitimacy in the European Union* (Oxford, OUP, 2003); Smith, 'The Evolution and Application of EU Membership Conditionality' in M Cremona (ed), *The Enlargement of the European Union* (Collected Courses of the Academy of European Law, OUP, 2003); M Cremona, 'EU Enlargement: Solidarity and Conditionality', forthcoming in *EL Rev*.

[12] Commission Communication to the Council and European Parliament on the Stabilisation and Association process for countries of South-Eastern Europe, 26 May 1999, COM (1999) 235.

[13] The term is used the Preambles to the Stabilisation and Association Agreements with FYROM and Croatia, as well as by the European Council at Feira, 19–20 June 2000, Presidency Conclusions at para 67. See also Phinnemore, 'Stabilisation and Association

works both ways and has resulted in increased levels of commitment and obligation from the EU as well as from its third country interlocutors.

The success of enlargement 'creates legitimate expectations in the EU's future neighbours'.[14] Can the logic that enlargement increases peace, security and prosperity be sustained indefinitely, or is it 'ultimately in contradiction with the logic of cohesion', as Kok suggests?[15] Prodi has argued that to 'go on enlarging forever' would create a danger of 'watering down the European political project', turning the EU into a continent-wide Free Trade Area.[16] The old question of widening versus deepening is raising its head again. Experience seems to show that these aspirations are not as inter-dependent as had been thought, at least in the either-or sense that some have suggested; they depend on different rationales and have tended to co-exist. But sustainability remains a question.

The issue of legitimate expectations and the future borders of the EU (and Europe) is naturally sharpest among the enlarged Union's neighbours. In addition to its existing borders with Bulgaria and Turkey, the EU now has five new borders with Croatia, Serbia, Romania, Ukraine and Belarus. Its border with Russia has extended (taking in the Kaliningrad enclave), and it will have a new presence in the Southern and Eastern Mediterranean through Malta and Cyprus. Although enlargement will increase the security of the Union, it will also bring it closer to troubled areas.[17] And the EU itself, by insisting on the erection by the new Member States of new border requirements, including visa regimes, may exacerbate tensions with its new neighbours, at the same time as stressing the importance of good neighbourly relations.[18]

The new Members will bring with them experience (positive and negative), history and expertise in their relations with the EU's new neighbours, and they will have their own priorities and objectives. In its recent Communication on the Western Balkans the Commission proposes that the expertise of the new Member States in institution-building and legislative approximation should be mobilised, as they have 'recent successful experience of transition and of pre-accession preparations'.[19]

Agreements: Europe Agreements for the Western Balkans?' (2002) 8 *European Foreign Affairs Review* 77.

[14] Prodi, above note 9.
[15] W Kok, *Enlarging the European Union: Achievements and Challenges*, Report to the European Commission, EUI, 19 March 2003, at 64.
[16] Prodi, above note 9.
[17] J Solana, 'A Secure Europe in a Better World', paper for the European Council, Thessaloniki, 19–20 June 2003, SO 138/03.
[18] Borissova, 'The Adoption of the Schengen and the Justice and Home Affairs Acquis: The Case of Bulgaria and Romania' (2003) 8 *European Foreign Affairs Review* 105.
[19] Commission Communication 'The Western Balkans and European Integration', 21 May 2003, COM(2003) 285 final, at p 8; see further discussion in section 4 below. This sentiment was also expressed by the Council in its Thessaloniki Agenda, adopted by the Council on 16 June 2003.

This link between the enlargement, and pre-accession, experience and the need to develop and enhance its policies towards its new neighbours is at the heart of recent Union thinking on its Proximity Policy. The Commission, supported by the Council and European Council, is seeking not only to draw upon its experience of economic transition but to go further and to use the policies and instruments which have proved successful in the context of enlargement (conditionality, the Accession Partnership, Action Plans, and regular reports). In doing so it hopes to repeat the trick of enhancing stability and security within a wider circle of neighbours — a key foreign policy objective — by promoting political and economic development and regional integration. However, the hard fact of sustainability is clearly demonstrated by the distinction made between the countries of the Western Balkans, designated 'potential candidates' on the one hand,[20] and Russia, the Western NIS and the Southern Mediterranean on the other, for whom a 'new neighbourhood policy' is envisaged.[21]

## THE 'EUROPEAN VOCATION' OF THE POTENTIAL CANDIDATES IN SOUTH-EAST EUROPE

Initial references at the time of the Stability Pact to the 'European vocation' of the Western Balkans and their 'perspective of EU membership'[22] have now become more definite. Since the European Council Conclusions at Feira in June 2000[23] the Western Balkan states have regularly been referred to as 'potential candidates', and this term also appears in the Preambles of the Stabilisation and Association Agreements already concluded with FYROM and Croatia:

> Recalling the European Union's readiness to integrate to the fullest possible extent [Croatia/FYROM] into the political and economic mainstream of

[20] The Western Balkans covers Albania, Bosnia-Herzegovina, Croatia, former Yugoslav Republic of Macedonia (FYROM) and Serbia and Montenegro.

[21] The Western NIS (WNIS) covers Ukraine, Moldova, Belarus. The Southern Mediterranean covers those countries that participate in the Barcelona Process, apart from the candidate States Cyprus, Malta and Turkey (viz. Algeria, Egypt, Israel, Jordan, Lebanon, Morocco, Palestinian Authority, Syria and Tunisia). Libya has also been included by the Council although not yet a formal member of the Barcelona Process.

[22] Report to the European Council on EU Action in support of the Stability Pact and South-Eastern Europe, presented to the European Council by the Finnish Presidency and the European Commission, Helsinki, 10–11 December 1999, Press Release 13814/99. In its 2nd Report on Progress towards Accession by each of the candidate countries, 13 October 1999, Composite Paper Part V.2, the Commission refers to the 'ultimate vocation' of membership for these countries. See also Commission Communication on the Stabilisation and Association Process COM(99) 235, 26 May 1999. See further M Cremona, 'Creating the New Europe: The Stability Pact for South-Eastern Europe in the Context of EU-SEE Relations' *CYELS, Vol II 1999* (Oxford, Hart Publishing, 2000) 463.

[23] European Council at Feira, 19–20 June 2000, Presidency Conclusions, para 67.

Europe and its status as a potential candidate for EU membership on the basis of the Treaty on European Union and fulfilment of the criteria defined by the European Council in June 1993, subject to the successful implementation of this Agreement, notably regarding regional co-operation.

Since 1999, EU relations with the Western Balkans have been conducted within the framework of the Stabilisation and Association Process (SAP), the central elements of which are the Stabilisation and Association Agreements (SAAs) and the CARDS assistance programme.[24] In the wake of the European Council decisions on enlargement taken in Copenhagen in December 2002, a number of policy initiatives have been taken during 2003 with a view to enhancing the SAP.[25] In addition to the Commission's Annual Report on the SAP, and the Council's Conclusions on its Annual Review of the SAP,[26] the Commission produced a Communication on the Western Balkans in May 2003,[27] and the Council adopted the 'Thessaloniki Agenda' which was then endorsed by European Council in Thessaloniki in June. Following the European Council meeting, an EU-Western Balkans Summit was held, out of which emerged the Thessaloniki Declaration affirming the region's 'privileged relationship' with the EU.

The introduction to the Commission Communication is headed 'The Western Balkans and the Challenge of Enlargement', significantly and probably deliberately echoing the Commission's highly influential 1992 paper 'Europe and the Challenge of Enlargement'.[28] The theme of the Communication is the enhancement of the SAP in the light of enlargement, using the experience of the current enlargement process.[29] The core proposal, adopted by the Council, is for new 'European Partnerships' (echoing the Accession Partnerships[30]) which would identify short and

[24] Commission Communication on the Stabilisation and Association Process COM(99) 235, 26 May 1999. Council Regulation 2666/2000/EC on Community Assistance for Reconstruction, Democratisation and Stabilisation (CARDS) OJ 2000 L 306/1.

[25] The Brussels European Council in March 2003 invited 'the Council and the Commission to examine ways and means, based also on the experience from the enlargement process, to further strengthen the Union's Stabilisation and Association Policy towards the region.' (Presidency Conclusions para 84).

[26] Commission's First Annual Report on The Stabilisation and Association process for South East Europe, 4 April 2002, COM(2002) 163; Commission's Second Annual Report on The Stabilisation and Association process for South East Europe, 26 March 2003, COM(2003)139 final; the Council's annual review of the SAP, endorsing the Commission's Report, was adopted by the External Relations Council on 16 June 2003.

[27] Commission Communication on Western Balkans and European Integration of 21 May 2003, COM (2003) 285.

[28] EU Bulletin Supplement 3/92.

[29] For the pre-accession strategy see M Maresceau, 'Pre-Accession' in M Cremona (ed), *The Enlargement of the European Union* (Collected Courses of the Academy of European Law, OUP, 2003).

[30] For Accession Partnerships, see Regulation 622/98/EC on assistance to the applicant States in the framework of the pre-accession strategy, and in particular on the establishment of Accession Partnerships OJ L 85/1.

medium term priorities for reform and act as a check list to measure progress. Priorities would be established (both for action by the SAP State and for assistance under the CARDS programme[31]) and progress assessed using the Commission's own assessments in its Annual Reports. Again an echo of the pre-Accession Progress Reports, these Reports have developed out of the regular country reports on the Western Balkans that the Commission has produced since the introduction of the regional policy based on conditionality in 1997, together with its Annual Reports on the SAP process. They will therefore combine specific Western Balkans conditionality with the Copenhagen criteria. In the preparation of the new European Partnerships consultations with the country concerned, using SAA structures such as the Joint Committees, will lead to a Commission proposal and Council Decision (the same procedure as for Accession Partnerships). The associate countries will then produce detailed national plans for the implementation of the partnerships, modelled on the accession states' National Programmes for the Adoption of the Acquis. The first Partnerships will be proposed to the Council at the time of the next SAP Annual Report (March-April 2004).[31a]

These Partnerships are intended to be the cornerstone of the new enhanced SAP, but they would be supplemented by other initiatives also borrowed from the pre-accession strategy such as 'twinning',[32] TAIEX assistance,[33] and participation in some Community programmes such as education, research and energy.[34] Other policy areas covered by the Commission's Communication on the Western Balkans include cooperation in Justice and Home Affairs (including visa and migration policy, action against organised crime and trafficking and projected agreements with Europol), trade policy (including support for a regional FTA, and for the extension of cumulation of origin), development of SMEs (a proposal that the Western Balkan countries might commit to the European Charter for

[31] The Commission proposes an increase in the CARDS budget of Euro 200 million for 2004–06.

[31a] For commission proposals for European Partnerships, see *http://europa.eu.int/comm/external_relations/see/docs/index.htm#eip*.

[32] Twinning is an institution-building exercise which involves the secondment of member states' civil service personnel to accession states in order to share experience and transfer know-how.

[33] The TAIEX (technical assistance information exchange) office provides technical assistance to candidate countries in the process of adoption of the acquis and implementation and enforcement of Community law, including documentation, information and advice, workshops and study visits.

[34] See Commission Communication on 'Participation of candidate countries in Community programmes, agencies and committees', COM (1999) 710. Accession states participate in the Socrates programme for student mobility, for example, and in the EC Framework Programmes for Research and Development. On energy, see also Commission Communication on the development of energy policy for the enlarged EU, its neighbours and partner countries, 13 May 2003, COM(2003)262. For the Western Balkans, participation in Community programmes will be based on framework agreements to be negotiated which each country.

Small Enterprises), and regional cooperation (including refugee return, the possibility of visa-free movement and regional energy markets). The dual emphasis is thus on enhanced security at a regional level and support for economic development within the Western Balkan partners, against a background of closer integration with the EU.

The Thessaloniki Agenda, while endorsing and adopting these Commission policy proposals and an increase in financial support, is an important political statement of Union policy towards the region. Although only two of these countries have so far formally applied for membership, it can be seen as the *de facto* start of a pre-accession process. The Agenda speaks of the Balkans as 'an integral part of a unified Europe' and invites them to follow the same road to membership as the current accession States. This route will be guided by the Copenhagen criteria and what the document calls SAP conditionality, with a reference to the conclusions of the Zagreb Summit of November 2000.

One commentator has predicted that 'the Western Balkans are the region where EU enlargement can be used to make the CFSP a success'.[35] The Thessaloniki Agenda seeks to extend CFSP cooperation, including the extension of political dialogue to those states which do not yet have contractual relations with the EU (Serbia/Montenegro and Bosnia-Herzegovina), and inviting the SAP states to align themselves with EU CFSP measures, including common positions and declarations,[36] and informal meetings with the Political and Security Committee on crisis management issues. The objective is thus to extend the cooperative base, and to build a network of support for the EU's foreign policy beyond its borders. The aim is to increase Europe's security by binding the countries of Europe together, seeking to develop a common world-view alongside efforts at regional cooperation and economic development. The Thessaloniki Summit launched the EU-Western Balkans Forum, bringing together the EU Member States, the acceding and candidate states, and the SAP states, together with key regional players such as the UN's Special Representative in Kosovo. It endorsed the Thessaloniki Agenda as 'our shared agenda'.

In spite of the significant parallels there are also some significant differences between the Western Balkans Agenda and pre-accession for the fifth enlargement. First, the EU's relations with the Western Balkans are structured around the framework of the SAP, which itself built on the so-called

[35] Vachudova, 'Strategies for Democratization and European Integration in the Balkans' in M Cremona (ed), *The Enlargement of the European Union* (Oxford, OUP, 2003) 141, 160.

[36] Current practice is for the 'Acceding Countries Cyprus, the Czech Republic, Estonia, Hungary, Latvia, Lithuania, Malta, Poland, the Slovak Republic and Slovenia, the Associated Countries Bulgaria, Romania and Turkey and the EFTA countries Iceland, Liechtenstein and Norway, members of the European Economic Area' to align themselves to CFSP declarations.

'regional approach' dating from 1996, and the Stability Pact. The emphasis on a regional approach affects objectives as well as structures, also combining what the Council calls the principles of 'own merits' and 'catch up': in other words an individualised approach to conditionality. Thus, apart from the regional structures created by the SAP there is greater emphasis on regional cooperation, including regional free-trade and the possibility of achieving visa-free movement within the region.[37] Second, a version of conditionality will be applied which includes not only the Copenhagen criteria but in addition the specific Western Balkans conditionality developed and applied since 1997.[38]

## THE WIDER EUROPE: NEW NEIGHBOURHOOD POLICY

Commission Progress Reports on the candidate States from 1999 onwards have contained references to the enlarged EU's relations with its neighbours. Earlier Reports emphasise the benefits of enlargement to the wider region. In Strategy Papers attached to the country Reports in 2001[39] and 2002[40] the outlines of a more substantive 'proximity policy' begin to emerge. They include the creation of a wider free trade area encompassing the EU and its neighbours, progressive alignment with the rules and regulatory framework of the EU's internal market, cooperation on migration issues[41] and border management. Existing policy structures (the Euro-Med Partnership and the Partnership and Cooperation Agreements) will be linked together in a policy for a Wider Europe — or a New Neighbours policy — in an attempt to achieve a more coherent approach.

Since April 2002 the New Neighbours initiative has regularly appeared on the agenda of the Council. An initial joint position paper by Solana and Patten was discussed in September 2002 and a Commission Communication was published in March 2003.[42] In June 2003 the Council adopted Conclusions based on the Commission's proposals, and these were

[37] In suggesting this the Council does not acknowledge the obstacles presented by the Union's own visa policy, which will compel countries that wish to align themselves with that policy — itself a feature of the Agenda — to impose visa requirements on other countries within the region, such as Serbia/Montenegro.

[38] This includes full implementation of UNSCR 1244, the Dayton/Paris agreements and the Ohrid and Belgrade agreements, and cooperation with the ICC and ICTY.

[39] Commission Strategy Paper, 13 November 2001, 'Making a Success of Enlargement'.

[40] Commission Strategy Paper, 9 October 2002, 'Towards the Enlarged Union'.

[41] See Commission Communication, 'Integrating Migration Issues in the EU's Relations with Third Countries', COM (2002)703 final, and the Proposal for a Regulation establishing a programme for financial and technical assistance to third countries in the area of migration and asylum, COM (2003)355 final.

[42] Commission Communication, 'Wider Europe — Neighbourhood: A New Framework for Relations with our Eastern and Southern Neighbours', 11 March 2003, COM(2003)104.

endorsed by the European Council in Thessaloniki. The overall objective is to counterbalance possible fears that the future borders of the Union will become a new dividing line in Europe, and 'to create a ring of stability and safety around us,'[43] a 'ring of friends' from Morocco to Russia and the Black Sea.[44]

The mechanisms for achieving this objective may be summarised as the offer of an enhanced relationship with the EU based on the EEA model, that would be 'as close to the Union as can be without being a member'[45] and the use of instruments derived from the pre-accession process, including agreed reform targets, Action Plans and a strong element of conditionality.

The current proposal is that the new neighbourhood policy should not replace the existing framework for relations with Russia, the Western NIS and the Southern Mediterranean, including existing bilateral agreements, Common Strategies, the Barcelona Process and the Northern Dimension initiative. However the possibility of new enhanced agreements will be considered, 'on the basis of evaluation of the implementation of existing agreements, and taking into account the principle of differentiation'[46] (in other words, applying conditionality). This is particularly important for Russia and the WNIS whose existing Partnership and Cooperation Agreements do not at present establish a free trade area with the EU. A possible new legal base for these agreements is presented by the draft Constitutional Treaty, which in Title VIII 'The Union and its immediate environment' (placed immediately before Title IX on Union Membership and accession procedures) contains a new Article I-56:

> 1. The Union shall develop a special relationship with neighbouring States, aiming to establish an area of prosperity and good neighbourliness, founded on the values of the Union and characterised by close and peaceful relations based on cooperation.
> 2. For this purpose, the Union may conclude and implement specific agreements with the countries concerned in accordance with Article III-222. These agreements may contain reciprocal rights and obligations as well as the possibility of undertaking activities jointly. Their implementation shall be the subject of periodic consultation.

The idea of shared values as the basis for the neighbourhood relationship is not new. It can be found in the European Council statements at Copenhagen in December 2002, and is repeated in the recent June 2003

[43] Kok, above note 7, 14 and 64.
[44] Prodi, above note 9. See also Commission Communication, 'Wider Europe — Neighbourhood: A New Framework for Relations with our Eastern and Southern Neighbours', 11 March 2003, COM(2003)104, at p 4.
[45] Commission Communication COM(2003)104, at p 10.
[46] Council Conclusions on Wider Europe — New Neighbourhood, 16 June 2003, para 9.

Council Conclusions, in which the Council stated that the overall goal of the new policy would be to create an 'area of shared prosperity and values'. The reference to the values of the Union in draft Article I-56 reflects Article I-2 which states that the Union 'is founded on the values of respect for human dignity, liberty, democracy, equality, the rule of law and respect for human rights.' These are the values also listed by the Council as underpinning the new neighbourhood policy.[47] Is this talk of shared values a substitute for a more concrete offer (ie Union membership)? Or is it a sign of the political conditionality that will underpin the relationship?

The Commission's Communication and Council Conclusions are firmly based on conditionality: increased market access is offered in return for political and economic reform, together with cooperation in policy areas such as transport, the environment and security. The ultimate possibility is of an extension of Internal Market freedoms and regulatory structures to Russia, the Western NIS and the Southern Mediterranean, but this is very much a long-term objective, to be worked towards by stages.

The Communication stresses the differences between these different partners (Russia, the WNIS and the Southern Mediterranean), differences not only in their geo-political situation and economic and political development, but also in the history of their relations with the EU. For example the emphasis on free trade and regional integration in the Mediterranean policy contrasts with the non-preferential and more limited Partnership and Cooperation Agreements and existing bilateral relations with the WNIS. But there are mutual interests, characterised by the Commission in terms of proximity (to the EU), prosperity and poverty. Proximity suggests an emphasis on border issues, including security, customs, border management and energy and communications networks. The reduction of poverty and creation of shared prosperity suggest an emphasis on economic growth and development, trade and investment, but also on political reform.

These interests are reflected in the main elements of the planned new policy. On the one hand the EU proposes the development of free trade agreements and support for WTO membership (the current applicant countries are Russia, Ukraine, Algeria, Lebanon, Syria), trade-related technical assistance and the promotion of investment, including the development of SMEs and business-to-business dialogue. On the other hand, the EU would like to see cooperation on lawful migration including local border traffic, long-stay visas, visa free regimes, integration of lawful residents, and readmission agreements. Integration into European networks for transport, energy, telecommunications is also on the agenda, including progress towards a harmonised regulatory environment, compatible infrastructures and research collaboration. The EU's wider security interests are reflected

[47] Council Conclusions, 16 June 2003, para 2.

in the extension of the policy to cover the CFSP and ESDP, including crisis management, conflict resolution and internal post-conflict reconstruction. The wide scope of the initiative, drawing together political, economic, cultural and security issues, is reminiscent of the Euro-Med Barcelona Process, but with a stronger implementation framework (based on conditionality) and commitment to a deeper level of integration as the ultimate long-term goal.

The incentives offered by the EU will include financial and technical assistance. In current policy statements, the emphasis is on coordination and interaction between existing financial instruments and with other financial agencies. However the Commission is to consider a new financial instrument (the Neighbourhood Instrument) which would build on existing programmes (such as TACIS, PHARE, CARDS, MEDA and INTERREG) and which would focus on cross- and trans-border issues.[48]

The policy will use models based on pre-accession processes which are judged to have worked. These would supplement rather than replace existing frameworks, just as pre-accession did not replace Europe Agreement structures for the candidate states. What Prodi has called 'sharing everything but institutions'[49], does not preclude the creation of new (maybe joint) institutions although the emphasis on existing structures suggests that the institutional frameworks of the Partnership and Cooperation Agreements, Euro-Mediterranean Agreements and the Barcelona Process are likely to provide a starting point. Over the longer term, and if the new policy develops in the direction envisaged by the Commission, the experience of the EEA illustrates the difficulty of managing deep integration in the absence of shared law-making institutions.

The different starting points of the neighbouring states will entail different speeds and timetables, and although the Commission wishes to enhance the coherence of its policy, both Commission and Council are also committed to the differentiation that both the differing starting points and conditionality imply. The policy will be structured around 'a differentiated framework, which responds to progress made by the partner countries in defined areas',[50] and based on Action Plans containing targets, timetables and benchmarks. The idea is that benchmarks will be concrete and objectively-testable, offering greater predictability and certainty than what the Commission calls 'traditional conditionality'. They will set specific targets, including implementation of international commitments (such as OSCE

[48] The Commission Communication also suggests clarifying the criteria for macro-financial assistance and mobilising EIB and EBRD support for infrastructure investment and private sector development, and an increased role for the EBRD in Russia and the WNIS: Com (2003)104 final, p 14–15. See also Commission Communication, 'Paving the way for a New Neighbourhood Instrument', COM (2003) 393 final, 1 July 2003.
[49] Prodi, above note 9.
[50] Council Conclusions on Wider Europe — New Neighbourhood, 16 June 2003, para 5.

and Council of Europe standards), economic reform targets and timetables for legal approximation.

Action Plans and benchmarks would be agreed by the Council, acting on proposals from Commission, after consultation with partner countries (thus following the Accession Partnership model). The Commission suggested that the Action Plans would supersede Common Strategies as the 'main policy document' for these countries.[51] The Council does not follow this suggestion although it categorises the Action Plans as 'key policy instruments' and in terms that echo the purpose of Common Strategies:

> Action Plans ... should be political documents, building on existing agreements and setting out clearly the over-arching strategic policy targets, common objectives, political and economic benchmarks used to evaluate progress in key areas, and a timetable for their achievement which enable progress to be judged regularly.[52]

The Actions Plans are to be launched from 2004, starting with Ukraine, Moldova and the Southern Mediterranean countries with Association Agreements.

Essentially the Union's proposal is to harness the pre-accession processes including Plans, targets, conditionality and regular monitoring in order to achieve a high level of integration on the EEA model, strengthened cooperation on border management and common management of cross-border and regional issues. The Commission's Communication endorses a comment by Prodi, 'If a country has reached this level, it has come as close to the EU as it is possible to be without being a member.'[53] The question is whether the structures will work in the absence of membership as a target.

## THE PRE-ACCESSION MODEL WITHOUT ENLARGEMENT

Comparing these recent policy initiatives towards the Western Balkans and the Eastern and Southern Neighbours, we find similar structures (based on pre-accession instruments) but with different goals. And this difference is precisely the problem for the EU. As the circle of members, candidates and

[51] COM(2003)104 at p 17. Common Strategies, based on Art 13 TEU, have been adopted in relation to Russia, Ukraine and the Mediterranean. On Common Strategies, see C Hillion, 'Common Strategies and the Interface Between EC External Relations and the CFSP: Lessons of the Partnership Between the EU and Russia' in A Dashwood and C Hillion (eds), *The General Law of EC External Relations* (London, Sweet & Maxwell, 2000); E Denza, *The Intergovernmental Pillars of the European Union* (Oxford, OUP, 2002) 290–93.
[52] Council Conclusions on Wider Europe — New Neighbourhood, 16 June 2003, para 7.
[53] Com (2003)104 final, p 10, citing Prodi, op cit note 9.

prospective candidates grows wider, anything less than a promise of membership is now regarded as second best.

What does this mean for future EU foreign policy? Can the EU repeat its success? Will the instruments of enlargement, deployed in a wider context, succeed in achieving its goals of security and stability, its 'circle of friends', or is this only possible where enlargement itself is an instrument of policy? Will the 'pre-accession' model for progress being suggested work in the absence of the real incentives, and competitive dimension, caused by the goal of accession?

The perception of legitimacy, both of the policies themselves and in the distinctions and differentiations they make, is important; 'doubts about the legitimacy of the EU's decisions to include or exclude states could damage the credibility of the borders of the EU.'[54] The EU should not raise expectations (including the prospect of membership) that it is not prepared to meet.[55] But it is probably dangerous to seek to 'draw the boundaries' of the EU, in part because perceptions can change quite rapidly in response to new situations: the position of the Western Balkans is a clear example of this. The Wider Europe neighbourhood policy seeks to avoid this dilemma by disassociating itself from the question of membership: it does not promise membership but it does not preclude it either, and 'should be seen as separate from the question of possible EU accession'.[56] Again the EEA is a model here, with its neutrality towards membership, but what worked for the EFTA States may not work for the Union's new neighbours: the current accession states of central and eastern Europe were concerned that any move towards accession to the EEA would merely be used as an excuse to delay full EU membership.[57] In discussing the New Neighbourhood policy, the Council deflects the question of membership by referring to Article 49 of the Treaty on European Union. The implication is that the accession process, initiated by the prospective candidate state, will take its course according to Treaty-based procedural stages. This is to ignore the enormous political impact of categorising some — but not other — neighbouring countries as potential candidates.

The challenge will be to find ways to include the neighbours and potential candidates in the ongoing process of the Europeanization of foreign policy, so that those States are more participants than recipients of

[54] Sjursen and Smith, 'Justifying EU Foreign Policy: The Logics Underpinning EU Enlargement', Arena Working Papers, No 01/1; *http://www.arena.uio.no/*.

[55] Kok has pointed out the dangers posed by disillusioned neighbours with reference to the possibility of a failure by current Members to ratify the new accessions: Kok, above note 5, 17.

[56] COM(2003)104 at p 5; Council Conclusions on Wider Europe — New Neighbourhood, 16 June 2003, para 2.

[57] S Peers, 'An Ever Closer Waiting Room? The Case for Eastern European Accession to the EEA' (1994) 19 *CML Rev* 187.

EU policy-making. In the Communication on the Western Balkans, the Commission refers to the development of a 'shared agenda for European integration', but this is only part of the picture. Strengthening foreign policy cooperation beyond European integration is also envisaged, especially through inviting Western Balkans countries to associate themselves with CFSP common positions and other decisions. There is a prospect of developing common external policy initiatives within the wider Neighbourhood region on issues such as transport, environment, migration, as well as security, peacekeeping and crisis management. 'A shared neighbourhood implies burden-sharing and joint responsibility for addressing the threats to stability created by conflict and insecurity.'[58] The language of burden-sharing and joint responsibility implies the existence of solidarity based on shared values.[59] Such a relationship cannot be summoned into existence by a word or a policy statement, but will need to be built step by step and based on practical and reciprocal commitment.

A primary purpose of the new initiatives we have been considering here is to enlist the neighbouring States into sharing the EU's objectives of stability and security. Enlargement, as a policy instrument, will achieve this through a process of absorption. With the Western Balkans the EU is following a similar, though steeper, road. The difficulties still faced by some of those countries will put a great deal of strain on the delicate balance between inclusiveness and differentiation that has somehow been maintained over the fifth enlargement. That balance has been based on the assurance of the irreversibility of the enlargement process. Without that assurance, or the promise of membership, success in the process of developing shared objectives — not to mention achieving them — will depend very much on the Neighbourhood states accepting the new goal, the Neighbourhood Policy, as worthwhile in itself and not merely an unwillingness on the part of the Union to engage in a debate over the boundaries of Europe, or a vehicle for promoting an EU agenda.

[58] COM(2003)104, 12.
[59] M Cremona, 'EU Enlargement: Solidarity and Conditionality', forthcoming in *EL Rev*.

# 24

# *The European Employment Strategy and the Challenges of Enlargement*

SAMANTHA VELLUTI

*Another major consideration on our side is the need to reform the EES to reflect the reality of an enlarged Union. (...) It will certainly lead to wider diversity between national labour market situations within the EU. An issue that should be fully considered.*[1]

## INTRODUCTION

THIS CHAPTER CONSIDERS the social dimension of Central European enlargement and addresses the question of how effective the implementation of the European Strategy for Employment (EES) can be in the context of economies that are still in the process of moving from a 'central planning system' to a mainly 'neo-liberal driven system'. In particular, I examine *how* and the *extent* to which the labour markets of the future Member States are adapting to the EES and the results obtained by Central and Eastern European Countries (CEECs) in comparison to the current EU Member States in achieving the objectives of the Strategy. The study also assesses whether the EES is well suited for CEECs' labour markets. The paper concludes by maintaining that the future Constitutional Treaty should include a series of new provisions that strengthen the current framework of the EES and which create the conditions for improving the distribution of competence between the European Union (EU) and the Member States and also between vertical and horizontal levels of policy-making in the area of EC social policy.

[1] Anna Diamantopoulou, Employment and Social Affairs Commissioner, Informal Labour and Social Affairs Council, Burgos, 18–19 January 2003.

The first part of the chapter provides the framework of study, *ie* the legal and political scenario, and identifies the main issues and questions, which are posed by enlargement particularly with regard to the conceptualisation of EU law and governance in the area of social policy *sensu lato*.

The second part considers the measures adopted in CEECs and assesses the extent to which the latter have been progressively adjusting their institutional and political systems to the EES. In this context the study focuses on the implementation of labour market and social policies in the new Member States as explained in *ad hoc* national reports, *ie* the Joint Assessment Papers (JAPs) and in the recent Commission Communication *Progress on the implementation of the Joint Assessment Papers on employment policies in candidate countries*.

The third part evaluates whether the EES and its implementation through the Open Method of Co-ordination (OMC) represents the appropriate policy instrument for CEECs' labour markets and employment situation by way of analysing the Strategy's strengths as well as its weaknesses.

The fourth and final part of the chapter looks at the evaluation of the first five years of implementation of the Strategy by the Commission and its re-design for the future and suggests a series of amendments to Title VIII and Title XI of the EC Treaty.

## INTRODUCTION: LAW AND POLICY IN AN ENLARGED UNION

The current enlargement is a further step towards European integration and it epitomises the European Union (EU) *raison d'être*: to encourage peace, stability, democracy and prosperity throughout Europe by way of integrating states and people.

This enlargement process, however, differs from its predecessors for many reasons. Whether in terms of number of new states, population, geographic expansion, linguistic diversity, or social and economic heterogeneity, not only *vis-à-vis* the current Member States but also among themselves, this enlargement represents a historic momentum in that it has yielded the idea of a reunified Europe but chiefly because it shifts the EU to a new scale of activity, *ie* a continental scale of operation.[2] Furthermore, it may be conceived as a move from a specific EU foreign policy to the making of a European common policy. In this context, Tulmets departs from an emphasis on the unilateral aspect of enlargement and maintains that it

[2] Report of Wim Kok to the European Commission, *Enlarging the European Union, Achievements and Challenges*, Robert Schuman Centre for Advanced Studies, European University Institute, 26 March 2003, p 8.

should be seen as a 'mutually constitutive process'[3] in which candidate countries have had a pro-active role in the programming and implementation of assistance programmes, *eg* PHARE[4] and Twinning projects.[5] In fact, the novelty of this fifth enlargement is reflected in the way the EU has been developing in recent years a 'new widening method' based upon classical elements of former enlargements and new features of policy-making and interest mediation.[6]

Prior to the 2002 Copenhagen European Council the focal point was the process of accession *per se*, *ie* 'how and when will the new countries join?' Now the focus is on 'what happens after they join?', 'how can decisions be taken?' and 'what overall European strategy do we need for an enlarged EU?'

The inherent paradox of the European integration process is that it is taking place apace but at the same time also too slowly. There is the need to balance the process of 'widening' (enlargement) with the process of 'deepening' (reform). Even without enlargement, the EU needs a profound review of its decision and policy-making process. The institutional reforms decided at Nice in fact did not entail a fundamental review of the EU decision-making system. In addition to the criteria for new members — the three 'Copenhagen criteria' — the EU laid down in 1993 a fourth criterion for enlargement: 'the Union's own capacity to absorb new members, while maintaining the momentum of European integration'.[7] The furthering of the enlargement process, therefore, has acted as a catalyst for change and self-reform.[8] This explains why questions of identity, governance and

[3] E Tulmets, 'The EU PHARE/Twinning Programme as a Socialisation Instrument in the Enlarging Europe: Between Organisational Impact and Transfer of Norms', paper presented at the 33rd UACES Annual Conference, Newcastle-upon-Tyne, 2–4 Sept 2003.

[4] PHARE ('Pologne-Hongire, Aide à la Reconstruction Economique') was launched in July 1989 to fund and support institutional, administrative and economic change in these two countries and subsequently extended to all CEECs.

[5] The Twinning exercise was introduced in 1997 as a new institution–building instrument in order to help CEECs improve their administrative capacities and strengthen their institutions. It consists in the long-term secondment of one or more Pre-Accession Advisors (PAA) from a Ministry or other approved body in a given member state to work on projects in the corresponding Ministry of a candidate country. It may also include short-term expertise, training and specific services. See EC Commission, *Twinning in Action*, (CEC, 2001).

[6] M Steffens, *The EU's Acquis as an Evolving Transformation Framework for the CEE: From the Classical to the New Enlargement Method*, paper presented at the 33rd UACES Annual Conference, Newcastle-upon-Tyne, 2–4 September 2003.

[7] The EU accepts conditionally eventual membership of the CEECs provided that the CEECs have: a) stable institutions (guarantee of democracy, rule of law, human rights, minority rights); b) functioning market economy and capacity to cope with competitive pressures inside the EC; c) ability to adopt the *acquis*; accepted aims of political, economic and monetary union. Presidency Conclusions of the Copenhagen European Council — 21–22 June 1993.

[8] See Report of the Working Group on the Eastern Enlargement of the European Union, *Preparing the EU and Its Institutions foe Enlargement*, Policy Papers, RSC No 99/7, p 14.

(democratic) legitimacy as well as 'institutional engineering' have been at the forefront of the Community's top agenda and why the next IGC aims at achieving a comprehensive institutional reform and political re-organisation with the ratification of the Constitutional Treaty.[9]

Before I embark on the analysis of the EES and the challenges of enlargement it is important to emphasise the different functions that European law has had within the fifty years of existence of the European Community. Bermann explains this effectively.[10] In the 1950s since European law was conceived chiefly as a means of attaining largely economic objectives, the law was conceived as 'law that *emerged from* the Community's legislative, administrative and judicial processes rather than law that *accounted for and explained* those processes.'[11] European law has since then gradually evolved into being more than merely instrumental to the pursuit of the Internal Market and to Europeanisation and increasingly seen as exemplifying the various processes and phases of European integration and governance. In fact post Maastricht, the legal debates have focused mainly on constitutionalism issues, democratic deficit, European citizenship, transparency, subsidiarity and human rights.

What is striking about this enlargement is that the very same factors, *ie* political, economic and social, which make it in many ways unprecedented, have not only fostered the completion of the constitutional project but also re-assigned an instrumental function to European law in order to enable it to perform problem-solving tasks and to *shape* the EU decision and policy- making processes.[12]

Another important development concerns the very nature of EU law. The area of social policy *sensu lato* is illustrative. Recent actions and strategies by EU Institutions in this area reveal an increase in the use of complementary[13] or rather alternative methods of regulation to the Community Method that eschew traditional forms of law, enhance diversity and pave the way towards what I define as a 'transverse form of policy-making.'[14] This new process draws upon a trans-national multi-tiered form of governance and basis of

[9] The draft of the Constitutional Treaty was endorsed by the governments of the fifteen Member States at the European Council meeting in Thessaloniki, June 2003. Presidency Conclusions, Thessaloniki European Council, 19 and 20 June 2003.

[10] G Bermann, 'Law in an Enlarged European Union' (2001) 14(3) *EUSA Review* 1–5.

[11] *Idem.*

[12] *Idem.*

[13] EC Commission White Paper on *EU Governance*, COM(2001) 428, pp 20–22.

[14] Confront this definition with the broader notions of 'flexibility' or 'differentiated integration process.' See EC Commission 'Targeted Socio-Economic Research, I- Guidance note relating to the work programme 1996,' pp 4 and 10, (Luxembourg: Office for Official Publications of the European Communities) where the concept of 'transversality' is used to highlight the interaction between the different elements/themes of the Fourth Framework programme (1994–98); N Walker, 'Sovereignty and Differentiated Integration in the European Union' (1998) 4(4) *European Law Journal* 355–88.

self-regulation,[15] co-regulation,[16] voluntary networks and more specifically on the interaction of actors distributed across the various levels of policy-making. It is articulated upon 'co-operative and horizontal' forms of subsidiarity and proximity.

With regard to the new Member States it is unquestionable that the approximation of their legal systems to the *acquis communautaire* is a legal obligation.[17] In fact the horizontal provisions on the approximation of laws in Europe Agreements (EAs)[18] represent a core part of the latter.[19] The conformity of CEECs domestic legal systems with the body of EU rules was one of the conditions for the accession of these countries to the EU.[20]

Approximation and harmonisation of laws are often used as synonyms. In the context of enlargement these terms have a different meaning in that the term approximation describes the process by which candidate countries as third countries are voluntarily approximating their legal systems to an external legal regime, *ie* the EU. Hence, a different situation from harmonisation whereby EU legislation has a binding effect on the current Member States' legal systems.[21] Moreover, the obligation to approximate the legal system to the *acquis communautaire* is an obligation *to act*, not an obligation of *results*. According to Piontek the 'approximation process entails an obligation to incorporate the respective Community rules into the legal order of the associated country to the *fullest extent possible* as an important condition of membership in the Union.'[22] The investigation is undertaken precisely in this broader framework of voluntary self-reform.

[15] EC Commission White Paper on *EU Governance*, COM(2001) 428, p 20 where self-regulation is referred to as one of the complementary tools to legislation.

[16] 'Co-regulation combines binding legislative and regulatory action within actions taken by the actors most concerned, drawing on their practical expertise;' EC Commission White Paper on *EU Governance*, COM(2001) 428, p 21, where the Commission has also outlined the conditions for its application.

[17] For a detailed analysis, see A Ott and K Inglis, *Handbook on European Enlargement: A Commentary on the Enlargement Process* (The Hague, TMC Asser Press, 2002) 631–39.

[18] Europe Agreements (EAs) are formal bi-lateral agreements between the EU and the candidate countries, which cover a variety of issues. EAs may be defined as association agreements (AAs), which present the classical elements of a trade agreement supplemented by a 'political dialogue'. See U Sedelmeier and H Wallace, 'Eastern Enlargement', in W and H Wallace (eds), *Policy-Making in the European Union* (Oxford, CUP, 2000) 435–40.

[19] The EAs provide for two broad categories of provisions regarding approximation: a) horizontal provisions in chapters specifically devoted to approximation (*lex generalis*); b) vertical provisions contained in different provisions of the agreements (*lex specialis*).

[20] See, above, n 7.

[21] See A Evans, 'Voluntary Harmonisation in Integration between the European Community and Eastern Europe' (1997) 22 *European Law Review* 201.

[22] See E Piontek, 'Central and Eastern European Countries in Preparation for Membership in the European Union — a Polish Perspective' (1997) 1 *Yearbook of Polish European Studies* 73, emphasis added.

For the purposes of the negotiations for membership, the body of EU rules has been divided into thirty-one chapters, of which five concern labour market and social policies.[23]

The following sections are going to take into consideration issues regarding negotiation chapter 13 (social policy and employment), chiefly two broad issues. First, I am going to examine to what extent the new Member States can adequately embrace the corpus of existing social ('hard' and 'soft') law and which policy instruments may be appropriate to enable this approximation process. Secondly, I am going to look at the legal and institutional reforms necessary to accommodate an enlarged Union. These two issues are addressed within the analysis of the EES as a new form of governance.

## PREPARING FOR THE *ACQUIS COMMUNAUTAIRE*: LABOUR MARKETS AND EMPLOYMENT POLICIES IN CEECS

Social conditionality requires the implementation of the *hard acquis* of EU health and safety rules, a range of EU social legislation, *eg* on working time, parental leave, equal opportunities, mechanisms for social dialogue, and the *soft acquis*, which entails a shift from social law and legislative initiatives towards policies aimed at fostering employment creation, social protection and social inclusion and which are implemented on the basis of non-binding legal instruments. The EES is laid down in the Employment Title of the EC Treaty, Title VIII, and it is an important part of the Community social *acquis*. There is thus an obligation upon CEECs to implement the EES.

The new Member States have been defining labour market and employment policies in line with European standards and progressively adjusting institutions and policies to the EES in order to allow the full implementation of the Employment Title as from accession. To this end, in 1999 the EU Commission initiated a co-operation process on employment with these countries, which also aimed at ensuring that both the present EU financial support for accession and the preparation for ESF implementation would focus on supporting the identified employment policy priorities.[24] Moreover,

[23] *ie*, Chap 2 (freedom of movement of persons), chap 3 (freedom to provide services), chap 13 (social policy and employment), chap 18 (education and training), chap 21 (regional policy and coordination of structural instruments). See EC Commission, Report on the results of the negotiations on the accession of Cyprus, Malta, Hungary, Poland, the Slovak Republic, Latvia, Estonia, Lithuania, the Czech Republic and Slovenia to the European Union, available on-line at: *http://europa.eu.int/comm/enlargement/index_en.htm*.

[24] See Commission Staff Working Paper, *Supporting Document to the Communication 'Progress in the implementation of the Joint Assessment Papers on employment policies in candidate countries'*, Brussels, SEC (2003) 200.

at the European Council in Stockholm in 2001 it was decided that the future Member States should be actively involved in the goals and procedures of the Lisbon Strategy. The National Plan for the Adoption of the *Acquis* requires that CEECs take responsibility for drawing up long-term market strategies, as a basis for the detailed annual action plan, which has to be drawn up each year under the EES.[25] Several of the these countries have drawn up employment action plans containing programmes that are structured on the basis of the EES. Moreover, CEECs and the EU Commission have been analysing the key challenges for employment policies in the JAPs on the basis of studies funded by the EU Commission in co-operation with the European Training Foundation. At the beginning of 2002 seven CEECs had been evaluated.[26]

These countries and the EU Commission have subsequently agreed to monitor the implementation of the JAP commitments. Shortly after the signature of the JAPs the main commitments have been discussed in technical seminars between the EU Commission and representatives of different Ministries, regional authorities, the Public Employment Services (PES) and the social partners to encourage policy action.[27] In late Spring 2002, the JAPs were reviewed in a second round. This reviewing process helped to identify strategic challenges, some of which are also shared with the current members states.[28]

Studies conducted on of CEECs[29] show that:

— Sectoral characteristics of employment are quite different from those in the current EU Member States. In fact in CEECs agriculture and industry have a much higher share of total employment. The restructuring process has severely damaged the industrial sector, which has led to high levels of unemployment. The service sector now represents the main source of new jobs;

[25] See European Commission, *Towards the Enlarged Union. Report on the Progress Towards Accession by Each Candidate Countries*, (Brussels, CEC, 2002).
[26] The first JAPs were signed with the Czech Republic, Slovenia, Poland and Estonia in 2000 and early 2001, followed by Hungary, Slovakia and Lithuania in late 2001/early 2002 and by Romania, Bulgaria in Autumn 2002. The JAP with Latvia has been signed in early 2003.
[27] European Commission, Communication from the Commission to the Council, the European Parliament, the Economic and Social Committee and the Committee of the Regions, *Progress on the implementation of the Joint Assessment Papers on employment policies in candidate countries*, COM(2003) 37 final.
[28] European Commission to the Spring European Council in Brussels, *Progress on the Lisbon Strategy*, COM(2003) 5 final.
[29] H Khol and H-W Platzer, 'Labour relations in central and eastern Europe and the European social model' (2003) 1 *Transfer* 26 *et seq*; M Celin, 'European Employment Strategy: the right answer for candidate countries?' (2003) 1 *Transfer* 88; Editorial 'Employment in the European Union candidate countries' (2003) 350 *European Industrial Relations Review* 22–27.

— Labour relations in CEECs are developing along nationally characteristic lines and are showing considerable variations. A comparison of structural developments in labour relations in eight CEECs at company, sectoral and national levels shows that change is difficult to achieve. Significant common features, except for Slovenia, are the overall weak and fragmented structures at company level, with widespread absence of a sectoral level of action and organisation and a pronounced emphasis on the state, which also characterises tripartism at national level; educational and training levels are generally lower than those of current EU Member States;
— Labour productivity levels vary widely due to the specificities of each of the CEECs;
— Long-term unemployment as a consequence of structural and economic reform, which affects marginalized groups, such as minorities,[30] the disabled, the low-skilled, older workers, and people living in remote regions. The restructuring process has also entailed an increase of informal employment;
— Education and vocational training levels are in most cases lower than those in most current EU countries;
— High levels of regional and social disparities;
— Inefficiency of PES to adapt to the new economic and social scenario and their incapacity to create new jobs. This emerged during the transition period;
— Lack of national financial resources for implementing effective labour market and employment policies.

Furthermore, in most cases the drafting of the JAPs has been a purely administrative exercise with a lack of political commitment from most governments of the candidate countries.

In its report on progress on the implementation of the JAPs the EU Commission maintains that, despite significant differences, CEECs have made progress in transforming their labour markets and in adjusting policies to EU standards.[31] The report has identified the following strategic priorities for the labour markets of these countries:

— Increase labour supply, employment rates, particularly in the service sector, together with productivity rates and skill levels;[32]

[30] The Roma minority is the most marginalized minority in the CEECs with extremely high levels of unemployment even *vis-à-vis* the nationals of these countries.
[31] European Commission, Communication on *Progress on the implementation of the Joint Assessment Papers on employment policies in candidate countries*, COM(2003) 37 final.
[32] In 2001 the overall employment rate was 56.8% well below the EU average, 63.8%, and the Lisbon targets.

— Restructure the CEECs' economic system and the labour markets by way of taking into consideration the specificities and levels of adaptability of CEECs to change;
— Linked to the former, reduce the reliance on agriculture and traditional industrial sectors.

In summary, CEECs are undergoing enormous upheaval in their economic, political, institutional and socio-cultural structures. In fact the process of re-nationalisation, which follows the implementation of the *acquis communautaire* and the shift towards a mainly neo-liberal driven economic system will entail high costs of change in the short and medium term. In the Kok Report on enlarging the EU, it is maintained that 'even in the most positive of scenarios, the economic convergence of the new Member States with the present members will be a long-term process — a matter of decades. The costs and benefits will not necessarily occur in the same period; costs associated with increased competition and adjustment may come sooner.'[33] In most CEECs, economic policy measures and structural reforms have been enacted with the desire to join the European Union and in the future also the Economic and Monetary Union (EMU).[34] The main issue is how convergence will be achieved. Enlargement may in fact alter the balance between costs and benefits of the EU with a probable increase of the former. In addition, in the new enlarged European Union the risks of asymmetric shocks will increase.

In addition to the economic impact of enlargement, various changes regarding the constitutional, institutional, legal and political traditions of CEECs are required. In fact one of the major difficulties encountered by CEECs is not only represented by the approximation of laws to the *acquis communauataire per se* but also by the interpretation and incorporation of the 'mode of legal reasoning, which has evolved within the EU, as well as the institutional patterns of interaction — between national and European legal systems — which have marked its development'[35] together with the acceptance of the supremacy and direct effect of EU law and the adjudicatory primacy of the European Court of Justice (ECJ) by the national constitutional and legal systems. A further issue is the relationship between the reform of the EU Treaties, the requirement of unanimous ratification of the

[33] See Report of Wim Kok, above n 2, 37–38.
[34] All acceding countries will take over and implement the body of EU rules regarding EMU upon accession with the status of a country with a derogation under Art 122 of the EC Treaty (Art III-86 of the draft Constitutional Treaty). For an analysis of CEECs and joining the EMU, see Report of the Working Group on the Eastern Enlargement of the European Union, *Implications of the Euro for Enlargement*, RSC Publication, Policy Paper 99/3.
[35] See Report of the Working Group on the Eastward Enlargement of the European Union, *Preparing for the Acquis Communautaire*, RSC Policy Paper, No 98/6; A Ott and K Inglis, above n 18, 209–20.

EU Treaty amendments under the current Member States' constitutional procedures[36] and the constitutional systems of CEECs, which could represent 'constitutional barriers' to the full completion of the approximation process.[37]

## IS THE DYAD EES/OMC THE RIGHT ANSWER FOR CEECS?

Following the above analysis, what is the (potential) contribution of the EES to EU governance in an enlarged Union?

Enlargement may pose a new challenge to the reinforcement of the existing body of European social law and policy in the current EU and its extension to new Member States. In addition, the 2004 enlargement distinguishes itself from previous enlargements in terms of growing diversity. However, the EU has already been developing the integration process in line with 'diversity'.[38] Given the costs of implementation, the impact of EMU and of the Stability and Growth Pact (SGP), differentiation and flexibility represent appropriate regulatory tools, which would respect the various states' capacities and specificities. The policy instruments employed in the context of the OMC, as opposed to an implementation *tout court*, could well represent a leverage for the introduction of new measures in the area of social policy in CEECs whilst respecting their national characteristics and, at the same time, allow the EU to promote the adoption of structural policy measures aimed at modernising and improving the *European social model*.[39] Furthermore, the 2002 Copenhagen European Council reconfirmed the 'principle of differentiation' based on each countries' own merits.

The above begs the question of how can differentiation, the OMC and similar modes of governance enable the EU as a whole to anticipate and capitalise on change. What follows is a brief analysis of how the EES operates and its implementation through the OMC, which I have therefore called 'dyad EES/OMC.'

The dyad EES/OMC is an iterative process based on open participation in the implementation of policies, consensus building, exchange of best practices and information, use of benchmarking and more broadly co-operation and co-ordination within a multi-tiered framework of governance.[40] Moreover, the constraints on Member States, is not legal in nature since

36 See Art 48 TEU. Compare with Art IV-7 of the draft Constitutional Treaty.

37 See A Albi, 'Referendums in Eastern Europe: The Effects on Reforming the EU Treaties and on the Candidate Countries' Positions in the Convention', RSC No 2002/65.

38 See, above section I.

39 European Commission, Communication from the Commission to the Council, the European Parliament, the Economic and Social Committee and the Committee of the Regions, *Social Policy Agenda*, COM(2000) 379 final, p 24.

40 See J Scott and DM Trubek, 'Mind the Gap: Law and New Approaches to Governance in the European Union,' (2002) 8(1) *European Law Journal* 6–8. The authors identify and

this new regulatory mode lacks of a system of sanctions and enforcement procedures; it is rather a moral and political constraint.

The EES aims at achieving six major objectives regarding both the European and the national level of policy-making:[41]

i legitimacy of Community action;
ii promotion of policy learning;
iii efficiency of policy-making at the European and national level;
iv increase of policy co-ordination among all levels of government;
v promotion of greater inter-action between different policy areas;
vi promotion of trans-national forms of governance whilst maintaining a certain degree of convergence.

The first objective, legitimacy, has always been pursued by the EU Institutions in the difficult achievement of promoting further integration in policy areas, which have traditionally been considered as pertaining to the national domain.

From this perspective the EES does not represent an entirely new mode of governance. Rather it may be defined as constituting a *tertium genus* in that it presents elements of continuity with previous methods of policy-making in the field of social law and contemporaneously representing an innovative and qualitative break from the past.

The difficult task of promoting further convergence whilst respecting the diversity of the various labour market and industrial relations systems (objective vi) was already undertaken with the Agreement on Social Policy annexed to the Maastricht Treaty (ASP). The aim of the latter was to introduce a multi-tiered level of policy and decision-making at the Community level, complementing the use of different regulatory tools, such as directives and non-binding legal instruments and to co-ordinate these new methods of regulation with the Member States' different modes of legislation and/or policies.[42] The result was the power assigned to the social partners to negotiate European framework agreements, which could become European law, the formal consultation of the social partners in the drafting of social

describe succinctly six factors, which have fostered the increase in the use of 'new governance' instruments.

[41] See DM Trubek and J Mosher, 'New Governance, EU Employment Policy, and the European Social Model,' in *Symposium: Responses to the European Commission's White Paper on Governance*, sections 5–6. Available at: *http:www.jeanmonnetprogram.org/papers/01/0100501.html*. See also J Goetschy, 'The European Employment Strategy, Multi-level Governance and Policy Co-ordination: Past, Present and Future,' in Zeitlin and Trubek (eds), *Governing work and welfare in a new economy: European and American experiments* (Oxford, OUP, 2003).

[42] In most Member States, such as France, Spain, Germany and Italy social issues were also or mostly dealt through non-legislative regulatory tools such as collective agreements.

policy directives and finally the possibility of implementing directives by way of national collective agreements rather than legislation.

The Treaty of Amsterdam added further impetus to differentiation and subsidiarity with the adoption of a common strategy for employment and with a European collective bargaining system formalised in Title XI.[43]

These reforms were expected to increase the legitimacy of Community action in the social policy area by adding further importance to the interests of civil society and secondly by increasing the participation of Member States in the modernisation of the *European Social Model*.[44] Within the EES the objective is to integrate Member States policies with the EPGs in a medium and long-term perspective, with results, which are to increase at the end of every cycle and which transcend short-term policies and can therefore more effectively solve the unemployment problem across Europe.[45] Goetschy posits that 'the EES is a way to 'depoliticize' the unemployment problem from its immediate national contingencies and to address it in a longer-term perspective.'[46] The very existence of the EES, with its EPGs and its NAPs, shows that efforts are being made to integrate the various levels of governance both at the European and national level, strengthening the co-ordination of national and European social policies and ultimately increasing the efficiency of social regulation (objectives iii and iv).

The EES has in fact several cardinal features:

a) most of the policies must be carried out at the national or local level. There is relatively little direct action by the EC Institutions and bodies, the only exception being the (modest) use of the European structural funds to support the implementation of the EES;
b) the primary role of the EU Institutions is to provide a general framework of the strategy, to develop specific guidelines, establish a monitoring system and finally to make annual recommendations to the Member States, where necessary;
c) the institutional and legislative reforms are established and implemented at the national or local level.

43 Arts 136–140 EC (Arts III-98 of the draft Constitutional Treaty).

44 See Presidency Conclusions of the Nice European Council, 7, 8, and 9 December 2001, Annex I, para 11, for a definition of *European Social Model*, and Communication from the Commission to the Council, the European Parliament, the Economic and Social Committee and the Committee of the Regions, *Social Policy Agenda*, COM(2000) 379 final, for the meaning of *modernisation of the European Social Model.*

45 J Goetschy, 'The European Employment Strategy, Multi-level Governance and Policy Co-ordination: Past, Present and Future,' in Zeitlin and Trubek (eds), *Governing work and welfare in a new economy: European and American experiments* (Oxford, OUP, 2003).

46 See J Goetschy, 'The European Employment Strategy: Genesis and Development,' (1999) 5(2) *European Journal of Industrial Relations* 132.

The EES has also brought a change in the objectives of the EU agenda. Previous EU social policy and legislation was in fact oriented to labour market policies linked to the completion of the internal market and to the creation of EMU, without taking into account core issues of national social policies. On the contrary, the EES aims at addressing issues, which directly affect national employment policies and industrial relations systems. This is explained by the fact that 'the more nationally sensitive a subject and the more difficult to resolve at national level, the more likely are Member States to become involved in an EU co-ordination procedure.'[47] Syrpis maintains that 'in performance legitimacy terms, the focus has shifted away from the completion of the internal market, towards the re-distributive implications of European integration.'[48] Another feature of the EES is that it integrates separate policy domains[49] (objective v). This can be seen already in the selection of the four areas, which are to represent the four Pillars on which the EPGs are adopted.[50] The EPGs and the NAPs both illustrate that the EES has already identified a series of areas where the independent operation of the various actors involved and policy boundaries are to be substituted by strict co-operation, co-ordination and with the implementation of horizontal, preventative and active measures and initiatives at all levels.

Moreover, even in areas that are covered by the EPGs, the EES does not always demand convergence: many of the guidelines leave the states with a substantial level of discretion with regard to the ways of adopting the concerning measures. It may be argued therefore that the EES does aim at achieving convergence, but it is mostly convergence of results rather than policies. In this regard, the EES presents the same intrinsic logic of a Directive. In fact, although Directives are part of EC secondary 'hard' law they are only binding 'as to the result to be achieved, upon each member state to which it is addressed, leaving to the national authorities the choice of form and methods.'[51] The difference between the two regulatory methods lays in the fact that whereas the EES is a deliberative form of governance, Directives are, on the contrary, based on a diplomatic operational mode.[52] Secondly, as a soft law instrument, the

[47] *Ibid*, 133.
[48] See P Syrpis, 'Legitimising European Governance: Taking Subsidiarity Seriously within the Open Method of Co-ordination' EUI Working Paper, 2002.
[49] See S Ball, 'The European Employment Strategy: The Will but not the Way?' (2001) *Industrial Law Journal* 359–66; P Syrpis, 'Smoke Without Fire: The Social Policy Agenda and the Internal Market,' (2001) 30(3) *Industrial Law Journal* 271–88.
[50] Previously, measures aimed at fostering entrepreneurship, at promoting vocational (re-)training of workers and at strengthening gender mainstreaming were not only dealt with by different authorities, institutions and bodies but were also regulated separately.
[51] See Art 249(3) EC. In the draft Constitutional Treaty Directives have been substituted by 'European framework laws', see Art 32, Title V of Part I.
[52] *Contra*, J Goetschy, 'The European Employment Strategy: Genesis and Development,' (1999) 5(2) *European Journal of Industrial Relations* 132. The author argues in fact that in

EES does not provide any kind of legal sanctions in the event of a member state failing to meet the EPGs objectives. This can be partially explained by the fact that in most cases the EPGs do not provide quantified targets. It would thus be hard to establish whether a member state, given its economic and social structure, has achieved the objectives established by the EPGs. Even in cases where the target to be achieved has to correspond to the average of the three best performing Member States[53] it would appear politically incorrect for the EU Commission and the Council to impose legal sanctions to those Member States, which fail to achieve quantified targets since the industrial relations system and the labour market of each country are extremely varied. This explains why, the use of recommendations and the adoption of incentive measures by the Council designed to encourage co-operation between Member States and to support their action in the field of employment through initiatives aimed at developing exchanges of information and best practices appear far more successful in promoting structural reforms in the Member States.

Another objective of the EES is the promotion of policy learning. Teague maintains that alternative regulatory and deliberative methods, which promote policy learning and innovation, are preferable to the more traditional modes of governance.[54] Some scholars argue that this is an area where the EES has been most successful.[55]

The amendments introduced in the EPGs, in particular in the guidelines for 2001,[56] are evidence of the fact that overall the EES is fostering policy learning and innovation. While some are an attempt to refine the previous EPGs, the most recent guidelines introduce new objectives and targets.[57] Some of the changes inserted in the EPGs exemplify the fact that the learning process is gradually affecting policy development and the preliminary

the case of directives the diplomatic mode of interaction prevails and there is a lack of deliberative process, which on the contrary typifies the EES.

[53] This is the case for example of G 2, regarding the Employability Pillar.

[54] See P Teague, 'Deliberative Governance and EU Social Policy,' 2001 7(1) *European Journal of Industrial Relations* 7–26.

[55] See M Ferrara, A Hemerijk and M Rhodes, *The Future of Social Europe: Recasting Work and Welfare in the New Economy* (Oxford, OUP, 2001); DM Trubek and J Mosher 'New Governance, EU Employment Policy, and the European Social Model' in *Symposium: Responses to the European Commission's White Paper on Governance*, sections 5 & 6. Available at: *http:www.jeanmonnetprogram.org/papers/01/0100501.html.*

[56] Five so-called 'horizontal objectives' have been introduced. For a detailed analysis see, C Degryse and P Pochet, 'Social Developments in the European Union, Second Annual Report,' OSE and ETUI, Brussels, 2001, 16–19, [online]. Available at: *http://www.ose.be/en/default.htm.*

[57] See Council Decision, on Guidelines for Member States' employment policies for the year 2001, of 19 January 2001, OJEC, L22/18, 24.1.2001, G 1 and 10 (public services) and G 4; G 9, G 3, G 5.

results achieved so far suggest that more changes will be made also at the national level in the following years.[58]

The Dolowitz and Marsh model develops a framework to analyse the process of policy transfer.[59] The model conceives policy transfer as a dependent variable and looks either at the main elements of policy transfer or at the reasons for learning. The model shows that policy transfer may also be treated as an explanatory variable but it cannot alone be the only variable explaining policy development. This is because there is not enough evidence to confirm that policy transfer has been successful in promoting policy diffusion.

The submission of NAPs by Member States in cooperation with the social partners, in accordance with common objectives and indicators established in the annual EPGs, and the evaluation made by the European Institutions through the Joint Employment Report (JER) and the Assessment Report on Implementation (ARI) is illustrative of the way the 're-regulation' or 're-nationalisation process'[60] operates in practice. The implementation of the EES, therefore, entails, on the one hand, the Europeanisation of social policy and, on the other hand, it increases the importance of national social pacts. The EES in fact promotes the creation of new employment and labour market paradigms through the exchange of best practices and benchmarking and by linking various areas of social policy together both from a supply and demand-side perspective.

Recent case studies, which assessed the implementation of the EES at the national level, however, reveal a less optimistic picture of the EES. The case studies conducted have been confronted first of all with research methodological problems. Reliable data sources are scarce and not uniform and the availability of information varies between countries. In particular, information on Southern Mediterranean countries has been insufficiently detailed and the NAPs are a mere reformulation of national programs. Added to this, the difficulty also consisted in assessing the data available, *ie* cross-country comparisons have been hard to make due to the different national labour market patterns.

As regards to the causal link between the EES and the national employment and labour market policies the case studies have showed that

[58] See Commission Staff Working Paper, *Assessment of the Implementation of the 2001 Employment Guidelines, Supporting Document to the Joint Employment Report 2001*, SEC(2001) 1398; see also European Commission, *Employment in Europe 2001, Recent Trends and Prospects*. Available at: http://europa.eu.int/comm/employment_social/empl&esf/docs/empleurope2001_en.pdf.

[59] See D Dolowitz and D Marsh, 'Learning from Abroad: The Role of Policy Transfer in Contemporary Policy-Making' (2000) 13(1) *Governance* 5–24.

[60] See S Sciarra, 'Global or Re-nationalised? Past and Future of European Labour Law' in F Snyder (ed), *The Europeanisation of Law: The Legal Effects of European Integration* (Oxford, Hart Publishing, 2000) 270–71.

the EPGs and national social policies either aimed at achieving similar objectives or, on the contrary, had different targets. The second step was to assess the effective implementation of the Strategy at the national level. In the case of non-convergence of policy objectives the research studies were conducted in order to provide some valuable proposals of reform in line with the EPGs. The countries selected for the case studies were France, Sweden, Denmark and Spain, each representing different labour markets' performances and political practices.[61]

The case studies showed that the level of 'policy distance' between a given national context and the European objectives determines the level of European influence on the national level. Moreover, the whole process was mostly administered at the ministerial level, *ie* Ministry of Economy and Finance and Social Affairs. In fact even though the participation of social partners in these two countries is higher compared to other countries, the case studies revealed that their involvement is still more formalistic and passive — 'more a matter of information than real consultation or negotiation with the government' — than in the domestic level of policy-making. Case studies showed that the EES is insufficient *per se* due to particular political patterns and to the existence of persisting structural problems. With regard to the involvement of the social partners in the adoption and implementation of the NAPs, most social partners have reported positively on the Luxembourg Process. The role of the social partners, however, is still unsatisfactory still being far from proper negotiation and consultation with the government. This situation contrasts with the EPGs, where the social partners are given a key role in the modernisation of work organisation and in lifelong learning measures.[62] Moreover, the NAPs reveal that it is mostly national confederations that are involved in the process and little information is provided on the extent of the social partners' participation at the sectoral level.[63] Lafoucrière argues that the effective implementation of the EPGs regarding adaptability can only be guaranteed by the wider use of a 'positive social dialogue,' *ie* by introducing more specific guidelines, which are currently too vague and by defining more clearly an active role of the social partners in the EES.[64]

[61] See C De La Porte and P Pochet (eds), *Building Social Europe through the Open Method of Co-ordination* (Brussels, PIE-Peter Lang, 2002).

[62] See G13, G14 and G15. See also G6 (combating emerging bottlenecks); G17 (equal opportunities) G18 (reconcile work and family life) and Horizontal Objectives B (Quality of Work); C (Lifelong Learning Strategy) D (partnership) and F (common structural indicators).

[63] See Keller and Bansbach, 'Social Dialogues: an interim report on recent results and prospects,' (1999/2000) *Industrial Review Journal Annual Review* 84.

[64] See C Lafoucrière, 'The European Employment Strategy — The Third Pillar: Adaptability,' ETUI, DWP 2000.01.03, p 31; see also 22–24 and 29–31.

One final point regards the obligation that Member States have to exchange best practices. With the beginning of the second annual cycle of the NAPs, Member States have been required to present examples of best practices. The achievement of such a target has been quite scant. Although the JER lists a few examples of best practices, the method used for the share of best practices consists in the review of the NAPs of those Member States that have not given enough details of best practices, which are then circulated to all Member States. Despite the measures adopted by the EU Commission, it is still necessary to review these learning policy mechanisms in order to make them more effective.

The EES therefore has various weaknesses that are inherent in its soft law nature. First, the very nature of the EES as a non-binding legal instrument does not allow for the accurate assessment of the results achieved given that national measures might not refer to the EPGs for their adoption and that many elements of the EES are already part of national policy programs. Secondly, the subordination of the EES implementation to the economic and political situation within the various Member States combined with its soft law nature does not guarantee its further development in moments of economic recession or political instability. Moreover, the paucity of specific procedural rules and detailed guidelines, the scant information on the operationalisation of the exercise of benchmarking — particularly on how parameters and structural indicators are selected and applied, the absence of a clear definition of the distribution of competence, particularly at the national level, and finally the lack of a system of legal or formal sanctions in the event of non-alignment of a given member state with the EPGs seriously undermine the legitimacy and the effectiveness of the Strategy as a form of deliberative supra-nationalism considering that the guidelines are normative in character. Moreover, both the EU Parliament and the Committee of the Regions have been given a minor consultative role in the overall implementation[65] and the ECJ is absent from the process.

Hodson and Mayer emphasise 'the opacity and complexity of the institutional framework'[66] and argue that the EES/OMC 'may not provide a durable alternative to the traditional EU model.'[67]

A preliminary evaluation may be made from the previous analysis. If we balance the pros and cons of the EES for its future application to the future Member States we may argue that its overall implementation would be quite successful as a policy learning instrument given the

[65] See E Szyszczak, 'The New Paradigm for Social Policy: A Virtuous Circle?' (2001) 38 *CML Rev* 1141.

[66] See D Hodson and I Maher, 'The Open Method of Co-ordination as a new mode of governance: The case of soft economic policy co-ordination' (2001) 39(4) *JCMS* 730–32.

[67] *Idem.*

flexibility of the process. Having said this a few caveats need to be made. The content of the EPGs would have to be reviewed in order to take into account the economic and social specificities of CEECs, which would also require, *inter alia*, a stronger link between the EES and regional, structural and social cohesion policies. This objective could be achieved by way of strengthening EU assistance programmes between the 'old' and the 'new' Member States.

## THE RE-DESIGN OF THE EES BY THE EU COMMISSION

Following the Barcelona European Council,[68] which called for a strengthening of the EES, the EU Commission issued a series of Communications. In the Communication *Taking Stock of Five Years of the European Employment Strategy* it reviewed the experience of five years of the EES and broadly outlined a re-design of the EES for the future.[69]

Ten topics were the subject of the evaluation:

- Prevention and policies of activation to employment;
- Tax reforms and benefits;
- Lifelong learning;
- Social inclusion;
- Administrative simplification and the self-employed;
- Creation of jobs in services, at local level and in social economy;
- Taxation;
- Modernising work organisation;
- Equal opportunities;
- Changes in policy-making.

The Communication identified four main issues for the reform of the EES:

- the need to set clear objectives in response to the policy challenges;
- the need to simplify the policy guidelines without undermining their effectiveness;
- the need to improve governance and partnership in the execution of the strategy and;
- the need to ensure greater consistency and complementarity with respect to other relevant EU processes.

[68] See Presidency Conclusions of the Barcelona European Council of 15 and 16 March 2003.
[69] Communication from the Commission to the Council, the European Parliament, the Economic and Social Committee and the Committee of the Regions, *Taking Stock of Five Years of the European Employment Strategy*, COM(2002) 416 final.

The EU Commission further developed the objectives outlined in this Communication in a subsequent Communication on the future of the EES where it provided examples of concrete objectives, targets and considerations and suggestions for possible new targets.[70] In addition, it streamlined the EPGs and BEPGs with a shift towards a more medium and longer-term approach.[71] The aim of the new process is to improve coherence and complementarity between the various processes and instruments, foster the participation and involvement of the EU Parliament, the national Parliaments, a better consultation of social partners and civil society and increase the transparency of policy co-ordination.

In April 2003 the EU Commission presented a *Guidelines Package*, which included formal proposals of BEPGs and EPGs and the annual recommendations to the Member States, which would cover a three-year period up to 2006. In particular, the guidelines are only to be issued on an annual basis if they have to stress the importance of possible major new developments. Likewise and consistent with the Cardiff process (structural reform) and pursuant to the Lisbon Strategy, the Internal Market Strategy (IMS),[72] which accompanies the *Guidelines Package*, considers internal market matters until 2006 and will be subject to changes during this three-year period only if necessary. Following the June European Council[73] and its consideration of the current situation in the economic and social fields, the Council will adopt the BEPGs,[74] the EPGs[75] and the Employment Recommendations to Member States.[76]

## A REVISED EES IN VIEW OF ENLARGEMENT

The amendments made to the EES are to be welcomed, but they only represent *ad hoc* remedies, the effectiveness of which is debatable. In order to further the constitutionalisation of the new trans-national processes it is necessary to go one step beyond, *ie* strengthen the legal base of the EES and

[70] Communication from the Commission to the Council, the European Parliament, the Economic and Social Committee and the Committee of the Regions, *The future of the European Employment Strategy (EES) 'A strategy for full employment and better jobs for all'*, COM(2003) 6 final.

[71] Communication from the Commission on *Streamlining the Annual Economic and Employment Policy Co-ordination Cycles*, COM(2002) 487 final.

[72] For information on the implementation of the IMS, http://europa.eu.int/comm/internal_market/en/update/strategy/.

[73] See Presidency Conclusions of the Thessaloniki European Council, 19 and 20 June 2003.

[74] See Commission Recommendation on the Broad Guidelines of the Economic Policies of the Member States and the Community (for the 2003–2005 period), COM(2003) 170 final.

[75] See Council Decision of 22 July 2003 on *Guidelines for the Employment Policies of the* Member States, (2003/578/EC).

[76] See Council Recommendation of 22 July 2003 on the *Implementation of* Member States' *Employment Policies*, (2003/578/EC).

introduce a horizontal provision for the OMC in the Constitutional Treaty. This presupposes a clear hierarchy of legal acts and distribution of competence within the EU, between the latter and the Member States and within the national arena between the different levels of policy-making. The European Convention has certainly contributed to this in the draft Constitutional Treaty.[77]

With regard to the strengthening of the legal base of the EES, in another article I have proposed a series of amendments to Title VIII and XI of the EC Treaty[78] in order to link soft law instruments to the Community Method.[79] The difficulty of creating a new institutional framework is due to the intrinsic difference between Title VIII and Title XI of the EC Treaty. In fact whereas Title VIII is a vertical consolidation of a number of years of political thinking initiated by the EU Commission and often endorsed by the Member States through soft law measures, Title XI, on the contrary, represents a horizontal consolidation of accepted judicial and political practice and it illustrates the dichotomy between sensitive and non-sensitive areas of Community intervention in EC Social Policy.[80] In recent years, however, the adoption of various Directives in the area of EC Labour Law confirms and reinforces what is being maintained in this paper.[81]

Firstly, Article 128 EC[82] should be amended in order to include both European and national social partners. With regard to the European social partners, Article 128(2) EC should be linked to Article 138(2) and (3) EC.[83] Secondly, Article 128(2) EC should also be amended in order to enhance the role of the EU Parliament, the Economic and Social Committee and the Committee of the Regions in the adoption of the Employment Guidelines. Thus, the legislative procedure regarding the adoption of the EPGs should be changed so that the EU Parliament rather than being consulted by the

[77] See Part I Titles III on the Union's competences, Title V on the Exercise of Union competence and Title VI on the Democratic life of the Union of the Draft Constitutional Treaty.

[78] In the draft Constitutional Treaty Title VIII and XI have been renumbered Section I, 'Employment' and Section II, 'Social Policy', of Chapter III, 'Policies in other specific policy areas', of Title III, 'Policies and Internal Action', of Part III, 'The Policies and functioning of the Union'. See European Convention, *Draft Treaty establishing a Constitution for Europe*, CONV 820/1/03, REV 1, Brussels, 27 June 2003 (01.07).

[79] See S Velluti, 'Towards the Constitutionalisation of New Forms of Governance: A Revised Institutional Framework for the European Employment Strategy' (2003) 22 *Yearbook of European Law* 353–405.

[80] See E Szyszczak, 'The Evolving European Employment Strategy,' in J Shaw (ed), *Social Law and Policy in an Evolving European Union* (Oxford, Hart Publishing, 2000) 197.

[81] See N Bruun, 'The European Employment Strategy and the 'Acquis Communitaire' of Labour Law' (2001) 17(3) *International Journal of Comparative Labour Law and Industrial Relations* 309–24, who exhaustively illustrates and explains the relationship between the EES and EC Labour Law.

[82] Art III-95 in the draft Constitutional Treaty.

[83] Art III-100 in the draft Constitutional Treaty.

Council should *act together* with the Council in the adoption of the EPGs. The legislative route to be used would be the co-decision procedure, pursuant to Article 251 EC.[84] Within this context amendments should be made to the last sentence of paragraph 2 in order to eliminate the implicit subjection of the EPGs to the BEPGs. This amendment would be in line with the new objective of improving consistency and complementarity between the two processes. Thirdly, Article 128(3) EC should be reviewed to include the participation of the social partners in the elaboration and implementation of the NAPs at the national level and to include the concertation between European, national, sectoral and enterprise social partners. Fourthly, Article 128(4) EC should be amended in order to include the EU Parliament, the Economic and Social Committee and the Committee of the Regions.

With regard to the OMC some of the Working Groups of the European Convention made various propositions that have not been included in the draft Constitutional Treaty but which, nevertheless, ought to be mentioned, as their inclusion would have introduced more transparency and legal certainty. In this context the OMC is conceived as being instrumental in bringing about domestic change and in paving the way towards the constitutionalisation of new values and principles.

Most of the members of the Working Group VI on *Economic Governance* suggested the inclusion of basic objectives, procedures and limits of the OMC in the Constitutional Treaty, in a way which would not undermine the flexibility of the method and which would not have the effect of replacing or circumventing the Community method.[85] In addition, they suggested widening the consultation process particularly with the social partners. Similarly, the Working Group XI on *Social Europe* proposed the insertion of a horizontal provision in the Treaty to be incorporated in the Constitutional Treaty, within the Chapter on the EU instruments, which constitute non-legislative measures.[86] The Group further recommended introducing some procedural rules regarding the OMC implementation. In particular, the OMC would have been used each time following a decision of the Council on the basis of an EU Commission proposal with the notification of the EU Parliament and the consultation of national parliaments, regional and local authorities, social partners and civil society. Moreover, the Committee on Employment and Social Affairs of the European Parliament proposed that the EES/OMC should be integrated with the

[84] Art III-298 in the draft Constitutional Treaty.

[85] See European Convention, *Final Report of Working Group VI on Economic Governance*, CONV 357/02, WG VI 17, Brussels, 21 October 2002.

[86] See European Convention, Final Report of Working Group XI on Social Europe, Brussels, 30 January 2003, CONV 516/03, WG XI 9, Part VII.

national policy-making procedure and in particular that NAPs should be adopted by the national parliament concerned on the basis of a government bill.[87]

## CONCLUSION

This chapter has focused on the social dimension of Central Eastern Enlargement and analysed the new Member States' labour markets, employment situation and the extent to which these states have adequately embraced the body of existing social ('hard' and 'soft') law and which policy instruments could be appropriate to enable this approximation process. After an evaluation of the strengths and weaknesses of the dyad EES/OMC, the chapter has suggested a series of amendments to Title VIII and XI of the EC Treaty for the establishment of a new institutional framework for the EES, which introduces a clear distribution of competences and lays out the conditions for the judicial enforceability of social rights now reinforced by the EU Charter of Fundamental Rights. These amendments strengthen the institutional architecture of the EES by way of introducing the rule of law approach with a clear distribution of competence and thus improving the efficiency of the decision-making process in an enlarged EU.

[87] See European Parliament, Committee on Employment and Social Affairs, Working Document *on the impact evaluation and future of the European Employment Strategy-Overview of technical analysis*, DT\463273EN.doc.

25

# *The EU Charter of Fundamental Rights: Is it a New Accession Condition for the Candidate Countries Especially in Light of the Post-Nice IGC?*

JENÖ CZUCZAI[1]

*This Charter is a symbol of the transition from an economic Europe to a political Europe and a message for the applicant countries.*

Ms Paciotti

## INTRODUCTION

THE EU CHARTER of Fundamental Rights[2] (hereinafter: the Charter) is an important development in the European constitutionalisation process and certainly a significant newly-emerged cornerstone in the democracy-building process in a reunited Europe.[3] The Charter

[1] This paper is a summary of two presentations recently delivered on the topic explored below at two different Conferences. One was held in Cambridge on 12–13 July 2002 under the organisation of the CELS with the title of '*EU Enlargement: A Legal Approach*'. The other was organised by the IALS, University of London on 25–27 June 2003 in London (the W G Hart Workshop 2003) on *'EU Law for the 21st Century: Rethinking the New Legal Order'*. The author expresses his personal thanks to Takis Tridimas and Christophe Hillion for their contribution to the birth of this paper. The usual disclaimer applies.

[2] See official text in OJ 18.12.2000 C–364/1 *et seq*. It should be noted that this paper follows the numbering of the original Charter of the Nice European Council Summit. However, the author is aware of the fact that the Convention adopted the Draft Treaty establishing a Constitution for Europe, see below. I will make special reference to this version only if found necessary.

[3] See J Schwarze: 'A German view on the European Charter of Fundamental Rights' in *CYELS* 2000 (Oxford, Hart Publishing, 2001) 407 *et seq*.

has a special message (or maybe even messages) for the acceding new Member States. It is the main purpose of this chapter to look at and to explore in more detail what these possible impacts and in some cases particular challenges the Charter can/will bring for the new-comers.[4]

First of all it should be recalled from the Charter that:

> The provisions of this Charter are addressed to the institutions and bodies[5] of the Union with due regard for the principle of subsidiarity and to the Member States *only when they are implementing Union law.*
>
> Article 51(1)[6]

This means that the candidate countries (current and future, outgoing or incoming), for sure, will have to take the Charter into account in the context of their preparation for acceding to the EU. Such a conclusion can be derived from the fact in the above-referred article 51 of the Charter that the provisions of the Charter are also addressed to the Member States. The main questions, however in my view, are: to what extent and in what sense the Charter is addressed to the acceding new Member States? In answering to these questions, we should bear in mind that *the current candidate countries will be able to implement the EU law*[7] only after accession. Does this mean that anyone could conclude from this that *strictu sensu* in legal terms *'the current candidate countries, therefore, are not addressed by the Charter at all?'*[8] This is also a question, which will be answered in this paper.

[4] See W Sadurski, 'Charter and Enlargement'(2002) 3 *ELJ*, 340–62, in particular 348–53.

[5] In *the draft Treaty establishing a Constitution for Europe* (hereinafter DCT), there is a change under this para 51, namely that the 'agencies of the Union' are also addressed. See CONV 850/03, 18 July 2003.

[6] See Lord Goldsmith QC, 'A Charter of Rights, freedoms and principles'(2001) 38 *CML Rev* 1201–16. Lord Goldsmith concludes in this article: '*…the Charter will not impose on Member States any obligation when they are acting within their areas of national competences.*' (1205). See also JB Liisberg, 'Does the EU Charter of Fundamental Rights threaten the supremacy of Community law?'(2001) 38 *CML Rev*, 1171–99.

[7] I would like to mention that it is pity that there is no interpretative provision at all in the Charter for example in terms of what is to be meant by 'EU law'? Especially in comparison with the fact that in the main part of the Charter (I-VI Chapters) exclusively the term of 'Community law' or just simply the term of 'law' is used.

[8] In this context it is important to mention that in the Preamble of the Charter there is written: '*The peoples of Europe, in creating an ever closer union among them, are resolved to share a peaceful future based on common values*', which means that the Charter is in the broadest sense also addressed to all peoples of Europe (including even those which live even not in applicant states from an EU law point of view. See in more details J Czuczai, 'Challenges of the Charter for the Candidate Countries in Central and Eastern Europe'(2002) 3 *Europa 2002* 460–55.

SOME PRELIMINARY OBSERVATIONS

**What are the Purposes of the Charter from a Pre-accession Dimension?**

Before answering to this question, I think that we should address the following preliminary questions to ourselves: why the Charter was in fact drawn up?[9] What are/can be the main purposes of the Charter?[10] And is the Charter a political document or something else? Lord Goldsmith has admirably summarized the answer to these questions:

> The purpose of the Charter, as conceived, was therefore to make the existing rights, which the EU ought to respect, more visible. To my mind, that was for two reasons. First, the purpose was to deepen and strengthen the culture of rights and responsibilities in the EU. Bringing together in a single document, endorsed by Member States and Community institutions a proclamation of existing rights will have a powerful effect in reinforcing in the minds of administrators, governments and legislators the rights that the citizens possess and the need to respect them. The second purpose was to remedy this lack of clarity in the protection of human rights by declaring clearly which were the rights, freedoms and principles the Union is to respect. There is, however, it will readily be seen some tensions between the two objectives, which lies at the heart of some of the drafting difficulties encountered.

I also think that these purposes — if one wishes as messages — should be well-understood/received in the next years to come in the acceding new Member States too (not talking about future candidate countries).

What was the opinion of the European Commission on the nature and the effects of the Charter?[11] (1):

> At the end of the day it is clear that the Charter will not replace national constitutions in the area within its cope in respect for fundamental rights at

[9] See an interesting approach to this question found in JHH Weiler, Does the EU truly need a Charter of Rights?' (2000) 6:2 *EL Rev* 55–98. In the same issue see also C Engel, 'The European Charter of Fundamental Rights: A Changed Political Structure' (2000) 6:2 *EL Rev* 151–71. Further literature can be found in AF Kellermann, JW de Zwaan and J Czuczai, (eds), *EU Enlargement: The Constitutional Impact at EU and National Level* (The Hague, Asser Press, 2001) 15–36, especially the contributions made by R Errera and H Ballin, and for the implications of the Charter in candidate states, Evgeni Tanchev's contribution.

[10] An official answer to this question can be found in the Charter'Preamble itself: '*To that end it is necessary to strengthen the protection of fundamental rights in the light of changes in society, social progress and scientific and technological development by making those rights more visible in a Charter*'.

[11] As we know the Charter was not given legally binding effect by the European Council summit, held in December 2000 in Nice. It was decided in Nice that the legal status of the Charter should be addressed by the Convention, convened by the Laeken Summit, and finally decided by the Post-Nice next IGC, which was convened on the 4th October 2003.

> national level. And it is clear that the relationship between the Union primary law, which would include the Charter if it is incorporated into the Treaties, and national law will remain unchanged......The Charter will offer a clear guide for the interpretation of fundamental rights by the Court of Justice which in the current situation has to use disparate, sometimes uncertain, sources of inspiration......it is highly likely that the Court of Justice will seek inspiration in it, as it already does in other fundamental rights instruments. It can reasonably be expected that the Charter will become mandatory through the Court's interpretation of it as belonging to the general principles of Community law', (2) 'It is ... preferable, for the sake of visibility and certainty as to the law, for the Charter to be made mandatory in its own right and not just through its judicial interpretation. In practice, the real question is when and how it should be incorporated in the Treaties?[12]

I think that the candidate countries should rely on this legal analysis, issued by the Commission, as far as the *de lege lata* as well as *de lege ferenda* legal effect of the Charter is concerned.

## How has the Charter been Received by the ECJ?

The Charter's real significance in European jurisprudence was properly addressed, in my view, by Avocat General Mischo's Opinion in a recent preliminary ruling proceeding:[13]

> I know that the Charter is not legally binding, but it is worthwhile referring to it given that it constitutes the expression, at the highest level , of a democratically established political consensus on what must today be considered as the catalogue of fundamental rights guaranteed by the Community legal order.[14]

In this conclusion of the AG on the Charter's judicial implications, I would give special emphasis to the words *'must be considered'* and the

[12] See 'Communication from the Commission on the legal nature of the Charter of Fundamental Rights of the EU', Brussels, 11.10.2000, COM (2000) 644 final, pp 5–6.

[13] See Joined cases C-20/00 and C-64/00 *Booker Aquaculture Ltd Trading as Marine Harvest Mc Connell & Hydro Seafood GSP Ltd v The Scottish Ministers*, AG's opinion delivered on 20 September 2001, not yet decided. The case relates the possible application of Article 17 of the Charter on the right to property. In the meantime remarkable ECJ judicial *acquis* has occured in the context of the Charter, but non of them has moved further then AG Mischo in his quoted Opinion above: See for example, Cases T-54/99 *Max-Mobil*, Judgement of 30 January 2002, and T-177/01 *Jégo-Quéré*, Judgement of 3 May 2002, or see AG Tizzano's Opinion in C-173/99 BECTU /2001/ ECR I-4881 or AG Léger's Opinion in *Council v Heidi Hautala* Case C-353/99, /1999/ ECR II-2489, appeal pending before the ECJ; or AG Tesauro's Opinion in *Netherlands v EP and Council*, joined cases C-159/2001-197/2001 et al (not yet decided).

[14] Lord Goldsmith sees similar function to be devoted to the Charter by the ECJ (*'The Charter will be a useful guiding resource'*). He makes reference to the experiences gained earlier in the way EC jurisprudence had approached the Social Charter, for example — above note 6, 1215.

words *'catalogue of fundamental rights guaranteed by the Community legal order'*.

## The Charter and the Copenhagen Membership Criteria of 1993?

The last point to be raised under this heading is how all the above can be understood in the context of the so-called Copenhagen membership criteria, laid down in June 1993? It is beyond doubt that: (i) the Charter can be brought under the scope of the first so-called political criterion which stipulates: *'an applicant country shall assure the stability of institutions guaranteeing democracy, rule of law, respect for human rights, respect for and protection of minority rights'* (ii) it should be seen that since Copenhagen neither the European Council nor the Commission has given in fact a more-detailed guidelines on what is to be meant by this first political criterion in contents (especially on what is to be meant under 'respect for human rights'). The wording of this criterion has, therefore, remained very vague for obvious political reasons. It is also clear that there was no screening chapter on the so-called 'constitutional *acquis* of the EU'[15] within the Accession IGC, which means that there is no 'screened *acquis*'on this, that would have been made clear to the candidates in this respect[16], (3) it is also clear, however, that the Charter has been made, at least indirectly, part of the so-called 'accession *acquis* of the Union'[17] by the Presidency's opening speech, delivered on 31st March 1998 in Brussels on the occasion of launching the Eastward Accession IGC. Made part of the accession *acquis* either by making reference to the political statements, made by the European Council summits, or by reference to the judicial *acquis* developed by the ECJ, both being considered by the Presidency as being essential elements of the accession EU *acquis*, constantly developing. Therefore it has remained opened that whether in the second and the third-way of enlargement, how the screening process will be organised (or maybe reorganized) by the European Commission in this respect?

[15] See C Delcourt, 'The *acquis communautaire*: has the concept had its day?' (2001) 38 *CML Rev* 829.

[16] Although we do have documents on this criterion, adopted by the European Parliament (eg the Oostlander's Report etc) and we have a table of international legal instruments on human rights prepared by the Commission in the recourse of preparing the annual progress reports on the candidates. See in more detail J Czuczai, 'The legal alignment process with the constantly evolving constitutional *acquis* of the EU in Central and Eastern Europe' (2002) II:I *Europa 2002*, 3–11.

[17] See J Czuczai, 'Challenges stemming from the process of what is called "approximation of laws" in Central and Eastern Europe' in A Nikodem (ed), *Implications of the Enlargement of the EU* (Budapest, Bibó István College of Law, 1998) 53–59.

## WHAT MESSAGES CAN THE CHARTER BRING FOR/FORWARD TO THE CANDIDATE COUNTRIES (CURRENT AND FUTURE)?

### How is the Permanent Practice of the ECtHR at Present Implemented by the Ordinary and Administrative Courts in the Candidate Countries? What Can We Conclude from This?

The first obvious message is associated with the ECtHR and its implementation practice in those states which are signatories to the Convention. According to its Preamble, the Charter reaffirms rights resulting from the European Convention on Human Rights [18] and Fundamental freedoms (ECtHR), the Social Charters, *as well as those resulting from the* jurisprudence of the ECJ and *of the ECtHR*.[19] We should not forget about the fact that all the candidate countries — with which accession negotiations are under operation or were concluded in December 2002 in Copenhangen — are members to the ECHRs from Central and Eastern Europe. Now let me recall again something from Lord Goldsmith:

> The ECtHR continued to play a special part in the ECJ's approach to the fundamental-rights protection to such an extent that in the Bosphorus case, AG Jacobs was able to say that '...For practical purposes the Convention can be regarded as Community law and can be invoked as such both in this Court and in national courts where community laws are in issue...[20]

My main questions would be, therefore, in relation to the candidates and considering the possible political message of the Charter in the light of all said above: to what extent and how frequently is the case law of the ECtHR invoked now before national courts in the candidate countries? Are there references made to the case law of the ECtHR in the judgements being issued by the candidates' national courts in concrete legal disputes in which for example human rights — having link to the Convention — are an issue? Who controls this in the context of the pre-accession phase and as far as the preparedness of the candidates is assessed in light of the first political criterion of Copenhagen?

### EU Citizenship: A Challenging Exercise?

Second possible message: I think that what will be really new for the candidate countries is the so-called *'Treaty-based EU Citizens' rights'* part

[18] See as an excellent comparative analysis on this: K Lenaerts and EE de Smijter, 'A Bill of Rights for the EU' (2001) 38 *CML Rev* 273–300.
[19] OJ 2000, C 364/1 of 18.12.2000.
[20] Cited from Lord Goldsmith above note 6, 1203.

of the Charter. These rights are embodied in Chapter V of the Charter (Articles 39–46). Why will this be new for the new-comers? Because the citizens of the would-be Member States can understand the scope, the merit, and the significance of these rights, just after their accession, when they will have really become citizens of the EU too. That means that the Charter in this respect can be a great challenge for the peoples of the acceding CEECs especially from a psychological and sociological point of views.[21] Also it can be considered as a message, forwarded to the peoples of the candidates; and in terms of that they shall be well-prepared after accession to cope with the new challenges that will be stemming from the legal institution of 'EU citizenship'.

## The Role of National Law in Light of EU Fundamental Rights' Protection

Finally in my view no problem can occur for the candidate countries with the below-mentioned rights/freedoms of the Charter since they are '*recognized, in accordance with the national laws governing the exercise of these rights*'.[22] Why? Because this textual wording in the Charter means that the national constitutional traditions and prevailing legal limitations for instance in terms of exercising these rights can be preserved by the would-be Member States too, after accession.[23] These rights are, for example, the

[21] A special intellectual challenge will be for the candidates (current and future as well) to 'absorb' in practice the real meaning of Art 41 of the Charter which is about the 'right to good administration at EU level'. I think that first of all they need to understand what is meant by 'good administration' in their own countries (and in their own legal culture) and then to develop perceptions of the same notion at the EU level. It should be mentioned that the Convention technically revised this provision of the Charter as follows:

> Art II-41. Right to good administration. 1. Every person has the right to have his or her affairs handled impartially, fairly and within reasonable time by the Institutions, bodies and agencies of the Union. 2. This right includes:(a) the right of every person to be heard, before any individual measure which would affect him or her adversely is taken, (b) the right of every person to have access to his or her file, while respecting the legitimate interests of confidentiality and of professional and business secrecy, (c) the obligation of the administration to give reasons for its decision. 3. Every person has the right to have the Union make good any damage caused by its Institutions or by its servants in the performance of their duties, in accordance with the general principles common to the laws of the Member States. 4. Every person may write to the Institutions of the Union in one of the languages of the Constitution and must have an answer in the same language.

I want to underline the significance of this right in the Charter, because in this context the right is not addressed in the ECHR.

[22] The DCT further strengthened this under the new text of Art II-52, especially under Art II-52, point 5–6.

[23] For more detailed analysis on the 'general and specific limitations by reference according to the Charter', see for example D Triantafyllou, 'The European Charter of Fundamental Rights and the "Rule of Law": Restricting Fundamental Rights by Reference' (2002) 39 *CML Rev* 53–64. See also R Alonso Garcia, 'The General Provisions of the Charter of

following in the Charter: Article 9 (Right to marry and right to found a family);[24] Article 10.2 (Freedom of thought, conscience and religion); or Article 16 (Freedom to conduct a business, but limited to EC law too); Art 27 (Workers' rights to information and consultation within the undertaking, but limited to EC law too); Art 28 (Right of collective bargaining and action, but limited to EC law too); Art 30 (protection in the event of unjustified dismissal , but limited to EC law too); Art 34 (Social security and social assistance, but limited to EC law too) etc). But — and we shouldn't forget about this! — approximation of laws is still a task to be done in order to make national laws fully compatible with the existing and constantly developing Union *acquis* (including the Union constitutional *acquis* too!) in all the fields, just referred to above.

## SOME REFLECTIONS ON THE CONTENT OF THE CHARTER FROM THE POINT OF VIEW OF THE ACCEDING CENTRAL, EASTERN AND SOUTHERN EUROPEAN COUNTRIES

*(i)* In my view, the most significant challenge will be the proper implementation of Article 21 of the Charter on non-discrimination, and in more general terms of the EU non-discrimination *acquis* in the would-be Member States. There are special grounds based on which any kind of discrimination is prohibited in the EU and which *causae speciales* in my opinion are yet totally under-developed in Central, Eastern and Southern Europe in terms of that any discrimination on such grounds being provided with efficient legal protection against before courts, like eg age, disability, genetic features, sexual orientation.[25] These special grounds are differently approached by the acceding new Member States for historical, socio-political, economical and many other reasons. These mentally prevailing gaps, or one could say, obvious discrepancies in human way of thinking in the different parts of the reuniting Europe should be given, in my view, much more attention in the future, otherwise the

Fundamental Rights of the EU' (2002) 8:4 *ELJ* 492–514, or M La Torre, 'The Law Beneath Rights' Feet: Preliminary Investigation for a Study of the Charter of Fundamental Rights of the EU' (2002) 8:4 *ELJ* 515–35.

[24] But see comments on this latter especially in the light of the judgement and the AG opinion in joined cases C-122–125/1999 PD v Council, decided on 31 May 2001 (not yet reported).

[25] See on this whole heading in more detail J Czuczai, 'Challenges Stemming from the European Charter of Fundamental Rights for the Economic Transformation Process in the Candidate Countries of Central and Eastern Europe' in Duschanek and Griller (eds), *Grundrechte für Europa, Die Europaische Union nacht Nizza* (Wien/New York, Springer, 2002) 123–30.

level of protection of fundamental rights in the enlarged EU will surely not be equal.

*(ii)* The second main challenge will be brought, as I can see now, by the different understanding of social and economic rights in the Charter and in the candidate countries in Central, Eastern and Southern Europe (Main provisions that can be reflected by this consideration: Articles 15.2, 15.3, 23.1, 33, 34.3, 35, 45 (with 15.2), 45.2). As far as the social and economic rights are concerned (for example: full employment-related) in the Charter, special attention should be devoted in the future to the budgetary and financial aspects of the effective implementation of these rights in the current and future new Member States in particular bearing in mind that they have just gone through a very complex and demanding economic transformation process in Central, Eastern and Southern Europe, which transition process is even today far away not yet completed.[26]

*(iii)* Other rights, freedoms and principles that can be also of some significance in terms of future tensions which problems might occur in the candidate countries with regard to their efficient implementation after accession are for example Article 38 of the Charter (on consumer protection), Article 11.2 (freedom and pluralism of the media), Article 12.2 (EU level political parties) etc. The reasons behind these possible tensions are wide-ranging, some of them, however, are of political nature (like in the field of public media) and/or human, mental one (like for example in the field of consumer protection, where we shouldn't forget about that this is a brand-new area of the legal system of the transition countries in Central, Eastern and Southern Europe. For almost 45 years even the legal term of 'consumer(s)' didn't exist in the previous communist regime, then how we could perceive at all about their rights? Therefore more tolerance and most importantly time and budget are needed for the acceding new Member States to gradually catch up in the future with the proper implementation of this Charter-based rights on EC cosumer policy). Finally I think that the budgetary aspects are also not properly taken into account in terms of the acceding new Member States when addressing the above-mentioned rights or freedom especially from an effective enforcement point of view.

[26] See J Czuczai, 'Transition from State Economy to Market Economy — The Hungarian Experiences' in Apirat Petchsiri et al (eds), *Comparative Regional Integration — ASEAN and the EU* (Monograph series Vol II 2002, Chulalongkorn University, Bangkok, 160–83).

*(iv)* Another problematic provision of the Charter can be Article 9 from the view-point of the current legal culture of the acceding CEECs. This article stipulates that: '*The right to marry and the right to found a family shall be guaranteed in accordance with the national laws governing the exercise of these rights*'. The current laws in force in the candidate countries are still very rigid on this matter, especially as regards homosexuals.[27]

*(v)* Similarly to the problem, mentioned above in terms of non-discrimination, I should also recall Article 26 of the Charter. It stipulates: *The Union recognises and respects the rights of persons of disabilities to benefit from measures designed to ensure their independence, social and occupational integration and participation in the life of the Community*.' The approach to the persons of disabilities should be given still a progressive reorientation in the near future in the candidate countries. Special attention should be also devoted to this Charter provision and in fact its implementation-related barriers in the new Member States from a budgetary and institution-building point of view too.

*(vi)* Finally I think that another challenge can be for the candidate countries (or acceding new Member States) in terms of what is stipulated in Article 47 of the Charter (Right to an effective remedy and to a fair trial). It reads as follows: '*3. Legal aid*[28] *shall be made available to those who lack sufficient resources in so far as such aid is necessary to ensure effective access to justice*'. I don't know, to be honest, when this legal aid system will be put in effective operation in all the new Member States (just think about the budgetary implications of this?). In Hungary it doesn't exist yet, for example, in praxi.

## FUTURE POSSIBLE IMPACTS OF THE CHARTER FOR THE FIRST WAVE OF ENLARGEMENT, WITH SPECIAL REGARD TO THE OUTCOME OF THE CONVENTION AS WELL AS FOR THE SECOND WAVE OF THE EASTWARD ENLARGEMENT PROCESS UNDER-WAY

*(i)* I am convinced that the Charter should be finally incorporated into the new Constitutional Treaty on the EU.[29]

[27] See for example the Declaration of the Government of the Republic of Poland concerning public morality attached to the Acts of Accession, as Declaration No 39.

[28] Please note that this type of 'legal aid', covered by the Charter, is obviously relevant to all those legal areas being outside the criminal law — governed fields.

[29] As known, in the meantime the Convention accepted the Draft Treaty establishing a Constitution for Europe (Hereinafter reffered: DCT). See: CONV 850/03, issued on

However, it should be revised with special regard to minority rights (sources are available, just think about the relevant instruments developed by the Council of Europe etc), which is a crucial issue in Central, Eastern and Southern Europe.[30] In this respect, I expect the Convention (by now IGC) to come out with

18 July 2003, Brussels. The relevant article is Article 7 which reads as follows: 'Fundamental Rights: 1. *The Union shall recognise the rights, freedoms and principles set out in the Charter of Fundamental Rights which constitutes Part II of the Constitution. 2.The Union shall seek accession to the European Convention for the Protection of Human Rights and Fundamental Freedoms. Such accession shall not affect the Union's competences as defined in the Constitution.3. Fundamental Rights, as guaranteed by the European Convention for the Protection of Human Rights and Fundamental Freedoms, and as they result from the constitutional traditions common to all Member States, shall constitute general principles of the Union's law*'. And then the Charter follows in Part II of the DCT almost totally unchanged as compared to its version adopted in Nice in December 2000. Yet, it should be also noted that the President of the Convention officially submitted the DCT to the Greek Presidency on 19–20 June 2003 in Thessaloniki. See: Presidency Conclusions, Point I/1–7 articles, especially article 5, which reads as follows: 'The European Council decided that the text of the DCT *is a* good basis for starting in the Intergovernmental Conference (IGC). It requests the future Italian Presidency to initiate, at the Council meeting in July, the procedure laid down in Article 48 of the Treaty in order to allow this Conference to be convened in October 2003. The Conference should complete its work and agree the Constitutional Treaty as soon as possible and in time for it to become known to European citizens before the June 2004 elections for the European Parliament. *The acceding States will participate fully in the IGC on an equal footing with the current Member States. The Constitutional Treaty will be signed by the Member States of the enlarged Union as soon as possible after 1 May 2004. 7. The three candidate countries — Bulgaria and Romania, with whom accession negotiations are underway, and Turkey — will take part in all meetings of the Conference as observers*' The next IGC on the DCT has started on 4th October 2003. It is clear that there is no discussion among the Member States on Part II of the DCT in terms of content, so it is highly like that the Charter in content will be adopted by the forthcoming IGC and therefore incorporated into the new EU Constitutional Treaty as it stands now in the DCT.

[30] It should be noted that in many national constitutions in Central, Eastern and Southern Europe, minority rights are specifically addressed at constitutional level (!) clearly separated from the general Human (or Fundamental) Rights' Chapters in the respective constitutions concerned. See for example: *1992 Slovakian Constitution* even in the Preamble, the following is stipulated: 'We, the Slovak Nation.......*Together with members of national minorities and ethnic groups living on the territory of the Slovak Republic,* ...Thus we, the citizens of the Slovak Republic have ... adopted this Constitution: ...' and then in Title 2 (Fundamental Rights and freedoms) under Section IV. (The Rights of National Minorities and Ethnic Groups) special provisions are about minority rights in the Slovakian Constitution (see: articles 33–34!). Another example is the recently adopted new Constitutional Charter of the State Union of Serbia and Montenegro (February 17, 2003) Article VIII–IX, which specifically addresses — among the human rights and freedoms — the 'minority rights' too! Then, on 28 February 2003 a Charter of Human and Minority Rights and Civil Liberties was adopted and attached to the Constitutional Charter in Serbia and Montenegro. See, Official Gazette of Serbia and Montenegro No 6 of 2003. Moreover in Serbia and Montenegro, there is a Minister for Human and Minority Rights in Office (See Art 45 of the Constitutional Charter) which is unique.

[31] As known, it will be the 2nd Part of the DCT, as well as no change can be expected to be made about the current version of the Charter despite the fact that many acceding Member States — especially Hungary — have indicated that she would like to make modifying proposals to the DCT in this respect. This means that the minority rights won't be treated separately

a slightly revised text on the Charter, or at least Article 2 of the DCT, in this respect.[31]

*(ii)* I also think that in the framework of the on-going IGC the candidates — meaning (i) the new Member States from 1 May 2004, (ii) the so-called second-wave 'candidates' (Romania, Bulgaria and Turkey) and in my view (iii) the remaining potential 'candidates' (for example, Croatia, Serbia and Montenegro in the near future etc)[32] — should be somehow made able to better contribute to the scope and the merit of the possibly revised version of the Charter (or the European constitutionalisation process in more general terms, certainly in different forms depending on the quality of the respective candidacies). This is an important condition for them to be able to secure/represent efficently in the reformulation process of the Charter in particular their own constitutional traditions and permanent practice, developed eg by the constitutional courts in the respective candidate countries with special regard to the protection of fundamental rights and freedoms.

## CONCLUSIONS

*(i)* Concerning my final conclusion on the question put into the title of this intervention, namely whether the Charter is a new accession condition for the candidates, my answer is that in legal terms for sure, no! In a political sense, I think, yes, but it is already deemed to be interpreted as a post-accession condition, not as a pre-accession condition (obviously in view of the acced-

in the Charter, only as one of the special grounds for prohibition on any kind of discrimination (See Art II-21.1 of the DCT). Therefore in the current EU this national minority rights' issue is understood to be a matter of individual rights, completely ignoring the fact that there are also well — known in european law so-called collective rights of national minorities, which should be somehow addressed at EU level too (if not for other reasons than because of the obvious political need for keeping the level of protection of national minorities' rights not harmed by enlargement after accession already in an enlarged EU).

[32] In this respect, I think, that the above-referred point II.7 in the Presidency Conclusions adopted by the European Council in Thessaloniki on 19–20 June 2003, should be somehow revisited and reconsidered in view of that if Turkey is invited to be an observer at the IGC then based on which reasons, for example, Croatia shouldn't be also invited to take the same observer's status in the next IGC!? I think this is a valid question in political terms for sure in spite of the fact that legally speaking I know that in formal sense Croatia is not yet a 'canidate country' whereas Turkey is at least a 'virtual candidate country'. But, many experts say that Croatia will join the EU earlier than Turkey. If this statement is true, then I think that my question is also a practically correct and legitimate one, which ought to be answered by the Presidency in office somewhen.

ing new Member States in CEE). This means that in practical terms the 'current candidates' should look at the Charter as a post-screening exercise with the purpose to get- on their side- a more detailed description about the first membership criterion of the Copenhagen Summit (namely what concerns: '*the applicant countries shall assure stability of the institutions guaranteeing … respect for and protection of human rights*'). The Charter gave a better clarification on what 'human rights' are to be meant by under this membership criterion at EU level! However there is still a great loophole in the Charter, in that no interpretative guidance has been given, at least at EU level, about what concerns the term '*minority rights*' in the same sentence of the Copenhagen European Council decision quoted above![33] This shortage should be corrected in my view in the framework of the IGC.[34] This is specifically true for 'the second-way and third-way candidates', for whom the Charter or the *de lege ferenda* Part II of the DCT can be even made more easily a 'pre-accession condition' making thus their preparatory tasks even more demanding and compliacted in the forthcoming future!

*(ii)* I may also agree with Lord Goldsmith's following conclusion:

> I believe the Charter lacks the precision of language necessary to allow it legal force……So whilst it should be acceptable and valuable as a political statement, my own view is that this text is not suitable for incorporation into the Treaties whether directly or by cross-reference.[35]

In my view, no real progress has been made in this context within the Convention, unfortunately. Hopefully, the on-going IGC will somehow and somewhat remedy this problem, especially if we want a 'Constitution for Europe' as legally enforcable, or in other words a 'living one' instead of a 'Constitution for Europe' on paper, the latter type of which has been already so much experienced by the peoples living in Central, Eastern and Southern Europe for more than 40 years (since before the Berlin Wall came down).

[33] See J Czuczai's contribution in *EU enlargement. The Constitutional impact….'* op cit, 411–22.

[34] I am convinced about that this issue cannot be covered only by the present Article 21 in the Charter (under non-discrimination). This issue should be given a separate chapter in the revised version of the Charter in order that minority rights could be regulated in a more qualitative domension in the future.

[35] See Lord Goldsmith above note 6, 1215.

This means from the viewpoint of 'the current — but also the future — candidate countries that since the Convention suggested that the Charter should be incorporated into the Treaty by the Post-Nice IGC, then I think, its textual wording should be by all means revisited (in order to make it more legalistic/'better codified') before the incorporation. This is therefore a task remaining for the IGC.[36] In this respect, as explored above, it seems not reasonable and realistic to my mind to let the ECJ through its case law carry out the legalization process of the Charter. I think that the ECJ — based on the last almost three years' experiences — has clearly rejected the invitation to become a second human rights' court in Europe as well as to take up more and more tasks and duties stemming from the Charter in terms of subsequent constitutional judicialisation.

*(iii)* Finally I think that from a legal certainty point of view, the current candidate countries can welcome the following statement made by the Charter: 'This Charter doesn't establish any new power or tasks for the Community or for the Union, or modify powers and tasks defined by the Treaties.' This was in Article 51(2), which was redrafted by the Convention as follows: '*This Charter doesn't extend the field of application of Union law beyond the powers of the Union* or establish any new power or task for the Union, or modify powers and tasks defined in the other Parts of the Constitution' (Article II-51.2 of the DCT). In terms of content however, it remained in fact unchanged or legally even more-restricted thus defending (current and future) Member States' sensitivities.[37]

[36] This requirement can be further strengthened by the fact that the DCT will — for the first time in the history of the EU — incorporate the 'primacy doctrine' into the Constitutional Treaty (Article 10.1. of the DCT).

[37] See also the revised Art II-52 of the DCT.

# Index


access to documents:
  Amsterdam Treaty 44
  and democracy 45
  exceptions 45–47
  public interest exception 45–46
access to justice 122, 123, 125, 209, 221
  *see also* right to effective remedy
accountability:
  Commission 48–50
  and EU courts 47–53
  European Council 154–55
  European Ombudsman 50–52
  expert groups 52–53
  governance principle 148
  national parliaments 153
  public authorities 135
  watchword 136, 150
*acquis communautaire* 192, 299, 380, 381, 400, 419–24, 441
*Acte Clair* 200
administration:
  administrative cooperation 325
  annulment of actions 32–33
  and European Ombudsman 50
  principles 48
  right to sound administration 48
Advocates General, appointment 118
agencies, judicial review of actions 125
agriculture, shared competence 68
Algeria 409
alienation 112
Amsterdam Treaty:
  CFSP 263, 279, 281
  common commercial policy 323
  employment 426
  immigration 348, 349, 378, 378–79
  Social Policy Agreement 55, 426
  Subsidiarity Protocol 70
  and transparency 44
Ankara Agreement 283
annulment actions:
  access to justice 122, 209
  administrative acts 32–33
  amendment of treaties 110
  classes of applicants 110
  decisions 28–29
  directives 22–23, 29, 55, 212
  draft Constitution 40–41, 111–12, 114, 117, 120–29, 209–18, 220
  ECJ jurisdiction 115
  and equality before the law 110
  implementing regulations 122
  interim orders 219
  judicial creativity 187
  *locus standi see locus standi* in EU courts
  or actions for damages 23–24, 26
  privileged applicants 110
  regulatory acts 28, 121, 213–14
  sanctions 220
  self-executing regulations 40
  subsidiarity 120
  TWD rule 220
anti-dumping 14–15, 21, 22, 340–42
arrest warrants 286
asylum:
  accelerated procedures 387
  access to labour market 350
  common policy 347
  competence 347, 388
  current practice 348–55
  death penalty 374
  definition of refugees 346, 352, 356, 362–63
  directives 350, 351, 356, 361–62, 365–75, 375, 388
  draft Constitution 347–48
  and ECJ jurisdiction 129
  and enlargement 377–80
  family reunion 364
  generalised violence 374
  Geneva Convention *see* Refugee Convention
  harmonization of standards 345–58
  and human rights 345, 359–66
  international law 361, 362–66
  member states, from 379

*asylum continued*
mutual recognition 345–55
new members' policies 384–89
new members' statistics 385
obligations on applicants 350
persecution 369–70, 372–74, 375
Phare Programme 386, 392, 417
preliminary references 220
procedures 350–51
real risk 366, 368, 375
reception conditions 346, 350
responsibility for applications 349–50
Romas 379–80
safe countries of origin 350–51, 379–80, 384, 387
serious harm 369, 370–72, 373, 374
standard of proof 365–69
subsidiary protection 363–64, 367, 373, 374, 375
UNHCR guidelines 363, 365, 369, 370
well-founded fear 365–66, 368, 375
Austria 136, 351, 380, 382, 383, 386
Aznar Protocol 378–79

Balkans 289, 398, 401, 402, 403–7, 411–13
Baltic countries 384, 391
Barcelona Process 410
Bathing Water Directive 231, 232–33
bees 317–18
Belarus 389, 390, 402
Belgium 35, 176, 364, 379
Bermann, G 418
Birds Directives 229–30, 233–34, 314
Blair, Tony 275, 279
border controls 346, 348, 356, 378, 391–93
Bosnia-Herzegovina 406
Bristol 231
Brundtland Report 304
Bulgaria 377, 380, 393, 400, 402, 448
Bush, George W 275

Canada 332, 333, 336
CARDS 405, 410
Carrington, Lord 262
Cartagena Protocol 294, 297, 298
Cassese, A 268
Central and Eastern European Countries:
asylum policies 384–89
border controls 391–93
and Charter of Fundamental Rights 443–48
consumer protection 445
control of migration 383–95
EES/ OMC dyad 424–32
and European Employment Strategy 415–16
immigration from 352, 377–83
labour relations 422
new members 377
and non-discrimination 444
restructuring economic systems 423
social and economic rights 445
sovereignty 259
traditional sectors 421, 423
training 422
unemployment 421, 422
Charter of Fundamental Rights:
and access to EU courts 63
*acquis communautaire* 441
annexation, 102–3
Cologne meeting 95
derogations 100
and enlargement 437–50
horizontal provisions 99–102
imprecision 449
incorporation into EU constitution 97–105, 115, 140, 446–47
interpretative guidance 449
and judicial review 49
message to new members 442–44
methods of incorporation 102–5
minority rights 446–47, 449
and national laws 443–44
purposes 439–40
recognition 103–5
replication of other instruments 98–99
revision 97–98, 446–48, 450
right to effective remedy 25, 109, 214
scope 100, 438, 450
social and economic rights 445
status 95–96, 440–41
Chirac, Jacques 279
CITES 294
civil protection, competence 68, 325
comitology 81–83, 84, 85, 86, 143

Commission:
accountability 50, 148–49
accountability to EP 150
achievements 151
discretionary powers 48
and enlargement 400
EP approval 146
expert groups 52–53
governance 148–49, 151, 157
history 144–52
and implementing acts 88
legislative initiative 80
legitimacy 53, 151
and non-legislative acts 81
number of Commissioners 144, 145
and participation 84
powers 147
President 143, 144, 146, 149
reorganisations 147, 148–50
reviewability 48–50, 210
and right to effective remedy 36–37
role 143–52
Santer Commission 59, 148
technocracy 150, 151
voting rights 149
WTO participation 327–28
Committee of the Regions 71
Common Agricultural Policy 309
common commercial policy:
dismantling 297
and Doha Round 326–27
draft Constitution 322–26
exclusive competence 67, 326, 327, 329, 337, 342
and external agreements 326
and multilateral trade agreements 326–27
qualified majority voting 297
WTO participation 326–27
Common Foreign and Security Policy:
Amsterdam Treaty 263, 279, 281
Commissioner for External Affairs 271
common and single 259–60
competence 68, 266–67
constraints on member states 269–70
development 279
draft Constitution 259–72, 300–1, 399
ECJ jurisdiction 128–29, 216, 264
and enlargement 397–413
High Representative 270
implementing acts 215
incrementalism 276–77, 280
intergovernmental procedure 263, 264, 274
and Iraq 275
Maastricht Treaty 262–63, 267, 279, 281
and member states 282
model 278
objectives 398–99
paradox 277–79, 281–84
procedural mechanisms 277
and sovereignty 264–66
*sui generis* nature 277, 280, 286
and terrorism 286
Union Minister for Foreign Affairs 270–71
common good 292, 294
competences of Union:
categories of competence 67–68
competence creep 66
complementary competences 67, 325
draft Constitution 1, 65, 66–68, 141
ECJ role 115
exclusive competences 67–68
expectations and results 66–67
fundamental principles 70
generally 65–73
implied powers 69
*Kompetenz-Kompetenz* 72–73, 91–92
and legitimacy 65
Nice remit 271
proportionality 92–93
shared competences 66, 68
simplicity 68–69
and subsidiarity 65, 67, 68, 69–72, 92–93
unanswered questions 72–73
and WTO accession 322, 325
competition 21, 67, 242
Constitution for Europe:
annexation of Charter of Rights 102–3
asylum 347–48
border controls 346
common commercial policy 322–26
competences 1, 65, 66–68, 141
constitutional review 115, 210–18

*Constitution for Europe continued*
Convention 149
Court of Justice *see* European Court of Justice
debate 259, 271
defence policy 279
democracy 76, 416
draft Treaty 1
employment 435
and EU structure 263–64
foreign policy 259–72, 279, 281, 300–1, 399
functionality 2
fundamental rights 96–97
hierarchy of norms 40, 76–79, 214
immigration 347–48
incorporation of Charter of Rights 97–105, 115, 446–47
incorporation of ECHR 105–9
interpretation, preliminary rulings 130
judicial cooperation 348
legitimacy 2, 17
*locus standi see locus standi* in EU courts
mandate 271–72
objective and subjective sense 9
and ordinary people 9–11
principles 76, 132, 136, 140, 336, 416
process 10, 11
separation of powers 76, 116
simplification 272
and sites of governance 13–15
and sovereignty of member states 264–66
subsidiarity 132, 336
uncertainties 272
constitutional culture 10–11
constitutional review 89, 89–90, 115
constitutionalism:
empirical study 194–207
and evidence 203–4
formalism 196–205, 207
and functionality 204–5
global constitution 12
issues 2–5
law and non-law roles 190–92, 207
and preliminary references 193–96
socialising the law 203–4
thick law 199, 206–7
consumer protection 445
copyright 332, 335
COREPER 45, 160
corruption 59
COSAC 162
Cottier, T 331
Court of First Instance 21, 116, 210–18
courts *see* Court of First Instance; EU courts; European Court of Justice
Cremona, M 298
Croatia 389, 402, 403, 448
culture, competence 68, 325
customs union, exclusive competence 67
Cyprus 284, 377, 378, 401, 402
Czech Republic 176, 377, 384, 386

damages:
action for damages or annulment 23–24, 26
liability of European Ombudsman 50–51
state damages *see* state liability for breach of EU law
De Gaulle, Charles 143
death penalty 374
decisions:
annulment actions 122
draft Constitution 76, 78
European implementing decisions 215
non-legislative acts 215
defence *see* European Security and Defence Policy
defence industries 287–88
deliberative democracy 181–82
Delors, J 143, 147
democracy:
and access to documents 45
constitutional objective 76
deliberative models 181–82
democratic deficit 151
and EU courts 17, 53–63
EU institutions 33–34
EU objective 76, 132, 416
and founding treaties 150–51
framework agreements 54–58
and legitimacy 159, 173–74
national parliaments 153, 154–56
pluralism of forms 136
Denmark 43–44, 141, 162, 260, 383, 386, 430
development cooperation 216

Diamantopoulou, Anna 415
Dicey, AV 256
Dillon, S 298
direct effect doctrine 191, 223, 224–28
directives:
annulment actions 22–23, 29, 55, 212
direct effect doctrine 191, 223, 224–28
discretion of member states 223, 228–37, 241, 249–50
failure to implement, 127
implementation 29–30
legality review 223–37
nature 22–23, 29
reform 40–41, 77, 79
disability rights 446
discretion:
implementation of directives 223, 228–37, 241, 249–50
public bodies 237
discrimination:
gender discrimination 241
language requirements 247–49
and new members 444
persecution 370
race discrimination 371
victimisation 251
Dolowitz, D 429
domestic remedies rule 30–31, 37, 108–9
Dooge Committee 147

Eastern Europe *see* Central and Eastern European Countries
Economic and Monetary Union (EMU) 423, 424
economics, and the law 203–4
education, competence 68, 325
embassies 261
empire, and globalisation 11–13
employment:
*acquis communautaire* 420–24
draft Constitution 435
EES and enlargement 415–36
EES/ OMC dyad 424–32
hard and soft law 420, 427–28, 431, 434
Joint Assessment Papers 421–23
Joint Employment Report 429
unemployment 426
endangered species 317
energy, shared competence 68
enlargement:
and asylum 377–80, 384–89
Aznar Protocol 378–79
and border controls 378, 391–93
and Charter of Fundamental Rights 437–50
conditionality 400, 401–2, 409, 420, 448
control of migration 383–95
criteria 417, 441
economic migration 380–83
EES re-design 433–36
employment *acquis communautaire* 420–24
and European Employment Strategy 415–36
foreign policy instrument 397–413
foreign policy objectives 398–401
future members 377
Joint Assessment Papers 416, 421–23
law and policy 416–20
legitimacy 412
magnet effect 401–3
and migration 377–83
new borders 402
new members 377
new neighbourhood policy 403, 407–11, 412–13
and non-discrimination 444
pre-accession model without enlargement 411–13
pre-accession process 400, 401
scale 416–17
second-class citizens 382
South-East Europe 403–7
Stabilisation and Association Agreements 403–4
Stabilisation and Association Process 401, 403, 404
success 397, 401
sustainability 402
transitional arrangements 381–83
and visa requirements 389–91
width and depth 402, 417–18
environmental assessments 229, 231
environmental protection:
balancing objectives 309–10

*environmental protection continued*
EU approach 304, 306–10, 313–17, 317
EU key objective 306
and free trade 304–19
global issue 291
implementation of directives 229–36, 237–38
legal instruments 216
proportionality 307, 309, 310, 314–15, 316
shared competence 68
and sustainable development 304
and WTO 294, 304, 311, 312–14, 315–17
Equal Treatment Directive 241, 245, 247, 251
*erga omnes* obligations 293
errors of law, implementation of directives 229–37
Estonia 377, 387
ETA 379
ethnic Hungarians 389, 390
ethnic Poles 389, 390
EU courts:
access 17, 63–64
and accountability 47–53
and democracy 53–63
legitimising role 43–63
*locus standi see locus standi* in EU courts
tiers 116
and transparency 43–47
Euro-Med Partnership 407, 410
European Armaments, Research and Military Capabilities Agency 289
European Central Bank 130, 210
European Convention on Human Rights:
and access to EU courts 63–64
and asylum 350, 366, 370–71
death penalty 374
derogation 379
EU accession to 95, 105–9
EU status 442
living instrument 371
purpose 101
right to effective remedy 109
European Corps of Border Guards 392
European Council:
accountability 154–55
autonomy 154
and delegated legislation 83
legislative role 80, 81
presidencies 150, 161–62
reviewability 210
transparency, lack of 155, 161
European Court of Justice:
constitutional character 191
Discussion Circle 114
draft Constitution
amendments of ECJ Statute 131
appeal rights 117
Article 28 115–17
CFSP jurisdiction 128–29
constitutional jurisdiction 113, 140
generally 113–32
High Court 116
intellectual property jurisdiction 131
judicial appointments 114, 118–20, 140
judicial panels 131
judicial tenure 119
jurisdiction 128–29, 140, 216
language 116
*locus standi* 117, 120–29
sanctions 126–27, 140
specialised courts 116
structure of courts 116
subsidiarity jurisdiction 133–35
Supreme Court of the Union 113, 141
and fundamental rights 135–39
interpretation of international treaties 298–99
judicial creativity 175, 185, 187, 306
jurisdiction 71, 342–43
*locus standi see locus standi* in EU courts
non-compliance with judgments, sanctions 126–27, 140
preliminary rulings *see* preliminary rulings
primary objective test 297
role 113, 115
and subsidiarity 34, 40, 71, 133–35, 168
workload 30–31, 123
European Employment Strategy:
EES/ OMC dyad 424–32
and enlargement 415–36
exchange of best practices 431

features 426, 427
implementation 429–32
implementation by new members 420–24
new mode of governance 425, 427–28
objectives 425, 427, 428, 433, 435
policy learning 428–29
provisions 420
re-design 432–36
soft law 427–28, 431 434
and unemployment 426
weaknesses 431
European Ombudsman 50–52
European Parliament:
accountability of Council to 155
approval of Commissioners 146
and common foreign policy 264
and delegated legislation 83
and democratic deficit 151
and ECJ 118, 119
and external relations 299
financing elections 18–19, 54
lack of popular support 155
legislative role 80, 81
*locus standi* in EU courts 18–20
low electoral turnout 148, 155
Nice Treaty 20
political groups 60–62
reviewability of acts 57–63, 210
role 55
European political consciousness 174
European Security and Defence Policy:
development 279–81
failed 1950 attempt 276
generally 273–89
and NATO 280, 281, 282–84
paradox 281–84
political background 273–76
role 287–88, 289
and territorial integrity 281–82
way forward 284–88
European Union:
competences *see* competences of Union
draft Constitution *see* Constitution for Europe
Draft Treaty Establishing EU 146
enlargement *see* enlargement
legal personality 265
principles 416
regional governance model 296, 321
structure 261–64
three-pillar structure 262, 263
trade and non-economic values 304–6
transnational governance 296
world role 11–13, 275, 282, 289
and WTO *see* WTO
European Union law:
alternative methods 418–19
constitutional provisions 76–79
direct effect 191, 223, 224–28
European framework laws 40–41, 76, 77, 79, 80, 86, 87, 127, 214, 215
European laws 40–41, 76, 77, 79, 80, 86, 214, 215
functions 418
hierarchy *see* hierarchy of norms
implementing acts 79, 85–88
integration into UK law 201–2
and judicial persuasion 205–6
judicial review 18–43, 89, 115, 210–18
legislative acts 77–80, 115, 215
nature 418–19
non-legislative acts 80–8, 115, 215
regulatory acts 121–22, 213–14, 217
state and EU law 90–93
state liability *see* state liability for breach of EU law
supremacy 90–91, 141, 191, 192, 199, 267–69
and WTO law, 344
expert groups, judicial review 52–53
external relations *see* foreign policy

*Factortame* case 196, 201
fair trial 109, 214, 446
fishing policy 24, 68, 122
food safety 298
foreign policy:
CFSP *see* Common Foreign and Security Policy
common and single 259–60
constitutional constraints on member states 269–70
development of EU policies 291–302
draft Constitution 259–72, 279, 281, 300–1, 399
and enlargement 397–413
and EU structure 260–64
and free trade 297

*foreign policy continued*
hierarchy of values 298
issues 5–8
Laeken Declaration 2
Nice Treaty 299
objectives of enlargement 398–401
test of sovereignty 260–61
formalism 196–205, 207
fortress Europe 298
framework laws 40–41, 76, 77, 79, 80, 86, 87, 127, 214, 215
France 256, 275, 298, 335–36, 364, 379, 386, 430
*Francovich* case:
actions for damages 37
and direct effect 225
flowchart 257
and parallel remedies 242–46
principle 239–57
public and private law 255–56, 257
and remedy defaults 246–49
unified approach 249–55
fraud 59
free movement of goods:
competence 68
and environmental protection 306–9
and language requirements 247–49
state liability in damages 247–49
free movement of workers 346, 381–83
free trade:
and environmental protection 306–19
and external relations 297
means to an end 311
and non-economic values 298, 303–6
Front National 61
functionality, and constitutionalism 204–5
fundamental rights:
asylum policy 345, 359–69
Charter *see* Charter of Fundamental Rights
compatibility of EU acts with 28
competence 101, 108
constitutional protection 95–112
domestic remedies rule 108
and EU legal order 187–88
and free trade 304–6
human rights challenge 140–41
human rights v fundamental freedoms 135–39
margins of appreciation 100–1
persistent breach 101–2
preliminary rulings 107–8, 109
respect for 44
social and economic rights 445
and sustainable development 304
and *Wednesbury* 238
FYROM 403

GATS 312, 333
GATT *see* WTO
gender discrimination 241
Geneva Convention on Refugees *see* Refugee Convention
Germany:
asylum 351, 359, 362, 386
border controls 392
and competences of Union 66, 69
economic migration 380, 382, 383
fusion of states 261
and Iraq 275
Maastricht judgments 141, 175, 178, 263
re-admission agreements 395
reunification 380
global legal pluralism 13–15
globalisation 11–12, 178–79, 291, 292, 292–99, 343
GMOs 340
Goetschy, J 426
Goldsmith, Lord 439, 442, 449
Goodwin-Gill, G 373
governance:
Commission 148–49, 151
European political consciousness 174
global legal pluralism 13–15
good governance 399
meaning 148
new forms 291
principles 148
regional governance 296, 321
transnational governance 178–79, 291, 293–99, 418–19
Greece 176, 281n, 282–83, 383
Groupe Technique des Députés Indépendants 61

Habermas, J 178–79, 181, 183, 207
Habitats Directive 230, 233, 234, 235

Hallstein, W 143, 151
Hamilton, Alexander 190
Hardt, M 11, 12
Hartley, T 175
Hathaway, J 369
health protection 68, 291, 312, 325
hierarchy of norms:
adherence 216
criteria 75–76
current lack of 33
draft Constitution 40, 76–79, 214
European regulations 80–84
generally 75–93
implementing acts 85–88
and inter-institutional relations 88–90
*Kompetenz-Kompetenz* 72–73, 91–92
legislative acts 79–80, 115, 215
non-legislative acts 78–88, 115, 215
primacy of EU law 90–91, 141, 191, 192, 199, 267–69
state and EU law 90–93
High Court 116
Hodson, D 431
*Hormones* case 14, 339, 344
Hull estuary 230–31
human rights *see* fundamental rights
humanitarian operations 279
Humber estuary 231
Hungary 176, 377, 384, 389, 390, 391, 446
Hurwitz, A 373
Hussein, Saddam 275

Iceland 351
identity 174, 260
Iglesias, R 40, 191
IMF 295
immigration:
common policy 347, 378
competence 347, 359
control of new members' migration 383–95
current practice 348–55
directives 351–55
draft Constitution 347–48
Eastern Europe Agreements 352
and ECJ jurisdiction 129
economic migration from new members 380–83
employment 353–54
and enlargement 377–78, 380–83
expulsion decisions 355–56
family reunion 351, 353
and globalisation 291
harmonisation of standards 345–55, 358–59
illegal immigration 354–55, 378, 391–93
long-term residence 351–53
mutual recognition 345–55
preliminary references 220
re-admission agreements 355, 394–95
restrictions on new members 378–83
returns to new member countries 394–95
students 353
trafficking in persons 355
transitional arrangements 381–83
Turkish immigrants 352
visas *see* visas
volunteers 353
implementation:
annulment actions 122, 213
categories of measures 215
and direct effect 224–28
errors of law 229–37
hierarchy of norms 85–88
legality review 223–37
requirement 122–23
state damages *see* state liability for breach of EU law
state discretion 228–37
India 341
industry, competence 68, 325
inhuman or degrading treatment 371, 373
institutions of the EU
*see also* specific institutions
efficiency 159
legitimacy 159
meaning 130
preliminary rulings 130
roles 145
and subsidiarity 165
intellectual property 131, 322, 323, 332–33, 335
interim orders 35, 219
internal market, shared competence 68

international law:
  and ECJ 298–99
  and globalisation 292–99
  rules 272
  supremacy 268
international organisations,
  powers 329
interpretation principles 202
INTERREG 410
Iran, sanctions 262
Iraq, war 275
Ireland 148, 176, 383

Jenkins, R 145
judges 35–36, 118–20
judicial cooperation 129, 215, 348
judicial review:
  and accountability 47–53
  acts of EU agencies and
    bodies 125
  assertions of competence 73
  Commission decisions 48–50
  and constitutional culture 10
  decentralisation 117, 123
  and democracy 53–63
  discretionary powers 237
  EU measures *see* annulment actions
  European Ombudsman's
    decisions 50–52
  European Parliament acts 57–63
  expert groups 52–53
  legitimising role of EU courts 43–63
  limits 45
  *locus standi see locus standi* in
    EU courts
  state discretion under
    directives 223–37
  subsidiarity infringement 133–35
  and transparency 43–47
  warnings to institutions 63
justice, shared competence 68

Kaliningrad 391, 402
Kinnock, N 145
Kok Report 423
Kok, W 397, 400, 402
*Kompetenz-Kompetenz* 72–73, 91–92

Laeken agenda 1, 3, 96
Laeken Declaration:
  co-decision procedure 157
  delimitation of powers 65
  EU world role 275
  external relations 2, 271
  legitimacy 159, 167
  national parliaments 159
  nature 114
  transparency 118–19
landfill 227
Latvia 377, 387
Lebanon 409
legal aid 446
legal certainty 125
legal culture 11
legal personality EU 265
legality review:
  direct effect doctrine 224–28
  discretion case law 228–37
  environmental
    protection 229–36, 237–38
  errors of law 229–37
  generally 223–37
  state discretion under
    directives 223–37
  terminology 225
legislation *see* European Union law
legitimacy:
  and access to EU courts 17, 33
  Commission 151
  and competences of Union 65
  constitutional objective 76, 136
  decision-making processes 53
  and democracy 159, 173–74
  EES 425
  enlargement 412
  Laeken Declaration 159
Leila 281
Lester, Lord 108
liberalism 12, 136
Lista Bonino 61
Lithuania 377
*locus standi* in EU courts:
  amendment of treaties 39, 110
  annulment actions
    classes of applicants 110
    directives 22–23
    domestic remedies 30–31, 37
    and equality before the law 110
    European Parliament 18–20
    generally 18–43, 109–12
    implementing acts 42
    individual
      applicants 20–43, 110–112
    individual concern 26–27,
      37–39, 59, 89–90, 110, 123, 218
    judicial creativity 187

regulatory acts 111
reinterpretation of criteria 37–38
requirements 22
and Constitution for Europe 41–42
constitutional review 89–90
and Convention 39–40, 42
draft Constitution
annulment actions 111–12, 114, 117, 120–29, 209–18
challenging decisions 122
challenging regulatory acts 121–22
direct concern 212–13
individual concern 121, 122, 218
limited liberalisation 123
restriction 140
Luxembourg Accords 1966 143

Maastricht Treaty:
and British courts 263
common foreign policy 262–63, 267, 279, 281
defence 280
and Denmark 43–44, 141, 260
ECJ penalties 126
external relations 297
and Germany 141, 175, 178, 263
problems 147
social policy 425
three pillar structure 262–63
MacCormick, N 172
Macedonia 403
Madison, James 190
Maher, I 431
Malta 377, 378, 402
marine conservation, exclusive competence 67, 68
marriage, right to 445–46
Marsh, D 429
MEDA 410
member states:
asylum from 379
constitutional values 139
defence industries 287–88
discretion, implementation of directives 223, 228–37
environmental protection 306
harmonization of standards 345–55
identification with 174
membership of WTO 329
new members *see* enlargement
non-compliance with ECJ, sanctions 126–27, 140
normative priority 172–75, 176
parliaments *see* national parliaments
post-sovereignty 172
respect for identity 260
suspension 101–2
WTO disputes 333–35
WTO participation 336–40
minority rights 446–47, 449
mobile phones 47
Moldova 411
monetary instruments, regulators 12
monetary policy, exclusive competence 67
Monnet, J 150, 151
Montenegro 406, 448
Moracsik, A 183, 184
mutual recognition, asylum and immigration 345–55

national parliaments:
early peripherality 153–54
and EU democracy 154–56
Laeken Declaration 159
monitoring subsidiarity 163–66
political control 132
post-Constitution role 166–69
Protocol 157, 158, 159, 160–61
role 154–56
scrutiny 156–57
scrutiny reserve 157–62
Working Group 159–60
national security, and immigration 355
NATO 259, 269, 275, 280, 282–84
necessity 315–16
Negri, Antonio 11, 12
neighbourhood policy 403
neo-liberalism 291
Netherlands 383, 386
New Zealand 370
Nice Declaration 65, 96, 159
Nice Treaty:
co-decision procedure 157
common commercial policy 323
defence policy 279
and ECJ 114
and European Parliament 20
external relations 299
and Ireland 148
and state representation 176
trade policy 298

NIS 403, 408, 409
Nitrates Directive 231, 232, 235–36
non-legislative acts 78–88, 115, 215
Norway 351
nutrition 291

OLAF 58–59
olive farmers 27
openness *see* transparency
opinions 76, 78
ordinary people, and
 Constitution 9–11
over-population 291

Paciotti, Ms 437
parental leave 55, 57
participation, social
 partners 55–57, 425, 434, 435
partnership and cooperation
 agreements 407, 409, 410
patents 332, 333, 335
Patten, Christopher 271, 397, 407
peace 416
peacekeeping 279
persecution 369–70, 372–74, 375
Phare Programme 386, 392, 417
pharmaceutical licensing 236–37
pluralism, global legal
 pluralism 13–15
Poland 377, 380, 386, 389, 390,
 391, 394
police cooperation 129
political control, national
 parliaments 132
political cooperation 262–64
politics, and law 194, 207
Portugal 176, 335, 383
post-sovereignty 172
Powell, Colin 281
precautionary principle 53
Prechal, S 225, 226–27, 228
preliminary rulings:
 asylum and immigration 220
 challenging EU Regulations 25
 draft Constitution 114, 128, 129–31
 empirical evidence 194–205
 human rights 107–8, 109
 interpretation of Constitution 130
 role 192–93
presidencies, rotation 161–62
Prodi, R 149, 150, 275, 400,
 402, 410, 411
Product Liability Directive 241
proportionality:
 and access to documents 46
 and competences of Union 92–93
 draft Constitution 336
 environmental protection 307,
 309, 310, 314–15, 316
 function 166–7, 202
 fundamental rights 139, 310
 and legislation 77
 principle 132, 202–3
 Protocol 132–35
 Tobacco Advertising Directive 238
prosperity 416
protocols, purpose 103
Proximity Policy 403
public bodies:
 accountability 135
 discretionary powers 237

qualified majority voting 264, 297

Rawls, J 180–81
recommendations 76, 78
Refugee Convention:
 application by member
 states 350
 definition of refugee 352, 362–63
 Eastern European members 385
 EU compliance with 358
 New York Protocol 361
 status 364
refugees *see* asylum
regional integration 10
regulations:
 annulment actions 24–28, 33,
 38–39, 121–22
 delegated regulations 41, 42,
 80–84, 86, 88, 215
 draft Constitution 40–41,
 76, 78, 79
 European implementing
 regulations 215
 non-legislative acts 215
 regulatory
 acts 121–22, 213–14, 217
remedies:
 annulment actions, draft
 Constitution 220
 domestic remedies
 rule 30–31, 37, 108–9
 reform of EU system 109–12
 right *see* right to effective remedy
residence permits 347, 349

right to effective remedy:
against EU agencies/ bodies 125
Charter of Fundamental Rights 25, 109
draft Constitution 220
EC Treaty 25
ECHR 109
enforcement mechanisms 36–40
EU compliance 109
exhaustion of alternative remedies 243
and *locus standi* in EU courts 23, 25–31
and new members 446
role of Commission 36–37
state liability *see* state liability for breach of EU law
right to fair trial 109, 214, 446
right to marry 445–46
Romania 377, 380, 384, 389, 393, 400, 402, 448
Romas 379–80
Russia 390, 391, 398, 402, 403, 408, 409

Santer, J 59, 148
Scharpf, F 183
Schengen Agreement 176, 348–49, 354, 355, 356, 383, 388, 391–93
Schengen Information System 392
Scientific Committee for Animal Nutrition (SCAN) 52, 53
scientific committees 52–53
Scotland 201, 261
Scrutiny Reserve Resolution 157–58
security *see* European Security and Defence Policy
security, competence 68
separation of powers 33, 76, 116
September 11 attacks 285, 287, 288
Serbia 389, 402, 406, 448
services, and CCP 322, 323–24, 326
Sheerness 230
Shellfish Waters Directive 234, 238
simplification objective 75–76, 93
Single European Act 262, 306
Slovakia 377, 380, 389, 391
Slovenia 377, 386, 389
social contract 180–82
social partners 55–57, 425, 434, 435
Social Policy Agreement 54, 55
Solana, J 270, 399, 407
South-East Europe 403–7, 409, 411
sovereignty:
criteria 260–61
debate 259
and EU constitution 264–66
and EU defence policy 279–80
and globalisation 11–12
post-sovereignty 172
Soviet Union 13, 389
Spain 281, 379, 383, 386, 430
special areas of conservation 230, 234, 235
special protection areas 230, 233–34
sports, competence 68, 325
SPS Agreement 294, 298, 312, 314
stability 416, 441
Stability and Growth Pact 424
standardisation 292, 294
state aids, *locus standi* 21
state liability for breach of EU law:
exhaustion of alternative remedies 243
flowchart 257
*Francovich* 37, 239–57
new remedy 35
parallel remedies 242–46
principles 239–42
public and private law 255–56, 257
remedy defaults 246–49
right to remedy 240
unified approach 249–55
states:
competing sites of governance 13
EU members *see* member states
external relations 261
model 10–11
test of sovereignty 260–61
students, immigration 353
subsidiarity:
annulment actions 120
and Commission powers 147
and competences of Union 65, 67, 68, 69–72, 92–3
definition 163, 165
draft Constitution 132, 336
early warning system 165, 166, 168
and ECJ 34, 40, 71, 133–35, 168
institutions 72
key objective 132
monitoring 163–66
perceptions 201–2

*subsidiarity continued*
Protocol 132–35, 163, 164, 165, 166–69
Working Group 163–66, 167
subsidies, EU and WTO 14–15
sustainable development 303–4, 311, 319
Sweden 364, 383, 386, 430
Switzerland 351
Syria 409
Syrpis, P 427

TACIS 410
TAIEX assistance 405
taxation 186, 240–41
TBT Agreement 294, 298, 312, 314
Teague, P 428
technocracy 150, 151
terrorism 64, 285–86, 291
Thessaloniki Agenda 404, 406, 407
Tindemans Report 144, 145
tobacco 22, 29, 47, 238
torture/ inhuman or degrading treatment 371, 373
trade *see* common commercial policy; free trade
trade marks 212
trafficking in persons 355
training, competence 68
transnational governance 178–79, 291, 418–19
transparency:
access to documents 44–47
and ECJ appointments 118–19
and EU courts 17, 43–47
European Council 155
governance principle 136, 148, 150
and legitimacy 159
WTO dispute settlement process 331
transport, shared competence 68
treaties:
deliberative democracy models 180–81
ECJ interpretation 298–99
EU treaty making capacity 265
extent of state consent 176
idealised negotiations 179–88
imagining outcomes 184–88
inadequacy 175–79
majoritarian approach 179–80
opt-outs 295
unanimous agreement to amendments 177
Trianon, Treaty of 389
Tridimas, T 198
TRIPS 312, 334–35
Tulmets, E 416–17
Turkey 275, 281n, 282–83, 352, 401, 402, 448
twinning projects 417

Ukraine 389, 390, 398, 402, 409, 411
UN 259, 269, 275
UNCLOS 294, 337
UNHCR 363, 365, 369, 370, 379
United Kingdom:
administrative law 256
asylum case law 369, 370
asylum policy 359, 364
border controls 392
circulars 231
and competences of Union 66
constitutionality 197
EC accession 268
empirical study 194–207
and enlargement 383
and EU foreign policy 267
and European legal language 202
European scrutiny committees 154, 155, 158, 159
integration of EU law 201, 202
interim injunctions 35
and Iraq 275
Lappel Bank 230
and Schengen Agreement 176
scrutiny reserve 157–62
United Nations 259, 269, 275
United States:
anti-dumping 342
Constitution 72–73, 190, 260
EC-WTO IP disputes 332–33
hegemony 11, 12
and Iraq 275
New Deal 12
non-delegation doctrine 84
social constitutional re-alignment 204
WTO disputes with EU member states 333
unjust enrichment 241

Vesterdorf, CFI President 40, 43
victimisation 251
Vietnam 261

virginiamycin 52
visas:
  current practice 348–49
  draft Constitution 347
  and ECJ jurisdiction 129
  and enlargement 389–91
  harmonisation 346, 349, 356
  preliminary references 220

war on terrorism, legality 64
Warbrick, C 261
waste, 307
Waste Directive 227
Weber, M 9
Weiler, JHH 100
Western NIS 403, 408, 409
WHO 294
World Bank 295
WTO:
  anti-dumping 14
  applicant countries 409
  Article XX 311–12, 315, 317
  complainants 330
  conflicts with other treaties 294
  cooperation principle 328–30, 337
  co-ordinated governance 293
  decision-making and EU 327–30
  and direct effect 298, 299, 342–43
  dispute settlement system 311, 322, 330–32
  Doha Round 326–27
  EC accession 322, 326
  and environmental protection 311
  and EU autonomy 342
  and EU code of conduct 337–40, 343
  EU complaints to 330–33
  EU compliance improvement 340–43
  EU disputes 330–36
  EU implementation 13–15
  EU member state participation 336–40
  EU participation 327–36
  EU respondent in disputes 333–36
  exceptions 311–12, 318
  and globalisation 343
  *Hormones* case 14, 339, 344
  international standards 294
  non-economic interests, 311–12
  non-legislative powers 329
  SPS Agreement 294, 298, 312, 314
  and sustainable development 311
  TBT Agreement 294, 298, 312, 314
  Trade Barriers Regulations 330, 331–32, 339
  trade v non-economic interests 304–6
  trade-environment disputes 312–13, 315–19
  zeroing methodology 342

youth, competence 68, 325
Yugoslavia 278, 384